SOCIALIST THOUGHT
A DOCUMENTARY HISTORY

REVISED EDITION

EDITED BY
ALBERT FRIED AND
RONALD SANDERS

COLUMBIA UNIVERSITY PRESS
NEW YORK

Columbia University Press Morningside Edition
Columbia University Press
New York   Chichester, West Sussex

Morningside Edition with new preface
Copyright © 1992 Columbia University Press
Copyright © 1964 Albert Fried and Ronald Sanders

Library of Congress Cataloging-in-Publication Data
Socialist thought : a documentary history / edited by Albert Fried and
    Ronald Sanders.—Rev. ed.
        p.   cm.
    Includes bibliographical references.
    ISBN 0-231-08264-9 (cloth) : —ISBN 0-231-08265-7 (paper)
    1. Socialism—History—18th century.   2. Communism—History—
18th century.   I. Fried, Albert.   II. Sanders, Ronald.
    HX36.S65   1993
    335—dc20   92-4481
                                                                    CIP

SOCIALIST THOUGHT

of Jimmy Carter's administration measures the enormity of America's decline.

Only the intense national desire to resurrect past glories explains the astonishing phenomenon that immediately followed—the Reagan years. The "Reagan Revolution" attempted to bring back the prosperity of old by unleashing business enterprise, lowering taxes on the rich, reducing or abolishing government regulations, and escalating the Cold War. To accomplish the latter, a series of offensives from Central America to Cambodia the "evil empire" were begun and a race started to develop the most sophisticated weapon systems known. The popularity of the "Reagan Revolution" is evident from the margin of victory in his second electoral victory (every state but one) and his successor's vow to preserve it inviolate.

To all appearances, America was delivered, its pride and self-esteem rehabilitated. The United States and her allies had been successful in the Gulf War and the Soviet Union had come to an inglorious end. It is too soon to tell whether or not it was the stepped-up arms race and the strain it placed on scarce resources that brought the contradictions of Soviet society to a head. It is safe to assume that the breakdown would have sooner or later because the Soviet Union could not have continued competing with the West, keeping its allies in tow, and subsidizing friendly, impoverished third world nations. Between 1989 and 1991, every country within the Soviet sphere broke free and changed governments. East Germany joined with West Germany and ceased to exist. In fact, the Soviet Union itself ceased to exist, the constituent republics going their own way. The United States had won the Cold War.

But, while Communist or Marxist-Leninist governments may be on the run, they have not disappeared. Even though it encourages free market, self-enrichment, and foreign investment, China still adheres to the Bolshevik principles adumbrated in this book. Vietnam, Cuba, and North Korea, still have Communist governments. Not only do Marxist-Leninist parties vie for power in other states but, under

The United States was saddled with huge military obligations and defense spending; these countries were not. Also, Third World nations that the West had once completely subjugated began to assert themselves. By establishing an international cartel, oil rich Middle East states raised the price of oil and then demonstrated their puissance by instituting an embargo that brought about a crisis which Americans had never experienced in peacetime—shortages of heating oil and gasoline and rationing at the pump. Americans began to question if their existence depended on the whim of desert sheiks.

4. **Communist Advances.** Perhaps most ominous was not only the recovery of America's inveterate foe, the Soviet Union, but its steady advance. By the 1970s, the Soviets had practically achieved parity with the United States in the number of nuclear weapons and delivery systems. This disturbing fact was acknowledged when the United States signed the Strategic Arms Limitation Treaty (SALT), the first such agreement between the superpowers. Despite this agreement, the Cold War continued to worsen for America. The year South Vietnam fell, the Portuguese lost their remaining colonies of Angola and Mozambique to pro-Communist guerillas, and the Ethiopian government of Hailie Selassie, once America's staunch ally, fell to army officers who established a Soviet-style people's republic. Four years later, a revolution in Nicaragua with Marxist-Leninist overtones ousted the America-backed dictator, Anastas Samoza. At the same time fighting broke out in El Salvador and Soviet troops invaded Afghanistan to shore up the country's faltering Communist regime. The Shah of Iran, America's closest Middle East friend, fled before a fundamentalist and violently anti-American uprising. Within months of the successful uprising, Americans held hostage in Tehran were paraded before the world and an American military rescue attempt proved to be an embarrassment.

The contrast between the ebullience and golden hours of John F. Kennedy's presidency and the foreboding mood

PREFACE TO
THE MORNINGSIDE EDITION

Almost thirty years ago, Ronald Sanders and I conceived this book, a documentary account of the intellectual side of Western socialism from the Enlightenment to our own day. For two young men just out of graduate school (we met at Columbia University), this was, if I may say so myself, an audacious undertaking, daunting project. We did it because, students and followers of socialism ourselves, we were convinced that such a book might reach a sizable audience. The quality paperback, "revolution" was gaining strength now that college enrollments were growing and courses routinely used paperbacks. Judging by the success of *SOCIALIST THOUGHT*, which was published in January 1964, the book did meet that need. It stayed in print for twenty years and probably would have stayed longer but for the new economics of publishing.

Putting the book together in the spring and summer of 1963, Ronald Sanders and I could never have envisioned the amazing concatenation of events that have since transformed the world, the socialist world in particular. Their magnitude and depth greatly surpass anything we described in our original introduction.

Back then, life, all in all, was very satisfying for us Americans. Thanks to massive government spending on military and space programs, we were riding high under President Kennedy. Regardless of the cost, America was committed to reaching the moon ahead of the Soviet Union. The economy, having just experienced a recession, embarked on what proved to be one of the great booms in American history, a decade of full employment. Meanwhile, the country still wore the glow of its stupendous triumph over the Soviet Union in the Cuban missile crisis. Of course, there were problems: the threat of revolution in Latin America; the inability of the American sponsored South Vietnamese government to defeat, or at the very least contain, Communist backed revolutionaries; and the indeterminate character of recently liberated countries. Yet, who could quarrel with the prevailing assumption, here and abroad, that this was indeed the "American Century?"

Over the next two decades, this optimism and confidence turned to disquietude and malaise. Could the "American Century" have been an illusion? A checklist of adversities shows how the nation's fortunes had shifted.

1. **Internal Convulsions.** President Kennedy's assassination occurred just as the civil rights movement was entering its radical phase, a time marked by demands for greater economic and social equality. The civil rights upsurge inspired other movements, other forms of mass protest, and other forms of rebellion. The most virulent of these was the response to the seemingly endless Vietnam war. All of these movements merged in a gigantic critique of institutions and life styles which had hitherto been sacrosanct. Authority, politics, the family, sex roles, the virtue of patriotism, and the supposed evils of communism came into question.

2. **Battlefield Defeat.** The anti-war protests represented the counterpoint of the Vietnamese Communists' resistance to the American onslaught which tested their ability to absorb unspeakable punishment. In the spring of 1975, ten years after the war started, it was the United States that abandoned the fight under the most humiliating circumstances. Almost 60,000 Americans had died in vain.

3. **Economic Blows.** In the meantime, two events of global significance deeply affected American life. Japan and Western Europe (especially Germany) became powerful enough to dispute American economic hegemony.

CONTENTS

new names, they are still a force in the former communist states in Eastern Europe. As for the post-industrial West, including France and Italy where Communist parties once thrived, what we wrote in 1963 holds true today. Industrialization, the ability to create wealth and distribute it to larger and larger segments of society, is the nemesis of Bolshevism. And our description of the socialist prospect in the industrial or post-industrial world also still holds true today. That is, in every country except the United States, reform-minded socialists form governments, participate in them, or serve as their main opposition.

What Ronald Sanders and I did not anticipate in 1963 was the extraordinary resurgence of traditional, old-line capitalism. Not only did this happen in the United States ("Reaganism"), it happened in Great Britain ("Thatcherism") and more modestly in Germany, France, Italy and the Scandinavian countries. With the same conservative party running the country since the late 1940s, Japan also belongs in this company. And yet, more than ever do we say that a viable democracy tends to drive politics to the center and general consensus. Although "Thatcherism" and its variants is the exception to this rule, it is normal for conservatives in power to uphold and occasionally advance welfare state programs and, thus, neutralize the socialist or liberal left. And socialists, eager to win middle class support, tend to discipline labor and unions and promote a climate favorable to business. The center draws the major parties into its gravitational field.

Since this book was first published, new challenges and opportunities for socialism have arisen. Ever since its appearance in the early 19th century, the socialist movement has embodied the ideal of economic equality. The end of class oppression would liberate the proletariat and the proletariat would liberate humanity as a whole. How best to end oppression and build the institutions of liberation was what distinguished one set of socialists from another— communitarians from Marxists, orthodox Marxists from revisionists, etc. However, in the past few decades, calls for

a radical alteration of the status quo in behalf of oppressed
or ignored groups have come from quarters unassociated
with the working class. Socialists may have implied feminism, environmentalism, and equal rights for racial minorities, homosexuals, lesbians, the insulted, and the injured
but that was as far as it went. It was all quite vague and
amorphous. There was, moreover, disturbing evidence to
the contrary. Feminisms, environmentalists, racial and
ethnic minorities, disaffected students, artists, and intellectuals did not exactly receive hearty applause from workers, trade unions, and the socialist or communist parties
purporting to represent them. Patriarchal, authoritarian,
and racist attitudes were deeply rooted in working class
culture. And a conflict of interest often arose between labor and ecologists, the notably "Green" movement, over
regulating industrial development. For their part, communist governments, in their unconcern for the environment,
proved as ruthless as the worse capitalist exploiters. Conversely and inexplicably from the socialist standpoint is
that feminism, environmentalism, and the demands for racial, sexual, and gender equality have flourished luxu-
riantly in the citadel of economic reaction, the very place
where socialism has been a practical nullity—the United
States.

The liberation movements that transcend economic im-
peratives and working class constituencies have, as we
said, also provided socialism with an opportunity to renew
itself. For, if socialism presumes to represent the community at large over and against individual rapacity, it will
keep faith with its fundamental and time-honored principles and demonstrate that it can adapt itself to changing
circumstances and changing conceptions of freedom.

The new chapter (Chapter XI) that has been added to
this edition reflects the attempt to broaden the scope of
socialist thought and to bring about a unity between the
received tradition and recent liberation movements. The
selections of course give only a sample of the literature; an
entire volume would scarcely do it justice. I am certainly

aware of what has been omitted. Schools of Marxist interpretations, for example, have proliferated in universities of
the world and cross-fertilized with schools of psycho-
analysis, philosophy, gender studies, literary theory, semi-
otics, economic history, and the like. The number of books
dealing with every facet of the socialist experience has
grown exponentially since *SOCIALIST THOUGHT* was
published. I would suggest that the interested reader con-
sult *A DICTIONARY OF MARXIST THOUGHT*, edited by
Tom Bottomore (Cambridge: Harvard University Press,
1983). Despite its Marxist rubric, this work ranges far and
wide over the socialist landscape while supplying a list of
suggested readings after each entry and a comprehensive
33 page bibliography.

I am sorry that Ronald Sanders did not live to see *SO-
CIALIST THOUGHT* reappear in such a handsome edition
and with the imprimatur of such a fine house. The prospect
that it will again fill a need and once more make available
documents translated from the French and German which
are found nowhere else would have pleased him immensely. This new preface, written in the spirit of our
collaboration, I dedicate to his memory.

Albert Fried
October 1992

PREFACE

To the following friends, whose help lightened our task, we owe gratitude and thanks: Dr. David Golding, who gave trenchant advice and criticism; Miss Edith Firoozi, who applied her considerable skill to help correct the manuscript and proofs; and Misses Emily Bernstein and Shareen Blair, who helped prepare the manuscript.

We should like to express our appreciation to Miss Kay Dunn, our editor at Anchor Books, for her indispensable advice at every stage in the creation of this work.

We are also indebted to the following translators: Benjamin Tucker for Proudhon's *What Is Property?*; the Foreign Languages Publishing House of the U.S.S.R. for the writings of Marx, Engels, Plekhanov, Lenin and Stalin; E. Peters for Lassalle's *The Working Men's Progress*; Edith C. Harvey for Bernstein's *Evolutionary Socialism*; A. M. Simon for Kautsky's *The Road to Power*; H. J. Stenning for Kautsky's *Dictatorship of the Proletariat*; and Max Shachtman for Trotsky's *The New Course*. Ronald Sanders translated the selections from Morelly, Rousseau, Babeuf, Saint-Simon, the Saint-Simonians, Blanqui, Blanc, Fichte, Hess, Bakunin, Jaurès, and Millerand. Many of the excerpts are reproduced as they were originally printed, and this preservation of the original style accounts for some variations in spelling and punctuation.

Chapter I

INTRODUCTION

Histories of socialism traditionally find themselves having to begin with an impossible task: that of defining socialism. The task is particularly difficult in the United States because we have little or no socialist tradition here, with the result that the word "socialism" usually takes on any of a number of under-privileged connotations, ranging from the fairly harmless—a quaint historical curiosity or a beautiful but hopeless dream—all the way to the widespread popular conception of it as some form of evil. Consequently, any work on socialism in this country is put upon promptly to defend itself, to provide immediate and concrete justification of its theme.

But socialism defies succinct definitions. It is a living and conscious organism, constantly growing and redefining itself. There are numerous "definitions" of socialism by socialists, but these are of course subjective interpretations. And yet any one of these yields more meaning than any more or less scientific definition. One could not ask, for example, for a more comprehensive and justly impartial definition than the one provided by Webster's *New International Dictionary* (2nd edition):

A political and economic theory of social organization based on collective or governmental ownership and democratic management of the essential means for the production and distribution of goods; also, a policy or practice based on this theory. Socialism aims to replace competition by co-operation and profit seeking by social service, and to distribute income and social opportunity more equitably than they are now believed to be distributed.

This definition is adequate in the same sense that it would be

adequate, say, to give a definition of "man" in broadly biological terms, laying stress upon the fact of intelligence as
distinguishing him from other primates. Such a definition
would be minimally correct, but it would have little to do with
any of the questions about the nature of man that have concerned philosophers for centuries. To understand more one
must study him in a wide sampling of his ramifications.

The attempt to define socialism, then, will be the task not
of this brief introduction, but of this entire book, which is
still altogether too brief. Socialism is a set of aspirations developing through history, as varied in its manifestations as are
the lives and characters of the people who have expressed
socialist ideas. To one coming to the subject for the first time,
the incredible range of these conceptions will perhaps be the
most striking aspect. Some socialists are so committed to a rigorous use of state power to achieve their ends that they must
be considered as more or less totalitarian, or, at any rate, quasi-
totalitarian, but others are radically anti-authoritarian and
some of these even want to eliminate the state altogether.
Some are revolutionary (*émeutiste* would be a better word)
and others are parliamentary; some are oracles of class struggle
and others of class collaboration; some believe in the abolition
of private property and others are not even opposed to the
profit principle; and so on. Indeed, the variety is so great that
one might be tempted to ask, is there any such thing as socialism at all?

And the answer is yes, in the same sense, let us say, as there
is an English Constitution that yielded up a Magna Carta in
one era and socialized medicine in another, or a Christian tradition that produced both a St. Francis and a Cotton Mather:
there is a continuous idea moving through all of these ramifications, as compelling and imperishable as it is mysterious
and protean. If we are to understand it, we must follow its
growth.

An examination of the subject can be made simpler, perhaps, if a few general principles are borne in mind. In the first
place, socialism belongs only to the present era in history, the
era that began with the American and French revolutions.

Much has been made by some writers of the fact that glimmerings of the socialist idea can be seen as far back as the Old Testament and ancient Greek philosophy, and these can certainly be looked upon as significant precursors and sources of inspiration for socialism. But socialism properly belongs to the age of democratic ideologies that began at the end of the eighteenth century. Like the liberal ideology which was its parent, socialism was engendered by the worldly moralism of the Western European philosophers of the seventeenth and eighteenth centuries, a moralism that was catalyzed into action, and hence into belief in the possibility of imminent and sweeping reform, by the French Revolution.

But unlike classical liberalism (another term that defies easy definition), socialism was a reaction *against* the industrial revolution. It came, rather, out of a crisis in classical liberalism which, with its great stress on individual liberty, had come to manifest itself in the area of economic activity under the celebrated slogan, *laissez faire, laissez passer.* This certainly meant freedom for businessmen, but, as the huge industrial consolidations of Manchester and Lyons came into being, it also meant a new kind of servitude for the thousands of men, women and children who spent most of their waking hours in these factories, receiving the merest subsistence wage. The socialists of the early nineteenth century shared the liberal ideal of freedom, but they were led to a more complex formulation of it than had hitherto prevailed. They were forced into a paradox: in order to find a way of providing the maximum freedom for all men, they had to think in terms of restricting freedom, at least in any sense of the word that resolved itself into the *laissez faire* conception. Their own era was providing them with the intellectual equipment for such an undertaking; the romantic movement was enshrining the paradox as a form of truth superior to the geometric formulations of previous generations, including the concept of *laissez faire* itself.

Socialism, specifically a response to the Industrial Revolution, was an attempt not only to redistribute wealth more equitably, but to rediscover the way to freedom in a world governed by the industrial system. Because of the problems from which it first arose and with which it continues to deal,

its orientation is primarily economic. But this does not mean
that socialism should be taken as mainly an economic theory
or tradition of theories. It is rather, in a sense, anti-economic;
it aims, in an era in which men have become burdened, and
often as much victimized as served, by a vast economic structure, to put the economic forces in their place, to subordinate
them to human life and place them at the service of man.
Socialists have not always been opposed to the existence of
machine industry; some have been, but this was more often
true of the extreme wing of the nineteenth-century socialist
movement that was called communism (in the pre-Soviet sense
of the word, of course), than of the mainstream of the movement. Marx, for example, was aware of the enormous potential that machine industry contained for making mankind prosperous; he opposed only the system by which it was owned
and administered. For most socialists the goal is a transformation in the organization and ownership of industry.

However, the socialist seeks to transform more than the material organization of society. He seeks above all a change of
consciousness—this was true even of Marx, who was at heart
an inveterate moralist, even though he tried to disparage moral
sentiments. The socialist seeks to rid man of what Karl
Polanyi has called the "market mentality," the inclination to
view human life in terms of the exchange of commodities. Believing that human creativity cannot be fully realized as long
as it is conceived of as something for sale, the socialist en-
visions a community of mankind that is free because all men
give freely; that is above all *human* because love and work
are not thwarted and fragmented but are one, within themselves and with each other. Perhaps this is only a dream, but it
graces mankind to have such a dream in its midst.

The three important dates in the history of socialism are
1789, 1848, and 1914–18. In other words: the French Revolution, which launched socialism along with every other nineteenth-century ideology; the abortive revolutions of 1848,
which marked the divide between "utopian" and "scientific"
socialism; and World War I, which inflicted a deep wound on
socialism that has been festering ever since. It is with these

chronological divisions in mind that we have assembled this book of socialist documents.

We have begun the story in eighteenth-century France where the radical Enlightenment produced a philosophy of egalitarianism, best exemplified in the writings of Morelly and Rousseau. Morelly, in his *Code of Nature,* created a utopian communist society that no one, including the author, accepted as a serious possibility at the time. But it was the first such scheme proposed by a modern philosopher, and it contained all the assumptions on which utopian plans for the future would be built. Rousseau's attack on property rights and social injustice in his *Discourse on the Origin of Inequality* cut deeper than Morelly's because it addressed itself to a contemporary problem, and it was widely read. Rousseau was no socialist (the word did not exist then), but his moral idealism was to be the basis of the socialist ethic. Law, said Rousseau, is made for the good of society as a whole, not for the privileged few.

More than any other single man, "Gracchus" Babeuf effected the transition from the radical Enlightenment to the era of socialism that followed the French Revolution. Babeuf, convinced that the Revolution had been betrayed, led a small conspiracy to overthrow the French regime in 1796. To his mind communism was the only legitimate offspring of the Revolution, and he intended to impose its claim. The participants in the Conspiracy of Equals were being punished, he argued at his trial, only because they conscientiously attempted to follow Rousseau's precepts. The selections from Babeuf trace his change within a ten-year period from an impetuous son of the Enlightenment to the first communist revolutionary in modern history.

The next two generations in France worked out the implications of Babeuf's example. In the course of doing so they raised socialism to a conscious ideal, designed to protect society as a whole from the predators and idlers who contribute nothing to it. In the rich body of socialist thought that flowered in the 1830s and 1840s, a period when the industrial middle class, in rapid ascendancy, was creating social inequalities of appalling magnitude, two theories stood out above the rest:

Saint-Simon's (and with his that of the Saint-Simonians, a group of followers who flourished after his death) and Fourier's. Both men, in quite different ways, laid down nostrums for a just, rational society, organized by and for those who perform useful labor. Utopian socialists, however, never succeeded in answering the question, how and by whom was socially useful labor to be determined?

Industrial capitalism flourished in England decades before it did in France, and it is therefore not surprising that the first nineteenth-century utopian socialist was the Englishman Robert Owen. In many ways he was also the most successful. The New Lanark community, which he founded and presided over, lasted longer than any community of its kind in the Old World and inspired a number of similar experiments in the New. Owen's socialism, though it derived much from French revolutionary thought, harked back to a native radical tradition which had always affirmed that the fruits of labor belonged to those who produced them.

These utopian schemes and communities adhered to no movement or class; they emanated from the minds of individual men and took root in small, isolated sects. They were less practical than other forms of socialism that sprang up before 1848—socialisms that adhered to a class and sought political power. Blanqui, for example, was a revolutionary who led conspiracies against the French government in the tradition of the Jacobins and the Babouvists. But Blanqui never had a significant organization behind him. More important were the socialists who were connected with the working class. In France, Louis Blanc advocated giving the voting franchise to workers so that they could use the state in their own behalf. Similarly, in England, the Chartists came forward with proposals to extend the franchise to the working class and to reform the procedure for electing members of Parliament. Proudhon differed from the other working-class socialists. He had no faith in the state and thought the workers should rely on their own resources, form their own economic and political solidarities, and resist central authority. Proudhon reflected a deeply rooted French tradition of working class insularity and self-sufficiency that was to last well into the twentieth century.

In the proliferation of disparate ideas and movements before 1848 socialism displayed a good deal of vigor and self-confidence. But the unsuccessful revolutions of 1848 and 1849 made it clear that it needed more than energy and hope to prevail. By 1850 nearly every species of socialism had disappeared like chaff in the wind. A pall of conservatism, lasting two decades, fell upon the whole continent. When it lifted, as a new period of insurgency got under way in the 1860s, Marxism emerged as the most serious challenge ever to confront the power of industrial capitalism.

Marx was the first outstanding German socialist. There had been several lesser German socialists before him, the most notable of whom, Moses Hess, had anticipated the line of thinking that Marx carried much further and developed much more systematically. Germany's radical tradition had been forged in philosophy, not in politics. Conflicts had been fought in the realm of consciousness, not in the world of action. As it turned out this was not all for the worse. The power and depth of German philosophy was assimilated through Marx into the mainstream of European socialism.

While Marxism was establishing itself as the leading socialist ideology in the West, it was being challenged, with varying degrees of effectiveness from country to country, by anarchism and anarcho-syndicalism. According to Marx, the centralization of political power that capitalism brought about increased the possibility of proletariat revolution. Once the proletariat had seized state power, Marx believed, it would proceed to abolish the bourgeoisie—and therefore itself—as well as the state; for without a bourgeoisie the state as a coercive instrument would no longer have any reason to exist. Michael Bakunin, the founder of the anarchist movement and Marx's contemporary, was willing to accept everything Marx said except the notion that the state would "wither away" *after* socialism rather than before it. To Bakunin the state was not the effect but the cause of oppression; only the state prevented man from returning to his natural condition of unlimited freedom. Differences between Marx and Bakunin flared up at the time of the First International and abated only with Bakunin's death in 1876. For many years the two revolutionary ideologies competed with each other for the loyalties of the Europan proletariat. Bakunin scored some initial successes in industrially underdeveloped countries and above all in countries lacking centralized political traditions. But in time socialists even in these countries tended more and more to regard the great German Socialist Party, which was entirely Marxist, as their model.

Anarchism was too volatile to be an ideology. Its adherents agreed only on the need to do away with the state; they disagreed on how this should be done and what the future society should be like. Anarchism went in two directions, one violent, the other legal and peaceful. Widespread acts of anarchist terror outraged the public and justified the belief that it was nothing more than love of disorder and libertinism. But Prince Peter Kropotkin, the best-known anarchist after Bakunin, was the least violent of men, and his philosophy of "mutual aid" and of autonomous communities proved congenial to many who were otherwise unsympathetic to anarchism.

Anarchism was also central to the theory of syndicalism which sprang up in the trade union movements of France, Italy, Spain, and even Britain before and during World War I. Syndicalism proposed to bypass the state altogether by basing the whole legal and political order upon the free association of independent trade unions. It found an exceptional advocate in the Frenchman Georges Sorel, who justified violent strikes because they strengthened the solidarity of labor against the world at large. In England the syndicalist idea was transmuted by intellectuals into Guild Socialism, which caused a brief stir when it received the support of some unions during the war. By the mid-1920s Guild Socialism had run its course. In fact, the whole anti-collectivist heritage of socialism that had begun with Proudhon and Bakunin was disappearing everywhere at this time. Only in Spain—which avoided the war —did anarcho-syndicalism retain any strength into the 1930s. Today no significant school of socialists questions the legitimacy of the state.

Before Marx socialists had believed, as had the radicals of the French Revolution and the philosophers of communism before them, that ideally the state embodied the will and was the supreme moral agent of society as a whole. The rule of law, and with it the expansion of the state, was the best hope of the people against rule by the predatory interests. Now, it is obvious that liberal idealism—as we may call the doctrine that regards the state as the expression of the general will—opposed the Marxist concept of the state as nothing but the executive arm of the ruling class, although it professed similar ends of freedom and equality. Liberal idealism naturally contradicted every other important Marxist principle: it denied that class struggle and violent revolution were necessary or desirable, that the proletariat occupied a privileged place in history, and that any class commanded higher loyalty than the general will of the nation.

But as the nineteenth century wore on, the advent of political democracy in Western Europe began drawing Marxism and liberalism closer together. Democracy meant that the power of the state was accessible to any party that could obtain a majority or a plurality of the votes. Where it was stable, democracy irresistibly drove all political movements toward the center and in this sense justified the liberal idea of the general will. It was a German socialist, Ferdinand Lassalle, who first conceived of working class socialism in terms of liberal ideals. As the spokesman of German labor in the 1860s, he hailed the democratic state as the unity of the nation and the proletariat. But Lassalle's counsel could not mean much in a country that then lacked even the rudiments of political democracy. In democratic Britain Fabian Socialism came into prominence soon after its founding in 1884, vowing its kinship with liberalism and its belief in the efficacy of slow change. In France Alexandre Millerand led a reform socialist movement in the 1890s that hardly differed from Fabianism. While the great Jean Jaurès did not go as far as Millerand in the direction of reform, he did sanction it. In his own philosophical system Jaurès subordinated Marxism to the larger moral context of the French nation.

With the appearance of Eduard Bernstein's revisionism in the late 1890s, liberal reform penetrated the very citadel of Marxism. Bernstein concluded that Marx's principles and pre-

dictions needed to be overhauled because they were proving
untrue—thanks largely to the democratic state. Bernstein's importance lay in the fact that he himself had been a noted
Marxist and that as such he threw down the gauntlet to the
German Socialist Party, the largest and best organized socialist party in the world and orthodox Marxist through and
through. Actually Bernstein was speaking for a significant
and fast-growing element in the party, which for some time
had been practicing reform. Nonetheless the party continued
to profess adherence to pure Marxism through the writings of
its noteworthy theoretician, Karl Kautsky.

Clearly, then, in the two decades before World War I European socialism, though apparently more Marxist than ever,
was working its way toward an accommodation with liberalism, whether it cared to admit it or not. Even Russia felt the
winds of change. Russian Marxism had been gaining adherents
at an accelerating rate since its founder, Georgi Plekhanov,
had begun writing in the early 1880s. By the turn of the century, however, Plekhanov was saying that since Russia would
first have to go through a long capitalist incubation before
socialism was possible, socialists must wait and patiently build
up a democratic party. He was opposed in this by Lenin, his
onetime disciple, who proceeded to build his own elite organization of dedicated and disciplined revolutionaries. Lenin's Bolshevik Party (as distinguished from Plekhanov's Menshevik Party) did not pretend to democracy and eschewed any
possibility of stable reconciliation with groups or parties less
revolutionary than itself.

From a Marxist viewpoint, the situation in Europe on the
eve of World War I was paradoxical. The largest and most
uncompromisingly revolutionist "proletariat" party existed in
a country that was industrially backward. The paradox grew
into an historical contradiction when the Bolsheviks overthrew the constitutional government in October, 1917, and
actually established a proletariat dictatorship. Karl Kautsky,
the onetime hierophant of orthodox Marxism, was quick to see
its implications. Kautsky had considered absurd the Bolshevik
claim that the bourgeois stage of history had been accomplished in Russia between February and October of 1917.

Russia was at the pre-Marxist level on the scale of social evolution. How was it possible, asked Kautsky, for the dictatorship to be a proletariat one? How could Russia of all places lay claim to socialism?

The logic of Bolshevism ran its course as Kautsky had feared it would. Under Lenin, during and after the Revolution, the party could claim that its dictatorial rule consciously expressed the popular will, and that it was the only safe guide to the future. Even with this justification the party took upon itself a fearful responsibility. Its leaders believed that, having mastered history, they could be saved from the fate to which all previous dictatorships had succumbed. Thus assured, they made the party omnipotent over all of society. Whoever controlled the party inherited greater power than any Czar had ever possessed. By 1924, the year of Lenin's death, this leviathan had come under the domination of Joseph Stalin, the party secretary, who, appreciating its possibilities, went on to become one of the great tyrants of history.

His first and most dangerous opponent was Trotsky, the best known Bolshevik after Lenin. Trotsky upheld the pure ideals of the Revolution and sought to goad the party into living up to them. The Revolution had to be "permanent," he insisted, if these ideals were not to be run into the ground. By "permanent revolution" he meant instituting plans for rapid industrialization, favoring the proletariat over the peasants, and affirming the party's solidarity with revolutionary movements in other countries. Stalin defended his retrenchment policies by the novel theory of "socialism in one country," according to which socialism was possible in Russia alone, through the alliance of peasants and proletariat and without reference to its immediate chances elsewhere. It was a simple matter for Stalin to characterize Trotsky as a man who had no faith in the great Russian people and who was willing therefore to sacrifice them on the altar of world revolution. Trotsky may have spoken for the spirit of Bolshevism; Stalin spoke for the fact of Bolshevism. On certain fundamentals, they were in agreement. With Stalin, Trotsky assumed as an article of faith that the party was supreme and that it alone had the right to exist. Trotsky fell foul of the dictator and paid the conse-

quences: he was declared an enemy of the party, was evicted
from the country as a traitor, and after eleven years of exile,
was murdered by the dictator's assassin.

Between the wars, adherence to Communism meant obedience to Russia's national interest, for, according to Stalin, socialism and Russia were one and the same. Nevertheless, from
the mid-'30s to the end of World War II, Communists and
democratic socialists intermittently closed ranks against the
paramount danger of fascism. Since then, however, their antipathy has been more intense than ever. Communist parties
have been reduced to nullities in every Western European
democracy save Italy and France. Even in those countries their
strength has been diminishing in recent years, and the possibility of revolution can be discounted. In every other Western
country, democratic socialists—and they either hold power
or form the opposition—can be hardly distinguished from liberals in their social philosophy. (See the excerpt from C. A.
R. Crosland's book, *The Future of Socialism,* a fairly representative statement of socialist thinking in Europe today.)
But while orthodox Marxism is practically extinct and Communists have reduced Marx to empty formulae (Antonio
Gramsci, a selection of whose writings is given below, is an
exception to this), interest in Marx has grown among small
groups of intellectuals, especially in France and Germany,
who are drawn to his early writings on alienation and freedom.

Since World War II socialist or Communist governments
have arisen in countries other than Russia and Western Europe. There are Communist countries in the Balkans, in Eastern Europe, and in Asia which no longer recognize Russian
Communism as their model. Yugoslavia and Poland have developed their own forms of Communism. China has become
Russia's competitor and someday may aspire to be Russia's
master. In the non-Communist world, the new countries in
Africa and Asia have evolved socialisms of their own that are
strange or exasperating to Communists and Western social
democrats alike. There is today an immense variety of socialisms, but what they all have in common is their attachment to
the ideal of social equality to which Europe gave birth over a
century and a half ago.

In the collection of documents below we have attempted to provide only the most rudimentary sketch of the history of socialism. In no other way could we do justice to the subject within the brief compass of a single volume. We are aware of what we have omitted. There are at least ten more socialists whom we would have included had we been able to. Two major considerations governed our choices: the historical significance of the document and its intrinsic value. Most often both were present. But in the case, say, of Stalin's *Foundations of Leninism*, the historic significance is considerable and the intrinsic value negligible. On the other hand Marx's *Economic and Philosophical Manuscripts of 1844* (which was not known to exist until the 1930s) has considerable intrinsic value and negligible historic significance.

The criterion of judgment is of course subjective, and we have given more space to some writers than to others because we believe them to be more important. For this reason we give greatest attention to the utopian socialists and to Marx. They brought socialist thought to its highest pitch of creativity. Since Marx socialism has produced very few original thinkers, though it has—it goes without saying—produced many important ones. Socialism has become an ideology—a relation of ideas to political power—but this, after all, is what its founding fathers had hoped it would become.

Chapter II

EARLY FRENCH COMMUNISM

Although modern socialism did not properly begin until after 1800, it nevertheless had distinct forbears in the preceding century, the age of the *philosophes* and the French Revolution. New ideas of social reform were scattered throughout the growing liberal ideology of eighteenth-century France. Many of us are inclined to look upon the French liberalism of that time in terms of the Anglo-American tradition, which placed a more exclusive stress upon *political* liberty and democracy, and which subscribed to John Locke's conception of property as a natural right that was to be held inviolable by a free society. But many French liberals of the eighteenth century came to view property as an institution that ought to be subject to social regulation—as did Jefferson, for that matter, who was as much influenced by the French tradition as he was by the English. In the Revolutionary scheme of "liberty, equality, fraternity," many Frenchmen took "equality" to be the keystone. And the conception of equality was often enough not simply the American one, which on the whole extended only to the abolition of social and juridical distinction between classes; to Babeuf and some of his predecessors it meant equality of wealth as well.

A modern reader might be tempted to conclude that the men who held to this ideal would have sought to establish a strong central authority. How else could wealth have been equalized in a country the size of eighteenth-century France? But nothing could have been more alien to the libertarian ideal of the French social reformers of the eighteenth and nineteenth centuries; far from being authoritarians (Robespierre to the contrary notwithstanding), most of them harbored a

rather strong anarchist inclination. They were perhaps inconsistent in this (although anarchism and socialism, so apparently incompatible when considered rationally, have persisted
in appearing side by side in the ideologies of various groups
and individuals, right down to the present day), but their conception was far more feasible in terms of the relatively primitive economy of eighteenth-century France than it would be
in terms of the France of today. The citizen of a modern industrial state has to look upon his national economy as a vast,
complex and highly interdependent structure, but to a contemporary of Rousseau it could still seem relatively simple,
and be considered primarily in terms of the ownership and
cultivation of the land. Even the ideology of industrialism in
the nineteenth century originated in part, through Adam
Smith, with the agrarian economics of the French physiocrats.

There is a deeply ingrained French tradition, which still
survives in rural France, of looking upon every head of a
household as a potential owner, or at least cultivator, of some
individual portion of the land, however small; the earth is a
potential network of such parcels. It is one of the strongest
traditions of individual ownership, and hence one of the most
robust sources of individualism and even anarchism, in the
world. Often enough, its political expression is the conservatism of the yeoman property-holder against any form of economic consolidation, whether capitalist or socialist. But it can
easily veer over into a conception of socially regulated property, and from there into a kind of communism. If every man
is entitled to have a portion of the land under his care, then he
should not be deprived of his portion in order that others may
have more than they need. Hence, a Robespierre will conclude
that the holdings must be distributed by society as a whole,
but this is not far from the notion of a Babeuf, who says that
the holdings are not to be private *property* at all.

The critique of property that arose with the liberalism of
eighteenth-century France was not, then, geared to the industrial system at all. Aside from advocating that private
property be eliminated, it had no economic orientation.
Rather, the concern of such a characteristic communist thinker

of the era as Morelly was entirely moral, and the abolition of private ownership was for him simply the focal point of a rationalized social and political structure that would then bring about the moral regeneration of man. For these reasons, Emile Durkheim argues that the communism of eighteenth-century France, like that of such earlier theorists as More, Campanella, and Plato, was not really socialism at all. The good society these men envisaged belonged to another world, and that is why the classic treatises on communism were usually written in the form of a fabulous narration of a voyage to an imaginary utopia.

But the communist theories of eighteenth-century France were different from their predecessors in certain crucial ways. There is in Morelly's *Code of Nature* a heightened passion, an air of outrage, that perhaps did not seem significant at the time, but that can be viewed in retrospect as signs of the coming storm. More important in this respect were the frequency and persistence of communist writings. The utopias of the past had been scattered and isolated works; the France of the eighteenth century produced a steady stream of these writings. Something was in the air; a tradition was being formed. Even the man recognized in his own day as one of the great living moralists, Jean Jacques Rousseau, began the mature phase of his work with a critique of private property. One gets the feeling that many of Rousseau's readers were simply literary gentlemen, cavaliers of the *salon,* whose appreciation of the ideas of a Morelly or a Rousseau was primarily aesthetic. It gratified their sensibilities to read of schemes for a better world, but the programs were visionary and remote, and one did not have to be troubled by the notion of their becoming a reality. The moral earnestness of the slightly rough-edged lower-class Protestant from Geneva was smoothed over into mere sensibility by the atmosphere of the Paris *salons.* But there was nothing in the dour atmosphere of provincial France a generation later to neutralize Babeuf's earnestness. The harshness of poverty and social humiliation provided energy for his ideas; the catalyst of the Revolution transformed this disciple of Rousseau, Morelly, and the communist dreamers of the eighteenth century into the first modern social revolutionary.

MORELLY

Babeuf frequently referred to Diderot, the celebrated encyclopedist, as one of his major sources of inspiration. His writings quoted extensively from the book that he thought the most important of Diderot's works, the *Code of Nature*. This he did on good authority, since the complete edition of Diderot's works published in Amsterdam in 1773 included the *Code of Nature*. Nineteenth-century scholars discovered, however, that the author was not Diderot, but an obscure tutor named Morelly who lived in the town of Vitry-le-François, in northwestern France. His first name, the dates of his birth and death, where he was born, and other elementary biographical details, are not known. All that is certain is that he was the author of several philosophical works, and of an epic poem in rhymed hexameter couplets called the *Basiliad*, which told of a communist utopia in a far-away land. This work was sharply criticized, and Morelly wrote the *Code of Nature* in an attempt to give a systematic philosophical justification of his communist ideas.

The philosophical position expressed in the treatise is imbued with the prevailing rationalism of the mid-eighteenth century, uncritically and almost naively expressed. But added to this is a moral vigor that gives the work its special qualities. The first three parts of the *Code* constitute an exhaustive critique of the evils of the irrationally constructed social system in which men live. Private property is frequently pointed out as the chief source of the trouble. In the last part the author attempts to set down the constitution of a good society. The following selection consists of three passages on property from the first three sections of the work, and a large selection from the constitution in Part Four.

Code of Nature (1755)

. . . The only vice that I perceive in the universe is *Avarice;* all the others, whatever name they be known by, are only variations, degrees, of this one; it is the Proteus, the Mercury, the basis, the vehicle, of all the vices. Analyze vanity, fatuousness, pride, ambition, duplicity, hypocrisy, dishonesty; break down most of our sophistic virtues into their component parts, and they all resolve themselves into this subtle and pernicious element, *the desire to have.* You will even find it at the bottom of disinterestedness.

Now, would this universal plague, this slow fever, *private interest,* ever have been able to take hold if it had found no sustenance, nor even the slightest dangerous ferment?

I believe that no one will contest the justness of this proposition: that *where no property exists, none of its pernicious consequences could exist.* . . .

The true medium of all political or moral demonstration, and the primary cause of all disorder

. . . I dare to conclude here that it is almost mathematically demonstrable that all division of goods, whether equal or unequal, and that all private *property* from among these portions is, in all societies, what Horace calls "material for the highest evil." All moral and political phenomena are the effects of this pernicious cause; through it can be explained and resolved all *theorems* or *problems* about the origin or advancement of, the connection or affinity between, the different virtues and vices, disorders and crimes; about the true motives behind good or bad actions; about all the resolutions or perplexities of the human will; about the depravity of the passions; about the ineffectuality of precepts and laws that are meant to contain them; about the very *technical* faults in these lessons; finally, about all the monstrous productions that come from the aberrations of the mind or the heart. I say that the grounds for all these defects can be seen in the general tendency of legislators to allow the primary link of all sociability to be broken by the usurpation of the resources that should belong in common to all humanity. . . .

That which should remove from man any idea of moral evil

It is therefore certain that this moral principle, "Do good in order to receive good," takes precedence among men over the other maxim, "do not do to others what you would find distasteful if done to you." Now, if you were to take away property, and the blind and pitiless self-interest that accompanies it, you would cause all the prejudices and errors that they sustain to collapse. There would be no more resistance, either offensive or defensive, among men; there would be no more furious passions, ferocious actions, notions nor ideas of *moral evil*. If any were to remain, or if some vestige of it were to re-emerge, this would only be the result of the merest accident, one of the smallest consequence. Minor oppositions of will, obfuscating ever so slightly the light of reason among the opponents, would, far from weakening the domination of natural beneficence, only cause men to have a greater sense of its importance. In a word, there would be only a few small discords in society; it would quickly recover its harmony, and proceed to do far less to trouble this harmony than it would do to prevent it from fading away. . . .

Model of Legislation that Conforms to the Intentions of Nature

I am giving this sketch of laws as a sort of appendix, outside the body of the work itself, since it is unfortunately all too true that to form a republic of this sort would be just about impossible at the present time.

Any sensitive reader will be able to judge from the text, which requires no long commentaries, how many miseries mankind would be spared by the exercise of these laws. I have just proven that it would have been easy for the first legislators to see to it that the peoples of the world were spared the knowledge of any other laws: if my proofs are complete, then I have achieved my objective.

I do not have the temerity to pretend to reform mankind; but I claim at least courage enough to be able to speak the truth untroubled by the outcries of those who bring truth into question because their concern is to deceive mankind, or at least to let it remain entangled in the errors by which they themselves have been duped.

Sacred and Fundamental Laws that would tear out the roots of vice and of all the evils of a society

I. Nothing in society will belong to anyone, either as a personal possession or as capital goods, except the things for which the person has immediate use, for either his needs, his pleasures, or his daily work.

II. Every citizen will be a public man, sustained by, supported by, and occupied at the public expense.

III. Every citizen will make his particular contribution to the activities of the community according to his capacity, his talent and his age; it is on this basis that his duties will be determined, in conformity with the *distributive* laws.

Distributive or Economic Laws

I. In order that everything be carried out in good order, without confusion or trouble, every nation will be enumerated and divided into *families, tribes* and *cities*, and, if the number of cities is large enough, into *provinces* as well.

II. Each tribe will be made up of an equal number of families, each city of an equal number of tribes, and so on.

III. As the nation grows, the tribes and cities will be expanded proportionately, but only until the point is reached where it will be possible to form, out of the additional population, a new city or cities as populous as the original ones.

IV. The number *ten* and its multiples will be the terms of all public division of things and persons; in other words, all enumerations of things, all classifications, weights, measures, etc., will be made up of decimal parts.

V. For each occupation, there will be so and so many *tens*, or so and so many *hundreds*, of workers, in proportion to the difficulty of the work, and in proportion to what is necessary to provide for the needs of a given city without overtiring the workers.

VI. In order to regulate the distribution of the products of nature and art, it should first of all be noted that some products are *durable,* which is to say that they can be preserved, or that they remain usable for a long time. Among the products of this sort are: (1) those that are in daily and general use, (2) those that are in general use, but not all the time, (3) those that are constantly in use by at least one or a few persons at a time, and are used by everybody in the long run, (4) those that are never of either general or constant use: these latter are made by specific agreements for individual tastes. Now, all these durable products will be gathered together in public stores in order to be distributed to all the citizens, daily or at some other specified interval in the case of the first three categories of products, or on request, in the case of the fourth category.

VII. It should also be noted that there is an order of products of nature and art that are *perishable.* These things will be brought to the public places and distributed there by those assigned in advance to the production and preparation of goods of this sort.

VIII. The quantities of the products of every variety will be determined, and will then be apportioned, either according to the number of citizens of each city, or according to the number of those who use the particular product; the durable products will be publicly distributed according to the same rules, and their surplus will be placed in reserve.

IX. In the case of the provisions that are made only on request, whether they be of a general or particular use, if the supply begins to run out before all orders have been filled, even if it is apparent that only one citizen will be deprived of his share, then all distribution of the product will be suspended, or else it will be apportioned in greatly reduced quantities, until the lack has been corrected. But particular care must be taken to prevent mishaps of this sort in the case of goods in general use.

X. The surplus provisions of each city or province will be distributed among those in which there is danger of a shortage, or will be held in reserve for future cases of need.

XI. In accordance with the *sacred laws,* nothing will be sold or exchanged between citizens. Someone who needs, for example, greens, vegetables or fruits, will go to the public square, which is where these items will have been brought by the men who cultivate them, and take what he needs for one day only. If someone needs bread, he will go to the baker and get the quantity that he needs for some specified period, and the baker will go to the public store to get the amount of grain that he needs for the quantity of bread that he has to prepare, whether for one day or several. Whoever needs an article of clothing will get it from the man who makes such articles, while the clothing-maker will get his fabrics from the man who manufactures them, and the manufacturer of fabrics will, in turn, get his raw material from the public store, where it will have been brought by those who cut or gather it: and so on, for all things that are to be distributed to heads of families, for their use and that of their children.

XII. If the nation helps a neighboring or foreign nation by sending it some of its goods, or is helped in this way by some other nation, this commerce alone will be by the method of exchange, and will be carried out through the intermediary of citizens whose transactions will be public; but scrupulous care must be taken to see to it that such commerce does not introduce private property of any sort into the republic.

Agrarian Laws

I. Every city will have a stretch of cultivable land that will be as contiguous and as uniform as possible, that will not be held either as a whole or in part as private property by anyone, and that will be sufficient for the subsistence of the inhabitants.

II. If a city is situated in an arid region, then only crafts will be practiced there, and the neighboring cities will provide what is necessary for the subsistence of its inhabitants: but this city will nevertheless have, like every other community, its corps of agricultural workers, who will work either in the city's own territory wherever there are arable places, or in the agricultural areas of the neighboring cities.

III. Every citizen between the ages of twenty and twenty-five, without exception, will be required to do agricultural work, unless some infirmity renders him unable to do so. . . .

Edile Laws

I. Since the number of families in a tribe will not exceed a certain amount, or at least will exceed it by very little, and the number of tribes in a city will never exceed a certain amount by more than a margin of one, the area of every city will be very nearly the same.

II. The public stores for all supplies and the public assembly rooms will be erected, in the form of a uniform and pleasant structure, around a great, even-sided, town square.

III. Outside this quadrangle will be the neighborhoods of the city, distributed at regular intervals, equal in size, of the same shape, and uniformly divided up into streets.

IV. Each tribe will occupy a neighborhood, and each family will have spacious and comfortable lodgings within it; all these buildings will be uniform.

V. All the neighborhoods of the city will be laid out in such a way that they can be expanded whenever necessary without disturbing the regularity of the arrangement, and these expansions will not exceed certain limits.

VI. Some distance away, around the various neighborhoods of the city, arcades will be built, housing the workshops of every mechanical profession in which the corps of workers exceeds ten in number.

VII. Beyond this belt of workshops will be erected another circle of buildings to house persons who are employed in agriculture and related occupations. These buildings will also serve as workshops for these occupations, or as barns, store-rooms, stables, or tool-sheds, in whatever number these things are required by the particular city.

VIII. Beyond all these ranges of buildings, some distance away and in the most felicitous possible location, will be erected a spacious and comfortable building, in which every citizen who is ill will be lodged and cared for.

IX. Not far away, a comfortable retreat for all aged and infirm citizens will be erected.

X. Somewhere else, in the most unpleasant and barren location that can be found, will be erected a building surrounded by high walls, divided into small cells and enclosed

in iron bars, in which all those who deserve to be separated
from society for a time will be incarcerated. . . .

Police Laws

I. In every occupation, the oldest and most experienced will
take turns every five days, according to seniority, in supervising five or ten of their companions, and will demand no
more nor less work of them than they would demand of themselves.

II. In every occupational group, there will be one master
for every ten or twenty workers, and it will be his task to instruct them, inspect their work, and report on their work and
conduct to the chief of the corps, who will be chosen annually. Every master will hold his position for life, and will
take his turn at being chief of the corps.

III. No one will be master in an occupation sooner than one
year after he has completed his agricultural service and returned to his original occupation, that is, not before he is
twenty-six years of age. . . .

V. At the age of ten, every citizen will begin learning the
occupation toward which he is inclined, and of which he seems
to be capable without excessively straining himself: at the age
of fifteen or eighteen he will be married: between the ages of
twenty and twenty-five, he will perform one of the agricultural
occupations: at twenty-six he will become a master either in
his original occupation, if he returns to it, or in an agricultural
occupation, if he chooses to remain in one. But, if he decides to
take up an entirely different line of work, he cannot become a
master until the age of thirty. At the age of forty, every citizen
who has not by then become a master in some trade will be a
free-lance worker, which is to say that, without being exempt
from doing work altogether, he will nevertheless not be forced
to do any work other than what he chooses, or any task other
than what he imposes upon himself; he will be the master of
his own free hours. . . .

VII. The chiefs of each occupation will indicate the hours
of rest and of work, and will designate which jobs have to be
performed.

VIII. Every fifth day will be a public day of rest; for this reason, the year will be divided into seventy-three equal parts; every leap year, one of the days of rest will be doubled.

IX. Public festivals will always begin on a day of rest, and will last six days, counting the day on which they begin.

X. The festivals will be celebrated immediately after the first plowing, before the beginning of the harvest, after the picking of the various fruits, and at the beginning of each year. During this last festival, all marriages will be performed, and the annually appointed chiefs of cities and of occupational groups will take up their posts.

Sumptuary Laws

I. At the age of thirty, every citizen will be allowed to dress according to his taste, but not in any excessively fancy way. He will take his nourishment within his family circle as before, without intemperance or gluttony. The senators and chiefs are authorized by this law to punish all excesses in this matter, and they are themselves to give an example of moderation to others.

II. The young people between the ages of twenty and thirty will be dressed uniformly within each occupation, in apparel that is both clean and appropriate to their particular work. Each corps will be distinguished by some color appropriate to the principal object of its work, or by some other distinguishing mark.

III. Every citizen will have both a work suit and a holiday suit, each of them modestly and appropriately adorned; the attire will be no more splendid than what the republic can afford, and no ornament will be permitted that might make a person stand out from the others in preference or regard. All manifestations of vanity will be suppressed by the chiefs and the fathers of families.

Laws Pertaining to the Form of Government that would prevent all tyrannical domination

I. Every head of a family will become a senator at the age of fifty, and will have a deliberative and decisive voice in every regulation that must be made pursuant to the intentions of the laws that the Senate is to preserve.

II. The other chiefs of families or of professional corps will be consulted in the regulation of matters concerning their occupations.

III. Every family in a tribe will take its turn in providing a chief for the tribe, who will hold that position for the rest of his life.

IV. The tribal chiefs will take turns at being chief of the city for terms of one year.

V. Each city will have its turn in providing a chief for the province, which will be an annual appointment, made by turns from the chiefs of each of the tribes of the city. . . .

VI. Each province will have its turn in providing a chief for the entire state, who will hold that position for life. . . .

Laws of Administration and Government

I. The function of the Supreme Senate will be to examine the decisions and directives of the Senates of each city and to see to it that they contain nothing that could contradict the laws of the state, either in the present or the future, and that the measures taken for police purposes or for the economy are wise and in conformity with the intentions of the laws. In consequence of this examination, the Supreme Senate will confirm or reject these particular directives in whole or in part: whatever has been thus fixed as law for a single city will then be observed in all the others, and will be given the force of law by the acquiescence of the local Senates. . . .

IX. The annually appointed chiefs of cities and of provinces will occupy themselves only with their express functions; after the expiration of their terms, they will then be free to practice whatever profession they wish. . . .

X. Every senator, political chief, workshop overseer and master artisan will be respected and obeyed in matters pertaining to the common service of the country, just as fathers of families are respected by their children.

XI. The formula of every public directive will be: *Reason wills it, the Law commands it.* . . .

Conjugal Laws that would do away with all debauchery

I. Every citizen will be married as soon as he has reached

the marriageable age; no one will be exempt from this, at least as long as nature or health presents no obstacle.

II. The marriage ceremonies will be held publicly at the beginning of each year. The young people of both sexes will be brought together in the presence of the city Senate; every boy will choose the girl that pleases him and, after obtaining her consent, will take her as his wife.

III. The first marriage will be indissoluble for a period of ten years, after which divorce will be permitted, either at the consent of both partners in the marriage, or of one only. . . .

Educational Laws that would prevent the consequences of the blind indulgence of children by their parents

I. Mothers will nurse their own children if their health permits, and will not be exempted from this without unquestionable proof of their indisposition. . . .

IV. Within each tribe, all children reaching the age of five will be brought together, and the two sexes will be separately housed and fed in an establishment set aside for this purpose. Their food, clothing and elementary education will be uniform throughout the land, without any distinctions, in accordance with rules that will be set down by the Senate.

V. For periods of five days at a time, groups of parents will succeed one another in taking care of the children in these establishments with as much care as they would give to their own, under the supervision of the tribal chief. They will apply themselves to inspiring moderation and obedience in their charges, and will try to prevent, through the use of either gentle persuasion or mild punishment, all discords, caprices, or bad habits; they will treat all the children with absolute equality.

VI. As their reason begins to develop, the children will be instructed in the laws of the country. They will be taught to respect the laws, to obey their parents, the chiefs, and other mature persons. They will be shown how to get along with their equals, to cultivate friendship with them, and never to lie. They will be instructed in activities suitable to their age, and, from time to time, in games that will help them to mold their bodies and prepare them for mature work. Nothing will

be prescribed for them until they have first been made to see
its reasonableness. These first instructions will continue to be
cultivated by the masters, into whose care the children will be
entrusted upon their leaving the first phase of childhood.

VII. Those children who prove to be robust enough to start
learning, even before reaching the age of ten, the first princi
ples of the profession for which they have been judged suitable, will be sent to the public workshops for several hours
every day to begin their apprenticeship.

VIII. All children upon reaching the age of ten, will leave
the common paternal residence and go into workshops, where
they will be housed, fed and dressed, and where they will be
instructed by the masters and chiefs of the various professions,
whom they will obey as they would their own parents. They
will all receive common treatment in every corps and in every
workshop, where the two sexes will be separated and instructed in the occupations that suit them.

IX. The masters and mistresses, as well as the chiefs, in
each profession, will include moral instruction in the technical exercises that they give. As the children begin to develop
their rational faculties, some of them will begin to realize
that there is a divinity, and, having heard people speak of it,
they will begin to ask questions about this supreme being. In
answer to their questions, they will be made to understand
that this supreme being is the first and beneficent cause of
everything that they admire or find to be lovable and good.
Care will be taken not to give them any vague idea of this
ineffable being, nor to pretend to explain his nature with
terms that are void of sense: they will be told quite plainly
that the author of the universe can be known only by his
works, which proclaim him to be nothing other than a being
who is infinitely good and wise, and that one cannot compare
him to anything mortal. The young people will be made to
realize that the feelings of sociability present in man are the
sole oracles of divine intentions, and that it is in observing
these sentiments that one can come to realize what a god is.
They will be told that the laws are made in order to perfect
these sentiments, and in order to apply systematically what
these sentiments prescribe for the good of society.

X. All precepts, all maxims, all moral reflections, will be derived from the *Sacred and Fundamental Laws,* and always with respect to social unity and sympathy. All exhortations will emphasize the happiness of the individual as inseparably linked with the common good, and people will be encouraged to have the esteem and friendship of their fellow citizens and chiefs as the object of their endeavors.

XI. The chiefs and senators will watch carefully to see to it that the laws and rules for the education of children are everywhere exactly and uniformly observed, and to see to it above all that those faults of childhood that could tend to develop into *the spirit of private ownership (l'esprit de propriété)* are wisely prevented or corrected. They will also prevent the minds of the very young from becoming imbued with any ridiculous myth, tale or fiction.

XII. At the age of fifteen or sixteen, when the young people are married, they will leave the Public Academies and return to their paternal homes. . . .

Laws of Study that would prevent all aberrations of the human mind and all unworldly reveries

I. The number of persons engaged in the sciences, and in the arts that demand more sagacity, penetration, concentration, industriousness and talent than they do physical strength, will be determined, so many for each branch of study, and so many for each city. The citizens best suited for work of this type will be instructed in it from an early age, although this type of study will not exempt them from their term of agricultural work when they reach the age for it. Nobody, except for the prescribed number of masters and pupils in the arts and sciences, will be permitted to give his time to pursuits of this sort before reaching the age of thirty. At that age, those whose experience has perfected their understanding and developed their inclinations in the direction of some pursuit more elevated than the one in which they had previously been engaged, will be able to enter the arts or sciences.

II. There will be absolutely no moral philosophy other than that worked out within the system of laws. The observations and precepts of this science will rest exclusively on the utility and wisdom of these laws, on the satisfactions that come from ties of blood and friendship, on the mutual service and regard that unite the citizens, on the usefulness of work, on love, on all the general and special rules of good order and perfect concord. The study of this science will be common to all the citizens.

III. All metaphysics will reduce itself to what was said above concerning the divinity. As for man, it will be pointed out that he is endowed with reason, which is destined to make him sociable; that the nature of his faculties, as well as the natural principles of their operation, are unknown to us; that it is only the *processes* of this reason that can be observed and followed by the thoughtful application of that same faculty; and that we do not know what constitutes the basis and sustenance of this faculty within us, just as we do not know what becomes of this principle when we die. It could perhaps be said that this *principe intelligent* subsists even after life, but that it is useless to attempt to know a condition about which the author of nature has not instructed us in any palpable way: such will be the prescribed limits of speculations of this sort.

IV. Complete freedom will be allowed to the sagacity and penetration of the human mind in those speculative and experimental sciences that have as their object inquiry either into the secrets of nature, or into ways of perfecting the arts useful to society.

V. There will be a sort of public code for all the sciences, in which nothing beyond the limits prescribed by the laws will ever be added to metaphysics or to morals. Only discoveries in physics, mathematics, or mechanics, confirmed by reasoning and experiment, will be added to the code.

VI. The moral and physical beauty of nature, of the objects of the sciences, of the pleasures and satisfactions of living in society, and the honor of the citizens who have contributed in a distinguished manner to the perfecting of things, will be celebrated in oratory, poetry, and painting.

VII. Every local Senate will maintain a written record of the activities of chiefs and of citizens worthy of being com-

memorated; but care will be taken to see that these histories
are free of all exaggeration, flattery and, above all, of all falsification. The Supreme Senate will put all these histories together to compose the history of the whole nation.

VIII. Every chapter of these laws will be engraved separately on the necessary number of columns erected in the
public square of each city, and their intentions will always
be followed according to the proper, direct, and literal sense
of the text, the slightest alteration of which will never be
permitted. If some obscurity or ambiguity should be found
in any one of the laws, it will be necessary either to try to
explain it by some other law, or to determine the meaning
of this law once and for all, in the way most favorable to the
principles of the *Sacred and Fundamental Laws.*

JEAN JACQUES ROUSSEAU (1712–78)

Rousseau is the intellectual forebear of the radical strain
in the French Revolution, in its various manifestations from
middle-class Jacobinism to the communism of Babeuf. He
was not one of the eighteenth-century communists, and his
own predilections were probably as far from those of Babeuf
as they were from the militant authoritarianism of Robespierre. Rather, he was one of the most radical of individual-
ists. But the stress on the principle of community in his
great work, *The Social Contract,* and his earlier statements
about equality and the corrupting effects of private property
lent themselves to a communist interpretation of his ideas.
Babeuf had no doubt that he was simply implementing
Rousseau's theories.

Perhaps Rousseau's most important legacy to the men of
the French Revolution was the quality of high moral fervor
with respect to social questions that is to be found throughout his writings. Such apostles of the act of feeling as
Edmund Burke and Johann Gottlieb Fichte seemed to imagine that the ideology of the French Revolution was exclusively the product of the cerebrations of cold-hearted

rationalists; in fact, much of it came from a romantic puritan-
ism that differed from their own only in having a higher
degree of fierceness. Coming from such products of a Catholic
culture as Robespierre and Babeuf, this might have surprised
the Protestants Burke and Fichte, who presumably conceived of all French Catholicism in the unruffled image of
the Paris aristocracy. But they should have perceived a
kindred spirit in the Calvinist from Geneva, whose unflagging preoccupation with morality not only was present in
his propositions for a republic of virtue in *The Social Contract,* but had appeared as far back as his first major work,
the *Discourse on the Moral Effects of the Arts and Sciences,*
published in 1750. In this essay, which challenged the
assumption that the arts were conducive to moral perfection,
and in the *Discourse on the Origin of Inequality,* which appeared five years later, Rousseau formulated a major challenge to the most cherished notions of the Paris salon society
that had hitherto lionized him. His attitude foreshadowed
the bourgeois revolution against feudalism that was to come.

Rousseau's criticism of property, in the *Discourse on the
Origin of Inequality,* appeared in the same year as Morelly's
Code, but he did not draw conclusions anything like the
communist program of Morelly. Nevertheless, his work is of
greater import in the revolutionary socialist tradition than
the *Code of Nature.* Rousseau took an important step when
he attempted to draw upon the anthropological knowledge
of his time in order to reconstruct systematically the origins
of private property and to show how it caused the evils of
society to evolve. His anthropology was not sound, but his
way of looking at social questions in historical terms was
full of possibilities for the future. Babeuf inherited this primitive historical consciousness, which later developed into a
fundamental element in the revolutionary outlook during the
nineteenth century.

DISCOURSE ON THE ORIGIN OF INEQUALITY
AMONG MEN (1755)

SECOND PART

The first man who, after enclosing a plot of land, saw fit to say: "This is mine," and found people who were simple enough to believe him, was the true founder of civil society. How many crimes, wars, murders, sufferings and horrors mankind would have been spared if someone had torn up the stakes or filled up the moat and cried to his fellows: "Don't listen to this impostor; you are lost if you forget that the earth belongs to no one, and that its fruits are for all!" But there is much evidence to indicate that, by that time, things had already reached the point of being unable to go on as they had: for this idea of property, which depended upon many preceding ideas that could only make their appearance one after another, did not take shape in the human mind all of a sudden. There had to be many advances; people had to acquire a great deal of knowledge and technique, and transmit and augment it all from one era to the next, before this last point in the state of nature could be arrived at. . . .

As long as men were satisfied with their rustic cabins, as long as they confined themselves to sewing together with thorns or fishbones the pelts that they used as clothing, to adorning themselves with plumes and shells, to painting their bodies in various colors, to painting and embellishing their bows and arrows, to hewing with sharp stones a few fishing canoes and crude musical instruments; in a word, as long as they applied themselves to tasks that took no more than one person to perform them, and as long as the arts did not require the combined efforts of several hands, their lives were free, healthy, happy and good for as long as their nature would allow, and they continued to enjoy the fruits of an independent commerce among themselves. But the moment one man needed the help of another; when someone perceived it was useful to have the tools of two men; then equality disappeared. Property was introduced, work became

necessary, and the vast forests were changed into glowing
fields that had to be watered with the sweat of men, where
one could soon see slavery and misery germinating and
ripening along with the crops.

Metallurgy and agriculture, once they had been discovered, were the two arts that produced this great revolution. For the poet it was gold and silver, but for the philosopher it was iron and wheat that civilized mankind and
caused it to be lost. Thus, both these arts were unknown
to the savages of America, and that is why they have remained as they are; other peoples seem to have remained
barbarous even when they practiced one of these arts but not
the other. And perhaps one of the main reasons that Europe
has been the most constantly and thoroughly civilized part
of the world, even if not the earliest to be so, is that it is at
once the most abundant in iron and the most fertile in wheat
of all parts of the world. . . .

The invention of other arts was necessary to force mankind
to apply itself to the art of agriculture. As soon as men were
needed to smelt and forge iron, others had to provide them
with sustenance. As the number of foundry workers grew, the
number of those employed in providing the common subsistence diminished, even though the number of mouths to
feed remained the same; and, since the one group needed
the produce of agriculture in exchange for its iron, the other
group finally discovered the secret of employing iron to increase the amount of its produce. From this arrangement was
born, on the one hand, agriculture and plowing, and on the
other hand, the art of working metal and multiplying its uses.

From the cultivation of the land there necessarily followed
the partitioning of it, and from property, once acknowledged,
the first rules of justice: for, in order to render to each man
what is his, it is necessary that he be able to have something.
Furthermore, as men began to look toward the future and see
how much it was now possible for them to lose, every one of
them found reason to fear reprisal for the wrongs that he
might do others. This origin is the most natural, for it is impossible to conceive of property being born in any other way
than through manual labor; it is hard to see what more a man

can apply than his labor to appropriate things that he did not make in the first place. It is only labor which, giving the cultivator the right to the product of the land he has plowed, gives him therefore the right to the ground as well, at least until the harvest, and thus from year to year; this arrangement, which establishes continuous possession, easily transforms itself into property. Grotius says that when the ancients gave Ceres the epithet "Legislatress," and on one holiday celebrated the name of Thesmophoria in her honor, they were indicating that the partitioning of the land had produced a new sort of right: the right of property, which is different from the right that derives from natural law.

Things could have remained equal in this state of affairs if talents had been equal, and if, for example, the use of iron and the consumption of agricultural products had constantly maintained an exact balance. But the proportion that was maintained by nothing was soon disrupted. The stronger did more work; the more adroit drew greater advantage from what they had; and the more ingenious found ways of reducing their work-load. The plowman had more need of iron, and the blacksmith had more need of wheat, and, though they did an equal amount of work, one man earned a great deal, while another could scarcely earn a livelihood. This is how natural inequality surreptitiously deploys itself along with inequality of combination, so that the differences between men, developed by differences of circumstance, become more evident and more permanent in their effects, and thus begin to wield their influence in the same proportion over the destiny of individuals.

Once things have reached this point, it is easy to imagine the rest. I will not take time to describe the successive inventions of the other arts, the progress of languages, the development and expanding application of the various talents, the growing inequality of fortunes, or the use and abuse of wealth; nor will I describe all the details that follow from these, which anyone can easily fill in. I shall confine myself solely to having a look at mankind established in this new order of things.

Here we are then, with all our faculties developed, our

memory and imagination in play, our self-esteem at work,
our reason active, and our mind almost at the summit of
the perfection of which it is capable. Here we are with all our
natural qualities in action, and the rank and life-situation of
every man established, not only with respect to the quantity
of goods in his possession, and his power to serve or to do
harm, but also with respect to his mind, his beauty, his
strength or skill, his merit or talent. Because these qualities
were the only ones that could win any consideration, one
soon had either to have them or to be able to affect them.
To gain any advantage, one soon had to show himself as
something different from what he actually was. To be and
to seem became two entirely different things, and from this
distinction arose pomp and ceremony, deceitful trickery,
and all the vices that follow in their wake. On the other
hand, look what man became, as a result of a multitude of
newly developed needs, from the free and independent spirit
that he once had been: a subject creature, so to speak, in
the domain of all nature, and even with regard to his fellow
men, whose slave he became in a sense, even when he was
also their master. Rich, he needs their services; poor, he
needs their help, and even moderate means does not render a
man able to dispense with this help. He must seek incessantly
to interest others in his lot and make them realize, or at any
rate seem to realize, that it is in their interest to work for his
sake: a situation that makes him cunning and two-faced
with some, tough and domineering with others, and that
forces him to abuse all those whom he needs when he cannot
make them fear him, and when he does not find it in his interest to perform any useful service for them. Finally, consuming ambition, the ardor to raise one's relative fortune,
which is due less to a genuine need than to a desire to stand
out from the others, inspires in all men a dark inclination to
do harm to one another, and a secret jealousy that is all the
more dangerous because, in order to make its weapons more
effective, it often assumes the guise of benevolence. In a
word, competition and rivalry on the one hand, opposition
of interests on the other, and everywhere the hidden desire to
profit at the expense of others—all these evils are the initial

effect of property and the burgeoning inequality that comes
inevitably in its wake.

Before its representative symbols were invented, wealth
could scarcely have consisted of anything more than land and
animals, these being the sole real goods that man can possess. Now, when estates had grown so in number and extent
as to cover all the land and touch upon one another, it was
no longer possible to aggrandize oneself except at the expense of others. The supernumeraries, whom weakness or
indolence had prevented from acquiring some share of their
own, became poor without losing anything, because, as
everything changed around them, they themselves did not
change at all, so that they were obliged to receive or to rob
their subsistence from the rich. That is how domination and
servitude, or rapine and violence, depending upon the character of the people involved, came into being. The rich,
for their part, no sooner learned the pleasure of dominating,
than they soon disdained all others, and, making use of their
already acquired slaves to get new ones, they began to dream
only of subjugating their neighbors and placing them in
servitude: something like those hungry wolves who, once
they have tasted human flesh, repudiate all other kinds of
food, and henceforth want to devour only men.

Thus, as the most powerful or the most wretched made
out of their strength or their needs a sort of right to the
goods or services of others, a right that was equivalent,
according to them, to that of property, equality was destroyed, and this was followed by the most dreadful disorder.
Thus, usurpation by the wealthy, brigandage by the poor,
and the unbridled passions of all, smothered all natural pity
along with the still feeble voice of justice, and rendered men
avaricious, ambitious, and wicked. Between the right of the
strongest and the right of the first occupant there emerged
a perpetual conflict that terminated only in battles and
murders. Newborn society yielded to the most horrible state
of war: mankind, debased and desolate, unable either to
retrace its steps or to renounce the unhappy acquisitions it
had made, preoccupied, to its shame, only in abusing the

faculties that had been the glory of the human species, brought itself to the brink of ruin.

It was inevitable that men finally began to reflect upon such a wretched situation and upon the calamities by which they were being overwhelmed. The rich in particular were soon bound to feel how much of a disadvantage it was for them to be in a perpetual state of war, the costs of which they alone had to bear, and which subjected all men in common to the risk of life and property. Besides, however much they were able to color their usurpations in their own eyes, they were reasonably well aware that they were standing upon a precarious and abusive right, and that, since they had made their acquisitions only through force, force could just as easily take it all away from them, and they would have no grounds for complaint. Even those who had become rich solely through their own industry could not claim a much better title to their property. They could say as often as they wanted, "I am the one who built this wall; I have earned this plot of land through my own efforts." "Who allotted it to you?" someone might have answered them, "and by what right do you claim payment at our expense for work that we have not imposed upon you? Do you realize that a multitude of your brothers are perishing and suffering from need of what you have in excess, and that you must have the express and unanimous consent of all of mankind before you can be allowed to appropriate from the common subsistence anything beyond what you need to maintain yourself?" Deprived of all valid grounds upon which he might justify himself and of sufficient strength to defend himself; easily crushed by bandit hordes even though himself easily capable of crushing one person at a time; alone against everyone, and unable, because of mutual jealousies, to ally himself with his equals against enemies united by the common hope of pillage, the rich man, under the pressure of necessity, finally conceived the most clever project ever to enter the human mind: to turn to his advantage the strength of the very men who were attacking him, to make his adversaries into his defenders, to inspire them with different maxims and give them different institutions, ones that were as favorable to him as the principle of natural right was not.

With this aim in mind, after having opened the eyes of his neighbors to the horrors of a situation in which they were all arming themselves against one another, in which their possessions were becoming as onerous to them as their needs, and in which no one found any security either in poverty or in wealth, he easily found specious reasons to win them over to his purposes. "Let us unite," he said to them, "to guarantee the weak against oppression, to restrain the ambitious, and to assure to every man the possession of what belongs to him: let us establish rules of peace and justice to which everyone will be obliged to conform, from which no one will be exempted, that will make up in some way for the caprices of fortune, by submitting the weak and the powerful equally to mutual duties. In a word, instead of turning our strength against ourselves, let us merge it into a supreme power that will govern us in accordance with wise laws, protect and defend all the members of the association, repulse the common enemy, and maintain us in a condition of internal harmony."

It did not require even as much as the equivalent of this speech to win over men who were crude and easy to seduce, who furthermore had too many matters to untangle between themselves to be able to dispense with arbitrators, and too much avarice and ambition to do without masters for very long. They all rushed to have themselves placed in irons, believing that they were thereby assuring their liberty; for, though they were endowed with enough reason to be able to sense the advantages of a political establishment, they did not have experience enough to be able to foresee its dangers. Those most capable of foreseeing the possibility of abuse were precisely those who intended to profit by it; and even wise men saw that it was necessary to sacrifice one part of their liberty in order to preserve the other, just as a wounded man has his arm amputated so that the rest of the body can be saved.

Such was, or is likely to have been, the origin of society and of laws, which formed new obstacles for the weak and gave new strength to the rich, destroyed natural liberty be-

yond the possibility of its return, enshrined the law of property and inequality for all time, made an adroit usurpation
into an irrevocable right, and, for the sake of the profit of a
few ambitious men, henceforth subjected all mankind to
misery, labor and servitude. One can readily see how
the establishment of a single society rendered indispensable
the establishment of all the others, and how, in order to
form a united force, each must unify in its turn. Societies,
multiplying and expanding rapidly, soon covered the whole
surface of the earth, and it became impossible to find a
single corner of the universe where a man could break out
from under the yoke and withdraw from beneath the sword
that every man perpetually saw suspended over his head,
and that was so often brought wantonly into play. Civil law
having thus become the common rule for all the citizens,
the law of nature no longer applied anywhere except between
one society and another, where, under the name of the law
of nations, it was tempered by a few tacit conventions that
made commerce possible and took the place of the natural
compassion that is normally felt by one man for another but
almost entirely lost between nations—except where it is felt
by a few great cosmopolitan spirits who are not contained
by the imaginary barriers that separate the peoples of the
world, and who, following the example of the Sovereign
Being that created them, embrace all of mankind in their
benevolence.

The bodies politic, remaining thus in a state of nature
with respect to one another, soon began to feel the disadvantages that had caused private individuals to leave it, for
that state became even more deadly among these great
bodies than it previously had been among the individuals
composing them. This was the beginning of national wars,
battles, murders, reprisals, all of which shock reason and
cause nature to tremble, as well as of these horrible predilections that place among the virtues the honor of having caused
human blood to flow. The most honorable men learned to
consider it one of their duties to cut the throats of their fellows. Soon there was the spectacle of men slaughtering one
another by the thousands without knowing why they were

doing so; it came to pass that more murders were committed in a single day of battle, and more horrors in the taking of a single town, than had been committed in the state of nature throughout entire centuries, and over all the surface of the earth. Such are the first effects that can be perceived of the division of mankind into different societies. Let us return to their institutions.

I know that some have depicted the origin of political society in other terms, such as the conquests of the powerful, or the union of the weak; the choice between one or another of these causes has no bearing upon what I am trying to establish. Meanwhile, the account that I have given seems to me the most natural for the following reasons: (1) In the first case, because the right of conquest is not a right at all, it cannot be the foundation for any other; and so the conqueror and the conquered people remain in a perpetual state of war against one another, except if it should happen that the people, once their liberty had been restored, should choose the conqueror for their chief. Short of that eventuality, whatever capitulations had been made would be founded only upon violence, and would therefore be null and void; therefore there cannot be, in this hypothesis, either a true society or a body politic, or any law but that of the strong. (2) In the second case, these words *strong* and *weak* are equivocal; for, in the interval between the establishment of the right of property or of the first occupant and the establishment of political governments, the meaning of these terms is better rendered by the words *rich* and *poor*, because a man really has no way, before the existence of laws, of subjecting his equals other than to attack their property or make them part of his own property. (3) It would have been insane for the poor, having nothing to lose but their freedom, to give up willingly the only possession that remained to them, to receive nothing in return; but since the rich, on the other hand, are sensitive, so to speak, in all parts of their possessions, it would have been much easier for them to be harmed. They therefore had to take greater precautions to guarantee their security; and finally, it is reasonable to suppose that a thing has been invented by those to whom it is useful, rather than by those whom it wrongs.

The newly created government did not have a constant and regular form. The defects of philosophy and of experience prevented men from seeing any other problems than those immediately at hand, and nobody dreamed of dealing with any others except as they arose. Despite all the efforts of the wisest legislators, the political state always remained imperfect, because it was almost entirely the creation of chance, and because, since it had been badly begun, time could never correct the vices of its constitution merely by discovering defects and suggesting remedies. One constantly made adjustments, instead of beginning, as one ought to have done, by clearing the air and getting rid of all the old materials, as Lycurgus had done at Sparta, and then going on to put up a solid edifice. Society at first consisted only in several general conventions that all the individuals were committed to observe, and by which the community established its own security with regard to each individual. It took experience to show how weak such a constitution was, and how easy it was for offenders to avoid conviction or punishment for infractions when the public alone was to act as witness and judge; the law had to be eluded in a thousand ways, and trouble and disorder to multiply continuously, before people thought of conferring the dangerous burden of public authority upon private individuals, and of turning over to magistrates the task of seeing to it that the deliberations of the people were observed; for, to say that the chiefs were chosen before the confederation was created, and that the ministers of the laws existed before the laws themselves, is a supposition that cannot be taken seriously.

It would not be reasonable to suppose that the peoples were first thrown into the hands of an absolute master without conditions and without recourse, and that the first means of providing for the common security imagined by proud and indomitable men was that they should precipitate themselves into slavery. In truth, why did they hand themselves over to superiors, if not to obtain defense against oppression, protection for their property, for their lives, and for their freedom, these being the constitutive elements of their being, so to speak? Now since, in the relations between man and man, the worst thing that can happen to one is to find himself subject to the will of another, would it not have been contrary to common sense for men to let a leader deprive them of the very things they were seeking his help to protect? What could he have offered them in exchange for the concession of such a fine right? And if he had dared demand it of them under the pretext of defending them, would he not have immediately received the apologist's reply: "What more will the enemy do to us?" It is therefore incontestable—and this is the fundamental maxim of all political right—that the peoples set up chiefs to defend their liberty and not to reduce them to servitude. "If we have a prince," said Pliny to Trajan, "it is in order that he keep us from having a master." . . .

"GRACCHUS" BABEUF (1760–97)

AND THE CONSPIRACY OF THE EQUALS

On May 11, 1796, after almost two years of the moderate republican rule that had succeeded Robespierre's dictatorship and was to last until Napoleon's *coup d'état* in 1799, the leaders of a group that called itself the Society of the Pantheon were accused of plotting to overthrow the government and arrested. This "conspiracy of the equals," as it came to be called, was at first regarded as one of many plots uncovered during the period of the Directorate, and the government even treated it as a royalist conspiracy. But the leader of the group, the journalist François Noël Babeuf, who had indicated his choice of spiritual antecedents by styling himself "Gracchus," used the trial as an opportunity to denounce the decline of the Revolution, and to restate its aims in terms of a vision of communist egalitarianism. Babeuf was sentenced to death, along with Darthé, another of the group's leaders, and they were executed the following year; the others were sentenced to short terms and ultimately released. Among those whose lives were spared was an Italian named Buonarroti, a descendant of the family of Michelangelo, who went on to write an account of the conspiracy that transformed Babouvism into a legend. The book became a source of inspiration for such middle-class revolutionary movements as the Carbonari, as well as for socialist movements such as Chartism. Babeuf can be said to be the bridge between eighteenth-century communism and modern socialism.

There is another aspect of Babeuf besides his program in which he represents the furthest extreme of the French Revolution; he was among the humblest in social origin of those who achieved political eminence in this period. Not that he was from the very bottom of the social scale—such a thing could not have come about in eighteenth-century France, even at the time of the Revolution. His father was a *déclassé* ex-army major, who claimed to be able to trace his ancestry back to the founder of the village of Babeuf in Picardy, but who had been reduced for a time to working as a hired laborer. The Babeufs came of a line of independent peasant proprietors, in a part of France where yeoman traditions were strong—Robespierre, and possibly Morelly, were also from Picardy. By the time his son was born, on November 23, 1760, the elder Babeuf had obtained the modest post of a local tax-collector in the town of Saint-Quentin. The future conspirator for equality seemed to have no greater prospects than his father for any other life than that of a provincial functionary; after marriage to a servant girl at the age of twenty-two, he settled down as a struggling family man and clerk. His post was that of *commissaire à terrier*, a minor professional position widespread in provincial France at that time, which had as its primary function the task of keeping straight the archives and transactions of feudal estates. Babeuf thus came to know a great deal about feudal property and its abuses.

Even before the outbreak of the Revolution, he developed higher aspirations than prudence would have allowed him. He steeped himself in the writings of the *philosophes*, and came to think of himself as a man of letters. In 1785 in response to the annual prize question posed by the Academy of Arras, he submitted an essay on ways of improving the roads in the province of Artois. As it turned out, his essay was submitted too late to be eligible for that year, but the secretary of the Academy, a nobleman named Dubois de Fosseux, found it so interesting that he began a correspondence with its author. This remarkable exchange of letters, which continued for three years, provided Babeuf with his first opportunity to write down his ideas on a range of subjects—literature, politics, agriculture, and many others—that might be frightening in its scope to any but the eighteenth-century imagination. In these letters he first set down his glimmers of a radical egalitarian social vision, one that was apparently taken far more seriously by the earnest clerk than by his aristocratic correspondent. There is a tone in Babeuf's later letters indicating a growing impatience with the mere play of sensibility that the dialogue was becoming. He stopped writing altogether immediately after the death of his daughter. It needed only the catalyst of 1789 to turn him into a full-blooded agitator, first in Arras, where he was sentenced to a long prison term but managed to evade arrest, and then in Paris, where he became the editor of his own newspaper, the *Tribune of the People,* and the center of attraction for the group of radicals who were rounded up and imprisoned in May 1796.

The first of the following selections is a long letter to Dubois de Fosseux, in which Babeuf gives his views on the subject matter of two recent projects for reform that the nobleman had just described at length in several letters. One of these dealt with a communist utopia, which Dubois found noble but amusing—he referred to its author with irony as "the Reformer of the whole world"; the other was a proposal for a uniform civil code in France, something dear to the heart of a liberal rationalist like Dubois. In his reply, Babeuf expresses his own preference to the contrary, and presents the first systematic exposition of his communist ideas. The second selection is the manifesto delivered by Babeuf's associates in the Society of the Pantheon in April 1796, to announce their somewhat vaguely conceived revolutionary program. Its author was Sylvain Maréchal, a poet, whose radicalism apparently had more violent

propensities than did Babeuf's. Nevertheless Babeuf did not
repudiate the program, and positively endorsed the *Analysis
of the Doctrine of Babeuf,* written by other members of the
group, which appears here as the third selection. The final
selection is from Babeuf's defense at the trial; it is especially
remarkable for its confident affirmation that all of its author's
ideas had come out of the eighteenth-century French philosophical tradition. His argument carried no weight with the
court, but it was true, even if Babeuf's predecessors would not
necessarily have gone to the barricades for their beliefs.

Babeuf to Dubois de Fosseux:

July 8, 1787
    The system of the Reformer of the whole world, and the re-
flections of your correspondent concerning the reformation of
the Code, have provoked me today into further reflections,
through which I will undertake to examine what these different projects of reform have in common, and what they have
not.
    Both seem to be tenderly disposed toward the common
good. But, dream for dream, paradox for paradox, I hardly
know to which of the two thinkers I would accord preference.
Meanwhile, the aim of one of them covers far more ground
than that of the other. The Apostle of the Universal Code
seems to desire that men of all classes, in every country, be
accorded the same rights in the order of succession to property; and *that would be very good.* But the general Reformer
would like to obtain for all individuals, without distinction, an
absolutely equal portion of all the goods and advantages that
can be enjoyed in this mean world; and *that, it seems to me,
would be even better.*
    The inconsistency of our Customs is astonishing. But it
seems to me that when one goes back to the epoch in which
they were formed, one can no longer be surprised about anything that he sees. The men of those times, ignorant and barbaric, could have created only things in conformity with their
character. Exalted by the enthusiasm over their conquests,
they found themselves driven, as if by a natural outcome of
that inhuman inclination from which the incredible feudal sys-

tem had newly gathered its strength, to establish practices that
would serve to satisfy their ridiculous vanity.

A lucky brigand would be only half-satisfied when he had
succeeded in assuring himself a rich property. His gluttonous
pride would suffer when, looking into the future, he envisaged
this property being parceled out among all his descendants,
and saw that it could not thus suffice for very long to provide
for its possessor the foolish importance that blind fortune
ordinarily imparts, especially in the eyes of men guided by
prejudices like those with which men were generally smitten
in the era about which I am speaking.

To ward off this possible drawback, a new indignity was
conceived. It was necessary to smother the voice of kinship for
the sake of ostentation, and so almost the very means of subsistence were taken away from the younger sons in order to
load up the eldest with superfluities, and give him a pretended
illustriousness by passing on to him usurped goods and a name
that had once been odious.

This is the origin of the so-called "nobility," and of all these
revolting distinctions in every segment of society.

Whoever was less ferocious, less deceitful, or more unfortunate in combat, was placed at the service of others and
made the object of their contempt.

This, furthermore, was the source of those bizarre codes
that served as confirmatory titles for the usurpers, made it
legitimate for them to pillage, and rendered irrevocable the
confiscation of the goods of the families that were defeated.

Moreover, things were arranged in such a way as to prevent
these defeated families from ever rising again from this debasement, and to keep them, rather, in such a state that they
could never be regarded by the victorious class as constituting
anything but a most inferior class of humanity.

To satisfy both the pride and the great acquisitiveness of
this supposed nobility, it was set down that they need recognize as their principal heir only the oldest male among their
children, and that the younger children, and even those daugh-
ters that were older than the principal heir, would be considered only halves, quarters, or even very often only fifths, of a
child. Those who had, in the assemblies convoked for the pur-

pose of drawing up the codes, greater influence and authority because of their wealth, saw to it that the articles were formulated in accordance with their desires. This is the reason for the inconsistency and inconsequentiality of these productions that men sometimes cite as works of prudence and of the utmost fairness, and that really present only the most unequivocal proof of the passions that always guided them.

What, then, would a new code amount to if it contained no other change than that of *putting an end to the prohibition in one province of that which is legitimate in some other?* A very small palliative for a very great evil. It would not put a stop to these children being born poor and deprived, while those of my neighbor start gorging themselves from the moment that their eyes first see the light of day. It would not prevent this neighbor, bloated with his immense fortune, from looking down upon me with sovereign contempt for no other reason than that I am an unfortunate, crushed under the weight of indigence. It would not prevent the feudal heir of this high and mighty man from becoming a very fat lord of the manor, while his younger brother remains but a rather skinny fellow by comparison, or from forcing his sister, whose tender heart is a long way from disgusted at the prospect of tying the hymenal knot, to ensconce herself in a gloomy cloister, so that he can fatten himself still more. It would not prevent, etc., etc., and still a great deal more, etc.

But how I like the general Reformer! It is really too bad that he leaves unexplained the means he has in mind for bringing about his reforms. I hope that he can soon have his subscription filled, so that he can explain this matter to us. His plan covers all points, and I do not see, all things considered, that any punishable crime would remain in existence, once his arrangements had been brought about, except that of failing to participate in some way in the common effort for the good of all humanity. For all this to be achieved, kings would have to renounce their crown, and all titled persons would have to give up their dignities, posts and positions in society. But that would not suffice. For a major revolution to be wrought, there would have to be great changes. What is the meaning, after all, of all these dignified titles? Are they anything more than vain and chimerical expressions, invented by pride and confirmed by baseness? Must there be any distinctions at all between men? Why accord any greater dignity to him who carries a sword than to him who forges it? Did Nature, who gave predominance to our species, command that it submit to other laws than those drawn up for all the other species of animate beings? Did it desire that one individual be less well-fed, less well-clothed and less well-housed than another? Is it likely that this is the way things were done in the earliest ages of life on earth? Our most advanced knowledge of what were the natural customs of our brothers, the American Indians, before we discovered their peaceful country and began treating them so poorly, certainly would disprove any assertion to that effect.

The first man, says the author of *Emile*, who, after enclosing a plot of land, saw fit to say: "This is mine,"[1] was the initial author of all the evils that afflicted humanity. Jean Jacques said elsewhere that these evils opened the way for all the knowledge that we have acquired since that time. But he maintains that all we have acquired only renders us less happy than we were in the earliest state of nature; he seems, therefore, to want us to return to it, in order to obtain the highest well-being that can possibly be enjoyed.

It seems to me that our Reformer does better than the citizen of Geneva, whom I have sometimes heard called a dreamer. In truth, he dreamed well, but our man dreams better. Like the citizen of Geneva, he maintains that, since men are absolutely equal, they must not have any private possessions, but must enjoy everything in common, so that no one can, by the mere fact of birth, be either more or less rich, or be considered less worthy, than any of those around him. But far from sending us back into the woods, as M. Rousseau does, in order to live thus, to sate ourselves under an oak, refresh ourselves at the nearest stream, and then repose serenely under the same oak where we first found our food, instead of all this, our Reformer has us eat four good meals a day, dresses us most elegantly, and also provides those of us who are fathers of families with charming houses worth a thousand *louis* each.

[1] See the first line of the selection from Rousseau's *Discourse on the Origin of Inequality*, page 33.

This is a fine reconciliation between the worthy aspects of social life and those of the natural and primitive life.

Well, so be it, as far as I am concerned; I have decided to be one of the first emigrants to this new republic. I would not have any difficulty in adjusting myself to the new way of life, just so long as I can be happy and satisfied, without any fears concerning the well-being of my children or of myself. If, once settled there, I should pursue my interest in writing, I would be greatly pleased to find myself no longer looked down upon by those who, because they are in professions that are considered here in France to be more distinguished, believe themselves authorized to pay attention to me only when they wish to appear to announce their protection; and, for my part, it will not bother me in the slightest to treat as an equal the artisan who cuts my hair, or who manufactures my shoes. This must come to be so in fact. Are not artisans of this sort useful and necessary? If their taste or natural inclinations have led them to professions of this sort rather than to studying law, must they be viewed by society as individuals who are less interesting than those whose faculties or inclinations have led them to the magistrature? Not everyone can be a magistrate, and perhaps the person who has come to be one has suffered less than has some unfortunate laborer, to whom Nature was unkind, in learning the simplest occupation. Is it this poor man's fault that he did not receive more fortunate propensities at birth? Must he enjoy fewer advantages, just for this, than would have been his lot if he had been capable of presiding over the government of the Republic? He has only learned to knit? All right, then! He will make stockings for the farmers, for the cooks, for the wine-growers, for the fabric-makers, for the shoemakers, for the wig-makers, for the masons, for the men of law, etc.; and these men will in return procure for him bread, good food, wine, clothing, shoes, head-dress, lodging, and the general preservation of all his rights. There will be the same reciprocity through all the levels of society; and I hope that, in this way, everyone will be perfectly satisfied.

Several years ago, someone wrote against the excesses of luxury that were beginning to be apparent. He complained that the various ranks of society were becoming confused; that it was no longer possible to distinguish, by the style of dress, a great lord from an ordinary person, and he proposed, in order to put a stop to this supposed abuse, that a distinctive emblem be established that would become part of the dress and would be expressive and even explicative of each social rank, so that, for example, the nobleman would wear a representation of a sword, the grocer one of a loaf of bread, the salad-oil merchant a keg of anchovies, the poulterer a goose, the blacksmith an anvil, the tailor a pair of scissors, etc.

I hope that when our new republic is established, people will not bother themselves with such questions, since all useful functions in society (and there will certainly no longer be any but useful functions) will be equally honorable.

MANIFESTO OF THE EQUALS
BY SYLVAIN MARÉCHAL (APRIL 1796)

*De facto equality, the final goal
of the social art.* (Condorcet)

PEOPLE OF FRANCE!

For fifteen centuries you have lived as slaves, and have therefore been miserable. For the past six years you have scarcely been able to breathe, awaiting independence, happiness, and equality.

EQUALITY! The first desire of nature! The first need of man, and the principal bond that ties together all legitimate association! People of France! You have not been more favored than the other nations that vegetate on this unfortunate globe! Everywhere and at all times the poor human species, delivered over to cannibals of varying degrees of adroitness, has served as the plaything of ambitions, the grazing-ground of tyrannies. Everywhere and at all times man has been rocked to sleep with fine speeches: nowhere and at no time has he received the real thing along with the word. Since time immemorial it has been repeated to us hypocritically: *men are equal;* and since time immemorial the most debasing and widespread inequality has insolently weighed upon mankind. For as long as civil societies have existed, man's finest appanage has been acknowledged without protest, but so far it has not been realized even once: equality was nothing but a fine and sterile fiction of the law. Today, when it is being demanded in a stronger voice, we are told: "Be quiet, you poor wretches! *De facto* equality is nothing but a chimera, be satisfied with conditional equality: you are all equal before the law. You vulgar mob, what more could you need? What *we* need?" Legislators, governors, rich property-owners, now it is your turn to listen.

We are all equal, are we not? This principle remains incontestable, because nobody would seriously claim, unless he were willing to be considered mad, that it is night when it is really day.

Well, then, we henceforth lay claim to living and dying equal, as we were born. We want real equality or death; that is what we need.

And we will have it, this real equality, at any price. Woe to those whom we encounter standing between it and ourselves! Woe to those who would resist a vow thus pronounced!

The French Revolution is only the herald of another revolution, far greater, far more solemn, which will be the last of them all.

The People have marched over the bodies of the kings and priests who were allied against them. They will do the same to the new tyrants, to the new political Tartuffes who are now seated in the place of the old ones.

What is it, you ask, that we need above and beyond equality of rights?

We not only need that equality which is set down in the *Declaration of the Rights of Man and Citizen;* we want it right in our midst, under our own roofs. We consent to everything for the sake of this, and will renounce everything else in order to have this alone. Let all the arts perish, if necessary, as long as real equality remains to us!

Legislators and governors, you who have no more ingenuity than you have good faith, rich property-owners without insides, it is in vain that you try to neutralize our sacred undertaking by saying: "They are only trying to bring about that agrarian law that has been asked for more than once before."

Calumniators, you be quiet now, and in the silence of your confusion, listen to our aspirations, dictated by nature and founded upon justice.

The agrarian law, or the division of the land, was the immediately avowed desire of a few unprincipled soldiers, of a few mobs that were moved by their instinct rather than by reason. We are speaking of something more sublime and more equitable, the COMMON GOOD, or the COMMUNITY OF GOODS! No more individual ownership of the land: *the land belongs to no one.* We are demanding, we desire, communal enjoyment of the fruits of the earth: *the fruits belong to all.*

We declare ourselves unable any longer to tolerate a situation in which the great majority of men toil and sweat in the service and at the pleasure of a tiny minority.

For a long enough time now, for too long a time, less than a million individuals have had at their disposal what belongs to more than twenty millions of their fellows, of their equals.

Let it come to an end at last, this great scandal that our posterity will never believe! Disappear at last, revolting distinctions between rich and poor, great and small, masters and servants, governors and governed.

Let there be no differences between human beings other than those of age and sex. Since all have the same needs and the same families, there should be a common education and a common supply of food for all. Everyone is satisfied with having the sun and the air in common. Why could not the same portion and the same quality of food suffice for all?

But already the enemies of an order of things that would be the most natural one possible are declaiming against us.

Disturbers of the peace, they say to us, faction-mongers, you want only pillage and slaughter.

PEOPLE OF FRANCE,

We will waste no time in answering them, but first we want to say to you: the sacred undertaking that we are organizing has no other aim than to put an end to civil dissension and widespread suffering.

Never has a more immense scheme been conceived and put into effect. Every once in a great while, throughout history, a few sages, men of genius, have spoken of it in low and trembling voices. None of them has had the courage to speak the whole truth.

The moment for great measures has arrived. Evil is at its saturation point; it covers the face of the earth. Chaos, under the guise of politics, has reigned for too many centuries. Let everything now return to order and resume its proper place. Let the elements of justice and happiness be organized in response to the voice of equality. The moment has come to found the REPUBLIC OF EQUALS, this great refuge open to all men. The day of general restitution has arrived. Suffering families, come sit at the common table that Nature has set for all her children.

PEOPLE OF FRANCE,

The purest of all glories has therefore been reserved for you! Yes, it is you who are to be the first to offer this moving spectacle to the world.

Old habits, worn-out prejudices, will rise up anew to try to block the establishment of the REPUBLIC OF EQUALS. The organization of true equality, the only equality that will answer to all needs without demanding victims or sacrifices, will perhaps not please everybody at first. The selfish man, the ambitious man, will quiver with rage. Those who now possess unjustly will cry out against the injustice.

The loss of exclusive possessions, solitary pleasures, personal comforts, will arouse some lively regrets among a few individuals who have no regard for the sufferings of others. The lovers of absolute power, the vile pillars of arbitrary authority, will only reluctantly allow their haughty chiefs to be bent down to the level of true equality. Their nearsighted vision will have trouble penetrating into the imminent future, with its prospect of common welfare. But what can a few thousand malcontents do against a mass of completely happy men, who will be surprised that it took them so long to discover a felicity that had always been right under their noses?

On the morrow of this true revolution they will say to themselves in amazement: "What! It took so little to achieve the common welfare? We had but to want it. Ah! why did we

not want it sooner? Did it have to be spoken of over and over
again so many times?" Yes, most certainly; it takes only one
man on earth, more resolute and more powerful than his
fellows, than his equals, to upset the equilibrium; then crime
and misery return to the earth.

PEOPLE OF FRANCE,

What signs do you need in order to recognize an excellent
Constitution when you see one? The one founded entirely
upon *de facto* equality is the only one that can suit you and
satisfy all your desires.

The aristocratic charters of 1791 and 1795 simply rivet
down your chains instead of breaking them. The one of 1793
was a great *de facto* step toward real equality; never had anything come so near to real equality. Yet even this latter Constitution did not reach the goal and bring about the common
welfare, the great principle of which it nevertheless solemnly
consecrated.

PEOPLE OF FRANCE,

Open your eyes and your hearts to the fulness of felicity.
Recognize and proclaim along with us THE REPUBLIC OF
EQUALS.

ANALYSIS OF THE DOCTRINE OF BABEUF
BY THE BABOUVISTS (1796)

1. Nature has given every man an equal right to the enjoyment of all its goods.

2. The purpose of society is to defend this equality, which
is often attacked in the state of nature by the wicked and the
strong, and to increase, through universal cooperation, the
common enjoyment of the goods of nature.

3. Nature has imposed upon everyone the obligation to
work; no one has ever shirked this duty without having
thereby committed a crime.

4. All work and the enjoyment of its fruits must be in
common.

5. Oppression exists when one person exhausts himself
through toil and still lacks everything, while another swims
in abundance without doing any work at all.

6. No one has ever appropriated the fruits of the earth or of industry exclusively for himself without having thereby committed a crime.

7. In a true society, there must be neither rich nor poor.

8. Those rich men who are not willing to renounce their excess goods in favour of the indigent are enemies of the people.

9. No one may, by the accumulation of all the available means of education, deprive another of the instruction necessary for his well-being: instruction must be common to all.

10. The aim of the Revolution is to destroy inequality and re-establish the common welfare.

11. The Revolution is not finished, because the rich are absorbing all goods and are exclusively in command, while the poor are toiling in a state of virtual slavery; they languish in misery and are nothing in the State.

12. The Constitution of 1793 is the true law of Frenchmen, because the People have solemnly accepted it.

BABEUF'S DEFENSE

(FROM THE TRIAL AT VENDÔME, FEBRUARY–MAY 1797)

. . . After the 13th of Vendémiaire, I observed that the majority of the people, tired of a Revolution whose every fluctuation and movement had only brought death, had been— one can only say—royalized. I saw that in Paris the simple and uninstructed multitude had actually been led by the enemies of the people into a cordial contempt for the Republic. This multitude, who are capable of judging things only by their sensations, had been easily persuaded to make a comparison that goes something like this: What were we under royal domination, what are we under the Republic? The answer was entirely to the detriment of the latter. It was then quite simple to conclude that the Republic was something detestable and that monarchy was better. And I was unable to see anything in the new constitutional structure or in the attitudes of the men whose task it was to run the machinery of government that would bring people to like this Republic any more than they did. I said to myself: the Republic is lost, barring some stroke of genius that could save it; surely monarchism will not hesitate to regain its hold upon us. I looked around me and saw many people who were defeated, even among those patriots, once so fervent and courageous, who had made so many successful efforts to strengthen Liberty. The sight of universal discouragement, of—if I can go so far as to say this—absolute *muzzling* all around; then the sight of disarmament, the complete stripping away of all the guarantees that the people had once been given against any unwarranted undertakings on the part of those who govern them; the recent imprint of irons that almost all energetic men bore on their flesh; and what seemed to me the almost complete conviction of many people who were not able to offer very good reasons for their attitude, that the Republic might really, after all, be something other than a blessing; these various causes had very nearly brought all spirits to a state of total resignation, and everyone seemed ready to bend under the yoke. I saw no one who might be disposed to revive the courageous mood of earlier days. And yet, I told myself, the same ferment of zeal and of love for all men still exists. There are perhaps still ways of keeping this Republic from being lost. Let every man make an effort to summon back his strength; let every man do what he can. For my own part, I am going to do whatever I believe to be within my power.

I gave words to these feelings in my *Tribune of the People.* I said to everyone: Listen: Those among you who have apparently come around to feeling, as a result of a long series of public calamities, that the Republic is worthless and that the Monarchy might be preferable—you people are right, I swear it. I spelled it out in capital letters: WE WERE BETTER OFF UNDER THE KINGS THAN WE ARE UNDER THE REPUBLIC. But you must understand which Republic I mean by that. A Republic such as the one we see is totally worthless, without a doubt. But this, my friends, is not the true Republic. The true Republic is something that you do not yet even know about.

All right then, if you wish, I will try to tell you something about it, and I am almost certain that you will idolize it.

The Republic is not a word—not even several words—empty

of meaning. The words *Liberty* and *Equality*, which have continuously resounded in your ears, cast a spell over you in the early days of the Revolution because you thought that they would signify something good for the People. Now they mean nothing to you at all, because you see that they are only vain articulations and ornaments of deceitful formulas. You must be made to learn that in spite of all this, they can and must signify a good that is precious for the greatest number.

The Revolution, I went on in my discourse to the people, need not be an act totally without results. So many torrents of blood were not spilled merely to make the lot of the people worse than it had been before. When a people makes a revolution, it is because the play of vicious institutions has pushed the best energies of a society to such an extreme that the majority of its useful members can no longer go on as before. It feels ill at ease in the situation that prevails, senses the need to change it, and strives to do so. And the society is right to do so, because the only reason it was instituted in the first place was to make all its members as happy as possible: *The purpose of society is the common welfare.*

It is this formula, comprised within the first article of the covenant of the Year I of the Republic, that I have always held to as my own, and I will continue to do so.

The aim of the revolution also is the well-being of the greatest number; therefore, if this goal has not been achieved, if the people have not found the better life that they were seeking, then the revolution is not over, even though those who want only to substitute their own rule for somebody else's say that it is over, as you would expect them to. If the revolution is really over, then it has been nothing but a great crime.

So I strove to make people understand what the nature of the *common welfare*, which is the aim of society, or of the *welfare of the greatest number*, which is the aim of the Revolution, might be.

I inquired into the reasons why at certain given periods the greatest number were not more fortunate. This inquiry led me to the following conclusion, which I dared to print in one of my first issues after the 13th of Vendémiaire:

"There are periods in which the ultimate effect of the cruel social order is that the whole of the society's wealth is concentrated in the hands of a few. Peace, the natural state of things when all men are happy, is necessarily threatened at a time like this. The masses can no longer exist; they are completely dispossessed, and encounter only pitiless hearts among the caste that is hoarding everything. Effects such as these determine what will be the eras of those great revolutions predicted in books, in which a general upheaval of the system of property is inevitable, and in which the revolt of the poor against the rich is driven by such necessity that nothing can vanquish it."

I had observed that the principal enactors of the revolution before me also concluded that their goal had to be that of rectifying the evils of our old vicious institutions, and of bringing about the well-being of society.

I had even, in this matter, painstakingly collected the observations of one of our legislator-philosophers, who died in his prime. Pains have also been taken to turn this simple collection into a piece of evidence against me, even though it was obvious that it had been faithfully copied from well-known texts. . . . Since it is being used against me in its entirety, I will surely be permitted to extract a part of it in order to justify myself:

"The welfare of men is a new idea in Europe. . . . You cannot endure the existence of an unfortunate or of a poor man in the State. . . . Let Europe come to realize that you no longer wish to have either unfortunates or oppressors in the territory of France. . . . The unfortunate are the powers of the earth; they have the right to speak as masters to the governments that neglect them. . . . Need makes the people who labor dependent upon their enemies. Can you conceive of the existence of an empire whose social relationships are contrary in their tendencies to the form of government? . . ."

I reproduced these insights in the issues of my newspaper. I wanted to make the people realize what the result of the revolution had to be, what the republic had to be. I felt that I could perceive the people's response quite distinctly; they were ready to love such a republic. I even dared to flatter my-

self with the thought that it was my writings that had given
rise to the hope of bringing about the new republic, and that
had done so much to deroyalize the present one.

In whose eyes is this, thus far, not a good work?

You pressed your maxims too far, someone might tell me—
This is what we must decide.

The plaintiffs have described on page 78 of the supplement
of their *Exposé*, a document that has as its title: *Analysis of
the Doctrine of Babeuf*. There are a great many questions
concerning it in various parts of the record of the trial, and it
has been regarded as the *extreme* among all ideas of social
upheaval. Therefore, it will be useful to examine this work in
detail.

(*The* Analysis *follows. See page 55.*)

When I was cross-examined during the trial, I declared
that this document had not been drawn up by me, but, acknowledging that it was a fair analysis of the principles I had
proclaimed, I approved it, and consented to its being printed
and published. It was in effect a faithful summary of the doctrine that I had scattered throughout the various issues of my
newspaper.

This doctrine appears to play the essential and fundamental role in a conspiracy. It figures in the accusation under
the title, "Pillage of Property"; it is what terrifies the plaintiffs as they reproduce it in every odious form. They call it,
successively, "agrarian law," "brigandage," "devastation," "dis-
organization," "dreadful system," "horrible upheaval," "sub-
version of the social order," "atrocious project," the sole result
of which would necessarily be "the destruction of the human
species; the reversion to the savage state, a life of roaming
about in the woods, anyone who survived . . . the total abandonment of all culture, of all industry . . . nature left to
her own resources . . . the strong setting up their superiority
over the weak as the sole source of rights; men becoming, if
this doctrine is accepted, more ferocious than brute animals,
fighting furiously over every scrap of food that they come
upon. . . ."

This is most certainly the crux of the accusation. The other
points are only accessories or appendages to it. The ends jus-

tify the means. To reach a certain goal, one must vanquish everything that stands in the way. Now, as to the hypothesis of social change in question, whether one chooses to describe it, after the fashion of the plaintiffs, as subversive of the whole social order, or to characterize it, in chorus with the philosophers and the great legislators, as a sublime regeneration, it is indubitable that this change could not be brought about except by the overthrow of the established government and the suppression of everything in the way. These acts of upheaval and suppression would therefore be only the accessory, the necessary means for achieving the principal object, which is the establishment of what we and the philosophers call *the general or common welfare*, and what our accusers call *devastation and pillage*. It therefore stands proven as if mathematically, that the part of the accusation based upon my alleged resolve to found a system which has been appreciated in such greatly varying ways, is the principal and almost the sole part of the accusation, since the others are only branches emanating from it.

It follows from this, it seems to me, that we must necessarily examine the following questions: did I really preach such a system? If so, in what spirit did I preach it—in the form of mere speculation, or with the hope of conspiring to bring it about by force and in spite of the people? Has this system been genuinely proven bad and destructive? Has it never been preached by anyone but me? Was it not preached before me, and did anyone before this, including even the kings themselves, ever aspire to punish its foremost apostles?

Several of these questions will soon be resolved. The first in two words. I really did preach the system of the *common welfare;*—I mean by these words, *the welfare of all, the general welfare*. I said that the social code which established in its opening line that the welfare of men was *the sole purpose of society*, consecrated in this line the unassailable standard of all truth and of all justice. It entirely sums up the Law of Moses and the prophets. I defy anyone to maintain to me that men, when they form themselves into an association, can have any other purpose, any other desire, than the happiness of all. I defy anyone to argue that they would have consented to this union if they had been told that it would be made up of institutions that would soon place the burden of toil upon the greatest number, force them to sweat blood and die of hunger, in order that a handful of privileged citizens could be maintained in luxury and idleness. But meanwhile all this has come about, as if the eternal laws did not in any way proscribe it, and so I have the right, as I am a man, to reiterate my demand that we carry out the original compact, which, though tacitly conceived, I admit, was nevertheless written in ineffaceable letters into the fibre of every human heart. Yes, it is one voice that cries out to all: *the purpose of society is the common welfare.* This is the primitive contract; it needs no other terms to clarify its meaning; it covers everything, because all institutions must be made to flow from this source, and nothing can be allowed to degenerate from its standard.

As for the second question, I have preached the system of the welfare of all only as a simple philanthropic speculation, as a simple proposition to the people, depending entirely upon the condition of their acquiescence. One can see, then, how far I was from being able to realize such a scheme; for no man can, without deluding himself excessively, flatter himself that this acquiescence would be easy to obtain, and I can assure you that it is far easier to calculate all the obstacles that stand in the way of obtaining it, the endless opposition that would be encountered, and to judge all this insurmountable in advance.

In the course of my narration I will prove that I have done nothing to establish this system by force and in spite of the people.

In order to see if this system is really as bad, destructive and reprehensible as the plaintiffs make it out to be, citizen Jurors, you must weigh against their views some of the reasons that I offered in justification of it during the course of my propagandistic work. In addition to the *Analysis* already presented, which, as I have pointed out, I did not compose, but which I have nevertheless approved and adopted, I myself offered in one of my writings a *résumé* justifying this doctrine. I will present it to you faithfully, citizen Jurors. What I am about to give you is my frank and sincere confession. Considering the notion of "getting along" with your fellows in which everybody is steeped nowadays, there will perhaps be several things in what I am about to say to you that will appear shocking. But, I beg of you, do not become alarmed before hearing me to the end. It is my soul and my intentions that you must judge; it is upon the depths of my heart and the final meaning of my avowals that I hope you will want to fix your attention. I hope to make you realize that my reflections upon the basic principles of society have always been founded upon pure philanthropy. Here then, presented with the utmost confidence, is the declaration that I believe I must make to you, expressed exactly as it was in my writings, concerning the purposes and the motives of men when they form themselves into a civil order.

"The lot of the individual" (I said in my *Tribune of the People*, No. 35, page 102), "did not have to worsen when he passed from the natural to the social state.

"By its origins, the land belongs to no one, and its fruits are for everyone.

"The institution of private property is a surprise that was foisted upon the mass of simple and honest souls. The laws of this institution must necessarily bring about the existence of fortunate and unfortunate, of masters and slaves.

"The law of *heredity* is supremely abusive. It produces poor men from the second generation on. The two children of a man who is sufficiently rich divide up his fortune equally. One of them has only one child, the other has a dozen. Each of these latter children then has only one-twelfth of the fortune of the first brother, and one-twenty-fourth of that of the grandfather. This portion is not sufficient to provide a living. Some of them are obliged to work for their rich first cousin; thus emerge masters and servants from among the grandchildren of the same man.

"The law of *alienation* is no less unjust. This man who is already the master of others descended from the same grandfather pays arbitrarily for the labor that they are

obliged to do for him. This wage is still not enough to
enable them to subsist; they are obliged to sell their meager
portion of the inheritance to him upon whom they are now
dependent. Thus they have been expropriated; if they leave
any children, these poor waifs will have nothing but their
wits to rely on.

"A third cause hastens the emergence of masters and
servants, of the overly fortunate and the extremely unfortunate: it is the differences in wage and esteem that
mere opinion attaches to the different forms of production
and industry. A fantastic opinion of this sort leads people
to attribute to the work-day of someone who makes a
watch twenty times the value of that of someone who plows
a field and grows wheat. The result is that the watchmaker
is placed in a position whereby he acquires the patrimony
of twenty plowmen; he has therefore expropriated it.

"These three roots of public misfortune, all the progeny of
property—heredity, alienation and *the diversity of value that
arbitrary opinion, as sole master, is able to assign to the
various types of production and labor*—give rise to all the
vices of society. They isolate all the members of society;
they make of every household a little republic consecrated
to a murderous inequality, which can do nothing but con-
spire against the large republic."

When I arrived at these conclusions, citizen Jurors, and
found that I had to regard them as irrefutable truths, I was
soon led to derive the following consequences from them:

"If the land does not belong to anyone; if its fruits are
for all; if possession by a small number of men is the result
of only a few institutions that abuse and violate the fundamental law, it follows that this possession by a few is an
usurpation. It follows that, at all times, whatever an individual hoards of the land and its fruits beyond what he
needs for his own nourishment has been stolen from society."

And then, moving from consequence to consequence, believing firmly in the importance of not concealing the truth
from men, I came to the following conclusions, and published them:

"Everything that a member of the social body lacks of

what would suffice for his various needs on any given day, has been taken from him. He has been despoiled of his natural individual property by the hoarders of the goods of the community.

"*Heredity* and *alienation* are homicidal institutions.

"The superiority of talents and of efforts is only a chimera and a specious trap, which has always unduly served the schemes of the conspirators against the equality and welfare of men.

"It is both absurd and unjust to pretend that a greater recompense is due someone whose task demands a higher degree of intelligence, a greater amount of application and mental strain; none of this in any way expands the capacity of his stomach.

"No grounds whatever can justify pretension to a recompense beyond what is sufficient for individual needs.

"Such a pretension is nothing but a matter of opinion, in no way validated by reason, and perhaps—it remains to be seen—not even valid in accordance with a principle of force, at least of a force purely natural and physical in nature.

"It is only those who are intelligent who have fixed such a high price upon the conceptions of their brains, and if the physically strong had been able to keep up with them in regulating the order of things, they would no doubt have established the merit of the arm to be as great as that of the head, and the fatigue of the entire body would have been offered as sufficient compensation for the fatigue of the small part of it that ruminates.

"If this principle of equalization is not posited, then the most intelligent and the most industrious are given a warrant for hoarding, a title to despoil with impunity all those who are less gifted.

"Thus the equilibrium of well-being in the social state is destroyed, is overthrown, since nothing has been better proven than this maxim: *that one succeeds in having too much only by causing others not to have enough.*

"All our civil institutions, our reciprocal transactions, are nothing but acts of perpetual brigandage, authorized by barbarous laws, under whose sway we are occupied only in tearing each other apart.

"Our society of swindlers brings all sorts of vice, crime and misfortune in the wake of its atrocious primordial conventions, against which good men ally themselves in a vain attempt to make war upon them. In this they cannot be victorious because they do not attack the evil at its roots, because their measures are only palliatives drawn from the reservoir of false ideas created by our organic depravity.

"It is clear, then, from all that has been said, that everything owned by those who have more than their individual due of society's goods, is theft and usurpation.

"It is therefore just to take it back from them.

"Even someone who could prove that he is capable, by the individual exertion of his own natural strength, of doing the work of four men, and so lay claim to the recompense of four, would be no less a conspirator against society, because he would be upsetting the equilibrium of things by this alone, and would thus be destroying the precious principle of equality.

"Wisdom imperiously demands of all the members of the association that they suppress such a man, that they pursue him as a scourge of society, that they at least reduce him to a state whereby he can do the work of only one man, so that he will be able to demand the recompense of only one man.

"It is only our species that has introduced this murderous folly of making distinctions in merit and value, and it is our species alone that knows misfortune and privation.

"There must exist no form of privation but the one that nature imposes upon everyone as a result of some unavoidable accident, in which case these privations must be borne by everyone and divided up equally among them.

"The products of industry and of genius also become the property of all, the domain of the entire association, from the very moment that the workers and the inventors have created them, because they are simply compensation for earlier discoveries made through genius and industry, from which the new inventors and workers have profited within the framework of social life, and which have helped them to make their discoveries.

"Since the knowledge acquired is the domain of everyone, it must therefore be equally distributed among everyone.

"A truth that has been impertinently contested by bad faith, by prejudice, by thoughtlessness, is the fact that this equal distribution of knowledge among everyone would make all men nearly equal in capacity and even in talent.

"Education is a monstrosity when it is unequal, when it is the exclusive patrimony of a portion of the association: because then it becomes, in the hands of this portion, an accumulation of machinery, an arsenal of all sorts of weapons that helps this portion of society to make war against the other, which is unarmed, and to succeed thereby in strangling it, deceiving it, stripping it bare, and shackling it down to the most shameful servitude.

"There are no truths more important than those that one philosopher has proclaimed in these terms: 'Declaim as much as you wish on the subject of the best form of government, you will still have done nothing at all so long as you have not destroyed the seeds of cupidity and ambition.'

"It is therefore necessary that the social institutions be such that they eradicate within every last individual the hope that he might ever become richer, more powerful, or more distinguished because of his talents, than any of his equals.

"To be more specific, it is necessary *to bind together everyone's lot;* to render the lot of each member of the association independent of chance, and of happy or unfavorable circumstance; *to assure to every man and to his posterity, no matter how numerous it may be, as much as they need, but no more than they need;* and to shut off from everybody all the possible paths by which they might obtain some part of the products of nature and of work that is more than their individual due.

"The sole means of arriving at this is to establish a *common administration;* to suppress private property; to place every man of talent in the line of work he knows best; to oblige him to deposit the fruit of his work in the common store, to establish a simple *administration of needs,* which, keeping a

record of all individuals and all the things that are available
to them, will distribute these available goods with the
most scrupulous equality, and will see to it that they make
their way into the home of every citizen.

"This form of government, proven by experience to be
practicable, since it is the form applied to the 1,200,000 men
of our twelve Armies (what is possible on a small scale is
possible on a large scale as well), is the only one that could
result in unqualified and unalterable universal welfare: *the
common welfare, the aim of society.*

"This form of government," I continued, "will bring about
the disappearance of all boundary lines, fences, walls, locks
on doors, trials, thefts, and assassinations; of all crimes,
tribunals, prisons, gibbets, and punishments; of the despair
that causes all calamity; and of greed, jealousy, insatiability,
pride, deception, and duplicity—in short, of all vices. Furthermore (and the point is certainly essential), it will put an
end to the gnawing worm of perpetual inquietude, whether
throughout society as a whole, or privately within each of
us, about what tomorrow will bring, or at least what next
year will bring, for our old age, for our children and for
their children."

This, citizen Jurors, was the interpretation of the code of
nature with which my mind was occupied. I believed that I
could see everything that was written on the immortal pages
of this code. I brought these pages to light and published
them. Certainly it was because I loved my fellow man, and
because I was persuaded that the social system which I
conceived was the only one that could bring about his happiness, that I wanted so much to see him disposed to adopt it.
But I did not imagine—it would have been a most illusory
presumption—that I could have converted him to this idea:
it would have taken no more than a moment's contemplation
of the flood of passions now subjugating us in this era of
corruption that we have come upon, to become convinced
that the odds against the possibility of realizing such a
project are more than a hundred to one. Even the most
intrepid partisan of my system ought to be convinced of this.

All this, then, citizen Jurors, was, more than anything else, a consolation that my soul was seeking. Such is the natural and palpable inclination felt by every man who loves his fellows, who gives thought to the calamities of which they are the victims, who reflects that they themselves are often the cause of these afflictions, to examine in his imagination all the possible curative measures that could be taken. If he believes that he has found these remedies, then, in his powerlessness to realize them, he afflicts himself for the sake of those whom he is forced to leave to their suffering, and contents himself with the feeble compensation of tracing for them the outlines of the plan that he feels could end their woes for all time. This is what all our philosopher-legislators did, and I am at best only their disciple and emulator, when I am doing anything more than merely repeating, echoing, or interpreting them. Rousseau said: "I fully realize that one should not undertake the chimerical project of trying to form a society of honest men, but I nevertheless believed that I was obliged to speak the whole truth openly." When you condemn me, citizen Jurors, for all the maxims that I have just admitted stating, it is these great men whom you are putting on trial. They were my masters, my sources of inspiration—my doctrine is only theirs. From their lessons I have derived these maxims of "pillage," these principles that have been called "destructive." You are also accusing the monarchy of not having been quite as inquisitional as the government of our present Republic; you accuse them of not having prevented the corrupting books of a Mably, a Helvetius, a Diderot, or of a Jean Jacques Rousseau, from falling into my hands. All those who govern should be considered responsible for the evils that they do not prevent. Philanthropists of today! It is above all to you that I address myself. It is because of these philosophical poisons that I am lost. Without them, I would perhaps have had your morality, your virtues. Like you, I would have detested brigandage and the overthrow of the existing social institutions above all things; I would have had the tenderest solicitude for the small number of powerful men of this world; I would have been pitiless toward the suffering multitude. But no, I will not repent of having been educated at the school of the

celebrated men whom I have just named. I will not blas-
pheme against them, or become an apostate against their
dogmas. If the axe must fall upon my neck, the lictor will
find me ready. It is good to perish for the sake of virtue—

I was not being fanciful, citizen Jurors, when I said that
this trial would be the trial of all those philosophers whose
remains have been placed in the Pantheon, as long as you
would condemn us for our popular and democratic opinions,
out of which the principal count in the accusation has been
forged under the title, "project for pillaging all property."
These philosophers too, formulated and published such projects. Various fragments of their projects are in the volumes
that have been placed in evidence against us. And for this
reason I believe I have the right to suspect rather strongly
that the court is presuming to judge them along with us.
What else could be the meaning of those fragments in the
accusation that I am about to cite, which are the work of
the author of the *Social Contract?* . . . Let me read from
them:

"Before these terrible words *mine* and *thine* were invented; before the existence of this cruel and brutal species
of men called *masters,* and of that other species of rogues and
liars called *slaves;* before there were men so abominable as
to *dare to have too much while others were dying of
hunger;* before mutual dependence had forced them all to
become cunning and jealous traitors. . . . I would like someone to tell me what their vices and crimes could then possibly have consisted of. . . . I am told that people have been
long disabused of the chimera of a golden age. It should be
added that men have been long disabused of the chimera of
virtue!"

It says in the volume printed by the court that the draft
of this statement is written in Babeuf's hand. I tell you that
it is only a copy. The proof that I am about to give you of
this will perhaps suffice to place other such attributions in
question. The original is from the hand of Jean Jacques
Rousseau. I have no fear of compromising this new conspirator by mentioning him here, since he can be neither
harmed nor tainted by the judgement of this tribunal. I

therefore do not hesitate to say that it was he who presided over the Society of Democrats of Floréal; he was one of their principal instigators. But what is the date of this statement of his that I have cited? 1758. It is a response made by the philosopher to M. Bordes, Academician of Lyons, *having to do with the discourse on the sciences and the arts*. These words are therefore somewhat prior to the conspiracy that is now being examined. Oh! what does it matter? For that matter, this conspiracy dates its origins from a much earlier time. Poor Jean Jacques! . . .

Chapter III

UTOPIAN SOCIALISM

The period between the final overthrow of Napoleon in 1815 and the French Revolution of 1830 was largely one of conservative reaction. Many believed that the world which had preceded 1789 was being restored. But even during this period, the old feudal powers were already being replaced by the new feudality of business and finance; and although most reformers and revolutionaries were declaiming against the "restored" *ancien régime* in the language of classical liberalism, a few of them perceived that new problems, demanding new solutions, were emerging with the rise of industrialism.

The three founders of the modern socialist tradition—Henri Saint-Simon, Charles Fourier, and Robert Owen—were of the same generation. Saint-Simon, the oldest of the three, was born in 1760, Fourier in 1772, and Robert Owen a year earlier. They all reached maturity immediately before or during the time of the French Revolution, and saw the industrial system become a reality in a world in which it had not seemed to exist at the time they were born. Even their personal lives bear the earmarks of the great social changes that were taking place. Saint-Simon was a nobleman, a descendant of the great memoirist of the court of Louis XIV; he fought in the American War of Independence, won and lost a fortune by speculating during the French Revolution, and ultimately renounced his title as the symbol of a social order that was becoming extinct. Fourier was the *déclassé* son of a wealthy bourgeois family that lost its fortune during the Revolution, and he was forced to eke out his living as a commercial traveler. Owen's life represents the reverse side of these developments. Son of a humble Welsh artisan, he worked his way up to become a wealthy man and partner in the largest cotton-mill in Scotland while still in his twenties. All three were men thoroughly engaged in the task of living, and in very different ways, but they all came, quite independently, to feel a need to devote the major part of their energies to working out plans for the abolition of human misery.

It was Marx and Engels who styled them "utopian" socialists. The *Communist Manifesto* describes them as constituting the first wave of social reformers to be flung up by the Industrial Revolution and the emergence of a proletariat. According to Marx and Engels, the utopians recognized the need to improve the lot of the proletariat, but they did not yet recognize the possibilities for any initiative on the part of this new class, because it was still relatively undeveloped. Consequently they sought to improve conditions by addressing mankind in general, and appealing to its moral consciousness, rather than by speaking specifically to the working-class, and invoking its self-interest, as later generations of socialists were to do. Marx and Engels, who were seeking a much more tough-minded approach to the realization of social reform, regarded the old-fashioned morality of these three men as merely "utopian." But even granting that this characterization of them was largely correct, they were different from the men who were literally conceiving utopias in eighteenth-century France, in that they now addressed themselves systematically and often with great precision to a critique of the industrial system. Marx and Engels could not have developed their own theories if these men had not preceded them.

CLAUDE HENRI SAINT-SIMON (1760–1825)

The man who was born Claude Henri de Rouvroy, Comte de Saint-Simon, and who died in poverty surrounded by a group of young disciples who looked upon him as the prophet of a new religion, must be considered something of an eccen-

tric, as was Fourier, his younger contemporary. But, unlike
the latter, whose origins and behavior were utterly bourgeois,
Saint-Simon led a life as cavalier as the name he renounced.
As a boy, he once applied a burning coal to himself to cauter-
ize the bite of a mad dog. He fought with Lafayette in the
American War of Independence while still a very young
man, and later, during the French Revolution, he made and
lost a fortune by speculating in *assignats*. After a brief,
unsuccessful marriage, he sought in vain the hand of Mad-
ame de Staël, the most celebrated woman of the day, believing that the union of two such people as themselves
would have historical significance. Convinced from an early
age that he had a special destiny, he long had his valet
awaken him in the morning with the reminder, "Remember,
Monsieur le Comte, you have great things to do." He turned
to philosophy, according to his own account, after Charlemagne, from whom his family claimed descent, appeared to
him in a dream, and told him that his future successes as a
philosopher would be equivalent to Charlemagne's as a soldier and statesman.

In 1803 he published his first book, the *Letters from an
Inhabitant of Geneva*. In it, he set down his proposal that
the world be governed by a scientific elite; this hierarchical
conception of a world order continued to underly his thinking,
even as his ideas changed in other respects. At this time his
main interest was still natural rather than social science,
although political and social philosophy were certainly part
of his scheme; even his interest in natural science had more
of a turn in the direction of great technological schemes,
such as that of building a canal through the Isthmus of
Suez, than toward pure research. He was still very much the
eighteenth-century rationalist and encyclopedist (D'Alem-
bert had been his teacher for a time) in his conception of
the role and relationship of the sciences.

But this was the age of the Faustian imagination, and
Saint-Simon was one of its best representatives. From the
start, his life and thought showed a certain appetite for
infinity not completely true to the eighteenth century. For
one thing, he became one of the most loyal disciples of that
thoroughly nineteenth-century conception, historicism. French

historicism, like romanticism, arose largely under the impact of German developments, but both also had a native tradition. Saint-Simon's historicism always retained the cosmopolitan and rationalist spirit of Condorcet's, although his organic conception of historical development more closely resembled that of the Germans. He came to see History, not in Condorcet's terms of the advancement of the human mind through increasingly greater knowledge and control of the world, but rather as an integrated and evolving social structure. Human thought and the conditions of the social relationships in a given era were inextricably bound up with one another: in this view, he anticipated Marx and the sociology of knowledge. He also was the direct ancestor of the ideas of Auguste Comte, who worked as his secretary for a time, and who owed him more than he ever cared to admit.

Saint-Simon saw industrial and technological development as the focus of the social structure of his own era. Hence, the task of society was to adjust an obsolete social order, founded upon feudal relations, to the conditions of the industrial age; and the task of philosophy, above all, was to enable the human mind to make this adjustment, by focussing upon concrete social and technological problems. He wanted to turn philosophy away from its predilection for metaphysics in the direction of more worldly and scientific interests. He was thus the originator of positivism, although he never used the term.

None of this was necessarily socialistic, and it was not in the case of Comte, but for Saint-Simon the creation of a new social science and a new social order in accordance with its conceptions meant the creation of a society without poverty. Through the years, his emphasis increasingly became that of "the most rapid possible amelioration of the lot of the most numerous and poorest class." This did not mean that he favored the poor *in opposition* to the rich. Rather, he thought that both would benefit from the rational reorganization of society, that the improvements that would bring the greatest wealth to *les industriels* would also naturally be the ones that would do the most to improve the well-being of the poor. The only class that he opposed and regarded as doomed to extinction was that of the "idlers" (*les oisifs*, as he called

them)—in other words, his own class, the old feudal aristocracy, which no longer had any useful function in society, and
with which he had renounced all affiliation.

   The New Christianity was written in the last year of his
life; it was meant as the first part of a three-volume work,
but the latter two parts were never written. This work
represents a turn toward religiosity—an utterly unorthodox
brand, of course—that was perhaps sudden at this point in
Saint-Simon's life, but by no means a complete departure
from all that he had done before. Rather, it is the crown of
his life's work, and it presents a comprehensive summing-up
of his whole philosophical conception. The emphasis on
religion is in keeping with the times. The Restoration had
brought with it a revival of old regime luster, and Chateau-
briand, who was the first literary giant to emerge after the
great cultural hiatus that the Revolution had created, was
filling hearts with romantic yearning for the monarchism and
Christianity of former times. Even the young Victor Hugo,
later to be the Isaiah of republicanism, was a monarchist in
the 1820s. Saint-Simon, whose life is a kind of record of the
growth of romanticism, could not but feel the impact of
these developments. The positivist spirit had to find room
within itself for the reverberations of the heart; Saint-Simon
was performing a useful service for progressives by demon-
strating that conservatism did not have a monopoly on
beauty. He, too, returned to Christianity, but not to that
of either Protestants or Catholics. He attempts, in the dialogue
between a conservative and an innovator, to show the sources
of positivism in the ethic of primitive Christianity, although
it must be said that, by and large, he is simply founding a
religion of his own.

LETTERS FROM AN INHABITANT OF GENEVA TO HIS CONTEMPORARIES (1803)

FIRST LETTER

   I am no longer young. I have observed and reflected
through the course of a good deal of activity all my life, and

your happiness has been the aim of my labors. I have conceived a project which, it seems to me, could be of use to you, and I am now going to present it.

Hold a subscription before the grave of Newton; enroll everyone without distinction at whatever sum you choose.

Have each subscriber nominate three mathematicians, three physicists, three chemists, three physiologists, three men of letters, three painters and three musicians.

Renew both the subscription and the nominations every year, but allow every subscriber the unqualified liberty to renominate the same persons.

Divide the total amount received from the subscriptions among the three mathematicians, the three physicists, etc., who have received the most votes.

Ask the president of the Royal Society of London to receive the subscriptions for this year.

Next year and the years thereafter, charge the person who has subscribed the largest amount with this honorable function.

Require those who have been nominated to accept no positions, honors or money from any fraction among you, but let them rather continue to be the absolute masters of their own activities, and to employ their powers in whatever way they see fit.

Men of genius will thereby enjoy a recompense worthy of them and of you. This recompense will place them in the position which alone can provide them with the means of performing for you all the services of which they are capable. It will become the goal of the ambition of the most energetic spirits, and will turn them from possibly harmful pursuits to the pursuit of your tranquillity.

By this measure, you will at last provide those who are working for the advancement of your understanding with leaders, you will invest these leaders with immense esteem, and you will place a considerable pecuniary power at their disposal. . . .

THE NEW CHRISTIANITY
DIALOGUES BETWEEN A CONSERVATIVE AND AN INNOVATOR
(1825)

FIRST DIALOGUE

THE CONSERVATIVE: Do you believe in God?

THE INNOVATOR: Yes, I believe in God.

THE C.: Do you believe that the Christian religion has a divine origin?

THE I.: Yes, I believe that.

C.: If the Christian religion is of divine origin, it is in no way subject to improvement; meanwhile, you, through your writings, are stirring up artists, industrialists and men of learning to want to perfect this religion: you thereby enter into a contradiction with yourself, since your opinion and your belief turn out to be in opposition to one another.

I.: The opposition between my opinion and my belief that you believe you have observed is only apparent; one must make a distinction between what God Himself said and what the clergy has said in His name.

What God said is certainly not subject to improvement, but what the clergy has said in his name composes a science subject to improvement like any other human science. The theories of theology need to be renewed in certain epochs, just like those of physics, chemistry and physiology.

C.: What, then, is the part of religion that you consider divine? What is the part that you regard as human?

I.: God said: *All men must behave as brothers towards one another;* this sublime principle contains everything that is divine in the Christian religion.

C.: What! You reduce everything divine in Christianity to one sole principle?

I.: Of necessity God related everything to one sole principle. He necessarily deduced everything from the same principle; without this, His will concerning men would not have been systematic. It would be blasphemous to suppose that the Almighty had founded His religion on several principles.

Now, according to this principle, given by God to men for the governing of their conduct, they must organize their society in the way that would be the most advantageous for the greatest number of people. They must make it their goal in all their efforts, in all their activities, to ameliorate as promptly and as completely as possible the moral and physical existence of the most numerous class.

I say that the divine part of the Christian religion consists in this and in this alone.

c.: I admit that God gave only one principle to men; I grant that He commanded them to organize their society in such a way as to guarantee to the poorest class the promptest and most complete amelioration of their physical and moral existence. But I must point out to you that God left mankind with guides. Before ascending to heaven, Jesus Christ charged His apostles and their successors with the task of directing the conduct of men, indicating to them the ways in which they were to apply this fundamental principle of divine morality, so as to make it easier for them to draw the most just consequences from it.

Do you recognize the Church as a divine institution?

I.: I believe that God Himself founded the Christian Church; I am filled with the deepest respect and the greatest admiration for the conduct of the Fathers of this Church.

These leaders of the primitive Church explicitly preached the unity of all peoples. They tried to get them to live at peace with one another; they proclaimed positively and most energetically to the rich and powerful that it was their first duty to employ all their resources in bringing about the promptest possible amelioration of the physical and moral existence of the poor.

These leaders of the primitive Church produced the best book that has ever been published, the *Primitive Catechism*, in which they divided the activities of men into two classes, the good and the bad—that is, into those activities that conform to the fundamental principle of divine morality, and those contrary to this principle.

c.: Tell me more about your idea, and tell me if you regard the Christian Church as infallible.

i.: In cases where the Church has for its leaders the men
who are the most capable of guiding the forces of society
in the direction of the divine purpose, I believe that the
Church can then, without reservations, be considered infallible, and that society is acting wisely in allowing itself to
be led by it.

I consider the Fathers of the Church to have been infallible for the epoch in which they lived, whereas the clergy
today seems to me to be, of all the organized groups within
society, the one that is committing the greatest errors, the
errors that are the most harmful to society; the group whose
conduct is the most diametrically opposed to the fundamental principle of divine morality.

c.: As you see it, then, the Christian religion is in a very
bad state?

i.: Quite the contrary; never before has there been in existence such a great number of good Christians; but nowadays
almost all of them belong to the class of laymen. Since the
fifteenth century, the Christian religion has been losing its
unity of action. Since that time, a Christian clergy has not
existed. All the clergies that are seeking today to fasten their
opinions, their morals, their rituals and their dogmas onto the
moral principle that mankind received from God are heretical,
since their opinions, their morals, their dogmas and their rituals are more or less opposed to divine morality; the most
powerful clergy of all is also the one whose heresy is the
greatest of all.

c.: What will become of the Christian religion if, as you believe, the men charged with the task of teaching it have become heretics?

i.: Christianity will become the sole, universal religion; the
Asians and Africans will convert to it; the members of the
European clergy will become good Christians, and will abandon the various heresies that they profess today. The true
doctrine of Christianity, that is, the most general doctrine that
can be derived from the fundamental principle of divine morality, will be produced, and the differences in religious
opinions that exist right now will immediately come to an end.

The first Christian doctrine to appear in history gave society only a partial and quite incomplete organization. The rights of Caesar remained independent of the rights assigned to the Church. *Render unto Caesar the things that are Caesar's;* so goes the famous maxim that separated these two powers. The temporal power continued to base itself upon the law of the strongest, while the Church maintained that society should recognize as legitimate only those institutions that had the amelioration of the existence of the poorest class as their object.

The new Christian organization will derive its temporal as well as its spiritual institutions from the principle that *all men must behave as brothers toward one another*. It will direct all its institutions, whatever their nature, towards the advancement of the well-being of the poorest class.

c.: On what facts do you base this opinion? By what authority are you able to believe that a single moral principle will become the sole regulator of all human societies?

i.: The most general principle, the principle of divine morality, is the one that must become the sole moral principle; this is the consequence of its nature and origin.

The people of God, that people who received divine revelation before the appearance of Jesus, and who are the most widely spread out over the surface of the earth, have always felt that the Christian doctrine, founded by the Fathers of the Church, was incomplete. They have always maintained that a great era is yet to come, an era to which they have given the name *messianic*, in which the religious doctrine would be presented in all the universality of which it is capable; that it would govern equally the activities of the temporal and the spiritual powers, and that all the races of man would henceforth have only one single religion, one common organization.

At last I can see the new Christian doctrine clearly, and I am going to expound it. . . . I will begin by examining the different religions that exist today; I will compare their doctrines with the one that derives directly from the fundamental principle of divine morality.

ON THE DIFFERENT RELIGIONS

The New Christianity will be made up of branches nearly like those that compose the various heretical associations existing in Europe and America today.

The New Christianity will have, as the heretical associations do, its morality, its rituals and its dogma; it will have its clergy, and there will be leaders among this clergy. But, in spite of this similarity of organization, the New Christianity will have been purged of all presently existing heresies; the New Christians will regard the moral doctrine as the most important element of their religion; they will look upon ritual and dogma only as accessories, since it will be the principal aim of these things to fix the attention of the faithful in all social classes upon morality.

The entire moral doctrine of the New Christianity will be derived directly from this principle: *All men must behave as brothers toward one another;* and this principle, which belongs to primitive Christianity, will undergo a *transfiguration,* by which it will be presented as the principle that today must be the aim of all religious activity.

This regenerated principle will be presented in the following form: *Religion must direct society toward the over-all goal of the most rapid possible amelioration of the condition of the poorest class.*

The men who are to be the founders of the New Christianity and the leaders of the new Church, must be all those who are the most capable of contributing to the advancement of the well-being of the poorest class. The functions of the new clergy, basically, will be to teach the new Christian doctrine, which the leaders of the new Church will work unceasingly to bring to perfection.

. . . We will now compare this conception of a religious institution with the religions that exist in Europe and America; by this comparison we will easily make it evident that all the religions that profess to be Christian today are only heresies. . . .

On the Catholic Religion

The Catholic Association, Apostolic and Roman, has the largest number of adherents of all the European and American religious associations; it still has several major advantages over all the other sects to which the inhabitants of these two continents are attached.

It was the immediate successor to the Christian association, and this gave it a certain *veneer* of orthodoxy.

Its clergy inherited a large part of the riches that the Christian clergy had acquired in its numerous victories during the fifteen centuries in which it struggled to replace the aristocracy of birth with the aristocracy of talents, and to establish the religious supremacy of peaceful over military men.

The leaders of the Catholic Church preserved the sovereignty of the city that has had unbroken domination of the world for more than twenty centuries, first by the force of arms, and then by the omnipotence of divine morality; and it is in the Vatican today that the Jesuits are assembling the means to dominate all mankind by an odious system of mystification and trickery.

The Catholic Association, Apostolic and Roman, is incontestably very powerful still, although it has eroded considerably since the pontificate of Leo X, who was its founder. But the strength that this association possesses is only a material strength, and it is able to maintain itself only by means of trickery. Spiritual strength, moral strength, Christian strength, the kind of strength that loyalty and sincerity provide, is missing from it entirely. In a word, the Catholic, Apostolic and Roman religion is nothing but a Christian heresy; it is only a degenerate portion of Christianity. . . .

Let us now examine how the Sacred College has been composed since the time of Leo X, founder of the Catholic, Apostolic and Roman Church; let us examine the kind of learning that this college requires of those to whom it grants priesthood; let us see what moral and physical ameliorations the poor classes have undergone in the Ecclesiastical States, which are intended to stand as models to all other governments; and

finally, let us examine the content of the teaching given by
the Catholic clergy to the faithful of its communion.

I shall make my summing-up to the Pope . . . so that he
may answer clearly and without employing any mystical turns
of phrase, four accusations that I am now going to level against
the Catholic Church.

*I accuse the Pope and his Church of heresy on the follow-
ing count:*

*The teaching that the Catholic clergy gives the laymen of
its communion is vicious, and does not guide their conduct
onto the path of Christianity.*

The Christian religion proposes to its faithful as an earthly
goal, the most rapid possible amelioration of the moral and
physical existence of the poor. Jesus Christ promised eternal
life to those who would work the most zealously for the advancement of the well-being of the most numerous class. . . .

Go through the entire body of works written, with the
approval of the Pope and his Sacred College, on the Catholic
dogma; examine the whole body of prayers consecrated by
the leaders of the Church, to be read by the faithful, whether
laymen or ecclesiastics; and nowhere will you find the aim of
the Christian religion clearly spelled out. Ideas on morality
are found in small number in the Christian writings, and they
never form a body of doctrine. They are thinly scattered
throughout an immense quantity of volumes that are made
up, basically, of fastidious repetitions and a few mystical conceptions; conceptions that could in no way serve as a guide,
and that are, on the contrary, of such a nature as to cause the
principles of the sublime moral doctrine of the Christ to be
lost from view.

It would be unjust to level the accusation of incoherence
against the immense collection of Catholic prayers consecrated
by the Pope. One can perceive that the selection of these
prayers was guided by a systematic conception; one can recognize that the Sacred College has directed all the faithful
toward a common goal. It is evident, however, that this goal is
not the Christian one, but rather, the heretical one of persuad-
ing laymen that they are in no condition to guide themselves
by their own lights, and that they must let themselves be

guided by the clergy, *without the clergy necessarily being obliged to have a capacity superior to theirs.*

Every part of the ritual, as well as every principle of the Catholic dogma, clearly has it as its object to place laymen in a condition of the most absolute dependence upon the clergy. . . .

I accuse the Pope and the Cardinals of being heretics on this second count:

I accuse them of not possessing the knowledge that would render them capable of guiding their faithful onto the path of salvation;

I accuse them of giving a poor education to the seminarians, and of not demanding of those to whom they grant the priesthood the learning that they need to become worthy pastors, capable of properly leading the flocks that are to be confided to them.

. . . The Roman clergy was orthodox until the accession of Leo X to the papal throne, because until that time it was superior to laymen in all the sciences whose progress contributed to the advancement of the well-being of the poorest class. Since that time, it has become heretical, because it has no longer cultivated anything but theology, and has allowed itself to be surpassed by laymen in the fine arts, in the exact sciences, and in all activities pertaining to industrial capacity. . . .

I accuse the Pope of behaving as a heretic on this third count:

I accuse him of conduct as a ruler more contrary to the moral and physical interests of the indigent class among his temporal subjects than that of any laic prince toward the same class.

Travel through all of Europe, and you will see that the population of the Ecclesiastical States is the one that suffers the most vicious and anti-Christian administration of public needs.

Considerable stretches of the lands that constitute the domain of Saint Peter, which once produced abundant crops, have now become, through the negligence of the papal government, pestilential swamps.

A great part of the territory that has not yet become swampy remains uncultivated. . . .

All branches of industry have become paralyzed. The poor are out of work, and would die of hunger if the ecclesiastical establishments, the government, in other words, did not feed them. The poor, since they are fed by charity, are ill fed, thus, their existence is wretched in its physical aspect.

They are even more wretched in the moral aspect of their lives, because they live in idleness, which is the mother of all vices and of all the brigandage with which this unfortunate country is afflicted. . . .

I accuse the Pope and all those who are currently Cardinals, I accuse all the Popes and all the Cardinals who have ever lived since the fifteenth century, of being and of having been heretics on this fourth count:

I accuse them first of all of having consented to the formation of two institutions diametrically opposed to the spirit of Christianity: the Inquisition and the Jesuit order; I further accuse them of having accorded their protection to these two institutions almost without interruption since the aforementioned epoch. . . .

On the Protestant Religion

The European mind took a great leap forward in the fifteenth century; great discoveries and rapid advances, always toward a positive utility, were effectuated in all directions, and these discoveries and advances were almost entirely due to the efforts of laymen. . . .

In this epoch, the court of Rome lost a great deal of the support that it had hitherto received from the class of plebeians against that of the patricians, and from the class of commoners against the nobles and the feudal power.

The Divine Founder of Christianity had advised His disciples to work without rest to raise up the lower classes of society, and to lessen the importance of those invested with the right of command and of making the law.

Until the fifteenth century, the Church had pursued this Christian ideal with reasonable consistency; all the Popes and almost all the Cardinals had arisen from the class of plebeians, and they often came from families engaged in the lowliest occupations.

With this policy, the clergy had, through its perseverance, tended to diminish the importance and influence of the aristocracy of birth, and elevate the aristocracy of talents in its place.

At the end of the fourteenth century, the character of the sacred college changed completely. It renounced the Christian ideal in order to adopt an entirely worldly policy. The spiritual power ceased to fight against the temporal power; it no longer identified itself with the lower classes of society, it no longer strove to make them important, it no longer sought to elevate the aristocracy of talents above that of birth. It conceived a plan of action whose object was to preserve the importance of the Church Militant and the riches it had acquired, to enable it to enjoy these riches and to suffer no longer, without at the same time having to perform any useful function in society.

In order to achieve this aim, the sacred college placed itself under the protection of the temporal power. . . .

In his diplomatic relations with Charles V, Leo X conducted himself in the capacity of a prince of the house of Medici, rather than in that of a Pope. The result was that the Papacy ceased to inspire the Emperor with apprehension, and so Charles V, no longer feeling himself restrained by the ecclesiastical power, which was alone capable of setting up a barrier to the ambitions of lay princes, conceived the project of establishing a universal monarchy for his own benefit, a project that was renewed by Louis XIV and by Bonaparte, whereas none of the lay princes of Europe, from the time of Charlemagne until the sixteenth century, had attempted to carry it out.

Such was the state of the only religion existing in Europe at the time when Luther began his insurrection against the court of Rome.

The works of this reformer naturally divide themselves into two categories: the first, critical, addressing itself to the papal religion; the second, constructive, having as its object the establishment of a religion distinct from the one presided over by the court of Rome.

The first part of Luther's work was susceptible to being fully realized, as indeed, it eventually was. Luther's critique of the court of Rome, rendered a major service to civilization; without it, papism would have completely subjected the human mind to superstitious ideas and caused morality to be totally lost from view. We owe it to Luther that a spiritual power which was no longer attuned to the condition of society was dissolved.

But Luther could not combat ultramontane doctrines without trying to reorganize the Christian religion himself. It is in this second part of his reform, the organic part of his work, that Luther has left his successors much to do: the Protestant religion, such as was conceived by Luther, is still only a Christian heresy. Certainly Luther was right in saying that the court of Rome had abandoned the ideal handed on by Jesus to His apostles; certainly he was right in proclaiming that the ritual and the dogma established by the Popes were no longer appropriate for directing the attention of the faithful to Christian morality, and that they were, on the contrary, of such a nature that they could be considered as only accessory to religion. But he was not right in concluding, on the basis of these two incontestable truths, that morality should be taught to the faithful of his own era in the same way that the Church Fathers had taught it to their contemporaries; nor was he right in concluding that ritual should therefore be stripped of all the charms with which the fine arts are capable of enriching it. . . .

I accuse the Lutherans of being heretics on this first count:

I accuse them of having adopted a moral doctrine most inferior to what could be applied to Christians in the present state of their civilization.

Since European public opinion is favorable to Protestantism, whereas it is contrary to Catholicism, I must be severe in my demonstration of the Protestant heresy, and so I am obliged to deal with this question in a highly general way.

Jesus had charged His apostles and their successors with the mission of organizing mankind in the way most favorable to the amelioration of the condition of the poor. At the same time, He had recommended to His Church that they employ only gentleness, persuasion and demonstration to achieve their goal.

A great deal of time and varied effort were necessary to fulfill this task; therefore, one cannot be surprised if it has not yet been completed.

What aspect of this task was it Luther's lot to perform? How well did he acquit himself of it? These are the two matters that I must now examine. . . .

In the epoch when Jesus conferred upon His apostles the sublime mission of organizing mankind in the interest of the poorest class, civilization was still in its infancy.

Society was divided into two great classes: masters and slaves. The class of masters was divided into two castes: the patricians, who made the law and performed all the important functions, and the plebeians, who had to obey the law, even though they did not make it, and who generally performed only menial functions. Even the greatest philosophers of the time would not have been able to conceive of a social organization on any other basis.

No form of moral system as yet existed, since nobody had yet found a way to reduce all the principles of this science to one single principle.

No form of religious system as yet existed, since all the public forms of belief paid homage to a multitude of gods, and these inspired men to a variety of sentiments, many of them even opposed to one another.

The human heart had not yet in any way given rise to philanthropic sentiments. The sentiment most widespread among generous spirits was patriotism, and this was extremely circumscribed, because of the small size of territories, and because of the lack of importance of the masses in the nations of antiquity. One nation alone, the Roman, dominated all the others, and governed them arbitrarily.

The dimensions of this planet were not yet known, so that it would not have been possible to conceive of a general plan of amelioration for the territorial property of mankind.

In a word, Christianity, its moral doctrine, its ritual and

dogma, its partisans and ministers, had its beginning completely outside the social organization, as well as outside the usages and manners of society.

But by the time Luther brought about his reform, civilization had made great progress. Since the establishment of Christianity, society had changed its face completely, the social organization was founded on a new basis.

Slavery had been almost completely abolished. The patricians were no longer in exclusive possession of the right to make laws; they no longer performed all the important functions. The temporal power, blasphemous in its very essence, no longer dominated the spiritual power, and the spiritual power was no longer directed by the patricians. The court of Rome had become the first court of Europe; since the establishment of the papacy, all the Popes and almost all the Cardinals had come from the class of plebeians; the aristocracy of talents was surpassing the aristocracy of wealth and privilege.

Society possessed a religious and moral system all in one, since the love of God and of one's neighbor gave a unitary character to the most generous sentiments of the faithful.

Christianity had become the basis of social organization. It had replaced the law of the strongest; the right of conquest was no longer considered the most legitimate of all rights.

America had been discovered; and mankind, aware of the full extent of its territorial possessions, was in a position to make a general plan of the work that had to be done to obtain the greatest possible benefit from this planet.

The peaceful arts had been developed, and had acquired precision at the same time; the fine arts had just been reborn; the sciences of observation had just begun to emerge, along with industry.

The philanthropic sentiment, the true basis of Christianity, had replaced patriotism in all generous hearts. If all men did not yet behave as brothers toward one another, at least they admitted that they had to regard themselves as all children of one father.

Had Luther's reform been complete, he would have produced and proclaimed the following doctrine; he would have said to the Pope and the Cardinals:

"Your predecessors have sufficiently perfected the theory of Christianity; they have sufficiently propagated this theory, and Europeans have become sufficiently imbued with it: now it is with the general application of this doctrine that you must concern yourselves. The true Christianity must render men happy on earth as well as in heaven.

"You should no longer focus the attention of the faithful upon abstract ideas; it is, rather, through an appropriate application of sensual ideas, by combining them in such a way as to obtain for men the highest possible degree of felicity during their earthly lives, that you would succeed in establishing Christianity, the general, universal, and unique religion.

"You must no longer confine yourselves to preaching to the faithful that the poor are the beloved children of God; you must also employ, openly and energetically, all the means and powers acquired by the Church Militant to the prompt amelioration of the moral and physical existence of the most numerous class. The preliminary and preparatory tasks of Christianity have been completed; the task you now have to carry out is much more satisfying than those of your predecessors. This task consists in establishing the general and definitive Christianity, in organizing all mankind in accordance with the fundamental principle of divine morality.

"To accomplish your task, you must set forth this principle as the basis and purpose of all social institutions.

"The apostles were forced to recognize the power of Caesar; they had to say, 'Render unto Caesar the things that are Caesar's,' because, being unable to dispose of a force sufficient to fight against him, they had to avoid making themselves his enemy.

"But today, since the respective positions of the spiritual and temporal powers have been reversed, thanks to the achievements of the Church Militant, you must proclaim to Caesar's successors that Christianity will no longer acknowledge the right to command men, this right founded upon conquest, in other words, upon the law of the strongest. . . .

"The most favorable situation for ameliorating the existence of the poorest class as rapidly as possible would be one in which a great quantity of works demanding a high degree of human intelligence are to be carried out. You are capable of creating such a situation; now that the dimensions of our planet are known, you should have the industrialists, the artists and the men of learning draw up a general plan of works that would make the territorial possessions of mankind as productive and as rewarding as possible in all respects.

"The enormous number of works that you could set up immediately, would contribute more to the amelioration of the lot of the poor class than the most abundant charities ever could; and by this means, the rich, far from impoverishing themselves with pecuniary sacrifices, would be increasing their own wealth at the same time that they were improving the lot of the poor. . . ."

I accuse the Protestants of heresy on this second count:
I accuse them of having adopted a poor ritual.

The more society is perfected morally and physically, the more its intellectual and manual efforts are subdivided; thus, in the ordinary course of life, the attention of men is fixed more and more upon objects of special interest, corresponding to the extent that the fine arts, science and industry progress.

The result of this is, that the more society progresses, the more its religious rituals have to be perfected; for the object of religious ritual is to draw the attention of men regularly assembling on their days of rest to the interests common to all members of society, to the general interests of mankind.

The reformer Luther, and, after his death, the ministers of the Reformed churches, should therefore have sought all means of making ritual as appropriate as possible to direct the attention of the faithful to the interests that they have in common.

They should have sought the best means and most favorable circumstances to develop completely before the eyes of the faithful the fundamental principle of the Christian religion: *all men must behave as brothers toward one another,* to familiarize their minds with this principle, and get them into the habit of applying it in all their social relations, so as to keep them from losing sight of it entirely in the ordinary course of their lives, no matter how specialized may be the objects of their day-to-day activities.

Now, in order to attract men's attention toward some idea, whatever it may be, in order to push them firmly in a certain direction, one must employ either of two general methods. Either you must inspire terror in them by showing them the terrible woes that would result if they were to pursue a line of conduct other than the one along which you were urging them, or you must lure them with the prospect of satisfactions that would necessarily result from efforts they made in the direction you were indicating.

In order to produce the most decisive and useful activity along either one of these lines, you must combine all the means and resources that the fine arts have to offer.

The preacher who is called upon by circumstances to employ eloquence, which is foremost among the fine arts, must make his listeners tremble when he describes the dreadful lot that the man who has merited public disapproval finds in this life. He must actually show people the arm of God raised over the head of the man whose sentiments have not all been dominated by the ideal of philanthropy.

Or else he must develop the most generous and energetic sentiments in the souls of his listeners by making them feel with all their hearts the superiority of those satisfactions which are accompanied by public esteem over all other satisfactions.

The poets must supplement the efforts of the preachers; they must provide the religious service with poetic works that can be recited in chorus, so that all the faithful will be preachers in regard to one another.

The musicians must enrich the religious poetry with their accompaniments, and stamp it with a musical character that will penetrate deeply into the souls of the faithful.

The painters and sculptors should place within the temples works that will fasten the attention of Christians upon the most eminently Christian acts that men have performed in the past.

The architects should build the temples in such a way that, within their walls, preachers, poets and musicians, painters and sculptors, will readily be able to stir up feelings either of terror, or of hope and joy, in the souls of the faithful.

These clearly are the bases that must be provided for ritual, and the means that must be employed to make ritual useful to society.

What did Luther do in this matter? He reduced the ritual of the Reformed church to mere preachment; he made all Christian sentiments as prosaic as possible; he banished all the ornaments of painting and sculpture from his temples; he suppressed music, and gave preference to religious edifices whose structures were the least significant and therefore the least appropriate to the task of favorably disposing the hearts of the faithful towards passions for the public good. . . .

I now level against the Protestants a third accusation of heresy:

I accuse them of having adopted a poor set of dogmas.

. . . Four major disadvantages have resulted from the excessive emphasis that the Protestants have placed upon the Bible:

1. This study has caused them to lose sight of positive ideas and contemporary problems; it has given them a taste for pointless inquiries, and a great penchant for metaphysics. In northern Germany in particular, which is the seat of Protestantism, vagueness of ideas and feelings dominates all the writings of the most noted philosophers and most popular novelists.

2. This study spices the imagination with reminders of various shameful vices that the advancement of civilization has caused to disappear, such as bestiality and incest of all imaginable sorts.

3. This study focusses the attention upon political desires contrary to the public good; it drives those who are governed to want to establish in society an utterly impracticable equality; it keeps Protestants from working for the formation of a political system in which the most capable men in the sciences of observation, in the fine arts, and in the industrial combinations would care for the general interest: a special system that would be the best humanity could achieve, since it is the one that would contribute the most directly and efficaciously to

the moral and physical amelioration of the existence of the poor.

4. This study leads those engaged in it to regard it as the most important study of all. The result of this is the widespread formation of Biblical societies, which distribute millions of copies of the Bible to the public every year. . . .

I have had to criticize Protestantism with the greatest severity in order to make Protestants realize how incomplete Luther's reform was, and how inferior it is to the New Christianity; but, as I pointed out at the beginning of my examination of Luther's work, I am none the less aware of how profound, in spite of his numerous errors, was the service that he rendered society in the part of his reform devoted to criticism. Besides, my own critique was directed against that Protestantism that is regarded by Protestants as the definitive reform of Christianity; I had no intention of attacking Luther's polemical genius. When one considers the times in which he lived, the conditions under which he had to struggle, one feels that he did everything possible at the time to start a reform movement and persuade people to adopt it. By presenting moral doctrine, instead of ritual and dogma, as the aspect of Christianity that should command the attention of the faithful, even though the moral doctrine of Protestantism was not properly attuned to the understandings of modern civilization, Luther prepared the way for the new reform of the Christian religion. Nevertheless, one must not look upon the New Christianity as a perfection of Protestantism. The new formula under which I am presenting the original principle of Christianity is completely different in nature from any improvements that have hitherto been made in the Christian religion.

I will stop here. I think, sir conservative, that I have sufficiently expounded my ideas on the new Christian doctrine for you to be able, at least for the present, to make a preliminary judgement. Tell me whether or not you believe me imbued with the spirit of Christianity, and whether or not my efforts to rejuvenate this sublime religion are of a nature that will not alter its primitive purity.

THE CONSERVATIVE: I have followed your discourse with great attention. As you spoke, my own ideas became clearer,

my doubts disappeared, and I felt my admiration for the
Christian religion grow inside of me; my attachment to the
religious system that has civilized Europe has in no way prevented me from understanding that it is possible to improve it
still more, and you have won me over completely on this
point. . . .

I find your conclusion to be legitimate and of the utmost
importance. I regard myself, from this moment on, as a New
Christian, and I unite my efforts with yours in the propagation
of the New Christianity.

But, with that in mind, I have several observations to make
on the general nature of your efforts. The new formula under
which you represent the principle of Christianity includes your
entire system of social organization, a system founded at once
upon philosophical considerations from the sciences, the fine
arts, industry, and the religious sentiment that is the most
widespread in the civilized world, that of Christianity. Why,
then, have you not presented this system, this object of all
your reflections, first and foremost from the religious point of
view, from the point of view that is at once the most elevated
and the most popular? Why have you addressed yourself to
industrialists, scholars and artists, instead of going directly to
the people with a religious message? Do you want people to
say of you exactly what you say of Luther: "He has criticized
well, but has formulated his doctrine poorly"?

The intellectual powers of man are really quite frail; it is by
making them converge upon a single goal, by directing them
all toward the same point, that a great effect is achieved and
an important result obtained. Why do you begin by employing
your powers in criticism, instead of starting right out and
formulating a new doctrine? Why do you not attack the question of the New Christianity right from the outset? . . .

What obstacles could such a doctrine encounter? Those who
would find it to be in their interest to support it are infinitely
more numerous than those whose interest would be in preventing it from being carried out. The partisans of this doctrine
have nothing less than the principle of divine morality to stand
on, whereas their adversaries have no weapons with which to
oppose them but an accumulation of habits that come from an

era of ignorance and barbarism, sustained by the principles of Jesuitic egoism.

In short, I think that you should immediately begin propagating your new doctrine and preparing missions among all the civilized nations, in order to bring about its adoption.

THE INNOVATOR: The New Christians should develop the same character and follow the same procedures as the Christians of the Primitive Church; they should not employ any forces other than those of their intelligence in getting their doctrine adopted. It is solely by persuasion and demonstration that they should work for the conversion of Catholics and Protestants; by these means they will succeed in making those Christians who have been misguided by the Papal and Lutheran religions want to renounce the heresies with which these religions have become infected, and willingly adopt the New Christianity.

The New Christianity will, like primitive Christianity, be supported, advanced and protected by moral force and by the great power of public opinion; and, if the propagation of this religion should unfortunately occasion acts of violence or unjust condemnations, it would be the New Christians who would be the sufferers; for at no time whatsoever would anyone see them employing physical force against their adversaries. Never would they function as judges or executioners.

After I had found the way to rejuvenate Christianity by causing it to undergo a transfiguration in its fundamental principle, my first concern was, and had to be, to take all necessary precautions to see to it that the spread of this new doctrine would not incite the poor classes to acts of violence against the rich and against governments.

I had to address myself first to the rich and powerful, to see to it that they became favorably disposed toward the new doctrine, by making them realize that it was in no way contrary to their interests, since it clearly would be impossible to ameliorate the moral and physical existence of the poor classes by any other means than those that tend to advance the well-being of the rich classes.

I had to make artists, men of learning and the chiefs of industrial enterprises realize that their interests were essentially

the same as those of the great masses of people; that they
themselves belonged to the class of laborers at the same time
that they were its natural leaders; that the approbation of the
masses for the services these men rendered them was the sole
recompense worthy of their glorious efforts. I had to insist
strongly upon this point, since it is of the greatest importance,
and is the sole means of providing the nations with the sort
of guides that truly deserve their confidence, guides capable
of leading public opinion and enabling it to judge sanely what
political measures are either favorable or contrary to the interests of the greatest number. Finally, I had to make Catholics and Protestants see exactly when it was that they had
started down a false path, so as to facilitate the means of
bringing them back onto the true one. I must insist upon this
point, because the conversion of the Catholic and Protestant
clergies would provide the New Christianity with great
sources of strength. . . .

But it is not my aim merely to demonstrate the heresies of
the Catholics and the Protestants; it will not suffice for me, in
order to rejuvenate Christianity entirely, to make it triumph
over all the existing religious philosophies. I must also establish its scientific superiority over all the doctrines of the philosophers who stood outside any organized religion. I must
reserve the development of this idea for a later discourse; but
meanwhile, I shall give you a synopsis of the whole of the
work that I have in mind.[1]

Mankind has never ceased to progress, but it has not always proceeded in the same way or employed the same methods for adding to its knowledge and perfecting its civilization.
On the contrary, observation shows that it has proceeded,
from the fifteenth century to the present, in a manner quite
different from the one it followed from the establishment of
Christianity until that time.

From the time Christianity was established until the fifteenth century, mankind was occupied mainly with the coordination of its generous sentiments, with the establishment of
a single and universal principle, and with the founding of an

[1] Saint-Simon did not live to complete the projected second
and third parts of this work.—Ed.

institution that had as its goal the elevation of the aristocracy of talent over that of birth; so that it tended to cause all particular interests to submit to the general interest. During this entire period, all direct observations concerning private interests, particular facts and secondary principles, were neglected and decried by most thinkers, while the prevailing opinion on this point came to be that secondary principles had to be derived from general facts and from a universal principle. This opinion was based upon purely speculative notions, since the human intelligence has, in fact, no way of establishing generalizations so precise that it would be possible to derive from them, as direct consequences, all the particularities in existence.

It is to this important point that I have related all the observations I have presented in the course of this dialogue, in my examination of Catholicism and Protestantism.

Since the dissolution of the European spiritual power—the result of Luther's insurrection—since the fifteenth century, the human mind has repudiated the broad generalizations of the preceding era: it has turned to particularities and has occupied itself with the analysis of concrete facts and of the private interests of the different classes of society; it has striven to establish secondary principles that could serve as bases for the different branches of knowledge. During this second period, the opinion became established that the consideration of generalities, of general principles and the general interests of mankind, was nothing but a vague and metaphysical pursuit, incapable of contributing efficaciously to the progress of knowledge and the perfecting of civilization.

Thus, the human mind has followed, since the fifteenth century, a course opposite to the one it had followed up to that time; and certainly, the important and positive advances in all aspects of human activity that have resulted from this change irrevocably demonstrate how greatly deceived were our ancestors in the Middle Ages, when they deemed the study of particular facts and secondary principles, and the analysis of private interests, to be of mediocre utility.

But it is equally true that great evil has ensued for society as a result of the state of abandon in which men have left all

efforts relative to the study of general facts, principles and
interests since the fifteenth century. This desertion has given
rise to selfish sentiments, which have become dominant among
all classes and all individuals. These sentiments have facili-
tated Caesar's recovery of a large part of the political power
he had lost before the fifteenth century. To this selfishness
we must attribute the political illness of our era, an illness that
causes all those in our society who are usefully employed to
suffer; an illness that enables the Kings to absorb for their
personal use, and for the use of their soldiers and courtiers, a
large part of the earnings of the poor; an illness that allows
the royalty and aristocracy to pre-empt an enormous part of
the honor and esteem that really belong to the men of learning, the artists and the chiefs of the industrial enterprises, in
recognition of the services of direct and positive utility that
they render the social body.

It is therefore most desirable that those labors that have for
their object the perfecting of our knowledge relative to general
facts, general principles and general interests be promptly resumed, and that they be protected henceforth by society just
as carefully as those works which have the study of particular
facts, secondary principles and private interests for their object. . . .

I will end this first dialogue by telling you frankly what I
think about the Christian revelation.

We are certainly quite superior to our predecessors in those
sciences that have a positive and specialized utility; it is only
since the fifteenth century, and, in particular, since the beginning of the last century, that we have made great advances in
mathematics, physics, chemistry and physiology. But there is
one science that is even more important for society than physical and mathematical knowledge: the science that constitutes
society itself, that serves as its basis, moral science. Now,
moral science has followed a line of development entirely opposite to that of the physical sciences and mathematics. Its
fundamental principle was brought forth more than eighteen
hundred years ago, and, since that time, none of the inquiries,
even those by men of the greatest genius, have been able to
discover a principle superior in either generality or precision

to the one that was then given by the Founder of Christianity. Moreover, when society lost sight of this principle, when men ceased looking upon it as a general guide for their conduct, they promptly fell back under the yoke of Caesar, that is, under the empire of physical force, which this principle had subordinated to intellectual force.

I ask you now if the Intelligence that produced the regulative principle of mankind eighteen hundred years ago, and which thereby had produced this principle fifteen centuries before we began making important advances in the physical and mathematical sciences—I ask you if this Intelligence does not clearly have superhuman power, and if there exists a greater proof of Christian revelation.

Yes, I believe Christianity to be a divine institution, and I am persuaded that God grants special protection to those who devote their efforts to causing all human institutions to be submitted to the fundamental principle of this sublime doctrine. I am convinced that I myself am performing a divine mission when I remind the Peoples and the Kings of the true spirit of Christianity. And, fully confident of the special and divine protection that is being given to my efforts, I therefore feel hardy enough to make representations concerning their conduct to the Kings of Europe, who have formed a coalition, and have given this union the sacred name of *Holy Alliance;* I now address myself directly to them, and dare to say:

PRINCES,

What is the nature, what is the character, in the eyes of God and of Christians, of the power that you exercise?

What are the bases of the system of social organization that you are working to establish? What measures have you taken to ameliorate the moral and physical existence of the poor classes?

You call yourselves Christians, yet you continue to base your power upon physical force, so that you are still only the successors of Caesar, and you forget that true Christians propose, as the final outcome of their efforts, to annihilate completely the power of the sword, the power of Caesar, which, by its very nature, is provisional. . . .

Listen to the voice of God, which speaks to you through my

lips; become good Christians once again, and stop looking
upon armies, noblemen, heretical clergies and perverse judges
as your principal sources of sustenance. United under the banner of Christianity, you will be able to accomplish all the
duties that this banner imposes upon the powerful; remember
that it commands them to employ all their forces in advancing
as rapidly as possible the social well-being of the poor!

THE SAINT-SIMONIANS

In the last years of his life, Saint-Simon had begun to attract disciples from among the elite of the younger generation
in France, including a good number of the technology-
minded graduates of the new Ecole Polytechnique. One of the
most eminent of *polytechniciens*, August Comte, worked as
Saint-Simon's secretary for a time, and derived much of his
positivist system from the master's ideas. Another of Saint-
Simon's secretaries was the future historian, Augustin Thierry,
whom the old man adopted as his son. Neither remained with
him for long, but by the time of his death in 1825, he had
come to be surrounded by a substantial group of high-minded
and talented young disciples whose approach to Saint-Simonian ideas was beginning to take on the air of a religious cult.

Their religious turn of mind had of course been signaled by
the master himself in his last book, but within a few years of
his death their behavior went far beyond his intentions, and
they formed themselves into a quasi-monastic order. Retiring
to the estate of the young engineer, Barthélemy-Prosper Enfantin (1796–1864), who, after a period of rivalry with another of the disciples, Saint-Amand Bazard (1791–1832),
had achieved ascendancy over the group, they assumed a
monastic garb, and proceeded to observe continence and cel-
ibacy, awaiting the arrival of a female messiah. *La Mère*, as
she was called, was to appear from the Middle East, and
marry *le Père* (a position assumed by Enfantin himself), thus
establishing a mystical union of East and West, and heralding
the dawn of a new era of brotherhood and happiness for mankind. The Paris police had its doubts, however, about the

political and moral aims of the organization, and the upshot was that Enfantin was arrested and sent to prison for a year. After his release, he continued to pursue his aims as before, this time organizing an expedition to the Middle East, for the purpose of seeking out *la Mère*, and of setting up various huge and characteristically Saint-Simonian projects, such as a canal through the Isthmus of Suez. This latter scheme was subsequently taken over by Vicomte Ferdinand Marie de Lesseps, who had been a follower of Enfantin for a time. Back in France by 1839, his energy and resources spent, Enfantin was appointed a government commissioner for Algerian development; in later years he became a prominent railway director.

The most remarkable thing about the Saint-Simonians was precisely this element of formidable worldly and practical talent that prevailed throughout the group, despite its odd mysticism. A large number of these one-time pseudo-monks of Ménilmontant went on to become leading financiers and industrialists of the Second Empire; Napoleon III even regarded himself as something of a Saint-Simonian. It is fair to say that Saint-Simonianism was a major moral and psychological source of the industrial revolution in France.

All this makes it something of a question whether Saint-Simonianism can properly be called a socialist movement. But, in the first place, we are talking about a period in which the influence of Marxism had not yet become great enough to make it quite clear what socialist loyalties were to be. Toward "the most numerous and poorest class", the Saint-Simonians remained kindly disposed, though paternalistic. They were, however, opponents of the *laissez-faire* principle, being mainly what the French call *dirigiste*, an important thing in a country where a deeply entrenched spirit of small-scale proprietorship —the *petit-bourgeois* outlook, as Marx called it—formed a powerful obstacle in the way of large-scale industrial consolidations. In other words, it took a kind of state-socialist attitude to create an industrial system in France. Furthermore, a more orthodox socialist spirit appears in the early works of the Saint-Simonians, particularly when they were still under the influence of Bazard. He proposed, for example, the abolition of inheritance—something that Saint-Simon himself had never explicitly advocated, although it was a perfectly logical inference from his doctrine that every man should live by his own efforts and talents. Bazard was the principal author of the series of lectures, called *The Doctrine of Saint-Simon*, that the group delivered to the public in 1828–29. The following selection is the first lecture from that series.

EXPOSITION OF THE DOCTRINE OF SAINT-SIMON
FIRST SESSION: ON THE NECESSITY OF A NEW
SOCIAL DOCTRINE (DECEMBER 17, 1828)

Gentlemen,

Society today, considered as a whole, presents the aspect of two armed camps. In one of them are entrenched the few defenders of the two-sided religious and political organization of the Middle Ages; in the other, under the rather inappropriate heading of "partisans of new ideas," are arrayed all those who applauded or cooperated in the overthrow of the old edifice. It is into the middle of these two armies that we have stepped forth, bringing peace, proclaiming a doctrine that preaches not only *horror of bloodshed*, but the horror of battle as well, in whatever form it may disguise itself. *Antagonism*, between a spiritual and a temporal power, *opposition*, in honor of liberty, *competition*, for the greatest good for all—we do not believe in the eternal necessity of any of these machines of war; we do not acknowledge to "civilized humanity" any "natural right" that obliges and condemns it to tear its guts out.

Our Doctrine will, we have no doubt of it, dominate the future more completely than the beliefs of antiquity dominated their era, more completely than Catholicism dominated the Middle Ages; more powerful than its predecessors, it will extend its beneficent activity to the four corners of the earth. No doubt its appearance will stir up vigorous opposition, no doubt it will encounter numerous obstacles as it is propagated; we are prepared to vanquish the former, and we are sure that the latter will sooner or later be overthrown, for victory is certain when one is following the path of humanity's progress, which cannot be deprived of its law of perfectibility by the power of any man.

Barely emerged from a period abounding in disorder and strife, we have seen the gulfs in which the old beliefs and political powers were swallowed up close again. These beliefs and powers had ceased to be legitimate because they were no longer in harmony with the demands of the new society; it would seem, then, that the hearts of men, more tired than satisfied, would have been ready to open themselves with love to the law that will someday unite them all. But the recent memory of a fight to the death, and the revolutionary attitude that men still feel obliged to assume, are holding back this day of unity. Our petulant dispositions, our invidious hatreds constantly present the phantom of despotism to our spirits. In any body of beliefs or area of *common* action, our pride can see only a new yoke, similar to the one that has just been broken at the price of so many tears, so much blood and sacrifice. Anything that seems to have as its end the reestablishment of *order* and *unity* takes on, in our eyes so blinded by distrust, the appearance of an attempt to cause humanity to retrogress.

This permanent anarchy amidst which humanity is quarreling with itself, this universal loosening of social ties, seems to have disturbed a few thinkers; but most of them, dominated by incomplete scientific ideas, believe that there are not yet enough verified *facts*, enough *observations* garnered, for anyone to be able to produce a general Doctrine. For us the problem is solved. We have raised the angle of our vision high enough to see beyond the narrow limits of the present, and, penetrating into the past, we see that we were beleaguered, encumbered with facts; since having done so, we have not doubted that the time has come for a new *conception,* which will embrace and explain the various specialized bodies of work that have accumulated throughout so many years. It is with the confidence that profound conviction gives that we present this conception today. If it is false, if it is merely another in a line of vain systems, then it will not arouse any sympathy, and will leave the populations of the world wallowing in selfishness. But if it is true, if it is the fertile source from which our descendants will derive a well-being that has been refused us, then the sympathetic excitement that it will arouse in all hearts will be dazzling testimony to its legitimacy.

At no time must its value be judged by the effect it might *at first* produce among even the most cultivated spirits, for an obstacle to its popularity exists in their present outlook; that is, their haughty distrust of any sort of general idea, an attitude inspired by the narrow habits contracted in the study of specialties. Philosophical doctrines are generally regarded as completely ineffectual, as mere exercises in intellectual gymnastics, and people take pains to enumerate, in order to prove their sterility, the multitude of *philosophies* that are said to appear in every era. There is an element of truth in this line of argument, but there is also an error; we must examine both of these elements before moving on.

Yes, they are ineffectual, these reveries of *spiritualism* or of *materialism*, which reproduce themselves during every critical epoch in basically the same way, although under different forms. Yes, they are sterile, these aphorisms of moralists that have never given rise to an act of devotion, or given society a worthy man. But collections of maxims, sentences, scattered moral observations, a few systems concerned with the play of the intellectual faculties, their essence and their products— these are not philosophical conceptions. This name can be given only to a body of thought that embraces all the modes of human activity and gives a solution to all social and individual problems. It is enough to say that there have been no more doctrines worthy of this name than there have been periods in which mankind was in a general state. Now, the phenomenon of a regular social order has been present only twice in the series of civilizations to which we belong and which has come down to us in an uninterrupted chain of occurrences—in ancient times and in the Middle Ages. The new general state that we are announcing for the future will form the third link in this chain; it will not be identical with those that preceded it, but it will present striking analogies to them, with respect to *order* and *unity*. It will succeed the various periods of crisis that have been taking place among us for the past three centuries, and will present itself in the end as a consequence of the law of the development of humanity.

This law, revealed to the genius of *Saint-Simon,* and verified by him in the study of a long historical series, shows us two distinct and alternating states of society, the first, which we call the *organic state,* being the one in which all the facts of human activity are classified, foreseen, and ordered into a general theory; in which the aim of social activity is precisely defined. The second, which we have named the *critical state,* is that in which all communion of thought, all wholeness of action, all coordination, have ceased, and in which all society presents itself as only an agglomeration of isolated individuals at war with one another.

Each of these states has occupied two periods in history. An *organic state* preceded the era of the Greeks, this latter being what has been called a *philosophical era,* and what we will characterize more appropriately under the title of *critical epoch.* Later, a new doctrine was produced, which passed through various phases of self-elaboration and self-perfecting, and finally established its political power over the whole of the Occident. The constituting of the Church began a new *organic epoch,* which came to an end in the fifteenth century, at the moment when the reformers gave the first signal for the *critical epoch* that has continued down to the present day.

The *critical* epochs are made up of two distinct phases. During the first phase, an atmosphere of collective action reigns, which, confined at first only to the most worthy men, is soon propagated among the masses: its aim, premeditated for the originators, instinctive for the masses, is the *destruction* of the established order, which, for all its virtues, is what maintains everything repugnant. Accumulated hatred finally bursts forth and there soon remains nothing but ruins of old institutions to testify that this had once been a harmonious society. The second phase comprises the interval that separates the *destruction* of the old order from the *erection* of the new. In this period, the anarchy has ceased to be violent, but has become more profound: there is now a divergence between *feeling, reasoning* and *action.*

Such is the state of incertitude in the midst of which we have been cast adrift, and which the apostles of liberty have not been able to quell. They affect to regard this bastard sys-

tem of *guarantees*, improvised in response to the critical and
revolutionary needs of the last century, as definitive. They present all these declarations of the rights of man and citizen, and
all the constitutions founded upon such documents, as the last
word in social perfection; they assure us that it was for this
great conquest (a paltry one, indeed) that the world toiled
for several centuries. Point out to them the general malaise,
and they will reply with assurance that these disturbances are
the outcome of passing and accidental causes; they regard the
battle between the peoples and their leaders as the normal
condition of humanity, and find that, at last, society has nothing more to wish for, now that *distrust has become fixed and
regulated in the social order*. To back up modern theories, they
point to the rapid development of the sciences, and to the importance that industry has assumed; and if they maintain a
discreet silence about that way of life which alone has the capacity to speak to the heart and stir it, if they say nothing
about the *fine arts*, it is because they consider this form of
activity to be only a diversion, only a series of moving and
impressive images, the *useful purpose* of which is to charm
the hours of a fatuous and *onerous* idleness.

Let us therefore cast a rapid glance over the *sciences*, *industry* and the *fine arts*, and see if these three great organs of
society, considered as a *Collective Being*, carry out their functions with the ease, and above all with the harmony, that
alone maintains the health and vigor of the social body and
facilitates the developments to which it is susceptible. We will
then be much better able to appreciate what is the influence
of the present outlook on *individual* and *social* relations.

SCIENCES

Our century is smitten with a virtually religious admiration
for the scientific advances that it has seen take place; it cites
with satisfaction the great number of its scientists; and, if it
deigns to preserve some memory of the past, this is only to oppose the darkness to the light, slumber to full consciousness,
and thus to render itself a more brilliant homage. Let us examine this pretension as briefly as possible, and see if it is as
well-founded as one is led to believe at first glance.

Science is divided into two lines of activity—the perfecting of theories, and the application of them. Let us note in a general way from the outset, that most scientists almost totally neglect the first of these, to the advantage of the second. As for the very small number of scientists who work directly for the progress of scientific theory, they are all engaged in pursuing the line that was opened up at the end of the sixteenth century by *Bacon*. They accumulate experiments, dissect nature in its entirety, enrich science with new details, add more or less curious facts to those previously observed; almost all of them *verify*, almost all of them are armed with microscopes, so that the most minute phenomena will not escape their vigilant exploration. But who are the scientists who classify this disorderly pile of riches? Where are those who arrange the fruits of this abundant harvest? A few stacks are to be perceived here and there; but they are few and far between on the vast plain of science, and no great theoretical synthesis has been produced for more than a century now. If you ask what link unites celestial and molecular attraction, what general conception of the order of phenomena presides over the inquiries of scientists, and whether their purpose is to study, according to the acknowledged division, inorganic bodies or organic ones, not only do your questions remain unanswered, but nobody even seems to take the trouble to look for a reply. The branches of inquiry have been divided and subdivided, and this is undoubtedly a wise thing to do; but the links that once held them together and gave them a common direction have been broken, and now each separate branch of science, congratulating itself on what it calls its emancipation, follows its own unique path. And since the over-all *conception* held to by previous generations is no longer applicable to recent findings, scientists have concluded that their task is to give themselves over *exclusively* to inquiries based on *observation*, with the result that only isolated columns are being erected, instead of a uniform edifice.

Meanwhile, it will be pointed out, there exist academies to which are summoned all those men who, by their discoveries, have given indication of possessing great intellectual capacities; one is led to believe that the field of science is exploited most thoroughly and beneficially by these institutions. Yes, to be sure, there are academies, and the members included within their fold are all men of great learning; every one of them is learned in some science, and some are learned in several. This is not the place to question whether the spirit of coterie that has made its way into these academies has not sometimes influenced the choice of one or another nominee; that is one present-day abuse with which we are not concerning ourselves; but we will say of these bodies of learned men the same thing we have said of the sciences themselves: no over-all conception orchestrates their efforts. The members who compose these bodies come together in a single meeting-hall; but, having no ideas in common, they do not undertake any work in common; they all wear the same costume, but only their insignia has the quality of unity, for deep within them no sympathy of any sort calls them to each other. Each one goes his own way pursuing lines of inquiry that are assuredly most useful and interesting, but without troubling himself to see whether a related science has not done something that might illuminate his own research. A few physicists have abandoned *Newton's* explanation for that of *Huyghens,* but only the small corner of scientific work given over to physics has taken this change into consideration, so to speak. As for the *moral* and *political* sciences, they are not even represented in our Institute.

The result of this vicious organization of scientific groups, of this absence of any intellectual hierarchy, is that even the most respectable academy does not believe itself to have a mission exalted enough to permit it to look into the state of acquisitions already made and to be made, to formulate the problems that are important for it to solve, to appreciate the efforts required and the results obtained, in a word, to *direct* all efforts with rapidity and regularity, and with the aim of perfecting them. The academies are well able to offer a few shabby prizes in order to obtain the solution of this or that problem; but if the public does not respond to this appeal, as is sometimes the case, the problem is left unsolved indefinitely, and the step forward—undoubtedly an important one, since the program said it was—remains to be taken.

Such are the various causes to which the sterility of our academies must be attributed. The idea behind the founding of them was much more that of offering a recompense and a place of retreat to men who might pursue a scientific career with distinction, than that of creating working associations having it as their purpose to organize and centralize efforts. Thus, deprived of a real activating principle, having no authority to assign work and judge its products, they obtain nothing but almost insignificant results, even though their members are men of the highest capacities. What can they expect when they are composed exclusively of scientists engaged in specialized efforts, and mainly practical ones at that?

What we see going on before our eyes is the consequence of the faultiness of the order of things that we have just pointed out. In the absence of an official inventory of verified scientific discoveries, the various isolated scientists are exposed every day to the hazard of repeating experiments already made by others, the knowledge of which would, by sparing them efforts that are often as painful as they are useless, facilitate the advancement of their work. Let us note further that their security is not complete. The work of competitors pursues them; another man, perhaps, is working in the same field, and is *going to steal a march* (as they say); they must hide away, hurry, work precipitously and in isolation at experiments that require deliberation and combined effort. In a word, one can see being manifested the inconveniences of every sort that result from an organization of things that consigns the task of perfecting scientific theories to miscellaneous individual pursuits. The academy does not *command* progress, it is satisfied to *record* it.

We said that most scientists devote themselves to *practical* pursuits. Wherever the existence of scientists is not assured by some consideration provided by society, there will assuredly be an abandonment of works of pure *theory;* for, if a person is to devote himself to such efforts, chance must provide him with a fortune and with a great intellectual capacity at the same time—a double condition that is rarely fulfilled. Not that the government does not sometimes provide scientists with recompense; but, being as incompetent as it is possible to be, it

seeks at the same time to *use* them in schools, faculties, arse-
nals, etc., forever forcing them to use up in *practical* pursuits
time that is precious for *theoretical* ones. There remains, then,
the great and noble resource of *sinecures;* but who would
want to pay this price to obtain the advantage of working in
peace? What elevated spirit would consent to be provided
with a function that he does not carry out, when he feels a
genuine calling within himself? Why must the insulting word
favor intervene where the word *justice* belongs? Besides, in
exchange for such a *favor,* a power alien to science demands
of the scientist, reduced to the role of solicitor, a complete political and moral servitude, forcing him to choose between his
love for science—between the progress of the *human* intelligence, in other words—and his love for *himself.*

But you must believe, some will say, that society finds
ample compensations for the disadvantages that you have
pointed out; obliged to devote themselves to the application
of their ideas in order to live, scientists are undoubtedly improving prospects along these lines. This thought naturally
occurs; but if one tries to verify it by the facts, one finds that
the various functions are in general badly filled, and that there
are no prospects for improvement anywhere. Disgust and
boredom intermingle in any kind of work that a person does
not like; life plays out its course in a succession of regrets,
and great talents pass through the world and are extinguished
after having rendered only a feeble part of the services that
they could have performed. Let us suppose that a talented
engineer were called upon to cut, count, and spread piles of
stones along a highway; it is likely that he would perform
this task more poorly than would a man of more humble talents, while the much more important task that he could have
been called upon to perform would not have been carried out.
Since we are speaking of application, is it not evident that
the most important, the greatest, application of science should
be in *education?* Now, there exists today complete discord between scientists and teachers; one might say, quite literally,
that they do not speak the same language. No general steps
have been taken to see to it that the advances in science, as
each of them is made, pass immediately into the body of in-

struction; there does not exist, finally, any wide and reliable framework by which one can pass from *theory* to *practice*.

And so, without meaning to deprecate the efforts of men who have, by their diligence, well deserved the esteem of society, but who remain at a far remove from a *Descartes*, a *Pascal*, a *Newton*, or a *Leibniz;* without seeking to denigrate their works, which often presuppose an uncommon capacity, we are forced to acknowledge that no great philosophical vision dominates and coordinates the scientific conceptions of today. In the whole body of these conceptions, we can discover only a rich collection of specialized data; it is a museum of fine coins waiting for the hand that is to classify them. The disorder of minds has invaded the sciences themselves, and it can be said that they present the painful spectacle of a complete anarchy. To conclude, let us say that it is in the absence of a unified social vision that one must seek the cause of the illness, and in the discovery of such a unity that one will find the remedy.

INDUSTRY

The wonders of *industry* have perhaps been even more extolled than those of science: let us endeavor to appreciate the efforts made in this direction.

Here, as in the sciences, we do not seek to gainsay any of the advances that have been made. Obviously, the sciences, recently directed towards practical application, were bound to illuminate several branches of technology; it is no less clear that, profiting from all the efforts of our predecessors, we were bound to surpass them. The question, then, is not whether industry has made conquests—no one could appreciate its conquests more than we do; but what we are concerned with is to find out if its progress along the path of amelioration might not have been much more rapid than it was. We are therefore led to observe industry in its three major aspects: (1) the technological aspect; (2) the organization of labor, or, in other words, the division of the tasks of *production* with respect to the needs of *consumption;* and (3) the relationship between the *laborers* and the *owners of the instruments of labor.*

In the present advanced state of science and industry, industry is, in its technological aspect, a derivation of science, a direct application of its data to material production, rather than a simple collection of routine procedures more or less confirmed by experience. Meanwhile, nothing is organized in such a way as to enable industry to escape the narrow confines within which we see it still ensnared, to enable industrial *practice* to rise to the level of scientific *theory*. Everything here is still at the mercy of chance and scattered individual insight. The method of trial and error, often extremely time-consuming, often giving rise to unwarranted predilections, is virtually the only method those engaged in industry employ for the improvement of their techniques; furthermore, each industrialist is obliged to go through this method from start to finish for himself, since, thanks to the competitive system, each considers it to be in his interest to shroud his discoveries in mystery, so as to preserve his monopoly of them. When, as happens every now and then, a rapprochement between *theory* and *practice* does take place, it occurs fortuitously, in isolated instances, and always incompletely.

Undoubtedly various improvements have seen the light of day in spite of these obstacles; but would it be possible to ascertain how much they have cost? How many futile efforts, how many wasted investments, how many emotional agonies there have been, the fruits of which have not been reaped by the founders of the most worthy enterprises! In industry, as in science, we find only isolated efforts; the sole sentiment that dominates all its thinking is *selfishness*. The industrialist troubles himself very little about the interests of society. His family, his instruments of labor, and the personal fortune he is striving to attain—these, respectively, are his *humanity*, his *universe* and his *God*. In those who are pursuing the same career as he, he sees only enemies; he hovers over them in expectation, spying upon them, and the prospect of ruining them is his glory and happiness. Into what kind of hands, then, have most of the workshops and instruments of industry fallen? Have they been turned over to the men who would make the best possible use of them, in the interest of society? Certainly not. They are managed, in general, by incompetent directors, who have been guided in the choice of what they feel they must learn by *personal interest*—a fact that has not generally been noticed until now.

Faults no less grave are to be seen in the *organization of labor*. Industry is in possession of a theory, as we have said; one might therefore be led to believe that this theory would show how *production* and *consumption* can and must be harmonized in every instance. Now, it happens that this very theory is the principal source of disorder, and the economists seem to have set themselves the following problem:

"Given leaders who are more ignorant than those whom they govern; supposing, furthermore, that these leaders, far from favoring the advancement of industry, want to place obstacles in its way, and that their delegates are the born enemies of the producers; what, then, is the most suitable form of industrial organization for society?"

Laissez faire, laissez passer!—such has been the solution that has necessarily followed, the sole general principle that they have proclaimed. It is well enough known under what influence this maxim was produced; it dates itself. The economists believed that they had thus, with a stroke of the pen, resolved all questions concerning the *production* and *distribution* of wealth; they have consigned the realization of this broad precept to *personal interest*, not dreaming that each individual, no matter how profound his view, cannot, in the environment within which he lives, judge the whole of things, cannot see from the depths of the valley what can be discovered only from the highest summit. We are witnesses to the disasters that have already resulted from this *opportunist principle* (*principe de circonstance*) and if we were to cite the striking examples, they would crowd together to testify to the impotence of a theory that was supposed to fertilize industrial growth. If there are a few monopolies today, a few enterprises based on exclusive privilege, most of them owe their existence entirely to legislative dispensation. The fact is that liberty is widespread, and the maxim of the economists is generally the rule in France and England.

Well, then, what is the scene that we have before our

eyes? Each separate industrialist, without a guide, without
any compass but his *personal* observation, which is always
incomplete no matter how extensive his connections in the
world, seeks to instruct himself in the needs of consumption.
Rumor has it that a certain branch of production has good
possibilities: all efforts, all available funds, are steered in
that direction, everyone plunging in blindly. Nobody even
takes time out to ask himself what the proper measure of
the situation might be, what the necessary limits are. The
economists, meanwhile, applaud at the sight of this con-
gested road, since a huge number of opponents indicates to
them that the principle of *competition* is going to be widely
applied. Alas! What is the result of this battle to the death?
A few lucky ones are victorious—but it is a victory paid for
by the complete ruin of innumerable victims.

The inevitable consequence of this manner of production
that is so excessive in certain directions, of these incoherent
efforts, is that the equilibrium between production and
consumption is disturbed at every moment. Countless catas-
trophes result from this situation—these commercial crises
that arise and terrify speculators, and put a stop to the
execution of the worthiest projects. Then we are confronted
with the spectacle of honest and hard-working men going
down to ruin, a sight that undermines the morality of the
onlookers, for it leads one to the conclusion that one evidently
needs, in order to succeed, something more than honesty and
industriousness. People then become subtle, adroit, deceitful, and they even glory in being so. Once they have taken
this step, they are lost.

Let us now add that this fundamental principle, *laissez
faire, laissez passer,* presupposes a personal interest that is
always in harmony with the general interest, a supposition
that innumerable facts tend to refute. To choose one example
from a thousand, is it not evident that, if society in general
conceives its interest to be in the construction of steam
engines, the worker who makes his living by toiling with his
hands cannot join his voice to that of society? The answer to
this objection is well known. Printing, for example, is
cited, and it is pointed out that printing today occupies more

men than the task of copying ever did, as a result of society's having pursued the consequences of the invention of printing; and so it is said, *everything balances out in the end.* An admirable conclusion! And until this balancing-process has run its course, what do we do with the thousands of men who are starving? Will our calculations console them? Will they endure their misery with patience because the statistical tables assure them that they will have bread in a few years?

This is not to criticize mechanical progress, which should take every step that its genius inspires it to take; but, with some foresight, society could see to it that the conquests of *industry* are not like those of *war.* Funeral dirges ought not to be mixed in among the songs of joy.

The third aspect of industry that we want to examine is the relationship between the laborers and the owners of the instruments of labor, or capital. But this question is related to that of the constitution of property itself. . . . We will merely remark at this point that the lands, workshops, capital investments, etc., can be employed to the greatest possible advantage of production only on this one condition, that they be placed in the hands of those most able to make use of them, of those, in other words, who have a *capacity for industry.* Now, today, *capacity* by itself constitutes feeble grounds for claiming credit; in order to acquire something, you must already be in possession of something. The *accident of birth* blindly distributes the *instruments of labor,* whatever they may be, and if the inheritor, the idle property-owner, entrusts them into the hands of a capable worker, it goes without saying that the raw product, the major part of the earnings, goes to the incompetent or lazy proprietor.

What can we conclude from all the above, if not that the results we now so admire would be greatly surpassed, but without the woes to which we are daily witness, if the exploitation of the goods of the world were regularized, and if, therefore, a general conception were to preside over this exploitation? It is unity and wholeness, then, that we still lack. The leaders of society have cried, "Save your own skins!" and so each member of the whole separates himself, saying, "Every man for himself, God for *nobody!*"

THE FINE ARTS

Now that we have demonstrated the lack of a common purpose in the sciences and in industry, we need only look at the fine arts, to have embraced all the modes of human activity.

When one considers the ages of *Pericles, Augustus, Leo X, Louis XIV,* and then regards the nineteenth century, he can only laugh, and never dream of establishing a parallel; on this point at least, everyone is in agreement. It is true that the newspapers can try to console us in our disgrace by assuring us that we are eminently *positive,* but this is just a feeble excuse to those of us who know the meaning of that magical and so strangely abused adjective.

We also acknowledge that the fine arts are in a state of languor and degradation, but we attribute this to fundamental causes; and we find it of interest to go into these causes, as we will find it later to make an estimate of the true role of the *fine arts,* and the *extent* of what, as we see it, this term covers.

The fine arts are the expression of feeling, or, in other words, of the only one among the three states of being of mankind that, without the fine arts, would be lacking a language. Without the fine arts, there would be a lacuna in the life of the individual, as well as in the life of society. It is the fine arts that condition men toward social acts, that lead them to see their private interest in the general interest; they are the sources of devotion, of lively and tender affections. The claim that is made nowadays, with a kind of satisfaction, that they are inferior, is withering proof of the general aridity of feeling, in society as a whole as well as on the part of the individuals, that prevails at the present time. To what role are the fine arts reduced when they are regarded as a completely ineffectual form of expression, when they are so reviled as to be looked upon as merely a form of *recreation?*

There are two elements in all the fine arts: *poetry,* or *animation,* and *form,* or *technique.* Undoubtedly, it is the first that determines the second; meanwhile we have been witness to the disappearance of *poetry,* while the perfecting of *technique* has survived it. Nowadays, form is the almost exclusive preoccupation; the nature of affections, for which form was originally intended only as the interpreter, is scarcely considered. We appreciate a work of art independently of its action upon our sympathies—in other words, we envisage it in only one of its two aspects. This is the cause of the indifference in which the fine arts find us and allow us to remain. Let us add, in passing, that the true artists today, the men who are truly inspired, reflect only anti-social sentiments, for the only poetic forms that have any animation whatsoever are *satire* and *elegy*. It is true that elegy is the language of tender spirits these days; but both these forms equally attack social sentiments, whether by the impassioned expression of despair, or by the expression of contempt whose infernal mockery throws dirt upon everything that is pure and sacred. But, rather than dwell any longer upon a subject that opens the way so readily to a critique of the present time, let us move on and probe into the social relations in which we shall find, on both the individual and the general social levels, the cause of the decadence of the fine arts. There we shall also verify the order that might well have been expected, given the picture we have drawn of scientific and industrial activity.

We have already explained what is to be understood by the terms *organic epoch* and *critical epoch;* we have said that paganism until the time of Socrates and Christianity until the time of Luther formed two organic states. Now we will rapidly sketch some of their characteristics.

The fundamental basis of the societies of antiquity was *slavery*. War was the sole means that these peoples had of providing themselves with slaves, and therefore with those things that could satisfy the material needs of their lives. Among these peoples, the strongest men were the richest; their industry confined itself to pillage. Woe to the weak man who could not carry the weight of armor! The dominant thought of these peoples, their constant purpose, was *war;* all their passions, all their feelings, answered to the cry of war, and their strongest emotions were founded upon love of country and hatred of the foreigner. Even a mother would give thanks to the gods when the shield of her dead son was brought to her. Wherever one went in Greece or Italy, one heard only the sounds of battle; Rome ceased to be Rome when the temple of Janus was closed.

Need we be astonished, then, at the power of the fine arts in that era? A single passion dominated the hearts of all men, a common purpose guided them, one sole thought instilled them with devotion; and devotion and poetic inspiration are inseparable.

Later, when Christianity, prepared for by the school of Socrates, destroyed slavery; when, at the price of a thousand sorrows, the precepts of the Gospels, applied to politics under the name *Catholicism*, had given society a new organization, one that was in harmony with its needs, the faith became a *spiritual fatherland,* common to all the children of Christ. And, in spite of the hatred and selfishness of nations, the new fatherland caused a new love to be born; then, too, one saw the reappearance of great devotion and inspiration. Eight successive crusades in the short space of two centuries did not weaken the fervor of the peoples, and then came the centuries of Leo X and of Louis XIV to crown the great work of Catholicism and of the feudality, which, from then on, were to know only a few more moments of life, or rather, of agony; for, after fifteen centuries, the medieval organization was threatened everywhere.

The clergy, incapable of continuing the divine mission that it had begun, had abandoned the weak, whom it was supposed to protect, and had subordinated itself to the successors of Caesar. The nobility, who also had consecrated themselves, under the name of chivalry, to the defense of the weak, had become pensioners in the splendid antechambers of the great king; and the laity, gradually seizing hold of science and wealth, applied these powerful weapons and overthrew the blasphemous coalition that believed in the eternal validity of the exploitation of man by man.

This is not the place to describe the long struggle that *prepared* the complete liberation of man by abolishing serfdom. We all know the outcome of that struggle, which began at the end of the fifteenth century. We now stand amongst the ruins of medieval society, ruins which still live, and which still can be heard expressing regrets all around us. Our only purpose in recalling these facts has been to establish the distinctive character of our epoch, and confirm that we are in the midst of one of those epochs that we have designated by the term *critical*.

The distinguishing mark of all *critical* epochs, as of all times of great disorder, is *selfishness*. All beliefs are abolished, all common sentiments are extinguished, the sacred fire is no longer tended by anyone. The poet is no longer the divine singer, placed at the head of society to serve as interpreter to man, give him laws, repress his retrograde inclinations, reveal the joys of the future to him, and stir up and sustain his progressive march. No, the poet no longer produces anything but sinister chants. Sometimes he arms himself with the whip of satire, and his verve is breathed out in biting phrases; he gives voice to his passion against all humanity, and provokes men to defiance and hatred of their fellows. Sometimes, with a feeble voice, he sings in elegiac verses of the charms of solitude, abandons himself to the vagueness of revery, and depicts happiness as something to be found in *isolation*, and meanwhile, if anyone is seduced by these melancholy rhythms and flees his fellow men, he will find only despair. But this sort of language no longer has the power even to attract attention. At the end of a *critical* epoch, you can no longer stir a man by speaking to his heart; you must show him, rather, that his *fortune* is in danger. Just look at the most prominent social critics of today; when they wanted to popularize their systems, did they call upon our poets, our painters, our musicians? What could these people have done? They would have been able only to strike within us the chords that respond to individual desires. Our critics therefore invoked the phantom of the *feudality*, presenting them to us as armed and ready to recapture their feudal privileges with one hand, and, with the other, to snatch their property out of the hands of the "acquisitors of the national goods." More recently, when a redoubtable attack was leveled against the freedom of the press, against the "palladium of our liberties" (as it is called in the language

of the speaker's platform), did anyone have recourse, in the
name of its defense, to general moral considerations? Hardly.
Who is not aware of how paltry is the number of men who
are disposed to rally to the defense of what is called the
"general interest"? Something more positive was prudently
appealed to: petitions were drawn up in the interest of book-
sellers, printers, stationers, bookbinders, etc.

Ah! We might as well say it: the fine arts no longer have
a voice when society ceases to love; poetry is not the
interpreter of *egoism*. A true artist, to reveal himself, must
have a chorus that will echo his songs and receive his soul
when he pours it out.

But if social affections do not exist, can we say at least
that the individual affections are well-developed in compensation? Even though the present generation, whenever it
is accused of egoism, proudly takes refuge in this claim, it
nevertheless would have to have a great deal of individual
affection for the claim to be valid. How is that sweet tie, by
which one sex unites itself with the other in order to share
the joys and sorrows of life, formed in our time? We have all
been taught what a "good marriage" is, as distinguished from
what is called a "foolish marriage." Poor girls! You are put
up for auction like slaves; on holidays, you are dressed up,
so as to *increase your value;* and often your father, in his
shamelessness, places your charms in the balance, so that he
can get away with giving a little less money to the unworthy
spouse who is bargaining for you. Of course there are men—
and we say this with joy—who repudiate this odious trafficking,
but they are few in number, and are laughed at by the world.

One might be inclined to believe that paternal and filial
affections, which are born, so to speak, on the day that we
receive life, are not of such a nature as to debase themselves
like this. But all the sympathies are connected with one another, so that the causes that weaken some of them act
equally upon the others; in order to achieve its full development, a sentiment must realize itself in all its possible applications. Have we not seen philosophy coldly cast doubt
upon the reciprocal duties of parents and children? And

have inheritances never *assuaged regrets?* Have they never dried tears?

All these miseries and evils we observe with regret, but not with bitterness. We say that they are gnawing at society, and that they would annihilate it if they were inherent within it. In designating *egoism,* we have placed our finger upon the deepest wound of modern society; it reigns as master among nations as well as among individuals. During the Middle Ages one saw more than once, thanks to religious ties, the peoples of Europe rising up to march towards a common goal, in spite of national hatreds. The sovereigns of our own day have tried to establish an association among themselves, but their efforts have resulted only in a sort of parody of the past, decorated by the title of "Holy Alliance." This European pact, based upon narrow interests, conceived solely out of fear of the revolutionary movement, deprived of that breath of life that animated the confederation of old, could have had nothing but an ephemeral existence. It did not realize anything more than what had been vainly attempted in various epochs for the sake of assuring the maintenance of the European *equilibrium*—an insoluble problem as long as the peoples of Europe do not feel themselves united by a common purpose. Until such a time, the members of this great European family, bristling with defiance towards one another, confirmed in their individuality, hostile to any power that does not associate itself with their separate destinies (which they seek without knowing what they are), will not feel linked by a common sense of duty and a common moral law, as they did in the days of the spiritual brotherhood of Christians.

We have lamented the recent misfortunes of Italy and Spain; we have seen these peoples trying to liberate themselves and adopt a form of government that we pretend to love. What have we done for them? We made ineffectual *promises.* The Greeks, being massacred by the thousands, begged for our pity. Did we form a crusade? No, we had to hold banquets and concerts in order to squeeze a bit of sterile charity out of our surplus.

Do we hear people say that it was because of the governments that the bustling spirit of the European nations was repressed, and that, without the obstacles that they provided, we would have rushed to the rescue of our brothers and avenged their defeat? But what about America, that model country that does not have the banal excuse that she is constrained by her government—what did she do? To her dishonor, it must be pointed out that she entered into *trade* with the Turks, so as to *supply* them! Some parts of South America wanted to shake off the Spanish yoke that was still weighing upon them; did the United States, still full of her own bitter memories of the mother country, the United States, where the sounds of chains recently broken still echoed, did she do anything at all to facilitate the emancipation of her compatriots? No. Did she, finally, offer the Republic of Haiti the help of her financial resources, which could have paid that small country's ransom? No, always no. This free people who has, it is said, ridden itself of all the prejudices of old Europe; this people at the forefront of all peoples on the path of civilization, *protested* against the existence of a liberated people, of a nation of Negroes!

Ah! No doubt, this picture that we have just drawn of the present era would be heart-rending if it were the definitive portrait of the condition of humanity for all time. Fortunately, a better future is in store for man, and the present, in spite of its vices, is bursting with this future towards which all our hopes, all our thoughts, and all our efforts are turned.

Freedom was proclaimed in order to destroy a social order that was no longer feasible, and no idea could have been more powerful against hierarchies that were, in the estimation of the peoples, *justly torn apart*. But when the aim became, in Europe or in America, to apply this idea to the *construction of a new social order*, the state of things that we have just depicted was produced. People seemed to believe that the solution of the problem consisted in placing the word *less* in front of all the terms of the formula of the Middle Ages, and this strange solution engendered only *anarchy*; the publicists of our own era have merely echoed the philosophers of the eighteenth century, without realizing that they have an *inverse* mission to perform. They have continued their attacks with as much fury as if the enemy were still present, and they are exhausting themselves in a battle against a ghost.

Has the time come for the formulation of a New Social Doctrine? Everything indicates it—the depth of the evils that exist, the ineffectual protests of a few philanthropists, and the outcries of distress from among those of high intelligence. For several years now, M. Guizot, and above all, M. Cousin, have been announcing something other than the eighteenth century, which was long proclaimed as the last word in the progress of the human mind. Saint-Simon had occasion to address his thanks to the former. . . . As for the latter, he appeared several years ago, presenting the *conception of representative government*—in other words, the political state realized in the first quarter of the nineteenth century—as the definitive conclusion of philosophy. We who, for our own part, are adopting neither the Middle Ages nor constitutionalism, look forward beyond the confines of the present; and the present regime, even if it were modified or perfected, appears to us only provisional, for one can see that it is tainted with vice to its very foundation. We are in no way ungrateful towards the defenders of this system; we realize that they are setting up a salutary obstacle to the attempts on the part of the old interests to make us retrogress; they also serve as a counterweight to a fraction of society that would like to introduce disorder among the European population, whose greatest need is peace. But we expect nothing of their efforts in the direction of organizing the peoples; for criticism, the equal of any foe in time of war, has only the power to destroy, and it has now carried out its mission. The time is coming when the nations will abandon the banners of an unreflective and disorderly liberalism, in order to enter with love into a state of peace and well-being, to renounce distrust, and to recognize that a *legitimate power* can exist on the earth.

Through a careful examination of social relations, we have recognized that all the links that united men in the past have been broken, and we have expressed no regrets about it. We have not even wept upon seeing the sentiment

of love of fatherland die out, because this is in our eyes only
the egoism of nations, and because this unquestionably
pure sentiment, which has inspired so much noble dedica-
tion and so many generous sacrifices, must disappear in the
face of a sentiment that is purer, greater and more fruitful,
the *love of the universal family of man*. Will we still have to
fight off the ideas of *yoke*, of *despotism*, that the word
"power" ordinarily awakens in perturbed spirits? Ah! sirs,
join us in blessing the yoke that is self-imposed out of conviction, and that satisfies all the sentiments in the heart of
man. Bless a power whose single thought is to impel the
peoples along the path of progress and fertilize all the
sources of public prosperity. The doctrine we are proclaiming must take hold upon all mankind, and give a common
purpose, a harmony of direction, to the three great human
faculties. Through it, the sciences will march, harmonious
and united, along the path of their most rapid development;
industry, regulated in the interest of all, will no longer offer
the dreadful spectacle of an arena of combat; and the fine
arts, animated by a lively sympathy once again, will unfold
for us sentiments of enthusiasm founded upon a life *in
common*, whose gentle influence will make itself felt even
in the most secret joys of *private life*.

CHARLES FOURIER (1772–1837)

Although tradition has classified all of them under the
single heading of "utopian," Fourier and Owen really represent a very different kind of approach to socialism than do
Saint-Simon and his followers. What they all had in common
was a sense of the inadequacy of unadulterated liberalism
when it resulted in such caricatures of human liberty as the
slums of Manchester, but whereas for Fourier and Owen, as
well as for the social democratic movements of more recent times, the task was to redistribute liberty so that it
could be enjoyed by all, the Saint-Simonians were more
inclined to modify freedom and look upon it as being of
secondary importance. If Fourier and Owen found that

classical liberalism provided an inadequate solution to the problem of human happiness, their answer was that society should undertake to reorganize itself *voluntarily* along different lines; the Saint-Simonians, who had little faith in the democratic principle, saw the reconstructed society as emerging out of the rhythms of history under the guidance of an elite. In a sense, Marx's theories worked out a reconciliation of these two strains, although they divided again later within the Marxian tradition into Bolshevism and Western European social democracy.

The two pioneer planners of voluntarist communities had little else in common, except the fact that they were both rather eccentric. In this respect, Fourier was perhaps the more remarkable. Here was a quiet, even prissy bachelor, living out his life in furnished rooms on his meager earnings as clerk and commercial traveler, whose most evident passions were cats, good eating, and following military parades while beating time to the music. People were hardly likely to have taken him seriously whenever he announced that he had a plan to reform the world. At least none of the right people took him seriously: one of his most regular rituals in the course of a life notable for its regularity, was his returning home at exactly noon every day for many years, in order to be there to receive any rich benefactor who might respond to his advertisements for a contribution to help him found his community. Nobody ever came. But in the long run, Fourier's work did not go unnoticed. Fourierist societies began to be formed shortly before his death, and as early as 1832 an attempt was made to found a Fourierist community in France. The most ambitious enterprises of this sort were those undertaken in America in the 1850s, including the celebrated Brook Farm of Margaret Fuller, Channing, Hawthorne, and others.

The crux of Fourier's scheme was the principle of what he called *passional attraction*. The evils of the world existed because human beings were not permitted by "civilization" (a term that he never used with anything but scorn) to live in accordance with their passions. For many of the Fourierists, free love was prominent among the remedies to this problem, a fact that shocked such profoundly New England sensibilities as that of Hawthorne. Fourier certainly did not exclude this ideal, but it was not the crux of the matter. The main thing was work, most of "civilized" man's unhappiness was due to the fact that he was forced to do work that was detestable to him. And yet, Fourier observed, even man's spontaneous, recreational activities had potentialities for social usefulness; the only trouble was that society was organized wrongly, so that the things men *liked* doing had no functional place in the social organism. The answer, then, was to formulate a social order in which work should be nothing but play. One way of doing this, for example, would be to divide up all work in the phalanstery—the Fourierist community—into teams, which would compete with one another for honors; another way would be to utilize some of the normal passions of children, such as that of making things, or of imitating their elders. Above all—and here is one of the shrewdest parts of Fourier's scheme—no single job was to be performed for more than two hours at a time. This did not mean that the workday on the phalanstery was not to be a long one; it was to be longer than most, in fact, but its increased length was to be made possible by the fact that the variety and pleasantness of the work would make it not seem like work at all.

One must be careful about applying all the notions that go with the term "socialist" to Fourier; he was by all means a socialist (a word that, it must be stressed again, was barely in existence at the time), but not in every aspect of the word in its present-day meaning. The phalanstery, for example, was indeed to be a cooperative in which every member was to be a part owner, but that is not to say that there was not to be a distribution of the profits in the form of money among the members, or that all the shares were to be equal. True, the largest single share was to go to labor (five-twelfths according to one of his books, six-twelfths according to another—Fourier mixed an air of incredible exactitude with a pleasant disregard for consistency), but capital got the next largest (four-twelfths in both schemes), and talent got a poor third (three-twelfths or two-twelfths, as the case may be). This was a long way from the communist conceptions of the day, or even from the "from each according to his ability, to each according to his needs," ideal of Louis Blanc, who was not a communist. In fact, Fourier's main concern was not with the problem of distribution, but with that of production, since he felt that everybody would have enough if enough were produced. The phalanstery was to be the answer to the problem of production, not only by being organized in a way that would make its workers happy and therefore efficient, but by innovations in its physical plant. It is noteworthy that Fourier's good society is an almost entirely agricultural one; unlike socialists of the Marxian variety, he saw no value in the industrial system, and his response to its abuses was a wish to do away with it entirely.

Fourier's writings are both overly long and repetitious; it was therefore a great service that the French economist Charles Gide performed when he produced a one-volume edition of extracts from Fourier's writings for the Guillaumin "Petite Bibliothèque Economique." This was translated into English by Julia Franklin as *Selections from the Works of Fourier*, published by George Allen and Unwin, Ltd., of London. It is from this English translation that the following selections have been made. The initials at the end of each selection refer, with the volume and page numbers, to the works of Fourier as follows:

Q.M.—*Théorie des Quatre Mouvements*, 1 vol., 2nd edition, 1841.

N.M.—*Le Nouveau Monde Industriel et Sociétaire*, 1 vol., 3rd edition, 1848.

U.U.—*Théorie de l'Unité Universelle*, 4 vol., 2nd edition, 1838.

F.I.—*La Fausse Industrie*, 2 vol., 1835–36.

Man.—*Manuscrits de Fourier*, 1851.

OF THE ROLE OF THE PASSIONS

All those philosophical whims called duties have no relation whatever to Nature; duty proceeds from men, Attraction proceeds from God; now, if we desire to know the designs of

God, we must study Attraction, Nature only, without any regard to duty, which varies with every age, while the nature of the passions has been and will remain invariable among all nations of men.—(Q. M., 107.)

The learned world is wholly imbued with a doctrine termed MORALITY, which is a mortal enemy of passional attraction.

Morality teaches man to be at war with himself, to resist his passions, to repress them, to believe that God was incapable of organizing our souls, our passions wisely; that he needed the teachings of Plato and Seneca in order to know how to distribute characteristics and instincts. Imbued with these prejudices regarding the impotence of God, the learned world was not qualified to estimate the natural impulses or passional attractions, which morality proscribes and relegates to the rank of vices.

It is true that these impulses entice us only to evil, if we yield to them individually; but we must calculate their effect upon a body of about two thousand persons socially combined, and not upon families or isolated individuals: this is what the learned world has not thought of; in studying it, it would have recognized that as soon as the number of associates (sociétaires) has reached 1600, the natural impulses, termed attractions, tend to form series of contrasting groups, in which everything incites to industry, become attractive, and to virtue, become lucrative.—(N. M., 125.)

The passions, believed to be the enemies of concord, in reality conduce to that unity from which we deem them so far removed. But outside of the mechanism termed "exalted," emulatory, interlocked (engrenées) Series, they are but unchained tigers, incomprehensible enigmas. It is this which has caused philosophers to say that we ought to repress them; an opinion doubly absurd inasmuch as we can only repress our passions by violence or absorbing replacement, which replacement is no repression. On the other hand, should they be efficiently repressed, the civilized order would rapidly decline and relapse into the nomad state, where the passions would still be malevolent as with us. The virtue of shepherds is as doubtful as that of their apologists, and our utopia-makers, by thus attributing virtues to imaginary peoples, only succeed in proving the impossibility of introducing virtue into civilization.—(U. U., iii., 33.)

We are quite familiar with the five *sensitive* passions tending to Luxury,[1] the four *affective* ones tending to Groups; it only remains for us to learn about the three *distributive* ones whose combined impulse produces *Series*, a social method of which the secret has been lost since the age of primitive mankind, who were unable to maintain the Series more than about 300 years.—(Q. M., 118.)

The four *affective* passions tending to form the four groups of friendship, love, ambition, paternity or consanguinity are familiar enough; but no analyses, or parallels, or scales have been made of them.

The three others, termed distributive, are totally misunderstood, and bear only the title of VICES, although they are infinitely precious; for these three possess the property of forming and directing the series of groups, the mainspring of social harmony. Since these series are not formed in the civilized order, the three distributive passions cause disorder only. Let us define them.—(U. U., i., 145.)

10th. THE CABALIST is the passion that, like love, has the property of confounding ranks, drawing superiors and inferiors closer to each other. Everyone must recall occasions when he has been strongly drawn into some path followed with complete success.

For instance: electoral cabal to elect a certain candidate; cabal on 'Change in the stock-jobbing game; cabal of two pairs of lovers, planning a *partie carrée* without the father's knowledge; a family cabal to secure a desirable match. If these intrigues are crowned with success, the participants become friends; in spite of some anxiety, they have passed happy moments together while conducting the intrigue; the emotions it arouses are necessities of the soul.

Far removed from the insipid calm whose charms are extolled by morality, the cabalistic spirit is the true destination of man. Plotting doubles his resources, enlarges his

[1] Fourier means by this the five senses.—Ch. G.

faculties. Compare the tone of a formal social gathering, its moral, stilted, languishing jargon, with the tone of these same people united in a cabal: they will appear transformed to you; you will admire their terseness, their animation, the quick play of ideas, the alertness of action, of decision; in a word, the rapidity of the spiritual or material motion. This fine development of the human faculties is the fruit of the cabalist or tenth passion, which constantly prevails in the labors and the reunions of a passionate series.

As it always results in some measure of success, and as its groups are all precious to each other, the attraction of the cabals becomes a potent bond of friendship between all the sectaries (sectaires), even the most unequal.—(U. U., iv., 339.)

The general perfection of industry will spring, then, from the passion which is most condemned by the philosophers; the cabalist or dissident, which has never been able to obtain among us the rank of a passion, notwithstanding that it is so strongly rooted even in the philosophers themselves, who are the greatest intriguers in the social world.

The cabalist is a favorite passion of women; they are excessively fond of intrigue, the rivalries and all the greater and lesser flights of a cabal. It is a proof of their eminent fitness for the new social order, where cabals without number will be needed in every series, periodical schisms, in order to maintain a movement of coming and going among the sectaries of the different groups. . . .

12th. THE COMPOSITE.—This passion requires in every action a composite allurement or pleasure of the senses and of the soul, and consequently the blind enthusiasm which is born only of the mingling of the two kinds of pleasure. These conditions are but little compatible with civilized labor, which, far from offering any allurement either to the senses or the soul, is only a double torment even in the most vaunted of work-shops, such as the spinning factories of England where the people, even the children, work fifteen hours a day, under the lash, in premises devoid of air.

The composite is the most beautiful of the twelve passions, the one which enhances the value of all the others. A love is not beautiful unless it is a composite love, combining the charm of the senses and of the soul. It becomes trifling or deception if it limits itself to one of these springs. An ambition is not vehement unless it brings into play the two springs, glory and interest. It is then that it becomes capable of brilliant efforts.

The *composite* commands so great a respect, that all are agreed in despising people inclined to simple pleasure. Let a man provide himself with fine viands, fine wines, with the intention of enjoying them alone, of giving himself up to gormandizing by himself, and he exposes himself to well-merited gibes. But if this man gathers a select company in his house, where one may enjoy at the same time the pleasure of the senses by good cheer, and the pleasure of the soul by companionship, he will be lauded, because these banquets will be a composite and not a simple pleasure.

If general opinion despises simple material pleasure, the same is true as well of simple spiritual pleasure, of gatherings where there is neither refreshment, nor dancing, nor love, nor anything for the senses, where one enjoys oneself only in imagination. Such a gathering, devoid of the *composite* or pleasure of the senses and the soul, becomes insipid to its participants, and it is not long before it "grows bored and dissolves."

11th. THE PAPILLONNE [Butterfly] or *Alternating*. Although eleventh according to rank, it should be examined after the twelfth, because it serves as a link between the other two, the tenth and the twelfth. If the sessions of the series were meant to be prolonged twelve or fifteen hours like those of civilized workmen, who, from morning till night, *stupefy themselves* by being engaged in insipid duties without any diversion, God would have given us a taste for monotony, an abhorrence of variety. But as the sessions of the series are to be very short, and the enthusiasm inspired by the composite is incapable of being prolonged beyond an hour and a half, God, in conformity to this industrial order, had to endow us with the passion of *papillonnage*, the craving for periodic variety in the phases of life, and for frequent variety in our occupations. Instead of working twelve hours with a scant intermission for

a poor, dull dinner, the associative state will never extend its
sessions of labor beyond an hour and a half or at most two;
besides, it will diffuse a host of pleasures, reunions of the two
sexes terminating in a report, from which one will proceed to
new diversions, with different company and cabals.

Without this hypothesis of associative labor, arranged in
the order I have described, it would be impossible to conceive
for what purpose God should have given us three passions so
antagonistic to the monotony experienced in civilization, and
so unreasonable that, in the existing state, they have not even
been accorded the rank of passions, but are termed only vices.

A series, on the contrary, could not be organized without
the permanent co-operation of these three passions. They are
bound to intervene constantly and simultaneously in the serial
play of intrigue. Hence it comes that these three passions
could not be discerned until the invention of the serial mechanism, and that up to that time they had to be regarded as
vices. When the social order for which God has destined us
shall be known in detail, it will be seen that these pretended
vices, *the Cabalist, the Papillonne, the Composite*, become
there three pledges of virtue and riches; that God did indeed
know how to create passions such as are demanded by social
unity; that He would have been wrong to change them in
order to please Seneca and Plato; that on the contrary human reason ought to strive to discover a social condition which
shall be in affinity with these passions. No moral theory will
ever change them, and, in accordance with the rules of the
duality of tendency, they will intervene for ever to lead us TO
EVIL in the disjointed state or social limbo, and TO GOOD in
the *regime* of association or serial labor.—(U. U., iii., 405–
411.)

The seven "affective" and "distributive" passions depend
more upon the spirit than upon matter; they rank as PRIMI-
TIVES. Their combined action engenders a collective passion
or one formed by the union of the other seven, as white is
formed by the union of the seven colors of a ray of light; I
shall call this thirteenth passion *Harmonism* or *Unityism;* it is
even less known than the tenth, eleventh, and twelfth, of
which I have not spoken.

Unityism is the inclination of the individual to reconcile his own happiness with that of all surrounding him, and of all human kind, to-day so odious. It is an unbounded philanthropy, a universal good-will, which can only be developed when the entire human race shall be rich, free, and just.— (Q. M., 121.)

Questions regarding gallantry and the love of eating are treated facetiously by the Civilized, who do not comprehend the importance that God attaches to our pleasures. Voluptuousness is the sole arm which God can employ to master us and lead us to carry out his designs; he rules the universe *by Attraction and not by Force;* therefore the enjoyments of his creatures are the most important object of the calculations of God.—(Q. M., 237.)

I shall, in order to dispose others to share my confidence, explain the object of one of these impulses, accounted as vicious.

I select a propensity which is the most general and the most thwarted by education: it is the gluttony of children, their fondness for dainties, in opposition to the advice of the pedagogues who counsel them to like bread, to eat more bread than their allowance.

Nature, then, is very clumsy to endow children with tastes so opposed to sound doctrines! every child regards a breakfast of dry bread as a punishment; he would wish for sugared cream, sweetened milk—food and pastry, marmalades and stewed fruit, raw and preserved fruit, lemonades and orangeades, mild white wines. Let us observe closely these tastes which prevail among all children; on this point a great case is to be adjudged: the question to be determined is who is wrong, God or morality?

God, dispenser of attraction, gives all children a liking for dainties: it was in his power to give them a liking for dry bread and water; it would have suited the views of morality; why then does he knowingly militate against sound civilized doctrines? Let us explain these motives.

God has given children a liking for substances which will be

the least costly in the associative state. When the entire globe
shall be populated and cultivated, enjoying free-trade, exempt
from all duties, the sweet viands mentioned above will be
much less expensive than bread; the abundant edibles will be
fruit, milk-foods, and sugar, but not bread, whose price will
be greatly raised, because the labor incident to the growing of
grain and the daily making of bread is wearisome and little
attractive; these kinds of labor would have to be paid much
higher than that in orchards or confectioneries.

And as it is fitting that the food and maintenance of children
should involve less expense than those of their parents, God
has acted judiciously in attracting them to those sweetmeats
and dainties which will be cheaper than bread as soon as we
shall have entered upon the associative state. Then the sound
moral doctrines will be found to be altogether erroneous concerning the nourishment of children, as well as upon all other
points which oppose attraction. It will be recognized *that God
did well what he did,* that he was right in attracting children
to milk-foods, fruit, and sweet pastries; and that, instead of
foolishly losing three thousand years in declaiming against
God's wisest work, against the distribution of tastes and passionate attractions, it would have been better to study its aim,
by reckoning with all those impulses combined, which morality insults singly, under the pretext that they are hurtful to the
civilized and barbarous orders; this is true, but God did not
create the passions for the civilized and barbarous orders. If
he had wished to maintain these two forms of society exclusively, he would have given children a fondness for dry bread,
and to the parents a love of poverty, since that is the lot of the
immense majority of mankind in civilization and barbarism.
—(N. M., 23.)

In the civilized state, love of eating does not ally itself to
industry because the *laboring* producer does not enjoy the
commodities which he has cultivated or manufactured. This
passion therefore becomes an attribute of the idle; and
through that alone it would be vicious, were it not so already
by the outlay and the excesses which it occasions.

In the associative state love of eating plays an entirely opposite *rôle;* it is no longer a reward of idleness but of industry;

because there the poorest tiller of the soil participates in the consumption of choice commodities. Moreover, its only influence will be to preserve us from excess, by dint of variety, and to stimulate us to work by allying the intrigues of consumption to those of production, preparation, and distribution. Production being the most important of the four, let us first state the principle which must guide it; it is the generalization of epicurism. In point of fact:

If the whole human race could be raised to a high degree of gastronomic refinement, even in regard to the most ordinary kinds of food, such as cabbages and radishes, and everyone be given a competence which would allow him to refuse all edibles which are mediocre in quality or treatment, the result would be that every cultivated country would, after a few years, be covered with delicious productions; for there would be no sale for mediocre ones, such as bitter melons, bitter peaches, which certain kinds of soil yield, upon which neither melons nor peaches would be cultivated; every district would confine itself to productions which its soil is capable of raising to perfection; it would fetch earth for spots where the soil is poor, or perhaps convert them into forests, artificial meadows, or whatever else might yield products of good quality. It is not that the passionate Series do not consume ordinary eatables and stuffs; but they desire, even in ordinary things such as beans and coarse cloth, the most perfect quality possible, in conformity to the proportions which Nature has established in industrial attraction.

The principle which must be our starting-point is, *that a general perfection in industry will be attained by the universal demands and refinement of the consumers, regarding food and clothing, furniture and amusements.*—(N. M., 253.)

My theory confines itself to *utilizing the passions now condemned, just as Nature has given them to us and without in any way changing them.* That is the whole mystery, the whole secret of the calculus of passionate Attraction. There is no arguing there whether God was right or wrong in giving mankind these or those passions; the associative order avails itself of them without changing them, and as God has given them to us.—(U. U., iv., 157.)

Its mechanism produces co-incidence in every respect between individual interest and collective interest, in civilization always divergent.

It makes use of men as they are, utilizing the discords arising from antipathies, and other motives accounted vicious, and vindicating the Creator from the reproach of a lacuna in providence, in the matter of general unity and individual foresight.

Finally, it in nowise disturbs the established order, limiting itself to trial on a small scale, which will incite to imitation by the double allurement of quadruple proceeds and attractive industry.—(F. I., 497.)

OF EDUCATION

There is no problem upon which people have gone more astray than upon public instruction and its methods. Nature has, in this branch of social politics, taken a malign pleasure in all ages in confounding our theories and their exponents, from the time of the disgrace incurred by Seneca, the instructor of Nero, to that of the failures of Condillac and Rousseau, of whom the first fashioned only a political idiot and the second did not dare to undertake the education of his own children. —(U. U., iv., 1.)

It will be observed that in Harmony the only paternal function of the father is to yield to his natural impulse, to spoil the child, to humor all his whims.

The child will be sufficiently reproved and rallied by his peers. When an infant or little child has in the course of the day passed through half a dozen such groups and undergone their jokes, he is thoroughly imbued with a sense of his insufficiency, and quite disposed to listen to the advice of the patriarchs and venerables who are good enough to offer him instruction.

It will, after that, be of little consequence that the parents at the child's bed-time indulge themselves in spoiling him, telling him that he has been treated too severely, that he is really very charming, very clever; these effusions will only skim the surface, they will not convince. The impression has been made. He is humbled by the railleries of seven or eight groups of little ones which he has visited during the day. In vain will it be for the father and mother to tell him that the children who have repulsed him are barbarians, enemies of social intercourse, of gentleness and kindliness; all these parental platitudes will have no effect, and the child on returning to the infantile seristeries the following day will remember only the affronts of the day before; it is he who in reality will cure the father of the habit of SPOILING, by redoubling his efforts and proving that he is conscious of his inferiority.—(U. U., iv., 33.) . . .

Nature endows every child with a great number of instincts in industry, about thirty, of which some are primary or guiding and lead to those that are secondary.

The point is to discover first of all the primary instincts: the child will seize this bait as soon as it is presented to him; accordingly, as soon as he is able to walk, to leave the infant seristery, the male and female nurses in whose charge he is placed hasten to conduct him to all the workshops and all the industrial reunions which are close by; and as he finds everywhere diminutive tools, an industry in miniature, in which little tots of from two and a half to three years already engage, with whom he is anxious to associate, to rummage about, to handle things, at the end of a fortnight one may discern what are the workshops that attract him, what his industrial instincts.

The phalanx containing an exceedingly great variety of occupations, it is impossible that the child in passing from one to the other should not find opportunities of satisfying several of his dominant instincts; these will exhibit themselves at the sight of the little tools manipulated by other children a few months older than himself.

According to civilized parents and teachers, *children are little idlers;* nothing is more erroneous; children are already at two and three years of age very industrious, but we must know the springs which Nature wishes to put in action to attract them to industry *in the passionate series and not in civilization.*

The dominant tastes in all children are:

1. *Rummaging* or inclination to handle everything, examine everything, look through everything, to constantly change occupations;

2. Industrial *commotion,* taste for noisy occupations;

3. *Aping* or imitative mania.

4. Industrial *miniature,* a taste for miniature workshops.

5. Progressive attraction of the weak toward the strong.

There are many others; I limit myself to naming these five first, which are very familiar to the civilized. Let us examine the method to be followed in order to apply them to industry at an early age.

The male and female nurses will first exploit the mania for rummaging so dominant in a child of two. He wants to peer into every place, to handle and examine everything he sees. He is consequently obliged to be kept apart, in a bare room, otherwise he would destroy everything.

This propensity to handle everything is a bait to industry; to draw him to it, he will be conducted to the little workshops; there he will see children only two and a half and three years old using little tools, little hammers. He will wish to exercise his imitative mania, termed APING; he will be given some tools, but he will want to be admitted among the children of twenty-six and twenty-seven months who know how to work, and who will repel him.

He will persist if the work coincides with any of his instincts: the nurse or the patriarch will teach him some portion of the work, and he will very soon succeed in making himself useful in some trifling things which will serve him as an introduction; let us examine this effect in regard to an inconsiderable kind of labor, within the reach of the smallest children,—the shelling and sorting of green peas. This work which with us would occupy the hands of people of thirty, will be consigned to children of two, three, four years of age: the hall is provided with inclined tables containing a number of hollows; two little ones are seated at the raised side; they take the peas out of the shell, the inclination of the table causes the grains to roll towards the lower side where three tots are placed of twenty-five, thirty, thirty-five months, charged with the task of sorting, and furnished with special implements.

The thing to be done is to separate the smallest peas for the sweetened ragout, the medium ones for the bacon ragout, and the largest for the soup. The child of thirty-five months first selects the little ones which are the most difficult to pick out; she sends all the large and medium ones to the next hollow, where the child of thirty months shoves those that seem large to the third hollow, returns the little ones to the first, and drops the medium grains into the basket. The infant of twenty-five months, placed at the third hollow, has an easy task; he returns some medium grains to the second, and gathers the large ones into his basket.

It is in this third rank that the infant *débutant* will be placed; he will mingle proudly with the others in throwing the large grains into the basket; it is very trifling work, but he will feel as if he had accomplished as much as his companions; he will grow enthusiastic and be seized by a spirit of emulation, and at the third *séance* he will be able to replace the infant of twenty-five months, to send back the grains of the second size into the second compartment, and to gather up only the largest ones, which are easily distinguished.—(N. M., 181.)

If civilized education developed in every child its natural inclinations, we should see nearly all rich children enamored of various very plebeian occupations, such as that of the mason, the carpenter, the smith, the saddler. I have instanced Louis the XVI, who loved the trade of locksmith; an Infanta of Spain preferred that of shoemaker; a certain king of Denmark gratified himself by manufacturing syringes; the former king of Naples loved to sell the fish he had caught in the market-place himself; the prince of Parma, whom Condillac had trained in metaphysical subtilties, in the understanding of intuition, of cognition, had no taste but for the occupation of church-warden and lay-brother.

The great majority of wealthy children would follow these plebeian tastes, if civilized education did not oppose the development of them; and if the filthiness of the workshops and the coarseness of the workmen did not arouse a repugnance stronger than the attraction. What child of a prince is there who has no taste for one of the four occupations I have just mentioned, that of mason, carpenter, smith, saddler, and who would not advance in them if he beheld from an early age the work carried on in bright workshops, by refined people, who would always arrange a miniature workshop for children, with little implements and light labor?—(U. U., iii., 543.)

No attempt will be made, as is the case in existing educational methods, to create precocious little *savants*, intellectual primary school beginners, initiated from their sixth year in scientific subtleties; the endeavour will by preference be to secure mechanical precocity; capability in bodily industry, which, far from retarding the growth of the mind, accelerates it.

If one wishes to observe the general inclination of children of from four and a half to nine years of age, he will see that they are strongly drawn to all material exercises, and very little to studies; it is right then, that, in accordance with the desire of nature or attraction, the cultivation of the material should predominate at that age.

Why this impulse of childhood toward material exercises? Because Nature wishes, above all, to make man husbandman and manufacturer, to lead him to wealth before leading him to science.—(U. U., iv., 73, 74.)

The Phalanstery

The announcement does, I acknowledge, sound very improbable, of a method for combining three hundred families unequal in fortune, and rewarding each person,—man, woman, child—according to the three properties, *capital, labor, talent*. More than one reader will credit himself with humor when he remarks: "Let the author try to associate but three families, to reconcile three households in the same dwelling to social union, to arrangements of purchases and expenses, to perfect harmony in passions, character, and authority; when he shall have succeeded in reconciling three mistresses of associated households, we shall believe that he can succeed with thirty and with three hundred."

I have already replied to an argument which it is well to reproduce (for repetition will frequently be necessary here); I have observed *that as economy can spring only from large combinations, God had to create a social theory applicable to large masses and not to three or four families.*

An objection seemingly more reasonable, and which needs to be refuted more than once, is that of social discords. How conciliate the passions, the conflicting interests, the incompatible characters,—in short, the innumerable disparities which engender so much discord?

It may easily have been surmised that I shall make use of a lever entirely unknown, and whose properties cannot be judged until I shall have explained them. The passional contrasted Series draws its nourishment solely from those disparities which bewilder civilized policy; it acts like the husbandman who from a mass of filth draws the germs of abundance; the refuse, the dirt, and impure matter which would serve only to defile and infect our dwellings, are for him the sources of wealth.—(U. U., ii., 29.)

If social experiments have miscarried, it is because some fatality has impelled all speculators to work with bodies of poor people whom they subjected to a *monastic-industrial* discipline, chief obstacle to the working of the series. Here, as in everything else, it is ever SIMPLISM (*simplisme*) which misleads the civilized, obstinately sticking to experiments with combinations of the poor; they cannot elevate themselves to the conception of a trial with combinations of the rich. They are veritable Lemming rats (migrating rats of Lapland), preferring drowning in a pond to deviating from the route which they have decided upon.—(U. U., iii., 156.)

It is necessary for a company of 1,500 to 1,600 persons to have a stretch of land comprising a good square league, say a surface of six million square *toises* (do not let us forget that a third of that would suffice for the simple mode).

The land should be provided with a fine stream of water; it should be intersected by hills, and adapted to varied cultivation; it should be contiguous to a forest, and not far removed from a large city, but sufficiently so to escape intruders.

The experimental Phalanx standing alone, and without the support of neighboring phalanxes, will, in consequence of this isolation, have so many gaps in attraction, and so many passional calms to dread in its workings, that it will be necessary to provide it with the aid of a good location fitted for a variety of functions. A flat country such as Antwerp, Leipsic,

Orleans, would be totally unsuitable, and would cause many Series to fail, owing to the uniformity of the land surface. It will, therefore, be necessary to select a diversified region, like the surroundings of Lausanne, or, at the very least, a fine valley provided with a stream of water and a forest, like the valley of Brussels or of Halle. A fine location near Paris would be the stretch of country lying between Poissy and Confleurs, Poissy and Meulan.

A company will be collected consisting of from 1,500 to 1,600 persons of graduated degrees of fortune, age, character, of theoretical and practical knowledge; care will be taken to secure the greatest amount of variety possible, for the greater the number of variations either in the passions or the faculties of the members, the easier will it be to make them harmonize in a short space of time.

In this district devoted to experiment, there ought to be combined every species of practicable cultivation, including that in conservatories and hot-houses; in addition, there ought to be at least three accessory factories, to be used in winter and on rainy days; furthermore, various practical branches of science and the arts, independent of the schools.

Above all, it will be necessary to fix the valuation of the capital invested in shares; lands, materials, flocks, implements, etc. This point ought, it seems, to be among the first to receive attention; I think it best to dismiss it here. I shall limit myself to remarking that all these investments in transferable shares and stock-coupons will be represented.

A great difficulty to be overcome in the experimental Phalanx will be the formation of the ties of high mechanism or collective bonds of the Series, before the close of the first season. It will be necessary to accomplish the passional union of the mass of the members; to lead them to collective and individual devotion to the maintenance of the Phalanx, and, especially, to perfect harmony regarding the division of the profits, according to the three factors, *Capital, Labor, Talent.*

This difficulty will be greater in northern than in southern countries, owing to the difference between devoting eight months and five months to agricultural labor.

An experimental Phalanx, being obliged to start out with

agricultural labor, will not be in full operation until the month of May (in a climate of 50 degrees, say in the region around London or Paris); and, since it will be necessary to form the bonds of general union, the harmonious ties of the Series, before the suspension of field labor, before the month of October, there will be barely five months of full practice in a region of 50 degrees: the work will have to be accomplished in that short space.

The trial would, therefore, be much more conveniently made in a temperate region, like Florence, Naples, Valencia, Lisbon, where they would have eight to nine months of full cultivation and a far better opportunity to consolidate the bonds of union, since there would be but two or three months of passional calm remaining to tide over till the advent of the second spring, a time when the Phalanx, resuming agricultural labor, would form its ties and cabals anew with much greater zeal, imbuing them with a degree of intensity far above that of the first year; it would thenceforth be in a state of complete consolidation, and strong enough to weather the passional calm of the second winter.

We shall see in the chapter on hiatuses of attraction, that the first Phalanx will, in consequence of its social isolation and other impediments inherent to the experimental canton, have twelve special obstacles to overcome, obstacles which the Phalanxes subsequently founded would not have to contend with. That is why it is so important that the experimental canton should have the assistance coming from field-work prolonged eight or nine months, like that in Naples and Lisbon.—(U. U., iii., 427, 429.) . . .

Let us proceed with the details of composition.

At least seven-eighths of the members ought to be cultivators and manufacturers; the remainder will consist of capitalists, scholars, and artists.

The Phalanx would be badly graded and difficult to balance, if among its capitalists there were several having 100,000 francs, several 50,000 francs, without intermediate fortunes. In such a case it would be necessary to seek to procure intermediate fortunes of 60,000, 70,000, 80,000, 90,000 francs. The Phalanx best graduated in every respect raises social harmony and profits to the highest degree.—(U. U., iii., 431.)

One is tempted to believe that our sybarites would not wish to be associated with Grosjean and Margot; they are so even now (as I believe I have already pointed out). Is not the rich man obliged to discuss his affairs with twenty peasants who occupy his farms, and who are all agreed in taking illegal advantage of him? He is, therefore, *the peasant's associate*, obliged to make inquiries about the good and the bad farmers, their character, morals, solvency, and industry; *he does associate in a very direct and a very tiresome way* with Grosjean and Margot. In Harmony, he will be their indirect associate, being relieved of accounts regarding the management, which will be regulated by the regents, proctors, and special officers, without its being necessary for the capitalist to intervene or to run any risk of fraud. He will, therefore, be freed from the disagreeable features of his present association with the peasantry; he will form a new one, where he will not furnish them anything, and where they will only be his obliging and devoted friends, in accordance with the details given regarding the management of the Series and of reunions. If he takes the lead at festivals, it is because he has agreed to accept the rank of captain. If he gives them a feast, it is because he takes pleasure in acknowledging their continual kind attentions.

Thus the argument urged about the repugnance to association between Mondor and Grosjean, *already associated in fact*, is only, like all the others, a quibble devoid of sense.— (U. U., iv., 518.)

The edifice occupied by a Phalanx does not in any way resemble our constructions, whether of the city or country; and none of our buildings could be used to establish a large Harmony of 1,600 persons,—not even a great palace like Versailles, nor a great monastery like the Escurial. If, for the purposes of experiment, only an inconsiderable Harmony of 200 or 300 members, or a *hongrée* of 400 members is organized, a monastery or a palace (Meudon) could be used for it.

The lodgings, plantations, and stables of a Society conducted on the plan of Series of groups, must differ vastly from

our villages and country towns, which are intended for families
having no social connection, and which act in a perverse manner; in place of that class of little houses which rival each other
in filth and ungainliness in our little towns, a Phalanx con-
structs an edifice for itself which is as regular as the ground
permits: here is a sketch of distribution for a location favorable to development.

The central part of the Palace or Phalanstery ought to be
appropriated to peaceful uses, and contain the dining-halls,
halls for finance, libraries, study, etc. In this central portion
are located the place of worship, the *tour d'ordre,* the telegraph, the post-office boxes, the chimes for ceremonials, the
observatory, the winter court adorned with resinous plants,
and situated in the rear of the parade-court.

One of the wings ought to combine all the noisy workshops, such as the carpenter-shop, the forge, all hammer-work;
it ought to contain also all the industrial gatherings of children,
who are generally very noisy in industry and even in music.
This combination will obviate a great annoyance of our civilized cities, where we find some man working with a hammer
in every street, some dealer in iron or tyro on the clarionet,
who shatter the tympanum of fifty families in the vicinity.

The other wing ought to contain the caravansary with its
ballrooms and its halls appropriated to intercourse with outsiders, so that these may not encumber the central portion of
the palace and embarrass the domestic relations of the
Phalanx.—(U. U., iii., 447, 455.) · · ·

ATTRACTIVE LABOR

In the civilized mechanism we find everywhere composite
unhappiness instead of composite charm. Let us judge of it
by the case of labor. It is, says the Scripture very justly, a
punishment of man: Adam and his issue are condemned to
earn their bread by the sweat of their brow. That, already, is
an affliction; but this labor, this ungrateful labor upon which
depends the earning of our miserable bread, we cannot even
get it! a laborer lacks the labor upon which his maintenance
depends,—he asks in vain for a tribulation! He suffers a sec-

ond, that of obtaining work at times whose fruit is his master's
and not his, or of being employed in duties to which he is
entirely unaccustomed. . . . The civilized laborer suffers a
third affliction through the maladies with which he is generally stricken by the excess of labor demanded by his master.
. . . He suffers a fifth affliction, that of being despised and
treated as a beggar because he lacks those necessaries which
he consents to purchase by the anguish of repugnant labor.
He suffers, finally, a sixth affliction, in that he will obtain
neither advancement nor sufficient wages, and that to the
vexation of present suffering is added the perspective of future
suffering, and of being sent to the gallows should he demand
that labor which he may lack to-morrow.—(Man., 208.)

Labor, nevertheless, forms the delight of various creatures,
such as beavers, bees, wasps, ants, which are entirely at liberty
to prefer inertia: but God has provided them with a social
mechanism which attracts to industry, and causes happiness
to be found in industry. Why should he not have accorded us
the same favor as these animals? What a difference between
their industrial condition and ours! A Russian, an Algerian,
work from fear of the lash or the bastinado; an Englishman,
a Frenchman, from fear of the famine which stalks close to
his poor household; the Greeks and the Romans, whose freedom has been vaunted to us, worked as slaves, and from fear
of punishment, like the negroes in the colonies to-day.—(U.
U., ii., 249.)

Associative labor, in order to exert a strong attraction upon
people, will have to differ in every particular from the repulsive conditions which render it so odious in the existing state
of things. It is necessary, in order that it become attractive,
that associative labor fulfil the following seven conditions:

1. That every laborer be a partner, remunerated by divi-
dends and not by wages.

2. That every one, man, woman, or child, be remunerated
in proportion to the three faculties, *capital, labor,* and *talent.*

3. That the industrial sessions be varied about eight times
a day, it being impossible to sustain enthusiasm longer than
an hour and a half or two hours in the exercise of agricultural
or manufacturing labor.

4. That they be carried on by bands of friends, united spontaneously, interested and stimulated by very active rivalries.

5. That the workshops and husbandry offer the laborer the allurements of elegance and cleanliness.

6. That the division of labor be carried to the last degree, so that each sex and age may devote itself to duties that are suited to it.

7. That in this distribution, each one, man, woman, or child, be in full enjoyment of the right to labor or the right to engage in such branch of labor as they may please to select, provided they give proof of integrity and ability.

⋈ [2] Finally, that, in this new order, people possess a guarantee of well-being, of a minimum sufficient for the present and the future, and that this guarantee free them from all uneasiness concerning themselves and their families.

We find all these properties combined in the associative mechanism, whose discovery I make public.—(U. U., ii., 15.) . . .

In order to attain happiness, it is necessary to introduce it into the labors which engage the greater part of our lives. Life is a long torment to one who pursues occupations without attraction. Morality teaches us to love work: let it know, then, how to render work lovable, and, first of all, let it introduce luxury into husbandry and the workshop. If the arrangements are poor, repulsive, how arouse industrial attraction?

In work, as in pleasure, variety is evidently the desire of nature. Any enjoyment prolonged, without interruption, beyond two hours, conduces to satiety, to abuse, blunts our faculties, and exhausts pleasure. A repast of four hours will not pass off without excess; an opera of four hours will end by cloying the spectator. Periodical variety is a necessity of the body and of the soul, a necessity in all nature; even the soil requires alteration of seeds, and seed alteration of soil. The stomach will soon reject the best dish if it be offered every

[2] The sign ⋈, in the language of Fourier, serves to designate that which is "pivotal," that is to say, fundamental, in enumeration.

day, and the soul will be blunted in the exercise of any virtue if it be not relieved by some other virtue.

If there is need of variety in pleasure after indulging in it for two hours, so much the more does labor require this diversity, which is continual in the associative state, and is guaranteed to the poor as well as the rich.—(U. U., i., 147.)

The chief source of light-heartedness among Harmonians is the frequent change of sessions. Life is a perpetual torment to our workmen, who are obliged to spend twelve, and frequently fifteen, consecutive hours in some tedious labor. Even ministers are not exempt; we find some of them complain of having passed an entire day in the stupefying task of affixing signatures to thousands of official vouchers. Such wearisome duties are unknown in the associative order; the Harmonians, who devote an hour, an hour and a half, or at most two hours, to the different sessions, and who, in these short sessions, are sustained by cabalistic impulses and by friendly union with selected associates, cannot fail to bring and to find cheerfulness everywhere. . . .

The radical evil of our industrial system is the employment of the laborer in a single occupation, which runs the risk of coming to a stand-still. The fifty thousand workmen of Lyons who are beggars to-day (besides fifty thousand women and children), would be scattered over two or three hundred phalanxes, which would make silk their principal article of manufacture, and which would not be thrown out by a year or two of stagnation in that branch of industry. If at the end of that time their factory should fail completely, they would start one of a different kind, without having stopped work, without ever making their daily subsistence dependent upon a continuation or suspension of outside orders.—(F. I. [d. s.].)

In a progressive series all the groups acquire so much the more skill in that their work is greatly subdivided, and that every member engages only in the kind in which he professes to excel. The heads of the Series, spurred on to study by rivalry, bring to their work the knowledge of a student of the first rank. The subordinates are inspired with an ardor which laughs at all obstacles, and with a fanaticism for the maintenance of the honor of the Series against rival districts. In the heat of action they accomplish what seems humanly impossible, like the French grenadiers who scaled the rocks of Mahon, and who, upon the day following, were unable, in cold blood, to clamber up the rock which they had assailed under the fire of the enemy. Such are the progressive Series in their work; every obstacle vanishes before the intense pride which dominates them; they would grow angry at the word *impossible,* and the most daunting kinds of labor, such as managing the soil, are to them the lightest of sports. If we could to-day behold an organized district, behold at early dawn thirty industrial groups issue in state from the palace of the Phalanx, and spread themselves over the fields and the workshops, waving their banners with cries of triumph and impatience, we should think we were gazing at bands of madmen intent upon putting the neighboring districts to fire and sword. Such will be the athletes who will take the place of our mercenary and languid workmen, and who will succeed in making ambrosia and nectar grow upon a soil which yields only briers and tares to the feeble hands of the civilized.—(Q. M., 244.)

ROBERT OWEN (1771–1858)

Robert Owen's life forms a notable contrast with Fourier's. To Owen socialism was not a dream-world reserved for midnight literary labors; he made it his full-time work, even though he had first appeared before the public eye as a successful capitalist. His early years constitute a classic Anglo-American success story. Born the son of a humble saddlemaker in a village in Central Wales, he ended his formal schooling and went to work at the age of nine. After an apprenticeship spent mostly in drapers' shops, he borrowed some money and set up a small cotton spinning mill of his own in Manchester. He was then eighteen years old. He attracted attention, and was, a little over a year later, appointed manager of a large mill employing some five hundred workers. At the age of twenty-eight, already a wealthy man of widespread reputation, he became manager and part owner of the New Lanark mills, the largest in Scotland, and subsequently married the daughter of David Dale, the man from whom they were bought.

This might well have been a leveling-off point in any man's life, but for Owen it only cleared the way to loftier and more hazardous ambitions. He had apparently conceived early in life a plan for improving the lot of humanity. It was founded upon a challenge to the age-old notion that man is the maker of his own character. According to Owen's theory, men were made by their environments, and as long as the world remained the way it was, most men were going to be forced by conditions beyond their control to live in ignorance and poverty. It was a remarkable reaction against the prevailing myths of rugged individualism in the middle-class Britain of Owen's day, especially from one who was himself such a complete and successful rugged individualist.

He used his position to start turning New Lanark into a model community, not only by providing higher wages and better working conditions than were to be had anywhere else, but also by building comfortable homes for his workers, establishing free and modern schools for the children, and the like. These improvements not only satisfied a humanitarian impulse on his part, but also did justice to his partners' business instincts and even his own by making New Lanark pay handsomely, thus proving the now somewhat more widely accepted theory that a happy group of employees is also a more productive one. Yet every new and expensive improvement was met by objections from his partners, until he succeeded, in time, in buying them out and replacing them with a more disinterested group that included Jeremy Bentham. Throughout his twenty-five years as manager of New Lanark, Owen carefully scrutinized the morality as well as the happiness of his workers, for these two things went hand-in-hand for him (one is tempted to say that, in this respect, Owen was as British as Fourier was French), and ran the community in a highly paternalistic way. Almost until the end of the first period in his career as social reformer, many of the men of wealth and power in Britain could still look upon him as a generous and harmless philanthropist.

But in the years just prior to 1824, he was beginning to

show a more radical turn of mind. In his speeches and writings he had begun to advocate cooperative ownership, and was becoming a vehement critic of all organized religion; furthermore, the first stirrings of a popular movement were beginning to form around him. In this period he continued to prefer to deal directly and in his own private person with the men in power, but though he came to Members of Parliament with factory reform proposals and schemes for establishing cooperative villages throughout the country, he was getting no results. In 1824, he finally gave up on the Old World, and went to organize a cooperative community in New Harmony, Indiana, which he had just purchased from the Rappites. After five years of difficulty and frustration, he returned to England, to begin a new phase of his career.

Trade Unions had become legal upon the repeal of the Combination Acts in 1824, and working-class activity was now becoming articulate and forceful. The effect of Owenite ideas, still at their height, upon this burgeoning labor movement, was to make workers desire to establish cooperative villages on their own initiative. Thus the once paternalistic Owen became the source of inspiration for working-class agitation; he accepted this new role, and presided over the formation of the Grand National Consolidated Trades Union, which reached the height of its activity in the agitation over the New Poor Law in 1834. The continuing repressiveness of government policy caused the labor movement to fall into temporary inaction after that year, and it passed out of Owen's hands. But his influence in Britain did not die out immediately; as late as 1844, the Rochdale Pioneers founded a cooperative village based on Owenite principles. An inveterate projector of grand schemes and believer in the absolute rightness of his convictions, Owen played out the late years of his long life in a variety of fruitless activities, and in his very old age even turned to spiritualism. But his immense energy and scope make him one of the most remarkable figures of the nineteenth century, and he is generally accepted in England today as the founder of British socialism.

The following selection is an address delivered in 1816, upon the opening of an "Institution for the Formation of Char-

acter" at New Lanark. It shows the essentially moralistic
character of Owen's ideas, as well as the great emphasis his
socialist vision placed upon the education of the young.

An Address to the Inhabitants of New Lanark (1816)

We have met to-day for the purpose of opening this Institution; and it is my intention to explain to you the objects for
which it has been founded.

These objects are most important.

The first relates to the immediate comfort and benefit of all
the inhabitants of this village.

The second, to the welfare and advantage of the neighborhood.

The third, to extensive ameliorations throughout the British
dominions.

The last, to the gradual improvement of every nation in the
world.

I will briefly explain how this Institution is to contribute
towards producing these effects.

Long before I came to reside among you, it had been my
chief study to discover the extent, causes, and remedy of the
inconveniences and miseries which were perpetually recurring
to every class in society.

The history of man informed me that innumerable attempts
had been made, through every age, to lessen these evils; and
experience convinced me that the present generation, stimulated by an accession of knowledge derived from past times,
was eagerly engaged in the same pursuit. My mind at a very
early period took a similar direction; and I became ardently
desirous of investigating to its source a subject which involved
the happiness of every human being.

It soon appeared to me, that the only path to knowledge on
this subject had been neglected; that one leading in an opposite direction had alone been followed; that while causes
existed to compel mankind to pursue such direction, it was
idle to expect any successful result: and experience proves how
vain their pursuit has been.

In this inquiry, men have hitherto been directed by their inventive faculties, and have almost entirely disregarded the only guide that can lead to true knowledge on any subject—experience. They have been governed, in the most important concerns of life, by mere illusions of the imagination, in direct opposition to existing facts.

Having satisfied myself beyond doubt with regard to this fundamental error; having traced the ignorance and misery which it has inflicted on man, by a calm and patient investigation of the causes which have continued this evil, without any intermission from one generation to another; and having also maturely reflected on the obstacles to be overcome, before a new direction can be given to the human mind; I was induced to form the resolution of devoting my life to relieve mankind from this mental disease and all its miseries.

It was evident to me that the evil was universal; that, in practice, none was in the right path—no, not one; and that, in order to remedy the evil, a different one must be pursued. That the whole man must be re-formed on fundamental principles the very reverse of those in which he had been trained; in short, that the minds of all men must be born again, and their knowledge and practice commence on a new foundation.

Satisfied of the futility of the existing modes of instruction, and of the errors of the existing modes of government, I was well convinced that none of them could ever effect the ends intended; but that, on the contrary, they were only calculated to defeat all the objects which human instructors and governors had proposed to attain.

I found, on such a patient consideration of the subject as its importance demanded, that to reiterate precept upon precept, however excellent in theory, while no decisive measures were adopted to place mankind under circumstances in which it might be possible to put those precepts in practice, was but a waste of time. I therefore determined to form arrangements preparatory to the introduction of truths, the knowledge of which should dissipate the errors and evils of all the existing political and religious systems.

Be not alarmed at the magnitude of the attempt which this declaration opens to your view. Each change, as it occurs, will

establish a substantial and permanent good, unattended by
any counteracting evil; nor can the mind of man, formed on
the old system, longer interpose obstacles capable of retarding the progress of those truths which I am now about to unfold to you. The futile attempts which ignorance may for a
short time oppose to them, will be found to accelerate their
introduction. As soon as they shall be comprehended in all
their bearings, every one will be compelled to acknowledge
them, to see their benefits in practice to himself and to each
of his fellow-creatures; for, by this system, none, no not one,
will be injured. It is a delightful thought, an animating reflection, a stimulus to the steady prosecution of my purpose,
beyond—nay, far beyond—all that riches, and honor, and praise
can bestow, to be conscious of the possibility of being instru-
mental in introducing a practical system into society, the complete establishment of which *shall give happiness to every
human being through all succeeding generations.* And such I
declare was the sole motive that gave rise to this Institution,
and to all my proceedings.

To effect any permanently beneficial change in society, I
found it was far more necessary to *act* than to *speak*. I tried
the effect of the new principles on a limited scale in the southern part of the island. The result exceeded my most sanguine
anticipations; and I became anxious for a more enlarged field
of action. I saw New Lanark: it possessed many of the local
circumstances proper for my purpose; and this establishment
became at my disposal. This event, as many of you may
recollect, occurred upwards of sixteen years ago. Sixteen years
of action is not a short period: extensive changes are the result.
You have been witnesses of my proceedings here, from the
time I undertook the direction of the establishment to the present hour. I now ask, and I will thank you to make either a
public or a private reply,—have any of you discovered even
one of my measures that was not clearly and decisively intended to benefit the whole population? But I am satisfied
that you are all now convinced of this truth. You also know
some of the obstacles which were opposed to my progress; but
you know not a tithe of them. Yet, after all, these obstacles
have been few, compared with those which I expected and

was prepared to meet; and which I trust I should have overcome.

When I examined the circumstances under which I found you, they appeared to me to be very similar to those of other manufacturing districts; except with regard to the boarding-house, which contained the young children who were procured from the public charities of the country. That part of the establishment was under an admirable arrangement, and was a strong indication of the genuine and extensive benevolence of the revered and truly good man (the late David Dale of Glasgow) who founded these works and this village. His wishes and intentions towards you all were those of a father towards his children. You knew him and his worth; and his memory must be deeply engraven upon your hearts. Little indeed could he be conscious, when he laid the first stone of this establishment, that he was commencing a work, from whence not only the amelioration of his suffering countrymen should proceed, but the means of happiness be developed to every nation in the world.

I have stated that I found the population of this place similar to that of other manufacturing districts. It was, with some exceptions, existing in poverty, crime, and misery; and strongly prejudiced, as most people are at first, against any change that might be proposed. The usual mode of proceeding on the principles which have hitherto governed the conduct of men, would have been to punish those who committed the crimes, and to be highly displeased with every one who opposed the alterations that were intended for his benefit. The principles, however, upon which the new system is founded, lead to a very different conduct. They make it evident, that when men are in poverty,—when they commit crimes or actions injurious to themselves and others,—and when they are in a state of wretchedness,—there must be substantial causes for these lamentable effects; and that, instead of punishing or being angry with our fellow-men because they have been subjected to such a miserable existence, we ought to pity and commiserate them, and patiently to trace the causes whence the evils proceed, and endeavor to discover whether they may not be removed.

This was the course which I adopted. I sought not the punishment of any delinquent, nor felt anger at your conduct
in opposition to your own good; and when apparently stern
and decisive, I was not actuated by a single feeling of irritation against any individual. I dispassionately investigated the
source of the evils with which I saw you afflicted. The immediate causes of them were soon obvious; nor were the remote
ones, or the causes of those causes, long hid from me.

I found that those which principally produced your misery,
were practices you had been permitted to acquire—of falsehood, of theft, of drunkenness, of injustice in your transactions,
want of charity for the opinions of others, and mistaken notions, in which you had been instructed, as to the superiority
of your religious opinions, and that these were calculated to
produce more happiness than any of the opinions impressed
on the minds of an infinitely more numerous part of mankind.
I found, also, that these causes were but the effects of others;
and that those others might all be traced to the ignorance in
which our forefathers existed, and in which we ourselves have
continued to this day.

But from this day a change must take place; a new era
must commence; the human intellect, through the whole extent of the earth, hitherto enveloped by the grossest ignorance
and superstition, must begin to be released from its state of
darkness; nor shall nourishment henceforth be given to the
seeds of disunion and division among men. For the time is
come, when the means may be prepared to train all the nations
of the world—men of every color and climate, of the most
diversified habits—in that knowledge which shall impel them
not only to love but to be actively kind to each other in the
whole of their conduct, without a single exception. I speak not
an unmeaning jargon of words, but that which I know—that
which has been derived from a cool and dispassionate examination and comparison, during a quarter of a century, of the
facts which exist around us. And, however averse men may
be to resign their early-taught prejudices, I pledge myself to
prove, to the entire satisfaction of the world, the truth of all
that I have stated and all that I mean to state. Nay, such is my
confidence in the truth of the principles on which the system

I am about to introduce is founded, that I hesitate not to assert their power heartily to incline all men to say, "This system is assuredly true, and therefore eminently calculated to realize those invaluable precepts of the Gospel—universal charity, goodwill, and peace among men. Hitherto we must have been trained in error; and we hail it as the harbinger of that period when our swords shall be turned into ploughshares, and our spears into pruning-hooks; when universal love and benevolence shall prevail; when there shall be but one language and one nation; and when fear of want or of any evil among men shall be known no more."

Acting, although unknown to you, uniformly and steadily upon this system, my attention was ever directed to remove, as I could prepare means for their removal, such of the immediate causes as were perpetually creating misery amongst you, and which, if permitted to remain, would to this day have continued to create misery. I therefore withdrew the most prominent incitements to falsehood, theft, drunkenness, and other pernicious habits, with which many of you were then familiar: and in their stead I introduced other causes, which were intended to produce better external habits; and better external habits have been introduced. I say better *external* habits; for to these alone have my proceedings hitherto been intended to apply. What has yet been done I consider as merely preparatory.

This Institution, when all its parts shall be completed, is intended to produce permanently beneficial effects; and, instead of longer applying temporary expedients for correcting some of your most prominent external habits, to effect a complete and thorough improvement in the *internal* as well as *external* character of the whole village. For this purpose the Institution has been devised to afford the means of receiving your children at an early age, as soon almost as they can walk. By this means many of you, mothers of families, will be enabled to earn a better maintenance or support for your children; you will have less care and anxiety about them; while the children will be prevented from acquiring any bad habits, and gradually prepared to learn the best.

The middle room of the story below will be appropriated to

their accommodation; and in this their chief occupation will be to play and amuse themselves in severe weather: at other times they will be permitted to occupy the enclosed area before the building, for, to give children a vigorous constitution, they ought to be kept as much as possible in the open air. As they advance in years, they will be taken into the rooms on the right and left, where they will be regularly instructed in the rudiments of common learning; which, before they shall be six years old, they may be taught in a superior manner.

These stages may be called the first and second preparatory schools: and when your children shall have passed through them, they will be admitted into this place (intended also to be used as a chapel), which, with the adjoining apartment, is to be the general schoolroom for reading, writing, arithmetic, sewing, and knitting; all which, on the plan to be pursued, will be accomplished to a considerable extent by the time the children are ten years old; before which age, none of them will be permitted to enter the works.

For the benefit of the health and spirits of the children both boys and girls will be taught to dance, and the boys will be instructed in military exercises; those of each sex who may have good voices will be taught to sing, and those among the boys who have a taste for music will be taught to play upon some instrument; for it is intended to give them as much diversified innocent amusement as the local circumstances of the establishment will admit.

The rooms to the east and west on the story below, will also be appropriated in bad weather for relaxation and exercise during some part of the day, to the children who, in the regular hours of teaching, are to be instructed in these apartments.

In this manner is the Institution to be occupied during the day in winter. In summer, it is intended that they shall derive knowledge from a personal examination of the works of nature and of art, by going out frequently with some of their masters into the neighborhood and country around.

After the instruction of the children who are too young to attend the works shall have been finished for the day, the apartments shall be cleaned, ventilated, and in winter lighted and heated, and in all respects made comfortable, for the reception of other classes of the population. The apartments on this floor are then to be appropriated for the use of the children and youth of both sexes who have been employed at work during the day, and who may wish still further to improve themselves in reading, writing, arithmetic, sewing, or knitting; or to learn any of the useful arts: to instruct them in which, proper masters and mistresses, who are appointed, will attend for two hours every evening.

The three lower rooms, which in winter will also be well lighted and properly heated, will be thrown open for the use of the adult part of the population, who are to be provided with every accommodation requisite to enable them to read, write, account, sew, or play, converse, or walk about. But strict order and attention to the happiness of every one of the party will be enforced, until such habits shall be acquired as will render any formal restriction unnecessary; and the measures thus adopted will soon remove such necessity.

Two evenings in the week will be appropriated to dancing and music: but on these occasions every accommodation will be prepared for those who prefer to study or to follow any of the occupations pursued on the other evenings.

One of the apartments will also be occasionally appropriated for the purpose of giving useful instruction to the older classes of the inhabitants. For, believe me, my friends, you are yet very deficient with regard to the best modes of training your children, or of arranging your domestic concerns; as well as in that wisdom which is requisite to direct your conduct towards each other, so as to enable you to become greatly more happy than you have ever yet been. There will be no difficulty in teaching you what is right and proper; your own interests will afford ample stimulus for that purpose; but the real and only difficulty will be to unlearn those pernicious habits and sentiments which an infinite variety of causes, existing through all past ages, have combined to impress upon your minds and bodies, so as to make you imagine that they are inseparable from your nature. It shall, however, ere long be proved to you, that in this respect, as well as in many others, you and all mankind are mistaken. Yet think not, from what I have said, that I mean to infringe, even in the most slight degree, on the liberty of private judgment or religious opinions. No! they have hitherto been unrestrained; and the most effectual measures have been adopted by all the parties interested in the concern, to secure to you these most invaluable privileges. And here I now publicly declare (and while I make the declaration I wish my voice could extend to the ear, and make its due impression on the mind, of every one of our fellow-creatures), "that the individual who first placed restraint on private judgment and religious opinions, was the author of hypocrisy, and the origin of innumerable evils which mankind through every past age have experienced." The right, however, of private judgment, and of real religious liberty, is nowhere yet enjoyed. It is not possessed by any nation in the world; and thence the unnecessary ignorance, as well as endless misery, of all. Nor can this right be enjoyed until the principle whence opinions originate shall be universally known and acknowledged.

The chief object of my existence will be to make this knowledge universal, and thence to bring the right of private judgment into general practice; to show the infinitely beneficial consequences that will result to mankind from its adoption. To effect this important purpose is a part, and an essential part, of that system which is about to be introduced.

I proceed to show how the Institution is to contribute to the welfare and advantage of this neighborhood.

It will be readily admitted, that a population trained in regular habits of temperance, industry, and sobriety; of genuine charity for the opinions of all mankind, founded on the only knowledge that can implant true charity in the breast of any human being; trained also in a sincere desire to do good to the utmost of their power, and without any exception, to every one of their fellow-creatures, cannot, even by their example alone, do otherwise than materially increase the welfare and advantages of the neighborhood in which such a population may be situated. To feel the due weight of this consideration, only imagine to yourselves 2,000 or 3,000 human beings trained in habits of licentiousness, and allowed to remain in gross ignorance. How much, in such a case, would not the peace, quiet, comfort, and happiness of the neighborhood be destroyed! But there is not anything I have done, or purpose to do, which is not intended to benefit my fellow-creatures to the greatest extent that my operations can embrace. I wish to benefit all equally; but circumstances limit my present measures for the public good within a narrow circle. I must begin to act at some point; and a combination of singular events has fixed that point at this establishment. The first and greatest advantages will therefore center here. But, in unison with the principle thus stated, it has ever been my intention that as this Institution, when completed, will accommodate more than the children of parents resident at the village, any persons living at Lanark, or in the neighborhood anywhere around, who cannot well afford to educate their children, shall be at liberty, on mentioning their wishes, to send them to this place, where they will experience the same care and attention as those who belong to the establishment. Nor will there be any distinction made between the children of those parents who are deemed the worst, and of those who may be esteemed the best, members of society: rather, indeed, would I prefer to receive the offspring of the worst, if they shall be sent at an early age; because they really require more of our care and pity; and by well training these, society will be more essentially benefited, than if the like attention were paid to those whose parents are educating them in comparatively good habits. The system now preparing, and which will ultimately be brought into full practice, is to effect a complete change in all our sentiments and conduct towards those poor miserable creatures whom the errors of past times have denominated the bad, the worthless, and the wicked. A more enlarged and better knowledge of human nature will make it evident that, in strict justice, those who apply these terms to their fellow-men are not only the most ignorant, but are themselves the immediate causes of more misery in the world than those whom they call the outcasts of society. *They* are, therefore, correctly speaking, the most wicked and worthless; and were they not grossly deceived, and rendered blind from infancy, they would become conscious of the lamentably extensive evils, which, by their well-intended but most mistaken conduct, they have, during

so long a period, inflicted on their fellow-men. But the veil of
darkness must be removed from their eyes; their erroneous
proceedings must be made so palpable that they shall thenceforth reject them with horror. Yool they will reject with
horror even those notions which hitherto they have from infancy been taught to value beyond price.

To that which follows I wish to direct the attention of all
your faculties. I am about to declare to you the cause and the
cure of that which is called wickedness in your fellow-men.
As we proceed, instead of your feelings being roused to hate
and to pursue them to punishment, you will be compelled to
pity them; to commiserate their condition; nay, to love them,
and to be convinced that to this day they have been treated
unkindly, unjustly, and with the greatest cruelty. It is indeed
high time, my friends, that our conduct—that the conduct of
all mankind, in this respect, should be the very reverse of what
it has been; and of this truth, new as it may and must appear
to many of you, you shall, as I proceed, be satisfied to the
most complete conviction.

That, then, which has been hitherto called wickedness in
our fellow-men has proceeded from one of two distinct causes,
or from some combination of those causes. They are what is
termed bad or wicked—

First,—Because they are born with faculties and propensities
which render them more liable, under the circumstances, than
other men, to commit such actions as are usually denominated
wicked. Or—

Second,—Because they have been placed, by birth or by
other events, in particular countries; have been influenced
from infancy by parents, playmates, and others; and have
been surrounded by those circumstances which gradually
and necessarily trained them in the habits and sentiments
called wicked. Or—

Third,—They have become wicked in consequence of some
particular combination of these causes.

Let us now examine them separately, and endeavor to discover whether any, and which of them, have originated with
the individuals; and, of course, for which of them they ought

to be treated by their fellow-men in the manner those denominated wicked have to this day been treated.

You have not, I trust, been rendered so completely insane,
by the ignorance of our forefathers, as to imagine that the
poor helpless infant, devoid of understanding, made itself, or
any of its bodily or mental faculties or qualities: but, whatever
you may have been taught, it is a fact, that every infant has
received all its faculties and qualities, bodily and mental, from
a power and cause, over which the infant had not the shadow
of control.

Shall it, then, be unkindly treated? And, when it shall
be grown up, shall it be punished with loss of liberty or life,
because a power over which it had no control whatever,
formed it in the womb with faculties and qualities different
from those of its fellows?—Has the infant any means of deciding who, or of what description, shall be its parents, its playmates, or those from whom it shall derive its habits and its
sentiments?—Has it the power to determine for itself whether
it shall first see light within the circle of Christendom; or
whether it shall be so placed as inevitably to become a disciple
of Moses, of Confucius, of Mahomed; a worshipper of the
great idol Juggernaut, or a savage and a cannibal?

If then, my friends, not even one of these great leading and
overwhelming circumstances can be, in the smallest degree,
under the control of the infant, is there a being in existence,
possessing any claim even to the smallest degree of rationality,
who will maintain that any individual, formed and placed
under such circumstances, ought to be punished, or in any
respect unkindly treated? When men shall be in some degree
relieved from the mental malady with which they have been
so long afflicted, and sound judgment shall take the place of
wild and senseless imagination, then the united voice of mankind shall say, "No!" And they will be astonished that a contrary supposition should ever have prevailed.

If it should be asked,—Whence, then, have wickedness and
misery proceeded? I reply, *Solely from the ignorance of our
forefathers!* It is this ignorance, my friends, that has been, and
continues to be, the only cause of all the miseries which men
have experienced. This is the evil spirit which has had domin-

ion over the world,—which has sown the seeds of hatred and
disunion among all nations,—which has grossly deceived mankind, by introducing notions the most absurd and unaccount-
able respecting faith and belief; notions by which it has effectually placed a seal on all the rational faculties of man,—by
which numberless evil passions are engendered,—by which all
men, in the most senseless manner, are not only made enemies
to each other, but enemies to their own happiness! While this
ignorance of our forefathers continues to abuse the world,
under any name whatever, it is neither more nor less than a
species of madness—rank insanity—to imagine that we can
ever become in practice good, wise, or happy.

Were it not, indeed, for the positive evils which proceed
from these senseless notions, they are too absurd to admit of a
serious refutation; nor would any refutation be necessary, if
they did not from infancy destroy the reasoning faculties of
men, whether Pagans, Jews, Christians, or Mahomedans; and
render them utterly incompetent to draw a just conclusion
from the numberless facts which perpetually present themselves to notice. Do we not learn from history, that infants
through all past ages have been taught the language, habits,
and sentiments of those by whom they have been surrounded?
That they had no means whatever of giving to themselves
the power to acquire any others? That every generation has
thought and acted like preceding generations, *with such
changes only as the events around it, from which experience
is derived, may have forced upon it?* And, above all, are we
not conscious that the experience of every individual now
existing is abundantly sufficient, on reflection, to prove to himself that he has no more power or command over his faith and
belief than he possesses over the winds of heaven? nay, that
his constitution is so formed, that in every instance whatsoever, the faith or belief which he possesses has been given to
him by causes over which he had no control?

Experience, my friends, now makes these conclusions clear
as the sun at noonday. Why, then, shall we not instantly act
upon them? Having discovered our error, why shall we longer
afflict our fellow-men with the evils which these wild notions
have generated? Have they ever been productive of one

benefit to mankind? Have they not produced, through all past ages—are they not at this moment engendering, every conceivable evil to which man, in every nation of the world, is subjected? Yes; these alone prevent the introduction of charity and universal goodwill among men. These alone prevent men from discovering the true and only road which can lead to happiness. Once overcome these obstacles, and the apple of discord will be withdrawn from among us; the whole human race may then, with the greatest ease, be trained in one mind; all their efforts may then be trained to act for the good of the whole. In short, when these great errors shall be removed, all our evil passions will disappear; no ground of anger or displeasure from one human being towards another will remain; the period of the supposed Millennium will commence, and universal love prevail.

Will it not, then, tend to the welfare and advantage of this neighborhood, to introduce into it such a practical system as shall gradually withdraw the causes of anger, hatred, discord, and every evil passion, and substitute true and genuine principles of universal charity and of never-varying kindness, of love without dissimulation, and of an ever-active desire to benefit to the full extent of our faculties all our fellow-creatures, whatever may be their sentiments and their habits,—wholly regardless whether they be Pagans, Jews, Christians, or Mahomedans? For anything short of this can proceed only from the evil spirit of ignorance, which is truly the roaring lion going about seeking whom he may devour.

We now come to the third division of the subject, which was to show that one of the objects of this Institution was to effect extensive ameliorations throughout the British dominions. This will be accomplished in two ways—

First,—By showing to the master manufacturers an example in practice, on a scale sufficiently extensive, of the mode by which the characters and situation of the working manufacturers whom they employ may be very materially improved, not only without injury to the masters, but so as to create to them also great and substantial advantages.

Second,—By inducing, through this example, the British

legislature to enact such laws as will secure similar benefits
to every part of our population.

The extent of the benefits which may be produced by
proper legislative measures, few are yet prepared to form
any adequate idea of. By legislative measures I do not mean
any party proceeding whatever. Those to which I allude are,
—laws to diminish and ultimately prevent the most prominent
evils to which the working classes are now subjected,—laws
to prevent a large part of our fellow-subjects, under the
manufacturing system, from being oppressed by a much
smaller part,—to prevent more than one-half of our population from being trained in gross ignorance, and their valuable
labor from being most injuriously directed,—laws to prevent
the same valuable part of our population from being perpetually surrounded by temptations, which they have not
been trained to resist, and which compel them to commit
actions most hurtful to themselves and to society. The principles on which these measures are to be founded, being
once fairly and honestly understood, they will be easy of
adoption; and the benefits to be derived from them in practice to every member of the community, will exceed any
calculation that can be made by those not well versed in
political economy.

These are some of the ameliorations which I trust this
Institution will be the means of obtaining for our suffering
fellow-subjects.

But, my friends, if what has been done, what is doing,
and what has yet to be done here, should procure the
benefits which I have imperfectly enumerated, to this village,
to our neighborhood, and to our country, only, I should be
greatly disappointed; for I feel an ardent desire to benefit all
my fellow-men equally. I know not any distinction whatever.
Political or religious parties or sects are everywhere the fruitful sources of disunion and irritation. My aim is therefore to
withdraw the germ of all party from society. As little do I
admit of the divisions and distinctions created by any imaginary lines which separate nation from nation. Will any being,
entitled to the epithet intelligent, say that a mountain, a river,
an ocean, or any shade of color, or difference of climate,

habits, and sentiments, affords a reason sufficient to satisfy the inquiries of even a well-trained child, why one portion of mankind should be taught to despise, hate, and destroy another? Are these absurd effects of the grossest ignorance never to be brought to a termination? Are we still to preserve and encourage the continuance of those errors which must inevitably make man an enemy to man? Are these the measures calculated to bring about that promised period when the lion shall lie down with the lamb, and when uninterrupted peace shall universally prevail?—peace, founded on a sincere goodwill, instilled from infancy into the very constitution of every man, which is the only basis on which universal happiness can ever be stablished? I look, however, with the utmost confidence to the arrival of such a period; and, if proper measures shall be adopted, its date is not far distant.

What ideas individuals may attach to the term Millennium I know not; but I know that society may be formed so as to exist without crime, without poverty, with health greatly improved, with little, if any, misery, and with intelligence and happiness increased a hundred-fold; and no obstacle whatsoever intervenes at this moment, except ignorance, to prevent such a state of society from becoming universal.

I am aware, to the fullest extent, what various impressions these declarations will make on the different religious, political, learned, commercial, and other circles which compose the population of our empire. I know the particular shade of prejudice through which they will be presented to the minds of each of these. And to none will they appear through a denser medium than to the learned, who have been taught to suppose that the book of knowledge has been exclusively opened to them; while, in fact, they have only wasted their strength in wandering through endless mazes of error. They are totally ignorant of human nature. They are full of theories, and have not the most distant conception of what may or may not be accomplished in practice. It is true their minds have been well stored with language, which they can readily use to puzzle and confound the unlettered and inexperienced. But to those who have had an opportunity of examining the utmost extent of their acquirements, and of

observing how far they have been taught, and where their
knowledge terminates, the deception vanishes, and the fallacy of the foundation upon which the superstructure of all
their acquirements has been raised, at once becomes most
obvious. In short, with a few exceptions, their profound investigations have been about words only. For, as the principle
which they have been taught, and on which all their subsequent instruction proceeds, is erroneous, so it becomes impossible that they can arrive at just conclusions. The learned
have ever looked for the cause of human sentiments and
actions in the individual through whom those sentiments
and actions become visible,—and hitherto the learned have
governed the opinions of the world. The individual has
been praised, blamed, or punished according to the whims
and fancies of this class of men, and, in consequence, the
earth has been full charged with their ever-varying absurdities, and with the miseries which these absurdities hourly
create. Had it not been a law of our nature, that any impression, however ridiculous and absurd, and however contrary to fact, may be given in infancy, so as to be tenaciously
retained through life, men could not have passed through
the previous ages of the world without discovering the gross
errors in which they had been trained. They could not have
persevered in making each other miserable, and filling the
world with horrors of every description. No! they would
long since have discovered the natural, easy, and simple
means of giving happiness to themselves and to every human being. But that law of nature which renders it difficult
to eradicate our early instruction, although it will ultimately
prove highly beneficial to the human race, serves now but
to give permanence to error, and to blind our judgments.
For the present situation of all the inhabitants of the earth
may be compared to that of one whose eyes have been
closely bandaged from infancy; who has afterwards been
taught to imagine that he clearly sees the form or color of
every object around him; and who has been continually
flattered with this notion, so as to compel his implicit belief
in the supposition, and render him impenetrable to every
attempt that could be made to undeceive him. If such be the

present situation of man, how shall the illusion under which
he exists be withdrawn from his mind? To beings thus circumstanced, what powers of persuasion can be applied, to
make them comprehend their misfortune, and manifest to
them the extent of the darkness in which they exist? In what
language and in what manner shall the attempt be made?
Will not every such attempt irritate and increase the malady,
until means shall be devised to unloose the bandage, and
thus effectually remove the cause of this mental blindness?
Your minds have been so completely enveloped by this dense
covering, which has intercepted the approach of every ray
of light, that were an angel from heaven to descend and
declare your state, you would not, because so circumstanced
you could not, believe him.

Causes, over which I could have no control, removed in
my early days the bandage which covered my mental sight.
If I have been enabled to discover this blindness with which
my fellow-men are afflicted, to trace their wanderings from
the path which they were most anxious to find, and at the
same time to perceive that relief could not be administered
to them by any premature disclosure of their unhappy state,
it is not from any merit of mine; nor can I claim any personal
consideration whatever for having been myself relieved from
this unhappy situation. But, beholding such truly pitiable
objects around me, and witnessing the misery which they
hourly experienced from falling into the dangers and evils by
which, in these paths, they were on every side surrounded,
—could I remain an idle spectator? Could I tranquilly see
my fellow-men walking like idiots in every imaginable direction, except that alone in which the happiness they were in
search of could be found?

No! The causes which fashioned me in the womb,—the circumstances by which I was surrounded from my birth, and
over which I had no influence whatever, formed me with
far other faculties, habits, and sentiments. These gave me a
mind that could not rest satisfied without trying every possible expedient to relieve my fellow-men from their wretched
situation, and formed it of such a texture that obstacles of
the most formidable nature served but to increase my ardor,

and to fix within me a settled determination, either to overcome them, or to die in the attempt.

But the attempt has been made. In my progress the most
multiplied difficulties, which to me at a distance seemed
almost appalling, and which to others seemed absolutely
insurmountable, have on their nearer approach diminished,
until, at length, I have lived to see them disappear, like the
fleeting clouds of morning, which prove but the harbingers
of an animating and cheering day.

Hitherto I have not been disappointed in any of the ex-
pectations which I had formed. The events which have yet
occurred far exceed my most sanguine anticipations, and my
future course now appears evident and straightforward. It is
no longer necessary that I should silently and alone exert
myself for your benefit and the happiness of mankind. The
period is arrived when I may call numbers to my aid, and the
call will not be in vain. I well knew the danger which would
arise from a premature and abrupt attempt to tear off the
many-folded bandages of ignorance, which kept society in
darkness. I have therefore been many years engaged, in a
manner imperceptible to the public, in gently and gradually
removing one fold after another of these fatal bands, from
the mental eyes of those who have the chief influence in
society. The principles on which the practical system I contemplate is to be founded, are now familiar to some of the
leading men of all sects and parties in this country, and to
many of the governing powers in Europe and America. They
have been submitted to the examination of the most celebrated universities in Europe. They have been subjected to
the minute scrutiny of the most learned and acute minds
formed on the old system, and I am fully satisfied of their
inability to disprove them. These principles I will shortly
state.

Every society which exists at present, as well as every
society which history records, has been formed and governed
on a belief in the following notions, assumed as *first principles:*

First,—That it is in the power of every individual to
form his own character.

Hence the various systems called by the name of religion, codes of law, and punishments. Hence also the angry passions entertained by individuals and nations towards each other.

Second,—That the affections are at the command of the individual.

Hence insincerity and degradation of character. Hence the miseries of domestic life, and more than one-half of all the crimes of mankind.

Third,—That it is necessary that a large portion of mankind should exist in ignorance and poverty, in order to secure to the remaining part such a degree of happiness as they now enjoy.

Hence a system of counteraction in the pursuits of men, a general opposition among individuals to the interests of each other, and the necessary effects of such a system,—ignorance, poverty, and vice.

Facts prove, however—

First,—That character is universally formed *for*, and not *by*, the individual.

Second,—That *any* habits and sentiments may be given to mankind.

Third,—That the affections are *not* under the control of the individual.

Fourth,—That every individual may be trained to produce far more than he can consume, while there is a sufficiency of soil left for him to cultivate.

Fifth,—That nature has provided means by which population may be at all times maintained in the proper state to give the greatest happiness to every individual, without one check of vice or misery.

Sixth,—That any community may be arranged, on a due combination of the foregoing principles, in such a manner, as not only to withdraw vice, poverty, and, in a great degree, misery, from the world, but also to place *every* individual under circumstances in which he shall enjoy more permanent happiness than can be given to *any* individual under the principles which have hitherto regulated society.

Seventh,—That all the assumed fundamental principles on

which society has hitherto been founded are erroneous, and
may be demonstrated to be contrary to fact. And—

Eighth,—That the change which would follow the abandonment of those erroneous maxims which bring misery into
the world, and the adoption of principles of truth, unfolding
a system which shall remove and for ever exclude that
misery, may be effected without the slightest injury to any
human being.

Here is the groundwork,—these are the data, on which
society shall ere long be re-arranged; and for this simple
reason, that it will be rendered evident that it will be for
the immediate and future interest of every one to lend his
most active assistance gradually to reform society on this
basis. I say *gradually*, for in that word the most important
considerations are involved. Any sudden and coercive attempt which may be made to remove even misery from
men will prove injurious rather than beneficial. Their minds
must be gradually prepared by an essential alteration of
the circumstances which surround them, for any great and
important change and amelioration in their condition. They
must be first convinced of their blindness: this cannot be
effected, even among the least unreasonable, or those termed
the best part of mankind, in their present state, without
creating some degree of irritation. This irritation, must then
be tranquillized before another step ought to be attempted;
and a general conviction must be established of the truth of
the principles on which the projected change is to be
founded. Their introduction into practice will then become
easy,—difficulties will vanish as we approach them,—and,
afterwards, the desire to see the whole system carried immediately into effect will exceed the means of putting it into
execution.

The principles on which this practical system is founded
are not new; separately, or partially united, they have been
often recommended by the sages of antiquity, and by modern
writers. But it is not known to me that they have ever
been thus combined. Yet it can be demonstrated that it is
only by their being *all brought into practice together* that
they are to be rendered beneficial to mankind; and sure I

am that this is the earliest period in the history of man when
they could be successfully introduced into practice.

I do not intend to hide from you that the change will be
great. "Old things shall pass away, and all shall become new."

But this change will bear no resemblance to any of the
revolutions which have hitherto occurred. These have been
alone calculated to generate and call forth all the evil passions
of hatred and revenge: but that system which is now contemplated will effectually eradicate every feeling of irritation
and ill will which exists among mankind. The whole proceedings of those who govern and instruct the world will be
reversed. Instead of spending ages in telling mankind what
they ought to think and how they ought to act, the instructors and governors of the world will acquire a knowledge
that will enable them, in one generation, to apply the means
which shall cheerfully induce each of those whom they
control and influence, not only to think, but to act in such a
manner as shall be best for himself and best for every
human being. And yet this extraordinary result will take
place without punishment or apparent force.

Under this system, before commands are issued it shall
be known whether they can or cannot be obeyed. Men shall
not be called upon to assent to doctrines and to dogmas
which do not carry conviction to their minds. They shall not
be taught that merit can exist in doing, or that demerit can
arise from not doing that over which they have no control.
They shall not be told, as at present, that they must love
that which, by the constitution of their nature, they are compelled to dislike. They shall not be trained in wild imaginary
notions, that inevitably make them despise and hate all mankind out of the little narrow circle in which they exist, and
then be told that they must heartily and sincerely love all
their fellow-men. No, my friends, that system which shall
make its way into the heart of every man, is founded upon
principles which have not the slightest resemblance to any
of those I have alluded to. On the contrary, it is directly
opposed to them; and the effects it will produce in practice
will differ as much from the practice which history records,
and from that which we see around us, as hypocrisy, hatred,

envy, revenge, wars, poverty, injustice, oppression, and all
their consequent misery, differ from that genuine charity and
sincere kindness of which we perpetually hear, but which we
have never seen, and which, under the existing systems, we
never can see.

That charity and that kindness admit of no exception. They
extend to every child of man, however he may have been
taught, however he may have been trained. They consider
not what country gave him birth, what may be his com-
plexion, what his habits or his sentiments. Genuine charity
and true kindness instruct, that whatever these may be,
should they prove the very reverse of what we have been
taught to think right and best, our conduct towards him, our
sentiments with respect to him, should undergo no change;
for, when we shall see things as they really are, we shall
know that this our fellow-man has undergone the same kind
of process and training from infancy which we have experienced; that he has been as effectually taught to deem his
sentiments and actions right, as we have been to imagine
ours right and his wrong; when perhaps the only difference
is, that we were born in one country, and he in another. If
this be not true, then indeed are all our prospects hopeless;
then fierce contentions, poverty, and vice, must continue for
ever. Fortunately, however, there is now a superabundance
of facts to remove all doubt from every mind; and the principles may now be fully developed, which will easily explain
the source of all the opinions which now perplex and divide
the world; and their source being discovered, mankind may
withdraw all those which are false and injurious, and prevent
any evil from arising in consequence of the varieties of sentiments, or rather of feelings, which may afterwards remain.

In short, my friends, the New System is founded on
principles which will enable mankind to *prevent*, in the
rising generation, almost all, if not all of the evils and miseries which we and our forefathers have experienced. A correct
knowledge of human nature will be acquired; ignorance will
be removed; the angry passions will be prevented from
gaining any strength; charity and kindness will universally
prevail; poverty will not be known; the interest of each in-

dividual will be in strict unison with the interest of every individual in the world. There will not be any counteraction of wishes and desires among men. Temperance and simplicity of manners will be the characteristics of every part of society. The natural defects of the few will be amply compensated by the increased attention and kindness towards them of the many. None will have cause to complain; for each will possess, without injury to another, all that can tend to his comfort, his well-being, and his happiness.—— Such will be the certain consequences of the introduction into practice of that system for which I have been silently preparing the way for upwards of five-and-twenty years.

Still, however, much more preparation is necessary, and must take place, before the whole can be introduced. It is not intended to put it into practice here. The establishment was too far advanced on the old system before I came amongst you, to admit of its introduction, except to a limited extent. All I now purpose doing in this place is, to introduce as many of the advantages of the new system as can be put into practice in connexion with the old: but these advantages will be neither few nor of little amount. I hope, ere long, even under the existing disadvantages, to give you and your children far more solid advantages for your labor, than any persons similarly circumstanced have yet enjoyed at any time or in any part of the world.

Nor is this all. When you and your children shall be in the full possession of all that I am preparing for you, you will acquire superior habits; your minds will gradually expand; you will be enabled to judge accurately of the cause and consequences of my proceedings, and to estimate them at their value. You will then become desirous of living in a more perfect state of society,—a society which will possess within itself the certain means of preventing the existence of any injurious passions, poverty, crime, or misery; in which every individual shall be instructed, and his powers of body and mind directed, by the wisdom derived from the best previous experience, so that neither bad habits nor erroneous sentiments shall be known;—in which age shall receive attention and respect, and in which every injurious distinction

shall be avoided,—even variety of opinions shall not create
disorder or any unpleasant feeling;—a society in which individuals shall acquire increased health, strength, and
Intelligence, in which their labor shall be always advanta-
geously directed,—and in which they will possess every rational enjoyment.

In due time communities shall be formed possessing such
characters, and be thrown open to those among you, and to
individuals of every class and denomination, whose wretched
habits and whose sentiments of folly have not been too
deeply impressed to be obliterated or removed, and whose
minds can be sufficiently relieved from the pernicious effects
of the old system, to permit them to partake of the happiness of the new.

(The communities alluded to shall be more particularly
described in a future publication.)

Having delivered this strange discourse, for to many of you
it must appear strange indeed, I conceive only one of two
conclusions can be drawn by those who have heard it. These
are,—that the world to this day has been grossly wrong, and is
at this moment in the depth of ignorance;—or, that I am completely in error. The chances then, you will say, are greatly
against me. True: but the chances have been equally against
every individual who has been enabled to make any discovery
whatsoever.

To effect the purposes which I have long silently medi-
tated, my proceedings for years have been so far removed
from, or rather so much in opposition to, the common practices of mankind, that not a few have concluded I was insane.
Such conjectures were favorable to my purposes, and I did
not wish to contradict them. But the question of insanity
between the world and myself will now be decided; either
they have been rendered greatly insane,—or I am so. You
have witnessed my conduct and measures here for sixteen
years; and the objects I have had in progress are so far advanced that you can now comprehend many of them. You,
therefore, shall be judges in this case. Insanity is inconsistency. Let us now try the parties by this rule.

From the beginning I firmly proposed to ameliorate your

condition, the condition of all those engaged in similar occupations, and, ultimately, the condition of mankind, whose situation appeared to me most deplorable. Say, now, as far as you know, did I not adopt judicious measures to accomplish these purposes?

Have I not calmly, steadily, and patiently proceeded to fill up the outline of the plan which I originally formed to overcome your worst habits and greatest inconveniences, as well as your prejudices? Have not the several parts of this plan, as they were finished, fulfilled most completely the purposes for which they were projected? Are you not at this moment deriving the most substantial benefits from them? Have I in the slightest degree injured any one of you? During the progress of these measures have I not been opposed in the most determined and formidable manner by those whose interests, if they had understood them, would have made them active co-operators? Without any apparent means to resist these attempts, were they not frustrated and overcome, and even the resistance itself rendered available to hasten the execution of all my wishes? In short, have I not been enabled, with one hand, to direct with success the common mercantile concerns of this extensive establishment, and with the other hand to direct measures which now seem more like national than private ones, in order to introduce another system, the effects and success of which shall astonish the profound theologian no less than the most experienced and fortunate politician?—a system which shall train its children of twelve years old to surpass, in true wisdom and knowledge, the boasted acquirements of modern learning, of the sages of antiquity, of the founders of all those systems which hitherto have only confused and distracted the world, and which have been the immediate cause of almost all the miseries we now deplore?

Being witnesses of my measures, you alone are competent to judge of their consistency. Under these circumstances it would be mere hypocrisy in me to say that I do not know what must be your conclusions.

During the long period in which I have been thus silently

acting for your benefit and for the benefit of each of my fellow-men,—what has been the conduct of the world?

Having maturely contemplated the past actions of men, as they have been made known to us by history, it became necessary for my purpose that I should become practically acquainted with men as they now are, and acquire from inspection a knowledge of the precise effects produced in the habits and sentiments of each class, by the peculiar circumstances with which the individuals were surrounded. The causes which had previously prepared my mind and disposition for the work,—which had removed so many formidable difficulties in the early part of my progress,—now smoothed the way to the easy attainment of my wishes. By the knowledge of human nature which I had already acquired, I was enabled to dive into the secret recesses of a sufficient number of minds of the various denominations forming British society, to discover the immediate causes of the sentiments of each, and to trace the consequences of the actions that necessarily proceeded from those sentiments. The whole, as though they had been delineated on a map, were laid open to me. Shall I now at this eventful crisis make the world known to itself? Or shall this valuable knowledge descend with me to the grave, and you, our fellow-men, and our children's children, through many generations, yet suffer the miseries which the inhabitants of the earth have to this day experienced? These questions, however, need not be asked. My resolutions were taken in early life; and subsequent years have added to their strength and confirmed them. I therefore proceed regardless of individual consequences. I will hold up the mirror to man,—show him, without the intervention of any false medium, what he *is*, and then he will be better prepared to learn what he *may be*. Man is so constituted, that, by the adoption of proper measures in his infancy, and by steadily pursuing them through all the early periods of his life to manhood, he may be taught to think and to act in any manner that is not beyond the acquirement of his faculties: whatever he may have been thus taught to think and to do, he may be effectually made to believe is right and best for all mankind. He may also be taught (however few may think and act as he does), that all those who differ from him are wrong, and even ought to be punished with death if they will not think and act like him. In short, he may be rendered insane upon every subject which is not founded on, and which does not remain in never-varying consistency with, the facts that surround mankind. It is owing to this peculiarity in the constitution of man, that when he is born he may be taught any of the various dogmas which are known, and be rendered wholly unfit to associate with any of his fellow-men who have been trained in any of the other dogmas. It is owing to this principle that a poor human being duly initiated in the mysteries of Juggernaut, is thereby rendered insane on everything regarding that monster. Or, when instructed in the dogmas of Mahomedanism, he is thus rendered insane on every subject which has reference to Mahomed. I might proceed and state the same of those poor creatures who have been trained in the tenets of Brahma, or Confucius, or in any other of those systems which serve only to destroy the human intellect.

I have no doubt, my friends, you are at present convinced, as thoroughly as conviction can be formed in your minds, that none of you have been subjected to any such process;— that you have been instructed in that which is true;—that is evident. Pagans, Jews, Turks, every one of them, millions upon millions almost without end, are wrong, fundamentally wrong. Nay, you will allow, also, that they are truly as insane as I have stated them to be. But you will add,—"We are right, —we are the favoured of Heaven,—we are enlightened, and cannot be deceived." This is the feeling of every one of you at this moment. I need not be told your thoughts. Shall I now pay regard to you or to myself? Shall I be content and rest satisfied with the sufficiency which has fallen to my lot, while you remain in your ignorance and misery? Or shall I sacrifice every private consideration for the benefit of you and our fellow-men? Shall I tell you, and the whole of the civilized world, that, in many respects, none of these have been rendered more insane than yourselves,—than every one of you is at this moment; and that while these maladies remain uncured, you and your posterity cannot but exist in the midst of folly and misery?

What think you now, my friends, is the reason why you believe and not as you do? I will tell you. It is solely and merely because you were born, and have lived, in this period of the world,—in Europe,—in the island of Great Britain,— and more especially in this northern part of it. Without the shadow of a doubt, had every one of you been born in other times or other places, you might have been the very reverse of that which the present time and place have made you: and, without the possibility of the slightest degree of assent or dissent on your own parts, you might have been at this moment sacrificing yourselves under the wheels of the great idol Juggernaut, or preparing a victim for a cannibal feast. This, upon reflection, will be found to be a truth as certain as that you now hear my voice.

Will you not, then, have charity for the habits and opinions of all men, of even the very worst human beings that your imaginations can conceive? Will you not, then, be sincerely kind to them, and actively endeavour to do them good? Will you not patiently bear with, and commiserate, their defects and infirmities, and consider them as your relatives and friends?

If you will not,—if you cannot do this, and persevere to the end of your days in doing it,—you have not charity; you cannot have religion; you possess not even common justice; you are ignorant of yourselves, and are destitute of every particle of useful and valuable knowledge respecting human nature.

Until you act after this manner, it is impossible that you can ever enjoy full happiness yourselves, or make others happy.

Herein consists the essence of philosophy;—of sound morality;—of true and genuine Christianity, freed from the errors that have been attached to it;—of pure and undefiled religion.

Without the introduction of this knowledge into full and complete practice, there can be no substantial and permanent ameliorations effected in society; and I declare to you, that until all your thoughts and actions are founded on and governed by these principles, your philosophy will be vain, —your morality baseless,—your Christianity only calculated to mislead and deceive the weak and the ignorant,—and your professions of religion but as sounding brass or a tinkling cymbal.

Those, therefore, who with singleness of heart and mind are ardently desirous to benefit their fellow-men, will put forth their utmost exertions to bring this just and humane system of conduct forthwith into practice, and to extend the knowledge of its endless advantages to the uttermost parts of the earth;—*for no other principles of action can ever become universal among men!*

Your time now makes it necessary that I should draw to a conclusion, and explain what ought to be the immediate result of what I have stated.

Direct your serious attention to the cause why men think and act as they do. You will then be neither surprised nor displeased on account of their sentiments or their habits. You will then clearly discover why others are displeased with you,—and pity them. As you proceed in these inquiries, you will find that mankind cannot be improved or rendered reasonable by force and contention; that it is absolutely necessary to support the old systems and institutions under which we now live, until another system and another arrangement of society shall be proved by practice to be essentially superior. You will, therefore, still regard it as your duty to pay respect and submission to what is established. For it would be no mark of wisdom to desert an old house, whatever may be its imperfections, until a new one shall be ready to receive you, however superior to the old that new one may be when finished.

Continue to obey the laws under which you live; and although many of them are founded on principles of the grossest ignorance and folly, yet obey them,—until the government of the country (which I have reason to believe is in the hands of men well disposed to adopt a system of general improvement) shall find it practicable to withdraw those laws which are productive of evil, and introduce others of an opposite tendency.

With regard to myself, I have not anything to ask of you, which I have not long experienced. I wish you merely to think that I am ardently engaged in endeavoring to benefit you and your children, and, through you and them, to render to mankind at large great and permanent advantages. I ask not for your gratitude, your love, your respect; for on you these do not depend. Neither do I seek or wish for praise or distinction of any kind; for to these, upon the clearest conviction, I am not entitled, and to me, therefore, they could be of no value. My desire is only to be considered as one of yourselves,—as a cotton spinner going about his daily and necessary avocations.

But for you I have other wishes. On this day a new era opens to our view. Let it then commence by a full and sincere dismissal from your minds of every unpleasant feeling which you may entertain towards each other, or towards any of your fellow-men. When you feel these injurious dispositions beginning to arise,—for, as you have been trained and are now circumstanced, they will arise again and again,—instantly call to your recollection how the minds of such individuals have been formed,—whence have originated all their habits and sentiments: your anger will then be appeased; you will calmly investigate the cause of your differences, and you will learn to love them and to do them good. A little perseverance in this simple and easily-acquired practice will rapidly prepare the way for you, and every one around you, to be truly happy.

Chapter IV

THE EMERGENCE
OF THE PROLETARIAT

The Revolution of 1830 in France and the Reform Bill of 1832 in England signaled a renewal of social and political ferment. This new wave of activity, which reached its climax in the revolutions of 1848, was still largely dominated by exponents of middle-class liberalism rather than by social reformers, but the latter were now becoming prominent for the first time. Whereas Saint-Simon and Fourier had never been activists, and Owen had taken his time in becoming one, the new breed of socialists emerging in the 1830s and '40s were often precisely that. Blanqui, for example, was untiring in his attempts at a revolutionary seizure of power from 1830 onwards, and Louis Blanc set a new precedent for socialists by taking part in the revolutionary Provisional Government in Paris in 1848. Even men whose orientation was not primarily political, like Cabet and Considérant, set out actually to found the communist or socialist communities that they envisioned. Above all, the Chartist movement in England became, in some respects, the first labor party of modern times.

The major source of this change was the fact that a large and self-conscious industrial working class was now beginning to take shape in England and Western Europe. Industrialism was more advanced in England than elsewhere, and so the British labor movement was naturally the most highly developed. In France, action by the workingmen themselves remained sporadic prior to 1848, though quite significant all the same. The major strike at Lyons in 1831 is what turned the Jacobin Blanqui into a "proletarian," as he subsequently called himself. With rare exceptions, continental socialism in this period continued to be led by middle-class intellectuals, but the experiences of Lyons and the Chartist demonstrations had given a new shape to their vision. They saw themselves no longer as scattered and isolated moralists, but rather as the leaders of a great revolutionary mass-movement.

CHARTISM

The passing of the Owenite phase of the British labor movement in 1834 brought about an only temporary lull in its activities; by 1837, the movement to petition Parliament for working-class representation was well under way, culminating in the "People's Charter" of the following year. It was an authentic working-class movement, and politically minded enough to produce the Chartist National Convention, a workingmen's parliament that sat in London between 1838 and 1839; but, despite the presence of some inflammatory phrase makers among its leaders, Chartism was not a revolutionary movement, nor even an especially socialist one. Made up of several not overly compatible segments of the British labor movement, it was led, up until 1838 when the first National Petition was presented to Parliament, by the moderate London Workingmen's Association, dominated by William Lovett. Lovett was of working-class origin, but he was basically nothing more extreme than a British nineteenth-century radical, an apostle of universal suffrage. His movement largely absorbed the group that had drawn up the Birmingham Petition, which had expressed aspirations similar to those subsequently embodied in the People's Charter.

The third major segment that subscribed to the Petition of 1838 was less susceptible to moderation. Lancashire and Yorkshire had long been prominent centers of labor unrest, and working-class activity in these districts fell under the leadership of two fiery-tongued Irish journalists: James Bronterre O'Brien, who had done an English translation of Buonarroti's book on Babeuf's conspiracy, and Feargus O'Connor, a former member of Parliament who edited a newspaper called

The Northern Star. O'Connor's program was an unrealistic one calling for resettlement of the unemployed upon the land, but he commanded the greater influence of the two, and after Parliament had rebuffed the Petition of 1838, he became the leader of the Chartist movement, to the extent that it then had a leader. He led the presentation of subsequent petitions in 1842 and 1848, after which the movement played itself out. In the long run, the basically moderate demands of the Charter were almost all incorporated into the British parliamentary system. Furthermore, the experience of the Chartist movement had given a start to what was for a long time the most highly developed labor movement in the world.

The statement, embodying the six major points to be incorporated into the Charter, was drawn up at a meeting of the London Workingmen's Association in 1837, at the "Crown and Anchor" Tavern in London.

PETITION AGREED TO AT THE "CROWN AND ANCHOR" MEETING, FEBRUARY 28th, 1837

To the Honourable the Commons of Great Britain and Ireland. The Petition of the undersigned Members of the Working Men's Association and others sheweth—

That the only *rational use* of the institutions and laws of society is justly to protect, encourage, and support all that can be made to contribute *to the happiness of all the people.*

That, as the object to be obtained is mutual benefit, so ought the enactment of laws to be by mutual consent.

That obedience to laws can only be *justly enforced* on the certainty that those who are called on to obey them have had, either personally or by their representatives, the power to enact, amend, or repeal them.

That all those who are excluded from this share of political power are not justly included within the operation of the laws; to them the laws are only despotic enactments, and the legislative assembly from whom they emanate can only be considered parties to an unholy compact, devising plans and schemes for taxing and subjecting the many.

That the universal political right of every human being is

superior and stands apart from all customs, forms, or ancient usuage; a fundamental right not in the power of man to confer; or justly to deprive him of.

That to take away this sacred right from the person and to vest it in *property*, is a wilful perversion of justice and common sense, as the creation and security of property *are the consequences of society*—the great object of which is human happiness.

That any constitution or code of laws, formed in violation of men's political and social rights, are not rendered sacred by time nor sanctified by custom.

That the ignorance which originated, or permits their operation, forms no excuse for perpetuating the injustice; nor can aught but force or fraud sustain them, when any considerable number of the people perceive and feel their degradation.

That the intent and object of your petitioners are to present such facts before your Honourable House as will serve to convince you and the country at large that you do not represent the people of these realms; and to appeal to your sense of right and justice as well as to every principle of honour, for directly making such legislative enactments as shall cause the mass of the people to be represented; with the view of securing *the greatest amount of happiness to all classes of society.*

Your Petitioners find, by returns ordered by your Honourable House, that the whole people of Great Britain and Ireland are about 24 millions, and that the males above 21 years of age are 6,023,752, who, in the opinion of your petitioners, are justly entitled to the elective right.

That according to S. Wortley's return (ordered by your Honourable House) the number of registered electors, who have the power to vote for members of Parliament, are only 839,519, and of this number only 8½ in 12 give their votes.

That on an analysis of the constituency of the United Kingdom, your petitioners find that 331 members (being a *majority* of your Honourable House) are returned by *one hundred and fifty-one thousand four hundred and ninety-two registered electors!*

That comparing the whole of the male population above the age of 21 with the 151,492 electors, it appears that 1-40 of them, or 1-160 of the entire population, have the power of passing all the laws in your Honourable House.

And your petitioners further find on investigation, that this majority of 331 members are composed of 163 Tories or Conservatives, 134 Whigs and Liberals, and only 34 who call themselves Radicals; and out of this limited number it is questionable whether 10 can be found who are truly the representatives of the wants and wishes of the producing classes.

Your petitioners also find that 15 members of your Honourable House are returned by electors under 200; 55 under 300; 99 under 400; 121 under 500; 150 under 600; 196 under 700; 214 under 800; 240 under 900; and 256 under 1,000; and that many of these constituencies are divided between two members.

They also find that your Honourable House, which is said to be exclusively the people's or the Commons House, contain *two hundred and five persons who are immediately or remotely related to the Peers of the Realm.*

Also that your Honourable House contains 1 marquess, 7 earls, 19 viscounts, 32 lords, 25 right honourables, 52 honourables, 63 baronets, 13 knights, 3 admirals, 7 lord-lieutenants, 42 deputy and vice-lieutenants, 1 general, 5 lieutenant-generals, 9 major-generals, 32 colonels, 33 lieutenant-colonels, 10 majors, 49 captains in army and navy, 10 lieutenants, 2 cornets, 58 barristers, 3 solicitors, 40 bankers, 33 East India proprietors, 13 West India proprietors, 52 place-men, 114 patrons of church livings having the patronage of 274 livings between them; the names of whom your petitioners can furnish at the request of your Honourable House.

Your petitioners therefore respectfully submit to your Honourable House that these facts afford abundant proofs that you do not represent the numbers or the interests of the millions; but that the persons composing it have interests for the most part foreign or directly opposed to the true interests of the great body of the people.

That perceiving the tremendous power you possess over the lives, liberty and labour of the unrepresented millions—perceiving the *military* and *civil forces* at your command—*the revenue* at your disposal—the *relief of the poor* in your hands

—the *public press* in your power, by enactments expressly ex-
cluding the working classes alone—moreover, the power of
delegating to others the whole control of the *monetary ar-*
rangements of the Kingdom, by which the labouring classes
may be silently plundered or suddenly suspended from employment—seeing all these elements of power wielded by your
Honourable House as at present constituted, and fearing the
consequences that may result if a thorough reform is not
speedily had recourse to, your petitioners earnestly pray your
Honourable House *to enact the following as the law of these*
realms, with such other essential details as your Honourable
House shall deem necessary:—

A LAW FOR EQUALLY REPRESENTING THE PEOPLE OF
GREAT BRITAIN AND IRELAND

EQUAL REPRESENTATION

That the United Kingdom be divided into 200 electoral
districts; dividing, as nearly as possible, an equal number of
inhabitants; and that each district do send a representative to
Parliament.

UNIVERSAL SUFFRAGE

That every person producing proof of his being 21 years of
age, to the clerk of the parish in which he has resided six
months, shall be entitled to have his name registered as a
voter. That the time for registering in each year be from the
1st of January to the 1st of March.

ANNUAL PARLIAMENTS

That a general election do take place on the 24th of June
in each year, and that each vacancy be filled up a fortnight
after it occurs. That the hours for voting be from six o'clock
in the morning till six o'clock in the evening.

NO PROPERTY QUALIFICATIONS

That there shall be no property qualification for members;
but on a requisition, signed by 200 voters, in favour of any
candidate being presented to the clerk of the parish in which
they reside, such candidate shall be put in nomination. And
the list of all the candidates nominated throughout the district

shall be stuck on the church door in every parish, to enable voters to judge of their qualification.

VOTE BY BALLOT

That each voter must vote in the parish in which he resides. That each parish provide as many balloting boxes as there are candidates proposed in the district; and that a temporary place be fitted up in each parish church for the purpose of *secret voting*. And, on the day of election, as each voter passes orderly on to the ballot, he shall have given to him, by the officer in attendance, a balloting ball, which he shall drop into the box of his favourite candidate. At the close of the day the votes shall be counted, by the proper officers, and the numbers stuck on the church doors. The following day the clerk of the district and two examiners shall collect the votes of all the parishes throughout the district, and cause the name of the successful candidate to be posted in every parish of the district.

SITTINGS AND PAYMENTS TO MEMBERS

That the members do take their seats in Parliament on the first Monday in October next after their election, and continue their sittings every day (Sundays excepted) till the business of the sitting is terminated, but not later than the 1st of September. They shall meet every day (during the Session) for business at 10 o'clock in the morning, and adjourn at 4. And every member shall be paid quarterly out of the public treasury £400 a year. That all electoral officers shall be elected by universal suffrage.

By passing the foregoing as the law of the land, you will confer a great blessing on the people of England; and your petitioners, as in duty bound, will ever pray.

LOUIS AUGUSTE BLANQUI (1805–81)

The legacy left by Babeuf, or better, by Buonarroti in his book about the Babeuf plot, *Conspiration pour l'Egalité*, achieved its highest fulfillment in the work of Blanqui. The son of a former Girondin, Blanqui, while he was a student in Paris, became a member of the Carbonari, the international conspiratorial association of liberal revolutionaries that was largely inspired by Buonarroti. He went on to become a radical journalist, and was wounded in the Revolution of 1830. The Lyons strike of the following year helped give a socialist turn to his ideas, and by 1832, when he was sent to jail for his writings, he was calling himself a "proletarian." From then on his life was a succession of participation in revolutionary organizations, attempted seizures of power, and prison terms. By the time of his death at the age of seventy-six, he had spent more than thirty years in prison.

Although he was an intellectual by origin and professional affiliation, and had a large proportion of intellectuals among his followers, Blanqui was really a kind of socialist primitive, in keeping with the revolution-charged atmosphere of Paris at the time, which left little room for speculation. He had no clearly conceived plan for a socialist society. From time to time he talked about a future world of cooperative associations, and he claimed to be a republican, although he detested parliamentary government. The only clear and consistent element in his theories—and this was his important contribution to the socialist tradition—was his idea of the revolutionary dictatorship of the proletariat. But his conception of this was, unlike that of Marx or even of Lenin (as Lenin himself was careful to point out), in no way that of a mass uprising, but rather that of a small revolutionary group seizing power in the name of the proletariat. It was the elitist idea *par excellence*. As such, it proved in time to be more middle-class (even with its unflagging *émeutisme*) than almost any other French socialist movement. The Blanquists were an important element in the Paris Commune of 1871 (Blanqui himself was in prison at the time), but they did not command its large working-class element. Nevertheless, led by Edouard Vaillant after the death of Blanqui, they continued to be an important and distinct element in French socialist politics (even becoming parliamentary in the 1890s), until the unified socialist party of France was created in 1905.

The following selection, taken from the *Critique Sociale*, a posthumous collection of various of Blanqui's articles, *feuilletons* and broadsides, is as near to a systematic statement of his

views as Blanqui ever made. It includes primitive perceptions
of many notions that Marx was later to develop with greater
sophistication, such as the idea of surplus value. Also, it shows
clearly how French socialist thought was moving from the
traditional French conception of landed property to an understanding of capitalist property.

The Man Who Makes the Soup Should Get to Eat It
(1834, revised in the 1850s)

Wealth is the offspring of intelligence and of work, the soul
and the life of humanity. But these two forces can act only
with the help of a passive element, the soil, which they make
productive by their combined efforts. It would seem, therefore, that this indispensable instrument should belong to all
men. This is not at all the case.

A few individuals have seized upon the common earth by
ruse or by violence and, claiming possession of it, have established by laws that it is to be their property forever, and
that this right of property is to be the basis of the social constitution, that it is, in other words, to suppress and if necessary
absorb all human rights, even the right to live, if any of these
should be so unfortunate as to come into conflict with the
privileges of the few.

This right of property logically extended itself from the soil
to other instruments, namely the accumulated products of
labor, designated by the generic term, capital. Now, since
capital, which is sterile by itself, bears fruit only through
manual labor, and furthermore, since it is the material that
pre-eminently requires the application of social forces in order
for it to be worked, the majority excluded from the possession
of it is condemned to forced labor, to the profit of the possessing minority. Neither the instruments nor the products of
labor belong to the workers; they belong rather to the idlers.
The gluttonous branches absorb the sap of the tree, to the
detriment of the fertile shoots. The hornets devour the honey
created by the bees.

Such is our social order, founded by conquest, which has

194 SOCIALIST THOUGHT

divided mankind into victors and vanquished. The logical consequence of such an organization is slavery. Nor has it waited long to make its appearance. In effect, since the soil yields its value only through cultivation, the privileged have derived from the right of possessing the soil that of also possessing the human livestock that makes it fruitful. They have looked upon this livestock, in the first place, as the complement of their domain, and then, in the last analysis, as a personal property, independent of the soil.

Meanwhile, the principle of equality, etched in the hearts of men, which conspires through the centuries to destroy the exploitation of man by man in all its forms, delivered the first blow to the sacrilegious right of property by shattering domestic slavery. Privilege was reduced to the possession of men, no longer as transferable property, but as a non-transferable and inseparable annex of non-transferable landed property.

In the sixteenth century a barbarous recrudescence of oppression gave rise to Negro slavery, and even today the inhabitants of a land that is considered French retain men in their possession by the same rights that they keep clothing and horses. For that matter, there is less difference than meets the eye between the social condition of the colonies and that of our own country. After eighteen centuries of warfare between privilege and equality, the country that has been the theater and principal champion of the battle could not very well stand for slavery in all its naked brutality. But the fact exists without the name, and the right of property, for all that it is more hypocritical in Paris than in Martinique, is no less intractable or oppressive.

Servitude, in effect, does not consist solely in being a man's chattel or a serf attached to a plot of ground. A person is not free when he is deprived of the instruments of labor and must remain at the mercy of those privileged persons who detain him. It is this kind of monopolizing, and not one political constitution or another, that makes the masses into serfs. Hereditary transmission of the soil and of capital is what places the citizen under the yoke of the property-owners. The citizens have no freedom but that of choosing their masters.

This is undoubtedly the origin of the sardonic saying: "The

rich make the poor work." That is about right, just as planters make their Negroes work, but with a little more indifference towards human life. For the factory worker is not a piece of capital to be taken care of the way the slave is. His death is no loss; there are always many people rivalling one another to be his replacement. Wages, though barely sufficient to stave off death, have the virtue of causing the exploited flesh to proliferate; they perpetuate the line of the poor who serve the rich, thus continuing from generation to generation the twin heritage—opulence and misery, enjoyment and sorrow running parallel to one another—that constitutes the elements of our society. When the proletarian has suffered enough and leaves his successors to suffer after him, he is sent to a hospital, where his cadaver is given to science, as a means of studying ways to provide cures for the masters.

These are the fruits of the appropriation of the instruments of labor. For the masses, incessant toil, barely providing the day's pennies, constant uncertainty about tomorrow, and famine, if a caprice of anger or of fear should take these instruments away! For the privileged, absolute autocracy, the right of life and death! They can wait out a crisis, because their coffers are full. Before all their reserves could possibly be used up, forcing them to capitulate, the last plebeian would be dead.

Who does not recall the miseries of 1831[1], when capital went into hiding out of fear or the desire for revenge? From Holland, gazing out over their plates of cheese, the barons of the strongbox coldly contemplated the anguish of that crowd decimated by the hunger that was its reward for blood spilled in the service of the bourgeois vanities of its employers. Reprisals through striking are impossible.

The workers of Lyons have just tried. But at what a price! Sixty thousand men were forced to kneel before a few dozen factory owners and ask their pardon. Hunger smothered the revolt. But was not even this much of a desire to resist really a miracle? How much suffering it took to wear out the patience

[1] Blanqui is referring to the 1831 strike at Lyons, which was the first important mass demonstration by French industrial workers. —Ed.

of these people and stiffen them at last against oppression!

The poor man does not know the source of his ills. Ignorance, the daughter of subjection, makes him into the docile instrument of the privileged. Crushed by toil, a stranger to the intellectual life, what can he know about these social phenomena in which he plays the role of the beast of burden? Accepting as a benefaction whatever fraction of the fruit of his own labor someone deigns to allow him, seeing the hand that exploits him only as the hand that feeds him, he is always ready, at a signal from the master, to tear apart the audacious man who tries to show him a better destiny.

Alas! humanity goes forth wearing a blindfold, which it raises in order to take a brief glance at its route only every once in a great while. Each step on the path of progress crushes the guide who caused it to take that step. The Gracchi were torn to pieces by a mob aroused by the voices of the patricians. Christ expired on the cross surrounded by the joyous howling of the Jewish population, excited by the priests and the Pharisees, and, only lately, the defenders of equality[2] died on the scaffold of the Revolution through the stupidity and ingratitude of the people, who allowed calumny to execrate their memory. Even today, the beneficiaries of privilege instruct the people of France every morning in how to spit on the tomb of these martyrs.

How difficult it is for the proletariat to open its eyes and see its oppressors! If the workers at Lyons rose up as one man, it was only because the flagrant antagonism of interests no longer permitted even the most obstinate to harbor illusions to the point of blindness. The stores of hatred and ferocity usually hidden in the hearts of these merchants were then finally revealed. In the middle of impending carnage, cannons, caissons, horses and soldiers were brought in from every direction, all for the purpose of extermination. To return to their duty or to perish under grape-shot—these were the alternatives offered the rebels. The duty of the worker of Lyons, of the man-machine, is to weep from hunger as he works day and

[2] Babeuf and Darthé. See page 43.—Ed.

night to create fabrics of gold, of silk, and of tears, for the pleasures of the rich.

But such a harsh tyranny has its dangers—resentment, revolt. To conjure away the peril, there was an attempt to reconcile Cain with Abel. Starting with the premise that capital is necessary as an instrument of labor, someone arrived at the conclusion that there is a community of interests, and hence solidarity between the capitalist and the laborer. What artistic phrases were woven upon this fraternal canvas! The sheep is shorn only for the good of his health. It owes thanks for this. Our Aesculapii know how to sugar the pill.

These homilies still find their dupes, but not many. Every day, more light is shed upon this supposed association of the parasite and his victim. The facts have their own eloquence; they prove that there is a duel going on, a duel to the death between profit and wage. Who will succumb? A question of justice and of common sense. Let us examine it.

There can be no society without labor! By the same token, there can be no idlers who have no need of laborers. But why do the laborers need the idlers? Is capital productive in the hands of the workers only on condition that it not belong to them? Suppose the proletariat were to desert *en masse*, and transplant its homes and its working capacity to some distant clime. Would it perchance die from the absence of its masters? Would the new society be able to get started only by setting up lords of the soil and of capital, by delivering over the possession of all the instruments of labor to a caste of idlers? Is no social mechanism possible but this division into property-owners and wage-earners?

On the other hand, how interesting it would be to see how our proud suzerains would conduct themselves after being abandoned by their slaves! What would they do with their palaces, their workshops, their deserted fields? Either die of hunger in the midst of all this wealth, or put on humble clothing, grab a pickax and take their turn at humbly sweating over some plot of ground. How much land could the lot of them cultivate? I imagine that all these gentlemen put together would not need so much as a sub-prefecture.

But a nation of thirty-two million people is no longer able

to withdraw to an Aventine Hill. Let us therefore take up the
inverse hypothesis, the more feasible one. One fine morning
the idlers evacuate the soil of France, leaving it in the hands
of the laborers. A day of happiness and triumph! What an
immense relief for so many millions of breasts, rid of the
weight that was crushing them! How deeply this multitude
will breathe! Citizens, hear in your hearts the chant of deliverance!

Axiom: the nation is impoverished by the loss of a worker; it
is enriched by the loss of an idler. The death of a rich man is
a benefaction.

Yes! the right of property is declining. Generous spirits are
prophesying and calling for its downfall. The Essenian principle of equality has been gradually undermining it for centuries, through the successive abolition of the various forms
of servitude that formed the foundation of its power. It will
disappear one day along with the last privileges that serve as
a retreat and a refuge for it. The present and the past guarantee us this outcome. For humanity never stands still. It advances or retreats. Its forward movement leads it to equality.
Its retrograde movement leads back through all the degrees
of privilege to personal slavery, the last word in property
rights. European civilization would assuredly perish before
returning to that state. But by what cataclysm? A Russian
invasion? On the contrary, it is the North that will be invaded
by the principle of equality which, under the leadership of
the French, is conquering all nations. The future is not in
doubt.

Let us say at once that equality is not the division of the
land. Infinite partitioning of the soil would not basically
change the right of property. The kind of wealth that comes
from possessing the instruments of labor rather than from
doing one's own work, the genius of exploitation, left intact,
would soon restore social inequality through the reconstruction of great fortunes.

Only association, substituted for individual property ownership, will bring about the reign of justice through equality.
This is why the men of the future ardently desire to work out
the principles of association and present them to the world.

Perhaps we can also bring our group to make a contribution to this common effort.

PIERRE JOSEPH PROUDHON (1809–65)

Proudhon has lost a good deal of esteem in the twentieth century, even in France, where Proudhonian traditions have remained the most persistent; and yet, he must be regarded as one of the most important figures in the history of socialism. Not only was he, in the 1860s, the spiritual founder of the French labor movement, but even his appearance on the public scene, twenty years before, was in fact of inestimable importance, for the emerging revolutionary socialism of the 1840s needed just such a moral force as he came to represent. This quality of moral force was the important thing about Proudhon; even where his thinking was fuzzy (and Marx came to find it unforgivably so), his presence carried weight and his conviction was inspiring. Furthermore, he was the only major socialist in the France of the forties who was of working-class origin.

Actually he was of peasant birth—in early nineteenth-century France, this was still true of most workingmen. In the countryside near Besançon where he was born, his father owned a house and a small plot of land, but had to earn his living by laboring both as a cooper and a brewer in the employ of others. Pierre Joseph was apprenticed to a printer at an early age, and in this capacity he began his formidable self-education, interesting himself at first in the study of philology and of classical and semitic languages. His intellectual achievements attracted the attention of some of the small community of scholars in Besançon, and in 1831 he was awarded the Suard Pension, a three-year scholarship given to young men of the Franche-Comté who showed intellectual promise. He pursued his studies in Paris, and although he went south again for a time after the period of his scholarship had ended, he returned to Paris later to make it his home. He had to continue earning his living in various humble ways, but by the late 1830s he was doing a good deal of writing, and had published

two books, one on grammar. The appearance of his first
major socialist work, *What Is Property?*, in 1840, brought
him fame.

During the course of an immensely productive literary career, Proudhon never ceased coming up with unexpected
theories and programs but the underlying ideas expressed in
this early work remained the core of his social philosophy.
It expresses an attitude toward property which, in spite of the
famous opening statement, "Property is theft," is not really
hostile to its existence at all. What is "theft," as it emerges
through the often unduly involved argumentation, is the kind
of property that is held, for example, by an absentee capitalist or landlord, the productivity of which is in someone else's
charge. In other words, Proudhon is a throwback to that old
French yeoman tradition, according to which the ideal form
of society would be one consisting entirely of small individual
holdings, each worked by the proprietor alone. The *mutualist*
idea that Proudhon developed in subsequent works, was basically a program for maintaining a socially regulated system of
such small holdings, through the administration of mutual
aid—by freely extending credit, for example, without charging
interest.

Proudhon was at heart opposed to industrialism all his life,
and one might therefore be tempted simply to write him off
as an anachronism, except that he persistently criticized the
structure of capitalism itself, and continued to invoke the
class-consciousness of the proletariat. Not that he was precisely a revolutionary socialist; he was too averse to politics
to have any political programs, even revolutionary ones, and
he called himself an anarchist. But, with fine inconsistency,
he became the chief spokesman of the emerging Paris workers'
movement of the 1860s, even though its principal aim at the
time was to form a working-class political party. The inconsistency was appropriate, however, because the political
orientation of that same workers' movement proved after his
death to be anti-political, or anarchist, as were his own deepest
sentiments. This was the spirit that caused the French working-class members of the First International, later the heroes
of the Paris Commune, to form a faction around Bakunin in

opposition to Marx. This was not the first time that Marx had run afoul of Proudhon's ideas; as far back as 1846, his response to Proudhon's *System of Economic Contradictions, or the Philosophy of Poverty*, which Marx ironically entitled *The Poverty of Philosophy*, claimed that Proudhon's socialism was essentially the product of the *petit-bourgeois* mentality. This it may have been, but such, then, was the mentality of the French workingman.

The following selection is from the translation of *What Is Property?* made by the American anarchist, Benjamin R. Tucker.

What Is Property?
OR
An Inquiry Into the Principle of Right and of Government
(1840)

CHAPTER I

METHOD PURSUED IN THIS WORK—THE IDEA OF A REVOLUTION

If I were asked to answer the following question: *What is slavery?* and I should answer in one word, *It is murder*, my meaning would be understood at once. No extended argument would be required to show that the power to take from a man his thought, his will, his personality, is a power of life and death; and that to enslave a man is to kill him. Why, then, to this other question: *What is property?* may I not likewise answer, *It is theft*, without the certainty of being misunderstood; the second proposition being no other than a transformation of the first?

I undertake to discuss the vital principle of our government and our institutions, property: I am in my right. I may be mistaken in the conclusion which shall result from my investigations: I am in my right. I think best to place the last thought of my book first: still am I in my right.

Such an author teaches that property is a civil right born

of occupation and sanctioned by law; another maintains that
it is a natural right, originating in labor,—and both of these
doctrines, totally opposed as they may seem, are encouraged
and applauded. I contend that neither labor, nor occupation,
nor law, can create property; that it is an effect without a
cause: am I censurable?

But murmurs arise!

Property is theft! That is the war-cry of '93! That is the
signal of revolutions!

Reader, calm yourself: I am no agent of discord, no fire-
brand of sedition. I anticipate history by a few days; I disclose a truth whose development we may try in vain to arrest;
I write the preamble of our future constitution. This proposition which seems to you blasphemous—*property is theft*—
would, if our prejudices allowed us to consider it, be recognised as the lightning-rod to shield us from the coming
thunderbolt; but too many interests stand in the way! . . .
Alas! philosophy will not change the course of events: destiny
will fulfil itself regardless of prophecy. Besides, must not justice be done and our education be finished?

Property is theft! . . . What a revolution in human ideas!
Proprietor and *thief* have been at all times expressions as contradictory as the beings whom they designate are hostile! all
languages have perpetuated this opposition. On what authority, then, do you venture to attack universal consent, and give
the lie to the human race? Who are you, that you should
question the judgment of the nations and the ages?

Of what consequence to you, reader, is my obscure individuality? I live, like you, in a century in which reason sub-
mits only to fact and to evidence. My name, like yours, is
TRUTHSEEKER.[1] My mission is written in these words of the
law: *Speak without hatred and without fear; tell that which
thou knowest!* The work of our race is to build the temple of
science, and this science includes man and Nature. Now truth
reveals itself to all; to-day to Newton and Pascal, to-morrow
to the herdsman in the valley and the journeyman in the shop.
Each one contributes his stone to the edifice; and, his task

[1] In Greek, σκεπτικος, examiner; a philosopher whose business is
to seek the truth.

accomplished, disappears. Eternity precedes us, eternity follows us; between two infinites, of what account is one poor mortal that the century should inquire about him?

Disregard then, reader, my title and my character, and attend only to my arguments. It is in accordance with universal consent that I undertake to correct universal error; from the *opinion* of the human race I appeal to its *faith*. Have the courage to follow me; and, if your will is untrammelled, if your conscience is free, if your mind can unite two propositions and deduce a third therefrom, my ideas will inevitably become yours. In beginning by giving you my last word, it was my purpose to warn you, not to defy you; for I am certain that, if you read me, you will be compelled to assent. The things of which I am to speak are so simple and clear that you will be astonished at not having perceived them before, and you will say: "I have neglected to think." Others offer you the spectacle of genius wrestling Nature's secrets from her, and unfolding before you her sublime messages; you will find here only a series of experiments upon *justice* and *right*, a sort of verification of the weights and measures of your conscience. The operations shall be conducted under your very eyes, and you shall weigh the result.

Nevertheless, I build no system. I ask an end to privilege, the abolition of slavery, equality of rights, and the reign of law. Justice, nothing else: that is the alpha and omega of my argument: to others I leave the business of governing the world.

One day I asked myself: Why is there so much sorrow and misery in society? Must man always be wretched? And not satisfied with the explanations given by the reformers—these attributing the general distress to governmental cowardice and incapacity, those to conspiracies and *émeutes*, still others to ignorance and general corruption—and weary of the interminable quarrels of the tribune and the press, I sought to fathom the matter myself. I have consulted the masters of science; I have read a hundred volumes of philosophy, law, political economy, and history; would to God that I had lived in a century in which so much reading had been useless! I have made every effort to obtain exact information, compar-

ing doctrines, replying to objections, continually constructing
equations and reductions from arguments, and weighing
thousands of syllogisms in the scales of the most rigorous logic.
In this laborious work, I have collected many interesting facts
which I shall share with my friends and the public as soon
as I have leisure. But I must say that I recognised at once
that we had never understood the meaning of these words,
so common and yet so sacred: *Justice, equity, liberty;* that
concerning each of these principles our ideas have been utterly
obscure; and, in fact, that this ignorance was the sole cause,
both of the poverty that devours us, and of all the calamities
that have ever afflicted the human race. . . .

Is political and civil inequality just?

Some say yes; others no. To the first I would reply that,
when the people abolished all privileges of birth and caste,
they did it, in all probability, because it was for their advantage; why then do they favour the privileges of fortune more
than those of rank and race? Because, say they, political inequality is a result of property; and without property society
is impossible: thus the question just raised becomes a question
of property. To the second I content myself with this remark:
If you wish to enjoy political equality, abolish property;
otherwise, why do you complain?

Is property just?

Everybody answers without hesitation, "Yes, property is
just." I say everybody, for up to the present time no one who
thoroughly understood the meaning of his words has answered no. For it is no easy thing to reply understandingly to
such a question; only time and experience can furnish an
answer. Now, this answer is given; it is for us to understand
it. I undertake to prove it.

We are to proceed with the demonstration in the following
order:—

I. We dispute not at all, we refute nobody, we deny nothing; we accept as sound all the arguments alleged in favor of
property, and confine ourselves to a search for its principle,
in order that we may then ascertain whether this principle is
faithfully expressed by property. In fact, property being defensible on no ground save that of justice, the idea, or at least the

intention, of justice must of necessity underlie all the arguments that have been made in defense of property; and, as on the other hand the right of property is only exercised over those things which can be appreciated by the senses, justice, secretly objectifying itself, so to speak, must take the shape of an algebraic formula. By this method of investigation, we soon see that every argument which has been invented in behalf of property, *whatever it may be,* always and of necessity leads to equality; that is, to the negation of property.

The first part covers two chapters: one treating of occupation, the foundation of our right; the other, of labor and talent, considered as causes of property and social inequality.

The first of these chapters will prove that the right of occupation *obstructs* property; the second that the right of labor *destroys* it.

II. Property, then, being of necessity conceived as existing only in connexion with equality, it remains to find out why, in spite of this necessity of logic, equality does not exist. This new investigation also covers two chapters: in the first, considering the fact of property in itself, we inquire whether this fact is real, whether it exists, whether it is possible; for it would imply a contradiction, were these two opposite forms of society, equality and inequality, both possible. Then we discover, singularly enough, that property may indeed manifest itself accidentally; but that, as an institution and principle, it is mathematically impossible. So that the axiom of the school—*ab actu ad posse valet consecutio:* from the actual to the possible the inference is good—is given the lie as far as property is concerned.

Finally, in the last chapter, calling psychology to our aid, and probing man's nature to the bottom, we shall disclose the principle of *justice*—its formula and character; we shall state with precision the organic law of society; we shall explain the origin of property, the causes of its establishment, its long life, and its approaching death; we shall definitively establish its identity with theft. And, after having shown that these three prejudices—*the sovereignty of man, the inequality of conditions, and property*—are one and the same; that they may be taken for each other, and are reciprocally convertible

—we shall have no trouble in inferring therefrom, by the principle of contradiction, the basis of government and right. There our investigations will end, reserving the right to continue them in future works.

The importance of the subject which engages our attention is recognized by all minds.

"Property," says M. Hennequin, "is the creative and conservative principle of civil society. Property is one of those basic institutions, new theories concerning which cannot be presented too soon; for it must not be forgotten, and the publicist and statesman must know, that on the answer to the question whether property is the principle or the result of the social order, whether it is to be considered as a cause, or an effect, depends all morality, and, consequently, all the authority of human institutions."

These words are a challenge to all men of hope and faith; but, although the cause of equality is a noble one, no one has yet picked up the gauntlet thrown down by the advocates of property; no one has been courageous enough to enter upon the struggle. The spurious learning of haughty jurisprudence, and the absurd aphorisms of a political economy controlled by property have puzzled the most generous minds; it is a sort of password among the influential friends of liberty and the interests of the people that *equality is a chimera!* So many false theories and meaningless analogies influence minds otherwise keen, which are unconsciously controlled by popular prejudice. Equality advances every day— *fit æqualitas.* Soldiers of liberty, shall we desert our flag in the hour of triumph?

A defender of equality, I shall speak without bitterness and without anger; with the independence becoming a philosopher, with the courage and firmness of a free man. May I, in this momentous struggle, carry into all hearts the light with which I am filled; and show, by the success of my argument, that equality failed to conquer by the sword only that it might conquer by the pen!

CHAPTER II

PROPERTY CONSIDERED AS A NATURAL RIGHT—
OCCUPATION
AND CIVIL LAW AS EFFICIENT BASES OF PROPERTY

Definitions

The Roman law defined property as the right to use and abuse one's own within the limits of the law—*jus utendi et abutendi re suâ, quatenus juris ratio patitur*. A justification of the word *abuse* has been attempted, on the ground that it signifies, not senseless and immoral abuse, but only absolute domain. Vain distinction! invented as an excuse for property, and powerless against the phrenesy of possession, which it neither prevents nor represses. The proprietor may, if he chooses, allow his crops to rot under foot; sow his field with salt; milk his cows on the sand; change his vineyard into a desert, and use his vegetable garden as a park: do these things constitute abuse or not? In the matter of property, use and abuse are necessarily indistinguishable.

According to the Declaration of Rights, published as a preface to the Constitution of '93, property "is the right to enjoy and dispose at will of one's goods, one's income, and the fruit of one's labor and industry."

Code Napoleon, article 544; "Property is the right to enjoy and dispose of things in the most absolute manner, provided we do not overstep the limits prescribed by the laws and regulations."

These two definitions do not differ from that of the Roman law: all give the proprietor an absolute right over a thing; and as for the restriction imposed by the code—*provided we do not overstep the limits prescribed by the laws and regulations*—its object is not to limit property, but to prevent the domain of one proprietor from interfering with that of another. That is a confirmation of the principle, not a limitation of it.

There are different kinds of property: 1. Property pure and simple, the dominant and seigniorial power over a thing: or, as they term it, *naked property.* 2. *Possession.* "Possession," says Duranton, "is a matter of fact, not of right." Toullier: "Property is a right, a legal power; possession is a fact." The tenant, the farmer, the commandité, the usufructuary are possessors; the owner who lets and lends for use, the heir who is to come into possession on the death of a usufructuary, are proprietors. If I may venture the comparison: a lover is a possessor, a husband is a proprietor.

This double definition of property—domain and possession —is of the highest importance; and it must be clearly understood, in order to comprehend what is to follow.

From the distinction between possession and property arise two sorts of rights: the *jus in re,* the right *in* a thing, the right by which I may reclaim the property which I have acquired, in whatever hands I find it; and the *jus ad rem,* the right *to* a thing, which gives me a claim to become a proprietor. Thus the right of the partners to a marriage over each other's person is the *jus in re;* that of two who are betrothed is only the *jus ad rem.* In the first, possession and property are united; the second includes only naked property. With me who, as a laborer, have a right to the possession of the products of Nature and my own industry—and who, as a proletaire, enjoy none of them—it is by virtue of the *jus ad rem* that I demand admittance to the *jus in re.*

This distinction between the *jus in re* and the *jus ad rem* is the basis of the famous distinction between *possessoire* and *petitoire*—actual categories of jurisprudence, the whole of which is included within their vast boundaries. *Petitoire* refers to every thing relating to property: *possessoire* to that relating to possession. In writing this memoir against property, I bring against universal society an *action petitoire:* I prove that those who do not possess to-day are proprietors by the same title as those who do possess; but, instead of inferring therefrom that property should be shared by all, I demand, in the name of general security, its entire abolition. If I fail to win my case, there is nothing left for us (the proletarian class and myself) but to cut our throats: we can ask nothing more from the justice of nations; for, as the code of procedure (art. 26) tells us in its energetic style, *the plaintiff who has been in non-*

suited in an action petitoire, is debarred thereby from bringing an action possessoire. If, on the contrary, I gain the case, we must then commence an *action possessoire,* that we may be reinstated in the enjoyment of the wealth of which we are deprived by property. I hope that we shall not be forced to that extremity; but these two actions cannot be prosecuted at once, such a course being prohibited by the same code of procedure. Before going to the heart of the question, it will not be useless to offer a few preliminary remarks.

1—*Property as a Natural Right*

The Declaration of Rights has placed property in its list of the natural and inalienable rights of man, four in all: *liberty, equality, property, security.* What rule did the legislators of '93 follow in compiling this list? None. They laid down principles, just as they discussed sovereignty and the laws; from a general point of view, and according to their own opinion. They did everything in their own blind way.

If we can believe Toullier: "The absolutely right can be reduced to three: *security, liberty, property.*" Equality is eliminated by the Rennes professor; why? Is it because *liberty* implies it, or because *property* prohibits it? On this point the author of "Droit Civil Expliqué" is silent: it has not even occurred to him that the matter is under discussion.

Nevertheless, if we compare these three or four rights with each other, we find that property bears no resemblance whatever to the other; that for the majority of citizens it exists only potentially, and as a dormant faculty without exercise; that for the others, who do enjoy it, it is susceptible of certain transactions and modifications which do not harmonize with the idea of a natural right; that, in practice, governments, tribunals, and laws do not respect it; and finally that everybody, spontaneously and with one voice, regards it as chimerical. . . .

Liberty is an absolute right, because it is to man what impenetrability is to matter,—a *sine quâ non* of existence; equality is an absolute right, because without equality there is no society; security is an absolute right, because in the eyes of every man his own liberty and life are as precious as another's. These three rights are absolute; that is, susceptible of neither increase nor diminution; because in society each associate receives as much as he gives,—liberty for liberty, equality for equality, security for security, body for body, soul for soul, in life and in death.

But property, in its derivative sense, and by the definitions of law, is a right outside of society; for it is clear that, if the wealth of each was social wealth, the conditions would be equal for all, and it would be a contradiction to say: *Property is a man's right to dispose at will of social property.* Then if we are associated for the sake of liberty, equality, and security, we are not associated for the sake of property; then if property is a *natural* right, this natural right is not *social*, but *antisocial*. Property and society are utterly irreconcilable institutions. It is as impossible to associate two proprietors as to join two magnets by their opposite poles. Either society must perish, or it must destroy property.

If property is a natural, absolute, imprescriptible, and inalienable right, why, in all ages, has there been so much speculation as to its origin?—for this is one of its distinguishing characteristics. The origin of a natural right! Good God! who ever inquired into the origin of the rights of liberty, security, or equality? They exist by the same right that we exist; they are born with us, they live and die with us. With property it is very different, indeed. By law, property can exist without a proprietor, like a quality without a subject. It exists for the human being who as yet is not, and for the octogenarian who is no more. And yet, in spite of these wonderful prerogatives which savour of the eternal and the infinite, they have never found the origin of property; the doctors still disagree. On one point only are they in harmony; namely, that the validity of the right of property depends upon the authenticity of its origin. But this harmony is their condemnation. Why have they acknowledged the right before settling the question of origin?

Certain classes do not relish investigation into the pretended titles to property, and its fabulous and perhaps scandalous history. They wish to hold to this proposition: that property is a fact; that it always has been, and always will be. With that proposition the *savant* Proudhon[2] commenced his "Treatise on the Right of Usufruct," regarding the origin of property as a useless question. Perhaps I would subscribe to this doctrine, believing it inspired by a commendable love of peace, were all my fellow-citizens in comfortable circumstances; but, no! I will not subscribe to it.

The titles on which they pretend to base the right of property are two in number: *occupation* and *labor*. I shall examine them successively, under all their aspects and in detail; and I remind the reader that, to whatever authority we appeal, I shall prove beyond a doubt that property, to be just and possible, must necessarily have equality for its condition.

2—*Occupation as the Title to Property*

It is remarkable that, at those meetings of the State Council at which the Code was discussed, no controversy arose as to the origin and principle of property. All the articles of Vol. II., Book 2, concerning property and the right of accession, were passed without opposition or amendment. Bonaparte, who on other questions had given his legists so much trouble, had nothing to say about property. Be not surprised at it: in the eyes of that man, the most selfish and wilful person that ever lived, property was the first of rights, just as submission to authority was the most holy of duties.

The right of *occupation,* or of the *first occupant,* is that which results from the actual, physical, real possession of a thing. I occupy a piece of land; the presumption is, that I am the proprietor, until the contrary is proved. We know that originally such a right cannot be legitimate unless it is reciprocal; the jurists say as much.

Cicero compares the earth to a vast theatre: *Quemadmodum theatrum cum commune sit, recte tamen dici potest ejus esse cum locum quem quisque occuparit.*

This passage is all that ancient philosophy has to say about the origin of property.

The theatre, says Cicero, is common to all; nevertheless,

[2] The Proudhon here referred to is J. B. V. Proudhon, a distinguished French jurist, and distant relative of the author.— *Translator*

the place that each one occupies is called *his own;* that is, it
is a place *possessed,* not a place *appropriated.* This comparison annihilates property; moreover, it implies equality. Can I,
in a theatre, occupy at the same time one place in the pit,
another in the boxes, and a third in the gallery? Not unless
I have three bodies, like Geryon, or can exist in different places
at the same time as is related of the magician Apollonius.

According to Cicero, no one has a right to more than he
needs: such is the true interpretation of his famous axiom—
suum quidque cujusque sit, to each one that which belongs to
him—an axiom that has been strangely applied. That which
belongs to each is not that which each *may* possess, but that
which each *has a right* to possess. Now, what have we a right
to possess? That which is required for our labor and consumption; Cicero's comparison of the earth to a theatre proves
it. According to that, each one may take what place he will,
may beautify and adorn it, if he can; it is allowable: but he
must never allow himself to overstep the limit which separates
him from another. The doctrine of Cicero leads directly to
equality; for, occupation being pure toleration, if the toleration is mutual (and it cannot be otherwise) the possessions
are equal.

Grotius rushes into history; but what kind of reasoning is
that which seeks the origin of a right, said to be natural,
elsewhere than in Nature? This is the method of the ancients:
the fact exists, then it is necessary, then it is just, then its
antecedents are just also. Nevertheless, let us look into it.

"Originally, all things were common and undivided; they
were the property of all." Let us go no farther. Grotius tells
us how this original communism came to an end through ambition and cupidity; how the age of gold was followed by the
age of iron, &c. So that property rested first on war and conquest, then on treaties and agreements. But either these treaties and agreements distributed wealth equally, as did the
original communism (the only method of distribution with
which the barbarians were acquainted, and the only form of
justice of which they could conceive; and then the question of
origin assumes this form: how did equality afterwards disappear?)—or else these treaties and agreements were forced

by the strong upon the weak, and in that case they are null; the tacit consent of posterity does not make them valid, and we live in a permanent condition of iniquity and fraud.

We never can conceive how the equality of conditions, having once existed, could afterwards have passed away. What was the cause of such degeneration? The instincts of the animals are unchangeable, as well as the differences of species; to suppose original equality in human society is to admit by implication that the present inequality is a degeneration from the nature of this society—a thing which the defenders of property cannot explain. But I infer therefrom that, if Providence placed the first human beings in a condition of equality, it was an indication of its desires, a model that it wished them to realize in other forms; just as the religious sentiment, which it planted in their hearts, has developed and manifested itself in various ways. Man has but one nature, constant and unalterable; he pursues it through instinct, he wanders from it through reflection, he returns to it through judgment; who shall say that we are not returning now? According to Grotius, man has abandoned equality; according to me, he will yet return to it. How came he to abandon it? Why will he return to it? These are questions for future consideration.

Reid writes as follows:—

The right of property is not innate, but acquired. It is not grounded upon the constitution of man, but upon his actions. Writers on jurisprudence have explained its origin in a manner that may satisfy every man of common understanding.

The earth is given to men in common for the purposes of life, by the bounty of Heaven. But to divide it, and appropriate one part of its produce to one, another part to another, must be the work of men who have power and understanding given them, by which every man may accommodate himself, *without hurt to any other.*

This common right of every man to what the earth produces, before it be occupied and appropriated by others, was, by ancient moralists, very properly compared to the right which every citizen had to the public theatre,

where every man that came might occupy an empty seat,
and thereby acquire a right to it while the entertainment
lasted; but no man had a right to dispossess another.

The earth is a great theatre, furnished by the Almighty,
with perfect wisdom and goodness, for the entertainment
and employment of all mankind. Here every man has a
right to accommodate himself as a spectator, and to perform his part as an actor; but without hurt to others.

Consequences of Reid's doctrine.

1. That the portion which each one appropriates may
wrong no one, it must be equal to the quotient of the total
amount of property to be shared, divided by the number of
those who are to share it;

2. The number of places being of necessity equal at all
times to that of the spectators, no spectator can occupy two
places, nor can any actor play several parts;

3. Whenever a spectator comes in or goes out, the places of
all contract or enlarge correspondingly: for, says Reid, *"the
right of property is not innate, but acquired"*; consequently,
it is not absolute; consequently the occupancy on which it is
based, being a conditional fact, cannot endow this right with
a stability which it does not possess itself. This seems to have
been the thought of the Edinburgh professor when he added:

> A right to life implies a right to the necessary means of
> life; and that justice, which forbids the taking away the
> life of an innocent man, forbids no less the taking from
> him the necessary means of life. He has the same right to
> defend the one as the other. To hinder another man's
> innocent labor, or to deprive him of the fruit of it, is an
> injustice of the same kind, and has the same effect as to
> put him in fetters or in prison, and is equally a just object
> of resentment.

Thus the chief of the Scotch school, without considering at
all the inequality of skill or labor, posits *a priori* the equality
of the means of labor, abandoning thereafter to each laborer the care of his own person, after the eternal axiom:
Whoso does well, shall fare well.

The philosopher Reid is lacking, not in knowledge of the principle, but in courage to pursue it to its ultimate. If the right of life is equal, the right of labor is equal, and so is the right of occupancy. Would it not be criminal, were some islanders to repulse, in the name of property, the unfortunate victims of a shipwreck struggling to reach the shore? The very idea of such cruelty sickens the imagination. The proprietor, like Robinson Crusoe on his island, wards off with pike and musket the proletaire washed overboard by the wave of civilization, and seeking to gain a foothold upon the rocks of property. "Give me work!" cries he with all his might to the proprietor: "don't drive me away, I will work for you at any price." "I do not need your services," replies the proprietor, showing the end of his pike or the barrel of his gun. "Lower my rent at least." "I need my income to live upon." "How can I pay you, when I can get no work?" "That is your business." Then the unfortunate proletaire abandons himself to the waves; or if he attempts to land upon the shore of property, the proprietor takes aim, and kills him. . . .

3—*Civil Law as the Foundation and Sanction of Property*

Pothier seems to think that property, like royalty, exists by divine right. He traces back its origin to God himself—*ab Jove principium*. He begins in this way:—

> God is the absolute ruler of the universe and all that it contains: *Domini est terra et plenitudo ejus, orbis terrarum et universi qui habitant in eo.* For the human race he has created the earth and all its creatures, and has given it a control over them subordinate only to his own. "Thou madest him to have dominion over the works of thy hands; thou hast put all things under his feet," says the Psalmist. God accompanied this gift with these words, addressed to our first parents after the creation: "Be fruitful, and multiply, and replenish the earth," etc.

After this magnificent introduction, who would refuse to believe the human race to be an immense family living in brotherly union, and under the protection of a venerable fa-

ther? But, heavens! are brothers enemies? Are fathers unnatural, and children prodigal?

God gave the earth to the human race: why then have I
received none? *He has put all things under my feet,*—and I
have not where to lay my head! *Multiply,* he tells us through
his interpreter, Pothier. Ah, learned Pothier! that is as easy to
do as to say; but you must give moss to the bird for its nest.

The human race having multiplied, men divided
among themselves the earth and most of the things upon
it; that which fell to each, from that time exclusively belonged to him. That was the origin of the right of property.

Say, rather, the right of possession. Men lived in a state of
communism; whether positive or negative it matters little.
Then there was no property, not even private possession. The
genesis and growth of possession gradually forcing people to
labor for their support, they agreed either formally or tacitly
—it makes no difference which—that the laborer should be
sole proprietor of the fruit of his labor; that is, they simply
declared the fact that thereafter none could live without working. It necessarily followed that, to obtain equality of products,
there must be equality of labor; and that, to obtain equality
of labor, there must be equality of facilities for labor. Whoever without labor got possession, by force or by strategy, of
another's means of subsistence, destroyed equality, and placed
himself above or outside of the law. Whoever monopolized
the means of production on the ground of greater industry,
also destroyed equality. Equality being then the expression of
right, whoever violated it was *unjust.*

Thus, labor gives birth to private possession, the right *in* a
thing—*jus in re.* But in what thing? Evidently *in the product,*
not *in the soil.* So the Arabs have always understood it; and so,
according to Cæsar and Tacitus, the Germans formerly held.
"The Arabs," says M. de Sismondi, "who admit a man's property in the flocks which he has raised, do not refuse the crop
to him who planted the seed; but they do not see why another,
his equal, should not have a right to plant in his turn. The
inequality which results from the pretended right of the first

occupant seems to them to be based on no principle of justice: and when all the land falls into the hands of a certain number of inhabitants, there results a monopoly in their favour against the rest of the nation, to which they do not wish to submit."

Well, they have shared the land. I admit that therefrom results a more powerful organization of labor; and that this method of distribution, fixed and durable, is advantageous to production: but how could this division give to each a transferable right of property in a thing to which all had an inalienable right of possession? In the terms of jurisprudence, the metamorphosis from possessor to proprietor is legally impossible; it implies in the jurisdiction of the courts the union of *possessoire* and *petitoire;* and the mutual concessions of those who share the land are nothing less than traffic in natural rights. The original cultivators of the land, who were also the original makers of the law, were not as learned as our legislators, I admit: and had they been, they could not have done worse: they did not foresee the consequences of the transformation of the right of private possession into the right of absolute property. But why have not those, who in later times have established the distinction between *jus in re* and *jus ad rem,* applied it to the principle of property itself? . . .

To sum up and conclude:—

Not only does occupation lead to equality, it *prevents* property. For, since every man, from the fact of his existence, has the right of occupation, and, in order to live, must have material for cultivation on which he may labor; and since, on the other hand, the number of occupants varies continually with the births and deaths,—it follows that the quantity of material which each laborer may claim varies with the number of occupants; consequently, that occupation is always subordinate to population. Finally, that, inasmuch as possession, in right, can never remain fixed, it is impossible, in fact, that it can ever become property.

Every occupant is, then, necessarily a possessor or usufructuary,—a function which excludes proprietorship. Now, this is the right of the usufructuary: he is responsible for the thing entrusted to him; he must use it in conformity with general utility, with a view to its preservation and development; he has no power to transform it, to diminish it, or to change its nature; he cannot so divide the usufruct that another shall perform the labor while he receives the product. In a word, the usufructuary is under the supervision of society, submitted to the condition of labor and the law of equality.

Thus is annihilated the Roman definition of property—*the right of use and abuse*—an immorality born of violence, the most monstrous pretensions that the civil laws ever sanctioned. Man receives his usufruct from the hands of society, which alone is the permanent possessor. The individual passes away, society is deathless.

What a profound disgust fills my soul while discussing such simple truths! Do we doubt these things to-day? Will it be necessary to again take arms for their triumph? And can force, in default of reason, alone introduce them into our laws?

All have an equal right of occupancy.

The amount occupied being measured, not by the will, but by the variable conditions of space and number, property cannot exist.

This no code has ever expressed; this no constitution can admit! These are axioms which the civil law and the law of nations deny! . . . . .

But I hear the exclamations of the partisans of another system: "Labor, labor! that is the basis of property!"

Reader, do not be deceived. This new basis of property is worse than the first, and I shall soon have to ask your pardon for having demonstrated things clearer, and refuted pretensions more unjust, than any which we have yet considered.

CHAPTER III

8—*That, from the Stand-point of Justice, Labor Destroys Property*

This proposition is the logical result of the two preceding sections, which we have just summed up.

The isolated man can supply but a very small portion of his wants; all his power lies in association, and in the intelligent combination of universal effort. The division and co-operation of labor multiply the quantity and the variety of products; the individuality of functions improves their quality.

There is not a man, then, but lives upon the products of several thousand different industries; not a laborer but receives from society at large the things which he consumes, and, with these, the power to reproduce. Who, indeed, would venture the assertion, "I produce, by my own effort, all that I consume; I need the aid of no one else"? The farmer, whom the early economists regarded as the only real producer—the farmer, housed, furnished, clothed, fed, and assisted by the mason, the carpenter, the tailor, the miller, the baker, the butcher, the grocer, the blacksmith, &c.,—the farmer, I say, can he boast that he produces by his own unaided effort?

The various articles of consumption are given to each by all; consequently, the production of each involves the production of all. One product cannot exist without another; an isolated industry is an impossible thing. What would be the harvest of the farmer, if others did not manufacture for him barns, wagons, ploughs, clothes, etc.? Where would be the *savant* without the publisher; the printer without the typecaster and machinist; and these, in their turn, without a multitude of other industries? . . . Let us not prolong this catalogue—so easy to extend—lest we be accused of uttering commonplaces. All industries are united by mutual relations in a single group; all productions do reciprocal service as means and end: all varieties of talent are but a series of changes from the inferior to the superior.

Now, this undisputed and indisputable fact of the general participation in every species of product makes all individual productions common; so that every product, coming from the hands of the producer, is mortgaged in advance by society. The producer himself is entitled to only that portion of his product, which is expressed by a fraction whose denominator is equal to the number of individuals of which society is composed. It is true that in return this same producer has a share in all the products of others, so that he has a claim upon all, just as all have a claim upon him; but is it not clear that this reciprocity of mortgages, far from authorizing property, destroys even possession? The laborer is not even possessor of his product; scarcely has he finished it, when society claims it.

"But," it will be answered, "even if that is so—even if the product does not belong to the producer—still society gives each laborer an equivalent for his product, and this equivalent, this salary, this reward, this allowance, becomes his property. Do you deny that this property is legitimate? And if the laborer, instead of consuming his entire wages, chooses to economise—who dare question his right to do so?"

The laborer is not even proprietor of the price of his labor, and cannot absolutely control its disposition. Let us not be blinded by a spurious justice. That which is given the laborer in exchange for his product is not given him as a reward for past labor, but to provide for and secure future labor. We consume before we produce. The laborer may say at the end of the day, "I have paid yesterday's expenses; to-morrow I shall pay those of to-day." At every moment of his life, the member of society is in debt; he dies with the debt unpaid:—how is it possible for him to accumulate?

They talk of economy—it is the proprietor's hobby. Under a system of equality, all economy which does not aim at subsequent reproduction or enjoyment is impossible—why? Because the thing saved, since it cannot be converted into capital, has no object, and is without a *final cause*. . . .

CHAPTER V

. . . Property, born of the reasoning faculty, intrenches itself behind comparisons. But, just as reflection and reason are subsequent to spontaneity, observation to sensation, and experience to instinct, so property is subsequent to communism. Communism—or association in a simple form—is the necessary object and original aspiration of the social nature, the spontaneous movement by which it manifests and establishes itself. It is the first phase of human civilization. In this state of society,—which the jurists have called *negative communism,*—man draws near to man, and shares with him the fruits of the field and the milk and flesh of animals. Little by little this communism—negative as long as man does not produce—tends to become positive and organic through the development of labor and industry. But it is then that the sovereignty of thought, and the terrible faculty of reasoning logically or illogically, teach man that, if equality is the *sine qua non* of society, communism is the first species of slavery.

To express this idea by a Hegelian formula, I will say: Communism—the first expression of the social nature—is the first term of social development,—the *thesis;* property, the reverse of communism, is the second term,—the *antithesis.* When we have discovered the third term, the *synthesis,* we shall have the required solution. Now, this synthesis necessarily results from the correction of the thesis by the antithesis. Therefore it is necessary, by a final examination of their characteristics, to eliminate those features which are hostile to sociability. The union of the two remainders will give us the true form of human association.

2—*Characteristics of Communism and of Property*

I. I ought not to conceal the fact that property and communism have been considered always the only possible forms of society. This deplorable error has been the life of property. The disadvantages of communism are so obvious that its critics never have needed to employ much eloquence to thoroughly disgust men with it. The irreparability of the injustice which it causes, the violence which it does to attractions and repulsions, the yoke of iron which it fastens upon the will, the moral torture to which it subjects the conscience, the debilitating effect which it has upon society; and, to sum it all up, the pious and stupid uniformity which it enforces upon the free, active, reasoning, unsubmissive personality of man, have shocked common sense, and condemned communism by an irrevocable decree.

The authorities and examples cited in its favour disprove it. The communistic republic of Plato involved slavery; that of Lycurgus employed Helots, whose duty it was to produce for their masters, thus enabling the latter to devote themselves exclusively to athletic sports and to war. Even J. J. Rousseau—confounding communism and equality—has said somewhere that, without slavery, he did not think equality of

conditions possible. The communities of the early Church did
not last the first century out, and soon degenerated into
monasteries. In those of the Jesuits of Paraguay, the condition of the blacks is said by all travellers to be as miserable
as that of slaves; and it is a fact that the good Fathers were
obliged to surround themselves with ditches and walls to
prevent their new converts from escaping. The followers of
Babeuf—guided by a lofty horror of property rather than by
any definite belief—were ruined by exaggeration of their
principles; the St. Simonians, lumping communism and inequality, passed away like a masquerade. The greatest danger to which society is exposed to-day is that of another
shipwreck on this rock.

Singularly enough, systematic communism—the deliberate
negation of property—is conceived under the direct influence
of the proprietary prejudice; and property is the basis of all
communistic theories.

The members of a community, it is true, have no private
property; but the community is proprietor, and proprietor
not only of the goods, but of the persons and wills. In consequence of this principle of absolute property, labor, which
should be only a condition imposed upon man by Nature,
becomes in all communities a human commandment, and
therefore odious. Passive obedience, irreconcilable with a
reflecting will, is strictly enforced. Fidelity to regulations,
which are always defective, however wise they may be
thought, allows of no complaint. Life, talent, and all the
human faculties are the property of the State, which has the
right to use them as it pleases for the common good. Private
associations are sternly prohibited, in spite of the likes and
dislikes of different natures, because to tolerate them would
be to introduce small communities within the large one, and
consequently private property; the strong work for the
weak, although this ought to be left to benevolence, and not
enforced, advised, or enjoined; the industrious work for the
lazy though this is unjust; the clever work for the foolish, although this is absurd; and, finally, man—casting aside his
personality, his spontaneity, his genius, and his affections—

humbly annihilates himself at the feet of the majestic and inflexible Commune!

Communism is inequality, but not as property is. Property is the exploitation of the weak by the strong. Communism is the exploitation of the strong by the weak. In property, inequality of conditions is the result of force, under whatever name it be disguised: physical and mental force; force of events, chance, *fortune;* force of accumulated property, etc. In communism, inequality springs from placing mediocrity on a level with excellence. This damaging equation is repellent to the conscience, and causes merit to complain; for although it may be the duty of the strong to aid the weak, they prefer to do it out of generosity,—they never will endure a comparison. Give them equal opportunities of labor, and equal wages, but never allow their jealousy to be awakened by mutual suspicion of unfaithfulness in the performance of the common task.

Communism is oppression and slavery. Man is very willing to obey the law of duty, serve his country, and oblige his friends; but he wishes to labor when he pleases, where he pleases, and as much as he pleases. He wishes to dispose of his own time, to be governed only by necessity, to choose his friendships, his recreation, and his discipline; to act from judgment, not by command; to sacrifice himself through selfishness, not through servile obligation. Communism is essentially opposed to the free exercise of our faculties, to our noblest desires, to our deepest feelings. Any plan which could be devised for reconciling it with the demands of the individual reason and will would end only in changing the thing while preserving the name. Now, if we are honest truth-seekers, we shall avoid disputes about words.

Thus, communism violates the sovereignty of the conscience and equality: the first, by restricting spontaneity of mind and heart, and freedom of thought and action; the second, by placing labor and laziness, skill and stupidity, and even vice and virtue on an equality in point of comfort. For the rest, if property is impossible on account of the desire to accumulate, communism would soon become so through the desire to shirk. . . .

3—*Determination of the third form of Society*
Conclusion

Then, no government, no public economy, no administration, is possible, which is based upon property.

Communism seeks *equality* and *law*. Property, born of the sovereignty of the reason, and the sense of personal merit, wishes above all things *independence* and *proportionality*.

But communism, mistaking uniformity for law, and levelism for equality, becomes tyrannical and unjust. Property, by its despotism and encroachments, soon proves itself oppressive and anti-social.

The objects of communism and property are good—their results are bad. And why? Because both are exclusive, and each disregards two elements of society. Communism rejects independence and proportionality; property does not satisfy equality and law.

Now, if we imagine a society based upon these four principles,—equality, law, independence, and proportionality,—we find:—

1. That *equality,* consisting only in *equality of conditions,* that is, *of means,* and not in *equality of comfort,*—which it is the business of the laborers to achieve for themselves, when provided with equal means,—in no way violates justice and *équité*.

2. That *law,* resulting from the knowledge of facts, and consequently based upon necessity itself, never clashes with independence.

3. That individual *independence*, or the autonomy of the private reason, originating in the difference in talents and capacities, can exist without danger within the limits of the law.

4. That *proportionality,* being admitted only in the sphere of intelligence and sentiment, and not as regards material objects, may be observed without violating justice or social equality.

This third form of society, the synthesis of communism and property, we will call *liberty*.[3]

[3] *Libertas, liberare, libratio, libra,*—liberty, to liberate, libration, balance (pound),—words which have a common derivation. Lib-

In determining the nature of liberty, we do not unite communism and property indiscriminately; such a process would be absurd eclecticism. We search by analysis for those elements in each which are true, and in harmony with the laws of Nature and society, disregarding the rest altogether; and the result gives us an adequate expression of the natural form of human society,—in one word, liberty.

Liberty is equality, because liberty exists only in society; and in the absence of equality there is no society.

Liberty is anarchy, because it does not admit the government of the will, but only the authority of the law; that is, of necessity.

Liberty is infinite variety, because it respects all wills within the limits of the law.

Liberty is proportionality, because it allows the utmost latitude to the ambition for merit, and the emulation of glory.

We can now say, in the words of M. Cousin: "Our principle is true; it is good, it is social; let us not fear to push it to its ultimate."

Man's social nature becoming *justice* through reflection, *équité* through the classification of capacities, and having *liberty* for its formula, is the true basis of morality,—the principle and regulator of all our actions. This is the universal motor, which philosophy is searching for, which religion strengthens, which egotism supplants, and whose place pure reason never can fill. *Duty* and *right* are born of *need*, which, when considered in connection with others, is a *right*, and when considered in connection with ourselves, a *duty*.

We need to eat and sleep. It is our right to procure those things which are necessary to rest and nourishment. It is our duty to use them when Nature requires it.

We need to labor in order to live. To do so is both our right and our duty.

We need to love our wives and children. It is our duty to protect and support them. It is our right to be loved in preference to all others. Conjugal fidelity is justice. Adultery is high treason against society.

We need to exchange our products for other products. It

erty is the balance of rights and duties. To make a man free is to balance him with others,—that is, to put him on their level.

is our right that this exchange should be one of equivalents; and since we consume before we produce, it would be our duty, if we could control the matter, to see to it that our last product shall follow our last consumption. Suicide is fraudulent bankruptcy.

We need to live our lives according to the dictates of our reason. It is our right to maintain our freedom. It is our duty to respect that of others.

We need to be appreciated by our fellows. It is our duty to deserve their praise. It is our right to be judged by our works.

Liberty is not opposed to the rights of succession and bequest. It contents itself with preventing violations of equality. "Choose," it tells us, "between two legacies, but do not take them both." All our legislation concerning transmissions, entailments, adoptions, and, if I may venture to use such a word, *coadjutoreries*, requires remodelling.

Liberty favours emulation, instead of destroying it. In social equality, emulation consists in accomplishing under like conditions; it is its own reward. No one suffers by the victory.

Liberty applauds self-sacrifice, and honours it with its votes, but it can dispense with it. Justice alone suffices to maintain the social equilibrium. Self-sacrifice is an act of supererogation. Happy, however, the man who can say, "I sacrifice myself."[4]

[4] In a monthly publication the first number of which has just appeared under the name of *L'Egalitaire,* self-sacrifice is laid down as a principle of equality. This is a confusion of ideas. Self-sacrifice, taken alone, is the last degree of inequality. To seek equality in self-sacrifice is to confess that equality is against nature. Equality must be based upon justice, upon strict right, upon the principles invoked by the proprietor himself; otherwise it will never exist. Self-sacrifice is superior to justice; but it cannot be imposed as law, because it is of such a nature as to admit of no reward. It is, indeed, desirable that everybody shall recognize the necessity of self-sacrifice, and the idea of *L'Egalitaire* is an excellent example. Unfortunately, it can have no effect. What would you reply, indeed, to a man who should say to you, "I do not want to sacrifice myself"? Is he to be compelled to do so? When self-sacrifice is forced, it becomes oppression, slavery, the exploitation of man by man. Thus have the proletaires sacrificed themselves to property.

Liberty is essentially an organizing force. To insure equality between men and peace among nations, agriculture and industry, and the centers of education, business, and storage, must be distributed according to the climate and the geographical position of the country, the nature of the products, the character and natural talents of the inhabitants, etc., in proportions so just, so wise, so harmonious, that in no place shall there ever be either an excess or a lack of population, consumption, and products. There commences the science of public and private right, the true political economy. It is for the writers on jurisprudence, henceforth unembarrassed by the false principle of property, to describe the new laws, and bring peace upon earth. Knowledge and genius they do not lack; the foundation is now laid for them.[5]

[5] The disciples of Fourier have long seemed to me the most advanced of all modern socialists, and almost the only ones worthy of the name. If they had understood the nature of their task, spoken to the people, awakened their sympathies, and kept silence when they did not understand; if they had made less extravagant pretensions, and had shown more respect for public intelligence,—perhaps the reform would now, thanks to them, be in progress. But why are these earnest reformers continually bowing to power and wealth,—that is, to all that is anti-reformatory? How, in a thinking age, can they fail to see that the world must be converted *by demonstration*, not by myths and allegories? Why do they, the deadly enemies of civilization, borrow from it, nevertheless its most pernicious fruits,—property, inequality of fortune and rank, gluttony, concubinage, prostitution, what do I know? theurgy, magic, and sorcery? Why these endless denunciations of morality, metaphysics, and psychology, when the abuse of these sciences, which they do not understand, constitutes their whole system? Why this mania for deifying a man whose principal merit consisted in talking nonsense about things whose names, even, he did not know, in the strongest language ever put upon paper? Whoever admits the infallibility of a man becomes thereby incapable of instructing others. Whoever denies his own reason will soon proscribe free thought. The phalansterians would not fail to do it if they had the power. Let them condescend to reason, let them proceed systematically, let them give us demonstrations instead of revelations, and we will listen willingly. Then let them organize manufactures, agriculture, and commerce; let them make labor attractive, and the most humble functions honourable, and our praise shall be theirs. Above all, let them throw off that Illuminism which gives them the appearance of imposters or dupes, rather than believers and apostles.

I have accomplished my task; property is conquered, never again to arise. Wherever this work is read and discussed, there will be deposited the germ of death to property; there, sooner or later, privilege and servitude will disappear, and the despotism of will will give place to the reign of reason. What sophisms, indeed, what prejudices (however obstinate) can stand before the simplicity of the following propositions:—

I. Individual *possession*[6] is the condition of social life; five thousand years of property demonstrate it. *Property* is the suicide of society. Possession is a right; property is against right. Suppress property while maintaining possession, and, by this simple modification of the principle, you will revolutionize law, government, economy, and institutions; you will drive evil from the face of the earth.

II. All having an equal right of occupancy, possession varies with the number of possessors; property cannot establish itself.

III. The effect of labor being the same for all, property is lost in the common prosperity.

IV. All human labor being the result of collective force, all property becomes, in consequence, collective and unitary. To speak more exactly, labor destroys property.

V. Every capacity for labor being, like every instrument of labor, an accumulated capital, and a collective property, inequality of wages and fortunes (on the ground of inequality of capacities) is, therefore, injustice and robbery.

VI. The necessary conditions of commerce are the liberty of the contracting parties and the equivalence of the products exchanged. Now, value being expressed by the amount of time and outlay which each product costs, and liberty being inviolable, the wages of laborers (like their rights and duties) should be equal.

[6] Individual possession is no obstacle to extensive cultivation and unity of exploitation. If I have not spoken of the drawbacks arising from small estates, it is because I thought it useless to repeat what so many others have said, and what by this time all the world must know. But I am surprised that the economists, who have so clearly shown the disadvantages of spade-husbandry, have failed to see that it is caused entirely by property; above all, that they have not perceived that their plan for mobilizing the soil is a first step towards the abolition of property.

VII. Products are bought only by products. Now, the condition of all exchange being equivalence of products, profit is impossible and unjust. Observe this elementary principle of economy, and pauperism, luxury, oppression, vice, crime, and hunger will disappear from our midst.

VIII. Men are associated by the physical and mathematical law of production, before they are voluntarily associated by choice. Therefore, equality of conditions is demanded by justice; that is, by strict social law: esteem, friendship, gratitude, admiration, all fall within the domain of *equitable* or *proportional* law only.

IX. Free association, liberty—whose sole function is to maintain equality in the means of production and equivalence in exchanges—is the only possible, the only just, the only true form of society.

X. Politics is the science of liberty. The government of man by man (under whatever name it be disguised) is oppression. Society finds its highest perfection in the union of order with anarchy.

The old civilization has run its race; a new sun is rising, and will soon renew the face of the earth. Let the present generation perish, let the old prevaricators die in the desert! the holy earth shall not cover their bones. Young man, exasperated by the corruption of the age, and absorbed in your zeal for justice!—if your country is dear to you, and if you have the interests of humanity at heart, have the courage to espouse the cause of liberty; Cast off your old selfishness, and plunge into the rising flood of popular equality! There your regenerate soul will acquire new life and vigor; your enervated genius will recover unconquerable energy; and your heart, perhaps already withered, will be rejuvenated! Everything will wear a different look to your illuminated vision; new sentiments will engender new ideas within you; religion, morality, poetry, art, language will appear before you in nobler and fairer forms; and thenceforth, sure of your faith, and thoughtfully enthusiastic, you will hail the dawn of universal regeneration! . . .

LOUIS BLANC (1811–82)

When the republicans finally had their day in February
1848, and overthrew the regime of Louis Philippe, they
needed the support of the Paris working classes, as had the
republicans of 1792. But, unlike the previous occasion, there
was now a self-conscious and articulate leadership among the
working-class who demanded, in addition to a republican
constitution, measures that would conform to their particular
interests. In response, the Provisional Government of 1848
established the Luxembourg Commission, a kind of loosely
organized Ministry of Labor, under the supervision of the
socialist journalist Louis Blanc.

Blanc's book, *The Organization of Labor*, first published in
1839, had advocated a system of "social workshops," of
industrial cooperatives owned by the workers themselves, to
be started with state subsidies. Blanc hoped to use the
Luxembourg Commission as a means for getting his project
under way, but members of the provisional government who
feared the establishment of a social republic were able to prevent his plans from being carried out. Instead, "national
workshops" were created, an assortment of public works
projects such as planting trees along the boulevards, which
were largely of dubious usefulness in a time of economic
crisis. By the end of May, the worsening relations between
the middle-class government and the restless Paris workers
were reaching a climax, and the government, unable to bear
indefinitely the expense of the "national workshops," dissolved
them. Their action resulted in an uprising by the Paris workers
in June, 1848, which led to the "June Day" bloody reprisals
against the rebels conducted in the streets by government
troops under the command of General Louis Eugène Cavai-
gnac. It was the first genuine civil war between the proletariat and the bourgeoisie. Louis Blanc, sensing personal
danger, had fled to England in May.

In his introduction to the 1848 edition of the *Organization
of Labor*, from which the following excerpt is taken, Blanc

advocates the use of political power to bring about the socialist transformation of society.

ORGANIZATION OF LABOR
(INTRODUCTION, 1848 EDITION)

. . . In order to obtain for the political reform program numerous adherents from among the people, it is indispensable
to show the people the relationship between the amelioration
of their lot, whether moral or material, and a change of power.
This is what the true friends or avengers of the people have
done in all eras. It is what was done in Rome long ago by
those men who, moved by a god-like pity at the sight of the
impoverished debtors being so cruelly persecuted, led the
multitude onto the Aventine Hill. It is what the immortal
Tiberius Gracchus was doing when, convinced of the usurpations of the Roman aristocracy, he cried out to those pallid
conquerors of the world: "You call yourselves masters of the
universe, and you have not a stone upon which you can rest
your heads." It is what the fisherman Masaniello was doing
in Naples in 1647 when, starving during the orgies of the
viceroy, he raised the cry, "No more *gabelles.*" And finally,
it is what was done fifty years ago by those fanatical philosophers, those valiant soldiers in the war of ideas who perished
in their task only because they had come too soon. The people have the right to ask of him who pretends to lead them
where it is that they are being led. Too often in the past
they have been called upon to agitate for the sake of words,
to fight in the darkness, to use up their energies in unworthy
self-sacrifices, and to spill their blood fortuitously in the path
of the ambitious, those tribunes of the evening who hail the
oppressors on the morrow!

But if it is necessary to become engaged in a program of
social reform, it is no less necessary to pursue one of political reform. For if the first is the *end,* the second is the *means.*
It is not enough to discover scientific processes appropriate
for inaugurating the principle of association and for organizing labor in accordance with the rules of reason, justice and
humanity. One must also find a way to realize the principle

that has been adopted, and to enable the processes that have been discovered through study to bear fruit. Now, power is organized force. Power depends upon chambers, tribunals, soldiers—in other words, upon the triple force of laws, judgements and bayonets. Not to use it as an instrument is to encounter it as an obstacle.

Besides, the emancipation of the proletarians is a most complicated task; it is involved with too many questions, it upsets too many habits, it is contrary, not in reality but in appearance, to too many interests, for anyone to believe seriously that it could be brought about by a series of partial efforts and isolated attempts. All the force of the State must be applied in this task. The proletarians lack the instruments of labor, which they need in order to emancipate themselves: the function of the government is to provide them with these. If we had to define the State as we see it, we would say that the State is the banker for the poor.

Now, is it true, as M. de Lamartine was not afraid to point out in a recent manifesto, that this conception "consists in seizing, in the name of the State, property and sovereignty over industries and labor, in suppressing all free will on the part of citizens who own property, who sell, buy, or consume; in arbitrarily creating or distributing products, in establishing maximum prices, in regulating wages, in completely substituting a dispossessed citizenry for an industrial and proprietary State?"

As God is our witness, we have never proposed anything of the sort! And if it is we that M. de Lamartine was pretending to refute, then he probably has not done us the honor of reading our work. What we ask, as will be seen further on, is that the State—once it has been democratically constituted— create social workshops, destined to replace the individual workshops gradually and without any sudden upheavals; we ask that the social workshops be governed by statutes incorporating the principle of association and having the form and power of law. But once it is founded and set in motion, the social workshop will be sufficient unto itself and will no longer have recourse to anything but its own organizing principle. After the first year, the associated laborers would freely choose administrators and leaders from among themselves; they would work out the division of the receipts among themselves; they would be occupied in discovering ways to expand the enterprise. How can anyone say that such a system opens the way to arbitrariness and tyranny? The State would found the social workshop, provide it with laws, and watch over the execution of those laws, to see that they are carried out for the good of everyone; but that would be the limit of its role. Is such a role, can such a role be tyrannical? Today, when the government arrests a thief who has been discovered in somebody's house, does anyone accuse the government of tyranny? Does anyone reproach it for having entered the domain of individual life, for having penetrated into the private affairs of families? Well, in our system, the State would be, with respect to the social workshops, only what it is today with respect to society as a whole. It would watch over the inviolability of the pertinent statutes, just as today it watches over the inviolability of the laws. It would be the supreme protector of the principle of association, without at the same time being allowed or enabled to absorb into itself the action of the associated laborers, just as today it is the supreme protector of the property principle, though it does not absorb into itself the action of the property-owners.

But are we for having the State intervene, at least from the standpoint of initiative, in the economic reformation of society? Have we avowed that our goal is to undermine competition, to withdraw industry from the regime of *laissez-faire, laissez-passer?* Most certainly, and far from denying it, we proclaim it aloud. Why? Because we want freedom.

Yes, freedom! That is what must be won; but real freedom, freedom for all, the freedom that is sought in vain wherever those immortal sisters, equality and fraternity, are absent.

If we were to ask why the freedom of the state of nature was judged false and destroyed, the first child who came along would be able to give us the right answer. The freedom of the state of nature was, *in fact*, only an abominable oppression, because it allied itself with inequality of strength, because it made the weak man the victim of the vigorous, the impotent man the prey of the agile. Now, in the present social regime, instead of the inequality of physical strength, we have inequality of the means of development; instead of the battle of body against body, we have that of capital against capital; instead of the abuse of physical superiority, we have the abuse of a superiority created by social conventions. In place of the weak we have the ignorant; in place of the impotent, the poor. Where, then, is freedom?

It most certainly exists for those who have the means of enjoying it and making it bear fruit, for those who own the soil, who have money, credit, and the thousand resources that culture and intelligence provide; these people have so much that they can even abuse it. But is it the same for that interesting and numerous class that has neither land, nor capital, nor credit, nor instruction—that has, in other words, nothing that would enable the individual to manage for himself and develop his faculties? And when society is thus divided, with immense strength on one side and immense weakness on the other, then competition is unleashed in its midst, competition that pits the rich against the poor, the wily speculator against the naive laborer, the client of some slick banker against the usurer's serf, the thoroughly accoutered athlete against the unarmed combatant, the nimble man against the paralytic! And this disorderly and permanent shock of power against impotence, this anarchy in the midst of oppression, this invisible tyranny unsurpassed in harshness by tyrannies that can be seen by the human eye—this is what they call freedom!

In other words, the son of a poor man, pulled by hunger off the road that takes him to school, forced to sell short his body and soul at the nearby spinning-mill in order to add a few pennies to the family earnings—this boy is free to develop his intelligence, if he wants to.

In other words, the worker, who will die if the debate goes on for too long, is free to discuss conditions with his employer! . . .

These days, it is said, nothing succeeds like success. This is true, and to say that the social order is characterized by such an aphorism is enough to condemn it. For all notions of justice and humanity are turned upside down when the more

ways of getting rich a person has the less he needs to use
them, while the fewer ways of escaping misery he possesses
the more miserable he is. Has the accident of birth thrown
you among us in a completely deprived condition? Toil,
suffer, die: no one allows credit to a poor man, and the doctrine of *laissez-faire* guarantees that he will be abandoned.
Were you born in the midst of opulence? Have a good time,
enjoy yourself, sleep: your money is making money for you.
Nothing succeeds like success!

But the poor man, you say, has the *right* to better his
position? So! and what difference does it make, if he has not
the *power* to do so? What does the *right* to be cured matter
to a sick man whom no one is curing?

Right, considered abstractly, is the mirage that has kept
the people in an abused condition since 1789. Right is the
dead metaphysical protection that replaced, for the people,
the living protection that was owed them. Right, sterilely
and pompously proclaimed in the charters, has only served to
mask whatever was unjust about the inauguration of a regime
of individualism, and whatever was barbarous about the
abandonment of the poor man. It is because freedom was
defined by the word "right" that people came to designate
men who were slaves of hunger, cold, ignorance, chance, as
"free" men. Let us say it then for once and for all: freedom
consists, not only in the RIGHTS that have been accorded,
but also in the POWER given men to develop and exercise
their faculties, under the reign of justice and the safeguard of
law.

And let it be noted that this is not a vain distinction; its
meaning is profound, its consequences are immense. For,
once it is admitted that a man must have the *power* to develop
and exercise his faculties in order to be really free, the upshot
is that society owes every one of its members both instruction,
without which the human mind *cannot* grow, and the instruments of labor, without which human activity *cannot*
achieve its fullest development. Now, how will society be
made to give suitable instruction and the necessary instruments of labor to every one of its members, if not by the intervention of the State? It is therefore in the name of freedom

that we are asking for the rehabilitation of the principle of authority. We want a strong government because, in the regime of inequality within which we are still vegetating, there are weak persons who need a social force to protect them. We want a government that will intervene in industry, because in an area where people make loans only to the rich, a social banker is needed who will lend to the poor. In a word, we are invoking the idea of power because the freedom of the future must be a reality.

For the rest, do not be deceived; this necessity for the intervention of governments is relative; it derives solely from this state of weakness, misery and ignorance into which earlier tyrannies have plunged the people. If the dearest hope of our hearts is not deceived, a day will come when a strong and active government will no longer be needed, because there will no longer be inferior and subordinate classes in society. Until then, the establishment of a tutelary authority is indispensable. The seed-bed of socialism can be fertilized only by the wind of politics.

O, rich men, you are deceived when you become aroused against those who dedicate their waking hours to the calm and peaceful solution of social problems. Yes, the sacred cause of the poor man is your cause too. A solidarity of heavenly origin binds you to their misery through fear and links you by your own interest to their future deliverance. Only their emancipation is capable of opening up to you the real treasure, that of tranquil joy, which you have not known as yet; the virtue of the principle of fraternity is precisely that, as it lessens the sorrows of the poor, it adds to your joys. "Watch out," you have been told, "watch out for the war of the have-nots against those who have." Ah! if this unholy war were really a possibility, what then would one be forced to think, good God! of the social order that had given rise to it? Miserable sophists! They do not perceive that this regime whose defense they discuss in whispers would be condemned beyond repeal if its danger really merited the stigma of their alarm! What, then! there would be such an excess of suffering among *those who have not*, such hatred in their souls, and such an impetuous desire to revolt in the depths of society, that to pronounce the word "fraternity," Christ's word, would be a terrible imprudence, and would serve as a signal for some new *Jacquerie!* No, rest assured, violence is to be feared only where discussion is not permitted. Order has no better protection than study. Thank heaven, people today understand that, if anger sometimes chastises evil, it is nevertheless incapable of bringing about good, that a blind and ferocious impatience would only pile up ruins under which the seeds of the ideas of justice and love would smother to death. It is not a question of taking wealth away; it is a question of fertilizing it so that it becomes universal. It is a question of raising the level of humanity for the good of all, without exception.

Chapter V

EARLY GERMAN SOCIALISM

France was the homeland of socialism until the appearance of Marx and Engels; England was the only other country that produced socialist ideas and activities of any prominence before 1848. For the most part, the few German socialists of any importance in the early nineteenth century took their cues from one or the other of these two countries—Weitling, for example, from French communism, and Rodbertus from Ricardian economics. There was little here to indicate that Germany was to become, in the last quarter of the nineteenth century, the virtual headquarters of the worldwide socialist movement.

Germany rose to predominance primarily because of the work of Marx and Engels, but these men did not emerge from nowhere. True, some of their principal ideas were of foreign origin: the critique of property and the conception of a revolutionary proletariat, for example, were both French, and their economics was largely derived from Ricardo. But the power of their doctrine comes from their having bound together these elements into a compelling philosophical system, and the philosophical base was utterly German. German philosophy prior to the 1830s had been, for the most part, too highly speculative to give rise to formulas for political action; on the occasions when it did turn to politics, it produced such conservative doctrines as Hegel's justification of the Prussian State. It was precisely this unworldly, and, for all practical purposes, conservative, quality of German philosophy that Marx sought to overcome—not, however, by abandoning that philosophy, but by adapting it to socialist revolutionary purposes. Marx was the first to make a complete and successful adaptation of this sort, but he was not the first to attempt it. Some of his philosophical predecessors undertook such an adaptation, and since their efforts provided the climate within which Marx worked, they constitute a significant minor phase in the history of European socialist thought.

JOHANN GOTTLIEB FICHTE (1762–1814)

In France, the era of belief in a universe of rationally constructed moral as well as physical laws culminated in the Revolution of 1789; in Germany, it reached its climax in the philosophy of Immanuel Kant. A pattern of action was established in France which, in a sense, remained the form in which that country dealt with crises between conviction and reality throughout the nineteenth century. Germany, on the other hand, was burdened with a problem of contemplation. The old conception of natural law had been based on the assumption that the human mind was capable of knowing the world of objects and the laws governing them exactly as they are in themselves. But Kant had now given systematic proof that the most the human mind could know was the experience of its own perceptions, which was subjective, and which, though of practical use in enabling men to get an approximate notion of the universe and hence establish some control in it, could never bring them to know the nature of *things in themselves*. Such a view could have led to a complete destruction of confidence in the value of action; the French, in effect, solved the problem by not worrying about Kant for the better part of a hundred years, and remained, because of their seeming ability to take action without reflection, the envy of their German neighbors. Kant tried to solve the problem by invoking the will and the sense of duty, by extension carrying the Protestant conscience to the extreme of saying that one's duty should be performed even if it might be ultimately futile.

In spite of this appeal to the sense of duty, German thought, not only in the realm of metaphysics, but in political and social theory as well, found itself in a bog. The German intellectual aspired passionately to freedom, and stood by impotently as he watched the French fight for it with increasing success in one revolution after another. Unable simply to act, he sought to solve the problem somewhere along the path of German philosophy. His task was cut out for him: it was to restore the yearning consciousness to the surrounding world, so that the paralyzing gap between thought and action that Kant had left could be closed.

Fichte was the first major figure who struggled for such a solution. This is not the place to discuss his metaphysics, which attempted somewhat unconvincingly to reconcile subject and object by relating them back to an all-encompassing entity that he called the Absolute Idea—a conception similar to Spinoza's, which got Fichte, like the great Jewish philosopher of Amsterdam, into trouble with the religious authorities. Fichte's successors later celebrated him as the founder of atheism. The important aspect of his system was his view that the fundamental task of the human consciousness was *activity* rather than reflection. To be active was the only way to fulfill one's nature, and hence to be truly free. But he gave better proof of this idea in his life—which was stormy for a philosopher, and remarkably full of conflict with the authorities for a German—than he did in his philosophy. The selection that follows, the preface to his more or less socialist work (the term applies only loosely; it is, at any rate, the first thing of any importance at all like a socialistic work to appear in Germany), *The Closed Commercial State*, explicitly deals with the problem of the gap between thought and action. The "socialism" of the book, which is more like an insulated and highly controlled state capitalism, is not the central thing here. More important is the problem that the author perceives will follow when one makes any kind of proposals for social and political reform. Even if the plan is a good one, what can be done to bring it into effect? This is the problem that was to haunt German liberalism with increasing persistence, until the Young Hegelians of the 1830s and '40s, and above all the young Karl Marx, began working out a solution.

The Closed Commercial State (1800)

PRELIMINARY EXPLANATION OF THE TITLE

The juridical state is made up of a closed mass of men who are subject to the same laws and to the same supreme coercive power. Now, this mass of men ought to be confined to mutual commerce and industry, between themselves and for themselves, and whoever is not subject to this same legislation and coercive power, ought to be excluded from any participation in these transactions. They would then form a *commercial state*, in fact, a *closed* commercial state, just as they now form a closed juridical state.

TO HIS EXCELLENCY
the most confidential minister of state of the Prussian
Kingdom
and Knight of the Order of the Red Eagle
Herr von Struensee,
From the author

May your excellency permit me to place before you, in accordance with the custom of the writers of dedications of former times, my thoughts about the purpose and chances for success of a work that I here publicly dedicate to you as a memento of my desire to do you honor.—Casaubonus, at the beginning of his edition of Polybius, freely discoursed with Henry IV about the study of the ancients, and about the usual prejudices regarding this study. Permit me then, your Excellency, to discourse thus freely with you, before the eyes of the public, on the relationship between the theoretician of politics and the practitioner.

The latter have in all eras granted to the former the right to expound their ideas on the organization and administration of states, without otherwise paying very much heed to these ideas and without having very seriously informed themselves on the subject of the Platonic republics and Utopian constitutions. To be sure, one must grant the reproach of *immediate* inapplicability that has always been made to the proposals of political theorists; and it is certainly no dishonor to the formulators of these proposals that they have only remained among themselves in an ideal world and have either ᵤuld us much, or demonstrated it with their deeds. For, just as it is certain that there is order, consequence and precision in their thoughts, so also is it certain that their prescriptions are appropriate only to the state of things that they have assumed or invented, to which their general rules can be applied, as in an arithmetic example. The practitioner of politics does not find this presumed situation directly around him, but finds rather something quite different. It is no wonder that he concludes that the prescription that has nothing to do with this immediate situation does not suit him.

But the philosopher, if he regards his science not as a mere game, but as something serious, will never concede or suppose the *absolute* inapplicability of his proposals; for, if such were the case, he would then undoubtedly turn his time to something more useful, instead of devoting it to something that he knows to be a mere game of ideas. He will maintain that, if his prescriptions are not immediately applicable when they are proposed in *purely theoretical* form, they nevertheless apply in their highest generality to *everything*, even though not to any *particular thing*, and that for an actual given situation, they *need only be made more specific*—just as a knowledge of the general relationship among the sides and angles of a triangle does not help a man to know the length or degree of a single side or angle in a field, so that he must always use some kind of measuring-stick and compass; but once he knows the general relationships in this particular situation, he can then arrive at the rest through *pure calculation*, instead of having to go through the task of measuring.

This process of further specifying the general rule that is to be applied to pure public law is what, in my opinion, *the* science which I am about to define consists of. I call this science *politics;* and I hold it to be the business of speculative philosophers *as such* (for it goes without saying that the practitioner of politics could just as easily be a speculative philosopher—and that perhaps the opposite could be true also). For a treatise that proclaims itself to be political, the accusation that its proposals are inapplicable, and proof that this is so, would be more dishonorable than would be the case for a work in public law. For truly, in my opinion, politics, which is certainly just a science and not a set of practical procedures, does not proceed from a particular state, for if it did, then there would be no general politics, but only particular politics for England, for France, for Prussia, and furthermore, only particularly for these states in the year 1800, and only particularly in the autumn of the year 1800, and so on. But politics proceeds rather from the situation which can be said to be common to just about all the states of the great European republic in this era. The practitioner of politics must always apply the ever-general rule in the particular situation, and must apply it a little differently in *every* particular situation; the general rule thus keeps coming nearer to the application.

If a political program were to be worked out on the basis of this idea, in conjunction with an exact comprehension of the present situation, and on the basis of solid principles of public right, with their exact consequences, it would not appear useless to anyone, in my opinion, except the pure empiric, who has no faith generally in ideas or calculations, but holds only to the affirmations of immediate experience. He would reject this program as containing no facts, but only ideas and suppositions of fact—in a word, because it would not be history. Such a politician has stored up in his memory a number of cases and successful measures that others have taken before him in similar situations. Whatever happens to him, he thinks of this or that situation which occurred in the past, and conducts himself like this or that politician, after dragging up one after another from the grave and setting them up anew for his own generation; he thus assembles his political career out of greatly varied fragments from very different men, without himself adding anything to it. One need only ask such a man, who was being imitated by the men who first applied the measures that are now being sanctioned and imitated by him, and upon what principle they relied in seizing upon those measures—previous experience, or calculation? One must remember that everything that is now old,

was at some time new, and that the human species could not
possibly have fallen so low in recent times that only memory
and the capacity for imitation have remained to it. He would
have to be shown that the progress of the human species,
which has taken place without his help and which he cannot
stop, has wrought so many changes that it has become necessary to work out measures entirely different from any that
had ever been thought of in previous times. One could hold
up in opposition to him an historical study that would perhaps be instructive, dealing with the question whether more
evil has been produced in the world by daring innovations, or
by a passive attachment to ancient measures that are no
longer either sufficient or applicable.

Whether the present treatise has lived up to the above-
mentioned demands for an examination of the foundations
of politics, the author will not attempt to answer by himself.
In the face of its proposal to close the commercial state in the
same fashion that the juridical state is closed, and of the
decisive means to this end—the elimination of *world* currency
and its replacement by *national* currencies—it is quite clear
that no state that does not *have to* accept this proposal will
want to do so, and that such a state will not have the promised
advantages of this measure; that the proposal would thus be
undecided upon, and, therefore, would never be carried out,
since whatever men cannot decide upon comes to be considered *impossible of execution*. The grounds for this unwillingness, well-thought out or not, will be that Europe has, in
the field of commerce, great advantages over the rest of the
world; that it takes the resources and products of the rest of
the world for itself, to an extent far greater than what its own
resources and products could provide; that each European
state, no matter how unfavorable may be its balance of trade
with the other European states, nevertheless derives some
advantage from this common exploitation of the rest of the
world, and never gives up the hope that it can swing the
balance of trade in its favor and thus derive a still greater advantage from the present arrangement. All these advantages
it would surely have to forsake if it were to step out of the
great European community of commerce. In order to do

away with this ground for unwillingness, it must be demonstrated that a relationship like that of Europe with the rest of the world, which is not founded upon right and equity, cannot possibly endure. This demonstration lies outside the limits of my present task. But even if it were carried out, someone could still say to me: "Until now, at least, this relationship has endured—the submission of the colonies to the mother countries has endured, the slave-trade has endured—and we shall not see any of them come to an end in our own lifetime. For as long as they last, then, let us take advantage of them; the era in which these things are to be abolished can work out for itself how to set things aright. The men of that time can try to see if they can profit in some way from your ideas. We can have no desire for your goal, and therefore have no need for any advice as to how to achieve it." I admit that I have no answer to this.

The author therefore resigns himself to the possibility that this project may remain a mere academic exercise without any success in the real world; a link in the chain of the system that he is developing little by little. He will be satisfied if, in making this system known to others, he gives them occasion to think more deeply about these matters, and perhaps leads one or two men from the spheres beyond which no one at present would ever want to go, to some useful and applicable discovery; and he limits himself to these aims quite specifically and after mature reflection. . . .

MOSES HESS (1812–75)

Eighteen-thirty was a year of disappointment for German liberals; the tocsin had sounded in Paris once again, and some other parts of Europe had responded, but nothing happened in Germany. Still, German intellectuals were answering the July Revolution in their own way: the revolution in philosophy was beginning.

By introducing the dynamism of history, Hegel had provided the most compelling material for escape from the paralyzing dualistic world that Kant had bequeathed. Subject and

object were alienated from one another, indeed, but not for
all time. The world-spirit and nature, pure idea and pure
matter, had become divorced from one another at the beginning of time, but only in order that they might achieve a
reconciliation at the end of history which, by the very experience of alienation or differentiation followed by the negation
of differentiation, would prove to be a higher state of freedom
than could ever have existed if spirit and matter had not become separated from one another in the first place. Individuality, in other words, could not have existed if there had been
no alienation of spirit and nature; and though the individual's
freedom is limited by this very alienated condition, it is this
condition that gives him the chance to realize freedom by overcoming this alienation, by negating it. All of reality is seen as a
mass of paradoxes, as Kant himself had recognized in his "antinomies," because of the contradiction in character between
subject and object, between spirit and nature; but, unlike
Kant, who did not introduce history into his perceptions, Hegel
maintained that all these contradictions were in the process of
working themselves out. History was the record of this process
of reconciliation, this overcoming of the gap between the spirit
and nature, in a series of reconciliations, both great and small.
The act of transcending a particular alienated situation, a
conflict between thesis and antithesis, as some of the Hegelians
called it, or between an affirmation and a negation, as Hegel
himself called it, was described either as the synthesis, or the
"negation of the negation." The entire process of affirmation,
negation, and negation of the negation is the Hegelian dialectic.

For Hegel and his disciples the historical struggle between
the spirit and its material environment manifested itself as
man's conflict with his own institutions. From the beginning
of human history, man had established institutions—social,
political, religious, aesthetic, etc.—which enabled him to come
to terms with the conditions in which he found himself. But
in all cases, these institutions were only partial realizations of
any reconciliation between man and his environment and, for
that matter, between man and himself. They were only partial realizations of the possibility of freedom, and because

they were only partial in nature, they were fraught with contradictions that had to be negated or transcended. History, then, was the record of these changing institutions, each new set of institutions being realized out of the transcendence of previously existing ones, and each new set being closer to a complete realization of freedom. For Hegel, the states of Western Europe in his own time represented the furthest realization of freedom, of reconciliation between the spirit and its environment, that man had ever seen. Not even non-Hegelians would have quarreled with this view. Unfortunately, Hegel regarded the Prussian state as being the most advanced specimen of the realization of freedom among the European states of the day.

This was the point at which a younger generation of German liberals, deeply impressed with Hegel's system—inebriated with the dialectic, one might even say—departed from the master. Most of them did not require any philosophy to perceive that the Prussian state was not in accordance with their ideals. But the Hegelian philosophy was too compelling, too full of possibilities for bringing Germany to terms at last with the nineteenth century, to allow it to fall just because of the master's politics. It was essential to rework the system, to make it accord with liberalism, without losing its tremendous force. This was the task of the Young Hegelians, or more particularly, of the element among them that came to be called the Left Hegelians.

A period of complex philosophical squabbling followed, dominated at first by such names as Bruno and Edgar Bauer, and Arnold Ruge; their work cannot be gone into here, although they were prominent elements in the atmosphere in which the young Karl Marx shaped his ideas. A more important figure was Ludwig Feuerbach, whose book *The Essence of Christianity* caused a small revolution among the Hegelians after its publication in 1841. Feuerbach opened the way to a more materialistic orientation for Hegelianism, a healthy antidote to the excessive concentration upon the world-spirit as the enactor of history that had led many of the Hegelians to scorn active politics, and content themselves with passive contemplation of cultural institutions, such as religion.

Marx's *Theses on Feuerbach* (see page 292), written in 1845, show how the influence of Feuerbach's materialism enabled him to take the first steps towards his own revolutionary philosophy. The Kantian problem was at last being solved by a philosophical reconciliation between theory and practice.

But Marx was not the first to work out such a reconciliation. The atmosphere of the early 1840s was filled with such efforts, and Marx was still, until 1845 at least, largely under the influence of some of his older contemporaries. Prominent among them was Moses Hess, six years older than Marx, and a socialist before Marx became one; Hess claimed, in fact, that it was he who had converted Engels to socialism. Hess's life was a remarkable strand in nineteenth-century German history. Born in an orthodox Jewish home and strictly educated within its traditions—Marx and others called him "the communistic rabbi"—he renounced religion and became an atheist in his twenties, turning to a kind of a pre-Zionism by the time he was fifty, when he wrote a book calling for the establishment of a Jewish state in Palestine. His socialist convictions never flagged, even when he became disillusioned with Marx's philosophy, which he had helped to form, and for a time had been dominated by.

By 1843, when he published his essay, *The Philosophy of the Act*, he had written two books in the philosophy of history, and had achieved eminence among the Left Hegelians. *The Philosophy of the Act*, which appears below in its entirety, is a difficult work, stuffed with the language of the German philosophy of the time—Fichte, Schelling, and Hegel are all present in large doses. But for all its apparent philosophical prolixity, the work is really a repudiation of philosophy, the product of impatience with German contemplativeness in the face of the French capacity for action, the product also, perhaps, of a Talmudic education, in which philosophy as something distinct from practical activity is virtually nonexistent. But Hess does not deny all that German philosophy has achieved; he says, rather, that France would benefit as much by incorporating the German philosophical revolution into her traditions as Germany would by incorporating the French social and political revolution into hers. His plea for

the unification of the French and German revolutionary movements is, in effect, the concrete form of his plea for unity of
thought and action. Thus, he goes a long way toward the kind
of reconciliation that Marx achieved two years later in the
Theses on Feuerbach. This essay by Hess forms a vital link between the German idealism of the early nineteenth century
and the historical materialism of the mature Marx.

THE PHILOSOPHY OF THE ACT (1843)

Only the first word of the Cartesian philosophy is true; it
was not really possible for Descartes to say *cogito ergo sum*,
but only *cogito*. The first (and last) thing that I perceive is
my own act of spirit, myself perceiving. The spirit, which is
life woken into self-consciousness, discovered its likeness to
itself, or identity, through the act of thinking about thinking.
All further perception is only an explication of this idea, which
is *the* idea *par excellence*. I know that I think, that I am spiritually active, or,—since there is no other kind of activity—that
I am active, but I do not know that I am. Not being, but the
act, is the first and last.

If we go on to an explication of this act, we find it to be
threefold: the thinking, the thought-about, and the identity
of these two, the "I". "I think" means: the "I" places itself (or
sets itself) before itself as another, but passes through this
reflection back to itself, in the same way that the discovery of
one's own life in a mirror is something that comes from the
outside. It perceives that the image in the mirror is its own.

The awakening of life to self-consciousness is a complicated
act. The simple saying of "I" does not constitute an identity.
Whoever says, I am I, or, I know that I am, knows nothing,
believes only in a mathematical point, is looking only into
blackness and seeing only what is not real—is seeing, that is,
the *difference* between the thinking and the thought about,
between the subject and the object, and is not seeing their
identity. The simple "I", the thinking in distinction from the
thought-about, is empty, has no content; there are no rational
grounds for this saying of "I"; it is hollow, not at all a *moi
raisonné*, a something thought about, but only a something

believed. Only the "I think" amounts to anything, that is, the likeness to itself of the one in the other. What the "I"-sayer believes, the "I", the identity, here becomes the imminent content of the act—against which the mathematical point, the black nothingness that calls itself Being, manifests itself in the middle of the activity as the fixed and frozen act of self-consciousness. The act thus becomes only half-realized, the thinking becomes arrested in the process of differentiation from the thought-about, which is really itself, so that the spirit runs its head against the wall, against the barrier that it has created and not broken through; it runs itself into a dead end. The act becomes frozen. The bridge, the steep passage-way from the thinking to the thought-about, is broken away, the artery that carries life itself is choked off. Living Becoming is turned into dead Being, and self-consciousness into theological consciousness, which now must lie its way out of black nothingness into pallid Being.

The reign of shadows begins. All of the thought-about remains a mere shadow, which shrivels up into a dark point beyond the realm of the thinking. Now that the thinking and the thought-about have been torn asunder, real life, the living "I", the self-conscious identity, makes its appearance outside of both; it is the unperceived, though believed or guessed at. This life that has been placed at a remove is an empty reflection of the empty "I", the shadow of a shadow, the theological God, the "Eternal Being," the "Absolute Spirit," and so on.

The self-conscious "I", from which all philosophy must proceed, because the "I think," which has been elevated above all proof and is impossible to prove (in this case, even doubting is an act of thinking), this *moi raisonné* of Descartes, is thus in no way a proof of abstract Being, but only a proof of thinking, of the act of the spirit. The "I think" has presented itself to us as the act, which is comprised of three moments that together constitute the "I"; but even this latter is not Being, and is neither the thinking nor the thought-about, but is rather the realization of an act: the movement of life imposing itself upon itself as another, or distinguishing itself from itself, but in either case perceiving its likeness to itself.

The "I" within is not something that stands still or is

quiescent, as the "I"-sayer thinks it is, but is rather something that is changing, is in constant motion, just as life, before it has been awakened to self-consciousness, is likewise constantly changing. Man is just like the "world's body," like everything that we see growing and moving, and this is true not only of the sensible part of his experience, but also of the spiritual part, his self-consciousness, which is constantly changing, is engaged in a constant activity of altering itself. The only thing that remains constant is this activity itself, or life. This constant altering of the "I" is necessary, because there is an "I" only so long as it goes on becoming another, in other words, only so long as it defines itself, limits itself, and perceives, in this act of the self becoming another, or limiting itself, its likeness to itself or free self-determination. Without this act there is no real "I", no identity, but rather either its act is unconscious (innocent, natural life), or it has split itself in two, and is a broken thread of life, a disrupted line, a black nothingness.

Reflection is like the Fates, cutting through the continuous thread of life with the shears of the understanding, disrupting all movement and choking off the breath. The "I" is an act of the spirit, an idea, which can comprehend itself only in change. The only thing that stands above change is the law that is involved in movement itself. The spirit perceives this law through the perception of its own life. In perceiving itself and its own activity, it is perceiving all activity, all life, with the same certainty. Life is activity. But activity is the recovery of an identity through the establishment and transcendence of its opposite, the producing of its likeness, its likeness to itself, through the breaking of the barrier within which the "I" is "not-I". Activity is, in a word, self-creation, the law of which is perceived by the spirit through its own act of self-creation.

Change, the differentiating of life, cannot be taken to be a change of the law of activity, an objective differentiating of life, but can be considered only a differentiating of self-consciousness. Reflection, which remains entirely within the head, turns things upside down and says: "Objective life is differentiated, but the 'I' remains constant." It seizes upon what is really the change of the "I", of self-consciousness, and views it as a change in the other, in the representation made by the

"I" (which is really itself). All its representations are looked upon as objective life, which is seen, naturally, as differentiating itself, as becoming something else at every moment, because the "I" itself is becoming something else at every moment, because the self-consciousness is a continuous chain of representations, because the idea, the one act of the spirit, is not fixed, but is movement, excitation, a constant rising and falling between the lowest form of self-consciousness (not in the usual meaning of this word) and its highest and most lucid form. The different states or excitations of the self-consciousness, which manifest themselves through time as different moments, stages, phases, and episodes, and in space as different examples or settings, are really the product of one and the same activity, which the self-consciousness recognizes in the end as its own. But reflection, the activity that can never arrive at likeness to itself, sees the opposite of reality everywhere. Objective life therefore seems to it to be differentiated, and the "I" (about which it *knows* nothing, but only *believes*) seems to be the constant, the immortal!

From every particular idea that is formed, from every stage of the self-consciousness, its opposite, its likeness as another, necessarily emerges, and indeed remains long enough for the particular idea to be able to explain itself. In other words, every essence duplicates itself until it has actually been created; it is active long enough, creative long enough, it lives long enough, to become reality. At that point, the duration of the particular idea, of this particular "I", comes to an end. "No," says reflection, "it is only then really beginning to live!" The spirit, which was nowhere able to find itself in life, which, whenever it saw its image in the mirror of life, was like the child who looked behind the mirror to see what was there and naturally never found anything but empty, black nothingness—this spirit, which, after it had produced, reflected and explicated itself, did not believe that it was seeing itself in the other, but thought that it was seeing something quite different from itself, at last looked again behind the mirror of life, to seek there what it ought to have found within itself. The poor devil who is constantly denying, but who never arrives, through the negation of the negation, at the breaking of limits, who has a retina that stands everything on its head, but no optic nerve to put it back on its feet again, tears with his careless hands the root, the hidden foundation of the tree of life, from the earth, and holds it up to the air, while pushing the treetop into the earth and thus preserving its rottenness. After removing his act from the spirit and making it into body, into a lifeless corpse, he wants to make this body eternal. He represents eternity to himself as the continuance through time of an unchanging body. He represents the particular "I", the temporal, as eternal, and the Eternal, the law, as a limited, particular, temporal "I". The essence of reflection is to turn thought into an absurdity.

The explication of a particular idea or act of the spirit, the working out of a particular stage of the self-consciousness, or of life, of humanity, one might say, is its transformation into reality, its individualization. The individual is the particular idea become other than itself, through which this idea becomes realized, establishes its identity. The individual is only the reality of the idea; it is generally only through the individual that life can arrive at self-consciousness, since no identity, no "I", is conceivable outside the act, as we have said earlier. The universal is intrinsically unreal, and is only an abstraction of the individual, which the idea reflects, and which is related to the idea, but takes shape not as the reality of it but as its reflection. The idea of life in general, the eternal law, "Absolute Spirit," "World-Spirit," "God," or by whatever names the Universal and the Eternal are either appropriately or inappropriately designated, is really only a thing that is changing, a thing becoming something else in the variety of things, in the individual, or, more correctly, in the endless succession of individuals, in the endless activity of things becoming something else or of things creating themselves. In other words, the universal comes out of the individual into its self-consciousness, and man, who perceives the idea of life, the universal, as his own life, is its highest or most thoroughly fulfilled reality.

All this, of course, is nothing new, and can be found in the works of all philosophers, especially the moderns. No new truths are being expounded here; rather, old ones are simply

being repeated, because what is to follow has these old truths
for its fundamental principles, and they cannot be repeated
often enough in an attempt to exorcise the theological consciousness, which has become arrested in the dead end of
reflection. The theological consciousness is the great lie, the
principle of all slavery (and domination), to which our species
remains subject for as long as the idea of life goes on being
alien to us, for as long as we have no perception of the self-
conscious act. At the present time, as the idea of life begins to
break a path for itself, the theological consciousness is binding
itself up with the existing material powers, with the institutions
that it originally called into being, so as to have their help
in its fight against the free act of the spirit—a most natural
alliance, an alliance of father and son, both defending their
house; a family alliance that should not be taken lightly!

So far, this family alliance has not had the attention that
it warrants from all sides. Either the son is forgotten in
exclusive attention to the father, or the father is overlooked
in the zeal to watch out for the son. The theological consciousness, religion, the father, is becoming known in this country
in all its mendacity, but people here bother and alarm themselves very little over politics, the son. In Germany, people
have almost forgotten politics in their concern over the religious dualism, and they have shown in recent times, now
that they are begining to trouble themselves about politics,
that they, as one might expect, know scarcely anything
about the modern social movement. They begin their republic
at the Year One, and consider it an heroic deed to bring into
Germany the slightest report about what seem to be the latest
doings in the political-social movement, no matter how abstract or narrow-minded is the point of view expressed.

In France, on the other hand, where they have unmasked
the son, the political dualism, people have remained at a
standstill in religious matters right down to the present day.
Proudhon, the most able leader that the contemporary social
movement has produced, speaks quite unctuously of "God,"
of the "Father," and his "Children," mankind, who are all
"Brothers"; he believes that he has done as much as possible
by dispensing with the "Priests," just the way the good old

Germans think they have set the political order aright by polemicizing against the king. But Proudhon does not allow himself to imagine, as a logical consequence of his position, that the kings and priests should be allowed to retain their old rights, or to recover them at will. Yet, the vague fantasies of God the Father and His little children are precisely what are exploited by the kings and priests, and used by them as a means of achieving domination. For the little children must have guardians, and among the sons of the father there can be only one first-born; thus there are unequal brothers, and nothing is more natural than that human society, when its relationship with its own essence comes to be conceived as that of a child in a family, should also want to be dominated by authority, and led along by the "venerable" reins of faith.

Who, then, has told our French philosopher, who protests so vigorously against all domination from without, that we have a father over us or outside us, that we are the children of another? His spirit, which feels or guesses at the identity, the unity, with its own essence, but does not clearly perceive it, represents this unity in the form of reflection, which stands before itself as another, outside of it. He takes this dichotomy to be real. But if it were real, it would mean that all men are in reality cut off from one another, rather than bound together, that they are different, not alike, opposed to one another, not united—and that, if they were to try to apply themselves, with their so very religious conceptions, to the problem of doing away with private property, they would turn out to be, in spite of all of Proudhon's protestations, opposed to crude material communism, and in favor, rather, of the most crude abstract communism, the monkish or Christian kind, in favor of the annihilation of all independence for the individual, in favor of the destruction of life or freedom. For they would have reached the point where they would either have to renounce or destroy the universal, which they represent as a heavenly power outside of themselves, a personality opposed to their own, or else would have to submit to it completely. Such submission would be an unbearable state of slavery which, when pursued to its logical extreme, would produce an impossible situation resembling that of the Middle Ages,

the era of the *juste-milieu*, during which earthly free will was
called into being and allowed to reign alongside the heavenly
tyranny, so that a constant battle was fought between the
representatives of the inauthentic individuals and the unreal
universal, between earthly and heavenly interests.

Either social freedom is based upon spiritual freedom, or
it is without foundation, and is thereby bound to become
transformed into its opposite, no matter how revolutionary
its opposition to the existing conditions that have come
down to us from the era of the *juste-milieu*. Out of the foundations of a Christian communism would emerge a Christian
Middle Ages, if it were thinkable that history, once having
reached the end of a line of development, could revert to an
earlier phase.

Clearly, the fighters for freedom are isolated on either side,
and are therefore not strong enough to stand up against their
opponents, who are united.

The lies of religion and politics must be unmasked relentlessly and with a single blow; the entrenchments, the enemy's
secret hiding places, the bridges of asses and of devils must
be burned down and annihilated. We fully realize that there
are lame and timid philosophers who, because the anger of
the act has been lost to them, poke about with their Diogenes
lanterns through the heaps of dirt that are the lies of religion
and politics, to see if they might possibly ferret out yet another
useful object. But it does no good to toil away picking shreds
out of the rubbish-heap of the past and throwing them into
the paper-mill of the dialectic so as to metamorphose them
into currency, when one must acknowledge all the while that
it is still the old familiar material in another form. The form
is the essence; the spirit must itself create its own products at
all times, and the Philistine, in order to be able to lay his hands
sooner upon the merchandise demanded of him, considers the
matter at an end, even if the product be out of his old lumber-
room, and looks upon it as something brand new that he will
sell at as fair a price as the old. The support that props up
the gaping masses can now once again be saved; the Philistines
shyly recoil before every original act of the spirit as they do
before an appearance of the Devil, until they gradually begin

to have some idea of it, and befriend it. What, then, is true in religion and politics? Indeed, truth slumbers inside them. But the slumber, rather than the truth, is the part that properly belongs to religion and politics. If truth were to awaken from its slumber, it would stop appearing in the form of the dualism of religion and politics.

Religion and politics are passageways from unconsciousness to the self-consciousness of the spirit. The religious dualism, the heavenly politics, is a product of reflection, of dichotomy, of misfortune—as is the political dualism, the earthly religion. Although reflection has no idea that it is the *pons asinorum* of the spirit, it nevertheless divines this fact, and this divination manifests itself in the form of reveries about a lost Golden Age, and later on in the form of prophecies about a better era to come, in which all fighting, antagonism and sin will come to an end. The Bible itself, this venerable document of the origin of our religion and politics that guides us with the most extreme naiveté into a theological dead end, allows Adam to hear the voice of a higher essence outside himself only after the fall. In its last section it prophesies a time of realization, in which all creatures will come together, no longer divided from one another and from their God. Christ is simply an anticipation of this time of realization. It is precisely for this reason that His role comes to an end at the moment when prophecy is no longer valid, because it has been fulfilled.

The state, like the Church, is the anticipation of the unity of social life. It is precisely because religion and politics hint at a future condition that they would never concede this condition to be in the present, because they would then do away with themselves. Yes, they must constantly postpone the presence of this future, because their role consists in hinting at a condition which, if realized, would bring this role to an end. In order that their lies not be browbeaten or denied by the truth, they must deny truth itself and turn it into falsehood. That is the greatest advantage won by religion and politics, although this is not their entire essence.

The essence of religion and politics consists, as has been said above, in allowing the real life, the life of the real individual, to become absorbed by an abstraction, by the "universal," which is nowhere real, and which is outside the individual himself. That idea sums up the history of these lofty twin sisters. Moloch is their prototype—human sacrifices everywhere establish the keynote of religious ritual and state ceremony. The "Absolute Spirit," which celebrates its reality in the "State," is a reproduction of the Christian God, who let His first-born Son be crucified, who was satisfied to build his Church out of martyrdom and upon a martyr, "upon this rock." The Christian God is a reproduction of the Jewish Moloch-Jehovah, to whom the first-born was sacrificed in order to be "atoned for," and who was appeased with money during the era of the *juste-milieu* of Judaism, when the first-born was "redeemed", and cattle were sacrificed instead of men. The original battle sacrifice everywhere was man, and when he later sought to be given "grace" again, or to be "redeemed," he got what he wanted only in the figurative sense. This is still the case today, and will be as long as religion and politics remain in control of him.

Religion and politics stood as a counterpoise to the crude materialism of the individuals, who, before they began to strive for self-consciousness, struggled against one another; religion and politics entered into life and established representatives of the general interest, who stepped in as the unreal truth of the untrue reality and opposed particular interests. The priests gave themselves over to the "service of God," and kings, aristocrats, and other sorts of selfish and ambitious men, as well as fools and frauds, gave themselves over to "service of the state," as the representatives of the "general" interest, drew out the sweat and blood of their underlings, and raised the cry that self-sacrifice is the highest act of virtue.

It is not necessary to repeat over and over again that the fine history of all religions and states was a necessity. As long as the peoples and individuals had not yet begun to strive for morality or self-realization, they had to be satisfied with allowing themselves to be treated like the good old cow; as long as they did not know how to govern themselves, they were governed by powers outside of themselves. That is clear. But it is also clear that religion and politics are the products of a situation appropriate only for cows, and that they themselves or their representatives are only the other side of the materialism that is dominating individuals and peoples. The priests and rulers cannot use the excuse that the peoples had made them necessary, any more than the individuals and peoples can somehow excuse their condition of slavery by pointing to their priests and rulers. Slavery and tyranny, abstract materialism and spiritualism, make their peace with one another, and the only deplorable people are those who do not perceive that there is no way out of this closed circle of servitude except a radical break with the past. This break the French and Germans have now achieved, the former by calling forth anarchy in politics, the latter by bringing about the same anarchy in religion. The main task now is to find the common ground from which this power of negation emerged on both sides. Without this common ground, all efforts are merely fragmentary and run themselves into their own opposition, as has actually been the case up until now in Germany and France.

Slavery has its own enclosed system; it has set up a well-ordered structure of lies that works as a block upon the still unborn freedom, a theoretical and practical block that is effective so long as freedom does not rise up and oppose it with the consequences of truth. Freedom becomes the surrounded phalanx of slavery, against which it will always be at a disadvantage so long as it does not carry out its own principles to their furthest consequences, as slavery had done with its principles. As long as dualism has not been overcome everywhere, in the spirit as in social life, freedom has not yet been victorious. The dualistic world-view necessarily had to come forth in history. But lies are none the less lies because of this. All of our history until now has been a necessary lie, so to speak. The Christ, in order to become a reality, had to appear as an individual among others, and thus above all in opposition to himself. The spirit evolves in opposition to itself.

History, which is nothing but this evolution of the spirit, could also not possibly have been anything in itself but the appearance of this opposition, and it should therefore not be surprising that, until now, only this opposition, the struggle of the individual with himself and with the universal, has come to the fore. The true individual—the self-conscious spirit, the free man, the true universal—had not taken shape as yet. The universal did not yet have any inner reality, since it is not real outside the individual. The individual appeared, in opposition to its essence, the universal, as the particular; the universal appeared, in opposition to reality, as abstraction—God, Priesthood, Pope, Church, State, Monarch, etc. And so a dichotomy came upon us, with the abstract universal on one side, and the material individual in opposition to it on the other, a dichotomy that is in itself nothing but an illusion created by falsehood, since the universal has no life without reality, and the particular has no spirit without truth. This dichotomy of the spirit has manifested itself, as I have said, in all history up until now. It achieved its highest peak in Christianity, the most fully realized religion, and in monarchy, the highest form of realization of the state. This is quite correct to say: Christianity is the true religion, and monarchy is the summit of all the forms of the state. In other words, the absolute religion and the absolute state are themselves nothing but the *absolutism* of the heavenly and earthly *tyrants* over *slaves.*

Domination and its opposite, subordination, are the essence of religion and politics, and the degree of perfection with which this essence manifests itself is the degree of perfection of religion and politics. In absolute religion and politics, the Lord is a lord of all. Universality manifests itself here as the negation of all individuality. All separate existences vanish before God and the monarch. God and the monarch are not themselves real individuals; they are exalted above all reality, are sacred persons, which is to say that they are not persons at all. The monarch, like God, is unthinkable majesty. Do not think about it, do not ask—just fall upon your knees! Abstraction can be pushed no further, and dualism, brought to these heights, can no longer maintain itself. It capsizes, and revolution and criticism begin.

The abstract universal must give way to the abstract individual; this, however, is no longer the natural individual, as was the case at the beginning of history, but the spiritual subject. From now on, not individual free will, but subjective freedom comes to the fore, not natural equality or the equal rights of individuals struggling in immediate opposition with one another, but the abstract rights of man or the equal right of the abstract personality, the reflected "I", the mathematical point. The majesty and sovereignty of the one has transformed itself into the majesty and sovereignty of everyone. Whereas previously the abstract universal ruled in the form of the one over the particular, and oppressed the individual, now the abstract individual rules in the form of the many over the universal, and oppresses the unity. In place of hierarchy and class structure, in place of fettered individuals, representation and the competition of individuals come forth.

Through the medium of this revolution an essentially new history emerges. The individual again begins with himself, history again begins at the Year One, and surges forward in fits and starts, in pendulum-swings of the spirit, along the path that leads from the anarchy of abstract freedom through slavery to the final point, where the striving for real freedom begins, as the law of negation begins to take shape along with the common ground from which this power of negation arose, to manifest itself on the one side as the subjective, and on the other as the objective, act of the spirit.

The revolution allowed the dualism to remain; the spiritual revolution, like the social (that is, the German revolution, like the French), really allowed everything to remain as it had been, at least so it would seem to any observer. Everything was "restored" to the way it had been; such had been the historical situation, and history is always right. What did the revolution achieve after all? Its freedom and equality, its abstract rights of man, turned out to be just another form of slavery. The other side of the scheme of opposition, the abstract individual, achieved domination, but the scheme itself, the opposition between domination and slavery, had not been overcome and discarded at all. The impersonal domination of justice, the self-domination of the spirit, which is like itself, had not done away with the domination of the one over the other. "The tyrants have only replaced one another, and tyranny has remained." The people, Proudhon says, were only the monkey of the kings. The kings were motivated in the making of their laws by the notion: For such is our pleasure (*Car tel est notre plaisir*).

But the people also wanted to have their pleasure for once, and to make laws. For fifty years now they have been making thousands of laws, and they still seem to get endless pleasure out of it. And we are paying extra for it—the people were only the monkey of the priest, Robespierre, who decreed the existence of a "highest essence," and stumbled into the role of a Pontifex Maximus. Our *Burschenschaften* students are good Christians, and they would like to be the means of anointing a pious Kaiser, another sort of Pope. Saint-Simonianism was simply an aping of hierarchy. The "Brahmans of logic" wanted to make their master into a second Christ, and they celebrated in him the "Second Coming of the Lord," or the Paraclete. The pious demagogues are incessantly carrying on their mischief in Germany and France, and one of them has ascended the throne. All possible freedoms are laid claim to on his behalf: freedom of trade and industry, of education and conscience. To what end? For the benefit of private interests and private opinions, which intend to strangle overlordship to death through the "free competition" of truth and justice! What is this democracy but the domination of the individual will under the name of "subjective" or "personal" freedom? How does it really differ from the domination of one person?

To be sure, the revolution is different from the *ancien régime*. A turning point in history has arrived, an even more important one than that time when the self-consciousness gave the first sign of life, and rose up to present itself as the universal, as distinguished from the particular—when the domination of kings and priests, the domination of Moloch, began. In other words, the individual is again laying claim to his rights, but now above all as the particular, not as the true universal. For now the opposition with itself in which the spirit finds itself is by nature intolerable; since it is no longer the unconscious, natural individual, but the conscious, spiritual subject, that finds itself in opposition to its own essence. It perceives the falsity of regarding itself as something separate, without being fully conscious of this perception; it knows that it is standing in a false distinction from the universal, but wishes to maintain this distinction all the same, because it still fears the "human putty" of the *ancien régime,* which it only barely negated and did not overcome. The specter of absolutism still keeps the individual from recovering consciousness. He embraces freedom in a delirious frenzy, and smothers it. Out of pure fear of falling back into the condition of "human putty," he makes himself into a stone, and throws himself with all his might against his opposite, the abstract universal, without realizing that he is thus keeping alive his mortal enemy, who is lying there close to death. The abstract universal has no more power, and is too senile to be able to oppress the individual or absorb the particular. But the particular willingly throws itself to the lions, and Moloch goes on swallowing it, like a sick man sucking up through a funnel the nourishment that someone is giving him in an effort to keep him alive a little longer.

Oppositions are the form in which the idea of life appears in the order of nature, so that there is no life where no opposition presents itself. But the life of nature does not consist in the realizing of freedom, and as long as the spirit is still joined to nature, there can be no talk of freedom. But the spirit and its proper world, the social life, man and mankind, finally arrive at the point of existing in likeness to themselves, the point where all the forms within which activity had previously been confined, and which had established themselves as habit and "second nature," are scattered, and do not remain as redundant activity—where the whole of determined nature transforms itself into free self-determination. German philosophy had long perceived this destination of the spirit entirely with respect to thought, and although the Philistines, seeing the whole stock of embodied ideas of which they finally had achieved some small grasp going up in smoke, raised the cry of "murder" over the arson that they thought was being committed, which seemed to "negate" everything for them, in reality very little was destroyed. And what happened here in relation to thought, happened in France in relation to social life.

The French social philosophers, Babeuf in his day, which was the time of Fichte, and more recently Proudhon, touched the igniting flame of the modern spirit to the structure of the old society, just as the German philosophers did to the structure of the old beliefs. But both the French and the German arsonists scarcely knew what they were after. The aim of socialism is nothing other than that of idealism which is this: to allow nothing to remain of the old activity of plunder. None of the forms within which this plunder had affixed itself until now can continue in the face of the free spirit, which now manifests itself only as active, and which does not stop with some result that has been won by someone and fix, embody and materialize it in order to store it up as "property" —which rather, as the real power over all things that are finite and determined, ever transcends them, and creates itself anew as an active force (each time in a different, particular way, to be sure). In this way does the free act distinguish itself from unfree work; for, in the condition of slavery, the very act of creation enchains what is created, whereas, in the condition of freedom, every limitation of which the spirit divests itself is not turned into determined nature, but is overcome, and thus turned into self-determination.

It is now the task of the philosophy of the spirit to become the philosophy of the act. Not only thought, but all human activity, must be brought to the point at which all oppositions fade away. The heavenly egoism, that is, the theological consciousness, against which German philosophy is now so zealously crusading, has thus far hindered us from stepping forth into the act. In this respect, Fichte went much further than our latest philosophy has gone. The young Hegelians, paradoxical as it may sound, continue to be enmeshed in the theological consciousness; for, although they have renounced the Hegelian "Absolute Spirit," which is a reproduction of the Christian God, although they have given up the Hegelian politics of Restoration and *juste-milieu,* and although they have finally negated the religious dualism, they nevertheless continue to set up the universal, or "State," against the individual, and they arrive at best at the anarchy of liberalism, that is to say, at the condition of limitlessness, from which they nevertheless fall back into the theological "State," because they have never really stepped forth into self-determination or self-limitation, but rather have remained in the self-centeredness of reflection. With them, social life has never overcome the attitude of reflection, the stage of self-centeredness. In this stage, the object of activity still appears to be really another, and the subject, in order to strive for the gratification of its selfhood, of its life, of its activity, must hold on to this object that has been torn from it as its "property", because it is otherwise threatened with the loss of its selfhood. It is in the form of material property that the notion of itself being active—no, of itself *having been* active—for its own sake, first occurs to the consciousness of the subject, which is still in the stage of reflection. Its act never manifests itself as present; it never lives in the present, but only in the past. It goes forth constantly deprived of its real property, its present act, because it does not yet have the capacity to manifest itself in its true form. It holds fast only to appearance, to the reflection of its property, of its activity, of its life, as if this reflection were its true life, its real property, its own act!

This is the curse that has weighed upon mankind throughout history until now: that men do not set up activity as an end in itself, but constantly conceive of its gratification as something separate from it, because all history up until now has presented itself as none other than the evolution of the spirit, which, in order really to evolve, must constantly rise up in opposition to itself. And just as this curse came into being with religion and politics, so it will also disappear after the domination of religion and politics is brought to an end, after the stage of reflection is overcome, and the reign of speculation, of the philosophical ethic, begins and takes hold of all of life.

The first words through which the God of reflection made himself known to man was that curse that the Bible loyally handed down to us in the form of the well-known saying: "In the sweat of thy face shalt thou eat bread." The first words through which the free spirit made itself known to man in opposition to the other was the famous dictum of Spinoza's *Ethics:* "What activity furthers and the love of life extols, is good." The work by "the sweat of thy face" has reduced man to slavery and misery; the "activity out of love" will make him free and happy.

Because men in Germany and France have so far not united with each other, but have striven after freedom isolated on either side, the result has been that a reaction has recently set in on both sides. On the French side, of course, where spiritual freedom has not yet been won, it has come from religion, while in Germany, on the other hand, where social freedom has been neglected, it has come from politics, or the states. In France we see the Clergy and the Legitimists steadily regaining power; here the Nobility and the Pietists are doing the same. There, it is the power of the state that has emerged from the revolution that feels itself threatened, here, it is the science that has come out of the Reformation. And because both revolutionary powers, in their one-sidedness or isolation, are without a strong base upon which to stand, they are led by a sense of their own weakness to placate and make concessions to the enemies whom they could destroy if they were united. In opposition to this tendency, as a result of the sense of deficiency in this matter that is now developing on both sides, a so-called radical party is emerging in both countries, to stand up against the reaction that has so far been victorious, in Germany in the form of the official learning, and in France in the guise of the official revolutionary government. This party does not wish to be known as a mediator and maker of concessions, because it is beginning to have an inkling of its real power, which resides in the fusion of the problems of spiritual freedom and social freedom.

In both countries, the radical party has come out against the official powers that emerged from the spiritual and social movement. Protestantism and the July Monarchy have now been attacked. Pierre Leroux, the French Arnold Ruge, is polemicizing against the *juste-milieu* government, just as his German equivalent is polemicizing against Protestantism, because they are beginning to see that these represent only a half-victory, as I have pointed out, and that they are really insufficient to destroy the enemy—and indeed are more likely to let themselves be overcome by it, in order to maintain the appearance of their existence. Consequently, an apparent alliance of radicalism with reaction emerges. This alliance is only an ironical one, to be sure, the character of which is made evident enough, for example, by Bruno Bauer's "trumpet blasts." Certainly the alliance between radicalism and the Legitimists in France is an old story by now, just as is the one in Germany between the radicals and the Pietists against the old rationalism. But now as they organize themselves to pursue practical goals, the irony fades into the background, and they show a stern mask to the world. To any but the most superficial observer, this alliance appears only all the more comical as a result. But because of this ironical alliance, the people allow themselves to be led out of the light, that is, back to religion, which here in Germany serves, by tacit agreement, as a common meeting-ground for both the radicals and the reactionaries. Just as it is the "State" that is exploited here in Germany, in the name of their opposing aims and by very different means, of course, by the philosophers and the Pietists (the one group using the material power of the State, the other employing the abstract Idea), so it is the "Church," religion, that is exploited in France.

The free act of the spirit is the common ground from which all the aspirations of the present time originate, and to which they return. It is therefore necessary to inquire into the very law of its structure and of its consequences. The basis of the free act is the *Ethics* of Spinoza, and the forthcoming philosophy of the act can be only a further development of this work. Fichte laid the groundwork for this further development, but German philosophy cannot break out of idealism on its own. In order for Germany to be able to attain socialism, it must have a Kant for the old social organism, just as it had for the old structure of thought. Without revolution, no new history can begin. As strong as was the approval of the French Revolution in Germany, its essence, which consisted in nothing less than tearing down the pillars upon which the old social life had stood, was just as strongly misunderstood everywhere. The value of negation was perceived in Germany in the realm of thought, but not in the realm of action. The value of anarchy consists in the fact that the individual must once again rely upon himself, and proceed from himself.

But Kant's philosophical criticism brought about this state

of anarchy nowhere but in the realm of thought, and so his
immediate successor, Fichte, laid the groundwork of modern
history only, once again, in the realm of thought, and not in
the realm of the whole life of the spirit, or free social activity.
In this respect, people were happy simply to appropriate "the
results of the French Revolution" for themselves. But nothing
more than that is done about it. In History, in the life of the
spirit, results mean nothing; it is only the carrying out of
legacies that is effective. The "realizing," not the "realization,"
is the important thing. With the "realization," the spirit has
nothing more to do, nothing new to realize, to work out and
strengthen. Simply to appropriate results is to place old
patches upon old clothes. People in Germany have become
satisfied with just this kind of patchwork as far as social life
is concerned, and they believe that they have thus wrought
justice. Only in France was the spirit given its due in the
matter of free social activity. From the anarchy of terrorism
stepped forth Babeuf, the French Fichte, the first communist,
who laid the groundwork for the further development of the
new ethic with respect to social activity, just as Fichte, the
first true atheist, laid the groundwork with respect to thought.
On the other hand, matters pertaining to thought were not
set right in France, and as much as people there strive to
appropriate the "results of German philosophy" for themselves, they have not been able to make any sense out of it
all, for the same reason that this appropriation of "results"
miscarried in Germany.

Man must begin with himself, with the "I", if he wants to
create, to be active. Just as the old History, the History of
nature, began with the first man, so must the new History, the
History of the spirit, begin with the original individual. Descartes made an unhappy attempt at this—he lost the thread,
as we have seen, with his second word. Spinoza did it all,
but history did not immediately come to terms with his
achievement; his *Ethics* lay in the earth bearing no fruit for
more than a century, until finally the two-edged sword of the
spiritual and social revolution cleared away the rubble that
was weighing down the buds of the modern era. Suddenly
there appeared two little shoots, whose roots no one had per-

ceived. Atheism and communism were taught, to the horror of the Philistines, by Fichte and Babeuf, in the two chief cities on either side of the Rhine, Berlin and Paris, and young people streamed to these places, seeking the inspiration of the new teachings. Atheism and communism! Let us examine this sapling.

The thing about it that most frightens people is its apparent lack of roots in any solid earth. Anarchy, upon which both atheism and communism are based, the negation of all domination in both spiritual and social life, seems at first to be the absolute annihilation of all definition, and thus of all reality. But it is only the process of the act becoming fixed by something outside itself, the domination of one thing over another, that anarchy strips away. So far is *self*-determination from being negated here, that it is rather the *negation* of it (brought about by the process of determination from the outside) that is being transcended. The anarchy created through the spirit is only a negation of limitation, not of freedom. It is not the limits that the spirit establishes *for itself* that anarchy clears away, for the limits that the spirit establishes for itself form the content of its free activity. Thus this establishing for itself, this determining of self, this limiting of self, is not something that can be negated by the free spirit; it can be negated only by the setting of limits from the outside.

When I believe in a power that is above or outside of my "I", I am thus limited from without. When I think in opposition to the object, and self-consciously create in accordance with the law of my spirit, I limit myself, without my being limited from without. In this way, I can determine myself in social life, and can be active in this or that determined way, without acknowledging a limit imposed from the outside on my activity—without having another to allow me my rights, or to limit me. How, then, now that anarchy is everywhere surging forth from communism and atheism, can we refashion the limitations from without into self-limitation, the outer God into an inner God, material property into spiritual property? To say it this way already makes it sound much less dreadful, and yet the atheists, communists and anarchists want nothing but this. It is what they *must* want, since they cannot desire the impossible.

In the meantime, we can perceive that the anarchists are not perfectly clear about what it is they want. The free individual who emerged from the revolution had no conception of his limits at first, but saw only his limitlessness; he did not see self-determination taking place within him, but saw only his complete lack of definition, his indeterminateness. He did not yet perceive that the true negation of the process of becoming defined from without consists in self-determination from within. The upshot of this was that he was unable to arrive at overcoming the limits imposed upon him from without, and anarchy turned into its opposite, the domination of the one over the other. People once again were forced to tolerate the limits from without, material property, the complete separation of individuals, because they did not understand that they had to set limits upon themselves, had to determine their own activity, had to enter into spiritual creativity, refashioning the "I" into its becoming-something-else, their activity into its being-for-itself. The terrorists and Babouvists cried out against the betrayal of the revolution, while two fine thinkers, Saint-Simon and Fourier, who saw what this betrayal necessarily had to produce, dedicated themselves to finding a remedy for the evil, and sought anew to define, to delimit, to give "organization" to the limitlessness of social activity, which the conflict of individualities made sharper in their time than it had been before.

The Kantians and Idealists were displaced here in a similar fashion, when Schelling and Hegel began to reflect upon how to restore the negated objective world. But in the midst of this zeal for "Restoration," people rediscovered the essence of revolution in spite of themselves. In order to restore the objective world, Saint-Simon went to the rescue of personal authority, Fourier to the rescue of material property, Schelling to that of feeling, and Hegel to that of Being—all determinations from without, which had been negated long before by the modern spirit.

Finally, the acknowledged new movement, the return to the point at which revolution emerges, began in both Germany

and France, in the macrocosm of the nations as in the micro-
cosm of the individuals. The Restoration king was driven out,
the Restoration philosopher, Hegel, died of cholera, the philosophers and socialists of the old school feebly flickered about
as always, unable to shed new light on anything. People finally
went back to the first heroes of the revolution, to Babeuf in
France and Fichte in Germany, so as to begin at the beginning and move forward without any sudden leaps. Proudhon
proceeds from anarchy, and the German philosophy proceeds
from self-consciousness. Atheism is again taught in Germany,
and communism in France; but people no longer swear by
indeterminateness; Proudhon, like Feuerbach, has accepted
the dialectical moment, but without employing it in the
restoration of the old, outside, negated objectivity. It is along
this path that freedom must be pursued, and will ultimately
be achieved.

Freedom is the overcoming of limits from the outside
through self-limitation, through the self-consciousness of the
spirit as an active agent, through the transcendence of natural
determinateness by self-determination. All history until now
has been what is encountered by thought and by social life,
this being the domain of the natural history of the spirit, just
as everything that we call the objective, material or physical
world is the domain of natural history itself. The only intrinsic difference between the history of mankind and the
history of nature is that in nature, for every self-limitation of
the spirit established, the object in which the spirit encounters
itself continues to exist, whereas for mankind every self-
limitation of the spirit is only a stage of development, and is
ultimately transcended. The true history of the spirit first begins at the point where all natural determination comes to an
end, where the spirit develops, self-consciousness calls out and
the act of the spirit is clearly perceived. With this perception
the reign of freedom begins, and we are standing at its portals
and knocking upon them now. This perception is the true key
to the kingdom, which has been withheld from us long enough
now by the Bishop of Rome. The German religious Reformation was the first to stretch out its arm to him, but the arm
was not long enough. In the meantime, however, the Reforma-

tion grew into German philosophy, while the French Revolution emerged by its side. With these two arms the European
peoples are tearing the key from the hands of its keeper; that
is certain! The unification of these efforts is now the principal
task. There is only one freedom, just as there is only one
spirit.

The common ground of social and spiritual freedom is morality, the highest good, the "perception of God," as Spinoza
puts it, or the self-consciousness of the "Absolute Spirit," as the
Hegelians ineptly put it. It is the spirit's consciousness of its
likeness to itself in its becoming something else, the overcoming of otherness as fixed, the transformation of determined
nature into self-determination. Without all this, neither
equality nor inner freedom is possible. All things are one, and
are equal. But this proves too much, and basically proves
nothing at all. If all things are equal, then even plants and
animals are equal to man, and Heine, the abstract pantheist,
can quite rightly make nonsense of the freedom and equality
of men (who are aristocrats alongside brute animals), as he
does from the ironic viewpoint of his *Atta Troll*, in which he
represents the communism of bears instead of men. Not only
our efforts to achieve freedom, not only communism, but every
earnest effort on the part of men, every moral act, is laughable
if all things are one.

Whoever knows no freedom other than limitlessness knows
no equality other than complete leveling out—pantheism and
communism in the sense of spiritualism. Whoever establishes
unity only as the negation of differentiation, and seeks idealism only through materialism, as the Christians did, whoever
does not have the power to attain abstract anarchy, like the
radicals of the stamp of Heine (this last knight of modern
Romanticism, this process of putrefaction of the Middle Ages),
must run himself into his opposite at every moment, and finally must settle for declaring that the world is out of joint,
because he has himself gone out of joint. This is a moral dis-
jointedness, into which the world collapsed when it drifted
away from itself in the time of Christ, negated all earthly
interests and proclaimed only heavenly ones. Communism and
anarchy rose to the surface at that time—the communism of

bears, that is, freedom as limitlessness—and worldliness or state power was transformed into spirituality. We would be beginning the history of the Middle Ages all over again, as I have already said, if we were to insist upon holding on to abstract communism and idealism.

This would be to repudiate one's rights not only in the history of religion, but in philosophy as well, not only in political history, but in socialism. German philosophy has already transcended the idealism of Fichte, just as French socialism has transcended the communism of Babeuf. We have once again lived out the history of the Middle Ages, this time spiritually. We will no longer say, all things are one; we will no longer say, all things are equal; least of all will we say any longer, everything is in opposition to everything else, everything is different from everything else. Instead we will say that the spirit renders everything one and in opposition, alike and different, at the same time; it creates its own opposite, the other, the world, in order for it to transcend this determination, this delimitation, every time, in order for it to pass back into itself and perceive that it is its own opposite, its own act, its own life, in order to conceive of itself, in other words, as living or acting—but not to create itself as material and fix itself in that state in which the free act would become an objective fact that limits it, in which the spiritual being-for-itself would become material property that throws away its likeness to itself, its morality, negates its freedom, freezes and confines the flow of its life, its movement.

Material property is the being-for-itself of the spirit transformed into a fixed idea. Because the spirit does not itself spiritually conceive its work, its working-out or working-away, as a free act, as its own life, but rather creates this work as a material other, it must therefore fix this other to itself, so as not to lose itself in infinity, so as to arrive at its being-for-itself. But property comes to an end and turns into spirit, which is what it should be (that is, into being-for-itself), when it realizes not the *forms* of the act but the result, the creation itself, as the being-for-itself of the spirit, when it realizes the phantom, the representation of the spirit, to be its own idea— in short, when it realizes its otherness as its being-for-itself,

and holds firmly on to this. It is the very quest for being, that
is, the quest to endure as determined individuality, as a de-
limited "I," as unending essence, that leads to greed. It is,
once again, the negation of all determination, the abstract I
and abstract communism, the outcome of the empty "thing-
in-itself" of Kantian criticism and of the revolution, of the
unsatisfied sense of duty, that led to being and having. This
is how auxiliary verbs became transformed into substantives.
This is how all verbs become substantives, and how everything that belongs to the changing periphery is made into
the permanent core; yes, this is how the world was stood upon
its head!

Freedom is morality; it is above all the fulfillment of the
law of life, of spiritual activity, as much in the narrow sense,
by which the act is called idea, as in the broader sense, by
which the idea is called act, with clear consciousness of this
law. Thus it is fulfillment, not as natural necessity or as determination by nature, as was the case for all living creatures
until now, but as self-determination. Without this morality,
no state of collectivism is conceivable; but also, no morality
is conceivable without collectivism. The riddle drawn out of
the closed circle of slavery can be solved by the spirit, and by
the spirit alone, through the progress of the dialectic, through
its history. History has already broken through the closed
circle of slavery. The revolution is the break from captivity,
from the condition of bigotry and oppression in which the
spirit found itself before it became self-conscious. But, as we
have seen, this anarchy only broke through the limits imposed
from the outside, without progressing further to self-determination or self-limitation, to morality. The revolution is still
incomplete, and it knows that it is still incomplete. Even so,
the anarchy could not stay as it was at the beginning, and
has in fact not stayed that way. And as we, the children of
the revolution, move on from it forward into morality, the
riddle is thus being solved.

The forerunners of the revolution foreshadowed this solving
of the riddle. Montesquieu had already said that the republic
is not possible without virtue. In this statement, as well as in
many others made by other men of that time, such as Jean

Jacques Rousseau, they had shown themselves to have a fair premonition of the idea of collectivity and morality that is now beginning to reign. But they did not clearly perceive it, and imagined that they were doing away with the conditions of the past with their words, which really lacked clearly defined and meaningful ideas. They thought that they were drawing a picture of what was to be done.

Like the word "republic," the word "virtue" has not been properly understood. *Res publica* and *virtus* are words without content, just as the ideal state of things that they described was without content. The content first had to be built up through history. Our morality is different from the virtue of the ancients, our freedom is not theirs; how could the future condition of society be like the ancient world? The conditions of old have been long since negated; Christianity transcended them, and the Middle Ages have transcended Christianity. Montesquieu committed an error in politics similar to the one that Luther, the forerunner of German philosophy, committed in religion. In its still blind strivings, the revolution sought to rehabilitate the situation of ancient times, just as the Reformation sought to revive primitive Christianity, whereas history had long since transcended these ancient conditions. They made this error because, though they had a consciousness of degeneration, of aberration, they did not know that the trouble had arisen in the transition from unconsciousness to the self-conscious spirit. Every early condition is an undeveloped shoot that must first perish in order for the seed to sprout into a full-grown tree, into a ripe and succulent fruit. Whoever wants to return to an earlier condition wants, in effect, to go through history all over again from the beginning.

This is the sort of thing that we want to abolish at last, and we must do so! What we want is something brand new, that has never existed before. We must first begin to develop it. Freedom and equality are beautiful words. We have made ourselves suffer for them, we have sacrificed ourselves for them, and it is for them that we will be resurrected, so that we can stand up and fight once more!

Chapter VI

MARX (1818–83) AND
ENGELS (1820–95)

Historians, by applying the term "utopian" to Marx's socialist predecessors, have in effect corroborated his judgment of them. Marx charged the utopians with being unscientific and ahistorical, with failing to root their ideas in the actual processes of social and historical change. He went on to predict (in 1848) that they would wither and die in the course of time, and indeed this happened very soon after Marx made his prediction. By "scientific" socialism Marx meant socialism based on the inevitable rise of the industrial proletariat to political power. Marx thought that he had come to grips with the fundamental truth of history and had laid moralizing and theory-mongering to rest once and for all.

In the decades following his death his ideas cut a wide swath across the continent of Europe. Capitalism evolved before men's eyes in precise accordance with the laws to which he alone had called attention, and there was good reason to believe in the inevitability of proletarian revolution. The strength of Marxism at that time was due to the support it attracted from the two classes—the proletariat and the intellectuals—that, for different reasons, felt most cruelly subjugated by the bourgeoisie. Marxism ingeniously joined the interests of both classes in a single theoretical system that each found compellingly persuasive.

Engels described Marxism as a synthesis of French revolutionism, German philosophy, and English political economy. In a sense this triad represents the order of Marx's own personal development. In the Rhineland, where Karl Marx was born (on May 5, 1818) and brought up, the influence of French revolutionary ideals was stronger than anywhere else in Germany, especially after Napoleon's troops departed and Prussia assumed control over the region in 1815. Marx's family certainly knew the benefits of French liberty. His father, who had been born in the ghetto, had been emancipated along with the other Jews by the Code Napoleon and was thus enabled to rise to prominence in his city of Trier, where he became a Christian. In his youth Marx was caught up by French ideals of liberty and wrote romantic poetry to celebrate them. His father thought that a "demon" had taken possession of him and wondered whether it would turn out to be "heavenly" or "Faustian."

At Berlin University, Marx joined the "Left Hegelians," who disciplined themselves in Hegel's philosophy even as they criticized its conservative social and religious implications. They subscribed to Hegel's logic, according to which progress in history arose from man's spiritual conflicts—conflicts that bore him along through higher and higher levels of consciousness culminating in absolute self-consciousness or the state of pure freedom. What they objected to was that Hegelian philosophy—which was predicated on incessant change and criticism—had been made into a mystical and metaphysical justification for Prussian absolutism. Like Marx, the Left Hegelians found their inspiration in French radical ideals which they hoped to combine with the best in German philosophy and so regenerate the spirit of their country.

The Left Hegelians, however, fought their battles in the realm of abstract thought, never descending to the level of politics. Ludwig Feuerbach, the most famous of them, brilliantly attacked Christianity from a materialist point of view, but there was no active or constructive political principle behind his critique. Other Left Hegelians were content to maintain the solitary integrity of critical thought; they despised action altogether. Moses Hess, however, did develop a form of philosophical socialism that regarded political activity as the highest good, but socialism itself remained, even for him, an abstract ideal (see *The Philosophy of the Act*, p. 249). It was at this point in the early 1840s that Marx undertook an intensive critique of German philosophy with the purpose of defining his own active commitment to socialism.

Marx emphatically broke with the Left Hegelians when he assumed that human activity consisted in the creation of material objects by the power of labor, not in ideas dreamt by philosophers. The working class was the agent and its labor the substance of history. Man lost his freedom, according to Marx, when he was deprived of the objects he had created and became dependent on those who owned them. The conflicts in history were therefore conflicts of economic classes corresponding to specific modes of production, such as slavery or feudalism or capitalism. The more advanced the mode of production, the more general or universal the conflict. Capitalism, the culmination of all previous modes of production, produced, in the conflict between bourgeoisie and proletariat, a conflict that engaged all of mankind. It followed that when the proletariat did away with capitalism, man—his labor no longer alienated from him—would cease to be subject to or to dominate other men. By 1847 Marx had worked out his critique of German philosophy and his own systematic theory, which he outlined for the first time the following year in the Communist Manifesto.[1]

The failure of the 1848 revolutions effectively destroyed the incipient socialist movement in Europe. Marx, who himself had taken part in the Rhineland uprising as the editor of a magazine, concluded that nothing could be hoped for until the proletariat emerged in full strength on the continent of Europe just as it already had emerged in England. Marx was aware that his conception of socialism remained incomplete or vulnerable, perhaps even utopian, until he mastered the economics of capitalism and disclosed exactly how capitalism created, in the proletariat, the condition of its own downfall. In this way he satisfied himself that he was a scientist, raising to consciousness the objective laws of society, and not merely a moralist imposing his arbitrary rules on it. He never saw the prophet in himself, nor ever conceived the possibility that beneath the scientist might lie the moralist.

From the time he went to England in 1849 until his death, he worked on Capital, exhaustively reading the literature of

[1] We have omitted the Communist Manifesto because it is available in many anthologies and cheap editions.

political economy at its source; for, until the end of the nineteenth century, the science of economics was almost exclusively an English science. Marx's strategy was to turn capitalism against itself, just as he had turned German philosophy and the tradition of French socialism against themselves. He had originally intended to finish *Capital* soon after arriving in England. The first volume, however, appeared more than fifteen years later, and he failed to complete the other two. The subject was much more than he had bargained for; more important, he never ceased being an active socialist, though he was no longer a revolutionary in the sense that he had been before 1848.

His activities as a socialist seemed to belie his theory of the breakdown of capitalism and of an inevitable proletariat revolution. He fully supported meliorist movements to secure a shorter work day, universal suffrage and factory reform, and he was the moving force in the First International (established in 1864 and dissolved in 1876), whose purpose was to protect labor in Europe and America. Within the organization he constantly fought against the followers of Proudhon and Bakunin who wanted labor to take a more active revolutionary role, though at the same time an anti-political one. These internecine quarrels helped to wreck the International, but for a while the organization did much to help its members, thanks largely to Marx's efforts.

Marx of course never ceased to believe in revolution, though he granted that democracy might preclude the need for violence. Nor did he explain what he meant by his famous phrase, "dictatorship of the proletariat." (Engels discussed its meaning, rather vaguely and ambiguously, in *Socialism: Utopian and Scientific*). It is clear, however, that Marx was slowly moving in a direction the next two generations of his followers would carry still further.

Friedrich Engels had, by 1844, independently arrived at the same conclusions on the historic function of the proletariat. From this time on the two men were fast friends and co-workers, until Marx's death in 1883. Engels, born in 1820 to a family of wealthy German textile manufacturers, was, for a long while, Marx's sole source of financial support, and it is

doubtful that Marx would have been able to go on had Engels
not assisted him and his hard-pressed family. Engels was a
talented, urbane, and remarkably erudite writer (he knew
oomo twonty languages and wrote authoritatively on all the
social and natural sciences) who popularized and supplemented Marx's ideas. He never pretended to originality, being
content to regard himself as Marx's helpmate. No one knew
Marx's mind, or reflected it, better than Engels, and his essays
on a variety of subjects are part of the original Marxist canon.
He put the unfinished manuscripts of *Capital* into shape and
published them as the second and third volumes. He died in
1895, having lived to see Marxism become the leading socialist ideology in Europe.

ECONOMIC AND PHILOSOPHICAL
MANUSCRIPTS OF 1844

The most audacious of the Left Hegelians, and the man
most responsible for shaping Marx's early development, was
Ludwig Feuerbach, whose *Essence of Christianity* was an
event in Germany when it appeared in 1841. In it Feuerbach
argued that the Christian religion stood in opposition to the
idea of Christ. Christ symbolized man's yearning for oneness
with himself, with other men and with nature. But Christianity, the religion of ministers and priests and elaborate
theologies, thwarted those needs—the needs that called it
forth in the first place—and so embodied man's alienation and
dependence. Freedom for Feuerbach, by which he meant
man's possession of himself and of all the natural objects that
fulfill his needs, could come only with the removal of Christianity as an organized religion.

Marx was drawn to Feuerbach's humanist naturalism, but
he found that Feuerbach had failed to indicate the concrete
conditions under which mankind was alienated. For Marx the
truth lay in socialism, for socialism understood man in his
concrete changing nature. Human needs, according to Marx,
could not be defined, as Feuerbach had defined them, apart
from action. In the course of satisfying his material needs
man creates fresh ones. Man is what his creative work, his

labor, makes him. Alienation, it follows from this, consists in man's dependence on the objects created by his own labor and therefore on the class which possesses them. Alienated man defines himself by money or property or things. The free man, on the contrary, transcends all definitions in the course of continually creating himself. A communist society, Marx concluded, would be a society of just such free men.

By 1844 Marx had clarified his thoughts on alienation and communism sufficiently to make them serve as the concrete basis for a general critique of German philosophy. He was then co-editor of the *Deutsch-Französische Jahrbücher*—so called because it aimed to bring together the "heart" of France and the "head" of Germany—and in it he intended to publish various manuscripts but only one number appeared, that of February 1844. Thus the *Economic and Philosophical Manuscripts* remained unknown to the world until they were discovered and published in the early 1930s.

▼ ▼ ▼

. . . The worker is related to the *product of his labor* as to an *alien* object. For on this premise it is clear that the more the worker spends himself, the more powerful the alien objective world becomes which he creates over-against himself, the poorer he himself—his inner world—becomes, the less belongs to him as his own. It is the same in religion. The more man puts into God, the less he retains in himself. The worker puts his life into the object; but now his life no longer belongs to him but to the object. Hence, the greater this activity, the greater is the worker's lack of objects. Whatever the product of his labor is, he is not. Therefore the greater this product, the less is he himself. The *alienation* of the worker in his product means not only that his labor becomes an object, an *external* existence, but that it exists *outside him*, independently, as something alien to him, and that it becomes a power on its own confronting him; it means that the life which he has conferred on the object confronts him as something hostile and alien.

Let us now look more closely at the *objectification*, at the production of the worker; and therein at the *alienation,* the *loss* of the object, his product.

The worker can create nothing without *nature,* without the sensuous external world. It is the material on which his labor is manifested, in which it is active, from which and by means of which it produces.

But just as nature provides labor with the *means of life* in the sense that labor cannot *live* without objects on which to operate, on the other hand, it also provides the *means of life* in the more restricted sense—i.e., the means for the physical subsistence of the *worker* himself.

Thus the more the worker by his labor *appropriates* the external world, sensuous nature, the more he deprives himself of *means of life* in the double respect: first, that the sensuous external world more and more ceases to be an object belonging to his labor—to be his labor's *means of life;* and secondly, that it more and more ceases to be *means of life* in the immediate sense, means for the physical subsistence of the worker.

Thus in this double respect the worker becomes a slave of his object, first, in that he receives an *object of labor,* i.e., in that he receives *work;* and secondly, in that he receives *means of subsistence.* Therefore, it enables him to exist, first, as a *worker;* and, second, as a *physical subject.* The extremity of this bondage is that it is only as a *worker* that he continues to maintain himself as a *physical subject,* and that it is only as a *physical subject* that he is a *worker.*

(The laws of political economy express the alienation of the worker in his object thus: the more the worker produces, the less he has to consume; the more values he creates, the more valueless, the more unworthy he becomes; the better formed his product, the more deformed becomes the worker; the more civilized his object, the more barbarous becomes the worker; the mightier labor becomes, the more powerless becomes the worker; the more ingenious labor becomes, the duller becomes the worker and the more he becomes nature's bondsman.)

Political economy conceals the alienation inherent in the nature of labor by not considering the direct relationship be-

tween the worker (labor) *and production*. It is true that labor produces for the rich wonderful things—but for the worker it produces privation. It produces palaces—but for the worker, hovels. It produces beauty—but for the worker, deformity. It replaces labor by machines—but some of the workers it throws back to a barbarous type of labor, and the other workers it turns into machines. It produces intelligence —but for the worker idiocy, cretinism.

The direct relationship of labor to its produce is the relationship of the worker to the objects of his production. The relationship of the man of means to the objects of production and to production itself is only a *consequence* of this first relationship—and confirms it. We shall consider this other aspect later.

When we ask, then, what is the essential relationship of labor we are asking about the relationship of the *worker* to production.

Till now we have been considering the alienation of the worker only in one of its aspects, i.e., the worker's *relationship to the products of his labor*. But the alienation is manifested not only in the result but in the *act of production—* within the *producing activity* itself. How would the worker come to face the product of his activity as a stranger, were it not that in the very act of production he was alienating himself from himself? The product is after all but the summary of the activity, of production. If then the product of labor is alienation, production itself must be active alienation, the alienation of activity, the activity of alienation. . . .

What, then, constitutes the alienation of labor?

First, the fact that labor is *external* to the worker, i.e., it does not belong to his essential being; that in his work, therefore, he does not affirm himself but denies himself, does not feel content but unhappy, does not develop freely his physical and mental energy but mortifies his body and ruins his mind. The worker therefore only feels himself outside his work, and in his work feels outside himself. He is at home when he is not working, and when he is working he is not at home. His labor is therefore not voluntary, but coerced; it is *forced labor*. It is therefore not the satisfaction of a need; it is merely a *means* to satisfy needs external to it. Its alien character emerges clearly in the fact that as soon as no physical or other compulsion exists, labor is shunned like the plague. External labor, labor in which man alienates himself, is a labor of self-sacrifice, of mortification. Lastly, the external character of labor for the worker appears in the fact that it is not his own, but someone else's, that it does not belong to him, that in it he belongs, not to himself, but to another. Just as in religion the spontaneous activity of the human imagination, of the human brain and the human heart, operates independently of the individual—that is, operates on him as an alien, divine or diabolical activity—in the same way the worker's activity is not his spontaneous activity. It belongs to another; it is the loss of his self.

As a result, therefore, man (the worker) no longer feels himself to be freely active in any but his animal functions—eating, drinking, procreating, or at most in his dwelling and in dressing-up, etc.; and in his human functions he no longer feels himself to be anything but an animal. What is animal becomes human and what is human becomes animal.

Certainly eating, drinking, procreating, etc., are also genuinely human functions. But in the abstraction which separates them from the sphere of all other human activity and turns them into sole and ultimate ends, they are animal.

We have considered the act of alienating practical human activity, labor, in two of its aspects. (1) The relation of the worker to the *product of labor* as an alien object exercising power over him. This relation is at the same time the relation to the sensuous external world, to the objects of nature as an alien world antagonistically opposed to him. (2) The relation of labor to the *act of production* within the *labor* process. This relation is the relation of the worker to his own activity as an alien activity not belonging to him; it is activity as suffering, strength as weakness, begetting as emasculating, the worker's *own* physical and mental energy, his personal life or what is life other than activity—as an activity which is turned against him, neither depends on nor belongs to him. Here we have *self-alienation,* as we had previously the alienation of the *thing.*

We have yet a third aspect of *alienated labor* to deduce from the two already considered.

Man is a species being, not only because in practice and in theory he adopts the species as his object (his own as well as those of other things), but—and this is only another way of expressing it—but also because he treats himself as the actual, living species; because he treats himself as a *universal* and therefore a free being.

The life of the species, both in man and in animals, consists physically in the fact that man (like the animal) lives on inorganic nature; and the more universal man is compared with an animal, the more universal is the sphere of inorganic nature on which he lives. Just as plants, animals, stones, the air, light, etc., constitute a part of human consciousness in the realm of theory, partly as objects of natural science, partly as objects of art—his spiritual inorganic nature, spiritual nourishment which he must first prepare to make it palatable and digestible—so too in the realm of practice they constitute a part of human life and human activity. Physically man lives only on these products of nature, whether they appear in the form of food, heating, clothes, a dwelling, or whatever it may be. The universality of man is in practice manifested precisely in the universality which makes all nature his *inorganic* body—both inasmuch as nature is (1) his direct means of life, and (2) the material, the object, and the instrument of his life-activity. Nature is man's *inorganic body*—nature, that is, in so far as it is not itself the human body. Man *lives* on nature—means that nature is his *body,* with which he must remain in continuous intercourse if he is not to die. That man's physical and spiritual life is linked to nature means simply that nature is linked to itself, for man is a part of nature.

In alienating from man (1) nature, and (2) himself, his own active functions, his life-activity, alienated labor alienates the *species* from man. . . .

In creating an *objective world* by his practical activity, in *working-up* inorganic nature, man proves himself a conscious species being, i.e., as a being that treats the species as its own essential being, or that treats itself as a species being.

Admittedly animals also produce. They build themselves nests, dwellings, like the bees, beavers, ants, etc. But an animal only produces what it immediately needs for itself or its young. It produces one-sidedly, while man produces universally. It produces only under the dominion of immediate physical need, while man produces even when he is free from physical need and only truly produces in freedom therefrom. An animal produces only itself, while man reproduces the whole of nature. An animal's product belongs immediately to its physical body, while man freely confronts his product. An animal forms things in accordance with the standard and the need of the species to which it belongs, while man knows how to produce in accordance with the standard of every species, and knows how to apply everywhere the inherent standard to the object. Man therefore also forms things in accordance with the laws of beauty.

It is just in the working-up of the objective world, therefore, that man first really proves himself to be a *species being*. This production is his active species life. Through and because of this production, nature appears as *his* work and his reality. The object of labor is, therefore, the *objectification of man's species life*: for he duplicates himself not only, as in consciousness, intellectually, but also actively, in reality, and therefore he contemplates himself in a world that he has created. In tearing away from man the object of his production, therefore, alienated labor tears from him his *species life*, his real species objectivity, and transforms his advantage over animals into the disadvantage that his inorganic body, nature, is taken from him.

Similarly, in degrading spontaneous activity, free activity, to a means, alienated labor makes man's species life a means to his physical existence.

The consciousness which man has of his species is thus transformed by alienation in such a way that the species life becomes for him a means.

Alienated labor turns thus:

(3) *Man's species being*, both nature and his spiritual species property, into a being *alien* to him, into a *means* to his *individual existence*. It alienates man's own body from

him, as it does external nature and his spiritual essence, his *human* being.

(4) An immediate consequence of the fact that man is alienated from the product of his labor, from his life-activity, from his species being is the *alienation of man* from *man*. If a man is confronted by himself, he is confronted by the *other* man. What applies to a man's relation to his work, to the product of his labor and to himself, also holds of a man's relation to the other man, and to the other man's labor and object of labor. . . .

The alienation of man, and in fact every relationship in which man stands to himself, is first realized and expressed in the relationship in which a man stands to other men.

Hence within the relationship of alienated labor each man views the other in accordance with the standard and the position in which he finds himself as a worker.

We took our departure from a fact of political economy—the alienation of the worker and his production. We have formulated the concept of this fact—*alienated* labor. We have analysed this concept—hence analysing merely a fact of political economy.

Let us now see, further, how in real life the concept of alienated labor must express and present itself.

If the product of labor is alien to me, if it confronts me as an alien power, to whom, then, does it belong?

If my own activity does not belong to me, if it is an alien, a coerced activity, to whom, then, does it belong?

To a being *other* than me.

Who is this being?

The *gods?* To be sure, in the earliest times the principal production (for example, the building of temples, etc., in Egypt, India and Mexico) appears to be in the service of the gods, and the product belongs to the gods. However, the gods on their own were never the lords of labor. No more was *nature*. And what a contradiction it would be if, the more man subjugated nature by his labor and the more the miracles of the gods were rendered superfluous by the miracles of industry, the more man were to renounce the joy of production and the enjoyment of the produce in favor of these powers.

The *alien* being, to whom labor and the produce of labor belongs, in whose service labor is done and for whose benefit the produce of labor is provided, can only be *man* himself.

If the product of labor does not belong to the worker, if it confronts him as an alien power, this can only be because it belongs to some *other man than the worker.* If the worker's activity is a torment to him, to another it must be *delight* and his life's joy. Not the gods, not nature, but only man himself can be this alien power over man.

We must bear in mind the above-stated proposition that man's relation to himself only becomes *objective* and *real* for him through his relation to the other man. Thus, if the product of his labor, his labor *objectified,* is for him an *alien,* hostile, powerful object independent of him, then his position towards it is such that someone else is master of this object, someone who is alien, hostile, powerful, and independent of him. If his own activity is to him an unfree activity, then he is treating it as activity performed in the service, under the dominion, the coercion and the yoke of another man. . . .

Communism is the *positive* expression of annulled private property—at first as *universal* private property. By embracing this relation as a *whole,* communism is:

(1) In its first form only a *generalization* and *consummation* of this relationship. It shows itself as such in a twofold form: on the one hand, the dominion of *material* property bulks so large that it wants to destroy *everything* which is not capable of being possessed by all as *private property.* It wants to abstract *by force* from talent, etc. For it the sole purpose of life and existence is direct, physical *possession.* The category of *laborer* is not done away with, but extended to all men. The relationship of private property persists as the relationship of the community to the world of things. Finally, this movement of counterposing universal private property to private property finds expression in the bestial form of counterposing to *marriage* (certainly a *form of exclusive private property*) the *community of women,* in

which a woman becomes a piece of *communal* and *common* property. It may be said that this idea of the *community of women* gives away the *secret* of this as yet completely crude and thoughtless communism. Just as the woman passes from marriage to general prostitution, so the entire world of wealth (that is, of man's objective substance) passes from the relationship of exclusive marriage with the owner of private property to a state of universal prostitution with the community. In negating the *personality* of man in every sphere, this type of communism is really nothing but the logical expression of private property, which is its negation. General *envy* constituting itself as a power is the disguise in which *avarice* re-establishes itself and satisfies itself, only in *another* way. The thoughts of every piece of private property —inherent in each piece as such—are *at least* turned against all *wealthier* private property in the form of envy and the urge to reduce to a common level, so that this envy and urge even constitute the essence of competition. The crude communism is only the consummation of this envy and of this levelling-down proceeding from the *preconceived* minimum. It has a *definite, limited* standard. How little this annulment of private property is really an appropriation is in fact proved by the abstract negation of the entire world of culture and civilization, the regression to the *unnatural* simplicity of the *poor and undemanding* man who has not only failed to go beyond private property, but has not yet even attained to it.

The community is only a community of *labor,* and an equality of *wages* paid out by the communal capital—the *community* as the universal capitalist. Both sides of the relationship are raised to an *imagined* universality—*labor* as a state in which every person is put, and *capital* as the acknowledged universality and power of the community. . . .

(2) Communism (α) of a political nature still—democratic or despotic; (β) with the annulment of the state, yet still incomplete, and being still affected by private property (i.e., by the alienation of man). In both forms communism already knows itself to be re-integration or return of man to himself, the transcendence of human self-alienation; but since it has not yet grasped the positive essence of private property, and

just as little the *human* nature of need, it remains captive to it and infected by it. It has, indeed, grasped its concept, but not its essence.

(3) *Communism* as the *positive transcendence of private property*, as *human self-alienation,* and therefore as the real *appropriation of the human* essence by and for man; communism therefore as the complete return of man to himself as a *social* (i.e., human) being—a return become conscious, and accomplished within the entire wealth of previous development. This communism, as fully-developed naturalism, equals humanism, and as fully-developed humanism equals naturalism; it is the *genuine* resolution of the conflict between man and nature and between man and man—the true resolution of the strife between existence and essence, between objectification and self-confirmation, between freedom and necessity, between the individual and the species. Communism is the riddle of history solved, and it knows itself to be this solution.

The entire movement of history is, therefore, both its *actual* act of genesis (the birth act of its empirical existence) and also for its thinking consciousness the *comprehended* and *known* process of its *coming-to-be.* That other, still immature communism, meanwhile, seeks an *historical* proof for itself—a proof in the realm of the existent—amongst disconnected historical phenomena opposed to private property, tearing single phases from the historical process and focusing attention on them as proofs of its historical pedigree (a horse ridden hard especially by Cabet, Villegardelle, etc.). By so doing it simply makes clear that by far the greater part of this process contradicts its claims, and that, if it has once been, precisely its being in the *past* refutes its pretension to being *essential.*

That the entire revolutionary movement necessarily finds both its empirical and its theoretical basis in the movement of *private property*—in that of the economy, to be precise—is easy to see.

This *material,* immediately *sensuous* private property is the material sensuous expression of *alienated human* life. Its movement—production and consumption—is the *sensuous* rev-

elation of the movement of all production hitherto—i.e.,
the realization or the reality of man. Religion, family, state,
law, morality, science, art, etc., are only *particular* modes of
production, and fall under its general law. The positive
transcendence of *private property* as the appropriation of
human life is, therefore, the positive transcendence of all
alienation—that is to say, the return of man from religion,
family, state, etc., to his *human,* i.e., *social* mode of existence.
Religious alienation as such occurs only in the realm of *consciousness,* of man's inner life, but economic estrangement is
that of *real life;* its transcendence therefore embraces both
aspects. It is evident that the *initial* stage of the movement
amongst the various peoples depends on whether the true
and for them *authentic* life of the people manifests itself
more in consciousness or in the external world—is more ideal
or real. Communism begins from the outset (*Owen*) with
atheism; but atheism is at first far from being *communism;*
indeed, it is still mostly an abstraction.

The philanthropy of atheism is therefore at first only *philosophical,* abstract, philanthropy, and that of communism is
at once *real* and directly bent on *action.*

We have seen how on the premise of positively annulled
private property man produces man—himself and the other
man; how the object, being the direct embodiment of
his individuality, is simultaneously his own existence for the
other man, the existence of the other man, and that existence
for him. Likewise, however, both the material of labor and
man as the subject, are the point of departure as well as the
result of the movement (and precisely in this fact, that they
must constitute the *point of departure,* lies the historical *necessity* of private property). Thus the *social* character is the
general character of the whole movement: *just as* society
itself produces *man as man,* so is society *produced* by him.
Activity and consumption, both in their content and in their
mode of existence, are *social: social* activity and *social* consumption; the *human* essence of nature first exists only for
social man; for only here does nature exist for him as a *bond*
with *man*—as his existence for the other and the other's existence for him—as the life-element of the human world; only

here does nature exist as the *foundation* of his own *human* existence. Only here has what is to him his *natural* existence become his *human* existence, and nature become man for him. Thus *society* is the consummated oneness in substance of man and nature—the true resurrection of nature—the naturalism of man and the humanism of nature both brought to fulfilment. . . .

THESES ON FEUERBACH (1845)

In the spring of 1845, Marx made more explicit his philosophical disagreements with Feuerbach in a series of ten "theses." Published by Engels for the first time in 1888 as an appendix to his book, *Ludwig Feuerbach and the End of Classical German Philosophy*, the theses have come to be acknowledged as an important statement of Marx's philosophy. It may be noted in passing that they bear close resemblance to John Dewey's philosophy of instrumentalism.

I

The chief defect of all hitherto existing materialism—that of Feuerbach included—is that the thing [*Gegenstand*], reality, sensuousness, is conceived only in the form of the *object* [*Objekt*] or of *contemplation* [*Anschauung*], but not as *human sensuous activity, practice*, not subjectively. Hence it happened that the *active* side, in contradistinction to materialism, was developed by idealism—but only abstractly, since, of course, idealism does not know real, sensuous activity as such. Feuerbach wants sensuous objects, really differentiated from the thought objects, but he does not conceive human activity itself as *objective* [*gegenständliche*] activity. Hence, in the *Essence of Christianity*, he regards the theoretical attitude as the only genuinely human attitude, while practice is conceived and fixed only in its dirty-judaical form of appearance. Hence he does not grasp the significance of "revolutionary," of "practical-critical," activity.

II

The question whether objective [*gegenständliche*] truth can be attributed to human thinking is not a question of theory but is a *practical* question. In practice man must prove the truth, that is, the reality and power, the this-sidedness [*Diesseitigkeit*] of his thinking. The dispute over the reality or non-reality of thinking which is isolated from practice is a purely *scholastic* question.

III

The materialist doctrine that men are products of circumstances and upbringing, and that, therefore, changed men are products of other circumstances and changed upbringing, forgets that it is men that change circumstances, and that the educator himself needs educating. Hence this doctrine necessarily arrives at dividing society into two parts, of which one is superior to society (in Robert Owen, for example).

The coincidence of the changing of circumstances and of human activity can be conceived and rationally understood only as *revolutionizing practice*.

IV

Feuerbach starts out from the fact of religious self-alienation, the duplication of the world into a religious, imaginary world and a real one. His work consists in the dissolution of the religious world into its secular basis. He overlooks the fact that after completing this work, the chief thing still remains to be done. For the fact that the secular foundation detaches itself from itself and establishes itself in the clouds as an independent realm is really to be explained only by the self-cleavage and self-contradictoriness of this secular basis. The latter must itself, therefore, first be understood in its contradiction and then, by the removal of the contradiction, revolutionized in practice. Thus, for instance, once the earthly family is discovered to be the secret of the holy family, the former must then itself be criticized in theory and revolutionized in practice.

V

Feuerbach, not satisfied with *abstract thinking*, appeals to *sensuous contemplation*, but he does not conceive sensuousness as *practical*, human-sensuous activity.

VI

Feuerbach resolves the religious essence into the *human essence. But the human essence is no abstraction inherent in* each single individual. In its reality it is the ensemble of the social relations.

Feuerbach, who does not enter upon a criticism of this real essence, is consequently compelled:

1. To abstract from the historical process and to fix the religious sentiment [*Gemüt*] as something by itself, and to presuppose an abstract—*isolated*—human individual.

2. The human essence, therefore, can with him be comprehended only as "genus," as an internal, dumb generality which merely *naturally* unites the many individuals.

VII

Feuerbach, consequently, does not see that the "religious sentiment" is itself a *social product,* and that the abstract individual whom he analyzes belongs in reality to a particular form of society.

VIII

Social life is essentially *practical.* All mysteries which mislead theory to mysticism find their rational solution in human practice and in the comprehension of this practice.

IX

The highest point attained by *contemplative* materialism, that is, materialism which does not understand sensuousness as practical activity, is the contemplation of single individuals in "civil society."

X

The standpoint of the old materialism is "*civil*" society; the standpoint of the new is *human* society, or socialized humanity.

XI

The philosophers have only *interpreted* the world, in various ways; the point, however, is to *change* it.

Marx to J. Weydemeyer (March 5, 1852)

A close friend of Marx, J. Weydemeyer, was a German revolutionist of 1848 who had moved to America (where he later became a high officer for the North in the Civil War).

▼ ▼ ▼

. . . And now as to myself, no credit is due to me for discovering the existence of classes in modern society, nor yet the struggle between them. Long before me bourgeois historians had described the historical development of this struggle of the classes, and bourgeois economists the economic anatomy of the classes. What I did that was new was to prove: (1) that the *existence of classes* is only bound up with *particular historical phases in the development of production;* (2) that the class struggle necessarily leads to the *dictatorship of the proletariat;* (3) that this dictatorship itself only constitutes the transition to the *abolition of all classes* and to a *classless society.* . . .

A Contribution to the Critique of Political Economy (1859)

Since becoming a socialist in the early 1840s Marx had been convinced that civil society rested on the foundation of economics and on the conflict of economic classes. He had sporadically taken up the study of English political economy, but his socialist activities had prevented him from analyzing capitalism in depth. The failure of the 1848 revolutions left no further doubt in his mind that socialism was possible only when a proletariat existed; which is to say only where there existed a highly developed system of capitalist production.

Marx moved to London in the fall of 1849 and remained there for the rest of his life. He spent most of his working day in the British Museum exhaustively studying economic literature, gathering material for a definitive analysis of capitalism. His work proceeded slowly. His terrible personal and family hardships, his involvement in socialist affairs and his fastidious standards of scholarship repeatedly delayed completion of his book. In 1859 he published *A Contribution to the Critique of Political Economy,* a prologue to the study of capitalism he intended to write. In the introduction to the *Critique* he described his development as a political economist. It is the best summary extant of his conception of history.

▼ ▼ ▼

. . . I was taking up law, which discipline, however, I only pursued as a subordinate subject along with philosophy and history. In the year 1842–43, as editor of the *Rheinische Zeitung,* I experienced for the first time the embarrassment of having to take part in discussions on so-called material interests. The proceedings of the Rhenish Landtag on thefts of wood and parcelling of landed property, the official polemic which Herr von Schaper, then *Oberpräsident* of the Rhine Province, opened against the *Rheinische Zeitung* on the conditions of the Moselle peasantry, and finally debates on free trade and protective tariffs provided the first occasions for occupying myself with economic questions. On the other hand, at that time when the good will "to go further" greatly outweighed knowledge of the subject, a philosophically weakly tinged echo of French socialism and communism made itself audible in the *Rheinische Zeitung.* I declared myself against this amateurism, but frankly confessed at the same time in a controversy with the *Allgemeine Augsburger Zeitung* that my previous studies did not permit me even to venture any judgment on the content of the French tendencies. Instead, I eagerly seized on the illusion of the managers of the *Rheinische Zeitung,* who thought that by a weaker attitude on the part of the paper they could secure a remission of the death sentence passed upon it, to withdraw from the public stage into the study.

The first work which I undertook for a solution of the doubts which assailed me was a critical review of the Hegelian philosophy of right, a work the introduction to which appeared in 1844 in the *Deutsch-Französische Jahrbücher,* published in Paris. My investigation led to the result that legal relations as well as forms of state are to be grasped neither from themselves nor from the so-called general development of the human mind, but rather have their roots in the material conditions of life, the sum total of which Hegel, following the example of the Englishmen and Frenchmen of the eighteenth century, combines under the name of "civil society," that, however, the anatomy of civil society is to be sought in political economy. The investigation of the latter, which I began in Paris, I continued in Brussels, whither I had emigrated in consequence of an expulsion order of M. Guizot. The general result at which I arrived and which, once won, served as a guiding thread for my studies, can be briefly formulated as follows: In the social production of their life, men enter into definite relations that are indispensable and independent of their will, relations of production which correspond to a definite stage of development of their material productive forces. The sum total of these relations of production constitutes the economic structure of society, the real foundation, on which rises a legal and political superstructure and to which correspond definite forms of social consciousness. The mode of production of material life conditions the social, political and intellectual life process in general. It is not the consciousness of men that determines their being, but, on the contrary, their social being that determines their consciousness. At a certain stage of their development, the material productive forces of society come in conflict with the existing relations of production, or—what is but a legal expression for the same thing—with the property relations within which they have been at work hitherto. From forms of development of the productive forces these relations turn into their fetters. Then begins an epoch of social revolution. With the change of the economic foundation the entire immense superstructure is more or less rapidly transformed. In considering such transformations a distinction should always be made between the material transformation of the economic conditions of production, which can be determined with the precision of natural science, and the legal, political, religious, aesthetic or philosophic—in short, ideological forms in which men become conscious of this conflict and fight it out. Just as our opinion of an individual is not based on what he thinks of himself, so can we not judge of such a period of transformation by its own consciousness; on the contrary, this consciousness must be explained rather from the contradictions of material life, from the existing conflict between the social productive forces and the relations of production. No social order ever perishes before all the productive forces for which there is room in it have developed; and new, higher relations of production never appear before the material conditions of their existence have matured in the womb of the old society itself. Therefore mankind always sets itself only such tasks as it can solve; since, looking at the matter more closely, it will always be found that the task itself arises only when the material conditions for its solution already exist or are at least in the process of formation. In broad outlines Asiatic, ancient, feudal, and modern bourgeois modes of production can be designated as progressive epochs in the economic formation of society. The bourgeois relations of production are the last antagonistic form of the social process of production—antagonistic not in the sense of individual antagonism, but of one arising from the social conditions of life of the individuals; at the same time the productive forces developing in the womb of bourgeois society create the material conditions for the solution of that antagonism. This social formation brings, therefore, the prehistory of human society to a close.

Friedrich Engels, with whom, since the appearance of his brilliant sketch on the criticism of the economic categories (in the *Deutsch-Französische Jahrbücher*), I maintained a constant exchange of ideas by correspondence, had by another road (compare his *The Condition of the Working Class in England in 1844*) arrived at the same result as I, and when in the spring of 1845 he also settled in Brussels, we resolved to work out in common the opposition of our view to the ideological view of German philosophy, in fact, to settle accounts with our erstwhile philosophical conscience. The resolve was carried out in the form of a criticism of post-Hegelian philosophy. The manuscript, two large octavo volumes, had long reached its place of publication in Westphalia when we received the news that altered circumstances did not allow of its being printed. We abandoned the manuscript to the gnawing criticism of the mice all the more willingly as we had achieved our main purpose—self-clarification. Of the scattered works in which we put our views before the public at that time, now from one aspect, now from another, I will mention only the *Manifesto of the Communist Party*, jointly written by Engels and myself, and *Discours sur le libre échange* published by me. The decisive points of our view were first scientifically, although only polemically, indicated in my work published in 1847 and directed against Proudhon: *Misère de la Philosophie,* etc. A dissertation written in German on *Wage Labour,* in which I put together my lectures on this subject delivered in the Brussels German Workers' Society, was interrupted, while being printed, by the February Revolution and my consequent forcible removal from Belgium.

The editing of the *Neue Rheinische Zeitung* in 1848 and 1849, and the subsequent events, interrupted my economic studies which could only be resumed in the year 1850 in London. The enormous material for the history of political economy which is accumulated in the British Museum, the favorable vantage point afforded by London for the observation of bourgeois society, and finally the new stage of development upon which the latter appeared to have entered with the discovery of gold in California and Australia, determined me to begin afresh from the very beginning and to work through the new material critically. These studies led partly of themselves into apparently quite remote subjects on which I had to dwell for a shorter or longer period. Especially, however, was the time at my disposal curtailed by the imperative necessity of earning my living. My contributions, during eight years now, to the first English-American newspaper, the *New York Tribune,* compelled an extraordinary scattering of my studies, since I occupy myself with newspaper correspondence proper only in exceptional cases. However, articles on striking economic events in England and on the Continent constituted so considerable a part of my contributions that I was compelled to make myself familiar with practical details which lie outside the sphere of the actual science of political economy.

This sketch of the course of my studies in the sphere of political economy is intended only to show that my views,

however they may be judged and however little they coincide
with the interested prejudices of the ruling classes, are the
result of conscientious investigation lasting many years. But
at the entrance to science, as at the entrance to hell, the de
mand must be posted:

> Qui si convien lasciare ogni sospetto;
> Ogni viltà convien che qui sia morta.[1]

INAUGURAL ADDRESS OF THE WORKINGMEN'S
INTERNATIONAL ASSOCIATION (1864)

Trade union activity on the Continent and in England
sprang up in the late '50s and early '60s. Simultaneously, a
series of international crises aroused Europe from its long
torpor: the Panic of 1857 was followed by the Crimean War
and then by the American Civil War, which, in cutting off
the supply of cotton to England, closed down many factories
and threw thousands out of work. Under these conditions
trade unions became increasingly political and international
in their outlook.

They had to be international because the lack of any organization to coordinate the policies of unions in different
countries had enabled businessmen to transfer cheap labor
from one country to another and so keep wages down to the
lowest competitive level. In 1862 and 1863 English and
French workers came together to discuss the possibility of
creating an international association. On September 28, 1864,
workers' deputies from different countries met in London's St.
Martin's Hall to map out further plans.

Marx had been officially listed as a German delegate to
this meeting but took no part in its formal sessions. Though he
favored creation of an international organization he hated organizational work. Nonetheless, he became more deeply involved, particularly as the committee assigned to draw up a
plan of action could not get started. In late October 1864,

[1] Taken from Dante's *The Divine Comedy*, Inferno, Canto III:
    Here must all misgiving be abandoned
    And here must die every cowardly thought.

Marx drafted an inaugural address and a body of rules that the committee accepted with few reservations. Both the address and the rules became the basis of the International Association.

The language of the Inaugural Address is less polemical than Marx's other more avowedly communist public statements. But it was not because Marx had become mellow and reformist. As he explained to Engels: "Time is necessary before the revived movement can permit itself the old audacious language. The need of the movement is: bold in matter, but mild in manner."

▼ ▼ ▼

. . . After the failure of the Revolutions of 1848, all party organisations and party journals of the working classes were, on the Continent, crushed by the iron hand of force, the most advanced sons of labor fled in despair to the Transatlantic Republic, and the short-lived dreams of emancipation vanished before an epoch of industrial fever, moral miasma, and political reaction. The defeat of the Continental working classes, partly owed to the diplomacy of the English Government, acting then as now in fraternal solidarity with the Cabinet of St. Petersburg, soon spread its contagious effects to this side of the Channel. While the rout of their Continental brethren unmanned the English working classes, and broke their faith in their own cause, it restored to the landlord and the money-lord their somewhat shaken confidence. They insolently withdrew concessions already advertised. The discoveries of new goldlands led to an immense exodus, leaving an irreparable void in the ranks of the British proletariat. Others of its formerly active members were caught by the temporary bribe of greater work and wages, and turned into "political blacks." All the efforts made at keeping up, or remodelling, the Chartist Movement, failed signally; the press organs of the working class died one by one of the apathy of the masses, and, in point of fact, never before seemed the English working class so thoroughly reconciled to a state of political nullity. If, then, there had been no solidarity of action between the

British and the Continental working classes, there was, at all
events, a solidarity of defeat.

And yet the period passed since the Revolutions of 1848
has not been without its compensating features. We shall here
only point to two great facts.

After a thirty years' struggle, fought with most admirable
perseverance, the English working classes, improving a mo-
mentaneous split between the landlords and money-lords, succeeded in carrying the Ten Hours' Bill. The immense physical,
moral and intellectual benefits hence accruing to the factory
operatives, half-yearly chronicled in the reports of the in-
spectors of factories, are now acknowledged on all sides. Most
of the Continental governments had to accept the English
Factory Act in more or less modified forms, and the English
Parliament itself is every year compelled to enlarge its sphere
of action. But besides its practical import, there was something
else to exalt the marvellous success of this working men's
measure. Through their most notorious organs of science, such
as Dr. Ure, Professor Senior, and other sages of that stamp,
the middle class had predicted, and to their heart's content
proved, that any legal restriction of the hours of labor must
sound the death knell of British industry, which, vampire like,
could but live by sucking blood, and children's blood, too. In
olden times, child murder was a mysterious rite of the religion of Moloch, but it was practised on some very solemn
occasions only, once a year perhaps, and then Moloch had
no exclusive bias for the children of the poor. This struggle
about the legal restriction of the hours of labor raged the
more fiercely since, apart from frightened avarice, it told indeed upon the great contest between the blind rule of the
supply and demand laws which form the political economy
of the middle class, and social production controlled by social
foresight, which forms the political economy of the working
class. Hence the Ten Hours' Bill was not only a great practical
success; it was the victory of a principle; it was the first time
that in broad daylight the political economy of the middle
class succumbed to the political economy of the working class.

But there was in store a still greater victory of the political
economy of labor over the political economy of property. We

speak of the co-operative movement, especially the co-operative factories raised by the unassisted efforts of a few bold "hands." The value of these great social experiments cannot be over-rated. By deed, instead of by argument, they have shown that production on a large scale, and in accord with the behests of modern science, may be carried on without the existence of a class of masters employing a class of hands; that to bear fruit, the means of labor need not be monopolised as a means of dominion over, and of extortion against, the laboring man himself; and that, like slave labor, like serf labor, hired labor is but a transitory and inferior form, destined to disappear before associated labor plying its toil with a willing hand, a ready mind, and a joyous heart. In England, the seeds of the co-operative system were sown by Robert Owen; the working men's experiments, tried on the Continent, were, in fact, the practical upshot of the theories, not invented, but loudly proclaimed, in 1848.

At the same time, the experience of the period from 1848 to 1864 has proved beyond doubt that, however excellent in principle, and however useful in practice, co-operative labor, if kept within the narrow circle of the casual efforts of private workmen, will never be able to arrest the growth in geometrical progression of monopoly, to free the masses, nor even to perceptibly lighten the burden of their miseries. It is perhaps for this very reason that plausible noblemen, philanthropic middle-class spouters, and even keen political economists, have all at once turned nauseously complimentary to the very co-operative labor system they had vainly tried to nip in the bud by deriding it as the utopia of the dreamer, or stigmatising it as the sacrilege of the socialist. To save the industrious masses, co-operative labor ought to be developed to national dimensions, and consequently, to be fostered by national means. Yet, the lords of land and the lords of capital will always use their political privileges for the defence and perpetuation of their economical monopolies. So far from promoting, they will continue to lay every possible impediment in the way of the emancipation of labor. Remember the sneer with which, last session, Lord Palmerston put down the advocates of the Irish Tenants' Right Bill. The House of Commons, cried he, is a house of landed proprietors. To conquer political power has therefore become the great duty of the working classes. They seem to have comprehended this, for in England, Germany, Italy, and France there have taken place simultaneous revivals, and simultaneous efforts are being made at the political reorganisation of the working men's party.

One element of success they possess—numbers; but numbers weigh only in the balance, if united by combination and led by knowledge. Past experience has shown how disregard of that bond of brotherhood which ought to exist between the workmen of different countries, and incite them to stand firmly by each other in all their struggles for emancipation, will be chastised by the common discomfiture of their incoherent efforts. This thought prompted the working men of different countries assembled on September 28, 1864, in public meeting at St. Martin's Hall, to found the International Association.

Another conviction swayed that meeting.

If the emancipation of the working classes requires their fraternal concurrence, how are they to fulfil that great mission with a foreign policy in pursuit of criminal designs, playing upon national prejudices, and squandering in piratical wars the people's blood and treasure? It was not the wisdom of the ruling classes, but the heroic resistance to their criminal folly by the working classes of England that saved the West of Europe from plunging headlong into an infamous crusade for the perpetuation and propagation of slavery on the other side of the Atlantic. The shameless approval, mock sympathy, or idiotic indifference, with which the upper classes of Europe have witnessed the mountain fortress of the Caucasus falling a prey to, and heroic Poland being assassinated by, Russia; the immense and unresisted encroachments of that barbarous power, whose head is at St. Petersburg, and whose hands are in every cabinet of Europe, have taught the working classes the duty to master themselves the mysteries of international politics; to watch the diplomatic acts of their respective Governments; to counteract them, if necessary, by all means in their power; when unable to prevent, to combine in simultaneous denunciations, and to vindicate the simple laws of morals and justice, which ought to govern the relations of private individuals, as the rules paramount of the intercourse of nations.

The fight for such a foreign policy forms part of the general struggle for the emancipation of the working classes.

Proletarians of all countries, Unite!

MARX TO L. KUGELMANN (OCTOBER 9, 1866)

The stronghold of the International was Geneva, Switzerland, and there the First Congress met on September 3, 1866. Marx—who did not attend—had drawn up a memorandum for the London delegation on coordinating the reform activities of working-class movements. The memorandum included no polemics or discussion of internecine controversies and it passed nearly intact. Marx had deliberately drawn it up this way in hopes of defeating the militant and agitative Proudhonists, whom he considered a threat to the organization. As Marx conceived it, the immediate purpose of the International was to secure piecemeal reforms for labor and not to engage in hopeless revolutionary rhetoric.

Kugelmann was not an active follower of Marx, but the two men corresponded extensively.

▼ ▼ ▼

. . . I had great fears for the first Congress at Geneva. On the whole, however, it turned out better than I expected. The effect in France, England and America was unhoped for. I could not, and did not want to go there, but wrote the program for the London delegation. I deliberately restricted it to those points which allow of immediate agreement and concerted action by the workers, and give direct nourishment and impetus to the requirements of the class struggle and the organization of the workers into a class. The Parisian gentlemen had their heads full of the emptiest Proudhonist phrases. They babble about science and know nothing. They scorn all *revolutionary* action, that is, action arising out of the class struggle itself, all concentrated social movements, and therefore also those which can be carried through by *political* means (for

instance, the *legal* shortening of the working day). Under the
pretext of freedom, and of anti-governmentalism or anti-
authoritarian individualism, these gentlemen, who for sixteen
years have so quietly endured the most miserable despotism,
and still endure it, actually preach ordinary bourgeois economy, only Proudhonistically idealized! Proudhon has done
enormous mischief. His sham criticism and sham opposition
to the Utopians (he himself is only a petty-bourgeois Utopian,
whereas in the Utopias of a Fourier, an Owen, etc., there is
the presentiment and imaginative expression of a new world)
attracted and corrupted first the *"jeunesse brillante,"* the students, and then the workmen, particularly those of Paris, who,
as workers in luxury trades, are strongly attached, without
knowing it, to the old rubbish. Ignorant, vain, presumptuous,
chattering, blusteringly arrogant, they were on the point of
spoiling everything, for they came to the Congress in numbers
which bore no relation whatever to the number of their
members. In the report I shall, incidentally, rap them on the
knuckles. . . .

ENGELS'S EXPLANATION OF *Capital* (1868)

Engels has written perhaps the most lucid brief summary
of the first volume of *Capital.* It appeared in the form of two
articles written in March 1868 for a German socialist weekly,
Die Demokratischer Wochenblatt.

▼ ▼ ▼

As long as there have been capitalists and workers on earth
no book has appeared which is of as much importance for the
workers as the one before us. The relation between capital and
labor, the axis on which our entire present system of society
turns, is here treated scientifically for the first time, and at
that with a thoroughness and acuity such as was possible only
for a German. Valuable as the writings of an Owen, Saint-
Simon or Fourier are and will remain—it was reserved for a
German to climb to the height from which the whole field of
modern social relations can be seen clearly and in full view

just as the lower mountain scenery is seen by an observer standing on the topmost peak.

Political economy up to now has taught us that labor is the source of all wealth and the measure of all values, so that two objects whose production has cost the same labor time possess the same value and must also be taken in exchange for each other, since on the average only equal values are exchangeable for one another. At the same time, however, it teaches that there exists a kind of stored-up labor, which it calls capital; that this capital, owing to the auxiliary sources contained in it, raises the productivity of living labor a hundred and a thousand fold, and in return claims a certain compensation which is termed profit or gain. As we all know, this occurs in reality in such a way that the profits of stored-up, dead labor become ever more massive, the capitals of the capitalists become ever more colossal, while the wages of living labor become constantly less and the mass of the workers living solely on wages becomes ever more numerous and poverty-stricken. How is this contradiction to be solved? How can there remain a profit for the capitalist if the worker receives in compensation the full value of the labor he adds to his product? Yet this ought to be the case, since only equal values are exchanged. On the other hand, how can equal values be exchanged, how can the worker receive the full value of his product, if, as is admitted by many economists, this product is divided between him and the capitalist? Economics up to now has been helpless in the face of the contradiction, and writes or stutters embarrassed phrases which say nothing. Even the previous socialist critics of economics have not been able to do more than to emphasize the contradiction; no one resolved it, until now at last Marx has traced the process by which this profit arises right to its birthplace and has thereby made everything clear.

In tracing the development of capital, Marx starts out from the simple, notoriously obvious fact that the capitalists increase the value of their capital through exchange: they buy commodities for their money and afterwards sell them for more money than they cost them. For example, a capitalist buys cotton for 1,000 talers and resells it for 1,100, thus "earn-

ing" 100 talers. This excess of 100 talers over the original
capital Marx calls *surplus value*. What is the origin of this
surplus value? According to the economists' assumption, only
equal values are unchanged and in the sphere of abstract
theory this, of course, is correct. Hence the purchase of cotton and its resale can just as little yield surplus value as the
exchange of a silver taler for thirty silver groschen and the re-
exchange of the small coins for a silver taler, a process by
which one becomes neither richer nor poorer. But surplus
value can just as little arise from sellers selling commodities
above their value, or purchasers buying them below their
value, because each one is in turn buyer and seller and things
would therefore again balance. Just as little can it arise from
buyers and sellers reciprocally overreaching each other, for
this would create no new or surplus value, but only divide the
existing capital differently among the capitalists. In spite of
the fact that the capitalist buys the commodities at their value
and sells them at their value, he gets more value out than he
puts in. How does this happen?

The capitalist finds on the commodity market under present
social conditions *a commodity* which has the peculiar property
that *its use is a source of new value, is a creation of new value,*
and this commodity is *labor power.*

What is the value of labor power? The value of every commodity is measured by the labor required for its production.
Labor power exists in the form of the living worker who requires a definite amount of means of subsistence for his
existence as well as for the maintenance of his family, which
ensures the continuance of labor power also after his death.
The labor time necessary for producing these means of
subsistence represents, therefore, the value of the labor
power. The capitalist pays this value weekly and purchases
for that the use of one week's labor of the worker. So far
messieurs the economists will be pretty well in agreement
with us as to the value of labor power.

The capitalist now sets his worker to work. In a certain
period of time the worker will have performed as much
labor as was represented by his weekly wages. Supposing
that the weekly wage of a worker represents three workdays,

then if the worker begins on Monday, he has by Wednesday evening *replaced* to the capitalist the *full value of the wage paid*. But does he then stop working? Not at all. The capitalist has bought his *week's* labor and the worker must go on working also during the last three week days. This *surplus labor* of the worker, over and above the time necessary to replace his wages, is the *source of surplus value*, of profit, of the steadily growing increase of capital.

Do not say it is an arbitrary assumption that the worker works off in three days the wages he has received, and works the remaining three days for the capitalist. Whether he takes exactly three days to replace his wages, or two or four, is to be sure quite immaterial here and hence varies according to circumstances; the main point is that the capitalist, besides the labor he pays for, also extracts labor that he *does not pay for*, and this is no arbitrary assumption, for the day the capitalist extracts from the worker in the long run only as much labor as he paid him in wages, on that day he will shut down his workshop, since indeed his whole profit would come to nought.

Here we have the solution of all those contradictions. The origin of surplus value (of which the capitalists' profit forms an important part) is now quite clear and natural. The value of the labor power is paid for, but this value is far less than that which the capitalist manages to extract from the labor power, and it is just the difference, the *unpaid labor*, which constitutes the share of the capitalist, or, more accurately, of the capitalist class. For even the profit that the cotton dealer made on his cotton in the above example must consist of unpaid labor, if cotton prices did not rise. The trader must have sold to a cotton manufacturer, who is able to extract a profit for himself from his product besides the 100 talers, and therefore shares with him the unpaid labor he has pocketed. In general it is this unpaid labor which maintains all the non-working members of society. The state and municipal taxes, as far as they affect the capitalist class, as also the ground rent of the land owners, etc., are paid from it. On it rests the whole existing social system.

It would, however, be absurd to assume that unpaid labor

arose only under present conditions where production is
carried on by capitalists on the one hand and wage-workers
on the other. On the contrary, the oppressed class at all
times has had to perform unpaid labor. During the whole
long period when slavery was the prevailing form of the
organization of labor, the slaves had to perform much more
labor than was returned to them in the form of means of
subsistence. The same was the case under the rule of serfdom
and right up to the abolition of peasant corvée labor; here in
fact the difference stands out palpably between the time
during which the peasant works for his own maintenance
and the surplus labor for the lord of the manor, precisely because the latter is carried out separately from the former.
The form has now been changed, but the substance remains
and as long as "a part of society possesses the monopoly of
the means of production, the laborer, free or not free, must
add to the working-time necessary for his own maintenance
an extra working-time in order to produce the means of subsistence for the owners of the means of production."

II

In the previous article we saw that every worker employed
by a capitalist performs two kinds of labor: during one part
of his working-time he replaces the wages advanced to
him by the capitalist, and this part of his labor Marx terms the
necessary labor. But afterwards he has to go on working and
during that time he produces *surplus value* for the capitalist,
an important part of which constitutes profit. That part of the
labor is called surplus labor.

Let us assume that the worker works three days of the week
to replace his wages and three days to produce surplus value
for the capitalist. Putting it otherwise, it means that, with a
twelve-hour working day, he works six hours daily for his
wages and six hours for the production of surplus value.
One can get only six days out of the week, or at most seven
even by including Sunday, but one can extract six, eight, ten,
twelve, fifteen or even more hours of work out of every
single day. The worker sells the capitalist a working day for

his day's wages. But, *what is a working day?* Eight hours or eighteen?

It is to the capitalist's interest to make the working day as long as possible. The longer it is, the more surplus value it produces. The worker correctly feels that every hour of labor which he performs over and above the replacement of the wage is unjustly taken from him; he learns from bitter personal experience what it means to work excessive hours. The capitalist fights for his profit, the worker for his health, for a few hours of daily rest, to be able to engage in other human activities as well, besides working, sleeping and eating. It may be remarked in passing that it does not depend at all upon the good will of the individual capitalists whether they desire to embark on this struggle or not, since competition compels even the most philanthropic among them to join his colleagues and to make a working time as long as theirs the rule.

The struggle for the fixing of the working day has lasted from the first appearance of free workers in the arena of history down to the present day. In various trades various traditional working days prevail; but in reality they are seldom adhered to. Only where the law fixes the working day and supervises its observance can one really say that there exists a normal working day. And up to now this is the case almost solely in the factory districts of England. Here the ten-hour working day (ten and a half hours on five days, seven and a half hours on Saturday) has been fixed for all women and for youths of thirteen to eighteen, and since the men cannot work without them, they also come under the ten-hour working day. This law has been won by English factory workers by years of endurance, by the most persistent, stubborn struggle with the factory owners, by freedom of the press, the right of association and assembly, as well as by adroit utilization of the splits in the ruling class itself. It has become the palladium of the English workers, it has gradually been extended to all important branches of industry and last year *to* almost *all trades,* at least to all those employing women and children. The present work contains most exhaustive material on the history of this legislative regulation of the working day in England. The next North German Reichstag will also have factory regulations to discuss and in connection therewith the regulation of factory labor. We expect that none of the deputies that have been elected by German workers will proceed to discuss this bill without previously making themselves thoroughly conversant with *Marx's* book. *There is much to be achieved here.* The splits within the ruling classes are more favourable to the workers than they ever were in England, because *universal suffrage compels the ruling classes to court the favour of the workers.* Under these circumstances, four or five representatives of the proletariat are *a power,* if they know how to use their position, if above all they know what is at issue, which the bourgeois do not know. And for this purpose, Marx's book gives them all the material in ready form.

We will pass over a number of further very fine investigations of more theoretical interest and will halt only at the final chapter which deals with the accumulation of capital. Here it is first shown that the capitalist mode of production, that is, that effected by capitalists on the one hand and wage-workers on the other, not only continually produces anew for the capitalist his capital, but at the same time also continually produces anew the poverty of the workers; thereby it is provided for that there always exist anew, on the one hand, capitalists who are the owners of all means of subsistence, all raw materials and all instruments of labor, and, on the other hand, the great mass of the workers, who are compelled to sell their labor power to these capitalists for an amount of the means of subsistence which at best just suffices to keep them able-bodied and to bring up a new generation of able-bodied proletarians. But capital does not merely reproduce itself: it is continually increased and multiplied—and thereby its power over the propertyless class of workers. And just as it itself is reproduced on an ever greater scale, so the modern capitalist mode of production reproduces the class of propertyless workers also on an ever greater scale and in ever greater numbers. ". . . Accumulation of capital reproduces the capital-relation on a progressive scale, more capitalists or larger capitalists at this pole, more wage-workers at that. . . . *Accumulation of capital is, therefore, increase of the pro-*

letariat." Since, however, owing to the progress of machinery, owing to improved agriculture, etc., fewer and fewer workers are necessary in order to produce the same quantity of products, since this perfecting, that is, this making the workers superfluous, grows more rapidly than even the growing capital, what becomes of this ever-increasing number of workers? They form an industrial reserve army, which, when business is bad or middling, is paid *below* the value of its labor and is irregularly employed or is left to be cared for by public charity, but which is indispensable to the capitalist class at times when business is especially lively, as is palpably evident in England—but which *under all circumstances* serves to break the power of resistance of the regularly employed workers and to keep their wages down. "The greater the social wealth . . . the greater is the relative surplus-population, or industrial reserve-army. But the greater this reserve-army in proportion to the active (regularly employed) labor-army, the greater is the mass of a consolidated (permanent) surplus-population, or strata of workers, whose misery is in inverse ratio to its torment of labor. The more extensive, finally, the lazarus-layers of the working-class, and the industrial reserve-army, the greater is official pauperism. This is the absolute general law of capitalist accumulation."

These, strictly scientifically proved—and the official economists take great care not to make even an attempt at a refutation—are some of the chief laws of the modern, capitalist, social system. But does this tell the whole story? By no means. Marx sharply stresses the bad sides of capitalist production but with equal emphasis clearly proves that this social form was necessary to develop the productive forces of society to a level which will make possible an equal development worthy of human beings for *all* members of society. All earlier forms of society were too poor for this. Capitalist production is the first to create the wealth and the productive forces necessary for this, but at the same time it also creates, in the numerous and oppressed workers, the social class which is compelled more and more to take possession of this wealth and these productive forces in order to utilize them for the whole of society—instead of their being utilized, as they are today, for a monopolist class.

Marx to F. Bolte (November 23, 1871)

By the late fall of 1871 the International Workingmen's Association was in rapid decline. Factional struggles had marked its history throughout, but none was so serious as that between Marx and Bakunin, the leading apostle of anarchism. Bakunin had many followers among the workers in France, Italy, Spain and Switzerland. Inveterate opponents of organization as such, these anarchists were everywhere a divisive force. The International also suffered a serious blow following the fall of the Paris Commune in 1871. Workers' organizations were thereafter suppressed or kept under careful surveillance by anxious governments throughout Europe. Membership fell off sharply, and relations between the General Council, which Marx dominated, and the separate organizations grew increasingly strained. As is obvious from the letter below, Marx had written off the International by late 1871. Its work, he believed, was done. By defining demands for economic reform it had prepared the working class for its ultimate goal, the conquest of political power. In 1872, at Marx's suggestion, the headquarters of the International was shifted to New York where it could be better protected from opposing factions. Four years later it expired.

▼ ▼ ▼

. . . The *International* was founded in order to replace the socialist or semi-socialist sects by a real organization of the working class for the struggle. The original Rules and the Inaugural Address show this at the first glance. On the other hand, the International could not have maintained itself if the course of history had not already smashed the sectarian system. The development of the system of socialist sects and that of the real workers' movement are always inversely proportional to each other. So long as the sects are (historically) justified, the working class is not yet ripe for an independent historic movement. As soon as it has attained this maturity all sects are essentially reactionary. Nevertheless what history has shown everywhere was repeated in the history of the International. The antiquated attempts to re-establish itself and maintain its position within the newly-achieved form.

And the history of the International was a *continual struggle on the part of the General Council* against the sects and amateur experiments which tried to maintain their position within the International itself against the real movement of the working class. This struggle was conducted at the *Congresses,* but far more in the private dealings of the General Council with the individual sections.

In Paris, as the Proudhonists (Mutualists) were co-founders of the Association, they naturally had the reins in their hands there for the first few years. Later, of course, collectivist, positivist, etc., groups were formed there in opposition to them.

In Germany—the Lassalle clique. I myself went on corresponding for two years with the notorious Schweitzer and proved irrefutably to him that Lassalle's organization is nothing but a sectarian organization and as such hostile to the organization of the *real* workers' movement striven for by the International. He had his "reasons" for not understanding this.

At the end of 1868 the Russian Bakunin entered the *International* with the aim of forming inside it a *second International* called the *"Alliance de la Démocratie Socialiste,"* *with himself as leader.* He—a man devoid of all theoretical knowledge—put forward the pretension of representing in this separate body the *scientific* propaganda of the International, and of making it the specialty of this *second International within the International.*

His program was a hash superficially scraped together from right and left—*EQUALITY of CLASSES* (!), *abolition of the right of inheritance* as the *starting-point* of the social movement (Saint-Simonistic nonsense), *atheism* as a *dogma* to be dictated to the members, etc., and as the main dogma (*Proudhonist*) *abstention from the political movement.*

This fable for children found favor in (and still has a certain hold on) Italy and Spain, where the real conditions of the workers' movement are as yet little developed, and among a few vain, ambitious and empty doctrinaires in Latin Switzerland and in Belgium.

For M. Bakunin, doctrine (the assembled rubbish he has begged from Proudhon, Saint-Simon, etc.) was and is a secondary affair—merely a means to his personal self-assertion. While he is a nonentity as a theoretician, he is in his element as an intriguer.

For years the General Council had to fight against this conspiracy (supported up to a certain point by the French Proudhonists, especially in the *South of France*). At last, by means of Conference resolutions 1, 2 and 3, IX and XVI and XVII, it delivered its long prepared blow.

Obviously the General Council does not support in America what it combats in Europe. Resolutions 1, 2, 3 and IX now give the New York committee legal weapons with which to put an end to all sectarian formations and amateur groups, and if necessary to expel them. . . .

The political movement of the working class has as its ultimate object, of course, the conquest of political power for the working class, and for this it is naturally necessary that a previous organization of the working class, arising from its economic struggles, should have been developed up to a certain point.

On the other hand, however, every movement in which the working class comes out as a *class* against the ruling classes and attempts to force them by pressure from without is a political movement. For instance, the attempt in a particular factory or even a particular trade to force a shorter working day out of the individual capitalists by strikes, etc., is a purely economic movement. On the other hand, the movement to force an eight-hour day, etc., *law* is a *political* movement. And in this way, out of the separate economic movements of the workers there grows up everywhere a *political* movement, that is to say, a movement of the *class*, with the object of achieving its interests in a general form, in a form possessing the virtue of being compulsory for society as a whole. If these movements presuppose a certain degree of previous organization they are themselves in like measure a means for the development of this organization.

Where the working class is not yet far enough advanced in its organization to undertake a decisive campaign against the collective power, that is, the political power, of the ruling classes, it must at any rate be trained for this by continual agitation against the ruling classes and adopting an attitude hostile to their policy. Otherwise it will remain a plaything in their hands, as the September Revolution in France showed, and as is also proved up to a certain point by the game Messrs. Gladstone and Co. have been successfully engaged in England even up to the present time.

ENGELS: SOCIALISM, UTOPIAN AND SCIENTIFIC (1877)

The rise of socialism in Germany attracted many intellectuals, among whom was an eccentric and pompous professor at the University of Berlin, Eugen Dühring. Dühring brought out several volumes in which he elaborated a gigantic synthesis of all knowledge, proving the inevitability of socialism. The work attracted much attention, particularly that part of it attacking Marx's economic theories. In 1877 Engels replied to Dühring in a long series of articles in the *Vorwärts*, the chief organ of the Socialist Party. These articles were immediately recognized as an important statement of Marxist philosophy and were brought out in a book, *Herr Dühring's Revolution in Science*. Later, the three chapters dealing with the historic evolution of socialism were published as a separate pamphlet, *Socialism: Utopian and Scientific*, of which an excerpt from Part III is given below.

▼ ▼ ▼

. . . Active social forces work exactly like natural forces: blindly, forcibly, destructively, so long as we do not understand, and reckon with, them. But when once we understand them, when once we grasp their action, their direction, their effects, it depends only upon ourselves to subject them more and more to our own will, and by means of them to reach our own ends. And this holds quite especially of the mighty productive forces of today. As long as we obstinately refuse to understand the nature and the character of these

social means of action—and this understanding goes against
the grain of the capitalist mode of production and its defenders—so long these forces are at work in spite of us, in
opposition to us, so long they master us, as we have shown
above in detail.

But when once their nature is understood, they can, in the
hands of the producers working together, be transformed
from master demons into willing servants. The difference is
as that between the destructive force of electricity in the
lightning of the storm, and electricity under command in
the telegraph and the voltaic arc; the difference between a
conflagration, and fire working in the service of man. With
this recognition, at last, of the real nature of the productive
forces of today, the social anarchy of production gives place
to a social regulation of production upon a definite plan,
according to the needs of the community and of each individual. Then the capitalist mode of appropriation, in which
the product enslaves first the producer and then the appro-
priator, is replaced by the mode of appropriation of the
products that is based upon the nature of the modern means
of production; upon the one hand, direct social appropriation,
as means to the maintenance and extension of production—
on the other, direct individual appropriation, as means of
subsistence and of enjoyment.

While the capitalist mode of production more and more
completely transforms the great majority of the population
into proletarians, it creates the power which, under penalty
of its own destruction, is forced to accomplish this revolution.
While it forces on more and more the transformation of the
vast means of production, already socialized, into state property, it shows itself the way to accomplishing this revolution.
*The proletariat seizes political power and turns the means of
production into state property.*

But, in doing this, it abolishes itself as proletariat, abolishes
all class distinctions and class antagonisms, abolishes also the
state as state. Society thus far, based upon class antagonisms,
had need of the state. That is, of an organization of the
particular class which was *pro tempore* the exploiting class,
an organization for the purpose of preventing any interference

from without with the existing conditions of production, and, therefore, especially, for the purpose of forcibly keeping the exploited classes in the condition of oppression corresponding with the given mode of production (slavery, serfdom, wage-labor). The state was the official representative of society as a whole; the gathering of it together into a visible embodiment. But it was this only in so far as it was the state of that class which itself represented, for the time being, society as a whole: in ancient times, the state of slaveowning citizens; in the Middle Ages, the feudal lords; in our own time, the bourgeoisie. When at last it becomes the real representative of the whole of society, it renders itself unnecessary. As soon as there is no longer any social class to be held in subjection; as soon as class rule, and the individul struggle for existence based upon our present anarchy in production, with the collisions and excesses arising from these, are removed, nothing more remains to be repressed, and a special repressive force, a state, is no longer necessary. The first act by virtue of which the state really constitutes itself the representative of the whole of society—the taking possession of the means of production in the name of society—this is, at the same time, its last independent act as a state. State interference in social relations becomes, in one domain after another, superfluous, and then dies out of itself; the government of persons is replaced by the administration of things, and by the conduct of processes of production. The state is not "abolished." *It dies out.* This gives the measure of the value of the phrase *"a free state,"* both as to its justifiable use at times by agitators, and as to its ultimate scientific insufficiency; and also of the demands of the so-called anarchists for the abolition of the state out of hand.

Since the historical appearance of the capitalist mode of production, the appropriation by society of all the means of production has often been dreamed of, more or less vaguely, by individuals, as well as by sects, as the ideal of the future. But it could become possible, could become a historical necessity, only when the actual conditions for its realization were there. Like every other social advance, it becomes practicable, not by men understanding that the existence of

classes is in contradiction to justice, equality, etc., not by
the mere willingness to abolish these classes, but by virtue
of certain new economic conditions. The separation of society into an exploiting and an exploited class, a ruling and
an oppressed class, was the necessary consequence of the
deficient and restricted development of production in former
times. So long as the total social labor only yields a produce
which but slightly exceeds that barely necessary for the
existence of all; so long, therefore, as labor engages all or
almost all the time of the great majority of the members of
society—so long, of necessity, this society is divided into
classes. Side by side with the great majority, exclusively bond
slaves to labor, arises a class freed from directly productive
labor, which looks after the general affairs of society: the
direction of labor, state business, law, science, art, etc. It is,
therefore, the law of division of labor that lies at the basis
of the division into classes. But this does not prevent this
division into classes from being carried out by means of
violence and robbery, trickery and fraud. It does not prevent
the ruling class, once having the upper hand, from consolidating its power at the expense of the working class, from
turning its social leadership into an intensified exploitation of
the masses.

But if, upon this showing, division into classes has a certain
historical justification, it has this only for a given period, only
under given social conditions. It was based upon the insufficiency of production. It will be swept away by the complete
development of modern productive forces. And, in fact,
the abolition of classes in society presupposes a degree of
historical evolution at which the existence, not simply of this
or that particular ruling class, but of any ruling class at all,
and, therefore, the existence of class distinction itself has
become an obsolete anachronism. It presupposes, therefore,
the development of production carried out to a degree at
which appropriation of the means of production and of the
products, and, with this, of political domination, of the monopoly of culture, and of intellectual leadership by a particular class of society, has become not only superfluous but

economically, politically, intellectually, a hindrance to development.

This point is now reached. Their political and intellectual bankruptcy is scarcely any longer a secret to the bourgeoisie themselves. Their economic bankruptcy recurs regularly every ten years. In every crisis, society is suffocated beneath the weight of its own productive forces and products, which it cannot use, and stands helpless, face to face with the absurd contradiction that the producers have nothing to consume, because consumers are wanting. The expansive force of the means of production bursts the bonds that the capitalist mode of production had imposed upon them. Their deliverance from these bonds is the one precondition for an unbroken, constantly accelerated development of the productive forces, and therewith for a practically unlimited increase of production itself. Nor is this all. The socialized appropriation of the means of production does away, not only with the present artificial restrictions upon production, but also with the positive waste and devastation of productive forces and products that are at the present time the inevitable concomitants of production, and that reach their height in the crises. Further, it sets free for the community at large a mass of means of production and of products, by doing away with the senseless extravagance of the ruling classes of today and their political representatives. The possibility of securing for every member of society, by means of socialized production, an existence not only fully sufficient materially, and becoming day by day more full, but an existence guaranteeing to all the free development and exercise of their physical and mental faculties—this possibility is now for the first time here, but *it is here.*

With the seizing of the means of production by society, production of commodities is done away with, and, simultaneously, the mastery of the product over the producer. Anarchy in social production is replaced by systematic, definite organization. The struggle for individual existence disappears. Then for the first time man, in a certain sense, is finally marked off from the rest of the animal kingdom, and emerges from mere animal conditions of existence into really human ones. The whole sphere of the conditions of life which environ man, and which have hitherto ruled man, now comes under the dominion and control of man, who for the first time becomes the real, conscious lord of Nature, because he has now become master of his own social organization. The laws of his own social action, hitherto standing face to face with man as laws of Nature foreign to, and dominating him, will then be used with full understanding, and so mastered by him. Man's own social organization, hitherto confronting him as a necessity imposed by Nature and history, now becomes the result of his own free action. The extraneous objective forces that have hitherto governed history pass under the control of man himself. Only from that time will man himself, more and more consciously, make his own history—only from that time will the social causes set in movement by him have, in the main and in a constantly growing measure, the results intended by him. It is the ascent of man from the kingdom of necessity to the kingdom of freedom.

Let us briefly sum up our sketch of historical evolution.

I. *Medieval Society*—Individual production on a small scale. Means of production adapted for individual use; hence primitive, ungainly, petty, dwarfed in action. Production for immediate consumption, either of the producer himself or of his feudal lord. Only where an excess of production over this consumption occurs is such excess offered for sale, enters into exchange. Production of commodities, therefore, only in its infancy. But already it contains within itself, in embryo, *anarchy in the production of society at large*.

II. *Capitalist Revolution*—Transformation of industry, at first by means of simple co-operation and manufacture. Concentration of the means of production, hitherto scattered, into great workshops. As a consequence, their transformation from individual to social means of production—a transformation which does not, on the whole, affect the form of exchange. The old forms of appropriation remain in force. The capitalist appears. In his capacity as owner of the means of production, he also appropriates the products and turns them into commodities. Production has become a *social* act. Exchange and appropriation continue to be *individual* acts, the acts of individuals. *The social product is appropriated by the individual capitalist.* Fundamental contradiction, whence arise all the contradictions in which our present-day society moves, and which modern industry brings to light.

A. Severance of the producer from the means of production. Condemnation of the worker to wage-labor for life. *Antagonism between the proletariat and the bourgeoisie.*

B. Growing predominance and increasing effectiveness of the laws governing the production of commodities. Unbridled competition. *Contradiction between socialized organization in the individual factory and social anarchy in production as a whole.*

C. On the one hand, perfecting of machinery, made by competition compulsory for each individual manufacturer, and complemented by a constantly growing displacement of laborers. *Industrial reserve army.* On the other hand, unlimited extension of production, also compulsory under competition, for every manufacturer. On both sides, unheard-of development of productive forces, excess of supply over demand, over-production, glutting of the markets, crises every ten years, the vicious circle: excess here, of means of production and products—excess there, of laborers, without employment and without means of existence. But these two levers of production and of social well-being are unable to work together, because the capitalist form of production prevents the productive forces from working and the products from circulating, unless they are first turned into capital —which their very superabundance prevents. The contradiction has grown into an absurdity. *The mode of production rises in rebellion against the form of exchange.* The bourgeoisie are convicted of incapacity further to manage their own social productive forces.

D. Partial recognition of the social character of the productive forces forced upon the capitalists themselves. Taking over of the great institutions for production and communication, first by joint-stock companies, later on by trusts, then by the state. The bourgeoisie demonstrated to be a superfluous class. All its social functions are now performed by salaried employees.

III. *Proletarian Revolution*—Solution of the contradictions. The proletariat seizes the public power, and by means of this transforms the socialized means of production, slipping from the hands of the bourgeoisie, into public property. By this act, the proletariat frees the means of production from the character of capital they have thus far borne, and gives their socialized character complete freedom to work itself out. Socialized production upon a predetermined plan becomes henceforth possible. The development of production makes the existence of different classes of society thenceforth an anachronism. In proportion as anarchy in social production vanishes, the political authority of the state dies out. Man, at last the master of his own form of social organization, becomes at the same time the lord over Nature, his own master —free.

To accomplish this act of universal emancipation is the historical mission of the modern proletariat. To thoroughly comprehend the historical conditions and thus the very nature of this act, to impart to the now oppressed proletarian class a full knowledge of the conditions and of the meaning of the momentous act it is called upon to accomplish, this is the task of the theoretical expression of the proletarian movement, scientific socialism.

ENGELS TO F. MEHRING (JULY 14, 1893)

By 1890 the philosophy of dialectical materialism had become central to European socialism, and many books were being published on it. Engels thought that many of Marx's followers were too rigidly mechanical and deterministic, over-emphasizing economic "facts" and neglecting "ideas." In an important letter—to the man who would one day write the best biography of Marx—Engels attempted both to explicate and to qualify the materialist conception of history.

▼ ▼ ▼

Today is my first opportunity to thank you for the *Lessing Legend* you were kind enough to send me. I did not want to reply with a bare formal acknowledgement of receipt of the book but intended at the same time to tell you something about it, about its contents. Hence the delay.

I shall begin at the end—the appendix on historical materialism, in which you have lined up the main things excellently and for any unprejudiced person convincingly. If I find anything to object to it is that you give me more credit than I deserve, even if I count in everything which I might possibly have found out for myself—in time—but which Marx with his more rapid *coup d'œil* and wider vision discovered much more quickly. When one has the good fortune to work for forty years with a man like Marx, one does not usually get the recognition one thinks one deserves during his lifetime. Then, if the greater man dies, the lesser easily gets overrated and this seems to me to be just my case at present; history will set all this right in the end and by that time one will have quietly turned up one's toes and not know anything any more about anything.

Otherwise there is only one point lacking, which, however, Marx and I always failed to stress enough in our writings and in regard to which we are all equally guilty. That is to say, we all laid, and *were bound* to lay, the main emphasis, in the first place, on the *derivation* of political, juridical and other ideological notions, and of actions arising through the medium of these notions, from basic economic facts. But in so doing we neglected the formal side—the ways and means by which these notions, etc., come about—for the sake of the content. This has given our adversaries a welcome opportunity for misunderstandings and distortions. . . .

Ideology is a process accomplished by the so-called thinker consciously, it is true, but with a false consciousness. The real motive forces impelling him remain unknown to him; otherwise it simply would not be an ideological process. Hence he imagines false or seeming motive forces. Because it is a process of thought he derives its form as well as its content from pure thought, either his own or that of his predecessors. He works with mere thought material, which he accepts without examination as the product of thought, and does not investigate further for a more remote source independent of thought; indeed this is a matter of course to

him, because, as all action is *mediated* by thought, it appears
to him to be ultimately *based* upon thought.

The ideologist who deals with history (history is here simply meant to comprise all the spheres—political, juridical,
philosophical, theological—belonging to *society* and not only
to nature) thus possesses in every sphere of science material
which has formed itself independently out of the thought of
previous generations and has gone through its own independent process of development in the brains of these successive generations. True, external facts belonging to one or
another sphere may have exercised a codetermining influence
on this development, but the tacit presupposition is that
these facts themselves are also only the fruits of a process of
thought, and so we still remain within that realm of mere
thought, which apparently has successfully digested even the
hardest facts.

It is above all this appearance of an independent history
of state constitutions, of systems of law, of ideological conceptions in every separate domain that dazzles most people.
If Luther and Calvin "overcome" the official Catholic religion
or Hegel "overcomes" Fichte and Kant or Rousseau with
his republican *contrat social* indirectly overcomes the constitutional Montesquieu, this is a process which remains
within theology, philosophy or political science, represents a
stage in the history of these particular spheres of thought and
never passes beyond the sphere of thought. And since the
bourgeois illusion of the eternity and finality of capitalist production has been added as well, even the overcoming of the
mercantilists by the physiocrats and Adam Smith is accounted
as a sheer victory of thought; not as the reflection in thought
of changed economic facts but as the finally achieved correct
understanding of actual conditions subsisting always and
everywhere—in fact, if Richard Coeur de Lion and Philip
Augustus had introduced free trade instead of getting mixed
up in the crusades we should have been spared five hundred
years of misery and stupidity.

This aspect of the matter, which I can only indicate here,
we have all, I think, neglected more than it deserves. It is the
old story: form is always neglected at first for content. As I

say, I have done that too and the mistake has always struck me only later. So I am not only far from reproaching you with this in any way—as the older of the guilty parties I certainly have no right to do so; on the contrary. But I would like all the same to draw your attention to this point for the future.

Hanging together with this is the fatuous notion of the ideologists that because we deny an independent historical development to the various ideological spheres which play a part in history we also deny them any *effect upon history*. The basis of this is the common undialectical conception of cause and effect as rigidly opposite poles, the total disregarding of interaction. These gentlemen often almost deliberately forget that once a historic element has been brought into the world by other, ultimately economic causes, it reacts, can react on its environment and even on the causes that have given rise to it. . . .

Chapter VII

ANARCHISM

Anarchism was never an organized movement, much less an ideology; there were almost as many forms of anarchism as there were anarchists. Some, Thoreau and Godwin for example, were non-socialists; others, like Tolstoy, were anti-socialist. All of them, socialist or not, opposed political force as such because they believed it regimented, corrupted and degraded men. They were convinced that men were naturally perfect and, in the absence of coercive institutions, would live in peace and harmony and be endlessly creative. For anarchists, the whole basis of conventional morality was false. Order came not from the formal and abstract instruments of law but from the free and spontaneous relationships between equals.

The diverse schools of socialist anarchism agreed on several additional principles: first, that ownership of property (or the unequal ownership of property) was chiefly responsible for political coercion; second, that the power of property should be abolished along with the state; and third, that collective associations of producers, distributers and consumers should be formed in the smallest communities possible and should grow increasingly large and comprehensive, eventually embracing all mankind.

Before anarchism socialists of whatever persuasion had generally defined freedom—following Rousseau—as obedience to the general will, the highest expression of one's own will. By obeying the general will one obeys oneself and is therefore free. This view resolved the traditional dichotomies in political thought between liberty and authority and between individual and society; after Rousseau it was possible to hold that authority *was* liberty when self-imposed. So the Jacobins argued in 1793, and so the utopian socialists maintained in justifying their own authoritarian schemes. Marx was a scathing critic of this conception of freedom. His own form of socialism envisioned the removal of all legal restraints from society—but not before the proletariat had seized the state and used it to abolish the bourgeoisie. Politically, then, socialist anarchism ran counter to every other school of socialism.

Socialist anarchism lasted from the 1860s through World War I. Only in Spain did it continue to have sizeable support thereafter. Proudhon had been the first socialist to clearly oppose the state as such. But support for his ideas had been limited to southern France, and it was not until Michael Bakunin's appearance in Western Europe in the early 1860s that anarchism as a revolutionary philosophy gained real strength in the working classes of France, Italy and Switzerland. Bakunin exercised the greatest influence where the state was most oppressive and most alien to the working class, as in France and Italy, or where regionalism was strongest, as in Switzerland. He found little support in the important industrial countries. In Britain the state was becoming democratic, and in Germany opposition to autocracy after unification in 1871 took the form of a disciplined socialist movement.

Bakunin, as man and thinker, reflected the inveterate anarchist tendency to slough off discipline and seek quick solutions. Many anarchists resorted to isolated acts of violence against state officials. Bakunin himself condoned terror and foolishly let himself be caught up in a Russian nihilist plot. Perhaps consistency required anarchists to resort to terror, for if they denied any alternative to perfection nothing was left for them except to eliminate those who held power, but terror was more sensational than effective. In any case only a few anarchists were violent, though even fewer were pacifists. Bakunin's most noteworthy disciple, the venerable Peter Kropotkin, was certainly no advocate of violence, and in fact wrote his books on the philosophy of anarcho-communism

mainly for a sympathetic audience of middle-class Englishmen.

In the 1890s anarchism sprouted afresh among the working classes of France, Italy and Spain. Syndicalism expressed
their traditional, uncompromising antipathy to the state and
to bourgeois institutions in general; their attitude was epitomized by Georges Sorel's *Reflections on Violence*. Syndicalism
was partly responsible for the development of Guild Socialism, the most significant anarchist movement in English
history, which, although it lacked the strength and militancy
of French syndicalism, enjoyed a brief vogue among certain
socialist intellectuals and trade unions. But with the end of
World War I Guild Socialism was finished, and so was
syndicalism, whose last citadels—Spain excepted—fell before
the combined forces of democracy, fascism and communism,
all of which rested on strong central governments.

MICHAEL BAKUNIN (1814–76)

Traditionally, Western European political thought has attempted to reconcile freedom and order, holding that both
are necessary because each is worthy only within limits. But
in the Russian tradition, this reconciliation has rarely been
achieved. Russian revolutionaries of the nineteenth century
yearned for absolute freedom because despotism was the
only kind of order they had experienced. This contrast between Russia and the West was nowhere better exemplified
than in the person of Michael Bakunin.

Bakunin's whole life was defined by rebellion and by the
search for absolute freedom. Born in 1814 to a distinguished
and cultured landowning family, he continually headed re-
bellions in his youth, first leading his brothers and sisters
against their father, and later encouraging his sisters (to
whom he was too deeply attached) to rebel against their
husbands. His hatred of authority remained personal and
immediate until he arrived in Germany in the early 1840s.
There, under the influence of the Left Hegelians, he decided
to spend the rest of his life fighting political and religious

oppressors. To the extent that socialist anarchism had a system it was traceable to him. He formulated something like a doctrine of beliefs as an afterthought to his revolutionary activities.

He was actively involved in the 1848 revolutions and managed to get jailed by the three most oppressive governments in Europe: Prussia, Austria, and Russia. Altogether, he spent eight years in prison, often under the cruelest possible conditions. While in the Peter Paul fortress he was forced to make a self-abasing confession to Czar Nicholas. He finally escaped from Siberia, where he had been sent as an act of leniency, and returned to Western Europe via Japan and the United States. Before his imprisonment he had advocated pan-Slavism on the theory that a union of Slavic peoples throughout Eastern Europe would bring down the Czar. He resumed this line of conspiracy in the early 1860s but soon gave it up at the first stirrings of revolt by the working class.

Bakunin's agents made headway among the workers of Switzerland, Italy, France and Spain who, though few in number, were impatient for results. By the mid-1860s he had a substantial following. His labor organizations rivalled Marx's International. In 1868 he joined the International in hopes of boring from within, and set off a struggle in the organization that contributed to its demise several years later. Marx fought Bakunin relentlessly, ridiculing his ideas but taking seriously their effect on the working class. To Marx, direct action by the working class was impotent and self-destructive. Finally, in 1872 Marx had Bakunin expelled—not that it mattered very much, since that very year the corpse of the International was sent to America for burial. Bakunin despised Marx whom he thought a typically arrogant and authoritarian German and the chief apostle of socialism from above.

Bakunin had simplified Marx's task when he allowed himself to be duped by the notorious Nechayev, the young Russian nihilist who scrupled at nothing, including murder, in leading his own conspiracy against the Czar. Attracted to conspiracies wherever he found them, Bakunin was completely taken in by Nechayev's and was made a fool of, to the great detriment of his movement. His influence declined rapidly in the 1870s primarily because working-class insurgency died down after the fall of the Paris Commune in 1871. He died in 1876, disappointed in the weakness of mankind

The power of Bakunin's personality was legendary. For a while he impressed even Marx. A superb speaker, he wrote fluently in several languages. But he was appallingly irresponsible in his private affairs. Very few could put up with his personal habits, and he tended to lose friends and supporters as quickly as he made them.

The following is taken from a series of articles he wrote in the spring of 1869 for the journal *Le Progrés* of Geneva.

To the Comrades
of the International Workingmen's Association
of Locle and Chaux-de-Fonds (1869)

FIRST LETTER

Friends and Brothers,

I feel the need, before leaving your mountains, to express to you once again in writing my profound gratitude for the fraternal reception you have accorded me. Is it not a wonderful thing that a man, a Russian, a one-time noble, completely unknown to you when he arrived here, found himself surrounded by hundreds of friends almost the very moment that he set foot in your country? Such miracles no longer happen these days, except at the hands of the *International Workingmen's Association,* and that for one simple reason: the International alone represents today the historical life, the creative power of the social and political future. Those who are united by a living body of thought, by a will and a great passion held in common, are truly brothers, even if they do not realize it themselves.

There was a time when the bourgeoisie, endowed with the same power of life and exclusively constituting the historical class, offered the same spectacle of fraternity and union, in its acts as well as its thoughts. It was the finest hour of this class, ever respectable to be sure, but since that time impotent, stupid and sterile; it was the epoch of its most energetic development. Such was the case before the great revolution of 1793; such was still the case, although to a much lesser degree, before the revolutions of 1830 and 1848. In those days the bourgeoisie had a world to conquer, a place to take up in society, and, organized for battle, intelligent, audacious, feeling itself strong because it bore the principle of right for everyone, it was endowed with an irresistible omnipotence. It alone made three revolutions against the monarchy, the nobility and the clergy united.

In this epoch the bourgeoisie too had created an international association, a universal and formidable one, the *Freemasons*.

It would be a substantial error to judge the Freemasonry of the last century, or even that of the first part of the present century, by what it is today. The bourgeois institution *par excellence*, Freemasonry, in its development, in its growing power at first and later in its decadence, represented in a way the development, power, and moral and intellectual decadence of the bourgeoisie. Today, fallen to the sad position of a senile old intriguer, it is a useless, sometimes malevolent and always ridiculous nullity, whereas, before 1830 and especially before 1793, having gathered together at its core, with very few exceptions, all the minds of the elite, the most ardent hearts, the proudest spirits, the most audacious personalities, it had constituted an active, powerful, and truly beneficial institution. It was the energetic incarnation and implementation of the humanitarian ideal of the eighteenth century. All those great principles of liberty, equality and fraternity, of reason and human justice, elaborated theoretically at first by the philosophy of that century, became in the hands of the Freemasons practical dogmas and the foundations of a new moral and political program, the soul of a gigantic enterprise of demolition and reconstruction. In that epoch, Freemasonry was nothing less than the universal conspiracy of the revolutionary bourgeoisie against the feudal, monarchical and divine tyranny. It was the International of the bourgeoisie.

It is known that all the principal actors of the first revolution were Freemasons, and that when this revolution broke out it was able to find, thanks to Freemasonry, friends and devoted and powerful collaborators in all other countries, a fact that was assuredly of great help in its victories. But it is equally clear that the triumph of the revolution killed Freemasonry, for once the revolution had largely fulfilled the aspirations of the bourgeoisie, and had enabled it to displace the old nobility, the bourgeoisie went on quite naturally, after having been an exploited and oppressed class for such a long time, to become in its turn a privileged class, a class of exploiters, oppressive, conservative and reactionary in nature, the most reliable friend and supporter of the State. After the *coup d'Etat* of the first Napoleon, Freemasonry became an imperial institution throughout a large part of the European continent.

The Restoration resuscitated it somewhat. Seeing itself threatened by the return of the Old Regime, forced to concede to the coalition of Church and nobility the place that it had conquered through the first revolution, the bourgeoisie became of necessity revolutionary once again. But what a difference between this reheated revolutionarism and the ardent and powerful revolutionarism that had inspired it at the end of the last century! In the old days the bourgeoisie had been of good faith, had believed seriously and naively in the rights of man, had been driven along and inspired by the genius of demolition and reconstruction, had been in full possession of its intelligence and at the height of its powers. It had as yet no fears that an abyss might be separating it from the people; it felt itself, believed itself, to be the people's representative, and it really was. But the Thermidorean reaction and the Conspiracy of Babeuf deprived it of this notion forever. The abyss that separates the toiling people from the exploiting bourgeoisie, from the dominant class that takes everything for itself, has opened, and it will take nothing less than the entire body of the bourgeoisie, their whole privileged existence, to fill it in again.

Furthermore, it was no longer the bourgeoisie in its entirety, but only a part of it that returned, after the Restoration, to the task of conspiring against the clerical and aristocratic regime, and against the legitimate monarchs.

In my next letter, I shall, if you will be so good as to permit me, develop my ideas on this last phase of constitutional liberalism and bourgeois carbonarism.

SECOND LETTER

I said in a preceding article that the reactionary, legitimist, feudal and clerical threat had incited a revival of the revolutionary spirit of the bourgeoisie, but that between this new spirit and the one that had animated it before 1793, there was an enormous difference. The bourgeois of the last century were giants, in comparison with whom even the most daring of the bourgeoisie of this century seem to be only pygmies.

To be assured of this, one has only to compare their programs. What was the program of eighteenth-century philosophy and of the great revolution? Neither more nor less than the integral emancipation of all humanity; the realization of the rights and real and complete liberty of every man, through the social and political equalization of all; the triumph of the human world over the wreckage of the divine one; the reign of justice and fraternity over the earth. The trouble with this philosophy and this revolution was that neither understood that the realization of human brotherhood was impossible so long as States existed, and that the real abolition of classes, the political and social equalization of individuals, will be possible only through the equalization of the economic means of education, instruction, labor, and life for everyone. Nevertheless, one cannot reprove the eighteenth century for not having understood this. Social science is not created and studied solely in books; it needs the great lessons of history, and we had to have the revolution of 1789 and 1793, we had to undergo the experiences of 1830 and 1848, to be able to arrive at this henceforth irrefutable conclusion: that any political revolution that does not have economic equality as its *immediate and direct* purpose is, from the standpoint of the rights and interests of the people, only a disguised and hypocritical reaction.

This most simple and evident truth was still unknown at
the end of the eighteenth century, and when Babeuf appeared
and posed the economic and social question, the power of
the revolution had already been exhausted. But this man retains the honor of having posed the greatest problem that
had ever been posed in history, that of the emancipation of
humanity in its entirety.

In comparison with this immense program, what goal do
we see pursued by the program of revolutionary liberalism in
the era of the Restoration and the July Monarchy? Its so-
called liberty—so dignified, so modest, so well-regulated, so
restrained—was conceived entirely for the modified tempera-
ment of a half-sated bourgeoisie who, weary of combat and
impatient to begin enjoying the fruits of its victories, felt itself
still threatened, only no longer from above, but now from
below, and watched with inquietude as these innumerable
millions of exploited proletarians, tired of suffering and preparing to demand their rights in return, massed together
like a huge black finger pointing towards the horizon.

At the beginning of the present century this rising specter,
later to be baptised the "red specter," this terrible ghost of
the rights of all men opposed to the privileges of a fortunate
class, this justice and reason of the people, which, as they
progress, should reduce to dust the sophisms of political
economy, of jurisprudence, of bourgeois politics and metaphysics, became at the moment of the triumph of the bourgeoisie in the modern world, the constant nemesis of its
pleasures, the diminishers of its confidence and its spirit.

And nevertheless, the social question was still nearly unknown during the Restoration, or rather, nearly forgotten.
True, there were a few great isolated dreamers, such as
Saint-Simon, Robert Owen and Fourier, whose genius or
great hearts had guessed at the necessity for a radical transformation of the economic organization of society. Around
each of them a small number of devoted and ardent disciples
grouped themselves, forming a number of small churches,
but they were as little known as their masters were, and
exercised no influence outside their own groups. There was
still the communist testament of Babeuf, transmitted by

his illustrious friend and colleague, Buonarrotti, to the most energetic proletarians, by means of a popular and secret organization, but this was still only a subterranean activity. Its manifestations did not make themselves felt until later, during the July Monarchy, and it was not perceived at all by the bourgeois class during the Restoration. The people, the masses of workers, remained quiet and did not demand anything for themselves.

It is clear that if the specter of political justice had any sort of existence at all in this epoch, it could only have been in the bad conscience of the bourgeois. Where did this bad conscience come from? Were the bourgeois who lived under the Restoration any more wicked than had been their fathers who made the revolution of 1789 and 1793? Not in the slightest! They were virtually the same men, but placed in another *milieu*, in the midst of different political conditions, enriched by a new experience, and therefore possessing a different conscience.

The bourgeois of the last century had sincerely believed that in emancipating themselves from the monarchical, clerical, and feudal yoke they would emancipate all the people along with them. And this naive and sincere belief was the source of their heroic audacity and all their marvelous power. They felt themselves united with all men, and, marching into battle, they carried the rights and the strength of all men within themselves. Thanks to these rights and to this power of the people that had been incarnated, so to speak, in their class, the bourgeois of the last century were able to scale the fortress of political power that their forefathers had coveted for so many centuries, and capture it. But at the very moment when they planted their banner upon it, a new realization entered their minds. As soon as they had conquered the source of power, they began to understand that their bourgeois interests had nothing in common with the interests of the masses, that, on the contrary, the two were radically opposed, and that the power and exclusive prosperity of the possessing class had to be supported by the misery and social and political dependence of the proletariat.

From then on, the relationship between the bourgeoisie

and the people was radically transformed, and even before
the workers had come to understand that the bourgeois were
their natural enemies, much more through necessity than
ill will, the bourgeois had already become conscious of this
fatal antagonism. This is what I call the bad conscience of the
bourgeois.

THIRD LETTER

The bad conscience of the bourgeois paralyzed, as I have
said, the whole intellectual and moral movement of the
bourgeoisie at the beginning of this century. Let me correct
myself—I shall replace the word *paralyzed* with another:
perverted. For it would be incorrect to say that there was any
paralysis in a spirit which, passing from theory to the application of the positive sciences, created all the miracles of
modern industry, and which, by discovering a new science
—statistics—and by pursuing political economy and historical
criticism of the development of wealth and civilization to
the point where their fullest possibilities could be realized,
established the basis for a new philosophy—socialism—which
from the standpoint of the exclusive interests of the bourgeoisie is nothing but a sublime suicide, the very negation
of the bourgeois world.

The paralysis did not arrive until later, after 1848, when
the bourgeoisie, terrified by the results of its earlier efforts,
consciously placed itself behind the times, and when, to
preserve its possessions, it renounced all thought and will,
submitted itself to the protection of the military, and gave
itself over, body and soul, to the most complete reaction. Since
that time it has done no more inventing, but rather has lost,
along with its courage, the very power of creation. It no
longer retains even the power or spirit of self-preservation,
for everything that it has done and continues to do for its
salvation pushes it inexorably toward the abyss.

Until 1848, the bourgeoisie was still full of spirit. To be
sure, this spirit no longer coursed with that vigorous sap
that had enabled it, between the sixteenth and eighteenth
centuries, to create a new world. This was no longer the

heroic spirit of a class that was highly audacious because it had to conquer everything: it was the prudent and reflective spirit of a new property owner who, after having acquired an ardently coveted possession, was determined to make it prosper and increase in value. The spirit of the bourgeoisie in the first half of this century can be characterized in particular by its almost exclusively utilitarian tendency.

The bourgeoisie has been reproached for this, and wrongly. I believe, on the contrary, that it has rendered a last great service to humanity by preaching, much more through example than through its theories, the cult of, or rather the respect for, material interests. Basically, such interests have always prevailed in the world, but until now they always manifested themselves under the cloak of a hypocritical or unhealthy idealism, which is precisely what always transformed them into malicious and iniquitous interests.

No one at all interested in the study of history could have failed to see that there was always some great material interest at the bottom of even the most abstract, the most sublime and idealistic theological and religious struggles. No war of races, nations, States or classes has ever been waged with any purpose other than domination, which is the condition and necessary guarantee of the possession and free use of goods. Human history, considered from this point of view, is nothing but the continuation of that great struggle for existence that, according to Darwin, constitutes the fundamental law of organic nature.

In the animal world, this battle takes place without ideas and without phases, and is furthermore without a solution; as long as the earth exists, the animal world will devour itself. This is the natural condition of its life. Human beings, carnivorous animals *par excellence*, began their history with this cannibalism. Today they tend towards universal association, and the collective production and use of goods.

But between these two points, what bloody and horrible tragedy! And we are not yet finished with this tragedy. After cannibalism came slavery, after slavery serfdom, after serfdom wage-labor, after which the terrible day of justice is to come, and only then, much later, the era of fraternity. These are

the phases through which the animal struggle for life is
transformed gradually, in history, into the human organization of life.

And, in the middle of this fratricidal combat of man
against man, amidst this mutual destruction, amidst this
reduction of men to servitude by a few who have maintained
themselves, under different names and forms, throughout the
centuries, what role did religion play? Religion has always
sanctified violence, and transformed it into right. It has
whisked away humanity, justice and fraternity into a fictitious
heaven, so as to leave room on earth for the reign of iniquity
and brutality. It has blessed successful brigands, and, in
order to increase their fortune even further, has preached
obedience and resignation to their innumerable victims, the
peoples. And, the more sublime the ideal adored in heaven
appeared to be, the more horrible became the reality on
earth. For it is in the nature of all idealism, whether religious
or metaphysical, to despise the real world, and, in despising
it, to exploit it; with the result that all idealism necessarily
engenders hypocrisy.

Man is matter, and cannot despise matter with impunity.
He is an animal, and he cannot destroy his own animality.
But he can and must transform and humanize it through
freedom, that is, through the combined action of justice and
reason, which in their turn have a grip upon freedom because
they are its products and highest expression. On the other
hand, every time that man has tried to abstract himself
from his animality, he has become its slave and its toy: witness
the priesthood of the most absurd and most idealistic religion
in the world, Catholicism.

Compare their well-known obscenity with their vow of
chastity; compare their insatiable covetousness with their
doctrine of the renunciation of the things of this world; and
you will agree that there exist no other beings so materialistic
as these preachers of Christian idealism. At this very moment,
what is the question that is troubling the whole Church most
of all? The preservation of its possessions, which everywhere
today stand in danger of being confiscated by that other
Church, that expression of political idealism, the State.

Political idealism is no less absurd, pernicious or hypocritical than the idealism of religion, and is, besides, only a different form of it, being its worldly and terrestrial expression and application. The State is the younger brother of the Church, and patriotism, that virtue and cult of the State, is only a reflection of the cult of the divine.

According to the precepts of the idealistic school, which is religious and political at the same time, the virtuous man must serve God and devote himself to the State. And it is this doctrine that bourgeois utilitarianism began to combat, using justice as a weapon, at the beginning of this century.

FOURTH LETTER

One of the greatest services rendered by bourgeois utilitarianism is, as I have said, to have killed the religion of the state, patriotism. Patriotism is, as we know, an ancient virtue, born within the Greek and Roman republics, where there had never been any real religion other than that of the State, nor any object of worship except the State.

What is the State? It is, the metaphysicians and doctors of law answer, the *public thing*, the collective goods and interests, the rights of everyone as opposed to the dissolving action of the interests and selfish passions of each individual. It is justice and the realization of morality and virtue on earth. Therefore the individual can perform no more sublime act or greater duty than to devote himself, sacrifice himself, to the ideal of dying for the sake of the triumph and the power of the State.

This, in a few words, is the whole of the theology of the State. Let us now see if this political theology does not, like the religious theology, hide under its very beautiful and poetic appearance quite common and quite dirty realities.

We will begin by analyzing the idea itself of the State, as its advocates represent it to us. This is the sacrifice of the natural liberty and interests of each component—of individuals, and of such comparatively small collective units as associations, communes and provinces—to the interests and freedom of everyone, to the prosperity of the great whole.

But what, in reality, is this everyone, this whole? It is the agglomeration of all the individuals and all the tightly knit human collectivities that compose it. But what actually be-comes of the whole at the moment when all individual and local interests have been sacrificed in order to compose it and coordinate themselves within it? It is not the living whole, that allows each one to breathe at his ease, and be-comes more fruitful, more powerful, and freer, the more widely it develops within itself the full liberty and prosperity of every man. It is not the natural human society that con-firms and augments the life of every man by the life of all. On the contrary, it is the immolation of every individual, as of all local associations, the destructive abstraction of living society, the limitation, or rather, complete negation of life and all the parts that compose the "everyone," for the so-called good of everyone. It is the State, the altar of political religion, upon which the natural society is always immo-lated: a devouring universality, living upon human sacrifices, like the Church. The State, I repeat, is the younger brother of the Church.

In order to prove this identity of Church and State, I beg the reader to be so good as to note that the one, like the other, is founded essentially upon the idea of the sacrifice of life and of natural right, and that both have the same prin-ciple as their point of departure: that of the natural wicked-ness of men, which can be vanquished, according to the Church, only by divine grace and the death of the natural man in God, and according to the State, only by law and the immolation of the individual upon the altar of the State. Both strive to transform man, the one into a saint, the other into a citizen. But the natural man must die, for the religions of the Church and of the State unanimously pronounce his sentence.

Such, in its ideal purity, is the identical theory of the Church and of the State. It is a pure abstraction; but all historical abstractions presuppose historical facts. These facts, as I said in my last article, are of an utterly real and brutal nature: their nature is violence, conquest, spoliation and reduction to servitude. Man is formed in such a way, that he cannot settle for merely acting, but must also explain and legitimize his acts before his own conscience and the eyes of the world. Religion came along, therefore, to bless the acts that had been performed, and thanks to this benediction, the iniquitous and brutal deed is transformed into right. Juridical science and political right are, as is well known, issues of theology first of all, and secondly of metaphysics, which is nothing but a disguised theology, a theology that makes the pretense of not being absurd and vainly strives to give its content a scientific aspect.

Let us now examine the role this abstraction, the State, parallel to the historical abstraction called the Church, has played and continues to play in real life, in human society.

The State is, as I have said, by its very principle an immense cemetery in which all manifestations of individual and local life, all the interests of the parts that together constitute society, come to sacrifice themselves, to die and be buried. It is the altar upon which real liberty and the well-being of peoples are immolated for the sake of political grandeur; and the more complete this immolation, the more perfect is the State. I conclude from this, and it is my conviction, that the Empire of Russia is the State *par excellence*, the State without rhetoric and without slogans, the most perfect State in Europe. Any State, on the other hand, in which the people can still breathe, is, from the standpoint of the ideal, an incomplete State, just as all the other Churches are, in comparison with the Roman Catholic Church, only partly realized as Churches.

The State is, as I have said, a voracious abstraction of the life of the people; but in order for an abstraction to come into being, develop and continue to exist in the real world, there must be a real collective body interested in its existence. This cannot be the great mass of the people, since they are precisely its victims; it must be a privileged body, the sacerdotal body of the State, the governing and political class that is to the State what the sacerdotal class of religion, the priesthood, is to the Church.

And what do we really see in all of history? The State has always been the patrimony of some privileged class, whether

sacerdotal, noble, or bourgeois, and, in the end, when all
the other classes have been used up, of a bureaucratic class.
The State descends or rises up, depending upon how you
look at it, into the condition of a machine. It is absolutely
necessary for its welfare that there be some privileged class
interested in its existence. And it is precisely the solidary
interest of this privileged class that we call *patriotism*.

PETER KROPOTKIN (1842–1921)

After Bakunin's death in 1876 anarchism presented a terrifying aspect to the world. In the 1880s and '90s no statesman
in Europe and America was safe from attack. The anarchist
ethic of individualism permitted acts of violence by persons,
as distinguished from those by governments—violence all
the more terrifying for its unpredictability. Though the
"propagandists of the deed" were small in number even
among anarchists, and completely disorganized—for anarchists never worked well together—they gave the movement
as a whole a bad name. Only a man possessing the simplicity of faith and high moral integrity of a Peter Kropotkin,
Bakunin's successor as the leading exponent of anarchism,
could have won the respect of the non-anarchist world. The
qualities evident in his person as well as in his voluminous
writings carried his influence well beyond the tiny circle of
his followers.

Like Bakunin, Kropotkin was a Russian aristocrat, a prince,
who threw up his privileges because his love of humanity
would not allow him to abide Czarist tyranny. He was a
first-rate geologist and naturalist, which may be the reason
he later made it one of his chief tasks to reconcile Darwinism
and anarcho-communism. The turning point in his revolutionary career came in 1872 when, in Switzerland, he fell
under Bakunin's influence, though he never joined the older
man in conspiratorial activities. Kropotkin actively propa-
gandized for anarchism, especially in France, where he spent
several years in jail, though he never committed or sanctioned
violence. Like so many other revolutionists before him, he

settled down in England after his release, wrote many books and became a well-known and respected member of the community. He moved to Russia following the Revolution in 1917 and, disillusioned by Bolshevism, died there in 1921.

With all anarchists, Kropotkin believed that man is good and that external authority is evil. He differed from the main body of anarchists in his emphasis on the natural solidarity, as contrasted with the natural individualism, of men. This instinct is the subject of his best known work, *Mutual Aid.* It was Kropotkin's deepest hope that a way could be found to bring city and country, factory and farm, into a harmonious working relationship. He was open-minded as to the means, insisting only that the state had to be abolished before any other measures could be undertaken.

Mutual Aid originally appeared in the British magazine *Nineteenth Century* in occasional issues between 1890 and 1896.

MUTUAL AID (1889–95)

MUTUAL AID AMONG ANIMALS

The conception of struggle for existence as a factor of evolution, introduced into science by Darwin and Wallace, has permitted us to embrace an immensely-wide range of phenomena in one single generalization, which soon became the very basis of our philosophical, biological, and sociological speculations. An immense variety of facts:—adaptations of function and structure of organic beings to their surroundings; physiological and anatomical evolution; intellectual progress, and moral development itself, which we formerly used to explain by so many different causes, were embodied by Darwin in one general conception. We understood them as continued endeavours—as a struggle against adverse circumstances—for such a development of individuals, races, species and societies, as would result in the greatest possible fulness, variety, and intensity of life. It may be that at the outset Darwin himself was not fully aware of the generality of the factor which he first invoked for explaining one series only of facts relative to the accumulation of individual variations in incipient species. But he foresaw that the term which he was introducing into science would lose its philosophical and its only true meaning if it were to be used in its narrow sense only—that of a struggle between separate individuals for the sheer means of existence. And at the very beginning of his memorable work he insisted upon the term being taken in its "large and metaphorical sense including dependence of one being on another, and including (which is more important) not only the life of the individual, but success in leaving progeny."

While he himself was chiefly using the term in its narrow sense for his own special purpose, he warned his followers against committing the error (which he seems once to have committed himself) of overrating its narrow meaning. In *The Descent of Man* he gave some powerful pages to illustrate its proper, wide sense. He pointed out how, in numberless animal societies, the struggle between separate individuals for the means of existence disappears, how *struggle* is replaced by *co-operation*, and how that substitution results in the development of intellectual and moral faculties which secure to the species the best conditions for survival. He intimated that in such cases the fittest are not the physically strongest, nor the cunningest, but those who learn to combine so as mutually to support each other, strong and weak alike, for the welfare of the community. "Those communities," he wrote, "which included the greatest number of the most sympathetic members would flourish best, and rear the greatest number of offspring." The term, which originated from the narrow Malthusian conception of competition between each and all, thus lost its narrowness in the mind of one who knew Nature.

Unhappily, these remarks, which might have become the basis of most fruitful researches, were overshadowed by the masses of facts gathered for the purpose of illustrating the consequences of a real competition for life. Besides, Darwin never attempted to submit to a closer investigation the relative importance of the two aspects under which the struggle for existence appears in the animal world, and he never wrote the work he proposed to write upon the natural checks to over-multiplication, although that work would have been the crucial test for appreciating the real purport of individual struggle. Nay, on the very pages just mentioned, amidst data disproving the narrow Malthusian conception of struggle, the old Malthusian leaven reappeared—namely, in Darwin's remarks as to the alleged inconveniences of maintaining the "weak in mind and body" in our civilized societies (ch. v.). As if thousands of weak-bodied and infirm poets, scientists, inventors, and reformers, together with other thousands of so-called "fools" and "weak-minded enthusiasts," were not the most precious weapons used by humanity in its struggle for existence by intellectual and moral arms, which Darwin himself emphasized in those same chapters of *Descent of Man.*

It happened with Darwin's theory as it always happens with theories having any bearing upon human relations. Instead of widening it according to his own hints, his followers narrowed it still more. And while Herbert Spencer, starting on independent but closely-allied lines, attempted to widen the inquiry into that great question, "Who are the fittest?" especially in the appendix to the third edition of the *Data of Ethics,* the numberless followers of Darwin reduced the notion of struggle for existence to its narrowest limits. They came to conceive the animal world as a world of perpetual struggle among half-starved individuals, thirsting for one another's blood. They made modern literature resound with the war-cry of *woe to the vanquished,* as if it were the last word of modern biology. They raised the "pitiless" struggle for personal advantages to the height of a biological principle which man must submit to as well, under the menace of otherwise succumbing in a world based upon mutual extermination. Leaving aside the economists who know of natural science but a few words borrowed from second-hand vulgarizers, we must recognize that even the most authorized exponents of Darwin's views did their best to maintain those false ideas. . . .

MUTUAL AID AMONG OURSELVES

The mutual-aid tendency in man has so remote an origin, and is so deeply interwoven with all the past evolution of the

human race, that it has been maintained by mankind up to
the present time, notwithstanding all vicissitudes of history. It
was chiefly evolved during periods of peace and prosperity;
but when even the greatest calamities befell men—when whole
countries were laid waste by wars, and whole populations
were decimated by misery, or groaned under the yoke of tyranny—the same tendency continued to live in the villages and
among the poorer classes in the towns; it still kept them together, and in the long run it reacted even upon those ruling,
fighting, and devastating minorities which dismissed it as sentimental nonsense. And whenever mankind had to work out
a new social organization, adapted to a new phasis of development, its constructive genius always drew the elements
and the inspiration for the new departure from that same ever-
living tendency. New economical and social institutions, in so
far as they were a creation of the masses, new ethical systems,
and new religions, all have originated from the same source,
and the ethical progress of our race, viewed in its broad lines,
appears as a gradual extension of the mutual-aid principles
from the tribe to always larger and larger agglomerations, so
as to finally embrace one day the whole of mankind, without
respect to its divers creeds, languages, and races.

After having passed through the savage tribe, and next
through the village community, the Europeans came to work
out in medieval times a new form of organization, which had
the advantage of allowing great latitude for individual initiative, while it largely responded at the same time to man's
need of mutual support. A federation of village communities,
covered by a network of guilds and fraternities, was called
into existence in the medieval cities. The immense results
achieved under this new form of union—in well-being for all,
in industries, art, science, and commerce—were discussed at
some length in two preceding chapters, and an attempt was
also made to show why, towards the end of the fifteenth century, the medieval republics—surrounded by domains of hostile feudal lords, unable to free the peasants from servitude,
and gradually corrupted by ideas of Roman Cæsarism—were
doomed to become a prey to the growing military States.

However, before submitting for three centuries to come, to

the all-absorbing authority of the State, the masses of the people made a formidable attempt at reconstructing society on the old basis of mutual aid and support. It is well known by this time that the great movement of the reform was not a mere revolt against the abuses of the Catholic Church. It had its constructive ideal as well, and that ideal was life in free, brotherly communities. Those of the early writings and sermons of the period which found most response with the masses were imbued with ideas of the economical and social brotherhood of mankind. The "Twelve Articles" and similar professions of faith, which were circulated among the German and Swiss peasants and artisans, maintained not only every one's right to interpret the Bible according to his own understanding, but also included the demand of communal lands being restored to the village communities and feudal servitudes being abolished, and they always alluded to the "true" faith—a faith of brotherhood. At the same time scores of thousands of men and women joined the communist fraternities of Moravia, giving them all their fortune and living in numerous and prosperous settlements constructed upon the principles of communism. Only wholesale massacres by the thousand could put a stop to this widely-spread popular movement, and it was by the sword, the fire, and the rack that the young States secured their first and decisive victory over the masses of the people.

For the next three centuries the States, both on the Continent and in these islands, systematically weeded out all institutions in which the mutual-aid tendency had formerly found its expression. The village communities were bereft of their folkmotes, their courts and independent administration; their lands were confiscated. The guilds were spoliated of their possessions and liberties, and placed under the control, the fancy, and the bribery of the State's official. The cities were divested of their sovereignty, and the very springs of their inner life— the folkmote, the elected justices and administration, the sovereign parish and the sovereign guild—were annihilated; the State's functionary took possession of every link of what formerly was an organic whole. Under that fatal policy and the wars it engendered, whole regions, once populous and wealthy, were laid bare; rich cities became insignificant boroughs; the very roads which connected them with other cities became impracticable. Industry, art, and knowledge fell into decay. Political education, science, and law were rendered subservient to the idea of State centralization. It was taught in the Universities and from the pulpit that the institutions in which men formerly used to embody their needs of mutual support could not be tolerated in a properly organized State; that the State alone could represent the bonds of union between its subjects; that federalism and "particularism" were the enemies of progress, and the State was the only proper initiator of further development. By the end of the last century the kings on the Continent, the Parliament in these isles, and the revolutionary Convention in France, although they were at war with each other, agreed in asserting that no separate unions between citizens must exist within the State; that hard labor and death were the only suitable punishments to workers who dared to enter into "coalitions." "No state within the State!" The State alone, and the State's Church, must take care of matters of general interest, while the subjects must represent loose aggregations of individuals, connected by no particular bonds, bound to appeal to the Government each time that they feel a common need. Up to the middle of this century this was the theory and practice in Europe. Even commercial and industrial societies were looked at with suspicion. As to the workers, their unions were treated as unlawful almost within our own lifetime in this country and within the last twenty years on the Continent. The whole system of our State education was such that up to the present time, even in this country, a notable portion of society would treat as a revolutionary measure the concession of such rights as every one, freeman or serf, exercised five hundred years ago in the village folkmote, the guild, the parish, and the city.

The absorption of all social functions by the State necessarily favoured the development of an unbridled, narrow-minded individualism. In proportion as the obligations towards the State grew in numbers the citizens were evidently relieved from their obligations towards each other. In the guild—and in medieval times every man belonged to some guild or fraternity—two "brothers" were bound to watch in turns a brother who had fallen ill; it would be sufficient now to give one's neighbour the address of the next paupers' hospital. In barbarian society, to assist at a fight between two men, arisen from a quarrel, and not to prevent it from taking a fatal issue, meant to be oneself treated as a murderer; but under the theory of the all-protecting State the bystander need not intrude: it is the policeman's business to interfere, or not. And while in a savage land, among the Hottentots, it would be scandalous to eat without having loudly called out thrice whether there is not somebody wanting to share the food, all that a respectable citizen has to do now is to pay the poor tax and to let the starving starve. The result is, that the theory which maintains that men can, and must, seek their own happiness in a disregard of other people's wants is now triumphant all round—in law, in science, in religion. It is the religion of the day, and to doubt of its efficacy is to be a dangerous Utopian. Science loudly proclaims that the struggle of each against all is the leading principle of nature, and of human societies as well. To that struggle Biology ascribes the progressive evolution of the animal world. History takes the same line of argument; and political economists, and their naïve ignorance, trace all progress of modern industry and machinery to the "wonderful" effects of the same principle. The very religion of the pulpit is a religion of individualism, slightly mitigated by more or less charitable relations to one's neighbours, chiefly on Sundays. "Practical" men and theorists, men of science and religious preachers, lawyers and politicians, all agree upon one thing—that individualism may be more or less softened in its harshest effects by charity, but that it is the only secure basis for the maintenance of society and its ulterior progress.

It seems, therefore, hopeless to look for mutual-aid institutions and practices in modern society. What could remain of them? And yet, as soon as we try to ascertain how the millions of human beings live, and begin to study their everyday relations, we are struck with the immense part which the mutual-aid and mutual-support principles play even now-a-days in human life. Although the destruction of mutual-aid institutions has been going on in practice and theory, for full three or four hundred years, hundreds of millions of men continue to live under such institutions; they piously maintain them and endeavour to reconstitute them where they have ceased to exist. In our mutual relations every one of us has his moments of revolt against the fashionable individualistic creed of the day, and actions in which men are guided by their mutual-aid inclinations constitute so great a part of our daily intercourse that if a stop to such actions could be put all further ethical progress would be stopped at once. Human society itself could not be maintained for even so much as the lifetime of one single generation. These facts, mostly neglected by sociologists and yet of the first importance for the life and further elevation of mankind, we are now going to analyze, beginning with the standing institutions of mutual support, and passing next to those acts of mutual aid which have their origin in personal or social sympathies. . . .

CONCLUSION

. . . It is especially in the domain of ethics that the dominating importance of the mutual-aid principle appears in full. That mutual aid is the real foundation of our ethical conceptions seems evident enough. But whatever the opinions as to the first origin of the mutual-aid feeling or instinct may be—whether a biological or a supernatural cause is ascribed to it—we must trace its existence as far back as to the lowest stages of the animal world; and from these stages we can follow its uninterrupted evolution, in opposition to a number of contrary agencies, through all degrees of human development, up to the present times. Even the new religions which were born from time to time—always at epochs when the mutual-aid principle was falling into decay in the theocracies and despotic States of the East, or at the decline of the Roman Empire—even the new religions have only reaffirmed that same principle. They found their first supporters among the humble, in the lowest, down-trodden layers of society, where the mutual-aid principle is the necessary foundation of everyday life; and the new forms of union which were introduced in the earliest Buddhist and Christian communities, in the Moravian brotherhoods and so on, took the character of a return to the best aspects of mutual aid in early tribal life.

Each time, however, that an attempt to return to this old principle was made, its fundamental idea itself was widened. From the clan it was extended to the stem, to the federation of stems, to the nation, and finally—in ideal, at least—to the whole of mankind. It was also refined at the same time. In primitive Buddhism, in primitive Christianity, in the writings of some of the Mussulman teachers, in the early movements of the Reform, and especially in the ethical and philosophical movements of the last century and of our own times, the total abandonment of the idea of revenge, or of "due reward"—of good for good and evil for evil—is affirmed more and more vigorously. The higher conception of "no revenge for wrongs," and of freely giving more than one expects to receive from his neighbours, is proclaimed as being the real principle of morality—a principle superior to mere equivalence, equity, or justice, and more conducive to happiness. And man is appealed to to be guided in his acts, not merely by love, which is always personal, or at the best tribal, but by the perception of his oneness with each human being. In the practice of mutual aid, which we can retrace to the earliest beginnings of evolution, we thus find the positive and undoubted origin of our ethical conceptions; and we can affirm that in the ethical progress of man, mutual support—not mutual struggle—has had the leading part. In its wide extension, even at the present time, we also see the best guarantee of a still loftier evolution of our race.

SYNDICALISM

French trade unionists shaped the doctrine of syndicalism between 1895 and World War I in protest against the encroachments of the state on the one hand and the growing tendency toward reformism within the socialist movement on the other. Despite its novel form, the protest kept faith with tradition. The anarchism of Proudhon and Bakunin had defined French working-class sentiment since the middle of the century, and it defined syndicalism as well. Syndicalists held that workers should control the industries in which they worked through their own trade unions and cooperatives. Each of these industrial syndicates should be autonomous, yet confederated with all the others. There would be no central government. Syndicalists further held that, in the absence of such a society, workers should express their solidarity and independence by direct action—the general strike.

The most famous and most extreme advocate of syndicalism, Georges Sorel, never personally had anything to do with trade unions or, for that matter, with any movement he defended. This freedom enabled him to anticipate, quite remarkably, some of the social movements—most notably fascism—that in time developed out of or were closely related to syndicalism. Sorel was born in Normandy in 1847 and, after receiving a private education there, attended the Ecole Polytechnique, where he distinguished himself in mathematics. He entered the civil service as an engineer and retired after the requisite twenty-five years, then promptly took up writing, and through innumerable books, established his place as a major social critic. Like Proudhon, Sorel had all the faults and virtues of the self-taught provincial: he read everything, assumed his ideas to be original discoveries and so enclosed them in the shell of dogma. He died in 1922, having lived long enough to bless the work of two favorites, Lenin and Mussolini.

Prior to his syndicalist phase Sorel had been a Marxist, and he never ceased to regard himself as one. What he disliked in Marxism was its abstract, intellectualist habits of thought and action. To his mind Marxist theory corresponded to the slow-moving stolid political organization that the German Socialist Party epitomized. To this intellectualism he opposed "intuitionalism" as Henri Bergson had explained it. "Intuitionalism" for Sorel took the form of a deliberately contrived myth that would inspirit the working class with iron solidarity and move it to take direct action by way of the general strike. This violent act was to be gratuitous; it was not to be undertaken with a view to consequences, for concern over consequences is intellectual and abstract.

Sorel's dislike of theory and patient planning led him to admire small conspiratorial groups who promised to effect radical social changes. He could thus support an extreme right-wing French nationalist movement at the same time that he defended trade union syndicalism and, after the war, could justify the activities of both Mussolini and Lenin because both led revolutionary conspiracies. As a thinker Sorel exercised little influence. Rather, he reflected the pre-war tendency of many socialists to embrace action at any cost in a world that had grown ruthlessly rational and ordered. They soon found in fascism a doctrine that better suited them.

REFLECTIONS ON VIOLENCE (1906)

. . . Every time that we attempt to obtain an exact conception of the ideas behind proletarian violence we are forced to go back to the notion of the general strike; and this same conception may render many other services, and throw an unexpected light on all the obscure parts of Socialism. In the last pages of the first chapter I compared the general strike to the Napoleonic battle which definitely crushes an adversary; this comparison will help us to understand the part played by the general strike in the world of ideas.

Military writers of to-day, when discussing the new methods of war necessitated by the employment of troops infinitely more numerous than those of Napoleon, equipped with arms much more deadly than those of his time, do not for all that imagine that wars will be decided in any other way than that of the Napoleonic battle. The new tactics proposed must fit into the drama Napoleon had conceived; the detailed development of the combat will doubtless be quite different from what it used to be, but the end must always be the catastrophic defeat of the enemy. The methods of military instruction are intended to prepare the soldier for this great and terrible action, in which everybody must be ready to take part at the first signal. From the highest to the lowest, the members of a really solid army have always in mind this catastrophic issue of international conflicts.

The revolutionary Syndicates argue about Socialist action

exactly in the same manner as military writers argue about war; they restrict the whole of Socialism to the general strike; they look upon every combination as one that should culminate in this catastrophe; they see in each strike a reduced facsimile, an essay, a preparation for the great final upheaval.

The *new school*, which calls itself Marxist, Syndicalist, and revolutionary, declared in favour of the idea of the general strike as soon as it became clearly conscious of the true sense of its own doctrine, of the consequences of its activity, and of its own originality. It was thus led to leave the old official, Utopian, and political tabernacles, which hold the general strike in horror, and to launch itself into the true current of the proletarian revolutionary movement; for a long time past the proletariat had made adherence to the principle of the general strike the *test* by means of which the Socialism of the workers was distinguished from that of the amateur revolutionaries.

Parliamentary Socialists can only obtain great influence if they can manage, by the use of a very confused language, to impose themselves on very diverse groups; for example, they must have working-men constituents simple enough to allow themselves to be duped by high-sounding phrases about future collectivism; they are compelled to represent themselves as profound philosophers to stupid middle-class people who wish to appear to be well informed about social questions; it is very necessary also for them to be able to exploit rich people who think that they are earning the gratitude of humanity by taking shares in the enterprises of Socialist politicians. This influence is founded on balderdash, and our bigwigs endeavour —sometimes only too successfully—to spread confusion among the ideas of their readers; they detest the general strike because all propaganda carried on from that point of view is too socialistic to please philanthropists.

In the mouths of these self-styled representatives of the proletariat all socialistic formulas lose their real sense. The class war still remains the great principle, but it must be subordinated to national solidarity. Internationalism is an article of faith about which the most moderate declare themselves ready to take the most solemn oaths; but patriotism also imposes sacred duties. The emancipation of the workers must be the work of the workers themselves—their newspapers repeat this every day,—but real emancipation consists in voting for a professional politician, in securing for him the means of obtaining a comfortable situation in the world, in subjecting oneself to a leader. In the end the State must disappear—and they are very careful not to dispute what Engels has written on this subject—but this disappearance will take place only in a future so far distant that you must prepare yourself for it by using the State meanwhile as a means of providing the politicians with tidbits; and the best means of bringing about the disappearance of the State consists in strengthening meanwhile the Governmental machine. This method of reasoning resembles that of Gribouille, who threw himself into the water in order to escape getting wet in the rain.

Whole pages could be filled with the bare outlines of the contradictory, comical, and quack arguments which form the substance of the harangues of our great men; nothing embarrasses them, and they know how to combine, in pompous, impetuous, and nebulous speeches, the most absolute irreconcilability with the most supple opportunism. A learned exponent of Socialism has said that the art of reconciling opposites by means of nonsense is the most obvious result which he had got from the study of the works of Marx. I confess my extreme incompetence in these difficult matters; moreover, I make no claim whatever to be counted among the people upon whom politicians confer the title of learned; yet I cannot easily bring myself to admit that this is the sum and substance of the Marxian philosophy.

The controversy between Jaurès and Clemenceau demonstrated quite clearly that our Parliamentary Socialists can succeed in deceiving the public only by their equivocation; and that, as the result of continually deceiving their readers, they have finally lost all sense of honest discussion. In the *Aurore* of September 4, 1905, Clemenceau accuses Jaurès of muddling the minds of his partisans "with metaphysical subtleties into which they are incapable of following him"; there is nothing to object to in this accusation, save the use of the word *Metaphysical;* Jaurès is no more a metaphysician than he is a lawyet or an astronomer. In the number of October 26 Clemen-

ceau proves that his opponent possesses "the art of falsifying
his texts," and he ends by saying, "It seemed to me instructive to expose certain polemical practices which we wrongly
supposed to be monopoly of the Jesuits."

Against this noisy, garrulous, and lying Socialism, which is
exploited by ambitious people of every description, which
amuses a few buffoons, and which is admired by decadents
—revolutionary Syndicalism takes its stand, and endeavours,
on the contrary, to leave nothing in a state of indecision; its
ideas are honestly expressed, without trickery and without
mental reservations; no attempt is made to dilute doctrines by
a stream of confused commentaries. Syndicalism endeavours
to employ methods of expression which throw a full light on
things, which put them exactly in the place assigned to them
by their nature, and which bring out the whole value of the
forces in play. Oppositions, instead of being glozed over, must
be thrown into sharp relief if we desire to obtain a clear idea
of the Syndicalist movement; the groups which are struggling
one against the other must be shown as separate and as compact as possible; in short, the movements of the revolted
masses must be represented in such a way that the soul of the
revolutionaries may receive a deep and lasting impression.

These results could not be produced in any very certain
manner by the use of ordinary language; use must be made of
a body of images which, *by intuition alone,* and before any
considered analyses are made, is capable of evoking as an undivided whole the mass of sentiments which corresponds to
the different manifestations of the war undertaken by Socialism against modern society. The Syndicalists solve this problem perfectly, by concentrating the whole of Socialism in the
drama of the general strike; there is thus no longer any place
for the reconciliation of contraries in the equivocations of the
professors; everything is clearly mapped out, so that only one
interpretation of Socialism is possible. This method has all the
advantages which "integral" knowledge has over analysis, according to the doctrine of Bergson; and perhaps it would not
be possible to cite another example which would so perfectly
demonstrate the value of the famous professor's doctrines.

The possibility of the actual realisation of the general strike has been much discussed; it has been stated that the Socialist war could not be decided in one single battle. To the people who think themselves cautious, practical, and scientific the difficulty of setting great masses of the proletariat in motion at the same moment seems prodigious; they have analysed the difficulties of detail which such an enormous struggle would present. It is the opinion of the Socialist-sociologists, as also of the politicians, that the general strike is a popular dream, characteristic of the beginnings of a working-class movement; we have had quoted against us the authority of Sidney Webb, who has decreed that the general strike is an illusion of youth, of which the English workers—whom the monopolists of sociology have so often presented to us as the depositaries of the true conception of the working-class movement—soon rid themselves.

That the general strike is not popular in contemporary England, is a poor argument to bring against the historical significance of the idea, for the English are distinguished by an extraordinary lack of understanding of the class war; their ideas have remained very much dominated by medieval influences: the guild, privileged, or at least protected by laws, still seems to them the ideal of working-class organisation; it is for England that the term *working-class aristocracy*, as a name for the trades unionists, was invented, and, as a matter of fact, trades unionism does pursue the acquisition of legal privileges. We might therefore say that the aversion felt by England for the general strike should be looked upon as strong presumptive evidence in favour of the latter by all those who look upon the class war as the essence of Socialism.

Moreover, Sidney Webb enjoys a reputation for competence which is very much exaggerated; all that can be put to his credit is that he had waded through uninteresting blue-books, and has had the patience to compose an extremely indigestible compilation on the history of trades unionism; he has a mind of the narrowest description, which could only impress people unaccustomed to reflection. Those who introduced his fame into France knew nothing at all about Socialism; and if he is really in the first rank of contemporary authors of economic history, as his translator affirms, it is because the intellectual level of these historians is rather low; moreover, many examples show us that it is possible to be a most illustrious professional historian and yet possess a mind something less than mediocre.

Neither do I attach any importance to the objections made to the general strike based on considerations of a practical order. The attempt to construct hypotheses about the nature of the struggles of the future and the means of suppressing capitalism, on the model furnished by history, is a return to the old methods of the Utopists. There is no process by which the future can be predicted scientifically, nor even one which enables us to discuss whether one hypothesis about it is better than another; it has been proved by too many memorable examples that the greatest men have committed prodigious errors in thus desiring to make predictions about even the least distant future.

And yet without leaving the present, without reasoning about this future, which seems for ever condemned to escape our reason, we should be unable to act at all. Experience shows that the *framing of a future, in some indeterminate time,* may, when it is done in a certain way, be very effective, and have very few inconveniences; this happens when the anticipations of the future take the form of those myths, which enclose with them, all the strongest inclinations of a people, of a party or of a class, inclinations which recur to the mind with the insistence of instincts in all the circumstances of life; and which give an aspect of complete reality to the hopes of immediate action by which, more easily than by any other method, men can reform their desires, passions, and mental activity. We know, moreover, that these social myths in no way prevent a man profiting by the observations which he makes in the course of his life, and form no obstacle to the pursuit of his normal occupations. . . .

The myth must be judged as a means of acting on the present; any attempt to discuss how far it can be taken literally as future history is devoid of sense. *It is the myth in its entirety which is alone important:* its parts are only of interest in so far as they bring out the main idea. No useful purpose is served, therefore, in arguing about the incidents which may

occur in the course of a social war, and about the decisive
conflicts which may give victory to the proletariat; even supposing the revolutionaries to have been wholly and entirely
deluded in setting up this imaginary picture of the general
strike, this picture may yet have been, in the course of the
preparation for the Revolution, a great element of strength,
if it has embraced all the aspirations of Socialism, and if it
has given to the whole body of Revolutionary thought a precision and a rigidity which no other method of thought could
have given.

To estimate, then, the significance of the idea of the general
strike, all the methods of discussion which are current among
politicians, sociologists, or people with pretensions to political
science, must be abandoned. Everything which its opponents
endeavour to establish may be conceded to them, without reducing in any way the value of the theory which they think
they have refuted. The question whether the general strike is
a partial reality, or only a product of popular imagination, is
of little importance. All that it is necessary to know is, whether
the general strike contains everything that the Socialist doctrine expects of the revolutionary proletariat.

To solve this question we are no longer compelled to argue
learnedly about the future; we are not obliged to indulge in
lofty reflections about philosophy, history, or economics; we
are not on the plane of theories, and we can remain on the
level of observable facts. We have to question men who take
a very active part in the real revolutionary movement amidst
the proletariat, men who do not aspire to climb into the middle
class and whose mind is not dominated by corporative prejudices. These men may be deceived about an infinite number
of political, economical, or moral questions; but their testimony is decisive, sovereign, and irrefutable when it is a question of knowing what are the ideas which most powerfully
move them and their comrades, which most appeal to them
as being identical with their socialistic conceptions, and
thanks to which their reason, their hopes, and their way of
looking at particular facts seem to make but one indivisible
unity.

Thanks to these men, we know that the general strike is

indeed what I have said: the *myth* in which Socialism is wholly comprised, *i.e.* a body of images capable of evoking instinctively all the sentiments which correspond to the different manifestations of the war undertaken by Socialism against modern society. Strikes have engendered in the proletariat the noblest, deepest, and most moving sentiments that they possess; the general strike groups them all in a co-ordinated picture, and, by bringing them together, gives to each one of them its maximum of intensity; appealing to their painful memories of particular conflicts, it colours with an intense life all the details of the composition presented to consciousness. We thus obtain that intuition of Socialism which language cannot give us with perfect clearness—and we obtain it as a whole, perceived instantaneously.

We may urge yet another piece of evidence to prove the power of the idea of the general strike. If that idea were a pure chimera, as is so frequently said, Parliamentary Socialists would not attack it with such heat; I do not remember that they ever attacked the senseless hopes which the Utopists have always held up before the dazzled eyes of the people. In the course of a polemic about realisable social reforms, Clemenceau brought out the Machiavelianism in the attitude of Jaurès, when he is confronted with popular illusions: he shelters his conscience beneath "some cleverly balanced sentence," but so cleverly balanced that it "will be received without thinking by those who have the greatest need to probe into its substance, while they will drink in with delight the delusive rhetoric of terrestrial joys to come" (*Aurore*, December 28, 1905). But when it is a question of the general strike, it is quite another thing; our politicians are no longer content with complicated reservations; they speak violently, and endeavour to induce their listeners to abandon this conception.

It is easy to understand the reason for this attitude: politicians have nothing to fear from the Utopias which present a deceptive mirage of the future to the people, and turn "men towards immediate realisations of terrestrial felicity, which any one who looks at these matters scientifically knows can only be very partially realised, and even then only after long efforts on the part of several generations." (That is what

Socialist politicians do, according to Clemenceau.) The more readily the electors believe in the *magical forces of the State*, the more will they be disposed to vote for the candidate who promises marvels; in the electoral struggle each candidate tries to outbid the others: in order that the Socialist candidates may put the Radicals to rout, the electors must be credulous enough to believe every promise of future bliss; our Socialist politicians take very good care, therefore, not to combat these comfortable Utopias in any very effective way.

They struggle against the conception of the general strike, because they recognise, in the course of their propagandist rounds, that this conception is so admirably adapted to the working-class mind that there is a possibility of its dominating the latter in the most absolute manner, thus leaving no place for the desires which the Parliamentarians are able to satisfy. They perceive that this idea is so effective as a motive force that once it has entered the minds of the people they can no longer be controlled by leaders, and that thus the power of the deputies would be reduced to nothing. In short, they feel in a vague way that the whole Socialist movement might easily be absorbed by the general strike, which would render useless all those compromises between political groups in view of which the Parliamentary regime has been built up.

The opposition it meets with from official Socialists, therefore, furnishes a confirmation of our first inquiry into the scope of the general strike. . . .

The study of the political strike leads us to a better understanding of a distinction we must always have in mind when we reflect on contemporary social questions. Sometimes the terms *force* and *violence* are used in speaking of acts of authority, sometimes in speaking of acts of revolt. It is obvious that the two cases give rise to very different consequences. I think it would be better to adopt a terminology which would give rise to no ambiguity, and that the term *violence* should be employed only for acts of revolt; we should say, therefore, that the object of force is to impose a certain social order in which the minority governs, while violence tends to the destruction of that order. The middle class have used force since the beginning of modern times, while the proletariat now

reacts against the middle class and against the State by
violence. . . .

GUILD SOCIALISM

Guild Socialism arose before World War I as an English
variation of the syndicalist movements that sprang up at the
same time in many other Western countries. It differed from
them in that it started from the top, a utopian scheme devised
by intellectuals. A number of Fabians, Christian Socialists,
anarchists, and young Oxford intellectuals came together in
London out of common belief that the individual worker was
losing his personality to large concentrations of economic
and political power and that the existing forms of socialism—
from Marxism through Fabianism—offered no alternative to
it. They did find an alternative, or a model, in the autonomous
medieval guild, with its emphasis on craftsmanship and group
solidarity. It remained for them to translate these ideals into
a realistic program.

This was done by Samuel Hobson, a journalist and busi-
nessman who, in a number of books and articles, conceived
of workers' guilds as the perfect instrument for running modern, large-scale industries. Each industry, according to
Hobson, would be organized by the appropriate guild, of
which the trade union would be the governing agent. The
state's function would be to preside over relations between
the trade unions representing their respective guilds. The government, lacking coercive power, would be a confederation
of industries. The resemblance to syndicalism was obvious
and conscious.

The trade unions themselves began to take up Hobson's
idea, and Guild Socialism became a serious challenge to the
state and to the insurgent Labor Party during World War I.
But the movement collapsed after the war, and its adherents
split into numerous factions, many of them going over to
communism. The chief cause of its demise was the fact that
the trade unions, seriously hurt by the depression of the early
'20s, could no longer support it. Moreover, the effect of the

War and of the Russian Revolution was destroying the syndicalist idea everywhere except Spain.

G. D. H. Cole was the best-known and most persuasive
exponent of Guild Socialism in its halcyon days. Born in
1889 he attended Oxford, where he belonged to the circle
of Guild sympathizers, and formally joined the movement in
1915. His *Guild Socialism Restated*, written in 1920, is the
best summary of its doctrine. Throughout his life Cole was
a prolific writer on many subjects in the social sciences. He
died in 1959, an honored Fabian (he was head of the Society between 1939 and 1946) and one of the important socialists of his time. His last work was the monumental *History
of Socialist Thought*.

GUILD SOCIALISM RESTATED (1920)

In the course of the last chapter the point was emphasised
that for the constructive task of social reorganisation more is
needed than a plan for the assumption of power by a social
class, however equipped. There is also needed a positive plan
of action for that class to pursue both in the course of and
after its assumption of power. Guild Socialism claims to
present the essential features of such a plan, based directly
upon the workers' own organisations and assigning to them
the leading rôle in the process of transformation.

As a necessary preliminary to the unfolding of this plan
we have now to pursue the second line of criticism suggested
in the preceding chapter, and to see wherein, even if we suppose the class character of existing Society to be eliminated,
its social structure still fails to satisfy the conditions of reasonable human association and government which we have laid
down as our fundamental assumptions. Of course, I do not
deny that many of the features of present-day social structure
which we shall have now to examine are indirectly the result
of its class basis; but they are such as might, in theory at
least, continue in existence after the abolition of social and
economic classes, and their continuance has indeed hitherto
been assumed to be desirable by many who call themselves
Socialists.

Under the present system, the supreme legislative control of policy is supposed to reside in Parliament, and the supreme executive power in a Cabinet which is supposed to be a sort of committee of the parliamentary majority in the House of Commons. Theoretically, the competence of Parliament knows no limits, and it can pass laws dealing with any subject under the sun. Moreover, as the body politic becomes more diseased, the number and diversity of the laws which it passes and the subjects with which it deals steadily increase. It is true that at the same time the real power of Parliament wanes, and its functions are largely usurped by the Cabinet acting as the trustee of the great vested interests. This, however, does not concern us; for we are studying Parliament and Cabinet as they appear, with other institutions such as the standing army and the national police, in the form of the modern State.

The theory of State omnicompetence has grown up gradually. Locke, a typical political philosopher of an earlier period, certainly regarded the State, not as "sovereign" in the sense now attaching to the term, but as strictly limited in function and capacity. There was a time, away back in the Middle Ages, when the State was only one of a number of social institutions and associations, all of which exercised, within their more or less clearly defined spheres of operation, a recognised social power and authority. During the period which followed the close of the Middle Ages, these other bodies were for the most part either swept away or reduced to impotence; but the effect of their disappearance was not, except to a limited extent for a time in the sixteenth and seventeenth centuries, the assumption of their powers by the State, but the passing of the social purposes which they had regulated outside the sphere of communal regulation altogether. Thus the ground was cleared for the unguided operation of the Industrial Revolution in the eighteenth and nineteenth centuries, and the vast structure of modern industrialism grew up without any attempt by Society, as an organised system, to direct it to the common advantage. This unregulated growth in its turn created the urgent need for intervention; and, all alternative forms of communal structure having been destroyed or submerged, it was the State which was called upon to intervene. Thus took place the vast extension of the sphere of State action, which, while it was partly protective in its origin, led to the confrontation of the pigmy man by a greater Leviathan, and produced a situation extremely inimical to personal liberty, of its real inroads upon which we are only now becoming fully sensible. As Mr. Belloc would say, it created the conditions in modern Society which are making for the Servile State.

The events of the last few years have opened the eyes of many to the real character of this development, and in particular have created a revolution in Socialist thought on the subject of the State. This is indeed a question on which Socialists have always been sharply divided; but the schools of Parliamentary Socialists, whether they have called themselves Marxian or not, have always, in opposition both to the industrial Socialists and to the catastrophic revolutionaries, been inclined to hold that Socialism would come about by the assumption by the people, or the workers, of the control of the State machine, that is by the conquest of parliamentary and political power. They have then conceived of the actual achievement of Socialism mainly by the use of this power for the expropriation of the rich, the socialisation of the means of production, and the re-organisation of industry under State ownership and under the full control of a Parliament dominated by Socialists. In fact, the only essential *structural* change to which they have looked forward, apart from the social and economic change involved in expropriation, is the completion of the present tendency towards State Sovereignty by the piling of fresh powers and duties on the great Leviathan.

If the fundamental assumptions on the basis of which we set out are right, this idea is certainly altogether wrong. For we assumed, not only that democracy ought to be fully applied to every sphere of organised social effort, but that democracy is only real when it is conceived in terms of function and purpose. In any large community, democracy necessarily involves representative government. Government, however, is not democratic if, as in most of the forms which pass for representative government to-day, it involves the substitution of the will of one man, the representative, for the wills of many, the represented. There are two respects in which the present form of parliamentary representation, as it exists in all "democratic" States to-day flagrantly violates the fundamental principles of democracy. The first is that the elector retains practically no control over his representative, has only the power to change him at very infrequent intervals, and has in fact only a very limited range of choice. The second is that the elector is called upon to choose one man to represent him in relation to every conceivable question that may come before Parliament, whereas, if he is a rational being, he always certainly agrees with one man about one thing and with another about another, or at any rate would do so as soon as the economic basis of present class divisions was removed.

The omnicompetent State, with its omnicompetent Parliament, is thus utterly unsuitable to any really democratic community, and must be destroyed or painlessly extinguished as it has destroyed or extinguished its rivals in the sphere of communal organisation. Whatever the structure of the new Society may be, the Guildsman is sure that it will have no place for the survival of the *factotum* State of to-day.

The essentials of democratic representation, positively stated, are, first, that the represented shall have free choice of, constant contact with, and considerable control over, his representative. The second is that he should be called upon, not to choose someone to represent him as a man or as a citizen in all the aspects of citizenship, but only to choose someone to represent his point of view in relation to some particular purpose or group of purposes, in other words, some particular *function*. All true and democratic representation is therefore *functional* representation.

The structure of any democratic Society must be in harmony with these essential principles. Where it employs the representative method, this must be always in relation to some definite function. It follows that there must be, in the Society, as many separately elected groups of representatives as there are distinct essential groups of functions to be performed. Smith cannot represent Brown, Jones and Robinson as human beings; for a human being, as an individual, is fundamentally incapable of being represented. He can only represent the common point of view which Brown, Jones and Robinson hold in relation to some definite social purpose, or group of connected purposes. Brown, Jones and Robinson must therefore have, not one vote each, but as many different functional votes as there are different questions calling for associative action in which they are interested.

It should be noted that the argument, up to the point to which we have at present carried it, does not suggest or prescribe any particular type of constituency or arrangement of the franchise. It does not lay down that men should vote by geographical, or that they should vote by occupational, constituencies, or that they should do both. All that we have yet established is that man should have as many distinct, and separately exercised, votes, as he has distinct social purposes or interests. But the democratic principle applies, not only to the whole body of citizens in a community in relation to each set of purposes which they have in common, but also and equally to each group of citizens who act in co-operation for the performance of any social function or who possess a common social interest. There are indeed two distinct kinds of bond which may link together in association members of the same community, and each of these bonds may exist either between all or between some of the members. The first bond is that of common vocation, the performance in common of some form of social service, whether of an economic character or not: the second bond is that of common interest, the receiving, using or consuming of such services. In the working-class world to-day, Trade Unionism is the outstanding example of the former type, and Co-operation of the latter.

In a democratic community, it is essential that the principle of self-government should apply to the affairs of every one of the associations arising out of either of these forms of common purpose. It is, from this point of view, immaterial whether a particular association includes all, or only some, of the whole body of citizens, provided that it adequately represents those who possess the common purpose which it exists to fulfil. Thus, the form of representative government or administration required for each particular service or interest will be that which most adequately represents the persons concerned in it.

But, it will be said, surely to a great extent everything is everybody's concern. It is certainly not the exclusive concern of the coal miners, or of the workers in any other particular industry, how their service is conducted; for everybody, including every other industry, is concerned as a consumer of coal. Nor is it by any means the exclusive concern of the teachers what the educational system is, or how it is administered; for the whole people is concerned in education as the greatest civic service. On the other hand, the coal industry clearly concerns the miner, and education concerns the teacher, in a way different from that in which they concern the rest of the people; for, whereas for the latter coal is only one among a number of commodities, and education one among several civic services, to the miner or the teacher his own calling is the most important single concern in social life.

This distinction really brings us to the heart of our problem, and to the great practical difference between Guild Socialism and other schools of Socialist opinion. For the Guildsman maintains that in a right apprehension of this distinction, and in the framing of social arrangements which recognise and make full provision for it, lies the key to the whole question at issue. It is absurd to deny the common interest which all the members of the community have, as consumers and users, in the vital industries, or as sharers of a common culture and code in such a service as education; but it is no less futile to deny the special, and even more intense, concern which the miners have in the organisation of their industry, or the teachers in the conduct of the educational system.

Nevertheless, there are schools of Socialist, or quasi-Socialist thought, which take their stand upon each of these impossible denials. The Collectivist, or State Socialist, who regards the State as representing the consumer, and the purely "Co-operative" idealist, who sees in Co-operation a far better consumers' champion, are alike in refusing to recognise the claim of the producer, or service renderer, to self-government in his calling. The pure "Syndicalist," or the pure "Industrial Unionist," on the other hand, denies, or at least used to deny, the need of any special representation of the consumers' standpoint, and presses for an organisation of Society based wholly on production or the rendering of service.

It is true that, in their extreme forms, both these antagonistic views are dying out, the pressure of each upon the other, and of Guild Socialism upon both, having compelled modification in both cases. But the ordinary State Socialist or Co-operative idealist to-day still stresses mainly the claim of the consumer and allows only a very subordinate and "discreetly regulated" freedom to the producer; while there are still many who lay nearly all the emphasis upon the producer, and give only a very grudging and half-hearted assent to the claims of the consumer for self-determination.

It has been the work of Guild Socialism to hold the balance between these two schools of thought, not by splitting the difference, but by pointing out that the solution lies in a clear distinction of function and sphere of activity. The phrase "control of industry" is in fact loosely used to include the claims of both producers and consumers; but it has, in the two uses, really to a great extent different meanings, and, still more, different associations. When the "Syndicalist" or the Guild Socialist speaks of the need for control by the producers, or when a Trade Union itself demands control, the reference is mainly to the internal conditions of the industry, to the way in which the factory or place of work is managed, the administrators appointed, the conditions determined, and, above all, to the amount of freedom *at his work* which the worker by hand or brain enjoys. When, on the other hand, a State Socialist or a Co-operator speaks of the need for "consumers' control," he is thinking mainly of the quantity and quality of the goods supplied, of the excellence of the distribution, of the price of sale—in short, of a set of considerations which, while they are intimately bound up with those which chiefly concern the producer, are still in essence distinct, and have to do far less with the internal conduct of the industry than with its external relations. They are, so to speak, its "foreign politics" as viewed by the foreigners.

Naturally, if these vital distinctions are not made, each of the claimants to "control of industry" is inclined to claim the whole, or at best to relegate the other to a quite subordinate position. Moreover, even when the distinction is clearly stated, there is a strong temptation for those who belong to either movement to claim too much for their own. The Guild Socialist endeavours to hold the scales fairly, and to decide, as far as the matter can be decided except in practice, what are the fair claims on each side.

In doing this, the Guildsman has not to face any problem of arbitrating between divergent interests. In a democratic Society, the whole body of consumers and the whole body of producers are practically the same people, only ranged in the two cases in different formations. There can be no real divergence of interests between them. It is a problem not, as in present-day Society, of economic warfare, but of reasonable democratic organisation on a functional basis.

The Guild Socialist contends, then, that the internal management and control of each industry or service must be placed, as a trust on behalf of the community, in the hands of the workers engaged in it; but he holds no less strongly that full provision must be made for the representation and safeguarding of the consumers' point of view in relation to each service. Similarly, he contends that general questions of industrial administration extending to all industries should, where they mainly concern the whole body of producers, be entrusted to an organisation representing all the producers; but he holds equally that the general point of view of all types of consumers must be fully represented and safeguarded in relation to industry as a whole. The mere detailed working out of this principle will occupy a considerable part of this book: and for the present it must be left in the shape of a generalisation. I claim, however, that, so far as it goes, it satisfies the conditions of democracy in a way which neither State Socialism, nor Co-operativism, nor Syndicalism, nor any alternative proposal hitherto brought forward is able to parallel.

This, however, may be dismissed by "practically-minded" people as a purely theoretical disquisition, and it is therefore advisable to state the case in a more practical way, by relating it closely to what was said in the last chapter concerning the changing psychology of the workers. Let us therefore ask ourselves whether, if all industry passed under the management of a "State," however democratic, or of a Co-operative Movement, however enlightened, the workers engaged in its various branches would have the sense of being free and self-governing in relation to their work. It is true that they would be voters in the democratic State, or members of the Co-operative Society, and would therefore, in a sense, be ultimately part-controllers in some degree of their conditions; but would they regard this as freedom, when, although their concern in the internal arrangements of their industry was far closer than that of others, they had at most only the same voice with others in determining them. Obviously, the answer is that they neither would, nor could be expected to, take any such view; for, by the time their share in determining conditions had gone its roundabout course through the consumers' organisation, it would have ceased to be recognisable as even the most indirect sort of freedom. Men will never recognise or regard as self-government in any association a system which does not give to them directly as a group the right of framing their common rules to govern their internal affairs, and of choosing, by their own decisions, those who are to hold office and authority in their midst.

This being so, no solution of the problem of industrial government is really a solution at all unless it places the rights and responsibilities of the internal conduct of industry directly upon the organised bodies of producers. On no other condition will men who have risen to a sense of social capacity and power consent to serve or to give of their best. Any other attempted solution will therefore break down before the unwillingness of the workers to produce, and will afford no way of escape from the *impasse* to which we have already been brought by the denial under capitalism of the human rights of Labor. It is our business, then, to accept unreservedly this claim of the producer, and at the same time to reconcile it with the consumer's claim that his voice shall also count. We shall see that there is nothing impossible or even difficult in this reconciliation.

Note.—In this chapter I have not challenged the correctness of the State Socialist claim that the State "represents the consumer."

I may say, however, here that I do not accept this contention, and therefore do not equate State with Co-operative management of industry. As, however, State Socialists and Co-operativists use the same arguments in favour of consumers' management, the difference between them does not arise in connection with this chapter.

Chapter VIII

REVISIONISM

In the decades following Marx's death industrialism relentlessly moved across the continent of Europe, polarizing society into bourgeois and proletariat classes. Marxist parties sprang up in every country, including those where anarchism was strong. The German Socialist Party emerged as the colossus of European socialism, and its growth kept pace with the phenomenal industrial growth of the country after German unification in 1871. It occupied an increasing number of seats in the local, state, and national legislatures, controlled immense trade unions, and was exceedingly well-disciplined and organized, acting in the belief that Marxian sociology provided irrefutable assurance of its ultimate triumph. As the dominant party in the Second International (created in 1889) it stamped its seal of authority on the socialist movement throughout the world.

But in the last decade of the nineteenth century ominous contradictions to Marxism began to appear. Industrialization was not bringing revolution. On the contrary, the United States and Britain—along with Germany the most highly industrialized countries in the world—had very small socialist parties and knew next to nothing about Marxism. In Britain the socialist Fabian Society did begin to impress segments of the middle class, but Fabianism was akin to radical liberalism and firmly anti-revolutionary. In France, reform increasingly took possession of the socialist movement, which was substantial in size. Though French socialism was divided, its main emphasis before World War I lay in the moderate position held by Jean Jaurès, its leading figure. It became apparent that wherever political democracy showed strength it tended either to neutralize the appeal of revolution, turning socialism into a form of radical liberalism, or to thwart its development altogether. (In the United States, for example, the Socialist Party never received more than seven percent of the popular vote.)

Since the early 1890s reform had also been corroding the foundation of the German Socialist Party, especially in the provinces, where socialists had been supporting the interests of small farmers. While this tendency to ally with kindred parties grew, the party leadership, through its chief spokesman and theoretician, Karl Kautsky, continued to exhort strict obedience to Marxist principles. Finally, in 1896, Eduard Bernstein, a leader of the party, publicly called for the radical revision of those principles and the acceptance of reform. Bernstein maintained that class conflict was diminishing, that capitalism was proving supple and strong and that socialism should be approached by piecemeal and parliamentary means. Through Kautsky, the party reaffirmed its orthodoxy over and over again, but by 1914 revisionism had become the working ideology of most of its members.

Neither revisionist nor orthodox socialists, however, addressed themselves to the real problem at hand. Their models of capitalism did not correspond to the German model. Bernstein had in mind British liberal democracy; Kautsky was thinking of Marx's sociology of history. Both assumed that economic relations were the basis of politics. What those relations were and what political measures one should take toward them constituted their points of disagreement. But in Germany the overwhelmingly dominant economic classes—namely, the bourgeoisie and the proletariat—were politically subordinate to the Kaiser and the Prussian military aristocracy. Germany, in other words, was an anachronism, and defied analysis in revisionist or orthodox Marxist terms. German socialists neglected to perform their paramount duty, that of fighting for a constitutional government. They were satisfied to interpret history, not create it. The German Socialist Party presented the spectacle of a party grown passive with size.

While the German regime became increasingly pugnacious and imperialist the socialists stood hopelessly by. The Kaiser's decision to go to war presented them with an accomplished fact. Most of them chose to support the regime (though Bernstein and Kautsky did not). The Second International collapsed, and with it the last hope of democratic socialist solidarity. Socialists in nearly every other country thereupon supported their governments in the war. In democratic countries the government and the socialists drew closer together. In autocratic, pre-industrial Russia, however, the war made it possible for a revolutionary socialist party to seize power. The contradiction in Marxism was thus complete.

FERDINAND LASSALLE (1825–64)

Ferdinand Lassalle has been the subject of many biographies since his death at the age of thirty-nine. Writer, political leader, champion of labor, famous lover, he was the most romantic figure in the history of socialism. The tragedy was that his immense talents were flawed by his colossal vanity and imprudence. He held vast and unchallenged influence over the German working class while he lived, but a decade after his death this influence had greatly diminished. Yet he may be considered the father of modern reform socialism. The political program that he framed in the 1860s and that the Marxists subsequently buried was resurrected under the name of revisionism at the turn of the century.

He was born Ferdinand Lasal (he added the three extra letters to give his name a French, hence revolutionary, ring) in Breslau to a family of wealthy Jewish merchants. At Berlin University, he, like Marx before him, came under the influence of Hegelian idealism—an influence to which he always remained subject. Out of hatred for aristocratic privilege, he threw himself into the most celebrated and complicated lawsuit of the time, siding with a countess who was involved in a divorce suit against her unfaithful husband. Lassalle won the case after struggling with it for nearly ten years, in the course of which he established his extraordinary public reputation. This reputation he placed in the service of socialism and soon emerged as the teacher and guide of the growing German labor movement. He died in 1864 after losing a duel fought for the hand of a girl half his age.

Lassalle's socialism was eclectic. It owed most to Marx (whom he acknowledged as his mentor), to the tradition of German idealism from Kant to Hegel and to French socialism, particularly that of Blanc and Proudhon. He advocated universal suffrage as the means by which the workers would force the state to turn over to them the whole fruit of their production. The working class, he believed, embodied the spirit of the people whose higher will was manifest in the state. Until it captured the state the working class could expect little from independent trade union activity. It was on this point that Lassalle, or rather the Lassalleans, and Marx vehemently disagreed. Lassalle, like Marx, assumed the existence of an Iron Law of Wages, according to which labor was inevitably driven down to the lowest level compatible with the maintenance of life. For Lassalle it therefore followed that labor could free itself only through the invincible power of the state. Marx, however, believed that the Iron Law could be broken by the action of labor itself. Marx had little faith in the state unless it responded directly to the interests of the working class; he had no faith whatever in the German state.

Marxists have since accused Lassalle of being a "state socialist." This is untrue: Lassalle exalted the social democratic state resting on popular suffrage, not the state as such. In this sense it is accurate to call him the precursor of revisionism. In any case German Marxists in particular owed much to Lassalle; he laid the groundwork for the huge German Socialist Party which came into being eleven years after his death. *The Working Class Program* was the written version of a speech delivered by Lassalle in Berlin in 1862 and illegally published as a pamphlet.

THE WORKING CLASS PROGRAM (1862)

. . . We have now seen, gentlemen, two periods of the world, each of which is dominated by the ruling idea of a particular class of the community which impresses its own principle on all the social arrangements of its time.

First the idea of nobility, or of the *possession of land* which forms the ruling principle of the Middle Ages, and permeates all its institutions.

This period closed with the French Revolution, although you will understand that, especially in Germany, where the change was not brought about by the people, but by very gradual and incomplete reforms introduced by the Government, numerous and important extensions of that first period of history have occurred, which even at the present day greatly hamper the progress of the Bourgeoisie.

We saw in the next place the period of history which begins at the eighteenth century with the French Revolution, which has for its principle *large private property*, or capital, and makes this into the privilege which pervades all the arrangements of society, and is the condition of participation in directing the will of the State and determining its aims.

This period also, little as outward appearances seem to show it, is virtually already closed.

On the 24th February 1848, the dawn of a new period of history appeared.

For on that day in France (that country in whose great struggles the victory or the defeat of freedom means victory or defeat for the whole human race) a revolution broke out which called a working man into the provisional Government, declared that the object of the State was the improvement of the lot of the working classes, and proclaimed the universal and direct right to the suffrage, by which every citizen who had attained his twenty-first year, without any reference to the amount of his property, received an equal share in the government of the State in the direction of its will and the determination of its aims.

You see, gentlemen, that if the Revolution of 1789 was the Revolution of the *Tiers état*, the *Third* class, it is now the *Fourth* class, which in 1789 was still enfolded within the third class and appeared to be identical with it, which will now raise its principle to be the dominating principle of the community, and cause all its arrangements to be permeated by it.

But here, in the domination of the fourth class comes to light this immense difference, that the fourth class is the last and the outside of all, the disinterested class of the community, which sets up and can set up no further exclusive condition, either legal or actual, neither nobility nor landed possessions nor the possession of capital, which it could make into a new *privilege* and force upon the arrangements of society.

We are *all* working men in so far as we have even the *will* to make ourselves useful in any way to the community.

This *Fourth* class in whose heart therefore *no* germ of a new privilege is contained, is for this very reason synonymous with the *whole human race. Its* interest is in truth the interest of the *whole of humanity*, its freedom is the freedom of humanity itself, and its domination is the domination of *all*.

Whoever therefore invokes the idea of the working class as the ruling principle of society, in the sense in which I have explained it to you, does not put forth a cry that divides and separates the classes of society. On the contrary, he utters a cry of *reconciliation*, a cry which embraces the whole of the community, a cry for doing away with all the contradictions in every circle of society; a cry of *union* in which all should join who do not wish for privileges, and the oppression of the people by privileged classes; a cry of *love* which having once gone up from the heart of the people, will *for ever remain the true cry of the people*, and whose meaning will make it still a *cry of love*, even when it sounds the war cry of the people.

We will now consider the principle of the working class as the ruling principle of the community only in three of its relations:—

(1) In relation to the formal means of its realisation.

(2) In relation to its moral significance.

(3) In relation to the political conception of the object of the State, which is inherent in that principle.

We cannot on this occasion enter upon its other aspects, and even those to which we have referred can be only very cursorily examined in the short time that remains to us.

The formal means of carrying out this principle is the universal and direct suffrage which we have already discussed. I say universal and *direct* suffrage, gentlemen, not that mere universal suffrage which we had in the year 1848. The introduction of two degrees in the electoral act, namely, original electors and electors simply, is nothing but an ingenious method purposely introduced with the object of falsifying as far as possible the will of the people by means of the electoral act.

It is true that even universal and direct suffrage is no magic wand, gentlemen, which is able to protect you from temporary mistakes.

We have seen in France two bad elections following one another, in 1848 and 1849. But universal and direct suffrage is the *only* means which in the long run of itself corrects the mistakes to which its momentary wrong use may lead. It is that spear which heals the wounds it itself has made. It is impossible in the long run with universal and direct suffrage that the elected body should be any other than the exact and true likeness of the people which has elected it.

The people must therefore at all times regard universal and direct suffrage as its indispensable political weapon, as the most fundamental and important of its demands.

I will now glance at the *moral* significance of the principle of society which we are considering.

It is possible that the idea of converting the principle of the *lower classes* of society into the ruling principle of the State and the community may appear to be extremely dangerous and immoral, and to threaten the destruction of morality and education by a "modern barbarism."

And it is no wonder that this idea should be so regarded at the present day since even public opinion, gentlemen—I have already indicated by what means, namely, the newspapers—receives its impressions from the mint of *capital*, and from the hands of the privileged wealthy Bourgeoisie.

Nevertheless this fear is only a prejudice, and it can be proved on the contrary, that the idea would exhibit the greatest advance and triumph of morality that the history of the world has ever recorded.

That view is a prejudice I repeat, and it is simply the prejudice of *the present time* which is dominated by privilege.

At another time, namely, that of the first French Republic

of the year 1793 (of which I have already told you that I cannot enter into further particulars on this occasion, but that it was destined to perish by its own want of definite aims) the opposite prejudice prevailed. It was then a current dogma that all the upper classes were immoral and corrupt, and that only the lower classes were good and moral. In the new declaration of the rights of man issued by the French convention, that powerful constituent assembly of France, this was actually laid down by a special article, namely, article nineteen, which runs as follows, "Toute institution qui ne suppose le peuple bon, et le magistrat corruptible, est vicieuse." "Every institution which does not assume that the people are good and the magistracy contemptible is vicious." You see that this is exactly the opposite to the happy faith now required, according to which there is no greater sin than to doubt of the goodwill and the virtue of the Government, while it is taken for granted that *the people* are a sort of tiger and a sink of corruption.

At the time of which we are speaking the opposite dogma had advanced so far, that almost every one who had a whole coat on his back was thought to be a bad man, or at least an object of suspicion; and virtue, purity, and patriotic morality were thought to be possessed only by those who had no decent clothes. It was the period of sansculottism.

This view, gentlemen, is in fact founded on a *truth*, but it presents itself in an *untrue* and *perverted* form. Now there is nothing more dangerous than a truth which presents itself in an untrue perverted form. For in whatever way we deal with it, we are certain to go wrong. If we adopt such a truth in its untrue perverted form, it will lead at certain times to most pernicious destruction, as was the case with sansculottism. But if we regard the whole statement as untrue on account of its untrue perverted form, then we are much worse. For we have rejected a *truth*, and, in the case before us, a truth without the recognition of which not a single sound step in our political life can be taken.

The only course that remains open to us, therefore, is to set aside the untrue and perverted form of the statement, and to bring its true essence into distinct relief.

The public opinion of the present day is inclined, as I have said, to declare the whole statement to be utterly untrue, and mere declamation on the part of Rousseau and the French Revolution. But even if it were possible to adopt the course of rejection in the case of Rousseau and the French Revolution, it is quite impossible to do so in the case of one of the greatest of German philosophers, the centenary of whose birth-day will be celebrated in this town next month: I allude to the philosopher Fichte, one of the greatest thinkers of all nations and times.

Even Fichte declares expressly in so many words, that the higher the rank the greater the moral deterioration, that— these are his very words—"Wickedness increases in proportion to the elevation of rank."

But Fichte did not develope the ultimate ground of this statement. He adduces, as the ground of this corruption, the selfishness and egoism of the upper classes. But then the question must immediately arise, whether selfishness does not also prevail in the lower classes, or why it should prevail less in these. Nay it must at first sight appear to be an extraordinary paradox to assert that less selfishness should prevail in the lower classes than in the higher who have a considerable advantage over them in education and training which are recognised as moralising elements.

The following is the true ground of what as I said appears at first sight to be extraordinary paradox.

In a long period in the past, as we have seen, the development of the people, which is the life-breath of history, proceeds by an ever advancing abolition of the privileges which guarantee to the higher classes their position as higher and ruling classes. The desire to maintain this, in other words their personal interest, brings therefore every member of the higher classes who has not once for all by a high range of vision elevated himself above his purely personal existence—and you will understand, gentlemen, that this can never be more than a very small number of exceptional characters—into a position thoroughly *hostile* in principle to the development of the people, to the progress of education and science, to the advance of culture, to all the life-breath and victory of historic life.

It is this opposition of the personal interest of the higher

classes to the development of the nation in culture which
evokes the great and necessary immorality of the higher
classes. It is a life, whose daily conditions you need only represent to yourselves, in order to perceive the deep inward deterioration to which it must lead. To be compelled daily to
oppose all that is great and good, to be obliged to *grieve* at its
successes, to rejoice at its failures, to restrain its further progress, to be obliged to undo or to execrate the advantages it has
already attained. It is to lead their life as in the country of an
enemy—and this enemy is the moral community of their *own
people*, amongst whom they live, and *for* whom to strive constitutes all true morality. It is to lead their lives, I say, as in
the country of an *enemy;* this enemy is their own people, and
the fact that it is regarded and treated as their enemy must
generally at all events be cunningly concealed, and this hostility must m re or less artfully be covered with a veil.

And to this we must add that either they must do all this
against the voice of their own conscience and intelligence, or
they must have stifled the voice by habit so as not to be oppressed by it, or lastly they must have never known this voice,
never known anything different and better than the religion
of their own advantage!

This life, gentlemen, leads therefore necessarily to a thorough depreciation and contempt of all striving to realise an
ideal, to a compassionate smile at the bare mention of the
great name of the Idea, to a deeply seated want of sympathy
and even antipathy to all that is beautiful and great, to a
complete swallowing up of every moral element in us, by the
one passion of selfish seeking for our own advantage, and of
immoderate desire for pleasure.

It is this *opposition*, gentlemen, between personal interest
and the development of the nation in culture, which the lower
classes, happily for them, are *without*.

It is unfortunately true that there is always enough of selfishness in the lower classes, much more than there should be,
but this selfishness of theirs, wherever it is found, is the fault
of single persons, of *individuals*, and not the inevitable fault of
the *class*.

A very reasonable instinct warns the members of the lower

classes, that so long as each of them relates himself only to himself, and each one thinks only of himself, he can hope for no important improvement in his position.

But the more earnestly and deeply the lower classes of society strive after the improvement of their condition as a class, the improvement of the *lot of their class,* the more does this personal interest, instead of opposing the movement of history and thereby being condemned to that immorality of which we have spoken, assume a *direction* which thoroughly accords with the development of the whole *people,* with the victory of the *idea,* with the advance of *culture,* with the living principle of history itself, which is no other than the development of *freedom.* Or in other words, as we have already seen, *its* interest is the interest of the entire human race.

You are therefore in this happy position, gentlemen, that instead of its being possible for you to be dead to the idea, you are on the contrary urged to the deepest sympathy for it by your own *personal interests.* You are in the happy position that the idea which constitutes your true personal interest, is one with the throbbing pulse of history, and with the living principle of moral development. You are able therefore to devote yourselves with *personal passion* to this historical development, and to be certain that the more strongly this *passion* grows and burns within you in the true sense in which I have explained it to you, the higher is the moral position you have attained.

These are the reasons, gentlemen, why the dominion of the fourth class in the State must produce such an efflorescence of morality, culture, and science, as has not yet been witnessed in history.

But there is yet another reason for this, one which is most intimately connected with all the views I have explained to you, and forms their keystone.

The fourth estate not only has a different formal political principle from that of the Bourgeoisie, namely, the universal direct franchise, instead of the census of the Bourgeoisie, and not only has through its position in life a different relation to moral forces than the higher classes, but has also—and partly in consequence of these—quite another and a different conception of the moral *object of the State* from that of the Bourgeoisie.

According to the Bourgeoisie, the moral idea of the State is exclusively this, that the unhindered exercise by himself of his own faculties should be guaranteed to each individual.

If we were all equally strong, equally clever, equally educated, and equally rich, this might be regarded as a sufficient and a moral idea.

But since we neither *are* nor *can be* thus equal, this idea is not satisfactory, and therefore necessarily leads in its consequences to deep immorality, for it leads to this, that the stronger, the cleverer, and the richer fleece the weaker and pick their pockets.

The moral idea of the State according to the working class on the contrary is this, that the unhindered and free activity of individual powers exercised by the individual is not *sufficient,* but that something *must be added* to this in a morally ordered community—namely, *solidarity* of interests, community and reciprocity in development.

In accordance with this difference, the Bourgeoisie conceive the moral object of the State to consist solely and exclusively in the protection of the personal freedom and the property of the individual.

This is a policeman's idea, gentlemen, a policeman's idea for this reason, because it represents to itself the State from a point of view of a policeman, whose whole function consists in preventing robbery and burglary. Unfortunately this policeman's idea is not only familiar to genuine liberals, but is even to be met with not unfrequently among so-called democrats, owing to their defective imagination. If the Bourgeoisie would express the logical inference from their idea, they must maintain that according to it if there were no such thing as robbers and thieves, the State itself would be entirely superfluous.[1]

[1] This idea of the State, which in fact does away with the State, and changes it into a mere union of egoistic interests, is the idea of the State as regarded by *liberalism,* and historically was produced by it. It forms by the power which it has necessarily obtained and which stands in direct relation to its superficiality, the true danger of spiritual and moral decay, the true danger, which threatens us at this day, of a "modern barbarism." In Ger-

Very differently, gentlemen, does the fourth estate regard the object of the State, for it apprehends it in its true nature.

History, gentlemen, is a struggle with nature; with the misery, the ignorance, the poverty, the weakness, and consequent slavery in which we were involved when the human race came upon the scene in the beginning of history. The progressive *victory* over this weakness—this is the development of freedom which history displays to us.

In this struggle we should never have made one step forward, nor shall we ever advance one step more by acting on the principle of *each one for himself, each one alone.*

It is *the State* whose function it is to carry on *this development of freedom,* this development of the human race until its freedom is attained.

The State is this unity of individuals into a moral whole, a unity which increases a million-fold the strength of *all* the individuals who are comprehended in it, and multiplies a million times the power which would be at the disposal of them *all* as individuals.

The object of the State, therefore, is not only to *protect* the personal freedom and property of the individual with which he is supposed according to the idea of the Bourgeoisie to have entered the State. On the contrary, the object of the State is precisely this, to place the individuals *through this* union in a position to attain to *such objects,* and reach such a *stage of existence* as they *never* could have reached as individuals; to make them capable of acquiring an amount of *education, power,* and *freedom* which would have been wholly unattainable by them as individuals.

Accordingly the object of the State is to bring man to positive expansion, and progressive development, in other words, to bring the destiny of man—that is the culture of which the

---

many happily it is strongly opposed by the ancient learning which has once for all become the indestructible foundation of German thought. From this proceeds the view "that it is necessary to enlarge the notion of the State to the fullest extent to which in my opinion it is possible to enlarge it, that the *State should be the organisation, in which the whole virtue of man should realise itself.*" (Augustus Boeth's address to his University of the 22nd March, 1862.)

human race *is capable*—into *actual existence;* it is the *training and development* of the human race to freedom.

This is the true moral nature of the State, gentlemen, its true and high mission. So much is this the case, that from the beginning of time through the very *force* of events it has more or less been carried out by the State without the exercise of will, and unconsciously even against the will of its leaders.

But the working class, gentlemen, the lower classes of the community in general, through the helpless condition in which its members find themselves placed as individuals, have always acquired the deep instinct, that this is and must be the duty of the State, to help the individual by means of the union of all to such a development as he would be *incapable* of attaining as an individual.

A State therefore which was ruled by the idea of the working class, would no longer be driven, as all States have hitherto been, unconsciously and against their will by the nature of things, and the force of circumstances, but it would make this moral nature of the State its mission, with perfect clearness of vision and complete consciousness. It would complete with *unchecked desire* and perfect *consistency,* that which hitherto has only been wrung in scanty and imperfect fragments from wills that were opposed to it, and *for this very reason*—though time does not permit me to explain in any detail this necessary connection of cause and effect—it would produce a soaring flight of the human spirit, a development of an amount of happiness, culture, well-being, and freedom without example in the history of the world, and in comparison with which, the most favourable conditions that have existed in former times would appear but dim shadows of the reality.

This it is, gentlemen, which must be called the working man's idea of the State, his conception of the object of the State, which, as you see is just as different from the bourgeois conception of the object of the State, as the principle of the working class, of the claim of *all* to direct the will of the State, or universal suffrage, is different from the principle held by the Bourgeoisie, the census.

The series of ideas which I have explained to you must be regarded as the idea of the working class. It is this that I had in view when I spoke to you, at the commencement of my lecture, of the connection of the particular period of history in which we live with the idea of the working class. It is *this* period of history beginning with February, 1848, to which has been allotted the task of bringing this idea of the State into actual existence. We may congratulate ourselves, gentlemen, that we have been born at a time which is destined to witness this the most glorious work of history, and that we are permitted to take a part in accomplishing it.

But on all who belong to the working class the duty of taking up an entirely new attitude is imposed, if there is any truth in what I have said.

Nothing is more calculated to impress upon a class a worthy and moral character, than the consciousness that it is destined to become a ruling class, that it is called upon to raise the principle of its class to the principle of the entire age, to convert *its idea* into the leading idea of the whole of society and thus to form this society by impressing upon it its own character. . . .

FABIAN SOCIALISM

As the nineteenth century began drawing to a close it was inevitable that England too should have a socialist movement —and it was just as inevitable that English socialism would be an original creation, distinct from the Continental sorts. The writings and preachings of such disparate reformers as Robert Owen, John Ruskin, William Morris, Charles Kingsley, T. H. Green, and the American Henry George had helped form the mind of the generation that came of age in the 1880s. They had eloquently driven home the point that *laissez-faire* capitalism was destroying the social and cultural life of the nation and that society would have to take measures at once to protect itself.

This was the view of the small group of young men—all in their twenties—who, in 1884, founded the Fabian Society. In the same year they recruited the two men who were to be the most famous apostles of Fabian Socialism, George Bernard

Shaw and Sidney Webb. Shaw, born in Dublin in 1856, was
then still an unsuccessful writer but was causing a stir in London as an exciting public speaker. Webb, twenty-five, a clerk
in the Colonial Office, was dazzling everyone in his circle with
his erudition in the social sciences. The early Fabians were
generally well-educated and came from the middle or shabby
genteel classes. Typically British, they were at once high-
minded, practical, and moderate. They chose the term Fabian
because the Roman general Fabius Maximus Cunctator deliberately procrastinated in the war against Hannibal. The Fabians might have subscribed to the lines of the poet Thomas
Gray:

> Let none object my lingering way
> I gain, like Fabius, with delay.

They disseminated their ideas by pamphlets and public debate and by "permeating" parties or groups, a method that
was most successful in the Liberal Party and later the Independent Labor Party. They concerned themselves with such
immediate practical problems as tax reform, women's rights,
the eight-hour day, education, local government, etc., and
learned to master the prosaic arts of economics and statistics.
Webb, rather than Shaw, embodied the soul of Fabian Socialism.

The Fabians assumed, as Marx had, that the logic of capitalism necessarily led to socialism. By socialism, however, they
meant gradual social control, where possible by local and co-
operative communities, over the means of production and distribution. In their view *laissez-faire* capitalism had become at
once unjust and inefficient. Perhaps too much, Fabians tended
to equate the two, finding special moral virtue in the art or
discipline of administration. They denied the existence of class
conflict. Far from exalting the proletariat, they would have
preferred a uniformly middle class society. Their economic
principles, drawn mostly from the writings of David Ricardo
and other liberal economists, were eclectic and unsystematic.
Their strength lay in their moral fervor and in their unusual
talents as writers, speakers, and men of affairs generally.

Fabian ideas called forth an immediate response from the

educated middle class of England. The movement spread rapidly very soon after its first book, *Fabian Essays in Socialism,* appeared in 1889. In 1890 the Society had 173 members; in 1893 it had 640 members and 74 chapters. For about ten years thereafter it steadily declined, but then sharply rose again. By the first decade of the twentieth century it had established deep and permanent roots in all levels of English society.

The excerpt is taken from a lecture delivered by Sidney Webb in 1888 and published six years later as Fabian Tract 15.

ENGLISH PROGRESS TOWARD SOCIAL DEMOCRACY (1894)

There are three stages through which every new notion in England has to pass: It is impossible: It is against the Bible: We knew it before. Socialism is rapidly reaching the third of these stages. "We are all Socialists now," said one of Her Majesty's late Ministers; and, in sober truth, there is no anti-Socialist political party. That which has long formed part of the unconscious basis of our practice is now formulated as a definite theory, and the tide of Democratic Collectivism is rolling in upon us. All the authorities, whatever their own views, can but note its rapid progress. If we look back along the line of history, we see the irresistible sweep of the growing tendency: if we turn to contemporary industrial development, it is there: if we fly to biological science, we do not escape the lesson: on all sides the sociologic evolution compels our adherence. There is no resting place for stationary Toryism in the scientific universe. The whole history of the human race cries out against the old-fashioned Individualism.

Economic Science, at any rate, will now have none of it. When the Editor of the new issue of the Encyclopædia Britannica lately required from some eminent Economist an article on Political Economy, fully representing the present position of that science, it was to an avowed Socialist that he addressed himself, and the article took the form of an elaborate survey of the inevitable convergence of all the economic tend-

encies towards Socialism. Professor Alfred Marshall's new
work will be as repugnant to Mr. Herbert Spencer and the
Liberty and Property Defence League as John Stuart Mill's
conversion was to his respectable friends. Have we not seen
Professor Sidgwick, that most careful of men, contributing an
article to the *Contemporary Review,* to prove that the main
principles of Socialism are a plain deduction from accepted
economic doctrines, and in no way opposed to them?

Indeed, those who remember John Stuart Mill's emphatic
adhesion to Socialism, both the name and the thing, in his
"Autobiography," cannot be surprised at this tendency of
economists. The only wonder is, that interested defenders of
economic monopoly are still able to persuade the British public that Political Economy is against Socialism, and are able to
make even Bishops believe that its laws "forbid" anything save
the present state of things.

It is, however, time to give a plain definition of Socialism, to
prevent any mistake as to meanings. Nothing is more common
than the statement, "I can't understand what Socialism is." But
this is sheer intellectual laziness. The word is to be found in
our modern dictionaries. The Encyclopædia Britannica contains exhaustive articles upon its every aspect. There are
enough Socialist lectures in London every week, good, bad,
and indifferent, to drive the meaning into every willing ear.

The abstract word "Socialism" denotes a particular principle
of social organisation. We may define this principle either
from the constitutional or the economic standpoint. We may
either put it as "the control by the community of the means of
production for public advantage, instead of for private profit,"
or "the absorption of rent and interest by the community collectively." Its opposite is the abandonment of our means of
production to the control of competing private individuals,
stimulated by the prospect of securing the rent and interest
gratuitously.

But this definition does not satisfy some people. They want
a complete description of a Socialist State, an elaborately
worked out, detailed plan, like Sir Thomas More's "Utopia" or
Gulliver's Travels. Such fancy sketches have, indeed, at times
been thrown off by Socialists as by all other thinkers; but with

the growing realisation of social evolution, men gradually cease to expect the fabrication of a perfect and final social state; and the dreams of Fourier and Cabet, like those of Godwin and Comte, become outworn and impossible to us. There will never come a moment when we can say, "*Now* let us rest, for Socialism is established": any more than we say, "*Now* Radicalism is established." The true principles of social organisation must already have secured partial adoption, as a condition of the continuance of every existing social organism; and the progress of Socialism is but their more complete recognition and their conscious adoption as the lines upon which social improvement advances.

Looking back over the record of human progress, we see one main economic characteristic underlying every form of society. As soon as production is sufficiently advanced to furnish more than maintenance, there arises, wherever two or three are gathered together, a fierce struggle for the surplus product. This struggle varies in outward form according to the time and circumstances, but remains essentially the same in economic character. The individuals or classes who possess social power, have at all times, consciously or unconsciously, made use of that power in such a way as to leave to the great majority of their fellows practically nothing beyond the means of subsistence according to the current local standard. The additional product, determined by the relative differences in productive efficiency of the different sites, soils, capitals, and forms of skill above the margin of cultivation, has gone to those exercising control over these valuable but scarce productive factors. This struggle to secure the surplus or "economic rent" is the key to the confused history of European progress, and an underlying, unconscious motive of all revolutions. The student of history finds that the great world moves, like the poet's snake, on its belly.

The social power which has caused this unequal division of the worker's product has taken various forms. Beginning, probably, in open personal violence in the merely predatory stage of society, it has passed in one field, through tribal war, to political supremacy, embodied, for instance, in a "Jingo" foreign policy, and at home in vindictive class legislation. A survival

in England at the present time is the severity of the punishment for trifling offences against property compared with that
for personal assaults; and its effect is curiously seen when the
legal respect for person and that for property are, to some extent, opposed to each other, as in the case of wife-beating.

The social power does not, however, always take the forms
of physical strength or political supremacy. From the Indian
medicine man and the sun-priests of Peru down to the Col-
lector of Peter's Pence and the Treasurer of the Salvation
Army, theological influences have ever been used to divert a
portion of the rent to spiritual uses, often nourishing (like the
meats offered to idols) whole classes of non-producers, many
of whom have been of no real spiritual advantage to the community.

But by far the most important means of appropriating the
surplus product has been in the organisation of labor. The industrial leader, who can oblige his fellows to organise their toil
under his direction, is able thereby to cause an enormous increase in their productivity. The advantages of co-operative
or associated labor were discovered long before they were
described by Adam Smith or Fourier; and human history is
the record of their ever-increasing adoption. Civilisation itself
is nothing but an ever-widening co-operation.

But who is to get the benefit of the increased productivity?
In all times this question has been decided by the political
condition of the laborer. The universally first form of industrial organisation is chattel slavery. At a certain stage in social
development there seems to have been possible no other kind
of industrial co-operation. The renunciation of personal independence is, as Darwin observed of the Fuegian, the initial
step towards civilisation.

As a slave, the worker obtained at first nothing but bare
maintenance at the lowest economic rate. Cato even advises
the Roman noble that the bailiff or foreman need not have so
large a ration as the other slaves, his work, though more
skilled, being less exhausting. On the other hand, the surplus
value was not yet differentiated into its component economic
parts, and went in an undivided stream of profit all to the
master.

Advancing civilisation, itself rendered possible only by chattel slavery, gradually made this form of servitude incompatible with intellectual and moral development, and inadequate to industrial needs. The slave became the feudal serf or the tribal dependent. As a chattel he had ceded all but his maintenance to his master: as a serf he rendered to his lord three or four days' unpaid labor per week, maintaining himself on the product of the rest.

The further development of the social organism proved no more favourable to feudalism than to chattel slavery; and the modern "free laborer" came into existence. But the economic servitude of the worker did not drop off with his feudal fetters. With the chains of innate status, there disappeared also its economic privileges; and the "free laborer" found himself, especially in England, in a community where the old common rights over the soil were being gradually but effectually extinguished. He became a landless stranger in his own country.

The development of competitive production for sale, and the industrial revolution of the past century, have made subsistence dependent, not merely upon access to the land, but upon the use, in addition, of increasingly large masses of capital, at first in agriculture, then in foreign trade, then in manufacture, and now, finally, also in distributive industries. The mere worker became steadily less and less industrially independent as his legal freedom increased. From an independent producing unit, he passed into a mere item in a vast industrial army, over the organisation of which he had no control. He was free, but free only to work at the market wage or to starve. Other resource he had none; and even now the freedom to work at all is denied to many at a time for varying periods, and we have the constantly recurring phenomenon of the unemployed. When it suits any person having the use of land and capital to employ the worker, he does so only on condition that two important deductions, rent and interest, can be made from the product for the gratuitous benefit of those possessing the legal ownership of land and capital. The reward of labor being thus reduced on an average by at least one third, the remaining eightpence out of the shilling is then shared between the various classes who *have* co-operated in the production, that is, the inventor, the managing employer, and the mere wage-worker—but in the competitive struggle it is shared in such a way that at least fourpence goes to a favoured set of educated workers numbering one-fifth of the whole, leaving four fifths to divide less than fourpence out of the shilling between them. We have the direct consequence in the social condition around us. A fortunate few, owing to their legal power over the instruments of wealth production, are able to command the services of thousands of industrial slaves whose faces they have never seen, without rendering any return whatever to them or to society. A larger body of persons contribute some labor, but are able, from their education or their cultivated ability, to choose occupations for which the competition wage is still high, owing to the relatively small number of possible competitors. These two classes together number only one-fifth of the whole. On the other side is the great mass of the people, the weekly wage-earners, four out of every five of the nation, toiling perpetually for less than a third of the aggregate product of labor, at an annual wage averaging at most £35 per adult, hurried into unnecessarily early graves by the severity of their lives, and dying, as regards, at least, one-third of them, destitute or actually in receipt of poor-law relief.

When we have bound the laborer fast to his wheel; when we have practically excluded the average man from every real chance of improving his condition; when we have virtually denied to him the means of sharing in the higher feelings and the larger sympathies of the cultured race; when we have shortened his life in our service, stunted his growth in our factories, racked him with unnecessary disease by our exactions, tortured his soul with that worst of all pains, the constant fear of poverty, condemned his wife and children to sicken and die before his eyes, in spite of his own perpetual round of toil—then we are aggrieved that he often loses hope, gambles for the windfall that is denied to his industry, attempts to drown his cares in drink, and, driven by his misery irresistibly down the steep hill of vice, passes into that evil circle where vice begets poverty, and poverty intensifies vice, until Society unrelentingly stamps him out as vermin. Thereupon we lay the flattering unction to our souls that it was his own fault, that

he had his chance; and we preach to his fellows thrift and
temperance, prudence and virtue, but always industry, that
industry of others which keeps the industrial machine in motion, so that we can still enjoy the opportunity of taxing it.
Nay, so that we may not lose his labor, we keep him when
we can from absolute starvation; and when the world has
taken his all, we offer him the pauper's dole. Nothing gives a
more striking picture of his condition than the official statistics
of our pauperism. We have clogged our relief with irksome
and humiliating conditions, so that the poor often die lingering deaths rather than submit to them. . . .

Those who believe it possible that the festering evils of
social ulceration can be cured without any fundamental
change in property relations, rely mainly on three leading remedies, Trade Unions, Co-operation, and a general recrudescence of a Christ-like unselfishness. What does the dry light of
science say to these homœopathic "pills against the earth-
quake"?

The belief in universal Trade Unionism as a means of
greatly and permanently raising wages all round must be at
once dismissed as involving a logical fallacy. Certainly, the
workers in some trades have managed to improve their economic position by strict Trade Unions. We are never allowed
to forget the splendid incomes earned by these aristocrats of
labor, a mere tenth of the whole labor class. But those who
merely counsel the rest to go and do likewise forget that the
only permanently effective Trade Union victories are won by
limitation of the numbers in the particular trade, and the excluded candidates necessarily go to depress the condition of
the outsiders. The Trade Unionist can usually only raise himself on the bodies of his less fortunate comrades. If all were
equally strong, all would be equally powerless—a point clearly
proved by Prof. Cairnes; and obvious to all Trade Unionists
themselves.

Co-operation is a more seductive means of escape: and most
social reformers cannot, even now, refrain from keeping alive
lingering hopes that some solution may here be found. But a
whole generation of experiment has done little more than show
the futility of expecting real help from this quarter. Less than

one four-hundredth part of the industry of the country is yet carried on by Co-operation. The whole range of industrial development in the larger industries seems against it; and no ground for hope in Co-operation as a complete answer to the social problem can be gained from economic science. . . .

There remains the ideal of the rapid spread of a Christ-like unselfishness. Of this hope let us speak with all the respect which so ancient a dream deserves. If it were realised it would, indeed, involve an upset of present property arrangements, compared with which Socialism is a mere trifle; yet science must perforce declare that the expectation of any but the slowest real improvement in general moral habit is absolutely without warrant. Forms of egoism may change, and moral habits vary; but, constituted as we are, it seems inevitable for healthy personal development that an at best instructed and unconscious egoism should preponderate in the individual. It is the business of the community not to lead into temptation this healthy natural feeling, but so to develop social institutions that individual egoism is necessarily directed to promote only the well-being of all. The older writers, led by Rousseau, in the reaction against aristocratic government, saw this necessary adjustment in absolute freedom. But that crude vision has long been demolished. "It is indeed, certain," sums up Dr. Ingram, "that industrial society will not permanently remain without a systematic organisation. The mere conflict of private interests will never produce a well-ordered commonwealth of labor."

Is there then no hope? Is there no chance of the worker ever being released from the incubus of what Mill called, "the great social evil of a non-laboring class, whose monopolies cause the taxation of the industrious for the support of indolence, if not of plunder?"

Mill tells us how, as he investigated more closely the history and structure of Society, he came to find a sure and certain hope in the Progress of Socialism, which he foresaw and energetically aided. We who call ourselves Socialists to-day in England, largely through Mill's teaching and example, find a confirmation of this hope in social history and economics, and see already in the distance the glad vision of a brighter day, when, practically, the whole product of labor will be the worker's and the worker's alone, and at last social arrangements will be deliberately based upon the Apostolic rule ignored by so many Christians, that if a man do not work, neither shall he eat.

But it must clearly be recognised that no mere charitable palliation of existing individualism can achieve this end. Against this complacent delusion of the philanthropist, Political Economy emphatically protests. So long as the instruments of production are in unrestrained private ownership, so long must the tribute of the workers to the drones continue: so long will the toilers' reward inevitably be reduced by their exactions. . . .

Where then is the Socialist hope?

In the political power of the workers. The industrial evolution has left them landless strangers in their own country; but the political evolution is about to make them its rulers. If unrestrained private ownership of the means of production necessarily keeps the many workers permanently poor without any fault on their part, in order to make a few idlers rich without any merit on theirs (and this is the teaching of economic science), unrestrained private ownership will inevitably go. In this country many successive inroads have already been made in it; and these constitute the Progress of Socialism.

Three hundred years ago, for fear of the horde of "sturdy beggars," which even hanging had failed to extirpate, the wise Cecil was led to institute the general system of poor relief, a deduction from rent and interest for the benefit of those who were excluded from directly sharing in them. But the industrial evolution had not yet made this condition universal; and little further progress was made in Socialism until the beginning of our century. Then, indeed, the acme of individualism was reached. No sentimental regulations hindered the free employment of land and capital to the highest possible personal advantage, however many lives of men, women, and children were used up in the process. Capitalists still speak of that bright time with exultation. "It was not five per cent. or ten per cent.," says one, "but thousands per cent. that made the fortune of Lancashire." But opinion turned against *Laissez-faire* fifty years ago. Mainly by the heroic efforts of a young nobleman, who lately passed away from us as Lord Shaftesbury, a really effective Factory Act was won; and the insatiate greed of the manufacturers was restrained by political power, in the teeth of their most determined opposition. Since then the progress has been rapid. Slice after slice has, in the public interest, been cut off the profits of land and capital, and therefore off their value, by Mines Regulation Acts, Truck Acts, Factory Acts, Adulteration Acts, Land Acts. Slice after slice has been cut off the already diminished incomes of the classes enjoying rent and interest, by the gradual shifting of taxation from the whole nation as consumers of taxed commodities to the holders of incomes above £150, the average family income of the Kingdom. Step by step political power and political organisation have been used for industrial ends, until a Minister of the Crown is the largest employer of labor in the country, and at least 200,000 men, not counting the army and navy, are directly in the service of the community, without the intervention of the profit of any middleman. All the public needs supplied by the labor of these public servants were at one time left to private enterprise, and were a source of legitimate individual investment of capital. Step by step the community has absorbed them, wholly or partially; and the area of private exploitation has been lessened. Parallel with this progressive nationalisation or municipalisation of industry, a steady elimination of the purely personal element in business management has gone on. The older economists doubted whether anything but banking could be carried on by joint-stock enterprise: now every conceivable industry, down to baking and milk-selling, is successfully managed by the salaried officers of large corporations of idle shareholders. More than one-third of the whole business of England, measured by the capital employed, is now done by joint-stock companies, whose shareholders could be expropriated by the community with little more dislocation of industry than is caused by the daily purchase of shares on the Stock Exchange.

Besides its direct supersession of private enterprise, the State now registers, inspects, and controls nearly all the industrial functions which it has not yet absorbed. The inspection is often detailed and rigidly enforced. The State in most of the larger industrial operations prescribes the age of the worker, the hours of work, the amount of air, light, cubic space, heat, lavatory accommodation, holidays, and meal-times; where, when, and how wages shall be paid; how machinery, staircases, lift-holes, mines, and quarries are to be fenced and guarded; how and when the plant shall be cleaned, repaired, and worked. Even the kind of package in which some articles shall be sold is duly prescribed, so that the individual capitalist shall take no advantage of his position. On every side he is being registered, inspected, controlled; eventually he will be superseded by the community, and he is compelled in the meantime to cede for public purposes an ever-increasing share of his rent and interest.

This is the rapid progress of "Collectivism" which is so noticeable in our generation. England is already the most Socialist of all European communities, though the young Emperor of Germany is now compelled by the uneasy ground swell of German politics to emulate us very closely. English Collectivism will, however, inevitably be Democratic—a real "Social Democracy" instead of the mere Political Democracy with which Liberals coquet. As the oldest industrial country, we are likely to keep the lead, in spite of those old-fashioned politicians who innocently continue to regard Socialism as a dangerous and absolutely untried innovation. Are there not still, in obscure nooks, disbelievers and despisers of all science? The schoolmaster never penetrates into *all* the corners in the same generation.

But some will be inclined to say, "This is not what we thought Socialism meant. We imagined that Socialists wanted to bring about a sanguinary conflict in the streets, and then the next day to compel all delicately nurtured people to work in the factories at a fixed rate of wages."

It is not only in the nursery that bogey-making continues to be a very general though quite unnecessary source of anxiety. Socialists do but foretell the probable direction of English social evolution; and it needs nothing but a general recognition of that development, and a clear determination not to

allow the selfish interests of any class to hinder or hamper it,
for Socialism to secure universal assent. All other changes will
easily flow from this acquiescent state of mind, and they need
not be foreshadowed in words.

"But will not Socialism abolish private property!" It will
certainly seriously change ideas concerning that which the
community will lend its force to protect in the personal enjoyment of any individual.

It is already clear that no really democratic government,
whether consciously Socialist or not, will lend its soldiers or
its police to enforce the "rights" of such an owner as Lord
Clanricarde. Even Matthew Arnold declared the position of
the mere landlord to be an "anachronism." "Landlordism" in
Ireland is admittedly doomed, and opinion in England is
rapidly ripening in favour of collective control over the soil.
The gradual limitation of the sphere of private property
which has been steadily taking place will doubtless continue;
and just as courts of justice, private mints, slaves, public offices,
pocket boroughs, votes, army commissions, post offices, telegraph lines, and now even continental telegraph cables landing
on English shores, have ceased to be permissible personal
possessions, so will the few remaining private gasworks, water-
works, docks, tramways, and schools be quickly absorbed, and
an end be also made to private railways and town ground-
rents. Ultimately, and as soon as may be possible, we look to
see this absorption cover all land, and at least all the larger
forms of industrial capital. In these, as Herbert Spencer
pointed out forty years ago as regards land, private ownership
will eventually no more be possible than it is now in a post
office or a court of justice, both of which were once valuable
sources of individual profit. Beyond the vista of this extension
of collectivism, it is at present unnecessary to look; but we
may at any rate be sure that social evolution will no more
stop there than at any previous stage.

This is the Progress of Socialism. To an ever growing number of students of history and science, its speedy acceleration
appears at once our evident destiny and our only hope. Political Economy, at least, whatever the economist may think of
Socialism, now recognises no other alternative. So long as

land and industrial capital remain in unrestrained private ownership, so long must "the subjection of labor to capital, and the enormous share which the possessors of the instruments of industry are able to take from the produce" inevitably continue, and even increase. The aggregate product may continue to grow; but "the remuneration of labor as such, skilled or unskilled, can never rise much above its present level."

The *only* effectual means of raising the material condition of the great mass of the people, is for them to resume, through their own public organisations, that control over their own industry which industrial evolution has taken from them, and to enter collectively into the enjoyment of the fertile lands and rich mines from which they are now so relentlessly excluded. This is the teaching of economic science; and, however little individual economists may relish the application, the workers are rapidly coming to appreciate it.

In this direction, too, is the mighty sweep and tendency of social evolution. Without our knowledge, even against our will, we in England have already been carried far by the irresistible wave. What Canute will dare to set a limit to its advance? One option we have, and one only. It is ours, if we will, to recognise a rising force, to give it reasonable expression, nay, within limits, even to direct its course. This is why we are Socialists, and why you must become so. For if the conscious intelligence of the natural leaders of the community lag behind the coming thought; if it ignore the vast social forces now rapidly organising for common action; if it leave poverty and repression and injustice to go on breeding their inevitable births of angry brutality and fierce revenge: then, indeed, social evolution may necessarily be once more accomplished by social cataclysm. From this catastrophe, our gradual adoption of Social Democracy is the path of escape.

JEAN JAURÈS (1859–1914)

Jean Jaurès was the outstanding French socialist in the halcyon years before World War I. He expressed more elo-

quently than anyone else the belief, prevalent among socialists at the time, that the future belonged to socialism. A
Marxist and an idealist who was convinced that history meant
progress, he occupied a place in the French political spectrum
roughly akin to Bernstein's in the German. But unlike the
German revisionist, Jaurès exercised an immense influence
over the Socialist Party of his country until he was struck down
by a nationalist fanatic in 1914.

He came to politics in his mid-twenties from a brilliant
career as a teacher and scholar. Born the same year as Henri
Bergson, he graduated from the Ecole Normale Supérieure in
philosophy at the same time Bergson did. He began his political career as a moderate republican but moved leftward
after entering the Chamber of Deputies in 1885. A man of
protean talents, Jaurès had no peer as an orator. He wrote a
towering history of the French Revolution from a Marxist-
idealist point of view, and founded one of the best socialist
papers in Europe, L'Humanité. His death was a great loss for
France and for socialism.

French socialism at the turn of the century was riven into
three factions: the reformers, led by Millerand; the Guesdistes,
followers of Jules Guesde, who favored a Marxist organization
on German lines; and the political syndicalists (as distinguished from the trade union syndicalists who eschewed politics). Jaurès was able to bring them together and frame a
platform—bristling with generalities—on which they could all
agree. Under these conditions and under his leadership the
French Socialist Party was unified in 1905.

Jaurès's ideal was to open the French working class to all
the magnificent possibilities of French culture. This had
been, he believed, the ideal of the Great Revolution, and it
remained for socialism to complete the task. Socialism for
Jaurès was based on moral truths such as Rousseau had found
in the democratic state. The moral development of mankind
was slow but inexorable. Economic justice would be achieved
by political means that were at once evolutionary and permanent. Disagreeing with the orthodox Marxists, who maintained
that ideals rested on an economic substratum, Jaurès also saw
through the conventional middle-class notion of a conflict be-

tween idealism and materialism. For him both came within the same moral imperative embodied to the highest degree in a state consecrated to equality among men.

His assassination was a cruel augur of the times. Assassinated with him were the exalted hopes, the limitless optimism of an age that he perhaps above all other men had reflected in his life and work.

IDEALISM IN HISTORY (1895)

First I want to caution you against an error that might arise from the fact that the subject I shall deal with here before you is one on which I spoke a few months ago. At that time I expounded the thesis of economic materialism, the interpretation and movement of history that was set forth by Marx; and I made an effort to justify Marx's doctrine, in such a way that it might have appeared that I accepted it without any qualification whatsoever.

This time, on the other hand, I want to demonstrate that the materialist conception of history does not preclude an idealist interpretation of it. And since one might, in this second part of my demonstration, lose sight of the arguments in all their force that I gave in favor of Marx's thesis, I ask you, so that there be no mistake about the whole of my thought on the subject, to correct, and complete each part of this exposition that we have been obliged to split in two by the other.

I demonstrated, last time, that one could interpret all the phenomena of History from the viewpoint of economic materialism, which, as I said then, is definitely not physiological materialism. Marx was as far as anyone could be from saying that all phenomena of the consciousness or of thought can be explained by simple groupings of molecular matter. This, in fact, is a hypothesis that Marx and, more recently Engels, regarded as metaphysical, and that has been repudiated as thoroughly by the scientific school as by the spiritualist one.

Nor is it what is sometimes called "moral materialism," which is the subordination of all of man's activity to the satisfaction of physical appetites and the search for individual well-being. On the contrary, if you will recall how Marx treats

the British utilitarian conception in his book *Capital,* if you
will recall with what disdain and contempt he speaks of
theoreticians of Utilitarianism like Jeremy Bentham, who
maintains that man always acts with a personal interest in
mind that is constantly sought after by him, you will see that
these two doctrines have nothing in common. Rather, one is
entirely the opposite of the other; for, precisely because Marx
held that the very modes of feeling and thought are determined in men by the essential form of the economic relationships of the society in which they live, he thereby introduced
into the individual's conduct social forces, collective forces,
historical forces, whose power transcends that of individual
and egoistic motives. What this means is that the essential in
history consists in economic relationships, in relationships of
production between man and man.

It is according to the way in which men are linked together
by one or another form of economic organization, that a society has this or that character, this or that conception of life,
this or that kind of morality, and gives one or another sort of
general direction to its enterprises. Furthermore, according
to Marx, men do not act in accordance with an abstract idea
of justice or right; they act because the social system that has
been formed among them out of the economic relations of
production is, at any given moment in history, an unstable
system, obliged to transform itself in order to yield its place to
other systems. It is the substitution of one economic system
for another, for example of slavery for cannibalism, that naturally brings along in its wake an equivalent transformation in
political, moral, aesthetic, scientific and religious conceptions:
in other words, the deepest and most significant well-spring
of historical energy is, according to Marx, the mode of organization of economic interests.

The term "economic materialism" can therefore be explained in this way: a man does not draw out of his own
brain a completely formed idea of justice; he does no more
than reflect within himself, within his cerebral substance, the
economic relations of production.

The idealist conception in relation to the materialist one,
exists in numerous forms. I will sum it up this way: it is the

conception according to which humanity has, at its point of departure, an initial presentiment of its destiny and development.

Before having the experience of history, before establishing this or that economic system, humanity carries within itself a preliminary idea of justice and right, and it pursues this preconceived ideal from one form of civilization to another, higher form. When humanity acts, it is not by the automatic and mechanical transformation of the modes of production, but under the obscurely or clearly felt influence of this ideal.

This takes place in such a way that the idea itself becomes the principle of movement and of action, and that, far from the intellectual conceptions being derived from economic facts, it is the economic facts that, little by little, translate and incorporate the ideal of humanity into reality and history.

Such is the conception of idealism in history, apart from the innumerable formulas that various religious or philosophical systems have given to it. Now, you will note that these two conceptions, apparently opposed to one another and even mutually exclusive, are really, in the contemporary consciousness, almost, I would say, enmeshed in one another and completely reconciled. There is in fact not a single idealist who would not concede that it is impossible to achieve a higher ideal of man without a preliminary transformation of the economic organism, and, on the other hand, there are very few adherents of the theory of economic materialism who do not allow themselves to appeal to the idea of justice and right, or who confine themselves to depicting the communist society of tomorrow as the necessary and fatal consequence of economic evolution. Rather, they continue to hail this communist society of tomorrow as a higher realization of justice and right.

Is there a contradiction here? Marx was always anxious to maintain the somewhat harsh integrity of his formula, and had nothing but jibes for those who believed that they were strengthening economic evolution and the socialist movement by appealing to the pure idea of justice; he had nothing but jibes for those who, in his own words, "wanted to throw over the reality of history, over the body of facts themselves, a sort of veil woven of the most immaterial threads of the dialectic, embroidered with flowers of rhetoric and soaked in sentimental dew."

It is our task to see if this reconciliation between the materialist and the idealist conceptions of history, which has been realized in fact in our country through instinct, is really alien to the socialist conscience. It is our task to see if it is theoretically and doctrinally possible, or if there is an insoluble contradiction in it, if we are obliged to make a decisive choice between the two conceptions, or if we can logically and reasonably consider them as two different aspects of a single truth. . . .

There is of course no need to remind those versed in the Marxian doctrine that Marx was the intellectual disciple of Hegel; he said so himself, proclaiming it in his introduction to *Capital* (and for the past few years, Engels, following that inclination that leads men who have lived a long time back to their origins, has apparently been making a more intense study of Hegel). It is a striking application of Hegel's formula of contradictions when Marx notes the antagonism of classes in the world today, the state of economic war that opposes the capitalist class to the proletarian class; because this antagonism was born under the capitalist regime, a regime of divisiveness and war, and is preparing the way for a new regime of peace and harmony. According to the ancient formula of Heraclitus that Marx was fond of citing: "Peace is only a form, an aspect of war; war is only a form, an aspect of peace." There is no need to hold up one in opposition to the other; the battle of today is the beginning of the reconciliation of tomorrow.

Modern thinking on the identity of opposites is summed up today in this other admirable conception of Marxism: Until now, humanity has been guided, so to speak, by the unconscious forces of history; until now, men have not acted on their own. Rather, economic evolution guides their acts; they believe themselves to be producing events, or imagine themselves to be vegetating and remaining always in the same place, but economic transformations are taking place without their even realizing it, and they are being unconsciously affected. In a way, humanity has been like a sleeping person afloat on a river, carried along by the flow without contributing to it, or at least without taking account of its direction, but waking up from time to time and perceiving that the surrounding countryside has changed.

Well, once the socialist revolution has become a reality, once the antagonism of classes has ceased, once the human community has become master of the principal means of production in order to direct them to the service of the known and acknowledged needs of men, then humanity will have been torn from the long period of unconsciousness in which it had resided for centuries, pushed along by the blind course of events, and will have entered upon the era in which man will no longer be subject to things outside himself, but will govern their movement instead. But this forthcoming era of full consciousness and clarity is possible only because of a long period of unconsciousness and obscurity.

If, at the dim beginnings of history, men had consciously tried to regulate the course of events and development of things, they simply would have set everything awry, wasted their resources for the future, and as a result of having too soon aspired to act with full consciousness, deprived themselves of the means of ever acting in full consciousness. It is as if a child were summoned too soon to the fully conscious life of reflective reason; deprived of the period of the unconscious evolution of the organic life and of the first manifestations of the moral life, he would then, as a result of having been forced to think in the first moments of life, be incapable of thinking thereafter.

For Marx, this unconscious life was the very condition of and preparation for the conscious life of tomorrow, and history was charged in this way with the task of resolving an essential contradiction. I ask you then, if one may not, if one must not, without violating the spirit of Marxism, press still further this method of the reconciliation of opposites, the synthesis of contradictory elements, and seek out the fundamental reconciliation of economic materialism with idealism, as applied to the development of history.

Notice in what spirit—and I must ask your pardon for these

long preliminaries, but one cannot resolve a particular question unless one's thought is based upon a general philosophical conception—notice in what spirit I seek this reconciliation of ＊＊＊＊＊＊＊ materialism with historical and moral idealism.

I am not trying to say that each has its place, that one part of history is governed by economic necessity, and another part is guided by a pure idea, by a concept—by the idea, for example, of humanity, of justice, or of right. I am not trying to place the materialist conception on one side of a partition, and the idealist conception on the other. I maintain that they must interpenetrate one another, the way that cerebral mechanism and conscious spontaneity interpenetrate one another in the organic life of man. . . .

Marx says: "The human brain does not produce an idea of right all by itself; such an idea would be vain and hollow. In all aspects of the life of humanity, even the intellectual and moral, there is only a reflection of economic phenomena in the human brain."

Well, I accept that. Yes, in all the development of the intellectual, moral, and religious life of humanity, there is only the reflection of economic phenomena in the human brain; yes, but there is at the same time the human brain, and therefore the cerebral preformation of humanity.

Humanity is the product of a long physiological evolution that preceded the historical one, and when man emerged, at the end of this physiological evolution, from animality, the state that was immediately below his own, he already had various predispositions and tendencies within this first brain of nascent humanity. . . .

I grant to Marx that all subsequent development would be nothing but the reflection of economic phenomena within the brain, but on condition that we agree that there were in this brain to begin with, through the aesthetic sense, through the faculty of imaginative sympathy, and through the need for unity, fundamental forces that intervene in the economic life.

Let us note, once again, that I am not juxtaposing the intellectual faculties with economic forces, that I am not trying to reconstitute that syndicate of historical factors that our eminent friend, Gabriel Deville, dispersed with such vigor a few months ago. No, I am not seeking such a juxtaposition, but I am saying that it is impossible that the observable economic phenomena penetrate the human brain without at the same time setting primitive faculties in motion. This is why I do not grant to Marx that religious, political and moral conceptions are solely the reflection of economic phenomena: there is within man such an interpenetration of the man himself and his economic *milieu* that one cannot separate the economic from the moral life. In order to subordinate one to the other, you must first abstract one from the other; now, this abstraction is impossible. You can no more cut historical humanity in two and dissociate its ideal life from its economic life, than you can cut a man in two and thereby dissociate his organic life from the life of his consciousness. Such is my thesis, which I find partially confirmed by Greek philosophy.

The Greeks did not begin by observing the economic antinomies, the laws that established order in the city, the opposition and reconciliation of the rich and the poor, and then go on to project their observations about the economic order onto the universe. No, rather they united economic and natural phenomena in a single view and a single conception. Look at Heraclitus, Empedocles, Anaximander; they observed the connections and contradictions between elements within single formulas, and noted that these elements *heat* and *cold, light* and *dark,* belonged to nature, or that the elements *healthy* and *sick* belonged to the physiological organism, or that the elements *perfect* and *imperfect, equal* and *unequal,* belonged to the intellectual life. They made a single table of these oppositions, borrowed either from nature or from society, and for Heraclitus, the same word, "Cosmos," expresses at one and the same time the order in the world resulting from the reconciliation of opposites, and the order in the city resulting from the reconciliation of factions. The Greek thinkers perceived the world order through the chaos of society in a single, unifying conception.

Since time prevents me from doing anything more than skimming lightly over the whole question, I will confine myself to addressing another request for an explanation to the

Marxist theoreticians, and ask them this: What judgment do you make, if you make one (and I'm sure you do), about the direction of economic movement and the direction of the movement of humanity?

It is not sufficient to say that one form of production succeeds another form—it is not sufficient to say that slavery succeeded cannibalism, that serfdom succeeded slavery, and that the collectivist or communist regime will succeed that of wage labor. No, you must say more than this. Is there evolution or progress? And if there is progress, what is the final and decisive idea by which the various forms of human development are measured? And, what is more, if you want to repudiate this idea of progress as being too metaphysical, then why has the movement of history gone from one form to another in the direction it has, from economic stage to economic stage, from slavery to serfdom, from serfdom to wage-labor, from wage-labor to the socialist regime, and not in some other direction? Why, by virtue of what source of energy—I won't say by virtue of what decree of Providence, because I remain attached to the materialist and positive conception of history—has the development of humanity proceeded in this fashion?

To me, the reason is easy to perceive, if you are willing to admit the activity of man as man, the activity of those human forces of which I have just spoken. The reason is that, precisely because the economic relations of production involve human beings, there is no single form of production that does not contain an essential contradiction within itself so long as the full freedom and solidarity of men have not been realized.

It was Spinoza who demonstrated admirably the fundamental contradiction within every tyrannical regime, every form of social and political exploitation of man by man, not by observing things from the standpoint of abstract right, but by showing that these situations presented a contradiction of fact. Either the tyranny will cause so much harm to those it oppresses that they will cease to fear the consequences of staging an insurrection, and so will rise up against the oppressor, or else, the oppressor, to prevent an uprising, will pay attention to some extent to the needs and instincts of his subjects, and will thus prepare them for freedom. And so, whatever course it takes, tyranny must disappear by virtue of the play of forces, *because these forces are men.*

This will be the same as long as the exploitation of man by man endures. It was Hegel, again, who said with marvellous precision: "The essential contradiction of all political or economic tyranny is that it is obliged to treat men as inert instruments, and men, no matter who they are, can never even conceive of descending to the condition of being mere machines." And let us note that this contradiction is at once a logical contradiction and a contradiction of fact.

It is a logical contradiction because there is an opposition between the very idea of man—that is, of a creature endowed with sensibility, spontaneity and the capacity for reflection— and the idea of a machine. It is a contradiction of fact because, when you use man as a tool that is alive in a way that you would use a tool that is not, you do violence to the very force that you are using, and thereby create a social mechanism that is discordant and precarious. Because this contradiction violates at the same time both man and the mechanical laws according to which a man's power can be utilized, the movement of history is at once an idealistic protest of the conscience against the regimes that debase man, and an automatic reaction of human forces against every unstable and violent social arrangement. What was cannibalism? It was a double contradiction: for, in obliging man to slaughter man even away from the excitation of combat, it did violence to man's primitive instinct of sympathy: moral contradiction;— and, furthermore, it made of man, who has a certain aptitude to produce through regulated labor, a sort of beast of prey not useful for anything but his flesh: economic contradiction. At that point, slavery had to be born, because the domestication of man did less violence to the instinct of sympathy, and better served the interests of the master, by getting from the man, through his labor, far more than he could give in his substance.

And one could easily make the same demonstration for slavery, for serfdom, or for wage-labor. One could then see that, since the whole movement of history results from the es-

sential contradiction between man and the use made of him,
that this movement tends in every one of its moments, as in
its over-all development, towards an economic order in which
man will bo made use of in a way that conforms to man.
Humanity gradually realizes itself through a succession of
economic forms that are more or less repugnant to its ideal.
And there is not only a necessary evolution in human history,
but an intelligible direction and a concept of the ideal as well.
So, through the whole course of the centuries, man has been
able to aspire toward justice only by aspiring toward a social
order less contradictory to himself than the existing one and
prepared by that existing order; thus the evolution of his
moral ideas is clearly regulated by the evolution of economic
forms. But at the same time, through the course of these successive configurations, humanity seeks out its nature and affirms itself, and whatever the diversity of *milieux*, of times, of
economic demands, it is the same breath of reproach and of
hope that escapes from the mouth of the slave, the serf, the
proletarian. It is the immortal breath of humanity, which is
the very soul of that which we call right. It is therefore not
necessary to oppose the materialist and the idealist conceptions of history to one another. They interweave in a single and
indissoluble line of development, because, if you cannot abstract man from economic relations, you also cannot abstract
economic relations from man, and history, at the same time
that it is a phenomenon unfolding in accordance with a mechanical law, is also an aspiration realizing itself according
to an ideal law.

And is it not the same, after all, for the whole evolution of
life as it is for historical evolution? Certainly life could not
have passed from one form to another, from one species to
another, except under the double action of *milieu* and the
immediately preceding biological conditions. The whole development of life is susceptible to the materialist explanation,
but at the same time one can say that the initial force of life
concentrated in the first living particles, as well as the general
conditions of our planetary existence, determined in advance
the general outlines, the plan, so to speak, of our life on this
planet. Thus, the innumerable beings that have evolved have,

at the same time that they were subject to a law, also collaborated through a secret aspiration in the realization of a plan of life. The development of physiological life as well as of historical life has thus been both idealist and materialist at the same time. And the synthesis that I am proposing to you therefore forms part of a more general synthesis that I can only point out, since there is no time to elaborate upon it.

But, to return to the economic question, didn't Marx himself really reintroduce the notion of the ideal, of progress, of right, into his historical conception? He did not merely proclaim the communist society as the necessary outcome of the capitalist order, but he demonstrated that it would put an end to the antagonism of classes that uses up the energies of humanity. He also demonstrated that, for the first time, man will enjoy a full and free life, that those who labor will have at the same time the lively sensibility of the worker and the tranquil vigor of the peasant, and that humanity will rise up, happier and nobler, on an earth that has been renewed.

Isn't this to recognize that the word "justice" has meaning, even within the materialist conception of history, and that the reconciliation that I am proposing is therefore already implicitly accepted by you?

ALEXANDRE MILLERAND (1859–1943)

Although German socialist reformers in the 1890s supported bourgeois programs, they never participated in bourgeois governments. French socialist reformers, led by Alexandre Millerand, were the first to exercise political power, a turning point in the history of European socialism. In the future socialists would not only join governments and even make them; they would, with Millerand, occasionally break strikes and suppress unions.

Millerand, born in Paris, came to the public's attention as a defense lawyer for a group of strikers at a time when strikes were still against the law. He was then a liberal, but, on being elected to the Chamber, moved steadily to the left. In 1896 he began to gravitate back to the right and continued to do so until he left politics altogether some forty-five years later. Prior to 1896 he had advocated sweeping reforms, including wholesale nationalization of industries. By 1899 he had joined the liberal republican cabinet of Waldeck-Rousseau as Minister of Commerce and put through some notable labor and welfare reforms. For the rest of his active political life he moved in and out of successive governments. During the war he formally broke with socialism and joined the conservative Nationalist Party. The high point of his career came in 1920 when he formed a government of his own, and, several months later, became President of the Republic.

Millerand set French socialism on the course of reform in a famous speech delivered to a socialist banquet at Saint-Mandé in 1896. Socialists had recently scored victories in municipal elections and the prospects for the future looked good—provided the different factions could be brought together. His purpose in the speech was to suggest to the assembled guests, among whom were all the leaders of French socialism, what policy the party should adopt. But three years later Millerand's own example—his joining a bourgeois government—was to split the party and delay its unification.

SAINT-MANDÉ PROGRAM (1896)

. . . A socialist candidate has accepted the obligation to withdraw in favor of any socialist candidate who has done better than he—wonderful! But how could one answer him if, seeing fit to speak up for himself, he denies his more fortunate competitor the right to be called a socialist? What should be the criterion for dealing with his claim? In other words, what is the minimum program that must be accepted by anyone who claims the title of socialist?

The question is certainly an important one. Without pretending in any way to set myself up as an authority, I ask your permission to set forth freely my own personal opinion on this subject.

At the point that the socialist party has reached in its development, it should, I think, for its own sake as well as out of a sense of duty, define its boundaries with the greatest possible precision. Where is the socialist party heading, and along what paths does it propose to achieve its aims? Is it true that it has the suppression of liberty and the confiscation of individual property as its objective, and that it plans to use force as its means?

These are the characteristics that all our adversaries, no matter who they are, have in mind when they picture the socialist party. But is it not immediately clear that all the points of this supposed definition—suppression of property, use of force—constitute the crudest antinomy, the most brutal contradiction of our doctrine and of the facts?

Cannot the socialist idea be summed up as the energetic determination to assure to every being in society the integral development of his personality? This necessarily implies two conditions, one following from the other: first, the appropriation by each individual of the things necessary to his security and development—of property, in other words; secondly, liberty, which is only a noble-sounding and hollow word if it does not have property as its safeguard and its base.

Furthermore, is not this very banquet, which has brought together this evening representatives of all the different shades of opinion in the socialist party, the most decisive affirmation of its tactics? And has any party in this country ever rendered greater homage to universal suffrage, and shown greater confidence in it, than has our own?

But it cannot be sufficient for us to stress these two facts, decisive as they ought to be in the eyes of all who judge us in good faith. We must push back our detractors as far as we can, we must oppose their criticisms point by point, we must see what is behind their declamations and perceive clearly what interests these men who have the words "liberty" and "property" incessantly on their tongues are striving to safeguard against us.

The picture of capitalist anarchy has often been drawn. To characterize such a regime in a word, it will suffice to point out that there is no security for anyone who lives under it. In such a regime, farmers, businessmen, industrialists, intellectual and manual laborers alike are subject to all kinds of

dangers. But collectivism maintains that it is from this very
excess of evil that salvation will burst forth.

Collectivism! I have pronounced this word fraught with
horror, the magic incantation of which is bound to cause all
the millions of workers of town and country who are no longer
frightened by the word "socialism" to line themselves up
against us.

I want to say only one thing about the collectivist idea:
it is neither the product of a dreamer's imagination, nor the
outcome of a philosopher's conceptions, but rather the recognition pure and simple of phenomena unfolding before our
eyes. No one makes collectivism, and no one ever will; it
makes itself every day—it is, if I may say it, the secretion of
the capitalist regime.

Under the double influence of the advancement of science
(of which the developments in technology are only the practical application) and the concentration of capital, the expropriation of small property-owners is taking place before our
eyes, along with the dissociation of work and property, and
the formation of a new feudal class. This class, accumulating
in its hands the ownership of the instruments of production,
could become by a slow but relentless progression the absolute master of the economic, political and moral life of the
entire population, who would thus be reduced to that modern
form of slavery called wage-labor.

Well, then! Collectivism claims that wage-labor will be no
more eternal than were those earlier forms of servitude and
human exploitation called slavery and serfdom.

Collectivism recognizes that the normal development of capitalist society consists in the substitution of the tyrannical
monopoly of a minority for the individual holding of property,
which is the condition and safeguard of liberty. It does not
rebel against this recognition, but yields to it. It does not pretend to turn back the centuries or to put a stop to the transformation of humanity: rather, it adapts itself to the rules of
this transformation. And, since it is a law of sociological evolution that all the means of production and exchange pass
from the form of individual property to that of capitalist property, all the aspirations of collectivism are adjusted to the view

that the way in which these immense capitalist properties
come into being, causing all small-scale, individual property
to wither and die, is also the way in which socialist property
will substitute itself for capitalist property.

And here I believe I am putting my finger on the characteristic feature of the socialist program.

In my opinion, whoever does not accept the necessary and
progressive substitution of social property for capitalist property is not a socialist. In other words, it is not just a question
of those three categories of the means of production and exchange that can be considered as classic: credit or the bank,
railroad transportation, mining. In addition to these, to take
an example which is certainly not farfetched, a certain industry is ripe at this moment for social appropriation because,
monopolized by a few, bringing enormous profits to those who
exploit it, characterized both by the perfection of its machinery and the intense concentration of its capital, it is perfectly designed to be fruitful and pliable material for social
exploitation: I am referring to the sugar refineries.

This is one example, and it is *only* one example. But really,
is it such a great novelty, this national administration that will
restore to everyone tomorrow the profit today unduly monopolized by a few? Is it not true that—the representatives of
socialist municipalities who are listening to me know this well,
for yesterday I even discovered an example of it in a commune of one of our Eastern departments that is not socialist
at all—is it not true that a number of small rural and urban
collectivities have already, by taking over the administration
of water, light, traffic, and public transportation and by providing agricultural machinery for common use, substituted
social for capitalist property in their own spheres?

And this progressive socialization of the diverse categories
of the means of production can bring only hope and joy to
millions of human beings thus called upon to raise themselves
from the condition of wage-earners to that of co-participants
in the wealth of society, through a progression that will be
regulated not by human caprices, but by the nature of
things.

It would be in vain for anyone to try to excite against the

socialist party the alarm of those favored few who still hold
in their own hands the instruments of production and the
integral product of their own labor. These men, the small
property-owners, are not only not threatened by the transformation that the socialist party is seeking, since their small
pieces of property could not be the object of social appropriation; but they would even benefit from the successive incorporation of the large industries into the social domain, as
would all the other members of society.

I say "successive incorporation." No socialist has ever
dreamed, in other words, of transforming the capitalist regime with a wave of a magic wand, or of starting with a clean
slate to construct a completely new society.

In an article on the evolution of collectivism, Vandervelde,
the great Belgian orator and thinker, warned his friends
against the danger of hasty and arbitrary constructions in an
era in which science is capable of upsetting the elements of
life itself at a single stroke, whether by completely transforming the conditions under which we obtain our nourishment,
as our great chemist Berthelot once envisaged, or by profoundly modifying industrial conditions through undreamed-
of applications of the transportation of power.

By using such language, citizens, our friend was only
bringing out the two aspects of socialism, its idealistic power
and its practical greatness at the same time. Our philosophers,
our ideologists—this is, used in its proper place, a fine and
just word—are constructing systems: collectivism is an ideal
and complete plan for society.

But if our vision is lofty, and ever grows loftier, we keep
our feet on the ground all the same; we maintain contact
with the resistant and solid earth. We do not in any way
substitute our imaginings for the realities amidst which we
move, and every one of our realizations aspires to be and
must be only the consequence and result of things already
accomplished. . . .

Yes, socialism aims to assure to every human being, by a
beneficial transformation of an entirely natural order, these
two advantages: liberty and property, of which men are
deprived by the capitalist regime. But in thus noting the goal

pursued by our party, I have already answered the ridiculous reproach so often repeated that it seeks the triumph of its ideals only through violent revolution.

Our eminent friend Gabriel Deville, whom the Fourth Arrondissement will send next Sunday to sit among us in the socialist group in the Chamber of Deputies, stated several days ago, with as much force as precision, that we could expect the transformation of society to come not from a minority in revolt, but from the conscious majority. Against whom, and for whose sake, would we have recourse to force? Republicans above all, we do not cherish the foolish idea of appealing to the illusory prestige of a pretender, or to a dictator's saber, in order to make our doctrines triumph.

We address ourselves only to universal suffrage; our ambition is to bring about through this means, the economic and political liberation of all. We demand only the right to persuade the electorate. And no one, I suppose, would attribute to us the foolish intention of resorting to revolutionary means against a Senate that could easily have been brought to reason by radical ministers animated by a less vacillating will.

No, in order to realize the immediate reforms that can alleviate the lot of the working class and thus make it better able to bring about its own emancipation, in order to begin, under the conditions determined by the nature of things, the socialization of the means of production, it is necessary and sufficient for the socialist party to pursue the conquest of public power through universal suffrage.

But at the same time that socialism strives to substitute social property for capitalist property within the commune, department and nation, it cannot lose sight of the general, international character that the very development of human knowledge and hence of human relations has stamped upon the social problem. Ah! I know how hypocritical our adversaries are when they try to exploit the international accord of the workers as an argument against us.

The same men who know no boundaries when it comes to negotiating fruitful accords between speculators of all nationalities have raised cries of outrage at the thought that laborers who do not speak the same language should get together to discuss their common interests. They do not hesitate, these patriots, to throw the question of patriotism into our internal quarrels when to do so serves to safeguard their cause. But the public's good sense has done justice to these impudent maneuverings. Surely here at this meeting, at which both the variety of our country's aspects and its unity of thought are so forcefully expressed, I have no need to reiterate that we have never had the unholy and foolish idea of breaking with, of separating ourselves, from this incomparable instrument of material and moral progress forged through the centuries that is called the French *patrie*.

No, nor shall we ever; neither when, several days from now, we receive with all the sympathy and respect that are his due, Liebknecht, the indefatigable fighter for the socialist idea, the valiant defender of right, who paid with his freedom in 1871 for his admirable protest against the crime of the annexation of Alsace-Lorraine that the Iron Chancellor was preparing, nor when we present ourselves in a few weeks at the London Congress of the International, shall we forget that we are Frenchmen and patriots at the same time that we are internationalists. Patriots and internationalists—these are the two titles under which our ancestors of the French Revolution allied themselves. . . .

EDUARD BERNSTEIN (1850–1932)

The German Social Democratic Party rose to prominence in the last two decades of the nineteenth century. In the Reichstag election of 1881 it received 312,000 votes; in 1890 it received 1,427,000 votes—one fifth of all the votes cast —and held thirty-five seats. During the same period, the trade unions that were subordinate to the party suddenly swelled with the influx of new members. Disciplined, tightly organized, reared on the orthodox teachings of Marx and Engels, the party was the power and pride and hope of the Second International. Germany's rapid proletarianization seemed to be bearing out all Marx's predictions, and the party felt confident of the future.

But its problems multiplied with its affluence. When its activities were suppressed by Bismarck's police in the 1880s, revolution seemed the only course open. But when the party became legitimate and gained electoral strength it was uncertain about what its course of action should be. Should it support friendly non-socialist parties for the sake of expediency and so compromise its revolutionary principles and impair its own chances for power? Should it remain aloof from all political involvements and wait for the moment to arrive when it could govern alone? The trouble with the latter position was that the party could not avoid dealing with problems requiring piecemeal solutions. To avoid them would have resulted in a loss of electoral strength and in the forfeiture of future claims to govern. In the state of Bavaria, for example, socialists favored a policy of aiding the small farmers, whose numbers were growing, not diminishing. Support for these farmers contradicted the canons of orthodox Marxism and the party's proletariat direction. The central leadership officially objected to the policy of agrarian "reformism." Nevertheless, the Bavarian socialists went ahead and supported the farmers in the 1890s, and socialists in other agricultural states soon followed them.

Though the party was in fact becoming increasingly reformist, it continued to profess adherence to orthodox Marxism. But the view that reformism was right and that it was Marxism that should change was put forth by the "revisionist" school of Eduard Bernstein. Bernstein, born in Berlin of Jewish parents in 1850, had risen to an important position in the party, thanks to his unusual gifts as a journalist. In 1881 following the promulgation of the anti-socialist laws, he fled Germany to live first in Switzerland for seven years, serving as editor of the party's newspaper (then under ban in Germany), and later in England for thirteen as its London correspondent. During his stay in London he shed the vestments of orthodox Marxism and put on those of his own making—even while remaining a close friend of Engels.

England was the main source of his revisionism. Bernstein

was impressed by the vigor of the English political democracy, by the strength of its trade unions, by the resilience of
its capitalism and, above all, by its Fabian movement. It
seemed to Bernstein that Marx's conception of historical
inevitability was proving untrue. The crises in capitalism
were growing less, not more, severe; the middle class was
growing, not diminishing in size; the standard of living of
all classes was rising, not falling; the democratic state responded more or less to the will of the people, it was not
simply the executive arm of the ruling class. Socialism, he
concluded, would arise through pragmatic reform, not with a
catastrophe resulting in proletariat dictatorship. Moral ideals
should be the guide of the future, not the *ignis fatuus* of economic necessity.

Bernstein first presented these disturbing ideas in 1896 in
the *Neue Zeit*, the chief theoretical organ of the German
Socialist Party. After a long and bitter debate, in the course
of which the party officially censured him, he presented his
case in the book that has become one of the classics of
democratic socialism, *Die Voraussetzungen der Sozialismus
und die Aufgaben der Sozialdemokratie*, published in 1899
and translated that year into English as *Evolutionary Socialism*. Bernstein's revisionism stirred up every socialist party in
the years preceding World War I. Bernstein still considered
himself a Marxist in his method of critical thinking and in
his ideal of a socialist commonwealth. His enemies, of course,
denied this and maintained that he had become an apostate,
but they could not deny that capitalism had been changing in
all the industrial countries, most notably in the democracies,
and that the old Marxist formulae described a world that no
longer existed.

The excerpt is taken from the introduction and conclusion of *Evolutionary Socialism*.

Evolutionary Socialism (1899)

. . . No one has questioned the necessity for the working
classes to gain the control of government. The point at issue
is between the theory of a social cataclysm and the question

whether with the given social development in Germany and the present advanced state of its working classes in the towns and the country, a sudden catastrophe would be desirable in the interest of the social democracy. I have denied it and deny it again, because in my judgment a greater security for lasting success lies in a steady advance than in the possibilitites offered by a catastrophic crash.

And as I am firmly convinced that important periods in the development of nations cannot be leapt over I lay the greatest value on the next tasks of social democracy, on the struggle for the political rights of the working man, on the political activity of working men in town and country for the interests of their class, as well as on the work of the industrial organisation of the workers.

In this sense I wrote the sentence that the movement means everything for me and that what is *usually* called "the final aim of socialism" is nothing; and in this sense I write it down again to-day. Even if the word "usually" had not shown that the proposition was only to be understood conditionally, it was obvious that it *could* not express indifference concerning the final carrying out of socialist principles, but only indifference—or, as it would be better expressed, carelessness—as to the form of the final arrangement of things. I have at no time had an excessive interest in the future, beyond general principles; I have not been able to read to the end any picture of the future. My thoughts and efforts are concerned with the duties of the present and the nearest future, and I only busy myself with the perspectives beyond so far as they give me a line of conduct for suitable action now.

The conquest of political power by the working classes, the expropriation of capitalists, are no ends in themselves but only means for the accomplishment of certain aims and endeavours. As such they are demands in the program of social democracy and are not attacked by me. Nothing can be said beforehand as to the circumstances of their accomplishment; we can only fight for their realisation. But the conquest of political power necessitates the possession of political *rights;* and the most important problem of tactics

which German social democracy has at the present time to
solve, appears to me to be to devise the best ways for the
extension of the political and economic rights of the German
working classes

The following work has been composed in the sense of
these conclusions.

I am fully conscious that it differs in several important
points from the ideas to be found in the theory of Karl Marx
and Engels—men whose writings have exercised the greatest
influence on my socialist line of thought, and one of whom
—Engels—honored me with his personal friendship not only
till his death but who showed beyond the grave, in his testa-
mentary arrangements, a proof of his confidence in me.

This deviation in the manner of looking at things certainly
is not of recent date; it is the product of an inner struggle
of years and I hold in my hand a proof that this was no
secret to Friedrich Engels, and moreover I must guard Engels from the suspicion that he was so narrow-minded as to
exact from his friends an unconditional adherence to his
views. Nevertheless, it will be understood from the foregoing
why I have till now avoided as much as possible giving to
my deviating points of view the form of a systematic and
detailed criticism of the Marx-Engels doctrine. This could
the more easily be avoided up till now because as regards the
practical questions with which we were concerned Marx and
Engels in the course of time considerably modified their
views.

All that is now altered. I have now a controversy with
socialists who, like me, have sprung from the Marx-Engels
school; and I am obliged, if I am to maintain my opinions,
to show them the points where the Marx-Engels theory
appears to me especially mistaken or to be self-contradic-
tory. . . .

CONCLUSION

. . . The return to the *Communist Manifesto* points here to
a real residue of utopianism in the Marxist system. Marx had
accepted the solution of the utopians in essentials, but had

recognised their means and proofs as inadequate. He therefore undertook a revision of them, and this with the zeal, the critical acuteness, and love of truth of a scientific genius. He suppressed no important fact, he also forebore belittling artificially the importance of these facts as long as the object of the inquiry had no immediate reference to the final aim of the formula to be proved. To that point his work is free of every tendency necessarily interfering with the scientific method.

For the general sympathy with the strivings for emancipation of the working classes does not in itself stand in the way of the scientific method. But, as Marx approaches a point when that final aim enters seriously into the question, he becomes uncertain and unreliable. Such contradictions then appear as were shown in the book under consideration, for instance, in the section on the movement of incomes in modern society. It thus appears that this great scientific spirit was, in the end, a slave to a doctrine. To express it figuratively, he has raised a mighty building within the framework of a scaffolding he found existing, and in its erection he kept strictly to the laws of scientific architecture as long as they did not collide with the conditions which the construction of the scaffolding prescribed, but he neglected or evaded them when the scaffolding did not allow of their observance. Where the scaffolding put limits in the way of the building, instead of destroying the scaffolding, he changed the building itself at the cost of its right proportions and so made it all the more dependent on the scaffolding. Was it the consciousness of this irrational relation which caused him continually to pass from completing his work to amending special parts of it? However that may be, my conviction is that wherever that dualism shows itself the scaffolding must fall if the building is to grow in its right proportions. In the latter, and not in the former, is found what is worthy to live in Marx.

Nothing confirms me more in this conception than the anxiety with which some persons seek to maintain certain statements in *Capital,* which are falsified by facts. It is just some of the more deeply devoted followers of Marx who have not been able to separate themselves from the dialectical

form of the work—that is the scaffolding alluded to—who do
this. At least, that is only how I can explain the words of a
man, otherwise so amenable to facts as Kautsky, who, when
I observed in Stuttgart that the number of wealthy people
for many years had increased, not decreased, answered: 'It
that were true then the date of our victory would not only
be very long postponed, but we should never attain our goal.
If it be capitalists who increase and not those with no possessions, then we are going ever further from our goal the
more evolution progresses, then capitalism grows stronger,
not socialism."

That the number of the wealthy increases and does not
diminish is not an invention of bourgeois "harmony economists," but a fact established by the boards of assessment
for taxes, often to the chagrin of those concerned, a fact
which can no longer be disputed. But what is the significance
of this fact as regards the victory of socialism? Why should
the realisation of socialism depend on its refutation? Well,
simply for this reason: because the dialectical scheme seems
so to prescribe it; because a post threatens to fall out of the
scaffolding if one admits that the social surplus product is
appropriated by an increasing instead of a decreasing number of possessors. But it is only the speculative theory that is
affected by this matter; it does not at all affect the actual
movement. Neither the struggle of the workers for democracy
in politics nor their struggle for democracy in industry is
touched by it. The prospects of this struggle do not depend
on the theory of concentration of capital in the hands of a
diminishing number of magnates, nor on the whole dialectical
scaffolding of which this is a plank, but on the growth of
social wealth and of the social productive forces, in conjunction with general social progress, and, particularly, in conjunction with the intellectual and moral advance of the
working classes themselves.

Suppose the victory of socialism depended on the constant
shrinkage in the number of capitalist magnates, social democracy, if it wanted to act logically, either would have to
support the heaping up of capital in ever fewer hands, or at
least to give no support to anything that would stop this

shrinkage. As a matter of fact it often enough does neither the one nor the other. These considerations, for instance, do not govern its votes on questions of taxation. From the standpoint of the catastrophic theory a great part of this practical activity of the working classes is an undoing of work that ought to be allowed to be done. It is not social democracy which is wrong in this respect. The fault lies in the doctrine which assumes that progress depends on the deterioration of social conditions. . . .

Similar conflicts exist with regard to the estimate of the relation of economics and force in history, and they find their counterpart in the criticism on the practical tasks and possibilities of the working class movement which has already been discussed in another place. This is, however, a point to which it is necessary to recur. But the question to be investigated is not how far originally, and in the further course of history, force determined economy and *vice versa*, but what is the creative power of force in a given society.

Now it would be absurd to go back to the prejudices of former generations with regard to the capabilities of political power, for such a thing would mean that we would have to go still further back to explain those prejudices. The prejudices which the utopians, for example, cherished rested on good grounds; indeed, one can scarcely say that they were prejudices, for they rested on the real immaturity of the working classes of the period as a result of which, only a transitory mob rule on the one side or a return to the class oligarchy on the other was the only possible outcome of the political power of the masses. Under these circumstances a reference to politics could appear only to be a turning aside from more pressing duties. To-day these conditions have been to some extent removed, and therefore no person capable of reflecting will think of criticising political action with the arguments of that period.

Marxism first turned the thing round, as we have seen, and preached (in view of the potential capacity of the industrial proletariat) political action as the most important duty of the movement. But it was thereby involved in great contradictions. It also recognised, and separated itself thereby

from the demagogic parties, that the working classes had
not yet attained the required maturity for their emancipation,
and also that the economic preliminary conditions for such
were not present. But in spite of that it turned again and
again to tactics which supposed both preliminary conditions
as almost fulfilled. We come across passages in its publications where the immaturity of the workers is emphasised
with an acuteness which differs very little from the doctrinair-
ism of the early utopian socialists, and soon afterwards we
come across passages according to which we should assume
that all culture, all intelligence, all virtue, is only to be found
among the working classes—passages which make it incomprehensible why the most extreme social revolutionaries
and physical force anarchists should not be right. Corresponding with that, political action is ever directed towards a
revolutionary convulsion expected in an imminent future, in
the face of which legislative work for a long time appears
only as a *pis aller*—a merely temporary device. And we look
in vain for any systematic investigation of the question of
what can be expected from legal, and what from revolutionary action.

It is evident at the first glance that great differences exist
in the latter respect. But they are usually found to be this:
that law, or the path of legislative reform, is the slower way,
and revolutionary force the quicker and more radical. But
that only is true in a restricted sense. Whether the legislative
or the revolutionary method is the more promising depends
entirely on the nature of the measures and on their relation
to different classes and customs of the people.

In general, one may say here that the revolutionary way
(always in the sense of revolution by violence) does quicker
work as far as it deals with removal of obstacles which a
privileged minority places in the path of social progress: that
its strength lies on its negative side.

Constitutional legislation works more slowly in this respect
as a rule. Its path is usually that of compromise, not the
prohibition, but the buying out of acquired rights. But it is
stronger than the revolution scheme where prejudice and
the limited horizon of the great mass of the people appear

as hindrances to social progress, and it offers greater advantages where it is a question of the creation of permanent economic arrangements capable of lasting; in other words, it is best adapted to positive social-political work.

In legislation, intellect dominates over emotion in quiet times; during a revolution emotion dominates over intellect. But if emotion is often an imperfect leader, the intellect is a slow motive force. Where a revolution sins by over haste, the every-day legislator sins by procrastination. Legislation works as a systematic force, revolution as an elementary force.

As soon as a nation has attained a position where the rights of the propertied minority have ceased to be a serious obstacle to social progress, where the negative tasks of political action are less pressing than the positive, then the appeal to a revolution by force becomes a meaningless phrase. One can overturn a government or a privileged minority, but not a nation. When the working classes do not possess very strong economic organisations of their own, and have not attained, by means of education on self-governing bodies, a high degree of mental independence, the dictatorship of the proletariat means the dictatorship of club orators and writers. I would not wish that those who see in the oppression and tricking of the working men's organisations and in the exclusion of working men from the legislature and government the highest point of the art of political policy should experience their error in practice. Just as little would I desire it for the working class movement itself.

One has not overcome utopianism if one assumes that there is in the present, or ascribes to the present, what is to be in the future. We have to take working men as they are. And they are neither so universally pauperised as was set out in the *Communist Manifesto*, nor so free from prejudices and weaknesses as their courtiers wish to make us believe. They have the virtues and failings of the economic and social conditions under which they live. And neither these conditions nor their effects can be put on one side from one day to another.

Have we attained the required degree of development of the productive forces for the abolition of classes? In face of

the fantastic figures which were formerly set up in proof of
this and which rested on generalisations based on the development of particularly favoured industries, socialist writers
in modern times have endeavoured to reach by carefully
detailed calculations, appropriate estimates of the possibilities
of production in a socialist society, and their results are very
different from those figures. Of a general reduction of hours
of labor to five, four, or even three or two hours, such as
was formerly accepted, there can be no hope at any time
within sight, unless the general standard of life is much
reduced. Even under a collective organisation of work, labor
must begin very young and only cease at a rather advanced
age, it is to be reduced considerably below an eight-hours'
day. Those persons ought to understand this first of all who
indulge in the most extreme exaggerations regarding the
ratio of the number of the nonpropertied classes to that of
the propertied. But he who thinks irrationally on one point
does so usually on another. And, therefore, I am not surprised
if the same Plekhanov, who is angered to see the position of
working men represented as not hopeless, has only the anni-
hilating verdict, "Philistine," for my conclusions on the impossibility at any period within sight of abandoning the
principle of the economic self-responsibility of those capable
of working. It is not for nothing that one is the philosopher
of irresponsibility.

But he who surveys the actual workers' movement will
also find that the freedom from those qualities which appeared
Philistine to a person born in the bourgeoisie, is very little
valued by the workers, that they in no way support the
morale of proletarianism, but, on the contrary, tend to make a
"Philistine" out of a proletarian. With the roving proletarian
without a family and home, no lasting, firm trade union
movement would be possible. It is no bourgeois prejudice,
but a conviction gained through decades of labor organisation, which has made so many of the English labor leaders
—socialists and non-socialists—into zealous adherents of the
temperance movement. The working class socialists know the
faults of their class, and the most conscientious among them,

far from glorifying these faults, seek to overcome them with all their power.

We cannot demand from a class, the great majority of whose members live under crowded conditions, are badly educated, and have an uncertain and insufficient income, the high intellectual and moral standard which the organisation and existence of a socialist community presupposes. We will, therefore, not ascribe it to them by way of fiction. Let us rejoice at the great stock of intelligence, renunciation, and energy which the modern working class movement has partly revealed, partly produced; but we must not assign, without discrimination to the masses, the millions, what holds good, say, of hundreds of thousands. I will not repeat the declarations which have been made to me on this point by working men verbally and in writing; I do not need to defend myself before reasonable persons against the suspicion of Pharisaism and the conceit of pedantry. But I confess willingly that I measure here with two kinds of measures. Just because I expect much of the working classes I censure much more everything that tends to corrupt their moral judgment than I do similar habits of the higher classes, and I see with the greatest regret that a tone of literary decadence is spreading here and there in the working class press which can only have a confusing and corrupting effect. A class which is aspiring needs a sound morale and must suffer no deterioration. Whether it sets out for itself an ideal ultimate aim is of secondary importance if it pursues with energy its proximate aims. The important point is that these aims are inspired by a definite principle which expresses a higher degree of economy and of social life, that they are an embodiment of a social conception which means in the evolution of civilisation a higher view of morals and of legal rights.

From this point of view I cannot subscribe to the proposition: "The working class has no ideas to realise." I see in it rather a self-deception, if it is not a mere play upon words on the part of its author.

And in this mind, I, at the time, resorted to the spirit of the great Königsberg philosopher, the critic of pure reason, against the cant which sought to get a hold on the working class movement and to which the Hegelian dialectic offers a comfortable refuge. I did this in the conviction that social democracy required a Kant who should judge the received opinion and examine it critically with deep acuteness, who should show where its apparent materialism is the lightest and is therefore the most easily misleading—ideology, and warn it that the contempt of the ideal, the magnifying of material factors until they become omnipotent forces of evolution, is a self-deception, which has been and will be exposed as such at every opportunity by the action of those who proclaim it. Such a thinker, who with convincing exactness could show what is worthy and destined to live in the work of our great champions, and what must and can perish, would also make it possible for us to hold a more unbiassed judgment on those works which, although not starting from premises which to-day appear to us as decisive, yet are devoted to the ends for which social democracy is fighting. No impartial thinker will deny that socialist criticism often fails in this and discloses all the dark sides of epigonism. I have myself done my share in this, and therefore cast a stone at no one. But just because I belong to the school, I believe I am justified in giving expression to the need for reform. . . .

KARL KAUTSKY (1854–1938)

Above all other men Karl Kautsky personified the high glory of the German Socialist Party before World War I. It naturally fell to him, as the spokesman of orthodox Marxism everywhere, authoritatively to answer the revisionist argument. Born in Prague (then part of the Austrian Empire) and educated at the University of Vienna, Kautsky founded the Marxist *Neue Zeit* in Stuttgart in 1883 and very soon after established his reputation as a leading Marxist exegete. With Engels's death in 1895 the diadem of leadership passed to him. He was the executor of Marx's papers and put out the fourth volume of *Capital*, which contained Marx's history of theories of surplus value. Until the Second International fell apart Kautsky's pronouncements on controversial questions carried heavy weight with socialists of all persuasions, from Bernstein to Lenin.

Reflecting the ambivalence of the party, Kautsky upheld the orthodox Marxist position at every theoretical turn; less and less, however, did that position represent the party's increasingly pragmatic politics. Kautsky mediated between the revisionists and reformists on the right and the uncompromising revolutionists on the left, putting forth no consistent plans of his own. Both the right and the left at least had clearly defined programs of action, though how successful either might have been had it dominated the party cannot be known. Kautsky, believing that the party had to gain a majority of votes before confronting the ruling classes, encouraged it to pursue its rigorously legal course. At the same time, he maintained his Marxist faith inviolate and looked to the inevitable proletarian revolution, though he never said how the revolution could or should be brought about.

Kautsky tended to take the idea of historical materialism more seriously than Marx did. The inexorable concentration of economic power in fewer and fewer hands was, he believed, a scientific fact that defined the ethics of socialism and the party's responsibilities. History would determine when the time was right for revolution. The party, thus governed by the sublime and deterministic patience that Kautsky exemplified, was neither effectively reformist nor truly revolutionary.

THE ROAD TO POWER (1909)

THE CONQUEST OF POLITICAL POWER

Friends and enemies of the socialists agree upon one thing, and that is that they constitute a REVOLUTIONARY party. But unfortunately the idea of revolution is many-sided, and consequently the conceptions of the revolutionary character of our party differ very greatly. Not a few of our opponents insist upon understanding revolution to mean nothing else but anarchy, bloodshed, murder and arson. On the other hand there are some of our comrades to whom the coming social

revolution appears to be nothing more than an extremely gradual, scarcely perceptible, even though ultimately a fundamental change in social relations, much of the same character
as that produced by the steam engine.

So much is certain: that the socialists, as the champions of
the class interests of the proletariat, constitute a revolutionary
party, because it is impossible to raise this class to a satisfactory existence within capitalist society; and because the
liberation of the working class is only possible through the
overthrow of private property in the means of production and
rulership, and the substitution of social production for production for profit. The proletariat can attain to satisfaction
of its wants only in a society whose institutions shall differ
fundamentally from the present one.

In still another way the socialists are revolutionary. They
recognize that the power of the state is an instrument of class
domination, and indeed the most powerful instrument, and
that the social revolution for which the proletariat strives cannot be realized until it shall have captured political power.

It is by means of these fundamental principles, laid down
by Marx and Engels in the Communist Manifesto, that the
socialists of today are distinguished from the so-called utopian
socialists of the first half of the last century, such as Owen
and Fourier. It also distinguishes them from those who, like
Proudhon, either treat the political struggle as unimportant,
or else reject it entirely, and who believe it possible to bring
about the economic transformation demanded by the interest
of the proletariat through purely economic means without
changing or capturing the power of the state.

In their recognition of the necessity of capturing political
power Marx and Engels agreed with Blanqui. But while
Blanqui thought it possible to capture the power of the state
by a sudden act of a conspiratory minority, and then to use
that power in the interest of the proletariat, Marx and Engels
recognized that revolutions are not made at will. They come
with inevitable necessity, when the conditions which render
them necessary exist, and are impossible so long as those conditions, which develop gradually, do not exist. Only where the
capitalist methods of production are highly developed is there

the possibility of using the power of the state to transform capitalistic property in the means of production into social property. On the other hand, the possibility of capturing and holding the state for the proletariat only exists where the working class has grown to great proportions, is in large part firmly organized, and conscious of its class interests and its relation to state and society.

These conditions are being constantly created by the development of the capitalist methods of production and the class struggle between capitalists and laborers growing therefrom. So it is that just as the continuous expansion of capitalism necessarily and inevitably goes on, so the inevitable antithesis to this expansion, the proletarian revolution, proceeds equally inevitably and irresistibly.

It is irresistible, because it is inevitable that the growing proletariat should resist exploitation, and that it should organize industrially, co-operatively and politically to secure for itself better conditions of life and labor, and greater political influence. Everywhere the proletariat develops these phases of activity whether it is socialistically minded or not. It is the mission of the socialist movement to bring all these various activities of the proletariat against its exploitation into one conscious and unified movement, that will find its climax in the great final battle for the conquest of political power.

This position, the fundamental principles of which were laid down in the Communist Manifesto, is today accepted by the socialist movements of all countries. Upon it rests the whole great international socialist movement of our time.

Meanwhile it is unable to proceed on its victorious way without finding doubters and critics within its own ranks.

To be sure, actual evolution has taken the road foretold by Marx and Engels. And the triumphant progress of socialism is due, next to the extension of capitalism and therewith of the proletarian class struggle, above all to the keen analysis of the conditions and problems of this struggle supplied by the work of Marx and Engels. . . .

More and more it becomes evident that the only possible revolution is a *proletarian* revolution. Such a revolution is impossible so long as the organized proletariat does not form a body large enough and compact enough to carry, under favorable circumstances, the mass of the nation with it. But when once the proletariat comes to be the only revolutionary class in the nation, it necessarily follows that any crisis in an existing government, whether of a moral, financial or military nature, must include the bankruptcy of all capitalist parties, which as a whole are responsible, and in such a case the only government that could meet the situation would be a *proletarian* one.

Not all socialists, however, draw these conclusions. There are some who, when an expected revolution does not come at the time set, do not draw the conclusion that industrial development may have altered the form and character of the coming revolution from what might have been expected from the experience of previous capitalist revolutions. On the contrary, they at once conclude that, under the changed conditions, revolutions are not to be expected, are not necessary, and indeed are hurtful.

On one side they conclude that a further extension of the achievements already gained—labor legislation, trade unions, co-operation—will suffice to drive the capitalist class out of one position after another, and to quietly expropriate it, without a political revolution, or any change in the nature of governmental power. This theory of the gradual growth into (*hineinwachsen*) the future state is a modern form of the old anti-political utopianism and Proudhonism.

On the other hand it is thought to be possible for the proletariat to obtain political power without a revolution, that is without any important transfer of power in the state, simply by a clever policy of co-operation with those bourgeois parties which stand nearest to the proletariat, and by forming a coalition government which is impossible for either party alone.

In this manner they think to get around a revolution as an outgrown barbaric method, which has no place in our enlightened century of democracy, ethics and brotherly love.

When this attitude is carried to its logical conclusion it throws the whole system of socialist tactics founded by Marx and Engels into the street. The two cannot be reconciled. To be sure that is no reason why such a position should be declared false without examination. But it is a reason why everyone who, after careful study has become convinced of its erroneous character, should energetically oppose it, and this not merely because of a difference of opinion, but because it means weal or woe to the struggling workers.

It is very easy to be led into false paths in discussing this question unless the boundaries of the subject are narrowly defined.

Therefore it is necessary to make clear, what has so often been stated before, that we are not discussing the question of whether labor legislation and similar laws in the interest of the proletariat, and unions and co-operatives are necessary and useful or not. There are no two opinions among us on that point. What is disputed is the view that the exploiter class, who control the power of the state, will permit such a development of these factors, as will amount to abolishing capitalist oppression, without first making such a resistance, with all the means at its disposal, that it can be abolished only through a decisive battle.

Furthermore this has nothing to do with the question of utilizing quarrels among capitalist parties in the interest of the proletariat. It was not for nothing that Marx and Engels fought the use of the phrase "reactionary mass," because it tended to conceal the antagonism that exists between different factions of the ruling class, which may well be very important in securing the progress of the working class. Laws for the protection of labor and the extension of the suffrage are largely due to such differences.

What is opposed is the idea of the possibility that a proletarian party can during normal times regularly combine with a capitalist party for the purpose of maintaining a *government* or a *governmental party*, without being destroyed by the insuperable conflicts which must exist. The power of the state is everywhere an organ of class rule. The class antagonisms between the workers and the possessing class are so great that the proletariat can never share governmental power with any possessing class. The possessing class will always demand, and its interest will force it to demand, that the power of the state shall be used to hold the proletariat down. On the other hand the proletariat will always demand that any government in which their own party possesses power, shall use the power of the state to assist it in its battle against capital. Consequently every government based upon a coalition of capitalist and working class parties is foredoomed to disruption.

A proletarian party which shares power with a capitalist party in any government must share the blame for any acts of subjection of the working class. It thereby invites the hostility of its own supporters, and this in turn causes its capitalist allies to lose confidence and makes any progressive action impossible. No such arrangement can bring any strength to the working class. No capitalist party will permit it to do so. It can only compromise a proletarian party and confuse and split the working class.

It was just such a condition that constantly postponed the revolution of 1848 and brought about the political collapse of the bourgeois democracy, and excluded any co-operation with it for the purpose of winning and utilizing political power.

However willing Marx and Engels were to utilize the differences between capitalist parties for the furtherance of proletarian purposes, and however much they were opposed to the expression "reactionary mass," they have, nevertheless, coined the phrase *"dictatorship of the proletariat,"* which Engels defended shortly before his death in 1895, as expressing the fact that only through purely proletarian political domination can the working class exercise its political power.

Even if an alliance between capitalist and working-class political parties is incapable of contributing to the development of proletarian power, and even if the progress of social reform and economic organization must be limited under the present conditions, and even if because of these facts the political revolution has NOT YET come, this does not give the slightest reason for concluding that therefore revolutions belong to the past and there never will be any in the future. . . .

ECONOMIC EVOLUTION AND THE WILL

The revisionists meet these conclusions with the claim that there is a much greater contradiction in Marx himself. They

allege that, as a thinker, he recognized no such thing as a free
will, but expected everything to come from inevitable economic evolution, which moves on automatically, but that as
a revolutionary fighter he sought in the strongest manner to
develop wills, and to appeal to the volition of the proletariat.
This proves Marx to be guilty of an irreconcilable contradiction between theory and practice, declare the revisionists,
anarchists and liberals in closest harmony.

In reality Marx is guilty of no such contradiction. It is a
product of the confusion of his critics—a confusion that is
incurable, since it recurs again and again. It rests in the first
place in the making of will and free will identical. Marx has
never failed to recognize the significance of the will and the
"tremendous role of human personality" in society. He has
only denied the freedom of the will, something very different.
This has been explained so often that it scarcely seems necessary to restate it here.

Furthermore, this confusion rests upon a most remarkable
conception of the meaning of economics and economic development. All these learned gentlemen seem to think that
because this evolution proceeds according to certain definite
laws it is automatic and spontaneous without the willing human personality. For them the human will is a separate
element *alongside of* and *above* economics. It adds to the
force and operates upon economics, "making otherwise" the
things produced by economics. Such a view is only possible
in minds that have only a scholastic conception of economics,
that have gathered their ideas entirely from books, and that
treat it purely intellectually, without the slightest vital conception of the actual economic process. Here, at least, the
proletariat is superior to them, and in spite of Maurenbrecher
and Eisner, is better capable of comprehending this process
and its historic role, than the capitalist theoretician to whom
economic practice is foreign, or than the capitalist practical
man to whom every theoretical interest is foreign, and who
has no conception of the necessity of understanding anything
more of economics than is essential to successful profit making.

All economic theory becomes mere mental gymnastics for
those who do not proceed from the knowledge that the motive
force back of every economic event is the human will. Cer-

tainly not a FREE will, not a will existing by itself (*Wollen an sich*), but a PREDETERMINED (*bestimmtes*) will. It is, in the last analysis, the WILL TO LIVE which lies at the basis of all economics, which appeared with life as soon as it was gifted with movement and sensation. Every expression of the will is, in the last analysis, to be traced back to the will to live.

Whatever especial forms this life impulse (*Lebenswille*) of an organism may take in individual cases depends upon the conditions of that life, taking the word condition in the widest possible sense, as including all the dangers and limitations of life, not merely the means of its sustenance. The conditions of life determine the character of its volition, the nature of its acts and their results. . . .

Class antagonisms are antagonisms of volitions. The will to live of the capitalists meets with conditions that force it to bend the will of the workers and to make use of it. Without this bending of the will there would be no capitalist profit, and no capitalist could exist. The will of the laborer to live, on the other hand, forces him to rebel against the will of the capitalist. Therefore the class struggle.

Thus we see that the will is the motive force of the whole economic process. It is the starting point and enters into every expression of that process. There is nothing more absurd than to look upon the will and economic phenomena as two factors independent of each other. It is a part of the fetish-like conception that confuses the economic process—that is, the forms of social co-operative and competitive labor of mankind—with the material objects of such labor, and that imagines that just as men make use of raw materials and tools to form certain objects according to their own ideas, so the "creative personalities" make use through their free will of the economic process to form "thus and so," certain definite social relations to suit their needs. Because the laborer stands outside of the raw material and tools, because he stands above them and rules them, these worshipers of the economic fetish, think that man stands outside the economic process, that he stands above it and rules it according to his free will.

There is no more ridiculous misunderstanding than this. Economic necessity does not mean absence of will. It springs from the necessity of the will to live of living creatures, and from the inevitable necessity arising therefrom to utilize the conditions of life that they meet. It is the necessity of a predetermined volition.

There could also be no greater perversion of the truth than the idea that a knowledge of economic necessity means a weakening of the volition, and that the will of the workers must be aroused by biographies of generals and other powerful willed men, and by lectures on the freedom of the will. When the people have once been persuaded that a thing exists, then it must exist and can be used by them! If you do not believe this take a look at our professors and other bourgeois intellectuals, who have had a course in Kant on one side, and worshiped the powerful willed Hohenzollerns on the other, and observe what a great inflexible will they have obtained by this means.

If the will to live, which is the foundation of all economic necessity, is not most powerful in the workers, if this will must first artificially be awakened in them, then is all our struggle in vain.

This does not by any means imply that human volition has no relation to consciousness and is not determined by it. The energy of the will to live, to be sure, does not depend upon our consciousness, but our consciousness does determine the *form* that it will express itself in in any given case, and the amount of energy that the individual will expend in any given form. We have seen that next to instinct consciousness rules the will and that the way in which it is directed depends upon in what manner and to what degree the consciousness recognizes the conditions of existence. Since the intellect differs with individuals it can react differently upon the same will to live under the same conditions of life. It is this difference that gives the appearance of freedom of the will and makes it look as though the form of the volition of the individual depended, not upon the conditions of life, but upon his own will.

It is not through edifying legends and speculations concerning the freedom of the will, but only through a broader insight into social relations that the proletarian will can be awakened and its energy directed into the channels most effective for the furtherance of proletarian interests.

The will to live is the fact from which we must always take our start that we must presume to exist The form which it takes and the intensity with which it expresses itself depend, with each individual, class, nation, etc., upon their knowledge of the actual conditions of life. Wherever two classes arise developing opposing wills, the conditions are presented for conflict.

We have to deal only with this latter situation.

The expression of the will as the spirit of conflict is determined by three things: First, by the *stake* for which the combatants are striving; second, by their *consciousness of strength;* third, by their *actual strength.*

The greater the stake of battle, the stronger the will, the more the fighters will dare, the more eager the sacrifice of every energy to attain that stake. But this holds true only when one is convinced that the forces at his disposal are sufficient to attain the prize. If this necessary self-confidence is lacking, the prize may be ever so alluring, it will still fail to release any volition, but will only arouse desires and longings, and no matter how intense these may be they will give birth to no actual deed, and for all practical purposes are completely useless.

The feeling of strength is again worse than useless when it is not based upon actual knowledge of its own and its opponents' powers, but depends upon pure illusions. Strength, without a feeling of strength, is dead, and arouses no volition. A feeling of strength without strength can, under certain circumstances, lead to actions that may overwhelm or destroy an opponent, weakening or bending his will. But permanent results are not to be obtained without actual strength. Undertakings that are carried through without actual strength, but whose success depends upon deceiving an opponent as to his real strength, are doomed to failure sooner or later, and the disappointment which they will bring with them will be all the greater in proportion as their first successes were brilliant.

When we apply what has just been said to the class struggle of the proletariat it shows us what must be the nature of the work of those who would fight with and for that class and how the socialist movement affects it. Our first and greatest task must be to increase the strength of the proletariat. Naturally we cannot increase this by wishing for it. At any definite period of capitalist society the strength of the proletariat is determined by economic conditions and cannot arbitrarily be increased. But the effect of its existing strength can be increased by preventing its waste. The unconscious processes of nature always seem extremely wasteful when looked at from the standpoint of our purposes. Nature, however, has no purposes to serve. The conscious mind of man sets purposes before him, and also shows him the way to attain these purposes without waste of strength, and with the least expenditure of purposeful energy possible.

This holds true also in the class struggle of the proletariat. To be sure, it proceeds in the beginning without the consciousness of the participants. Their conscious volition includes only their closest personal needs. The social transformations that proceed from the effort to satisfy these needs remain hidden from the fighters. As a SOCIAL process, therefore, the class struggle is for a long time an unconscious process. As such it is laden with all the waste of energy inherent in all unconscious processes. Only through a RECOGNITION of the social process, its tendencies or aims can this waste be ended, the strength of the proletariat concentrated, the workers brought together into great organizations united upon a common aim, with all personalities and momentary actions subordinated to the permanent class interests, and those interests, in turn, placed at the service of the collective social evolution. . . .

Chapter IX

BOLSHEVISM

Bolshevik governments today order the lives of a billion people in a land area of 15,000,000 square miles stretching continuously from the Elbe River to the China Sea. Bolshevism is the adaptation of Western Marxism to economically backward countries in accordance with principles first laid down by Lenin at the turn of the century. Although Russia before World War I bore little resemblance to the proletarian society that Marx expected would form the basis of socialism, Lenin planned a Marxist revolution there by establishing in Bolshevism a political movement that presumed to be the chosen instrument of history and the absolute measure of right. Since the October Revolution Bolshevism has undergone many changes, and it is possible today to speak of different Bolshevisms—Mao's, Tito's, Castro's, Gomulka's, perhaps others. We shall confine ourselves here to discussing and documenting three stages in the history of Bolshevik thought: its genesis in Russian Marxism; Lenin's formulation of it; and the struggle between Trotsky and Stalin that settled the fate of Russia and of world communism for three decades.

The father of Russian Marxism was Georgi Plekhanov, who broke with Narodism (the dominant revolutionary movement in Russia in the 1860s and 1870s) on concluding that Russia was slowly turning into a capitalist society and that a new revolutionary movement had to be based on that fact. To Plekhanov Narodism was the Russian equivalent of Western utopian socialism. He projected a Marxist program for the future on the assumption that Russia would ineluctably follow the path of Western industrialization. But he thought that Russian Marxists would have to wait for the capitalist stage of history to appear before they could act. Plekhanov and his friends who were to form the Menshevik Party had leaped ahead of the consciousness of their society, but in doing so had also leaped ahead of themselves.

Lenin went one decisive step further than Plekhanov. He organized an elite squadron of revolutionaries, the disciplined vanguard of the proletarian society of the future. In the name of Marxism Bolsheviks evolved a conspiratorial apparatus that gave them a freedom of action in Czarist Russia that the Mensheviks denied themselves. The Mensheviks, in the organization of their party, adhered to an uncompromisingly Western conception of Marxism. Lenin Russified Marxism so to speak. This Russification of Marxism took on momentum after the October Revolution and settled into a fixed dogma with Stalin.

In establishing absolute dictatorial rule after 1917, Bolsheviks conceived it their purpose to raise the Russian masses to their own level of consciousness. To accomplish this ambitious task meant, first, bringing the whole society under the unquestioning rule of the party, and, second, carrying that society into the future by whatever means necessary. But the regime bogged down somewhere between the first and second steps. By 1921 all opposition parties had been eliminated, or declared illegal, and all democratic institutions ruthlessly subordinated to the party. The country as a whole, however, could not keep in step; it was exhausted by hunger and by seven years of war and revolution. Accordingly, the Bolsheviks scaled down their demands. Lenin instituted the New Economic Policy in 1921, permitting small-scale capitalism in both agriculture and industry. Simultaneously, the party swelled with the addition of hundreds of thousands of men who were out of sympathy with its professed ideology. This was inevitable since it had vast administrative duties, and even its fiercest opponents were resigning themselves to the system. The party, in short, lost its revolutionary force.

But its power grew with its bureaucratic responsibilities. Under the circumstances, Joseph Stalin, who had been one of Lenin's right hand men since the inception of Bolshevism, emerged as the dictator of Russia, by the time of Lenin's death in January 1924, on the strength of his position as party secretary. Stalin saw the possibilities of total power that lay open to him and drove them to their ultimate limits. Stalin himself, as man and "thinker" symbolized the retrenchment, conservatism and dullness that set in after 1921 and characterized Russian society as a whole after 1924.

He stamped his own ideology on Bolshevism in the course of his struggle with Trotsky in the mid-1920s. Trotsky, in the name of "October," came out for a decisive move to the left, proposing that the party undertake a program of rapid industrialization, remove privileges from the peasants, thoroughly proletarianize itself and openly encourage revolutionary movements in other countries. In answer to these criticisms Stalin forged his doctrine of "socialism in one country," which proclaimed Russia's determination to build socialism alone, through the alliance of peasants and workers. With Stalin as its lawgiver, Bolshevism became an ideology of Russian self-sufficiency, and this in turn justified the cruel, fanatical industrialization begun in 1928.

For his opposition to Stalin, Trotsky was cut off from the party and, within four years, from Russian society altogether. Should he have expected a different fate? Was it possible for the party to remain democratic, to tolerate open criticism, when the rest of Russia had been reduced to silence? Trotsky was one of the architects of proletarian dictatorship. As late as May 1924, he uttered words that were to mock him for the rest of his tragic life:

> The party in the final analysis is always right, because the party is the only historic instrument given to the proletariat for the solution of its fundamental problems. . . . I know that one can not be right *against* the party. One can be right only with the party, and through the party, for history has created no other road for the realization of what is right. . . .

GEORGI PLEKHANOV (1857–1918)

Narodism (Populism) was the revolutionary movement that immediately preceded Marxism in Russia. The Narodniks

were young intellectuals who went "among the people," by
which they meant back to the peasants and their ideal communities. Though the group had few members, it embodied
a feeling widespread among Russian intellectuals at the time;
writers, poets and composers as well as revolutionaries discovered the purifying spirit of the people. The Narodniks wrote
and agitated but they had no precise program. They agreed
only on the need to free the peasants from subjection to the
Czar, to the aristocracy and to the rural capitalists.

In the late 1870s they split over tactics. One group, the
Chorny Peredyel (Black Redistribution) maintained the traditional Narodist policy of non-political agitation; the other,
calling itself Narodnaya Volya (People's Will), embarked on
a campaign of violence and terror. The most extraordinary
accomplishment of Narodnaya Volya, the assassination of
Czar Alexander II, also marked its permanent demise; it could
not hold up in the face of the terrible reprisals which followed.
The Chorny Peredyel group was itself divided over the
desirability of preserving peasant communes. A few, led by
Georgi Plekhanov, were convinced that the peasants should
be abandoned for the proletariat. Yet it was Marx himself who
wrote to one of Plekhanov's followers in 1881: "The analysis
given in *Das Kapital* offers no argument either for or against
the vitality of the rural commune, but the special study I have
made of it . . . has convinced me that this commune is the
point d'appui for the social regeneration of Russia." But Plekhanov, more of a Marxist than Marx, had come to a different
conclusion by 1883.

Plekhanov was typical of nineteenth-century Russian revolutionaries who looked to the West as their source of inspiration: he was an intellectual, he came from one of the better
classes and he spent most of his life in exile. The son of a small
landowner, he received a good education before joining the
Narodniks at the age of twenty. He was drawn to Marx,
whose works he studied in depth, while going "among the
people"—the working class in his case, rather than the peasants. In 1880, after two brief imprisonments, he left Russia,
not to return until 1917, the year before he died. With two
other ex-Narodniks he founded an organization in Geneva that
published Marxist literature, including his own, and so formed

the nucleus for what was to become the most successful revolutionary movement in Russian history.

Plekhanov broke with Narodism when he concluded that the proletariat constituted the people, that the scientific path to the emancipation of the proletariat required the break-up of peasant communes and that a permanent party organization, based on Marxist principles, must replace terror and violence, which had become exercises in futility. His *Socialism and the Political Struggle*, published in 1883, was the first important announcement of this position. During the next three decades he wrote an immense number of books and articles elaborating Marxist theory. After Engels's death in 1895 he was, with Kautsky, its leading "orthodox" exponent. But unlike most Marxist theoreticians he wrote on many subjects—law, economics, science, aesthetics, formal philosophy—in a style noted for its lucidity, wit, and polemical force.

SOCIALISM AND THE POLITICAL STRUGGLE (1883)

The present pamphlet may be an occasion for much misunderstanding and even dissatisfaction. People who sympathize with the trend of *Zemlya i Volya*[1] and *Chorny Peredyel*[2] (publications in the editing of which I used to take part) may reproach me with having diverged from the theory of what is called Narodism. The supporters of other factions of our revolutionary party may be displeased with my criticism of outlooks which are dear to them. That is why I consider a short preliminary explanation necessary.

The desire to work *among the people* and for the people, the certitude that "the emancipation of the working classes must be conquered by the working classes themselves"—this *practical* tendency of our Narodism is just as dear to me as it used to be. But its *theoretical* propositions seem to me, indeed, erroneous in many respects. Years of life abroad and attentive study of the social question have convinced me that the tri-

[1] *Land and Freedom*, published from November 1879 to April 1880.

[2] *Black Redistribution*, published from January 1880 to December 1881.

umph of a spontaneous popular movement similar to Stepan Razin's revolt or the Peasant Wars in Germany cannot satisfy the social and political needs of modern Russia, that the old forms of our national life carried within them many germs of their disintegration and that they cannot "develop into a higher communist form" except under the immediate influence of a strong and well-organized *workers'* socialist party. For that reason I think that besides fighting absolutism the Russian revolutionaries must strive at least to work out the elements for the establishment of such a party in the future. In this creative work they will necessarily have to pass on to the basis of modern socialism, for the ideals of Zemlya i Volya do not correspond to the condition of the industrial workers. And that will be very opportune now that the theory of Russian exceptionalism is becoming synonymous of stagnation and reaction and that the progressive elements of Russian society are grouping under the banner of judicious "Occidentalism."

I go on to another point of my explanation. Here I will first of all say in my defence that I have been concerned not with persons but with opinions, and that my personal differences with this or that socialist group do not in the least diminish my respect for all who sincerely fight for the emancipation of the people.

Moreover, the so-called terrorist movement has opened a new epoch in the development of our revolutionary party—the epoch of *conscious political struggle* against the government. This change in the direction of our revolutionaries' work makes it necessary for them to reconsider all views that they inherited from the preceding period. Life demands that we attentively reconsider all our intellectual stock-in-trade when we step on to new ground, and I consider my pamphlet as a contribution which I can make to this matter of criticism which started long ago in our revolutionary literature. . . .

The honour of giving new scope to our movement belongs beyond dispute to Narodnaya Volya. Everybody still recalls the attacks that the Narodnaya Volya trend drew upon itself. The writer of these lines himself belonged to the resolute opponents of this trend, and although he perfectly admits now that the struggle for political freedom has become a burning issue for modern Russia, he is still far from sharing all the views expressed in Narodnaya Volya publications. That does not prevent him, however, from acknowledging that in the disputes which took place in the Zemlya i Volya organization about the time of its split,[3] the Narodnaya Volya members were perfectly right as long as they did not go beyond our practical experience. That experience was already then leading to amazing and completely unexpected conclusions, although we did not dare to draw them precisely because of their unexpectedness. Attempts at the practical struggle "against the state" should already then have led fundamentally to the thought that the Russian "rebel" was compelled by the insuperable force of circumstances to direct his agitation not against the state generally, but only against the *absolute* state, to fight not the idea of state, but the idea of bureaucracy, not for the full economic emancipation of the people, but for the removal of the burdens imposed on the people by the autocracy of tsarism. Of course, the agrarian question lay at the root of all or nearly all manifestations of popular dissatisfaction. It could not be otherwise among an agricultural population, where the "power of the land" is felt in absolutely the whole make-up and needs of private and social life. This agrarian question kept crying out for a solution, but it did not rouse *political* discontent. The peasants waited calm and confident for this question to be solved from above: they "rebelled" not for a redistribution of the land, but against oppression by the administration, against the excessive burdens of the taxation system, against the Asiatic way in which arrears were collected, and so on and so forth. The formula which applied to a large portion of the cases of active protest was the "legal state," not "Land and Freedom" (Zemlya i Volya) as it seemed to everybody at the time. But if that was so, and if revolutionaries considered themselves obliged to take part in the scattered and ill-considered struggle of isolated communities against the absolute monarchy, was it not time they understood the meaning of their own efforts and directed

[3] In 1879 the Narodniks split into two groups: the Narodnaya Volya, which advocated terror, and the Chorny Peredyel, which opposed terror. Plekhanov belonged to Chorny Peredyel.

them with greater purposefulness? Was it not time for them
to call all the progressive virile forces of Russia to the struggle
and, having found a more general expression for it, to attack
absolutism in the very centre of its organization? In answering
these questions in the affirmative, the members of Narodnaya
Volya were only summing up the revolutionary experience of
previous years; in raising the banner of political struggle,
they only showed that they were not afraid of the conclusions
and consciously continued to follow the road which we had
stepped on to although we had an erroneous idea of where it
led to. "Terrorism" grew quite logically out of our "rebellious-
ness."

But with the appearance of Narodnaya Volya, the logical
development of our revolutionary movement was already entering a phase in which it could no longer be satisfied with
the Narodist theories of the good old time, i.e., a time innocent of political interests. Examples of theory being outgrown
by practice are not rare in the history of human thought in
general and of revolutionary thought in particular. When revolutionaries introduce some change or other into their tactics
or recast their program one way or another, often they do not
even suspect what a serious test they are giving the teachings
generally acknowledged among them. Many of them indeed
perish in prison or on the gallows, fully confident that they
have worked in the spirit of those teachings, whereas in substance they represent new tendencies which took root in the
old theories but have already outgrown them and are ready
to find new theories to express them. So it has been with us
since the Narodnaya Volya trend consolidated. From the
standpoint of the old Narodist theories, this trend could not
stand criticism. Narodism had a sharply negative attitude to
any idea of the state; Narodnaya Volya counted on putting
its social-reform plans into practice with the help of the state
machine. Narodism refused to have anything to do with "politics"; Narodnaya Volya saw in "democratic political revolution" the most reliable "means of social reform." Narodism
based its program on the so-called "ideals" and demands of
the peasant population; Narodnaya Volya had to address
itself mainly to the urban and industrial population, and con-

sequently to give an incomparably larger place in its program to the interests of that population. Briefly, in reality, the Narodnaya Volya trend was the complete and all-round denial of Narodism, and as long as the disputing parties appealed to the fundamental propositions of the latter, the "innovators" were completely in the wrong: their practical work was in irreconcilable contradiction with their theoretical views. It was necessary completely to reconsider these views, so as to give Narodnaya Volya's program singleness of purpose and consistency; the practical revolutionary activity of its supporters had to be at least *accompanied* by a theoretical revolution in the minds of our socialists; in blowing up the Winter Palace we had at the same time to blow up our old anarchic and Narodist traditions. . . .

Fortunately, the Russian socialists can base their hopes on a firmer foundation. They can and must place their hopes first and foremost in the working class. The strength of the working class—as of any other class—depends, among other things, on the clarity of its political consciousness, its cohesion and its degree of organization. It is these elements of its strength that must be influenced by our socialist intelligentsia. The latter must become the leader of the working class in the impending emancipation movement, explain to it its political and economic interests and also the interdependence of those interests and must prepare them to play an independent role in the social life of Russia. They must exert all their energy so that in the very opening period of the constitutional life of Russia our working class will be able to come forward as a separate party with a definite social and political program. The detailed elaboration of that program must, of course, be left to the workers themselves, but the intelligentsia must elucidate for them its principal points, for instance, a radical review of the present agrarian relations, the taxation system and factory legislation, state help for producer's associations, and so forth. All this can be done only by intensive work among at least the most advanced sections of the working class, by oral and printed propaganda and the organization of workers' socialist study groups. . . .

Thus, the struggle for political freedom, on the one hand,

and the preparation of the working class for its future independent and offensive role, on the other, such, in our opinion, is the only possible "setting of party tasks" at present. To bind together in one, two so fundamentally different matters as the overthrow of absolutism and the socialist revolution, to wage revolutionary struggle in the belief that these elements of social development will *coincide* in the history of our country *means to put off the advent of both*. But it depends on us to *bring* these two elements *closer together*. We must follow the splendid example of the German Communists who, as the *Manifesto* says, fight "with the bourgeoisie whenever it acts in a revolutionary way, against the absolute monarchy," and yet "never cease, for a single instant, to instil into the working class the clearest possible recognition of the hostile antagonism between bourgeoisie and proletariat." Acting thus, the Communists wanted "the bourgeois revolution in Germany" to "be but the prelude to an immediately following proletarian revolution."

The present position of bourgeois societies and the influence of international relations on the social development of each civilized country entitle us to hope that the social emancipation of the Russian working class will follow very quickly upon the fall of absolutism. If the German bourgeoisie *"came too late,"* the Russian has come still later, and its domination cannot be a long one. Only the Russian revolutionaries should not, in their turn, begin "too late" the preparation of the working class, a matter which has now become of absolute urgency.

Let us make a reservation to avoid misunderstandings. We do not hold the view, which as we have seen was ascribed to Marx's school rather than as it existed in reality, and which alleges that the socialist movement cannot obtain support from our peasantry until the latter has been turned into a landless proletarian and the village community has disintegrated under the influence of capitalism. We think that on the whole the Russian peasantry would show great sympathy for any measure aiming at the so-called "nationalization of the land." Given the possibility of any at all free agitation among the peasants, they would also sympathize with the socialists, who naturally would not be slow in introducing into their program the demand for a measure of that kind. But we do not exaggerate the strength of our socialists or ignore the obstacles, the opposition which they will inevitably encounter from that quarter in their work. For that reason, and *for that reason only*, we think that for the beginning they should concentrate their main attention on the industrial centres. The rural population of today, living in backward social conditions, is not only less capable of conscious political *initiative* than the industrial workers, it is also less *responsive* to the movement which our revolutionary intelligentsia has begun. It has greater difficulty in mastering the socialist teachings, because its living conditions are too much unlike the conditions which gave birth to those teachings. And besides, the peasantry is now going through a difficult, critical period. The previous "ancestral" foundations of its economy are crumbling, "the ill-fated village community itself is being discredited in its eyes," as is admitted even by such "ancestral" organs of Narodism as *Nedelya;* and the new forms of labor and life are only in the process of formation, and this creative process is more intensive in the industrial centres. Like water which washes away the soil in one place and forms new sediments and deposits in others, the process of Russian social development is creating new social formations by destroying the age-old forms of the peasants' relation to the land and to one another. These new social formations contain the embryo of a new social movement which alone can end the exploitation of Russia's working population. The industrial workers, who are more developed and have higher requirements and a broader outlook than the peasantry, will join our revolutionary intelligentsia in its struggle against absolutism, and when they have won political freedom they will organize into a workers' socialist party whose task will be to begin systematic propaganda of socialism among the peasantry. We say *systematic propaganda* because isolated opportunities of propaganda must not be missed even at present. It is hardly necessary to add that our socialists would have to change the distribution of their forces among the people if a strong independent movement made itself felt among the peasantry.

That is the "program" which life itself suggests to the Russian revolutionary socialist party. Will the party be able to carry out this program? Will it be prepared to give up its fantastic plans and notions, which, it must be admitted, have a great appeal to sentiment and imagination? It is as yet difficult to answer that question with certitude. . . .

LENIN (1870–1924)

In the 1890s—a decade of famine, industrial strikes and political repressions—a generation of Marxist revolutionaries sprouted from the seeds Plekhanov and his small group in Switzerland had been planting in Russian soil. The difference between the new and old generations of Marxists was evident as soon as they came together. The older men were theorists who had found hope in Marxism for the distant future following the bankruptcy of Narodism; the younger ones were active revolutionists concerned with immediate political problems. If Lenin, the outstanding representative of the new generation, deserves to be called an original thinker, it is because he fashioned Marxism into a technique for seizing power, and in the process created an ideology of tremendous force.

Though Ilya Nikolayevich Ulyanov, a successful superintendent of schools, had been more than content with his lot under the Czar, and though his family was a happy one, all his children turned out to be revolutionaries. Vladimir, the future Lenin, was a fine, conscientious student of science when his older brother, Alexander, was executed for plotting against the life of Czar Alexander III. Vladimir, then seventeen, witnessed the trial and execution. He was automatically expelled from school, and his mother, sisters and brothers—his father having died before Alexander was caught—were sent to live in a remote community. Becoming a confirmed revolutionist, he eschewed Narodism, read Plekhanov at the age of twenty, was imprisoned for a while in Siberia, mastered Marx, and in 1895 went into exile.

Thereafter, Lenin never swerved from the purpose of his life, to overthrow the Czar and create a proletariat dictator-

ship. To this purpose he bent all his energies, ruthlessly sub-
ordinating to it his intellectual, aesthetic and social interests.
His writing reflects this singlemindedness and vehemence. In
his polemics—which comprise nearly all his published work—
he gave no quarter; blow followed blow until he had pulver-
ized his adversary. His writings were without wit or literary
grace. They never strayed far from the teachings of Marx,
whose words he quoted as a theologian would quote the
Bible. One of his fellow revolutionaries described him in 1903:
"There is no other man who is so absorbed by the revolution
twenty-four hours a day, who has no thoughts but the
thoughts of the revolution, and who, even when he sleeps,
dreams of nothing but the revolution."

Through his initiative, the Marxist newspaper, *Iskra*
(Spark), was founded in 1901 with himself, Plekhanov, and
four others—evenly balanced between the two generations—as
editors. Lenin hoped that *Iskra*, though published in London,
would be the nucleus of a socialist organization, ruthlessly
centralized and purged of all moderates and compromisers.
He believed that a revolutionary elite, small in number, functioning in secret, drawn from all classes and carefully trained,
must direct all socialist activities in Russia.

Lenin systematically presented his theory on the question
of revolutionary leadership in a long essay, *What Is to Be
Done?*, published in March 1902. His subsequent theoretical
writings only ramified its central ideas. After 1902 he broke
with the other editors of *Iskra*, because they disagreed with
him over the organization of a revolutionary party. The break
became complete in 1903 when he founded the Bolshevik[1]
faction and organized it on the basis of the principles laid
down in *What Is to Be Done?*

What Is to Be Done (1902)

. . . The political struggle of Social Democracy is far more
extensive and complex than the economic struggle of the

---

[1] Meaning "majority"—a name derived from the fact that
when the Socialist Party split Lenin received the support of more
than half the delegates; the other faction, led by Plekhanov, retained the name Menshevik, meaning "minority."

workers against the employers and the government. Similarly (indeed for that reason), the organisation of the revolutionary Social Democratic Party must inevitably be of *a kind different* from the organisation of the workers designed for this struggle. The workers' organisation must in the first place be a trade union organisation; secondly, it must be as broad as possible; and thirdly, it must be as public as conditions will allow (here, and further on, of course, I refer only to absolutist Russia). On the other hand, the organisation of the revolutionaries must consist first and foremost of people who make revolutionary activity their profession (for which reason I speak of the organisation of *revolutionaries*, meaning revolutionary Social Democrats). In view of this common characteristic of the members of such an organisation, *all distinctions as between workers and intellectuals*, not to speak of distinctions of trade and profession, in both categories, *must be effaced*. Such an organisation must perforce not be very extensive and must be as secret as possible. Let us examine this threefold distinction.

In countries where political liberty exists the distinction between a trade union and a political organisation is clear enough, as is the distinction between trade unions and Social Democracy. The relations between the latter and the former will naturally vary in each country according to historical, legal, and other conditions; they may be more or less close, complex, etc. (in our opinion they should be as close and as little complicated as possible); but there can be no question in free countries of the organisation of trade unions coinciding with the organisation of the Social Democratic Party. In Russia, however, the yoke of the autocracy appears at first glance to obliterate all distinctions between the Social Democratic organisation and the workers' associations, since *all* workers' associations and *all* study circles are prohibited, and since the principal manifestation and weapon of the workers' economic struggle—the strike—is regarded as a criminal (and sometimes even as a political!) offence. Conditions in our country, therefore, on the one hand, strongly "impel" the workers engaged in economic struggle to concern themselves with political questions, and, on the other, they "impel" Social

Democrats to confound trade-unionism with Social Democracy. . . .

I assert that it is far more difficult to unearth a dozen wise men than a hundred fools. This position I will defend, no matter how much you instigate the masses against me for my "anti-democratic" views, etc. As I have stated repeatedly, by "wise men", in connection with organisation, I mean *professional revolutionaries*, irrespective of whether they have developed from among students or working men. I assert: (1) that no revolutionary movement can endure without a stable organisation of leaders maintaining continuity; (2) that the broader the popular mass drawn spontaneously into the struggle, which forms the basis of the movement and participates in it, the more urgent the need for such an organisation, and the more solid this organisation must be (for it is much easier for all sorts of demagogues to side-track the more backward sections of the masses); (3) that such an organisation must consist chiefly of people professionally engaged in revolutionary activity; (4) that in an autocratic state, the more we *confine* the membership of such an organisation to people who are professionally engaged in revolutionary activity and who have been professionally trained in the art of combating the political police, the more difficult will it be to unearth the organisation; and (5) the *greater* will be the number of people from the working class and from the other social classes who will be able to join the movement and perform active work in it.

I invite our Economists, terrorists, and "Economists-terrorists" to confute these propositions. At the moment, I shall deal only with the last two points. The question as to whether it is easier to wipe out "a dozen wise men" or "a hundred fools" reduces itself to the question, above considered, whether it is possible to have a mass *organisation* when the maintenance of strict secrecy is essential. We can never give a mass organisation that degree of secrecy without which there can be no question of persistent and continuous struggle against the government. To concentrate all secret functions in the hands of as small a number of professional revolutionaries as possible does not mean that the latter will "do the thinking for all" and that the rank and file will not take an active part in the *movement*. On the contrary, the membership will promote increasing numbers of the professional revolutionaries from its ranks; for it will know that it is not enough for a few students and for a few working men waging the economic struggle to gather in order to form a "committee," but that it takes years to train oneself to be a professional revolutionary; and the rank and file will "think," not only of amateurish methods, but of such training. Centralisation of the secret functions of the *organisation* by no means implies centralisation of all the functions of the *movement*. Active participation of the widest masses in the illegal press will not diminish because a "dozen" professional revolutionaries centralise the secret functions connected with this work; on the contrary, it will *increase* tenfold. In this way, and in this way alone, shall we ensure that reading the illegal press, writing for it, and to some extent even distributing it, will *almost cease to be secret work,* for the police will soon come to realise the folly and impossibility of judicial and administrative red-tape procedure over every copy of a publication that is being distributed in the thousands. This holds not only for the press, but for every function of the movement, even for demonstrations. The active and widespread participation of the masses will not suffer; on the contrary, it will benefit by the fact that a "dozen" experienced revolutionaries, trained professionally no less than the police, will centralise all the secret aspects of the work—the drawing up of leaflets, the working out of approximate plans; and the appointing of bodies of leaders for each urban district, for each factory district, and for each educational institution, etc. (I know that exception will be taken to my "undemocratic" views, but I shall reply below fully to this anything but intelligent objection.) Centralisation of the most secret functions in an organisation of revolutionaries will not diminish, but rather increase the extent and enhance the quality of the activity of a large number of other organisations, that are intended for a broad public and are therefore as loose and as non-secret as possible, such as workers' trade unions; workers' self-education circles and circles for reading illegal literature; and socialist, as well as democratic, cir-

cles among *all* other sections of the population; etc., etc. We
must have such circles, trade unions, and organisations everywhere in *as large a number as possible* and with the widest
variety of functions; but it would be absurd and harmful
to confound them with the organisation of revolutionaries, to
efface the border-line between them, to make still more hazy
the all too faint recognition of the fact that in order to "serve"
the mass movement we must have people who will devote
themselves exclusively to Social Democratic activities, and
that such people must *train* themselves patiently and stead-
fastly to be professional revolutionaries.

Yes, this recognition is incredibly dim. Our worst sin with
regard to organisation consists in the fact that *by our primitiveness we have lowered the prestige of revolutionaries in
Russia.* A person who is flabby and shaky on questions of
theory, who has a narrow outlook, who pleads the spontaneity of the masses as an excuse for his own sluggishness,
who resembles a trade-union secretary more than a spokesman of the people, who is unable to conceive of a broad and
bold plan that would command the respect even of opponents,
and who is inexperienced and clumsy in his own professional
art—the art of combating the political police—such a man is
not a revolutionary, but a wretched amateur!

Let no active worker take offence at these frank remarks,
for as far as insufficient training is concerned, I apply them
first and foremost to myself. I used to work in a study circle
that set itself very broad, all-embracing tasks; and all of us,
members of that circle, suffered painfully and acutely from
the realisation that we were acting as amateurs at a moment
in history when we might have been able to say, varying a
well-known statement: "Give us an organisation of revolutionaries, and we will overturn Russia!" The more I recall the
burning sense of shame I then experienced, the bitterer become my feelings towards those pseudo-Social Democrats
whose preachings "bring disgrace on the calling of a revolutionary," who fail to understand that our task is not to champion the degrading of the revolutionary to the level of an
amateur, but *to raise* the amateurs to the level of revolutionaries. . . .

To be fully prepared for his task, the worker-revolutionary must likewise become a professional revolutionary. Hence B—v is wrong in saying that since the worker spends eleven and a half hours in the factory, the brunt of all other revolutionary functions (apart from agitation) *"must necessarily* fall mainly upon the shoulders of an extremely small force of intellectuals." But this condition does not obtain out of sheer "necessity." It obtains because we are backward, because we do not recognise our duty to assist every capable worker to become a *professional* agitator, organiser, propagandist, literature distributor, etc., etc. In this respect, we waste our strength in a positively shameful manner; we lack the ability to husband that which should be tended and reared with special care. Look at the Germans: their forces are a hundredfold greater than ours. But they understand perfectly well that really capable agitators, etc., are not often promoted from the ranks of the "average." For this reason they immediately try to place every capable working man in conditions that will enable him to develop and apply his abilities to the fullest: he is made a professional agitator; he is encouraged to widen the field of his activity, to spread it from one factory to the whole of the industry, from a single locality to the whole country. He acquires experience and dexterity in his profession; he broadens his outlook and increases his knowledge; he observes at close quarters the prominent political leaders from other localities and of other parties; he strives to rise to their level and combine in himself the knowledge of the working-class environment and the freshness of socialist convictions with professional skill, without which the proletariat *cannot* wage a stubborn struggle against its excellently trained enemies. In this way alone do the working masses produce men of the stamp of Bebel and Auer. But what is to a great extent automatic in a politically free country must in Russia be done deliberately and systematically by our organisations. A worker-agitator who is at all gifted and "promising" *must not be left* to work eleven hours a day in a factory. We must arrange that he be maintained by the Party; that he may go underground in good time; that he change the place of his activity, if he is to enlarge his experience, widen his outlook, and be able to hold out for at least a few years in the struggle against the gendarmes. As the spontaneous rise of their movement becomes broader and deeper, the working-class masses promote from their ranks not only an increasing number of talented agitators, but also talented organisers, propagandists, and "practical workers" in the best sense of the term (of whom there are so few among our intellectuals who, for the most part, in the Russian manner, are somewhat careless and sluggish in their habits). When we have forces of specially trained worker-revolutionaries who have gone through extensive preparation (and, of course, revolutionaries "of all arms of the service"), no political police in the world will then be able to contend with them, for these forces, boundlessly devoted to the revolution, will enjoy the boundless confidence of the widest masses of the workers. We are directly *to blame* for doing too little to "stimulate" the workers to take this path, common to them and to the "intellectuals," of professional revolutionary training, and for all too often dragging them back by our silly speeches about what is "accessible" to the masses of the workers, to the "average workers", etc.

In this, as in other respects, the narrow scope of our organisational work is without a doubt due directly to the fact (although the overwhelming majority of the "Economists" and the novices in practical work do not perceive it) that we restrict our theories and our political tasks to a narrow field. Subservience to spontaneity seems to inspire a fear of taking even one step away from what is "accessible" to the masses, a fear of rising too high above mere attendance on the immediate and direct requirements of the masses. Have no fear, gentlemen! Remember that we stand so low on the plane of organisation that the very idea that we *could* rise *too* high is absurd! . . .

The objection may be raised that such a powerful and strictly secret organisation, which concentrates in its hands all the threads of secret activities, an organisation which of necessity is centralised, may too easily rush into a premature attack, may thoughtlessly intensify the movement before the growth of political discontent, the intensity of the ferment and anger of the working class, etc., have made such an attack possible and necessary. Our reply to this is: Speaking abstractly, it cannot be denied, of course, that a militant organisation *may* thoughtlessly engage in battle, which *may* end in a defeat entirely avoidable under other conditions. But we cannot confine ourselves to abstract reasoning on such a question, because every battle bears within itself the abstract possibility of defeat, and there is no way of *reducing* this possibility except by organised preparation for battle. If, however, we proceed from the concrete conditions at present obtaining in Russia, we must come to the positive conclusion that a strong revolutionary organisation is absolutely necessary precisely for the purpose of giving stability to the movement and of *safeguarding* it against the possibility of making thoughtless attacks. Precisely at the present time, when no such organisation yet exists, and when the revolutionary movement is rapidly and spontaneously growing, we *already observe* two opposite extremes (which, as is to be expected, "meet"). These are: the utterly unsound Economism and the preaching of moderation, and the equally unsound "excitative terror," which strives "artificially to call forth symptoms of the end of the movement, which is developing and strengthening itself, when this movement is as yet nearer to the start than to the end." And the instance of *Rabocheye Dyelo* shows that *there exist* Social Democrats who give way to both these extremes. This is not surprising, for, apart from other reasons, the "economic struggle against the employers and the government" can *never* satisfy revolutionaries, and opposite extremes will therefore always appear here and there. Only a centralised, militant organisation that consistently carries out a Social Democratic policy, that satisfies, so to speak, all revolutionary instincts and strivings, can safeguard the movement against making thoughtless attacks and prepare attacks that hold out the promise of success.

A further objection may be raised, that the views on organisation here expounded contradict the "democratic principle". Now, while the earlier accusation was specifically Russian in origin, this one is *specifically foreign* in character. And only an organisation abroad (the Union of Russian Social

Democrats Abroad) was capable of giving its Editorial Board instructions like the following:

> *Organisational Principle.* In order to secure the success-
> ful development and unification of Social Democracy,
> broad democratic principles of Party organisation must be
> emphasised, developed, and fought for; this is particu-
> larly necessary in view of the anti-democratic tendencies
> that have revealed themselves in the ranks of our Party.

We shall see in the next chapter how *Rabocheye Dyelo* combats *Iskra's* "anti-democratic tendencies." For the present, we shall examine more closely the "principle" that the Economists advance. Everyone will probably agree that "the broad democratic principle" presupposes the two following conditions: first, full publicity, and secondly, election to all offices. It would be absurd to speak of democracy without publicity, moreover, without a publicity that is not limited to the membership of the organisation. We call the German Socialist Party a democratic organisation because all its activities are carried out publicly; even its party congresses are held in public. But no one would call an organisation democratic that is hidden from every one but its members by a veil of secrecy. What is the use, then, of advancing "the *broad* democratic principle" when the fundamental condition for this principle *cannot be fulfilled* by a secret organisation? "The broad principle" proves itself simply to be a resounding but hollow phrase. Moreover, it reveals a total lack of understanding of the urgent tasks of the moment in regard to organisation. Everyone knows how great the lack of secrecy is among the "broad" masses of our revolutionaries. We have heard the bitter complaints of B—v on this score and his absolutely just demand for a "strict selection of members." Yet, persons who boast a keen "sense of realities" *urge*, in a situation like this, not the strictest secrecy and the strictest (consequently, more restricted) selection of members, but "the *broad* democratic principle"! This is what you call being wide of the mark.

Nor is the situation any better with regard to the second attribute of democracy, the principle of election. In politically free countries, this condition is taken for granted. "They are members of the Party who accept the principles of the Party program and render the Party all possible support," reads Clause 1 of the Rules of the German Social Democratic Party. Since the entire political arena is as open to the public view as is a theatre stage to the audience, this acceptance or non-acceptance, support or opposition, is known to all from the press and from public meetings. Everyone knows that a certain political figure began in such and such a way, passed through such and such an evolution, behaved in a trying moment in such and such a manner, and possesses such and such qualities; consequently, *all* party members, knowing all the facts, can elect or refuse to elect this person to a particular party office. The general control (in the literal sense of the term) exercised over every act of a party man in the political field brings into existence an automatically operating mechanism which produces what in biology is called the "survival of the fittest." "Natural selection" by full publicity, election, and general control provides the assurance that, in the last analysis, every political figure will be "in his proper place," do the work for which he is best fitted by his powers and abilities, feel the effects of his mistakes on himself, and prove before all the world his ability to recognise mistakes and to avoid them.

Try to fit this picture into the frame of our autocracy! Is it conceivable in Russia for all "who accept the principles of the Party program and render the Party all possible support" to control every action of the revolutionary working in secret? Is it possible for all to elect one of these revolutionaries to any particular office, when, in the very interests of the work, the revolutionary *must* conceal his identity from nine out of ten of these "all"? Reflect somewhat over the real meaning of the high-sounding phrases to which *Rabocheye Dyelo* gives utterance, and you will realise that "broad democracy" in Party organisation, amidst the gloom of the autocracy and the domination of gendarmerie, is nothing more than a *useless and harmful toy*. It is a useless toy because, in point of fact, no revolutionary organisation has ever practised, or could practise, *broad* democracy, however much it may have desired to do so. It is a harmful toy because any attempt to practise

"the broad democratic principle" will simply facilitate the
work of the police in carrying out large-scale raids, will perpetuate the prevailing primitiveness, and will divert the
thoughts of the practical workers from the serious and pressing task of training themselves to become professional revolutionaries to that of drawing up detailed "paper" rules for
election systems. Only abroad, where very often people with
no opportunity for conducting really active work gather, could
this "playing at democracy" develop here and there, especially in small groups. . . .

The only serious organisational principle for the active
workers of our movement should be the strictest secrecy, the
strictest selection of members, and the training of professional
revolutionaries. Given these qualities, something even more
than "democratism" would be guaranteed to us, namely, complete, comradely, mutual confidence among revolutionaries.
This is absolutely essential for us, because there can be no
question of replacing it by general democratic control in Russia. It would be a great mistake to believe that the impossibility of establishing real "democratic" control renders the
members of the revolutionary organisation beyond control altogether. They have not the time to think about toy forms of
democratism (democratism within a close and compact body
of comrades in which complete, mutual confidence prevails),
but they have a lively sense of their *responsibility*, knowing as
they do from experience that an organisation of real revolutionaries will stop at nothing to rid itself of an unworthy member. Moreover, there is a fairly well-developed public opinion
in Russia (and international) revolutionary circles which has
a long history behind it, and which sternly and ruthlessly pun-
ishes every departure from the duties of comradeship (and
"democratism", real and not toy democratism, certainly forms
a component part of the conception of comradeship). Take all
this into consideration and you will realise that this talk and
these resolutions about "anti-democratic tendencies" have the
musty odour of the playing at generals which is indulged in
abroad. . . .

STATE AND REVOLUTION (1917)

The Bolshevik Party was the only major socialist party in Europe to oppose its government's participation in the war. To Lenin the war was an imperialist war pure and simple, the distinction between democratic and autocratic capitalist power was fictitious, and true socialists owed their loyalty to the proletariat everywhere, not to any particular state. The disagreement between Lenin and the European social democrats over the war exposed their deeper differences over the nature of socialism and in particular over the question of state power. When the imperialist powers collapsed what kind of socialism would follow? What, from the viewpoint of socialism, were the means and ends of political power? Lenin answered these questions as the high priest of pure Marxism.

Though Marx had never ceased hoping for a communist commonwealth, the possibility of its realization had been too remote for him to speculate on its nature. But to Lenin the communist commonwealth was near at hand and so he set himself the task of determining how it should be brought about and what it should be like. Within the terms of his revolutionary idealism, Lenin was perfectly consistent. He differed with the European democratic socialists over the role of the state because he saw communism as an immediate possibility while they did not—even when they thought it an ultimate possibility. Nowhere are the differences between Lenin and other socialists more clearly brought out, and the mystique of Bolshevism better defined, than in Lenin's *State and Revolution*. It remains the authoritative Bolshevik statement on political theory.

He began writing *State and Revolution* at the end of 1916 with the intention of publishing it early the following year, but the February Revolution came and he stopped work on it until after the abortive Bolshevik uprising of July. He resumed writing it while in hiding in August and September 1917. A month later he was at the head of the government, and he never completed the last chapter of the book, which he brought out in 1918. He wrote in the postscript: "It is more

pleasant and useful to go through 'the experience of the revolution' than to write about it."

▼ ▼ ▼

. . . It is often said and written that the main point in
Marx's teachings is the class struggle; but this is not true. And
from this untruth very often springs the opportunist distortion
of Marxism, its falsification in such a way as to make it acceptable to the bourgeoisie. For the doctrine of the class struggle was created *not* by Marx, *but* by the bourgeoisie *before*
Marx, and generally speaking it is *acceptable* to the bourgeoisie. Those who recognize *only* the class struggle are not yet
Marxists; they may be found to be still within the boundaries
of bourgeois thinking and bourgeois politics. To confine Marxism to the doctrine of the class struggle means curtailing Marxism, distorting it, reducing it to something which is acceptable to the bourgeoisie. Only he is a Marxist who *extends* the
recognition of the class struggle to the recognition of the *dictatorship of the proletariat*. This is what constitutes the most
profound difference between the Marxist and the ordinary
petty (as well as big) bourgeois. This is the touchstone on
which the *real* understanding and recognition of Marxism is to
be tested. And it is not surprising that when the history of
Europe brought the working class face to face with this question as a *practical* issue, not only all the opportunists and reformists, but all the "Kautskyites" (people who vacillate
between reformism and Marxism) proved to be miserable
philistines and petty-bourgeois democrats who *repudiate* the
dictatorship of the proletariat. Kautsky's pamphlet, *The Dictatorship of the Proletariat*, published in August 1918, i.e., long
after the first edition of the present book, is a perfect example
of petty-bourgeois distortion of Marxism and base renunciation of it *in practice*, while hypocritically recognizing it *in
words* (see my pamphlet, *The Proletarian Revolution and the
Renegade Kautsky*, Petrograd and Moscow, 1918).

Present-day opportunism in the person of its principal representative, the ex-Marxist, K. Kautsky, fits in completely with
Marx's characterization of the *bourgeois* position quoted
above, for this opportunism limits the recognition of the class

struggle to the sphere of bourgeois relationships. (Within this
sphere, within its framework, not a single educated liberal will
refuse to recognize the class struggle "in principle"!) Opportunism *does not extend* the recognition of class struggle to
what is the cardinal point, to the period of *transition* from
capitalism to communism, to the period of the *overthrow* and
the complete *abolition* of the bourgeoisie. In reality, this period inevitably is a period of an unprecedentedly violent class
struggle in unprecedentedly acute forms and, consequently,
during this period the state must inevitably be a state that is
democratic *in a new way* (for the proletariat and the propertyless in general) and dictatorial *in a new way* (against the
bourgeoisie).

To proceed. The essence of Marx's teaching on the state has
been mastered only by those who understand that the dictatorship of a *single* class is necessary not only for every class society in general, not only for the *proletariat* which has overthrown the bourgeoisie, but also for the entire *historical period*
which separates capitalism from "classless society," from communism. The forms of bourgeois states are extremely varied,
but their essence is the same: all these states, whatever their
form, in the final analysis are inevitably *the dictatorship of the
bourgeoisie*. The transition from capitalism to communism certainly cannot but yield a tremendous abundance and variety
of political forms, but the essence will inevitably be the same:
the dictatorship of the proletariat. . . .

. . . Democracy for an insignificant minority, democracy
for the rich—that is the democracy of capitalist society. If we
look more closely into the machinery of capitalist democracy,
we shall see everywhere, in the "petty"—supposedly petty—details of the suffrage (residential qualification, exclusion of
women, etc.), in the technique of the representative institutions, in the actual obstacles to the right of assembly (public
buildings are not for "beggars"!), in the purely capitalist organization of the daily press, etc., etc.—we shall see restriction
after restriction upon democracy. These restrictions, exceptions, exclusions, obstacles for the poor, seem slight, especially
in the eyes of one who has never known want himself and has
never been in close contact with the oppressed classes in their

mass life (and nine-tenths, if not ninety-nine hundredths, of the bourgeois publicists and politicians are of this category); but in their sum total these restrictions exclude and squeeze out the poor from politics, from active participation in democracy.

Marx grasped this *essence* of capitalist democracy splendidly, when, in analyzing the experience of the Commune, he said that the oppressed are allowed once every few years to decide which particular representatives of the oppressing class shall represent and repress them in parliament!

But from this capitalist democracy—that is inevitably narrow, and stealthily pushes aside the poor, and is therefore hypocritical and false to the core—forward development does not proceed simply, directly and smoothly towards "greater and greater democracy," as the liberal professors and petty-bourgeois opportunists would have us believe. No, forward development, i.e., towards communism, proceeds through the dictatorship of the proletariat, and cannot do otherwise, for the *resistance* of the capitalist exploiters cannot be *broken* by anyone else or in any other way.

And the dictatorship of the proletariat, i.e., the organization of the vanguard of the oppressed as the ruling class for the purpose of suppressing the oppressors, cannot result merely in an expansion of democracy. *Simultaneously* with an immense expansion of democracy, which *for the first time* becomes democracy for the poor, democracy for the people, and not democracy for the moneybags, the dictatorship of the proletariat imposes a series of restrictions on the freedom of the oppressors, the exploiters, the capitalists. We must suppress them in order to free humanity from wage slavery, their resistance must be crushed by force; it is clear that where there is suppression, where there is violence, there is no freedom and no democracy.

Engels expressed this splendidly in his letter to Bebel when he said, as the reader will remember, that "the proletariat uses the state not in the interests of freedom but in order to hold down its adversaries, and as soon as it becomes possible to speak of freedom the state as such ceases to exist."

Democracy for the vast majority of the people, and suppression by force, i.e., exclusion from democracy, of the exploiters and oppressors of the people—this is the change democracy undergoes during the *transition* from capitalism to communism.

Only in communist society, when the resistance of the capitalists has been completely crushed, when the capitalists have disappeared, when there are no classes (i.e., when there is no difference between the members of society as regards their relation to the social means of production), *only* then "the state . . . ceases to exist," and it "*becomes possible to speak of freedom.*" Only then will there become possible and be realized a truly complete democracy, democracy without any restrictions whatever. And only then will democracy begin to *wither away*, owing to the simple fact that, freed from capitalist slavery, from the untold horrors, savagery, absurdities and infamies of capitalist exploitation, people will gradually *become accustomed* to observing the elementary rules of social intercourse that have been known for centuries and repeated for thousands of years in all copybook maxims; they will become accustomed to observing them without force, without compulsion, without subordination, *without the special apparatus* for compulsion which is called the state.

The expression "the state *withers away*" is very well chosen, for it indicates both the gradual and the spontaneous nature of the process. Only habit can, and undoubtedly will, have such an effect; for we see around us on millions of occasions how readily people become accustomed to observing the necessary rules of social intercourse when there is no exploitation, when there is nothing that rouses indignation, nothing that evokes protest and revolt and creates the need for *suppression*.

Thus, in capitalist society we have a democracy that is curtailed, wretched, false; a democracy only for the rich, for the minority. The dictatorship of the proletariat, the period of transition to communism, will for the first time create democracy for the people, for the majority, along with the necessary suppression of the minority—the exploiters. Communism alone is capable of giving really complete democracy, and the more complete it is the more quickly will it become unnecessary and wither away of itself.

In other words: under capitalism we have the state in the proper sense of the word, that is, a special machine for the suppression of one class by another, and, what is more, of the majority by the minority. Naturally, to be successful, such an undertaking as the systematic suppression of the exploited majority by the exploiting minority calls for the utmost ferocity and savagery in the work of suppressing, it calls for seas of blood through which mankind has to wade in slavery, serfdom and wage labor.

Furthermore, during the *transition* from capitalism to communism suppression is *still* necessary; but it is now the suppression of the exploiting minority by the exploited majority. A special apparatus, a special machine for suppression, the "state," is *still* necessary, but this is now a transitional state; it is no longer a state in the proper sense of the word; for the suppression of the minority of exploiters by the majority of the wage slaves of *yesterday* is comparatively so easy, simple and natural a task that it will entail far less bloodshed than the suppression of the risings of slaves, serfs or wage laborers, and it will cost mankind far less. And it is compatible with the extension of democracy to such an overwhelming majority of the population that the need for a *special machine* of suppression will begin to disappear. The exploiters are naturally unable to suppress the people without a highly complex machine for performing this task: but *the people* can suppress the exploiters even with a very simple "machine," almost without a "machine," without a special apparatus, by the simpler *organization of the armed masses* (such as the Soviets of Workers' and Soldiers' Deputies, let us remark, anticipating somewhat).

Lastly, only communism makes the state absolutely unnecessary, for there is *nobody* to be suppressed—"nobody" in the sense of a *class*, in the sense of a systematic struggle against a definite section of the population. We are not utopians, and do not in the least deny the possibility and inevitability of excesses on the part of *individual persons*, or the need to suppress *such* excesses. But, in the first place, no special machine, no special apparatus of suppression is needed for this; this will be done by the armed people itself, as simply and as readily as any crowd of civilized people, even in modern society, interferes to put a stop to a scuffle or to prevent a woman from being assaulted. And, secondly, we know that the fundamental social cause of excesses, which consist in the violation of the rules of social intercourse, is the exploitation of the masses, their want and their poverty. With the removal of this chief cause, excesses will inevitably begin to *"wither away."* We do not know how quickly and in what succession, but we know that they will wither away. With their withering away the state will also *wither away.*

Without indulging in utopias, Marx defined more fully what can be defined *now* regarding this future, namely, the difference between the lower and higher phases (levels, stages) of communist society. . . .

It will become possible for the state to wither away completely when society adopts the rule: "From each according to his ability, to each according to his needs," i.e., when people have become so accustomed to observing the fundamental rules of social intercourse and when their labor becomes so productive that they will voluntarily work *according to their ability.* "The narrow horizon of bourgeois right," which compels one to calculate with the coldheartedness of a Shylock whether one has not worked half an hour more than somebody else, whether one is not getting less pay than somebody else—this narrow horizon will then be crossed. There will then be no need for society to regulate the quantity of products to be received by each; each will take freely "according to his needs."

From the bourgeois point of view, it is easy to declare that such a social order is "sheer utopia" and to sneer at the socialists for promising everyone the right to receive from society, without any control over the labor of the individual citizen, any quantity of truffles, automobiles, pianos, etc. Even to this day, most bourgeois "savants" confine themselves to sneering in this way, thereby displaying both their ignorance and their mercenary defence of capitalism.

Ignorance—for it has never entered the head of any socialist to "promise" that the higher phase of the development of communism will arrive; whereas the great socialists, in *foreseeing* that it will arrive presuppose not the present productivity of labor *and not the present* ordinary run of people, who, like the seminary students in Pomyalovsky's stories, are capable of damaging the stocks of public wealth "just for fun," and of demanding the impossible.

Until the "higher" phase of communism arrives, the socialists demand the *strictest* control by society *and by the state* of the measure of labor and the measure of consumption; but this control must *start* with the expropriation of the capitalists, with the establishment of workers' control over the capitalists, and must be exercised not by a state of bureaucrats, but by a state of *armed workers.* . . .

The scientific difference between socialism and communism is clear. What is usually called socialism was termed by Marx the "first" or lower phase of communist society. In so far as the means of production become *common* property, the word "communism" is also applicable here, providing we do not forget that this is *not* complete communism. The great significance of Marx's explanations is that here, too, he consistently applies materialist dialectics, the theory of development, and regards communism as something which develops *out of* capitalism. Instead of scholastically invented, "concocted" definitions and fruitless disputes about words (what is socialism? what is communism?), Marx gives an analysis of what might be called the stages of the economic ripeness of communism.

In its first phase, or first stage, communism *cannot* as yet be fully ripe economically and entirely free from traditions or traces of capitalism. Hence the interesting phenomenon that communism in its first phase retains "the narrow horizon of *bourgeois* right." Of course, bourgeois right in regard to the distribution of articles of *consumption* inevitably presupposes the existence of the *bourgeois state,* for right is nothing without an apparatus capable of *enforcing* the observance of the standards of right.

It follows that under communism there remains for a time not only bourgeois right, but even the bourgeois state without the bourgeoisie!

This may sound like a paradox or simply a dialectical conundrum, of which Marxism is often accused by people who do not take the slightest trouble to study its extraordinarily profound content.

But as a matter of fact, remnants of the old surviving in the new confront us in life at every step, both in nature and in society. And Marx did not arbitrarily insert a scrap of "bourgeois" right into communism, but indicated what is economically and politically inevitable in a society emerging *out of the womb* of capitalism.

Democracy is of enormous importance to the working class in its struggle against the capitalists for its emancipation. But democracy is by no means a boundary not to be overstepped; it is only one of the stages on the road from feudalism to capitalism, and from capitalism to communism.

Democracy means equality. The great significance of the proletariats' struggle for equality and of equality as a slogan will be clear if we correctly interpret it as meaning the abolition of *classes*. But democracy means only *formal* equality. And as soon as equality is achieved for all members of society *in relation* to ownership of the means of production, that is, equality of labor and equality of wages, humanity will inevitably be confronted with the question of advancing farther, from formal equality to actual equality, i.e., to the operation of the rule, "from each according to his ability, to each according to his needs." By what stages, by means of what practical measures humanity will proceed to this supreme aim —we do not and cannot know. But it is important to realize how infinitely mendacious is the ordinary bourgeois conception of socialism as something lifeless, petrified, fixed once for all, whereas in reality *only* under socialism will a rapid, genuine, really mass forward movement, embracing first the *majority* and then the whole of the population, commence in all spheres of public and personal life.

Democracy is a form of the state, one of its varieties. Consequently, it, like every state, represents on the one hand the organized, systematic use of violence against persons; but on the other hand it signifies the formal recognition of equality of citizens, the equal right of all to determine the structure of, and to administer, the state. This, in turn, results in the fact that, at a certain stage in the development of democracy, it

first welds together the class that wages a revolutionary struggle against capitalism—the proletariat, and enables it to crush,
smash to atoms, wipe off the face of the earth the bourgeois,
even the republican bourgeois, state machine, the standing
army, the police and the bureaucracy, and to substitute for
them a *more* democratic state machine, but a state machine
nevertheless, in the shape of the armed masses of workers who
develop into a militia in which the entire population takes
part.

Here "quantity turns into quality": *such* a degree of democracy implies overstepping the boundaries of bourgeois society,
the beginning of its socialist reconstruction. If really *all* take
part in the administration of the state, capitalism cannot retain its hold. And the development of capitalism, in turn, itself
creates the *premises* that *enable* really "all" to take part in the
administration of the state. Some of these premises are: universal literacy, which has already been achieved in a number
of the most advanced capitalist countries, then the "training
and disciplining" of millions of workers by the huge, complex,
socialized apparatus of the postal service, railways, big factories, large-scale commerce, banking, etc., etc.

Given these *economic* premises it is quite possible, after the
overthrow of the capitalists and the bureaucrats, to proceed
immediately, overnight, to replace them in the *control* of production and distribution, in the work of *keeping account* of
labor and products by the armed workers, by the whole of
the armed population. (The question of control and accounting should not be confused with the question of the scientifically trained staff of engineers, agronomists and so on.
These gentlemen are working today in obedience to the wishes
of the capitalists; they will work even better tomorrow in obedience to the wishes of the armed workers.)

Accounting and control—that is the *main* thing required for
"arranging" the smooth working, the correct functioning of the
first phase of communist society. *All* citizens are transformed
here into hired employees of the state, which consists of the
armed workers. *All* citizens become employees and workers of
a *single* nationwide state "syndicate." All that is required is
that they should work equally, do their proper share of work,

and get equally paid. The accounting and control necessary for this have been *simplified* by capitalism to the extreme and reduced to the extraordinarily simple operations—which any literate person can perform—of supervising and recording, knowledge of the four rules of arithmetic, and issuing appropriate receipts.

When the *majority* of the people begin independently and everywhere to keep such accounts and maintain such control over the capitalists (now converted into employees) and over the intellectual gentry who preserve their capitalist habits, this control will really become universal, general, popular; and there will be no way of getting away from it, there will be nowhere to go."

The whole of society will have become a single office and a single factory, with equality of labor and equality of pay.

But this "factory" discipline, which the proletariat, after defeating the capitalists, after overthrowing the exploiters, will extend to the whole of society, is by no means our ideal, or our ultimate goal. It is but a necessary *step* for the purpose of thoroughly purging society of all the infamies and abominations of capitalist exploitation, *and for further* progress.

From the moment all members of society, or even only the vast majority, have learned to administer the state *themselves*, have taken this work into their own hands, have "set going" control over the insignificant minority of capitalists, over the gentry who wish to preserve their capitalist habits and over the workers who have been profoundly corrupted by capitalism—from this moment the need for government of any kind begins to disappear altogether. The more complete the democracy, the nearer the moment approaches when it becomes unnecessary. The more democratic the "state" which consists of the armed workers, and which is "no longer a state in the proper sense of the word," the more rapidly does *every form* of state begin to wither away.

For when *all* have learned to administer and actually do independently administer social production, independently keep accounts and exercise control over the idlers, the gentlefolk, the swindlers and suchlike "guardians of capitalist traditions," the escape from this popular accounting and control will inevitably become so incredibly difficult, such a rare exception, and will probably be accompanied by such swift and severe punishment (for the armed workers are practical men and not sentimental intellectuals, and they will scarcely allow anyone to trifle with them), that the *necessity* of observing the simple, fundamental rules of human intercourse will very soon become a *habit*.

And then the door will be wide open for the transition from the first phase of communist society to its higher phase, and with it to the complete withering away of the state. . . .

KARL KAUTSKY

It was fitting that the man who for thirty years had been the chief spokesman for orthodox Marxism should deliver as it were the official democratic socialist critique of the Bolshevik regime. Kautsky would not believe that the October Revolution was a Marxist revolution—not in a country so appallingly backward as Russia. He scoffed at the Bolshevik rationalization that Russia had gone through a bourgeois phase of development in eight months. To Kautsky the Bolshevik conception of proletariat dictatorship contradicted Marx's conception of it. In short, he accused the Bolsheviks of not being Marxists.

Kautsky's pamphlet of 1918, *Dictatorship of the Proletariat,* written after the Russian Constituent Assembly had been dissolved and after terror had begun on a wide scale, anticipated later developments in Russia with remarkable accuracy. He differed from other socialists—including revisionists—who believed that the dictatorship, at least in its most repressive aspects, would disappear as soon as the great crisis ended. Kautsky's polemic called forth a storm of Bolshevik vituperation, and communists have ever since referred to him as a "renegade."

During the war, Kautsky opposed the idea of splitting the Socialist Party, since he felt that the anti-war factions could eventually gain a majority within it. But after the split had taken place he joined the left wing Independent Socialdemocratic Party, thereby losing control of the journal, *Neue Zeit*, which he had founded 35 years before, to the majority Socialists. In 1924, he moved to Austria, but fled the Nazis in 1938, to Amsterdam. There he died a few months later.

DICTATORSHIP OF THE PROLETARIAT (1918)

. . . We have seen that the method of dictatorship does not promise good results for the proletariat, either from the standpoint of theory or from that of the special Russian conditions; nevertheless, it is understandable only in the light of these conditions.

The fight against Czarism was for a long time a fight against a system of government which had ceased to be based on the conditions prevailing, but was only maintained by naked force, and only by force was to be overthrown. This fact would easily lead to a cult of force even among the revolutionaries, and to over-estimating what could be done by the powers over them, which did not repose on the economic conditions, but on special circumstances. Accordingly, the struggle against Czarism was carried on secretly, and the method of conspiracy created the manners and the habits proper to dictatorship, and not to democracy.

The operation of these factors was, however, crossed by another consequence of the struggle against absolutism. We have already referred to the fact that, in contradistinction to democracy, which awakens an interest for wider relations and greater objects side by side with its constant preoccupations with momentary ends, absolutism arouses theoretical interest. There is to-day, however, only one revolutionary theory of society, that of Karl Marx.

This became the theory of Russian socialism. Now what this theory teaches is that our desires and capabilities are limited by the material conditions, and it shows how powerless is the strongest will which would rise superior to them. It conflicted sharply with the cult of mere force, and caused the social democrats to recognise that definite boundaries were set to their participation in the coming revolution, which, owing to the economic backwardness of Russia, could only be a middle-class one.

Then the second revolution came, and suddenly brought a measure of power to the socialists which surprised them, for this revolution led to the complete demobilisation of the army, which was the strongest support of property and middle class order. And at the same time as the physical support collapsed, the moral support of this order went to pieces, neither the church nor the intellectuals being able to maintain their pretensions. The rule devolved on the lower classes in the state, the workers and peasants, but the peasants do not form a class which is able itself to govern. They willingly permitted themselves to be led by a proletarian party, which promised them immediate peace, at whatever price, and immediate satisfaction of their land hunger. The masses of the proletariat rallied to the same party, which promised them peace and bread.

Thus the Bolshevist Party gained the strength which enabled it to seize political power. Did this not mean that at length the prerequisite was obtained which Marx and Engels had postulated for the coming of socialism, viz., the conquest of political power by the proletariat? In truth, economic theory discountenanced the idea that socialist production was realisable at once under the social conditions of Russia, and not less unfavorable to it was the practical confirmation of this theory, that the new regime in no way signified the sole rule of the proletariat, but the rule of a coalition of proletarian and peasant elements, which left each section free to behave as it liked on its own territory. The proletariat put nothing in the way of the peasants as regards the land, and the peasants put no obstacle in the way of the proletariat as regards the factories. None the less, a socialist party had become the ruler in a great state, for the first time in the world's history. Certainly a colossal and, for the fighting proletariat, a glorious event.

But for what can a socialist party use its power except to bring about socialism? It must at once proceed to do so, and, without thought or regard, clear out of the way all obstacles which confront it. If democracy thereby comes in conflict with the new regime, which, in spite of the great popularity which it so quickly won, cannot dispose of a majority of the votes in the empire, then so much the worse for democracy. Then it must be replaced by dictatorship, which is all the easier to accomplish, as the people's freedom is quite a new thing in Russia, and as yet has struck no deep roots amongst the masses of the people. It was now the task of dictatorship to bring about socialism. This object lesson must not only suffice for the elements in its own country which are still in opposition, but must also compel the proletariat of other capitalist countries to imitation, and provoke them to revolution.

This was assuredly a train of thought of outstanding boldness and fascinating glamour for every proletarian and every socialist. What we have struggled for during half a century, what we have so often thought ourselves to be near, what has always again evaded us, is at length going to be accomplished. No wonder that the proletarians of all countries have hailed Bolshevism. The reality of proletarian rule weighs heavier in the scale than theoretical considerations. And that consciousness of victory is still more strengthened by mutual ignorance of the conditions of the neighbor. It is only possible for a few to study foreign countries, and the majority believe that in foreign countries it is at bottom the same as with us, and when this is not believed, very fantastic ideas about foreigners are entertained.

Consequently, we have the convenient conception that everywhere the same imperialism prevails, and also the conviction of the Russian socialists that the political revolution is as near to the peoples of Western Europe as it is in Russia, and, on the other hand, the belief that the conditions necessary for socialism exist in Russia as they do in Western Europe.

What happened, once the army had been dissolved and the Assembly had been proscribed, was only the consequence of the step that had been taken.

All this is very understandable, if not exactly encouraging. On the other hand, it is not so conceivable why our Bolshevist comrades do not explain their measures on the ground of the peculiar situation in Russia, and justify them in the light of the pressure of the special circumstances, which, according to their notions, left no choice but dictatorship or abdication. They

went beyond this by formulating quite a new theory, on which
they based their measures, and for which they claimed universal application.

For us the explanation of this is to be found in one of their
characteristics, for which we should have great sympathy,
viz., their great interest in theory.

The Bolshevists are Marxists, and have inspired the proletarian sections coming under their influence with great enthusiasm for Marxism. Their dictatorship, however, is in contradiction to the Marxist teaching that no people can overcome the obstacles offered by the successive phases of their
development by a jump, or by legal enactment. How is it
that they find a Marxist foundation for their proceedings?

They remembered opportunely the expression, "the dictatorship of the proletariat," which Marx used in a letter written
in 1875. In so doing he had, indeed, only intended to describe
a political *condition,* and not a *form of government.* Now this
expression is hastily employed to designate the latter, especially as manifested in the rule of the Soviets.

Now if Marx had somewhere said that under certain circumstances things might come to a dictatorship of the proletariat, he has described this condition as one unavoidable
for the transition to socialism. In fact, as he declared, almost at
the same time that in countries like England and America a
peaceful transition to socialism was possible, which would only
be on the basis of democracy and not of dictatorship, he has
also shown that he did not mean by dictatorship the suspension of democracy. Yet this does not disconcert the champions of dictatorship. As Marx once stated that the dictatorship
of the proletariat might be unavoidable, so they announce that
the Soviet Constitution, and the disfranchising of its opponents, was recognised by Marx himself as the form of government corresponding to the nature of the proletariat, and in-
dissolubly bound up with its rule. As such it must last as long
as the rule of the proletariat itself, and until socialism is generally accomplished and all class distinctions have disappeared.

In this sense dictatorship does not appear to be a transitory emergency measure, which, so soon as calmer times have

set in, will again give place to democracy, but as a condition
for the long duration of which we must adapt ourselves.

This interpretation is confirmed by Theses 9 and 10 respecting the Social Revolution, which state:

"(9) Hitherto, the necessity of the Dictatorship of the Proletariat was taught, without enquiring as to the form it would
take. The Russian Socialist Revolution has discovered this
form. It is the form of the Soviet Republic as the type of the
permanent Dictatorship of the Proletariat and (in Russia) of
the poorer classes of peasants. It is therefore necessary to make
the following remarks. We are speaking now, not of a passing
phenomenon, in the narrower sense of the word, but of a particular form of the State during the whole historical epoch.
What needs now to be done is to organise a new form of the
State, and this is not to be confused with special measures directed against the middle class, which are only functions of a
special State organisation appropriate to the colossal tasks
and struggle.

"(10) The proletarian dictatorship accordingly consists, so
to speak, in a permanent state of war against the middle class.
It is also quite clear that all those who cry out about the violence of the Communists completely forget what dictatorship
really is. The Revolution itself is an act of naked force. The
word dictatorship signifies in all languages nothing less than
government by force. The class meaning of force is here important, for it furnishes the historical justification of revolutionary force. It is also quite obvious that the more difficult
the situation of the Revolution becomes, the sharper the dictatorship must be."

From the above it is also apparent that Dictatorship as a
form of government is not only to be a permanent thing, but
will also arise in all countries.

If in Russia now the newly-acquired general freedom is
put an end to again, this must also happen after the victory
of the proletariat in countries where the people's freedom is
already deeply rooted, where it has existed for half a century
and longer, and where the people have won it and maintained
it in frequent bloody revolutions. The new theory asserts
this in all earnestness. And stranger still it finds support not

only amongst the workers of Russia, who still remember the
yoke of the old Czardom, and now rejoice to be able to turn
the handle for once, even as apprentices when they become
journeymen rejoice when they may give the apprentices who
come after them the drubbing they used to receive themselves—no, the new theory finds support even in old democracies like Switzerland.

Yet something stranger still and even less understandable
is to come.

A complete democracy is to be found nowhere, and everywhere we have to strive after modifications and improvements.
Even in Switzerland there is an agitation for the extension
of the legislative powers of the people, for proportional representation and for woman suffrage. In America the power
and mode of selection of the highest judges need to be
very severely restricted. Far greater are the demands that
should be put forward by us in the great bureaucratic and
militarist states in the interests of democracy. And in the
midst of these struggles, the most extreme fighters raise their
heads, and say to the opponents: That which we demand
for the protection of minorities, the opposition, we only want
so long as we ourselves are the opposition, and in the minority.
As soon as we have become the majority, and gained the
power of government, our first act will be to abolish as far
as you are concerned all that we formerly demanded for
ourselves, viz., franchise, freedom of press and of organisation, etc.

The Theses respecting the Socialist Revolution are quite
unequivocal on this point:

"(17) The former demands for a democratic republic, and
general freedom (that is freedom for the middle classes as
well) were quite correct in the epoch that is now passed, the
epoch of preparation and gathering of strength. The worker
needed freedom for his Press, while the middle-class Press
was noxious to him, but he could not at this time put forward
a demand for the suppression of the middle-class Press.
Consequently, the proletariat demanded general freedom,
even freedom for reactionary assemblies, for black labour
organisations.

"(18) Now we are in the period of the direct attack on capital, the direct overthrow and destruction of the imperialist robber State, and the direct suppression of the middle class. It is therefore absolutely clear that in the present epoch the principle of defending general freedom (that is also for the counter-revolutionary middle class) is not only superfluous, but directly dangerous.

"(19) This also holds good for the Press, and the leading organisations of the social traitors. The latter have been unmasked as the active elements of the counter-revolution. They even attack with weapons the proletarian Government. Supported by former officers and the money bags of the defeated finance capital, they appear on the scene as the most energetic organisations for various conspiracies. The proletariat dictatorship is their deadly enemy. Therefore, they must be dealt with in a corresponding manner.

"(20) As regards the working class and the poor peasants, these possess the fullest freedom."

Do they really possess the fullest freedom?

The "Social Traitors" are proletarians and socialists, too, but they offer opposition, and are therefore to be deprived of rights like the middle-class opposition. Would we not display the liveliest anger, and fight with all our strength in any case where a middle-class government endeavoured to employ similar measures against its opposition?

Certainly we should have to do so, but our efforts would only have a laughable result if the middle-class government could refer to socialist precepts like the foregoing, and a practice corresponding with them.

How often have we reproached the liberals that they are different in government from what they are in opposition, and that then they abandon all their democratic pretensions. Now the liberals are at least sufficiently prudent to refrain from the formal abandonment of any of their democratic demands. They act according to the maxim; one does this, but does not say so.

The authors of the Theses are undeniably more honourable; whether they are wiser may be doubted. What would be thought of the wisdom of the German Social Democrats, if they openly announced that the democracy, for which they fight to-day, would be abandoned the day after victory. That they have perverted their democratic principles to their opposites, or that they have no democratic principles at all; that democracy is merely a ladder for them, up which to climb to governmental omnipotence, a ladder they will no longer need, and will push away, as soon as they have reached the top, that, in a word, they are revolutionary opportunists.

Even for the Russian revolutionaries it is a short-sighted policy of expediency, if they adopt the method of dictatorship, in order to gain power, not to save the jeopardised democracy, but in order to maintain themselves in spite of it. This is quite obvious.

On the other hand, it is less obvious why some German Social Democrats who are not yet in power, who furthermore only at the moment represent a weak opposition, accept this theory. Instead of seeing something which should be generally condemned in the method of dictatorship, and the disfranchising of large sections of the people, which at the most is only defensible as a product of the exceptional conditions prevailing in Russia, they go out of their way to praise this method as a condition which the German Social Democracy should also strive to realise.

This assertion is not only thoroughly false, it is in the highest degree destructive. If generally accepted, it would paralyse the propagandist strength of our party to the utmost, for, with the exception of a small handful of sectarian fanatics, the entire German, as also the whole proletariat of the world, is attached to the principle of general democracy. The proletariat would angrily repudiate every thought of beginning its rule with a new privileged class, and a new disfranchised class. It would repudiate every suggestion of coupling its demand for general rights for the whole people with a mental reservation, and in reality only strive for privileges for itself. And not less would it repudiate the comic insinuation of solemnly declaring now that its demand for democracy is a mere deceit.

Dictatorship as a form of government in Russia is as understandable as the former anarchism of Bakunin. But to understand it does not mean that we should recognise it; we must reject the former as decisively as the latter. The dictatorship does not reveal itself as a resource of a socialist party to secure itself in the sovereignty which has been gained in opposition to the majority of the people, but only as means of grappling with tasks which are beyond its strength, and the solution of which exhausts and wears it; in doing which it only too easily compromises the ideas of socialism itself, the progress of which it impedes rather than assists.

Happily, the failure of the dictatorship is not synonymous with a collapse of the revolution. It would be so only if the Bolshevist dictatorship was the mere prelude to a middle-class dictatorship. The essential achievements of the Revolution will be saved, if dictatorship is opportunely replaced by democracy.

TROTSKY (1879–1940)

It had been generally believed that Lenin's successor would be Leon Trotsky. Trotsky had led the October uprising in Petrograd, had headed the delegation which made peace with Germany at Brest-Litovsk and had organized and commanded the Red Army in the civil war. More than any other man, Lenin excepted, he had helped win and secure the Bolshevik Revolution. But his fall was spectacular; in 1925 —exactly a year after Lenin's death—he was stripped of his last government post; in 1926 he was thrown out of the Politburo; in 1927 he was cast out of the party; in 1928 he was sent to Siberia; and in 1929 he was exiled from Russia. He wandered for years across Europe until he found sanctuary in Mexico. There, on Stalin's orders, he was slain in 1940.

Born Lev Davydovich Bronstein near the south Russian city of Odessa, the only son of a prosperous Jewish farmer, he was a full-blown Marxist revolutionary by the age of eighteen. A brilliant writer even then, he came to the notice of Plekhanov and Lenin whom he later joined on the staff of *Iskra*. He was neither Menshevik nor Bolshevik, but he engaged in sharp polemical exchanges with Lenin—exchanges that were later used against him as proofs of his long-standing anti-Bolshevism. He took a leading part in the 1905 Revolution and, as president of the St. Petersburg Workers' Soviet (or Workers' Council) he nearly succeeded in toppling the government. After ten years of prison and exile he returned to Russia immediately on receiving word that the revolution had broken out.

In 1906 Trotsky had argued that Russia actually stood the best chance of having a proletarian revolution. This was so because while the Czarist regime was impossibly corrupt and the peasants slothful and disorganized, the proletariat, though relatively small in numbers, was concentrated, well-organized and close to the centers of power. This revolution would in the end fail, however, unless it triggered, and merged with, proletarian revolutions in the more advanced industrial countries of Western Europe. This theory gained notoriety as the theory of "permanent revolution." Events in 1917 seemed to bear it out and Lenin virtually adopted it as the basis of his strategy. In a real sense the October Revolution, both in theory and in execution, was Trotsky's.

After finishing his work for the Revolution he became the defender of its pure ideals. His theory of 1906 was still his model, and it explained for him why the sacrosanct ideals of October rapidly dissipated into jobbery, opportunism and inertia. He was alarmed by the swelling power of new classes of businessmen, farmers and government bureaucrats, by the stifling of criticism, by the spirit of selfishness and privilege that permeated every level of the party. All of this he was later to compress into the single term Stalinism. His first public attack on the system appeared in several articles he wrote for *Pravda*, in December 1923. These he expanded in a pamphlet, *The New Course*, published the following year.

Trotsky was caught in a tragic situation. He had no choice but to appeal to the party, although it was at the same time the chief object of his attacks. He was popular outside the party; inside it he had become anathema. Its functionaries were repelled by his unyielding revolutionary spirit, his cutting remarks, his intellectual aloofness, his disdain for mediocrity, and, not least, by the fact that he was a Jew. Stalin himself despised Trotsky for all of these reasons.

Yet Trotsky could not have appealed elsewhere without ceasing to be a Bolshevik. He believed no less than Stalin did that the Bolshevik Party alone embodied the future of all mankind. Once the party repudiated him he had nowhere to go. As an enemy of the party, he became, by the logic of proletarian dictatorship, an enemy of the state and of all history. Trotsky had always subscribed to this logic, and he did not question its validity, even after he became its victim.

The New Course (1924)

. . . The state apparatus is the most important source of bureaucratism. On the one hand, it absorbs an enormous quantity of the most active party elements and it teaches the most capable of them the methods of administration of men and things, instead of political leadership of the masses. On the other hand, it preoccupies largely the attention of the party apparatus over which it exerts influence by its methods of administration.

Thence, in large measure, the bureaucratization of the apparatus, which threatens to separate the party from the masses. This is precisely the danger that is now most obvious and direct. The struggle against the other dangers must under present conditions begin with the struggle against bureaucratism.

It is unworthy of a Marxist to consider that bureaucratism is only the aggregate of the bad habits of office holders. Bureaucratism is a social phenomenon in that it is a definite system of administration of men and things. Its profound causes lie in the heterogeneity of society, the difference between the daily and the fundamental interests of various groups of the population. Bureaucratism is complicated by the fact of the lack of culture of the broad masses. With us, the essential source of bureaucratism resides in the necessity of creating and sustaining a state apparatus that unites the interests of the proletariat and those of the peasantry in a perfect economic harmony, from which we are still far removed. The necessity of maintaining a permanent army is likewise another important source of bureaucratism.

It is quite plain that precisely the negative social phenomena we have just enumerated and which now nurture bureaucratism could place the revolution in peril should they continue to develop. We have mentioned above this hypothesis: the growing discord between state and peasant economy, the growth of the kulaks in the country, their alliance with private commercial-industrial capital, these would be—given the low cultural level of the toiling masses of the countryside and in part of the towns—the causes of the eventual counter-revolutionary dangers.

In other words, bureaucratism in the state and party apparatus is the expression of the most vexatious tendencies inherent in our situation, of the defects and deviations in our work which, under certain social conditions, might sap the basis of the revolution. And, in this case as in many others, quantity will at a certain stage be transformed into quality.

The struggle against the bureaucratism of the state apparatus is an exceptionally important but prolonged task, one that runs more or less parallel to our other fundamental tasks: economic reconstruction and the elevation of the cultural level of the masses.

The most important historical instrument for the accomplishment of all these tasks is the party. Naturally, not even the party can tear itself away from the social and cultural conditions of the country. But as the voluntary organization of the vanguard, of the best, the most active and the most conscious elements of the working class, it is able to preserve itself much better than can the state apparatus from the tendencies of bureaucratism. For that, it must see the danger clearly and combat it without let-up.

Thence the immense importance of the education of the party youth, based upon personal initiative, in order to serve the state apparatus in a new manner and to transform it completely. . . .

The more ingrown the party apparatus, the more imbued it is with the feeling of its own intrinsic importance, the slower it reacts to needs emanating from the ranks and the more inclined it is to set formal tradition against new needs and tasks. And if there is one thing likely to strike a mortal blow to the spiritual life of the party and to the doctrinal training of the youth, it is certainly the transformation of Leninism from a method demanding for its application initiative, critical thinking and ideological courage into a canon which demands nothing more than interpreters appointed for good and aye.

Leninism cannot be conceived of without theoretical breadth, without a critical analysis of the material bases of the political process. The weapon of Marxian investigation must be constantly sharpened and applied. It is precisely in this that tradition consists, and not in the substitution of a formal reference or of an accidental quotation. Least of all can Leninism be reconciled with ideological superficiality and theoretical slovenliness.

Lenin cannot be chopped up into quotations suited for every possible case, because for Lenin the formula never stands higher than the reality; it is always the tool that makes it possible to grasp the reality and to dominate it. It would not be hard to find in Lenin dozens and hundreds of passages which, formally speaking, seem to be contradictory. But what must be seen is not the formal relationship of one passage to another, but the real relationship of each of them to the concrete reality in which the formula was introduced as a lever. The Leninist truth is always concrete!

As a system of revolutionary action, Leninism presupposes a revolutionary sense sharpened by reflection and experience which, in the social realm, is equivalent to the muscular sensation in physical labor. But revolutionary sense cannot be confused with demagogical flair. The latter may yield ephemeral successes, sometimes even sensational ones. But it is a political instinct of an inferior type. It always leans toward the line of least resistance. Leninism, on the other hand, seeks to pose and resolve the fundamental revolutionary problems, to overcome the principal obstacles; its demagogical counterpart consists in evading the problems, in creating an illusory appeasement, in lulling critical thought to sleep.

Leninism is, first of all, realism, the highest qualitative and quantitative appreciation of reality, from the standpoint of revolutionary action. Precisely because of this it is irreconcilable with the flight from reality behind the screen of hollow agitationalism, with the passive loss of time, with the haughty justification of yesterday's mistakes on the pretext of saving the tradition of the party.

Leninism is genuine freedom from formalistic prejudices, from moralizing doctrinalism, from all forms of intellectual conservatism attempting to bind the will to revolutionary action. But to believe that Leninism signifies that "anything goes," would be an irremediable mistake. Leninism includes the morality, not formal but genuinely revolutionary, of mass action and the mass party. Nothing is so alien to it as functionary-arrogance and bureaucratic cynicism. A mass party has its own morality, which is the bond of fighters in and for action. Demagogy is irreconcilable with the spirit of a revolutionary party because it is deceitful: by presenting one or another simplified solution of the difficulties of the hour, it inevitably undermines the next future, weakens the party's self-confidence.

Swept by the wind and gripped by a serious danger, demagogy easily dissolves into panic. It is hard to juxtapose, even on paper, panic and Leninism.

Leninism is warlike from head to foot. War is impossible without cunning, without subterfuge, without deception of the enemy. Victorious war cunning is a constituent element of Leninist politics. But at the same time, Leninism is supreme revolutionary honesty toward the party and the working class. It admits of no fiction, no bubble-blowing, no pseudo-grandeur!

Leninism is orthodox, obdurate, irreducible, but it does not contain so much as a hint of formalism, canon, nor bureaucratism. In the struggle, it takes the bull by the horns. To make out of the traditions of Leninism a supra-theoretical guarantee of the infallibility of all the words and thoughts of the interpreters of these traditions, is to scoff at genuine revolutionary tradition and transform it into official bureaucratism. It is ridiculous and pathetic to try to hypnotize a great revolutionary party by the repetition of the same formulæ, according to which the right line should be sought not in the essence of each question, not in the methods of posing and solving this question, but in information . . . of a biographical character.

Since I am obliged to speak of myself for a moment, I will say that I do not consider the road by which I came to Leninism as less safe and reliable than the others. I came to Lenin fighting, but I came fully and all the way. My actions in the service of the party are the only guarantee of this: I can give no other supplementary guarantees. And if the question is to be posed in the field of biographical investigation, then at least it ought to be done properly.

It would then be necessary to reply to thorny questions: Were all those who were faithful to the master in the small matters also faithful to him in the great? Did all those who showed such docility in the presence of the master thereby offer guarantees that they would continue his work in his absence? Does the whole of Leninism lie in docility? I have no intention whatever of analyzing these questions by taking as examples individual comrades with whom, so far as I am concerned, I intend to continue working hand in hand.

Whatever the difficulties and the differences of opinion may be in the future, they can be victoriously overcome only by the collective work of the party's mind, checking up each time by itself and thereby maintaining the continuity of development.

This character of the revolutionary tradition is bound up with the peculiar character of revolutionary discipline. Where tradition is conservative, discipline is passive and is violated at the first moment of crisis. Where, as in our party, tradition consists in the highest revolutionary activity, discipline attains its maximum point, for its decisive importance is constantly checked in action. Thence, the indestructible alliance of revolutionary initiative, of critical, bold elaboration of questions, with iron discipline in action. And it is only by this superior activity that the youth can receive from the old this tradition of discipline and carry it on.

We cherish the traditions of Bolshevism as much as anybody. But let no one dare identify bureaucratism with Bolshevism, tradition with officious routine.

Certain comrades have adopted very singular methods of political criticism: they assert that I am mistaken today in this or that question because I was wrong in this or that question a dozen years ago. This method considerably simplifies the task.

The question of today in itself needs to be studied in its full contents. But a question raised several years ago has long since been exhausted, judged by history and, to refer to it again does not require great intellectual effort; all that is needed is memory and good faith.

But I cannot say that in this last respect all goes well with my critics. And I am going to prove it by an example from one of the most important questions.

One of the favorite arguments of certain circles during recent times consists of pointing out—mainly by indirection—that I "underestimate" the rôle of the peasantry. But one would seek in vain among my adversaries for an analysis of this question, for facts, quotations, in a word, for any proof.

Ordinarily, their argumentation boils down to allusions to the theory of the "permanent revolution," and to two or three bits of corridor gossip. And between the theory of the "permanent revolution" and the corridor gossip there is nothing, a void.

As to the theory of the "permanent revolution," I see no reason to renounce what I wrote on this subject in 1904, 1905, 1906, and later. To this day, I persist in considering that the thoughts I developed at that time are much closer, taken as a whole, to the genuine essence of Leninism than much of what a number of Bolsheviks wrote in those days.

The expression *"permanent revolution"* is an expression of Marx which he applied to the revolution of 1848. In Marxian, naturally not in revisionist but in revolutionary Marxian lit-erature, this term has always had citizenship rights. Franz Mehring employed it for the revolution of 1905–1907. The permanent revolution, in an exact translation, is the continuous revolution, the uninterrupted revolution. What is the political idea embraced in this expression?

It is, for us communists, that the revolution does not come to an end after this or that political conquest, after obtaining this or that social reform, but that it continues to develop further and its only boundary is the socialist society. Thus, once begun, the revolution (insofar as we participate in it and particularly when we lead it) is in no case interrupted by us at any formal stage whatever. On the contrary, we continually and constantly advance it in conformity, of course, with the situation, so long as the revolution has not exhausted all the possibilities and all the resources of the movement. This applies to the conquests of the revolution inside of a country as well as to its extension over the international arena.

For Russia, this theory signified: what we need is not the bourgeois republic as a political crowning, nor even the democratic dictatorship of the proletariat and peasantry, but a workers' government supporting itself upon the peasantry and opening up the era of the international socialist revolution.

Thus, the idea of the permanent revolution coincides entirely with the fundamental strategical line of Bolshevism. It is understandable if this was not seen eighteen or fifteen years ago. But it is impossible not to understand and to recognize it now that the general formulæ have been verified by full-blooded historical context. . . .

STALIN (1879–1953)

Joseph Stalin, Lenin's successor, was born Joseph Vissarionovich Djugashvili in the Georgian town of Gori. Brought up by his mother—his father, a penurious cobbler, died when Joseph was eleven—he worked hard as a youth until he was admitted to the theological seminary in Tiflis. But at the seminary he learned Marxism as well as theology and was expelled for personal disobedience. He joined the Bolshevik Party immediately after its founding in 1903 and before long came to Lenin's attention as a trustworthy and resourceful worker in the Caucases. After serving several jail terms and performing valuable strong-arm services for the party, he was made Lenin's chief lieutenant in Russia. After the October

Revolution he took his place alongside Lenin in the highest councils of party and state.

None of his colleagues in 1917, least of all Lenin, had any idea what kind of man he was or would be. They thought of him as Lenin's dedicated subordinate, a conscientious party functionary, a tough, plodding, unimaginative man who got things done and kept his own counsel; intellectually, he was no match for the coruscating writers and speakers who led the party. But Stalin's qualities were precisely those the party needed to meet the responsibilities that had suddenly fallen to it. No one in the Central Committee grudged Stalin his tasks because it never entered anyone's mind that he wanted —or that it was possible for him—to usurp all power.

But it was possible, perhaps inevitable. The Bolshevik Party after January 1918 (when it dissolved the Constituent Assembly) was the only legitimate political institution in Russia. It held all society in subjection to its revolutionary will and believed itself the repository of absolute truth. But the party's revolutionary will became increasingly subordinate to the needs of its bureaucracy, swelled to monstrous size. Authority and prestige henceforth were to go not to the revolutionary idealist but to the silent worker who descended into the sinks of organization. It was Stalin's genius to have seen this fact and to have acted upon it. As Commissar of Nationalities, then as Commissar of Worker's and Peasant's Inspection, and above all, as General Secretary of the party, he built an insuperable hierarchy of loyalties. By early 1923 Lenin was prepared to oust him from office as a dangerous opportunist. But before Lenin could do anything about it he suffered his third stroke, which incapacitated him until his death in January 1924.

Stalin the bureaucrat, not Trotsky the revolutionist, re-flected the mood of the Russian people in 1924. After a decade of suffering they had no wish to embark on further adventures, at home or abroad. Moreover, the hope of proletarian uprisings in Europe had grown dim. The com-munist revolutions in Bavaria and Hungary were memories; the last insurrection in Germany had been crushed the year before and there was little likelihood of another in the foreseeable future. At the same time the Soviet Union was gaining respectability among the nations of the world and learning to prize it.

Against this background, Stalin characterized Trotsky as a dangerous gambler who would throw away the gains already made at much sacrifice, in order to force catastrophic changes at home while carrying on bootless adventures abroad. To Trotsky's idea of "permanent revolution," Stalin opposed his own conception of "socialism in one country." Why, Stalin in effect asked, should the peasants and proletariat of Russia have to wait upon the rest of world? Russia was capable of building socialism alone, and the rest of the world would look to Russia for its example. "Socialism in one country" was Stalin's contribution to the dogma of Marxism-Leninism.

Ideologically, the real difference between "permanent revolution" and "socialism in one country" turned on a difference of emphasis. Trotsky also believed in first consolidating the revolution in Russia, and never suggested that it be sacrificed for revolutions abroad. And Stalin also professed to believe in the ultimate ideal of world revolution. But Trotsky denied that revolution in a single country, least of all in a backward one, could be complete, while Stalin affirmed that socialism would succeed in Russia even if nowhere else. Thus Stalin was not only defending retrenchment, he was defending—or so he made it seem—the soil and spirit of the homeland. Henceforth, communists of the Third International (Trotsky was to form a Fourth) would be distinguished by one criterion above all: loyalty to the Soviet Union.

The Foundations of Leninism (1924)

. . . 3. *The Party as the highest form of class organization of the proletariat.* The Party is the organized detachment of the working class. But the Party is not the only organization of the working class. The proletariat has also a number of other organizations, without which it cannot properly wage the struggle against capital: trade unions, cooperative societies, factory organizations, parliamentary groups, non-Party women's associations, the press, cultural and educa-

tional organizations, youth leagues, revolutionary fighting
organizations (in times of open revolutionary action), Soviets
of deputies as the form of state organization (if the proletariat
is in power), etc. The overwhelming majority of these organizations are non-Party, and only a certain part of them
adhere directly to the Party, or represent its offshoots. All
these organizations, under certain conditions, are absolutely
necessary for the working class, for without them it would
be impossible to consolidate the class positions of the proletariat in the diverse spheres of struggle; for without them
it would be impossible to steel the proletariat as the force
whose mission it is to replace the bourgeois order by the
socialist order. But how can single leadership be exercised
with such an abundance of organizations? What guarantee
is there that this multiplicity of organizations will not lead
to divergency in leadership? It might be argued that each of
these organizations carries on its work in its own special
field, and that therefore these organizations cannot hinder
one another. This, of course, is true. But it is also true that
all these organizations should work in one direction for they
serve *one* class, the class of the proletarians. The question
then arises: who is to determine the line, the general direction, along which the work of all these organizations is to
be conducted? Where is that central organization which is
not only able, because it has the necessary experience, to
work out such a general line, but, in addition, is in a position,
because it has sufficient prestige for that, to induce all these
organizations to carry out this line, so as to attain unity of
leadership and to preclude the possibility of working at cross
purposes?

This organization is the Party of the proletariat. . . .

4. *The Party as the instrument of the dictatorship of the
proletariat.* The Party is the highest form of organization of
the proletariat. The Party is the principal guiding force within
the class of the proletarians and among the organizations of
that class. But it does not by any means follow from this
that the Party can be regarded as an end in itself, as a self-
sufficient force. The Party is not only the highest form of
class association of the proletarians; it is at the same time an

instrument in the hands of the proletariat *for* achieving the
dictatorship when that has not yet been achieved and *for*
consolidating and expanding the dictatorship when it has already been achieved. The Party could not have risen so high
in importance and could not have overshadowed all other
forms of organization of the proletariat, if the latter were not
confronted with the problem of power, if the conditions of
imperialism, the inevitability of wars, and the existence of a
crisis did not demand the concentration of all the forces of
the proletariat at one point, the gathering of all the threads
of the revolutionary movement in one spot in order to overthrow the bourgeoisie and to achieve the dictatorship of
the proletariat. The proletariat needs the Party first of all as
its General Staff, which it must have for the successful seizure of power. It need hardly be proved that without a Party
capable of rallying around itself the mass organizations of
the proletariat, and of centralizing the leadership of the
entire movement during the progress of the struggle, the proletariat in Russia could never have established its revolutionary dictatorship.

But the proletariat needs the Party not only to achieve
the dictatorship; it needs it still more to maintain the dictatorship, to consolidate and expand it in order to achieve the
complete victory of Socialism.

"Certainly, almost everyone now realizes," says Lenin,
"that the Bolsheviks could not have maintained themselves
in power for two-and-a-half months, let alone two-and-a-half
years, unless the strictest, truly iron discipline had prevailed
in our Party, and unless the latter had been rendered the
fullest and unreserved support of the whole mass of the
working class, that is, of all its thinking, honest, self-sacrificing
and influential elements who are capable of leading or of
carrying with them the backward strata." (Vol. XXV, p. 173.)

Now, what does it mean to "maintain" and "expand" the
dictatorship? It means imbuing the millions of proletarians
with the spirit of discipline and organization; it means creating among the proletarian masses a cementing force and a
bulwark against the corrosive influences of the petty-bourgeois elements and petty-bourgeois habits; it means enhancing

the organizing work of the proletarians in re-educating and
remoulding the petty-bourgeois strata; it means helping the
masses of the proletarians to educate themselves as a force
capable of abolishing classes and of preparing the conditions
for the organization of socialist production. But it is impossible to accomplish all this without a party which is strong
by reason of its solidarity and discipline.

"The dictatorship of the proletariat," says Lenin, "is a
persistent struggle—bloody and bloodless, violent and peaceful, military and economic, educational and administrative—
against the forces and traditions of the old society. The force
of habit of millions and tens of millions is a most terrible
force. Without an iron party tempered in the struggle, without a party enjoying the confidence of all that is honest in
the given class, without a party capable of watching and
influencing the mood of the masses, it is impossible to conduct
such a struggle successfully." (Vol. XXV, p. 190.)

The proletariat needs the Party for the purpose of achieving and maintaining the dictatorship. The Party is an instrument of the dictatorship of the proletariat.

But from this it follows that when classes disappear and
the dictatorship of the proletariat withers away, the Party
will also wither away.

5. *The Party as the embodiment of unity of will, incompatible with the existence of factions.* The achievement
and maintenance of the dictatorship of the proletariat is
impossible without a party which is strong by reason of its
solidarity and iron discipline. But iron discipline in the Party
is inconceivable without unity of will, without complete and
absolute unity of action on the part of all members of the
Party. This does not mean, of course, that the possibility of
contests of opinion within the Party is thereby precluded.
On the contrary, iron discipline does not preclude but presupposes criticism and contest of opinion within the Party.
Least of all does it mean that discipline must be "blind." On
the contrary, iron discipline does not preclude but presupposes
conscious and voluntary submission, for only conscious discipline can be truly iron discipline. But after a contest of
opinion has been closed, after criticism has been exhausted

and a decision has been arrived at, unity of will and unity of action of all Party members are the necessary conditions without which neither Party unity nor iron discipline in the Party is conceivable.

"In the present epoch of acute civil war," says Lenin, "a Communist Party will be able to perform its duty only if it is organized in the most centralized manner, only if iron discipline bordering on military discipline prevails in it, and if its party centre is a powerful and authoritative organ, wielding wide powers and enjoying the universal confidence of the members of the Party." (Vol. XXV, pp. 282–83.)

This is the position in regard to discipline in the Party in the period of struggle preceding the achievement of the dictatorship.

The same, but to an even greater degree, must be said about discipline in the Party after the dictatorship has been achieved.

"Whoever," says Lenin, "weakens ever so little the iron discipline of the party of the proletariat (especially during the time of its dictatorship), actually aids the bourgeoisie against the proletariat." (Vol. XXV, p. 190.)

But from this it follows that the existence of factions is incompatible either with the Party's unity or with its iron discipline. It need hardly be proved that the existence of factions leads to the existence of a number of centres, and the existence of a number of centres connotes the absence of one common centre in the Party, the breaking up of the unity of will, the weakening and disintegration of discipline, the weakening and disintegration of the dictatorship. Of course, the parties of the Second International, which are fighting against the dictatorship of the proletariat and have no desire to lead the proletarians to power, can afford such liberalism as freedom of factions, for they have no need at all for iron discipline. But the parties of the Communist International, whose activities are conditioned by the task of achieving and consolidating the dictatorship of the proletariat, cannot afford to be "liberal" or to permit freedom of factions.

The Party represents unity of will, which precludes all factionalism and division of authority in the Party.

Hence Lenin's warning about the "danger of factionalism from the point of view of Party unity and of effecting the unity of will of the vanguard of the proletariat as the fundamental condition for the success of the dictatorship of the proletariat," which is embodied in the special resolution of the Tenth Congress of our Party "On Party Unity."

Hence Lenin's demand for the "complete elimination of all factionalism" and the "immediate dissolution of all groups, without exception, that had been formed on the basis of various platforms," on pain of "unconditional and immediate expulsion from the Party." (See resolution "On Party Unity.") . . .

ON THE PROBLEMS OF LENINISM (1924)

. . . Here is what Comrade Trotsky says concerning "permanent revolution":—

"It was during the interval between January 9 and the October strike of 1905 that I came to consider the revolutionary development of Russia under the aspect of what ultimately came to be known as the 'permanent revolution.' This rather abstruse designation was intended to convey the idea that the Russian revolution, though in the immediate future forced to realise certain bourgeois aims, could not stop at that. The revolution could not accomplish its immediate bourgeois tasks unless the proletariat had risen to power. Once the proletariat had seized power, it could not confine its activities within the framework of the bourgeois revolution. On the contrary; if the proletarian vanguard was to reap the harvest of its victory it must at the very outset make the most decisive inroads into the domains both of feudal and of capitalist property. Such action would have led to hostile collisions, not only with all bourgeois groups which had helped the revolution in its early stages, but likewise with the peasant masses whose co-operation had raised the proletariat to power. The contradictions inherent in the position of a workers' gov-

ernment functioning in a backward country where the
large majority of the population is composed of peasants, can only be liquidated on an international scale,
in the arena of a world-wide proletarian revolution."

So far Comrade Trotsky on the subject of the "permanent
revolution."

We need but compare this quotation with those extracts
from Lenin's works concerning the dictatorship of the proletariat which we quoted above, in order to understand the
depth of the abyss which separates Lenin's theory of the dictatorship of the proletariat from Trotsky's theory of permanent
revolution. . . .

The opportunists in every land maintain that the proletarian revolution can begin—if it ever does begin anywhere
according to their theories!—only in countries of advanced
industrial development, and that the chances of a victory for
socialism in such countries are increased in proportion to the
extent of their industrial development. Furthermore, they
deny the possibility of a victory for socialism taking place in
one country alone, especially if that country be at a stage of
backward industrial development. Now Lenin, already during
the days of the great war, basing his contention upon the law
of irregular development of imperialist States, contraposed
this theory of the opportunists by his own theory of the
proletarian revolution, which is: That socialism can be victorious in one country alone even when that country is in a
condition of backward capitalist development.

We all know that the October revolution entirely confirmed
Lenin's theory.

How does Comrade Trotsky's theory of "permanent revolution" stand in relation to Lenin's theory of the proletarian
revolution?

Let us consider Trotsky's work entitled "OUR REVOLU-
TION," published in 1906. Here we read:—

"In the absence of direct State support on the part of
the European proletariat the Russian working class will
not be able to keep itself in power and to transform its

temporary rule into a stable socialist dictatorship. No doubt as to the truth of this is possible."

What do these words signify? That the victory of socialism in one country alone (in Russia, for the nonce) is impossible without the "direct State support . . . of the European proletariat." Which is to say that so long as the European proletariat has not won to power no victory is possible.

Is there anything in common between this "theory" and Lenin's thesis of the possibility of a victory for socialism taking place "at the outset in a small number of capitalist countries, nay, even in one alone"?

Obviously, nothing at all!

We admit that Trotsky's pamphlet was written at a time (1906) when it was difficult to determine the character of our revolution, and the views expressed therein do not entirely correspond to the writer's views at a later date. Let us consider, therefore, another of Trotsky's pamphlets, "THE PROGRAM OF PEACE," which was published on the eve of the October revolution, 1917, and revised in 1924, was included in his book entitled "1917." In this essay, Comrade Trotsky criticises the Leninist theory of the proletarian revolution, and contraposes the slogan of the United States of Europe. He asserts that socialism cannot secure a victory in one isolated country, that a victory can only be secured as a result of the triumph of several European States (let us say, Great Britain, Russia, and Germany), grouped together as the United States of Europe. He confidently maintains that "a victorious revolution in Russia or in Great Britain is impossible without the revolution in Germany, and vice versa." He goes on to say:—

"The only concrete and historical objection to the slogan of the United States of Europe was formulated by the 'Sozialdemokrat' (the chief newspaper of the Bolsheviks at that date, and published in Switzerland). Here we read: 'Irregularity in political and economic development is the supreme law of capitalism.' From this the 'Sozialdemokrat' concludes that socialism may be victorious in one country alone, and that, consequently, it was not necessary to make the dictatorship of the proletariat dependent in each country upon the inauguration of the United States of Europe. It is an indisputable fact that the development of capitalism is irregular. But this irregularity is, itself, irregular. Certainly the degree of capitalist development is not the same in Great Britain, in Austria, in Germany, and in France. Nevertheless, in comparison with Africa or Asia, these countries represent capitalist 'Europe,' ripe for the social revolution. No country can afford to 'wait' for the others to join in the struggle; this is an elementary truth which it is well to reiterate, so that the idea of simultaneous international action be not replaced by the idea of international postponement and inaction. Without awaiting the others, we have to begin and continue the struggle on a national scale, urged on by the conviction that our initative will set the ball rolling in other lands. Should this not happen it would be futile to expect (and historical experience no less than theoretical considerations are there to prove the contention), for instance, that revolutionary Russia could hold its own in face of a conservative Europe, or that a socialist Germany could be maintained in isolation in the midst of a capitalist world." (Trotsky, Collected Works, Russian edition, vol. iii, part I, pp. 89–90.)

As will be seen, we have here, once more, the theory that the triumph of socialism must take place simultaneously in the leading countries of Europe. This theory conflicts with the Leninist theory of revolution and the victory of socialism in one country.

It goes without saying that in order to achieve the complete victory of socialism, in order to provide a full guarantee that the old order shall not be re-established, the combined efforts of the proletarians of many lands are needed. There can be no doubt that, if our revolution had not been supported by the European proletariat as a whole, the Russian proletariat could not have withstood the concerted attacks of its enemies. In like manner, without the co-operation of the Russian proletariat, the revolutionary movement in Western Europe would not have been able to develop as rapidly as it has since the advent of the dictatorship of the proletariat in Russia

What, in view of all this, is the significance of Comrade Trotsky's contention that revolutionary Russia cannot hold its own against conservative Europe?

First of all, Trotsky does not understand the inner strength of our revolution; secondly, he does not grasp the incalculable importance of the moral support to the Russian revolution contributed by the workers of the West and by the peasants of the East; in the third place, he is not aware of the cancer which is gnawing at the vitals of imperialism.

Carried away by his criticism of Lenin's theory of the proletarian revolution, Comrade Trotsky unconsciously deals himself a knock-out blow in his pamphlet "THE PROGRAM OF PEACE," which was first published in 1917 and subsequently reissued in 1924.

Maybe, however, that this pamphlet likewise no longer represents Trotsky's views? Let us, therefore, consider some of his more recent writings, those written after the victory of socialism in one country alone, i.e., in Russia. We will take the POSTFACE (1922) to the new edition of his "PROGRAM OF PEACE." This is what he writes:—

"In my 'PROGRAM OF PEACE' I repeat at frequent intervals my conviction that the proletarian revolution cannot be brought to a victorious conclusion in one country alone. This affirmation may seem to conflict with five years' experience in Soviet Russia. Such a conclusion would, however, be erroneous. The fact that a workers' State, in spite of its isolation and the backwardness of its development, has withstood the attacks of a world in arms, demonstrates the amazing strength of the proletariat, and goes to prove that the proletariat in other, more advanced countries, when it rises, will accomplish veritable marvels. But though we have as a State, been able to withstand political and military attacks, we have not yet succeeded in building up a socialist society, indeed we have not even begun doing so yet. . . . So long as the bourgeoisie rules in the other European States, we are obliged (in order to fight against economic isolation) to enter into agreements with the capitalist world; at the same time we can truthfully say that such agreements may, in the long run, help in the healing of this or that wound in the body economic, and may help us to go forward a pace or so; but a steady rise of socialist economy in Russia will not be possible until after the victory of the proletariat in the leading countries of Europe." (Trotsky, Collected Works, Russian edition, vol. iii, pp. 92–93.)

Thus does Trotsky, in his obstinate endeavour to save the theory of "permanent revolution" from irrevocable ruin, come into conflict with realities.

No matter what we may do, we have "not yet succeeded" in building up a socialist society; nay, more, "we have not even begun" doing so. Some of us, it appears, were nourished upon the hope of "agreements with the capitalist world," though these agreements, too, were incompetent to yield satisfactory results, seeing that "a steady rise of socialist economy" will remain impossible so long as the proletariat has not been victorious in "the leading countries of Europe."

Since there is as yet no victory of the proletariat in Western Europe, the Russian revolution has the alternative choice of rotting as it stands or degenerating into a bourgeois State. . . .

Lenin's theory of the proletarian revolution is the exact opposite of Trotsky's theory of "permanent revolution."

Lack of faith in the strength and capacity of our revolution, lack of faith in the strength and capacity of the Russian proletariat—these are the foundations of the theory of "permanent revolution."

Hitherto it has been usual to draw attention to only one aspect of the theory of "permanent revolution," namely, the lack of faith in the revolutionary possibilities of the peasant movement. Now we must supplement this by drawing atten-

tion to another aspect, namely, the lack of faith in the strength
and the capacity of the Russian proletariat.

In what way does Trotsky's theory differ from the prevalent theory of the mensheviks: a theory which holds that the
victory of socialism in one country (and especially in a backward country) is not possible unless victory of the revolutionary forces has already been achieved in the leading
countries of Western Europe?

In essence the two theories are identical.

There can be no doubt that Comrade Trotsky's theory of
"permanent revolution" is a variety of menshevism. . . .

Chapter X

CONTEMPORARY SOCIALISM:
TWO VIEWS

Since World War II Western socialism has become "revisionist" in all but two countries. Democratic socialists have drawn closer to the right than ever before; at the same time, their opponents—the traditional conservative and liberal parties —have moved to the left. In most Western countries a broad consensus exists among all the major parties. The exceptions, of course, are the communist parties of France and Italy, both resting on working class support, but the pull toward the center has begun to affect them too. The once haughty power of the French Communist Party has shrunk measurably. The Italian Communist Party, in retaining its strength, has at the same time grown more liberal and parliamentary.

Democratic socialism is confined to the West (and Israel). But today socialism is a world-wide ideology. Bolshevism burst out of Russia after World War II. Every country which came under Soviet rule in Eastern and Southern Europe felt its implacable fury. With the fall of China to the communists in 1949 an immense "Marxist-Leninist" empire, encompassing most of Asia, came into being. But in the course of time different forms of Bolshevism evolved within this empire and, in the case of Yugoslavia, even outside it. One may expect this evolution to continue and the rivalry between China and Russia to intensify, with what consequences no one can foresee.

Different species of socialism have also sprung up in the new countries of Asia and Africa. Generally, these new and indigenous socialisms fall within two broad categories: those tending toward a Western-type parliamentary democracy; and those tending toward communist or nationalist authoritarianism. Within these two extremes there are as many variations as there are countries, and one may be sure that neither Western democratic socialists nor Russian communists are satisfied with what they see.

We have chosen to restrict this chapter to two contemporary Western authors, the first an Italian Marxist, the second a British democratic socialist. The newer currents in world socialism deserve a book of their own.

ANTONIO GRAMSCI (1891–1937)

The father of Italian communism, Antonio Gramsci, is one of the very few creative Marxists of our time, the first Italian since Antonio Labriola to make a significant contribution to Marxist literature. The energies of Marxism have otherwise come almost entirely from Central and Eastern Europe. Gramsci's Marxism bears the imprint of Italy's cultural tradition. Through him Dante, Machiavelli, Vico, De Sanctis, and Croce merge with Marx into a "philosophy of action." Only in recent years has Gramsci come to the attention of a public outside Italy. During the Stalinist era communists anathematized his writings on the grounds that they contained heretical implications. His best known book, for example, *Materialismo Storia e la filosofia di Benedetto Croce*, attempts to reconcile Marxism and Crocean idealism. Now, little by little, he is being published by the Italian Communists and translated into other languages.

Gramsci was born in Sardinia of a poor family. He won a scholarship to Turin University where he distinguished himself in linguistics and philology. By 1917 he had become a Marxian socialist, then quickly rose to importance within the Italian Socialist Party and, in 1921, led the communist wing out of it. Gramsci proposed the establishment of workers' soviets in Italy to serve as the basis of revolution, but the idea was nipped in the bud by Mussolini. In 1926, while serving as Communist deputy in the impotent Italian parliament, he was arrested and sentenced to prison for twenty years. There his frail health deteriorated, though he continued to write, and he died in 1937.

MARXISM AND MODERN CULTURE (1926–37)

Marxism has been a potent force in modern culture and, to a certain extent, has determined and fertilised a number of currents of thought within it. The study of this most significant fact has been either neglected or ignored outright by the so-called orthodox (Marxists), and for the following reasons: the most significant philosophical combination that occurred was that in which Marxism was blended with various idealist tendencies, and was regarded by the orthodox, who were necessarily bound to the cultural currents of the last century (positivism, scientism), as an absurdity if not sheer charlatanism. (In his essay on fundamental problems, Plekhanov hints at this but it is only touched upon and no attempt is made at a critical explanation.) Therefore, it seems necessary to evaluate the posing of the problem just as Antonio Labriola attempted to do.

This is what happened: Marxism in fact suffered a double revision, was submitted to a double philosophical combination. On the one hand, some of its elements were absorbed and incorporated, explicitly and implicitly, into various idealist currents (it is enough to cite as examples Croce, Gentile, Sorel, Bergson and the pragmatists); on the other hand, the so-called orthodox, preoccupied with finding a philosophy which, from their very narrow point of view, was more comprehensive than a "simple" interpretation of history, believed they were being orthodox in identifying Marxism with traditional materialism. Still another current turned back to Kant (for example, the Viennese Professor Adler, and the two Italian professors, Alfredo Poggi and Adelchi Baratono). In general one can say that the attempts to combine Marxism with idealist trends stemmed mainly from the "pure" intellectuals, while the orthodox trends were created by intellectual personalities more obviously devoted to practical activity who were, therefore, bound (by more or less close ties) to the masses (something which did not prevent the majority from turning somersaults of some historico-political significance).

The distinction is very important. The "pure" intellectuals, as elaborators of the most developed ruling-class ideology, were forced to take over at least some Marxist elements to revitalise their own ideas and to check the tendency towards excessively speculative philosophising with the historical realism of the new theory, in order to provide new weapons for the social group to which they were allied.

The orthodox, on the other hand, found themselves battling against religious transcendentalism, the philosophy most widely spread among the masses, and believed they could defeat it with the crudest, most banal materialism, itself a not unimportant layer of common sense, kept alive more than was or is thought by that same religion which finds, among the people, its trivial, base, superstitious, sorcery-ridden expression, in which materialism plays no small part.

Why did Marxism suffer the fate of having its principal elements absorbed by both idealism and philosophical materialism? Investigation into this question is sure to be complex and delicate, requiring much subtlety of analysis and intellectual caution. It is very easy to be taken in by outward appearances and to miss the hidden similarities and the necessary but disguised links. The identification of the concepts which Marxism "ceded" to traditional philosophies, and for which they temporarily provided a new lease of life, must be made with careful criticism and means nothing more nor less than rewriting the history of modern thought from the time when Marxism was founded.

Obviously, it is not difficult to trace the clearly defined absorption of ideas, although this, too, must be submitted to a critical analysis. A classic example is Croce's reduction of Marxism to empirical rules for the study of history, a concept which has penetrated even among Catholics . . . and has contributed to the creation of the Italian school of economic-juridical historiography whose influence has spread beyond the confines of Italy. But most needed is the difficult and painstaking search into the "implicit," unconfessed, elements that have been absorbed and which occurred precisely because Marxism existed as a force in modern thought, as a widely diffused atmosphere which modified old ways of thinking through hidden and delayed actions and reactions. In this connection the study of Sorel is especially interesting, because through Sorel and his fate many relevant hints are to be found; the same applies to Croce. But the most important investigation would appear to be of Bergsonian philosophy and of pragmatism, in order to see in full how certain of their positions would have been inconceivable without the historical link of Marxism.

Another aspect of the question is the practical teachings on political science inherited from Marxism by those same adversaries who bitterly combated it on principle in much the same way that the Jesuits, while opposing Machiavelli theoretically, were in practice his best disciples. In an "opinion" published by Mario Missiroli in *La Stampa* when he was its Rome correspondent (about 1925), the writer says something like this: that it remains to be seen whether the more intelligent industrialists are not persuaded in their own minds that *Capital* saw deeply into their affairs and whether they do not make use of the lessons so learned. This would not be surprising in the least, since if Marx made a precise analysis of reality he did no more than systematise rationally and coherently what the historical agents of this reality felt and feel, confusedly and instinctively, and of which they had the greater awareness after his critical analysis.

The other aspect of the question is even more interesting. Why did even the so-called orthodox also "combine" Marxism with other philosophies, and why with one rather than another of those prevalent? Actually the only combination which counts is that made with traditional materialism; the blend with Kantian currents had only a limited success among a few intellectual groups. In this connection, a piece by Rosa Luxemberg on *Advances and Delays in the Development of Marxism* should be looked into; she notes how the constituent parts of this philosophy were developed at different levels but always in accordance with the needs of practical activity. In other words, the founders of the new philosophy, according to her, should have anticipated not only the needs of their own times but also of the times to come, and should have created an arsenal of weapons which could not be used because they were ahead of their times, and which could only be polished up again some time in the future. The explanation is somewhat captious since, in the main, she takes the fact to be explained, restates it in an abstract way, and uses that as an explanation. Nevertheless it contains something of the truth and should be looked into more deeply. One of the historical explanations ought to be looked for in the fact that it was necessary for Marxism to ally itself to alien tendencies in order to combat capitalist hangovers, especially in the field of religion, among the masses of the people.

Marxism was confronted with two tasks: to combat modern ideologies in their most refined form in order to create its own core of independent intellectuals; and to educate the masses of the people whose level of culture was medieval. Given the nature of the new philosophy the second and basic task absorbed all its strength, both quantitatively and qualitatively. For "didactic" reasons the new philosophy developed in a cultural form only slightly higher than the popular average (which was very low), and as such was absolutely inadequate for overcoming the ideology of the educated classes, despite the fact that the new philosophy had been expressly created to supersede the highest cultural manifestation of the period, classical German philosophy, and in order to recruit into the new social class whose world view it was a group of intellectuals of its own. On the other hand modern culture, particularly the idealist, has been unable to elaborate a popular culture and has failed to provide a moral and scientific content to its own educational programmes, which still remain abstract and theoretical schemes. It is still the culture of a narrow intellectual aristocracy which is able to attract the youth only when it becomes immediately and topically political.

It remains to be seen whether this manner of cultural "deployment" is an historical necessity and whether, always taking into account the circumstances of time and place, it has always been so in the past. The classic example, previous to the modern era, is undoubtedly the Renaissance in Italy and the Reformation in the Protestant countries. In *History of the Baroque Age in Italy* (p. 11) Croce writes: "In Italy, its mother and nurse, the Renaissance movement remained aristocratic, confined to select circles; it never broke out of court circles, never penetrated to the people, never became custom and 'prejudice', that is, collective acceptance and faith." The Reformation, on the other hand, "had this virtue of popular penetration but paid for it with the delay in its inner development, by a slow and often interrupted maturing of its vital seed." And on page 8: "And Luther, like the humanists, deprecates sadness and celebrates joy, condemns idleness and commands work but, on the other hand, is led to indifference and hostility to letters and scholarship, so that Erasmus was able to say: '*Ubicumque regnat Lutheranismus, ibi litterarum est interitus*'; and it is true, though not solely as a result of its founder's aversion, that German Protestantism was almost sterile in scholarship, criticism and philosophy for a couple of centuries. Italian reformers, especially the circle of Giovanni des Valdes and its friends, fused humanism and mysticism, combining the cult of scholarship with moral austerity without effort. Nor did Calvinism, with its hard concept of grace and its strict discipline, encourage free investigation and the cult of beauty; but, through interpreting and explaining and adapting the concept of grace to that of vocation, arrived at an energetic advocacy of the thrifty life, of the production and accumulation of wealth."

Lutheranism and Calvinism inspired a broad popular national movement over successive periods during which a higher culture was diffused. Italian reformers inspired no great historical events. It is true that the Reformation in its highest stage of development necessarily assumed Renaissance ways and, like it, spread also to non-Protestant countries where there had been no popular incubation; but the period of popular development made it possible for the Protestant countries tenaciously and successfully to resist the crusades by Catholic regiments, and it was in this way that the German nation was born as one of the most vigorous of modern Europe. France, which was torn by religious wars in which Catholicism apparently emerged victorious, experienced in the '70s a great popular reform through the Enlightenment, Voltairism and the Encyclopædists, which preceded and accompanied the 1789 revolution. Because it embraced the great mass of peasants as well, because it had a clearly defined lay base and tried to substitute for religion an absolutely lay ideology founded on national and patriotic ties, it was in fact a great intellectual and moral reform movement of the French people, more complete than German Lutheranism. But even it had no immediate flowering on a high cultural level, except in political science in the form of a positive science of law.

Marxism assumes this whole cultural past—the Renaissance and the Reformation, German Philosophy, the French Revolution, Calvinism and English classical political economy, lay liberalism and the historical thinking which rests at the foundation of the whole modern conception of life. Marxism crowns the whole movement for intellectual and moral reform dialecticised in the contrast between popular and higher culture. It corresponds to the nexus of Protestant Reformation plus French Revolution. It is philosophy which is also politics, and it is politics which is also philosophy. It is still passing through its popularising stage; to develop a core of independent intellectuals is no simple task but a long process with actions and reactions, agreements and dissolutions and new formations, both numerous and complex; it is the creation of a subordinate social group, without historical initiative, which is constantly growing but in a disorganized manner, never being able to pass beyond a qualitative stage which always lies this side of the possession of State power, of real hegemony over all of society which alone permits a certain organic equilibrium in the development of the intellectual group. Marxism itself has become "prejudice" and "superstition"; as it is, it is the popular aspect of modern historical thinking, but it contains within itself the principle for overcoming this. In the history of culture, which is broader by far than that of philosophy, whenever popular culture has flowered because there was a period of revolt and the metal of a new class was being selected out of the popular mass, there has always been a flowering of "materialism," while conversely the traditional classes have clung to spiritualism. Hegel, astride the French revolution and the Restoration, dialecticised the two streams in the history of thought: materialism and spiritualism, but his synthesis was "a man standing on his head." Those who followed after Hegel destroyed this unity and a return was made to materialist systems of thought on the one hand and on the other, to the spiritual. Marxism, through its founder, relived this whole experience from Hegel to Feuerbach and French materialism in order to reconstitute the synthesis of the dialectical unity—"man on his feet." The mutilation suffered by Hegelian thought was also inflicted on Marxism; on the one hand there has been a return to philosophical materialism and on the other, modern idealist thought has tried to incorporate into itself elements from Marxism which were indispensable to it in its search for a new elixir.

"Politically," the materialist concept is close to the people, to common sense; it is closely bound up with many beliefs and prejudices, with nearly all popular superstitions (sorcery, ghosts, etc.). This can be seen in popular Catholicism and especially in Greek Orthodoxy. Popular religion is crassly materialistic, while the official religion of the intellectuals tries to prevent the formation of two distinct religions, two separate strata, in order not to cut itself off from the masses, not to become officially what it is in actuality—the ideology of narrow groups. In this respect, Marxist attitudes must not be confused with those of Catholicism. While the one maintains a dynamic contact with the masses and aims continually to raise new strata of the masses to a higher cultural life, the other maintains a purely mechanical contact, an outer unity based on liturgy and on the cult which most obviously appeals to the masses. Many heretical movements were popular manifestations for a reform of the Church and were efforts to bring it closer to the people, to elevate the people. The Church reacted violently and created the Jesuit Order, armed itself with the decisions of the Council of Trent and organized a marvellous "democratic" apparatus for selecting its intellectuals, but only as single individuals and not as representatives of popular groups.

In the history of cultural developments it is essential to note especially the organisation of culture and also the persons through whom it takes concrete form. In G. de Ruggiero's *Renaissance and Reformation* the attitude of many of the intellectuals led by Erasmus is shown: in the face of the persecutions and articles, they yielded. Therefore the carriers of the Reformation were actually not the intellectuals but the German people as a whole. It is this desertion by the intellectuals when attacked by the enemy which explains the Reformation's "sterility" in the sphere of higher culture, until there gradually emerged a new group of intellectuals from among the masses of the people who remained faithful, and whose work culminated in classical philosophy.

Something similar has happened with Marxism up to the present; the great intellectuals formed in its soil were few in number, not connected with the people, did not come from the people but were the expression of the traditional middle classes to which many reverted during the great historical "turning points." Others remained, but in order to submit the new concept to systematic revision and not to win an independent development for it. The assertion that Marxism is a new, independent original concept and a force in the development of world history is the assertion of the independence and originality of a new culture in birth which will develop with the development of social relations. What exists at each new turn is a varying combination of the old and the new, creating a momentary equilibrium of cultural relationships corresponding to the equilibrium in social relationships. Only after the creation of the State does the cultural problem pose itself in all its complexity and tend towards a concrete solution. In every case, the attitude preceding the State can only be critical-polemical; never dogmatic, it must be romantic in attitude but with a romanticism that consciously aspires towards its own classical composition.

THE MODERN PRINCE (1926–1937)

Observations on some Aspects of the Structure of Political Parties in Periods of Organic Crisis

At a certain point in their historical life social groups detach themselves from their traditional parties; i.e. the political parties, in that given organisational form, with the particular men who constitute, represent and lead them, are no longer recognised as the proper expression of their class or fraction of a class. When these crises occur, the immediate situation becomes delicate and dangerous, since the field is open to solutions of force, to the activity of obscure powers represented by "men of destiny" or "divine" men.

How are these situations of opposition between "represented and representatives" formed, situations which from the field of the parties (party organisations in the strict sense of the parliamentary-electoral field, newspaper organisation), are reflected throughout the whole State organism, strengthening the relative position of power of the bureaucracy (civil and military), of high finance, of the Church, and in general of all the organisms which are relatively independent of the fluctuations of public opinion? In every country the process is different, although the content is the same. And the content is a crisis of hegemony of the ruling class, which comes about either because the ruling class has failed in some big political undertaking for which it asked, or imposed by force, the consent of the broad masses (like war), or because vast masses (especially of peasants and petty-bourgeois intellectuals) have passed suddenly from political passivity to a certain activity and put forward aims which in their disorganic complex constitute a revolution. One speaks of a "crisis of authority" and this in fact is the crisis of hegemony, or crisis of the State in all spheres.

The crisis creates immediately dangerous situations, because the different strata of the population do not possess the same capacity for rapid reorientation or for reorganising themselves with the same rhythm. The traditional ruling

class, which has a numerous trained personnel, changes men
and programs and reabsorbs the control which was escaping
it with a greater speed than occurs in the subordinate
classes; it makes sacrifices, exposes itself to an uncertain
future by making demagogical promises, but it maintains
power, strengthens it for the moment and makes use of
it in order to crush its opponent and disperse its leading
personnel, which cannot be very numerous or well-trained.
The transference of the effectives of many parties under
the banner of a single party which better represents and
embodies the needs of the entire class, is an organic and
normal phenomenon, even if its rhythm is very rapid and
almost like a thunderbolt in comparison with calm times:
it represents the fusion of a whole social group under a single
leadership which is alone considered capable of solving an
existing, predominant problem and removing a mortal danger.
When the crisis does not find this organic solution, but the
solution of a divine leader, it means that there exists a static
equilibrium (whose factors may be unequal, but in which
the immaturity of the progressive forces is decisive); that no
group, either conservative or progressive, has the force for
victory and that even the conservative group needs a master.

This order of phenomena is connected with one of the most
important questions relating to the political party; that is, to
the capacity of the party for reacting against the spirit of
habit, against the tendency to become mummified and anachronistic. Parties come into existence and are constituted organ-
isationally in order to lead the situation in historically vital
moments for their classes; but they are not always able to
adapt themselves to new tasks and new periods, they are not
always able to develop according to the development of the
complex relations of force (and hence relative position of their
classes) in the particular country or in the international field.
In analysing this party development it is necessary to distinguish: the social group; the mass of the party; the bureaucracy and High Command of the party. The bureaucracy is
the most dangerously habitual and conservative force; if it
ends up by constituting a solid body, standing by itself and
feeling independent from the masses, the party ends by be-

coming anachronistic, and in moments of acute crisis becomes emptied of all its social content, like an empty shell. One can see what happened to a number of German parties with the expansion of Hitlerism. The French parties are a rich field for this research; they are all mummified and anachronistic, historico-political documents of different phases of past French history, whose outworn terminology they repeat; their crisis might become even more catastrophic than that of the German parties. . . .

On Bureaucracy

(1) The fact that in the historical development of political and economic forms there has come to be formed a type of "career" functionary, technically trained for bureaucratic work (civil and military), has a primary significance in political science and in the history of State forms. Was it a matter of necessity or of a degeneration from self-government, as the "pure" liberals pretend? It is certain that every form of society and State has had its own problem of functionaries, its own way of presenting and solving it, its own system of selection, its own type of functionary to be educated. It is of capital importance to reconstruct the development of all these elements. The problem of the functionaries partly coincides with the problem of the intellectuals. But, if it is true that every new form of society and State has had need of a new type of functionary, it is also true that new ruling social groups have never been able to put aside, at least for a certain time, the traditional and established interests, that is, the formation of functionaries already existing and preconstituted at the time of their advent (especially in the ecclesiastical and military sphere). Unity of manual and intellectual work and a closer link between the legislative and the executive power (by which the elected functionaries concern themselves with the execution of State affairs as well as with control), can be inspiring motives for a new line in the solution of the problem of the intellectuals as well as for that of the functionaries.

(2) Connected with the question of the bureaucracy and its "best" organisation is the discussion of so-called "organic centralism" and "democratic centralism" (which, on the other

hand, has nothing to do with abstract democracy, since the
French Revolution and the Third Republic have developed
forms of organic centralism of which the absolute monarchy
and Napoleon I knew nothing). The real economic and political relationships which find their organisational form, their
articulation and function in the different manifestations of organic and democratic centralism in all fields, will have to be
researched into and examined: in State life (centralism, federation, union of federated States, federation of States or fed-
eral State, etc.); in inter-State life (alliances, various forms of
international political "constellations"); in the life of political
and cultural associations (Free Masonry, Rotary Club, Catholic Church); economic unions (cartels, trusts); in the same
country, in different countries, etc.

Polemics arose in the past (before 1914) about the German
predominance in the life of high culture and of some international political forces: was then this predominance real, or in
what did it really consist? It can be said: (a) that no organic
disciplinary link established this supremacy, which was therefore merely a phenomenon of abstract cultural influence and
very shaky prestige; (b) that this cultural influence did not in
any way concern effective activity, which vice versa was disconnected, local, without a unifying direction. One cannot
speak therefore of any centralism, neither organic nor democratic nor of any kind of mixture. The influence was felt and
sustained by small intellectual groups, without ties with the
popular masses; and precisely this absence of ties characterised the situation. Nevertheless, such a state of affairs is
worth examining because it is useful in explaining the process
which led to the formulation of the theories of organic centralism, which were a one-sided criticism by intellectuals of
disorder and dispersal of forces.

At the same time it is necessary to distinguish, in the
theories of organic centralism, between those which conceal
a precise program of the real predominance of one party over
everything (whether it is a party composed of a group, like
that of the intellectuals or made up of a "privileged" territorial group) and those which are a purely one-sided standpoint of sectarians and fanatics, and which, though they

may conceal a program of predominance (usually of a single individual, like that of Papal infallibility by which Catholicism was transformed into a kind of cult of the Pope), do not immediately appear to conceal such a program as a conscious political fact. The more correct name would be that of bureaucratic centralism. "Organicness" (*organicità*) can only come from democratic centralism which is "centralism" in movement, so to speak, that is, a continuous adjustment of the organisation to the real movement, a tempering of the thrusts from below with the command from above, a continuous intrusion of elements which emerge from the depths of the masses into the solid frame of the apparatus of rule, which assures continuity and the regular accumulations of experiences; it is "organic" because it takes account of the movement, which is the organic means for the revealing of historical reality and does not become mechanically stiffened in the bureaucracy, and, at the same time, it takes account of what is relatively stable and permanent or what at least moves in an easily foreseeable direction, etc. This element of stability in the State is embodied in the organic development of the central nucleus of the ruling group, just as happens on a more restricted scale in the life of parties. The prevalence of bureaucratic centralism in the State indicates that the ruling group is saturated, becoming a narrow clique which strives to perpetuate its selfish privileges by regulating or even suffocating the birth of opposing forces, even if these forces are homogeneous to the fundamental ruling interests (for example, in the protectionist systems in their struggle to the bitter end with economic liberalism). In parties which represent socially subordinate groups the element of stability is necessary in order to ensure hegemony not for privileged groups but for the progressive elements, organically progressive in comparison with other related and allied, but composite and wavering, forces.

In any case, it needs to be pointed out that unhealthy manifestations of bureaucratic centralism occurred because of a lack of initiative and responsibility below, that is, because of the primitive politics of the peripheral forces, even when these were homogeneous with the hegemonic territorial group (the phenomenon of Piedmontesism in the first decades of Italian unity). The formation of such situations can be extremely damaging and dangerous in international organisations (the League of Nations).

Democratic centralism provides an elastic formula, which lends itself to many embodiments; it lives to the extent to which it is continuously interpreted and adapted to necessity: it consists in the critical research into what is uniform in the apparent irregularity and on the other hand of what is distinctive and even contrasting in the apparent uniformity, in order to organise and connect closely together what is alike, but in such a way that the organising and connecting appears as an "inductive" and experimental necessity and not as the result of a rationalistic, deductive and abstractive process, that is, one which is peculiar to pure intellectuals (or pure asses). This continuous effort to separate the "international" and "unitary" element from the national and local reality is in fact concrete political action, the only activity which produces historical progress. It requires an organic unity between theory and practice, between intellectual groups and popular masses, between rulers and governed. From this point of view the formulæ of unity and federation lose a great part of their significance, while they preserve their poison in the bureaucratic conception, as a result of which we end up with no unity, but a stagnant marsh, superficially calm and "dumb," and with no federation, but a "sack of potatoes," i.e. a mechanical juxtaposition of individual "unities" without any link between them. . . .

C. A. R. CROSLAND (1918-)

The British Labour Party emerged from World War II the leading social democratic party in the world. The other great socialist parties in Europe—Sweden's excepted—had been weakened or ruined by fascism and war. The Labour Party, however, received an overwhelming vote of approval in 1945. Nowhere in the past had socialists been elected to power by such a commanding majority. The future appeared to be finally theirs.

The socialist government of Prime Minister Clement Attlee ruled for six years and passed two overwhelmingly important measures: it granted independence to India, thus dissolving the empire, and it enacted a program of comprehensive socialized medical care. For the rest, it was identified with lackluster austerity and moderation. In 1951 it was turned out of office, and it remained out for a longer period of time than had any other opposition party in modern British history. Even before it lost power the party split. The left wing, which had been led at first by the late Aneurin Bevan, blamed the party's low estate on its timidity and its failure to take seriously its avowed socialist principles. The right wing, dominant in the party, criticized its doctrinal rigidity, which was alienating the new middle class in Britain, and advocated a more liberal and open-minded form of socialism. This liberal socialism is perhaps best reflected in C. A. R. Crosland's book, *The Future of Socialism*, from which this selection is an excerpt.

Mr. Crosland's book also reflects the state of European democratic socialism in general in the post-war era. Outside France and Italy there are no Marxist parties of consequence; nor, for that matter, are there any left-wing parties of consequence in Western Europe and North America (again France and Italy excepted). By the same token, traditional forms of conservatism have been disappearing. All parties, in every democracy have been continuously gravitating toward the center.

In his books and essays C. A. R. Crosland has been an eloquent defender of the moderate socialist point of view in Britain. He was born in Sussex, studied at Trinity College, Oxford, and taught economics there for some time. He served as a Labour Member of Parliament between 1950 and 1955 and returned to Parliament in 1959.

THE FUTURE OF SOCIALISM (1956)

THE MEANING OF SOCIALISM

I. The Psychological Resistance to Revisionism

It is surely time, then, to stop searching for fresh inspiration in the old orthodoxies, and thumbing over the classic texts as though they could give oracular guidance for the future. The first need now, in R. H. Tawney's words, "is to treat sanctified formulae with judicious irreverence and to start by deciding what precisely is the end in view."

The need for a restatement of doctrine is hardly surprising. The old doctrines did not spring from a vacuum, or from acts of pure cerebration performed in a monastery cell. Each was the product of a particular kind of society, and of minds reacting to that society. Since this external factor was not constant and unchanging, the doctrines changed through time. And as society has changed again since before the war, so again a restatement of objectives is called for. The matter can be put quite simply. Traditional socialism was largely concerned with the evils of traditional capitalism, and with the need for its overthrow. But to-day traditional capitalism has been reformed and modified almost out of existence, and it is with a quite different form of society that socialists must now concern themselves. Pre-war anti-capitalism will give us very little help.

The traditionalists may comfort themselves by reflecting that this will not be the first time that socialism has been restated; nothing is more traditional in the history of socialist thought than the violent rejection of past doctrines. Marx expended prodigious energy in flaying the Utopian and Owenite brands of socialism that held the field before him. The Fabians used less vitriolic pens, but were as vehement in rejecting Marx as Marx had been in rejecting Owen. Neither owed anything significant to previous doctrine. Thus even revisionism is hallowed by an appeal to the past; and the common-sense view that the more is achieved, the less relevant traditional dogmas become, need not be thought heretical.

But it will, nevertheless, be unpopular. I am not thinking simply of the fact that people dislike new ideas, and hate to be jolted out of the old, familiar habits of mind: but of a more subtle reason why revisionism has, historically, always been resented. This is because many working-class militants, and still more some middle-class people who have espoused the workers' cause, feel their whole status and psychological security to depend on preserving a traditional, proletarian philosophy of class-struggle.

For the middle-class socialist, this is because he may think that he must prove himself more royalist than the king—that he must be combatively traditional and doctrinal in order to be accepted as a good comrade, to win the approval of the workers, and feel that he really "belongs" to their party; in politics, as in religion, the most rigid attachment to dogma is often to be found amongst the converts. And for the working-class activist, devoting his entire energies to the socialist movement, both his social status and emotional certainty depend on the conviction that militant struggle is necessary; it is only on this assumption that his life makes sense. Revisionism, by casting doubts on the need for militancy, or suggesting that the class-struggle is now rather out-of-date, challenges both his social and emotional security; if class-conscious anti-capitalism is obsolete, what is his status as a militant, and what his purpose in life? Hence the anger with which criticisms of militancy or class-struggle are often greeted.

Bernstein, the great socialist "revisionist," discovered this more than 50 years ago. Arthur Rosenberg wrote that "the practical advantages of the revisionist theory for the labor movement were far greater than those of official radicalism. . . . Nevertheless the majority of the International refused to acknowledge [its] logical justification and rejected it with impassioned vehemence. For the majority of the workers the gesture of protest and isolation with respect to the bourgeois state had become a vital necessity. Popular Marxism . . . endowed [them] with self-reliance, consolation, and hope for the future, almost reminding one of a religious movement. If they had accepted the proposals of the revisionists, however, [they] would have been compelled to renounce their Utopian

belief in the future and their vitally necessary class sentiment."
This instinctive clinging to class-consciousness can still be
found in the Labour Movement to-day.

And there is now an additional psychological reason for
resenting revisionism, stemming from the very success of the
socialist movement. M. Raymond Aron has correctly observed
that "Socialism has ceased in the West to be a myth because
it has become a part of reality"—not, of course, a complete
reality, but sufficiently so to be no longer a myth. Labour
Governments have been in power, and have found responsibility harsher and quite different from anything they expected;
while full employment and social security have destroyed the
rationale of much of the old emotional enthusiasm.

Revisionism draws attention to this new reality. It is an
explicit admission that many of the old dreams are either dead
or realised; and this brutal admission is resented. It is resented, first, because it destroys the old simplicity, certainty,
and unquestioning conviction. "The will to Socialism," wrote
G. D. H. Cole before the war, "is based on a lively sense of
wrongs crying for redress." And when the wrongs were so
manifest, we all knew what to do, and where the enemy was,
and what was the order of battle; it was exhilarating to fight
for such clear-cut and obviously righteous aims. But now the
certainty and simplicity are gone; and everything has become complicated and ambiguous. Instead of glaring and
conspicuous evils, squalor and injustice and distressed areas,
we have to fuss about the balance of payments, and incentives,
and higher productivity; and the socialist finds himself pin-
ioned by a new and unforeseen reality.

And the objective has become not only less clear-cut, but
also, after the reforms described in the first two chapters, less
urgent; hence it no longer excites the same crusading spirit.
But people want something to crusade about; and even the
partial fulfilment of a dream leaves a feeling of lassitude and
anti-climax. "Oh, how I should like to begin all over again!"
cries Olof in Strindberg's play at the moment when the Reformation triumphs; "it was not victory I wanted—it was the
battle"; and many socialists, deep down, feel much the same.
A people enjoying full employment and social security has

lost its dreams, and lost the need to struggle; and the activists in consequence feel restless and frustrated. That is why they resent revisionist thinkers who compel them to face the new reality, and try to delude themselves instead that all the old enemies—capitalist barons, Wall Street, exploiting profiteers —are still there, waiting to be attacked. 90% of resolutions at Annual Conference to-day are Quixotic tilts at objects still hopefully seen as "outrageous giants of that detested race"; unfortunately, there are too few Sancho Panças to point out that they are really only windmills.

II. The Confusion between Ends and Means

If we are to reformulate socialist doctrine, the first task is clearly to decide what precise meaning is to be attached to the word "socialism."

This is not an easy question to answer. The word does not describe any present or past society, which can be empirically observed, and so furnish unimpeachable evidence for what is or is not "socialism." Thus statements about socialism can never be definitely verified; and we cannot treat it as being an *exact* descriptive word at all. There is therefore no point in searching the encyclopaedias for a definitive meaning; it has none, and never could.

This can easily be seen by considering the numerous and, as the previous chapter showed, often inconsistent meanings attached to the word by people who have called themselves "socialists." Marx, defining it as the "nationalisation of the means of production, distribution, and exchange," meant something quite different from Proudhon, who defined it as consisting of "every aspiration towards the amelioration of our society." Sir William Harcourt, declaring in 1892 that "we are all socialists now," evidently had a different version from his contemporary Bradlaugh, to whom socialism meant that "the State should own all wealth, direct all labor, and compel the equal distribution of all produce." And any history of socialist thought will provide dozens of different definitions, some in terms of ownership, some of co-operation, some of planning, some of income-distribution; and it soon becomes simply a matter of subjective personal preference which is chosen as the "correct" one. Many definitions, moreover, are so vague as to be virtually meaningless; one can read almost anything, for example, into Sidney Webb's definition: "the economic side of the democratic ideal."

The confusion has become worse inasmuch as the word is also charged with a high degree of emotional content, and so has acquired a range of purely persuasive meanings. It is either used to denote or win approval, as in Hitler's National "Socialism" and "Socialism" in Eastern Europe, or when Left-wing weeklies attack a policy which they dislike as not being "Socialist"; or pejoratively, as when Right-wing Americans speak of "creeping Socialism."

But the worst source of confusion is the tendency to use the word to describe, not a certain kind of society, or certain values which might be attributes of a society, but particular policies which are, or are thought to be, means to attaining this kind of society, or realising these attributes. To rescue the word from these confusions, and the debasement referred to above, one must begin by asking what, if anything, is common to the beliefs of all, or almost all, of those who have called themselves socialists. The only constant element, common to all the bewildering variety of different doctrines, consists of certain moral values and aspirations; and people have called themselves socialists because they shared these aspirations, which form the one connecting link between otherwise hopelessly divergent schools of thought.

Thus the word first came on the modern scene with the early nineteenth-century Owenites, whom Marx contemptuously termed "Utopian" socialists. They based their "socialism" explicitly on an ethical view of society, a belief in a certain way of life and certain moral values. The means by which they thought this "good society" could be attained are irrelevant to-day; and in fact they were quickly challenged by other socialist schools of thought, since when a continuous debate has proceeded, with no agreement, about what constituted the most suitable means. This debate would have no particular interest to-day, but for the fact that all the protagonists tried to appropriate the word "socialism" to describe the particular means which they themselves favored.

Thus Marx appropriated it for the collective ownership of the means of production on the false assumption . . . that the pattern of ownership determined the character of the whole society, and that collective ownership was a sufficient condition of fulfilling the basic aspirations. And generally the word came to be applied to policies for the economic or institutional transformation of society, instead of to the ultimate social purposes which that transformation was intended to achieve; so one often hears socialism equated not only with the nationalisation of industry, but with government planning, or redistribution, or state collectivism. This of course is quite unhelpful, for although people may agree on ends, they may legitimately disagree about means. Moreover, the means most suitable in one generation may be wholly irrelevant in the next, and in any case (still more significant) a given means may lead to more than one possible end, as indeed has happened with each of the policies just mentioned.[1]

Thus if, for example, socialism is defined as the nationalisation of the means of production, distribution and exchange, we produce conclusions which are impossible to reconcile with what the early socialists had in mind when they used the word: such as, that Soviet Russia is a completely socialist country (much more so, for instance, than Sweden)—even though it denies almost all the values which Western socialists have normally read into the word. Similarly, if socialism is defined as economic collectivism or State control of economic life, then Nazi Germany would correctly have been called a socialist country. But in neither case would the end-result be described as socialism by most socialists; the means of nation-

[1] The use of the term "ends" and "means" might seem to imply a utopian or "blueprint" view of society—a belief that society might, or could, settle down to a stable, unchanging state, analogous to the classical "stationary" state of economics. And of course most early socialists did hold this view. But as used in the text, the word "end" is to be understood simply as describing principles or values, such as equality, or justice, or democracy, or co-operativeness, which might or might not be embodied in, or determine the character of, a particular society: and the word "means" as describing the essentially institutional changes required to realise, or at least promote, these values in practice. [Crosland].

alisation and planning have proved adaptable to more than
one purpose, which shows how unwise it is to identify the
means with the end.

Not only is it unwise, but it is also semantically and historically incorrect. The various schools of thought which have
called themselves, and been called by others, "socialist"—
Owenites and Marxists, Fabians and Christian Socialists, Syndicalists and Guild Socialists—have differed profoundly over
the right means; and no one means has a better title to the
label "socialist" than any other. The one single element common to all the schools of thought has been the basic aspirations, the underlying moral values. It follows that these embody the only logically and historically permissible meaning
of the word socialism; and to this meaning we must now
revert.

III. The Basic Socialist Aspirations

These ethical and emotional ideals have been partly negative—a protest against the visible results of capitalism—and
partly positive, and related to definite views about the nature
of the good society; though of course negative and positive
strands are often inter-twined.

Perhaps one can list them roughly as follows. First, a protest
against the material poverty and physical squalor which capitalism produced. Secondly, a wider concern for "social welfare"—for the interests of those in need, or oppressed, or
unfortunate, from whatever cause. Thirdly, a belief in equality
and the "classless society," and especially a desire to give the
worker his "just" rights and a responsible status at work.
Fourthly, a rejection of competitive antagonism, and an ideal
of fraternity and co-operation. Fifthly, a protest against the
inefficiencies of capitalism as an economic system, and notably
its tendency to mass unemployment. The first three formed
the basis of socialism as "a broad, human movement on behalf
of the bottom dog." The first and last were censures on the
material results of capitalism; while the other three stemmed
from an idealistic desire for a just, co-operative and classless
society.

(I have listed only the social and economic aspirations. But of course underlying them, and taken for granted, was a passionate belief in liberty and democracy. It would never have occurred to most early socialists that socialism had any meaning except within a political framework of freedom for the individual. But since this political assumption is shared by British Conservatives as well as socialists, no further reference is made to it.)

As thus formulated, even these basic aspirations are not all equally relevant to present-day society. Some are expressed in language adapted to conditions that no longer exist, and in particular are too negative in character. This is natural, for they were, in large part, a reaction against the actual results of pre-war capitalism; and with two million unemployed, widespread poverty and malnutrition, and appalling slums set against a background of flamboyant wealth amongst the richer classes, it was natural that the negative desire to abolish evils should outweigh more positive and detailed aspirations.

But to the extent that evils are remedied and injustices removed, negative statements become less and less appropriate. And they are seen to be inappropriate by the electorate, a growing section of which has no recollection of unemployment, or poverty, or dole-queues, and finds Labour propaganda which plays on the themes and memories of the 1930s quite incomprehensible. To a population which has lost its fears, and now has every hope of a rapidly rising standard of living, a negative protest against past wrongs is merely a bore.

Thus even when we go back to the basic aspirations, we still find the same, welcome, difficulty that the pace of change has overtaken the doctrine, and a re-formulation is needed. Of course if a Tory Government were to re-create all the old evils, matters would be simple. New thinking could be set aside "for the duration," and negative statements would again suffice. But it is not likely that the Tories will act so recklessly, or that mere periodic counter-attacks to regain lost positions will remove the need for a map of the new terrain.

How should we re-formulate these aspirations to-day in such a way as to preserve their basic emotional and ethical content, yet discarding what is clearly not germane to present-day conditions? Of the original five, the first and last are rapidly losing their relevance in a British context. Such primary poverty as remains will disappear within a decade, given our present rate of economic growth; and the contemporary mixed economy is characterised by high levels both of employment and productivity and by a reasonable degree of stability. In other words, the aspirations relating to the economic consequences of capitalism are fast losing their relevance as capitalism itself becomes transformed.

But the remaining three more positive ideals, described above as stemming either from a concern with the "bottom dog," or from a vision of a just, co-operative and classless society, have clearly not been fully realised. No doubt we should phrase them differently to-day, but their basic content is still perfectly relevant. We have plenty of less fortunate citizens still requiring aid; and we certainly have not got an equal or classless society, nor one characterised by "co-operative" social relations. . . .

IV. The Co-operative Aspiration

. . . To sum up, the co-operative aspiration has at least been partially fulfilled, in that society is much less aggressively individualistic and competitive than a century ago; and indeed the trend toward "sociability" is now so strong that we are more likely to be deprived of solitude than company. On the other hand we do not yet live in a co-operative utopia. Most people still work mainly for personal gain, and not for the social good; and the ideal of communal, co-operative participation has scarcely begun to be realised in industry.

Now there are one or two specific directions in which a clear choice exists between more or less competition—most notably in education. . . . There are one or two further directions in which a less clear choice exists between more or less communal activity, e.g. housing development and town planning. Furthermore, the *sense* of co-operation in industry may spread as management grows more progressive and enlightened; and a gradual increase in equality will itself . . . still further diminish the intensity of competition. But beyond this, at our present state of knowledge, we cannot go. We cannot assert definitely what would be the effect either on personal contentment, or attitudes to work, or the quality of our society, of a wholesale effort to suppress the motive of personal gain, or to elevate collective at the expense of individual relationships: nor can we even begin to see a feasible institutional framework within which these changes could be brought about: nor can we be sure that even if they were practicable, they might not lead to serious losses in other directions, such as privacy, individuality, personal independence, equality of opportunity, or the standard of living.

While, therefore, I realise that as a matter of verbal precision the co-operative ideal is certainly embraced by the word "socialism," and while I accept that it would clearly be in some sense "better" if there were a more general awareness of a common social purpose, I do not feel able, in what is intended to be a reasonably definite and practical statement of socialist aims, to include this as part of the goal. I shall no doubt be corrected by those with clearer views.

V. *The Welfare and Equality Aspirations*

The two remaining aspirations—the concern with social welfare, and the desire for an equal and classless society—still have a perfectly clear relevance. The first implies an acceptance of collective responsibility and an extremely high priority for the relief of social distress or misfortune, in contrast to the much lower priority which it would receive in a "free" economy guided mainly by an individualistic philosophy. This is the contemporary version of the traditional welfare and social-service philosophy of the Labour movement, and of the instinct to side automatically with the less fortunate and those in need.

There is plenty of residual social distress in Britain. It is now caused less by primary poverty, though this can still be found, than by secondary poverty, natural misfortune, physical or mental illness, the decline in the size of the family, sudden fluctuations in income, and deficiencies in social capital. These last, for all the high level of average personal spending, are still appalling—ugly towns, mean streets, slum houses, overcrowded schools, inadequate hospitals, understaffed mental institutions, too few homes for the aged, indeed a general, and often squalid, lack of social amenities.

The relief of this distress and the elimination of this squalor is the main object of social expenditure; and a socialist is identified as one who wishes to give this an exceptional priority over other claims on resources. This is not a matter of the overall vertical equality of incomes; the arguments are humanitarian and compassionate, not egalitarian. It is a matter of priorities in the distribution of the national output, and a belief that the first priority should always be given to the poor, the unfortunate, the "have-nots," and generally to those in need; from which follows a certain view about collective social responsibility, and thence about the role of the state and the level of taxation. This represents the first major difference between a socialist and a conservative.

The second distinctive socialist ideal is social equality and the "classless society." The socialist seeks a distribution of rewards, status, and privileges egalitarian enough to minimise social resentment, to secure justice between individuals, and to equalise opportunities; and he seeks to weaken the existing deep-seated class stratification, with its concomitant feelings of envy and inferiority, and its barriers to uninhibited mingling between the classes. This belief in social equality, which has been the strongest ethical inspiration of virtually every socialist doctrine, still remains the most characteristic feature of socialist thought to-day.

It is significant that these aspirations are not now primarily economic in character. The worst economic abuses and inefficiencies of modern society have been corrected; and this is no longer the sphere, as it has been for the greater part of the life of modern socialism, in which reforms are most urgently required. It is true, of course, that Britain still faces a serious economic problem—the problem of external solvency. But this is a problem common to both parties; and so far as specifically socialist policy is concerned, the battle is not mainly on this front.

It is also obvious that these ideals are much less pertinent to Britain, than to Britain's relations with the outside world. It is in the backward nations that the real poverty exists; and the inequality between those nations and Great Britain is far more glaring than the inequality between rich and poor in Britain.

That is why the most obvious fulfilment of socialist ideals lies in altering not the structure of society in our own country, but the balance of wealth and privilege between advanced and backward countries. This I do not discuss, for this book . . . is about the British domestic scene; and even within Britain these ideals are not yet fully realised. But socialists must always remember that inter-national now surpass inter-class injustices and inequalities.

VI. Is Socialism Still Relevant in Britain?

The ideals have so far merely been stated. They have not been justified in detail, nor any evidence adduced to show that their further fulfilment would definitely improve our society. All that has been argued is that they constitute "socialism" in the only legitimate sense of the word, and that they are not embodied in our present society to such an extent that most people would describe it as socialist.

A few people would, it is true, so describe it—not explicitly, but by implication. That is, they take the view that we are at, or anyway in sight of, the final objective. This of course is a plausible view only if we select those more modest aspirations which have largely been fulfilled, and define these, and these alone, as socialism. Thus if we were to say, as G. D. H. Cole once did before the war, that "the Socialist has two main enemies to fight—poverty and enslavement," it would follow that we now nearly have socialism in Britain, since we have very little poverty or enslavement.

Examples of such definitions can be found. Perhaps the most striking is the Frankfurt Manifesto of the reborn Socialist International in 1951, in which (after a preamble so vague as to be almost meaningless) the whole emphasis is placed on democratic planning, which is regarded as the basic condition of socialism. The purposes of planning are defined as "full employment, higher production, a rising standard of life, social security and a fair distribution of income and property"—purposes which (at least if one omits the one word "property") are either not peculiar to socialists, or else are largely achieved already in Britain and Scandinavia.

Now it is true that the planned full-employment welfare state, which has been the outcome of the first successful spell of Labour government, is a society of exceptional merit and quality by historical standards, and by comparison with pre-war capitalism. It would have seemed a paradise to many early socialist pioneers. Poverty and insecurity are in process of disappearing. Living standards are rising rapidly; the fear of unemployment is steadily weakening; and the ordinary young worker has hopes for the future which would never have entered his father's head. There is much less social injustice; the economy works efficiently; and the electorate, as the Labour Party discovered at the last election, is in no mood for large-scale change, and certainly not for the complete overthrow of the present system. Many liberal-minded people, who were instinctively "socialist" in the 1930s as a humanitarian protest against poverty and unemployment, have now concluded that "Keynes-plus-modified-capitalism-plus-Welfare-State"   works perfectly well; and they would be content to see the Labour Party become (if the Tories do not filch the role) essentially a party for the defence of the present position, with occasional minor reforms thrown in to sweeten the temper of the local activists.

Yet this is not socialism. True, it is not pure capitalism either; and it does fulfil some part of the traditional socialist aspirations, and to this extent has socialist features. Yet it could clearly be a great deal more socialist than it is—not, as people sometimes think, because it now has only 25% public ownership and is not fully planned down to the minutest detail, any more than Soviet society *is* more socialist because it has 100% public ownership and complete state planning: but simply because the traditional socialist ideals could be more fully realised than they are. To put the matter simply, we have won many important advances; but since we could still have more social equality, a more classless society, and less avoidable social distress, we cannot be described as a socialist country. . . .

One may at this stage briefly summarise, without attempting to justify, the reasons for wanting to move forward, and to alter what is admitted to be a prosperous and generally tolerable society; and the value judgments which underlie this wish. Lord Attlee recently remarked, looking back on his early days, that "I joined the socialist movement because I did not like the kind of society we had and I wanted something better." Why should anyone say the same to-day?

There are, I believe, three answers. First, for all the rising material standards and apparent contentment, the areas of avoidable social distress and physical squalor, which were referred to above, are still on a scale which narrowly restricts the freedom of choice and movement of a large number of individuals. Secondly (and perhaps more intractable), we retain a disturbing amount, compared with some other countries, of social antagonism and class resentment, visible both in politics and industry, and making society less peaceful and contented than it might be. Thirdly, the distribution of rewards and privileges still appears highly inequitable, being poorly correlated with the distribution of merit, virtue, ability, or brains; and, in particular, opportunities for gaining the top rewards are still excessively unequal.

This significant residue of distress, resentment, and injustice affords a *prima facie* justification for further social change—as I think, and shall argue, in a socialist direction. It may not justify the same *saeva indignatio* as mass unemployment and distressed areas before the war—rather a purposeful, constructive, and discriminating determination to improve an already improved society. But the belief that further change will appreciably increase personal freedom, social contentment, and justice, constitutes the ethical basis for being a socialist. . . .

Chapter XI

NEWER CURRENTS
IN SOCIALIST THOUGHT

By the 1960s, when the first edition of this book appeared, Western Europe had practically recovered from the destructive effects of World War II. In fact, it was on the verge of becoming America's economic competitor. It too was entering the post-industrial age, marked by a noticeable shift from a predominantly blue collar to a predominantly white collar work force; a shift, that is, to a higher ratio of professionals, technicians, and managers—the college educated.

Socialism thus faced a crisis as severe as the crises posed by revisionism around the turn of the century and the great schism caused by the Bolshevik Revolution. In one sense, it was the severest crisis to date because socialism now found itself compelled to deal with questions that always had been peripheral to its concerns. However widely one socialist tendency differed from another in terms of ideology and tactics, socialism has historically concentrated on economic and class issues. As a rule, the more radical the tendency—for example, orthodox Marxism before World War I and Marxist-Leninist after—the more it identified with the proletariat and poor farmers or peasants and favored revolution and party dictatorship. But the ranks of the proletariat had considerably diminished by the post-industrial age and poor farmers and peasants were becoming a thing of the past. Correspondingly, even in the countries where they had made a mark, as in France and Italy, Marxist-Leninist parties (communist and other) lost most of their power and influence. And, while it would be an

obvious exaggeration to claim that economic and class issues had become peripheral, there can be no doubt that
they lost much of their appeal. New demands for social
reform which included the extension of personal rights
and freedoms drew more and more popular appeal. Socialists could no longer blithely assert that the realization of
socialism would ipso facto guarantee equality for women
and racial and ethnic minorities and the creation of a healthy,
pleasant environment in which to live and work and enjoy
one's increasing leisure. No longer could socialists advocate patience and await the verdict of history; they had to
immediately address these issues and make them part of
the socialist canon.

The readings which follow give an idea of how, over the
past two decades, socialists have brought forth a new body
of theory, a synthesis of old and new. It must be emphasized that they tried to be consistent with the tradition
they inherited—the tradition that assumes that the welfare
of the community takes precedent over individual cupidity; that one's life chances should, with the community's
help, be maximized to the limits of one's capabilities; and
that each individual should be treated as an end rather
than as a means to an end.

The transformation of the rest of the world produced a
crisis, or series of crises, of quite another kind. The communist world which had once seemed impregnable suddenly collapsed under the weight of the radical reforms
instituted by Soviet President Michael Gorbachev. Single-
handedly fighting the Cold War against the United States
and the resurgent West had proven too burdensome for
such a comparatively backward nation, its heroic achievements not withstanding. The Warsaw Pact disintegrated
and its members began to abandon communism in the
process. The Soviet Union itself dissolved into separate,
autonomous republics, and Gorbachev was removed from
office. But the disappearance of communism has not meant
an end to socialism. The evidence so far indicates that as
Russia, Ukraine, Belorus, the Baltic states, Poland, Ro-

mania, Hungary, Bulgaria, and what used to be Czechoslo-
vakia and Yugoslavia turn more and more to the West, their
forms of socialism will presumably reflect the West's as
well. It is too soon to expect convincing theoretical models
to emerge from the socialisms that are beginning to take
root in what once was the communist East. None at least,
I have come across that are suitable for inclusion in this
edition.

And then there was the fate of the third world countries,
the industrially underdeveloped or developing countries
which had been under Western colonial rule until well
after World War II. Anti-colonial and national liberation
movements inspired hope that the poor and benighted
people would at least achieve a measure of true freedom—
not simply political independence but economic, social,
and cultural well-being. The third world called forth a
multiplicity of socialisms of their own but the results have
hardly borne out the bright promise of freedom. The poverty of underdevelopment or what is now neo-colonialism
has overwhelmed most of the third world and constitutes,
where most extreme, a "fourth" world of unspeakable misery and suffering. The relationship of these countries to
the affluent post-industrial ones is a matter of consuming
interest to socialists who regard the north-south divide to
be more important in the long run than the east-west divide that preoccupied them, obsessively so, during the
Cold War era.

ANDRÉ GORZ (1924–   )

André Gorz came to the world's attention in 1958 with
his existential treatise/novel, *The Traitor*, for which Sartre
wrote a long, encomiastic introduction. *The Traitor* contains many of the themes that Gorz would later pursue as
editor of Sartre's magazine, *Les Temps Moderne,* and as
author of numerous books and articles. He has been in the
forefront of the effort to discover a new vocation for the

socialist or Marxist tradition. He has sought to make socialism the bearer of personal freedom, a freedom for each
individual to choose, create, or recreate a life transcending
all the bounds that define it—gender, sexual orientation,
race, ethnicity, physical condition, and the like. Socialism
for Gorz must therefore concern itself above all with the
quality of one's life. How far he modified tradition is evident from the following excerpts from two of his books:
Farewell to the Working Class translated by Michael So-
nenscher (Boston: South End Press, 1982) and *Ecology
and Politics* translated by Patsy Vigderman and Jonathan
Cloud (Boston: South End Press, 1980).

Farewell to the Working Class
(nine theses for a future left)

This book is an essay in the fullest sense of the word. It
is an attempt to outline the perspectives and the themes
around which a Left endowed with a future rather than
burdened with nostalgia might re-emerge. It makes no
pretence to have answered all the questions it raises.

1. Its central theme is the liberation of time and the
abolition of work—a theme as old as work itself. *Work* has
not always existed in the way in which it is currently
understood. It came into being at the same time as capitalists and proletarians. It means an activity carried out: for
someone else; in return for a wage; according to forms and
time schedules laid down by the person paying the wage;
and for a purpose not chosen by the worker. A market
gardener "works"; a miner growing leeks in his back garden carries out a freely chosen activity.

"Work" nowadays refers almost exclusively to activities
carried out for a wage. The terms 'work' and 'job' have
become interchangeable: work is no longer something that
one *does* but something that one *has*. One "looks for work"
and "finds work" just as one "looks for" or "finds" a job.

Work is an imposition, a heterodetermined, heteronomous activity, perceived by most of those who either "have"

it or are "looking for" it as a nondescript sale of time. One
works "at Peugeot's" or "at Boussac's" rather than to make
cars or textiles. One "has" a good or a bad job according to
how much one earns—and only secondly according to the
nature of the task and its purpose. One can have a 'good'
job in the armaments industry and a 'bad' job in the health
service.

For both wage earners and employers, work is only a
means of earning money and not an activity that is an end
in itself. Therefore work is not freedom. Of course in any
sort of work, even on an assembly-line, a minimum of
freely given commitment is essential. Without it, everything grinds to a halt. But this necessary minimum of freedom is, at the same time, negated and repressed by the
organisation of work itself. This is why the notion that it is
necessary to free ourselves *in* our work as well as *from*
work, and *from* work as well as *in* our work, is as old as the
waged working class itself. During the heroic age of the
labour movement, the abolition of work and the abolition
of wage labour were goals between which no difference
was made.

2. The difference between wage labour and self-determined activity is the same as the difference between use-
value and exchange-value. Work is carried out essentially
for a wage—which serves to sanction the social utility of
the activity in question and entitles its recipient to a quantity of social labour equivalent to that which he or she has
sold. Working for a wage amounts to working in order to
purchase as much time from society as a whole as it has
previously received.

Self-determined activity, on the other hand, is not principally concerned with the exchange of quantities of time.
It is its own end, whether it takes the form of aesthetic
activity (like games, including love) or artistic creation.
When self-determined activity is one of production, it is
concerned with the creation of objects destined not for
sale, but to be consumed or used by the producers themselves or by their friends or relatives.

The abolition of work will only be emancipatory if it also allows the development of autonomous activity.

Thus the abolition of work does not mean abolition of the need for effort, the desire for activity, the pleasure of creation, the need to cooperate with others and be of some use to the community. Instead, the abolition of work simply means the progressive, but never total, suppression of the need to purchase the right to live (which is almost synonymous with the right to a wage) by alienating our time and our lives.

The abolition of work means the freeing or liberation of time. Freeing time—so that individuals can exercise control over their bodies, their use of themselves, their choice of activity, their goals and productions—represents a demand that has been translated in a regrettably reductive way by the phrase 'the right to idleness'. The demand to 'work less' does not mean or imply the right to 'rest more', but the right to 'live more'. It means the right to do many more things for ourselves than money can buy—and even to do some of the things which money at present *can* buy.

This demand has never been more urgent than now. This is so for a number of reasons which legitimate and reinforce one another.

3. The most immediately apparent of these reasons is that the abolition of work is a process already underway and likely to accelerate. In each of the three leading industrialised nations of Western Europe, independent economic forecasts have estimated that automation will eliminate 4–5 million jobs in ten years, unless there is a sharp reduction in the number of working hours as well as in the form and purpose of productive activity. Keynes is dead. In the context of the current crisis and technological revolution it is absolutely impossible to restore full employment by quantitative economic growth. The alternative rather lies in a different way of managing the abolition of work: instead of a society based on mass unemployment, a society can be built in which time has been freed.

A society based on mass unemployment is coming into

being before our eyes. It consists of a growing mass of the permanently unemployed on one hand, an aristocracy of tenured workers on the other, and, between them, a proletariat of temporary workers carrying out the least skilled and most unpleasant types of work.

The outlines of a society based on the free use of time are only beginning to appear in the interstices of, and in opposition to, the present social order. Its watchword may be defined as: let us work less so that we all may work and do more things by ourselves in our free time. Socially useful labour, distributed over all those willing and able to work, will thus cease to be anyone's exclusive or leading activity. Instead, people's major occupation may be one or a number of self-defined activities, carried out not for money but for the interest, pleasure or benefit involved.

The manner in which the abolition of work is to be managed and socially implemented constitutes the central political issue of the coming decades.

4. The social implementation of the abolition of work requires that we put an end to the confusion that has arisen under the influence of Keynesianism between the "right to work" and: the right to a paid job; the right to an income; the right to create use-values; the right of access to tools that offer the possibility of creating use-values.

The need to dissociate the right to an income from the 'right to a job' had already been stressed at the beginning of the second industrial revolution (that associated with taylorism). It was apparent then, as it is today, that the reduction in the number of working hours required to produce necessities called for new mechanisms of distribution independent of the laws of the market and the 'law of value'. If goods produced with a minimal expenditure of labour were to be purchased, it was necessary to supply the population with means of payment bearing no relation to the price of the hours of work they had put in. Ideas like those of Jacques Duboin in particular, concerning a social income guaranteed for life and a currency that cannot be accumulated, continue to circulate, mainly in Northern Europe.

Socialised distribution of production, according to need rather than effective demand, was for a long time one of the central demands of the Left. This is now becoming ever less the case. In itself, it can only lead to the state taking greater charge of individual lives. The right to a 'social income' (or 'social wage') for life in part abolishes 'forced wage labour' only in favour of a wage system without work. It replaces or complements, as the case may be, exploitation with welfare, while perpetuating the dependence, impotence and subordination of individuals to centralised authority. This subordination will be overcome only if the autonomous production of use-values becomes a real possibility for everyone.

Thus the division between "Left" and "Right" will, in the future, tend to occur less over the issue of the "social wage" than over the right to autonomous production. The right to autonomous production is, fundamentally, the right of each grass-roots community to produce at least part of the goods and services it consumes without having to sell its labour to the owners of means of production or to buy goods and services from third parties.

The right to autonomous production presupposes the right of access to tools and their conviviality. It is incompatible with private or public industrial, commercial or professional monopolies. It implies a contraction of commodity production and sale of labour power, and a concomitant extension of autonomous production based on voluntary cooperation, the exchange of services or personal activity.

Autonomous production will develop in all those fields in which the use-value of time can be seen to be greater than its exchange-value. In other words, it will develop in situations in which what one can do oneself in a given period of time is worth more than what one could buy by working the equivalent period of time for a wage.

Only if it is combined with effective possibilities for autonomous production will the liberation of time point beyond the capitalist logic, wage system and market relations. Effective possibilities for autonomous production cannot exist for everyone without a policy providing adequate collective facilities for that purpose.

4a. Autonomous productive activity is not to be confused with "housework". As Ivan Illich has shown, the notion of housework only appeared with the development of a type of sexual division of labour specific to industrialism. Industrialist civilisation has confined women in domestic activities that are not directly productive, so that men may spend all their working hours in factories and mines. As a result, women's activities in the household have ceased to be autonomous and self-determined. Women's work has become the precondition and subordinate appendage of male wage labour. Only the latter is considered important and essentially productive.

The notion that waged workers need to be relieved of domestic tasks, regarded as degrading and inferior, whereas waged work is supposedly "noble". This notion is specific to capitalist ideology. The only important thing is to get paid irrespective of the purpose, meaning or nature of the job. Hence the housewife's activities are considered to be degrading and inferior, whereas the same activities performed for a wage—in a nursery, an aeroplane or a nightclub—are held to be perfectly dignified and acceptable.

As the time spent working falls, leaving more free time, so heteronomously determined work tends to become secondary and autonomous activity dominant. A revolution in patterns of behaviour and a redefinition of values tend to endow domestic or family-based activities with a new dignity and lead to the abolition of the sexual division of labour. It is already underway in protestant societies. Women's liberation is not to be found in "wages for housework", but through association and cooperation between equals who, within the family or enlarged family, share all tasks both inside and outside the home and, where necessary, take turns at various tasks.

5. The abolition of work is neither acceptable nor desirable for people who identify with their work, define themselves through it and do or hope to realise themselves in

their work. Thus the 'social subject' of the abolition of work will not be the stratum of skilled workers who take pride in their trade and in the real or potential power it confers on them. The main strategic goal of this social stratum, which has always been hegemonic within the organised labour movement, will remain the appropriation of work, of the work tools and of power over production. Automation will always be perceived by skilled workers as a direct attack on their class insofar as it undermines workers' class power over production and eliminates the possibility to identify with one's work (or even to identify one's work at all). Thus their major concern will be to resist automation, rather than to turn its weapons against their attackers. Protecting jobs and skills, rather than seeking to control and benefit from the way in which work is abolished, will remain the major concern of traditional trade unionism.

This is why it is bound to remain on the defensive.

The abolition of work is, on the other hand, a central objective for all those who, whatever they may have learned, find that 'their' work can never be a source of personal fulfilment or the centre of their lives—at least for as long as work remains synonymous with fixed hours, pre-planned tasks, limited competence, regularity and assiduity over months and years, and the general impossibility of being active in several fields at the same time. All those who are "allergic to work", as Rousselet has put it, can no longer be considered to be marginals. They are not part of a subculture existing on the fringes of society, but represent a real or potential majority of those in 'active employment' who see 'their' work as a tedious necessity in which it is impossible to be fully involved.

This non-involvement is largely the result of the divergent changes on the cultural level on the one hand, and of the type of skills required by the majority of jobs on the other. Jobs have tended to become "intellectualised"— that is, to require mental rather than manual operations— without stimulating or satisfying intellectual capacities in

any way. Hence the impossibility for workers to identify
with "their" work and to feel that they belong to the working class.

I have used the term 'a non-class of non-workers' to
designate the stratum that experiences its work as an exter-
nally imposed obligation in which 'you waste your life to
earn your living'. Its goal is the abolition of workers and
work rather than their appropriation. And this prefigures
the future world. The abolition of work can have no other
social subject than this non-class. I do not infer from this
that it is already capable of taking the process of abolishing
work under its control and of producing a society based
upon the liberation of time. All I am asserting is that such
a society cannot be produced without, or in opposition to,
this non-class, but only by it or with its support. To object
that it is hard to see how a 'non-class' could 'seize power'
is beside the point. Its obvious incapacity to seize power
does not prove either that the working class *is* capable of
doing so (if it were, it would be obvious) or that power
should be *seized*, rather than dismantled, controlled, if not
abolished altogether.

6. The definition of the 'non-class of non-workers' as the
potential social subject of the abolition of work is not the
result of an ethical or ideological choice. The choice is not
between the abolition of work and the re-establishment of
well-rounded trades in which everyone can find satisfaction. The choice is: *either* a socially controlled, emancipatory abolition of work *or* its oppressive, anti-social abolition.

It is impossible to reverse the general trend (which is at
once social, economic and technological) and re-establish
the old crafts for everybody's benefit, so that autonomous
groups of workers may control both production and its
products and find personal fulfilment in their work. Inevitably, as the process of production becomes socialised, the
personal character of work is eroded. The process of socialisation implies a division of labour and a standardisation
and formalisation of tools, procedures, tasks and knowl-

edge. Even if, in accordance with recent rends, relatively small, decentralised units of production were to replace the industrial dinosaurs of the past, and even if repetitive, mindless work were abolished or (should this be impossible) distributed among the population as a whole, socially necessary labour would still never be comparable to the activities of craftsworkers or artists. It will never be a self-defined activity in which each individual or group freely determines the modalities and objectives of work and leaves its inimitable personal touch upon it. The socialisation of production inevitably implies that microprocessors or ball-bearings, sheet metals or fuels are interchangeable wherever they are produced, so that both the work and the machinery involved also have the same interchangeable characteristics everywhere.

This interchangeability is a fundamental precondition for reducing the length of working time and distributing socially necessary labour among the population as a whole. The old proposal—as old as the working-class movement itself—to reduce the number of working hours by 20 per cent by employing a corresponding proportion of additional workers implicitly presupposes that workers and work are more or less interchangeable. If 1,000 people on a 32-hour week are to do the work of 800 people working 40 hours, then the type of work must not call for irreplaceable personal skills.

Thus the depersonalisation, standardisation and division of labour constitute the prerequisites to both a reduction of working hours and its desirability. Each individual's work *can* be reduced because others are also capable of doing it, and it *should* be reduced so that each individual may do other, more personally satisfying and fulfilling things.

In other words, the heteronomous nature of work, which is the consequence of its socialisation and increased productivity, is also what makes the liberation of time and the expansion of autonomous acitivty both possible and desirable. It is a dangerous illusion to believe that 'workers' control' can make everyone's work gratifying, intellectually stimulating and personally fulfilling.

7. In any complex society, the nature, modalities and objectives of work are, to a large extent, determined by necessities over which individuals or groups have relatively little control. It is certainly possible to 'self-manage' workshops or to self-determine working conditions or to co-determine the design of machines and the definition of tasks. Yet as a whole these remain no less determined in a heteronomous way by the social process of production or, in other words, by society insofar as it is itself a giant machine. Workers' control (erroneously equated with workers' self-management) amounts in reality to self-determining the modalities of what has already been heteronomously determined: the workers will share and define tasks within the framework of an already existing social division of labour. They are not, however, able to define the division of labour itself nor, for example, the specifications of ball-bearings. They may eliminate the degrading characteristics of work, but they cannot endow it with the characteristics of personal creativity. What is at issue, then, is a form of alienation inherent not only in capitalist relations of production, but in the socialisation of the process of production itself: in the workings of a complex, machine-like society. The effects of this alienation can be attenuated, but never entirely eliminated.

The consequences of this situation are not entirely negative—provided that its ineradicable reality is accepted. Above all, it must be recognised that there can never be a complete identity between individuals and their socialised work and, inversely, that socialised work cannot always be a form of personal activity in which individuals find complete fulfilment. 'Socialist morality'—with its injunction that each individual be completely committed to his or her work and equate it with personal fulfilment—is oppressive and totalitarian at root. It is a morality of accumulation, which mirrors the morality of the bourgeoisie in the heroic age of capitalism. It equates morality with love of work, while at the same time depersonalising work through the processes of industrialisation and socialisation. In other words, it calls for love of depersonalisation—or self-sacrifice. It rejects the very idea of 'the free development of each individual as the goal and precondition of the free development of all' (Marx). It sets itself against the ethic of the liberation of time which originally dominated the working-class movement.

If individuals are to be reconciled with their work, it must be recognised that, even under workers' control, work is not and should not be the centre of one's life. It should be only one point of reference. The liberation of individuals and society, together with the regression of wage labour and commodity-based relationships, requires the domination of autonomous over heteronomous activity.

8. In describing the 'non-class of non-workers' as the (potential) social subject of the abolition of work, I am not claiming to put in place the working class, as defined by Marx, another class invested with the same type of historical and social 'mission'. The working class defined by Marx or marxists derives its theological character from being perceived as a subject transcending its members. It makes history and builds society through the agency of its unwitting members, whatever their intentions. The working class thus defined is a transcendent subject by which the workers are thought in their true being; but it remains unthinkable for the workers themselves, just as our body is unthinkable for the millions of its component cells or God is unthinkable for God's creatures. This is why the working class had and still has its priests, prophets, martyrs, churches, popes and wars of religion.

The non-class of those who are recalcitrant to the sacralisation of work, on the contrary, is not a 'social subject'. It has no transcendent unity or mission, and hence no overall conception of history and society. It has, so to speak, no god or religion, no reality other than that of the people who compose it. In short, it is not a class but a non-class. For this very reason it has no prophetic aura. It is not the harbinger of a new subject-society offering integration and salvation to its individual members. Instead it reminds individuals of the need to save themselves and define a social order compatible with their goals and autonomous existence.

This is the specific characteristic of all nascent social movements. Like the peasant movement, the protestant reformation and, subsequently, the working-class movement itself, the movement formed by all those who refuse to be nothing but workers has very strong libertarian overtones. It is a negation and rejection of law and order, power and authority, in the name of the inalienable right to control one's own life.

9. Of course, this right can only be affirmed if it corresponds to a power that individuals derive from their own existence rather than their integration into society—in other words, from their own autonomy. The building up of this autonomous power is, in the present phase, the central concern of the nascent movement. Since it is a fragmented and composite movement, it is by nature refractory towards organisation, programming, the delegation of functions or its integration into an already established political force. This is at once its strength and its weakness.

It is its strength because a different kind of society, opening up new spaces of autonomy, can only emerge if individuals set out from the very beginning to invent and implement new relationships and forms of autonomy. Any change in society presupposes an extra-institutional process of cultural and ethical change. No new liberties can be granted from above, by institutionalised power, unless they have already been taken and put into practice by people themselves. In the early phase of a movement, its suspicion towards institutions and established parties is a reflection of its reluctance to pose problems in traditional ways or to accept without question that debates on the management of the state by political parties, or the management of society by the state, are the last word on anything.

It is its weakness, however, because spaces of autonomy captured from the existing social order will be marginalised, subordinated or ghettoised unless there is a full transformation and reconstruction of society, its institutions and its legal systems. It is impossible to envisage the predominance of autonomous activities over heteronomous work in a society in which the logic of commodity production, profitability and capitalist accumulation remains dominant.

The predominance of autonomous activities is thus a political matter as well as an ethical and existential choice. Its realisation presupposes not only that the movement is able to open up new spaces of autonomy through its practice, but also that society and its institutions, technologies and legal systems can be made compatible with an expanded sphere of autonomy. The process of transforming society in accordance with the aims of the movement will certainly never be an automatic effect of the expansion of the movement itself. It requires a degree of consciousness, action and will. In other words it requires politics. The fact that the post-capitalist, post-industrial, post-socialist society envisaged here* cannot—and should not—be as

---

*In the traditional marxist schema socialism is a transitional stage towards communism. During this transition, the development and socialisation of the productive forces is to be completed; wage labour to be retained and even extended. The abolition of wage labour (at least as the dominant form of work) and market relations is, according to the schema, to be realised with the advent of communism.

In advanced industrial societies, socialism is already historically obsolete. As was recognised in the theses of the *Manifesto* group in Italy in 1969, political tasks have now gone beyond the question of socialism, and should turn upon the question of communism as it was originally defined.

The use of these terms is made difficult by the perversion and devaluation of the notions of 'socialism' and 'communism' by regimes and parties that claim to represent them. The crisis of marxism, which is reflected in these difficulties, should not, however, lead to forsaking analysis of capitalism, socialism, their crises and what lies beyond. The conceptual aparatus of marxism is

integrated, ordered and planned as preceding societies
have been, does not make it possible to dispense with the
problem of defining the workings, juridical bases and institutional balance of power to be found in this society. However non-integrated, diverse, complex, pluralistic and libertarian it may be, it will still remain one among a number
of possible choices of society and will have to be realised
by conscious action.

I do not know what form this action will take, or which
political force might be able to take it. I only know that
this political force is necessary, and that its relationship
with the movement will be—and should be—as strained
and conflictual as was that between the (anarcho-syndical-
ist) trade-union movement and the political parties of the
working class. The subordination of the one to the other
has always led to the bureaucratic sterility of both, especially when political parties have confused politics with
control of the state apparatus.

I have therefore deliberately left this question open and
unresolved. In the present phase, we must dare to ask
questions we cannot answer and to raise problems whose
solution remains to be found.

ECOLOGY AS POLITICS

(TWO KINDS OF ECOLOGY)

Ecology is like universal suffrage or the 40-hour week:
at first, the ruling elite and the guardians of social order
regard it as subversive, and proclaim that it will lead to the
triumph of anarchy and irrationality. Then, when factual
evidence and popular pressure can no longer be denied,
the establishment suddenly gives way—what was unthinkable yesterday becomes taken for granted today, and fundamentally nothing changes.

Ecological thinking still has many opponents in the board

irreplaceable, and it would be as childish to reject it wholesale as
to consider *Capital,* despite its unfinished and luxuriant condition, as revealed truth.

rooms, but it already has enough converts in the ruling elite to ensure its eventual acceptance by the major institutions of modern capitalism.

It is therefore time to end the pretense that ecology is, by itself, sufficient: *the ecological movement is not an end in itself, but a stage in the larger struggle.* It can throw up obstacles to capitalist development and force a number of changes. But when, after exhausting every means of coercion and deceit, capitalism begins to work its way out of the ecological impasse, it will assimilate ecological necessities as technical constraints, and adapt the conditions of exploitation to them.

That is why we must begin by posing the question explicitly: what are we really after? A capitalism adapted to ecological constraints; or a social, economic, and cultural revolution that abolishes the constraints of capitalism and, in so doing, establishes a new relationship between the individual and society and between people and nature? Reform or revolution?

It is inadequate to answer that this question is secondary, and that the main thing is not to botch up the planet to the point where it becomes uninhabitable. For survival is not an end in itself either: is it really worth surviving in a world "transformed into a planetary hospital, planetary school, planetary prison, where it becomes the principal task of spiritual engineers to fabricate people adapted to these conditions"? (Illich)

To be convinced that this is the world which the technocrats are preparing for us, one has only to consider the new "brainwashing" techniques being developed in the U.S. and Germany. Researchers attached to the psychiatric clinic of the University of Hamburg, following the work of American psychiatrists and psychosurgeons, are exploring ways of eliminating the "aggressiveness" which prevents people from accepting the most total forms of frustration— those of the prison system in particular, but also those of the assembly line, of urban crowding, of schooling, red tape, and military discipline.

We should do well, therefore, to define at the outset

what we are struggling for, as well as against. And we should do well to try to understand how, concretely, capitalism is likely to be affected and changed by ecological constraints, instead of believing that these will, in and of themselves, bring about its disappearance.

To do this we must first grasp what an ecological constraint means in economic terms. Consider the gigantic chemical plants of the Rhine valley: BASF in Ludwigshafen, AKZO in Rotterdam, or Bayer in Leverkusen. Each of these complexes represents a combination of the following factors:

• natural resources (air, water, minerals) that until now were considered without value and were treated as free goods, because they did not need to be *reproduced* (i.e., replaced);

• means of production (machines, buildings, etc.), i.e., fixed capital, which eventually become obsolete and must consequently be replaced (reproduced), preferably by more efficient and more powerful ones so as to give the firm an advantage over its competitors;

• labor power, which must also be reproduced (the workers must be housed, fed, trained, and kept healthy).

Under capitalism these factors are combined so as to yield the greatest possible amount of profit (which, for any firm interested in its future, means also the maximum control over resources, hence the maximum increase in its investments and presence on the world market). The pursuit of this goal has a profound effect on the way the different factors are combined and the weight given to each.

Corporate management is not, for instance, principally concerned with making work more pleasant, harmonizing production with the balance of nature and the lives of people, or ensuring that its products serve only those ends which communities have chosen for themselves. It is principally concerned with producing the maximum exchange value for the least monetary cost. And to do that it must give greater weight to the smooth running of the machines, which are costly to maintain and replace, than to the physical and psychic health of the workers, who are readily replaceable at low cost. It must give greater weight to lowering the costs of production than to preserving the ecological balances, whose destruction will not burden the firm financially. It must produce what can be sold at the highest prices, regardless of whether cheaper things might be more valuable to the community. Everything bears the imprint of these requirements of capital: the nature of the products, the production technologies, the working conditions, the size and structure of the plants.

But increasingly, and most notably in the Rhine valley, the human crowding and the air and water pollution are reaching the point where industry, in order to grow or even continue operating, is required to filter its fumes and effluents. That is, industry must now reproduce the conditions and resources which were previously considered part of nature and therefore free. This need to reproduce the environment has a chain of economic consequences: it becomes necessary to invest in pollution control equipment, thus increasing the mass of fixed capital; it is then necessary to ensure the amortization (i.e., the reproduction) of the purification installations, but the products of these installations (the restored properties of air and water) cannot themselves be sold for a profit.

In short, there is a simultaneous increase in capital intensity (in the "organic composition" of capital), in the cost of reproducing this fixed capital, and hence in the costs of production, without any corresponding increase in sales. One of two things must therefore occur: either the rate of profit declines or the price of the products increases.

The firm will, of course, seek to raise its prices. But it cannot get off so lightly: all of the other polluting firms (cement plants, steelworks, paper factories, refineries, etc.) will also seek to force the final consumer to pay higher prices for their goods. The incorporation of ecological constraints will in the end have the following results: prices will tend to rise faster than real wages, purchasing power

will be reduced, and it will be as if the cost of pollution
control had been deducted from the income available to
individuals for the purchase of consumer goods. The production of these goods will consequently tend to stagnate
or fall off; tendencies towards recession or depression will
be accentuated. And this diminution of growth and of production which, in another system, might be considered a
positive thing (fewer cars, less noise, more air to breathe,
shorter working days, and so on) will instead have entirely
negative effects: the polluting goods will become luxury
items, inaccessible to the majority but still available to the
privileged; inequality will intensify, the poor will become
relatively poorer and the rich richer.

Incorporating ecological costs, in short, will have the
same social and economic consequences as the oil crisis.
And capitalism, far from succumbing to this crisis, will
respond to it in the usual fashion: those groups financially
advantaged by the crisis will profit from the difficulties of
rival groups, will absorb them at a low cost and will extend
their control over the economy. The state will reinforce its
power over society: its technocrats will calculate "optimal"
norms of pollution control and of production, issue regulations, and extend the domain of "programmed" activity
and thus the scope of the repressive apparatus. Popular
resentment will be diverted with compensatory myths and
directed towards readily available scapegoats (racial or
ethnic minorities, migrant workers, young people, other
countries). The state will base its authority not upon consent but upon coercion; bureaucracies, police forces, armies, and private security forces will fill the vacuum left
by the disrepute of party politics and the fossilization of
political parties. Already, in France and elsewhere, we see
the signs of this decay all around us.

Doubtless, none of this is inevitable. But it is highly
probable, if capitalism is compelled to integrate ecological
costs *without being challenged* at all levels by alternative
social practices and an alternative vision of human civilization. The advocates of growth are right on one point:

within the framework of the existing society and consumption patterns—based on disparity, privilege, and the quest for profit—zero or negative growth can only mean stagnation, unemployment, and a widening gap between rich and poor. Within the framework of the existing mode of production, it is impossible to limit or suppress growth while simultaneously distributing goods more equitably.

Indeed, it is the nature of the goods themselves which most often prevents their equitable distribution—how can one equitably distribute supersonic air travel, Mercedes Benzes, pentihouse apartments with private swimming pools, or the thousands of new products, scarce by definition, which industry floods the market with each year in order to devalue older models and reproduce inequality and social hierarchy? And how can one "distribute equitably" university degrees, supervisory jobs, managerial roles, or tenured positions?

It is hard to avoid the recognition that the mainspring of growth is this generalized forward flight, stimulated by a deliberately sustained system of inequalities, which Ivan Illich calls "the modernization of poverty." As soon as a majority can aspire to what until then had been the exclusive privilege of the elite, this privilege (the high-school diploma, for example, or the automobile) is thereby devalued, the poverty line is raised by one notch, and new privileges are created from which the majority are excluded. Endlessly re-creating scarcity in order to recreate inequality and hierarchy, capitalist society gives rise to more unfulfilled needs than it satisfies: "the growth-rate of frustration largely exceeds that of production." (Illich)

As long as we remain within the framework of a cilization based on inequality, growth will necessarily appear to the mass of the people as the promise—albeit entirely illusory—that they will one day cease being "under privileged," and the limitation of growth as the threat of permanent mediocrity. It is not so much growth that must be attacked as the illusions which it sustains, the dynamic of ever-growing and ever-frustrated needs on which it is based, and the competition which it institutionalizes by inciting each individual to seek to rise "above" all others. The motto of our society could be: *That which is good for everyone is without value; to be respectable you must have something "better" than the next person.*

Now it is the very opposite which must be affirmed in order to break with the ideology of growth: *The only things worthy of each are those which are good for all; the only things worthy of being produced are those which neither privilege nor diminish anyone; it is possible to be happier with less affluence, for in a society without privilege no one will be poor.*

Imagine a society based on these criteria: the production of practically indestructible materials, of apparel lasting for years, of simple machines which are easy to repair and capable of functioning for a century or more. These are scientifically and technically accessible to us, along with a vast extension of community services and facilities (public transportation, laundromats, etc.), thus eliminating much of the need for fragile, expensive, and energy-wasting private machines.

Imagine collective dwellings—not, as they now are, blighted by the neglect of public space and the privatization of value, but as they might be if individual energies were to be released for the public good and vice versa. There could be two or three recreation rooms, playrooms for children, fully-equipped workshops and libraries, and accessible laundry areas. Would we still really require all of our individual equipment which lies idle much of the time? Would we still be eager to join the traffic jams on the freeways if there were comfortable, collective transport to recreation areas, bicycles and motorbikes readily available when required, an extensive network of mass transit for urban and suburban areas?

Imagine beyond this that the major industries, centrally planned, produced only that which was required to meet the basic needs of the population: four or five styles of durable shoes and clothing, three or four models of sturdy and adaptable vehicles, plus everything needed to provide the collective services and facilities. Impossible in a market economy? No doubt. Entailing massive unemployment? Not necessarily. We could have a 20-hour work week, providing we change the system. Uniformity, monotony, boredom? On the contrary, for imagine the following:

Each neighborhood, each town, would have public workshops equipped with a complete range of tools, machines, and raw materials, where the citizens *produce for themselves, outside the market economy*, the non-essentials according to their tastes and desires. As they would not work more than twenty hours a week (and possibly less) to produce the necessities of life, the adults would have time to learn what the children would be learning in primary school: not only reading and writing but also handicrafts of all kinds, sewing, leather-working, cabinet-making, masonry, metal-working, mechanics, pottery, agriculture—in short, all of the skills which are now commercially torn from us and replaced with buying and selling.

Are such proposals utopian? Why couldn't they become a political program? For such a "utopia" corresponds to the most advanced, not the most primitive, form of socialism—to a society without bureaucracy, where the market withers away, where there is enough for everyone, where people are collectively and individually free to shape their lives, where people produce according to their fantasies, not only according to their needs; in short, a society where "the free development of each is the condition for the free development of all." (Marx, *The Communist Manifesto*, 1848)

ZILLAH EISENSTEIN (1945–   )

Feminism prescribes no hard and fast ideological limits. A corporate executive who regards herself as conservative can justify her espousal of feminism as readily as a union organizer or apolitical lesbian. Thus, it is hardly surprising that socialism has come to acknowledge feminism as its

own and visa versa. Historically, from the time of the utopians onward, most socialists affirmed the equality of women
and some, Engels and August Bebel for example, wrote
extensively on the "woman question." Socialism also attracted sizeable numbers of suffragettes and communism
even raised the banner of women's rights. The Soviet Union
was the first country to grant divorce and abortion on demand. However, Stalin recinded these rights in the 1930s.
Simone deBouvoir, whose *Second Sex* was the pioneer
study of men's oppression of women, was an avowed socialist. However, it was not until the 1960s, when feminism arose as a movement in the United States, did its
relationship with socialism become truly joined. It was at
this time that women asserted themselves as an organized
force for change, a force which continues to gain momentum as they increasingly lay claim to rights hitherto denied
them.

So, it is only fitting that we should choose an American
scholar, Zillah Eisenstein, to set forth the theoretical basis
for unifying feminism and socialism. She teaches at Ithaca
College, has widely lectured, and has written extensively
on feminism in general. Among her books are *Feminism
and Sexual Equality: Crisis in Liberalism* (New York:
Monthly Review Press, 1984) and *Radical Future of Liberal Feminism* (New York: Longman, 1981). The following
is excerpted from her essay "Developing a Theory of Capitalist Patriarchy and Socialist Feminism," which introduced an anthology that she edited entitled *Capitalist Patriarchy and the Case for Socialist Feminism* (New York:
Monthly Review Press, 1978).

DEVELOPING A THEORY OF CAPITALIST PATRIARCHY AND
SOCIALIST FEMINISM
(INTRODUCTION)

Radical feminists and male leftists, in confusing socialist
women and socialist feminists, fail to recognize the politi-

cal distinction between being a woman and being a feminist. But the difference between socialist women and socialist feminists needs to be articulated if the ties between radical feminism and socialist feminists are to be understood. Although there are socialist women who are committed to understanding and changing the system of capitalism, socialist feminists are committed to understanding the system of power deriving from capitalist patriarchy. I choose this phrase, capitalist patriarchy, to emphasize the mutually reinforcing dialectical relationship between capitalist class structure and hierarchical sexual structuring. Understanding this interdependence of capitalism and patriarchy is essential to the socialist feminist political analysis. Although patriarchy (as male supremacy) existed before capitalism, and continues in postcapitalist societies, it is their present relationship that must be understood if the structure of oppression is to be changed. In this sense socialist feminism moves beyond singular Marxist analysis and isolated radical feminist theory.

Power is dealt with in a dichotomous way by socialist women and radical feminists: it is seen as deriving from either one's economic class position or one's sex. The critique of power rooted in the male/female distinction focuses most often on patriarchy. The critique of power rooted in the bourgeoisie/proletariat distinction focuses on capitalism. One *either* sees the social relations of production *or* the social relations of reproduction,[1] domestic *or* wage labor, the private *or* public realms, the family *or* the economy, ideology *or* material conditions, the sexual division of labor *or* capitalist class relations as oppressive. Even though most women are implicated on both sides of these dichotomies, *woman* is dealt with as though she were not. Such a conceptual picture of woman hampers the understanding of the complexity of her oppression. Dichotomy wins out over reality. I will attempt here to replace this dichotomous thinking with a dialectical approach.

The synthesis of radical feminism and Marxist analysis is a necessary first step in formulating a cohesive socialist feminist political theory, one that does not merely add together these two theories of power but sees them as interrelated through the sexual division of labor. To define capitalist patriarchy as the source of the problem is at the same time to suggest that socialist feminism is the answer. My discussion uses Marxist class analysis as the thesis, radical feminist patriarchal analysis as the antithesis, and from the two evolves the synthesis of socialist feminism.

THESIS WOMAN AS CLASS

1. Marx: Revolutionary Ontology and Women's Liberation

The importance of Marxist analysis to the study of women's oppression is twofold. First, it provides a class analysis necessary for the study of power. Second, it provides a method of analysis which is historical and dialectical. Although the dialectic (as method) is most often used by Marxists to study class and class conflict, it can also be used to analyze the patriarchal relations governing women's existence and hence women's revolutionary potential. One can do this because Marxist analysis provides the tools for understanding all power relations; there is nothing about the dialectical and historical method that limits it to understanding class relations. I will use Marx's analysis of class conflict, but I will also extract his method and apply it to some dimensions of power relations to which he was not sensitive. In this sense I am using Marx's method to expand our present understanding of material relations in capitalism to material relations in capitalist patriarchy.

These relations are illuminated by Marx's theories of exploitation and alienation. Since there has already been much discussion among socialist women and socialist feminists about the importance of the theory of exploitation to understanding woman's oppression, I will mention this only briefly. I will focus on the importance of Marx's dialectical revolutionary ontology as it is presented in his theory of alienation. Although his substantive discussion of alienation applies to women workers in the labor force and in qualified ways to nonpaid domestic workers as housewives, I am particularly interested in his method of analysis. By not reducing the analysis to class and class conflict as expressed in the theory of exploitation, the dialectical method present in the theory of alienation can be extended to the particular revolutionary potential of women. Essentially this means that although the theory of alienation is inclusive of exploitation it should not be reduced to it.

The theory of alienation and its commitment to "species life" in communist society is necessary to understanding the revolutionary capacity of human bēings. "Species beings" are those beings who ultimately reach their human potential for creative labor, social consciousness, and social living through the struggle against capitalist society, and who fully internalize these capacities in communist society. This basic ontological structure defines one's existence alongside one's essence. Reality for Marx is thus more than mere existence. It embodies within it a movement toward human essence. This is not a totally abstract human essence but rather an essence we can understand in historical contexts. "Species being" is the conception of what is possible for people in an unalienated society; it exists only as essence in capitalist society.

Without this conception human beings would be viewed as exploited in capitalist relations, but they would not necessarily be understood as potentially revolutionary. Exploitation, without this concept in the theory of alienation, would leave us with an exploited person. But because of the potential of species life in the individual, the exploited worker is also the potential revolutionary. Without the potential of species life we would have Aristotle's happy slaves, not Marx's revolutionary proletariat. And this potential exists in men and women, regardless of their position in the class structure or their relationship to exploitation. The actualizing of this potential, however, is differentiated according to one's class.

With his theory of alienation, Marx is critically probing
the nature of capitalism. By capitalism, Marx and Engels
referred to the entire process of commodity production. In
examining the exploitation inherent in this process, Marx
developed his theory of power. Power or powerlessness
derives from a person's class position; hence oppression is
a result of capitalist organization and is based in a lack of
power and control. Through productive labor capitalist society exploits the worker who creates surplus value for the
bourgeoisie. The surplus labor, which is inherent in profit,
is derived from the difference between the actual and
necessary labor time of the worker.

*Productive labor, in its meaning for capitalist produc-
tion, is wage-labor which, exchanged against the valuable
part of capital (the part of the capital that is spent on
wages), reproduces not only this part of the capital (or the
value of its own labor-power), but in addition produces
surplus-value for the capitalist . . . only that wage labor
is production which produces capital.*

The class structure, which manifests itself in social, political, and cultural forms as well, is economic at its base.
Society is divided into the bourgeoisie and the proletariat.
The basis of separation and conflict between the two is the
relation each one has to the modes of production; hence
the proletariat's exploitation, in which surplus value is
extracted from their productive labor, is their oppression.

This Marxist indictment of capitalist relations is subsumed into a revolutionary ontology of social and human
existence. It posits within each individual a dialectic between essence and existence which is manifested as revolutionary consciousness in society. Both the criticims of
class existence as alienating and exploitative and the revolutionary ontology of the theory make Marxist analysis critical to developing a feminist theory which incorporates
but moves beyond a theory of class consciousness.

When extended to women, this revolutionary ontology
suggests that the possibility of freedom exists alongside

exploitation and oppression, since woman is potentially more than what she is. Women is structured by what she is today—and this defines real possibilities for tomorrow; but what she is today does not determine the outer limits of her capacities or potentialities. This is of course true for the alienated worker. While a worker is cut off from his/ her creative abilities s/he is still potentially a creative being. This contradiction between existence and essence lies; therefore, at the base of the revolutionary proletariat as well as the revolutionary woman. One's class position defines consciousness for Marx, but, if we utilize the revolutionary ontological method, it need not be limited to this. If we wish to say that a woman is defined in terms of her sex as well, patriarchal relations define her consciousness and have implications for her revolutionary potential as a result. By locating revolutionary potential as it reflects conflicts between people's real conditions (existence) and possibilities (essence), we can understand how patriarchal relations inhibit the development of human essence. In this sense, the conception of species life points to the revolutionary potential of men and women.

The social relations defining the potential for woman's revolutionary consciousness are more complex than Marx understood them to be. Marx never questioned the hierarchical sexual ordering of society. He did not see that this further set of relations made species life unavailable to women, and hence that its actualization could not come about through the dismantling of the class system alone. Nevertheless, his writings on women are important because of his commitment to uncover the tensions between species life and capitalist alienated forms of social experience for both men and women. . . .

In conclusion, the analysis sketched by Marx and Engels in *The German Ideology*, and then further developed by Engels in *The Origin of the Family, Private Property, and the State*, reveals their belief that the family, at least historically, structured the division of labor in society, and

that this division of labor reflects the division of labor in
the sex act. Initially, the family structure defined the structure of society.

> According to the matterialistic conception, the de-
> termining factor in history is, in the final instance,
> the production and reproduction of immediate life.
> This, again, is of a two-fold character: on the one
> side, the production of the means of existence, of
> food, clothing and shelter and the tools necessary
> for that production; on the other side, the produc-
> tion of human beings themselves, the propagation
> of the species. The social organization under which
> the people of a particular historical epoch and a
> particular country live is determined by both kinds
> of production; by the stage of development of la-
> bour on the one hand and of the family on the other.

This perception is lost, however, in the discussion of the
family in capitalist society, for there the family comes to
be viewed as just another part of the superstructure, totally
reflective of class society, and relations of reproduction
become subsumed under the relations of production. The
point is not that the family doesn't reflect society, but that
through both its patriarchal structure and patriarchal ideology the family and the need for reproduction also *structure* society. This reciprocal relationship, between family
and society, production and reproduction, defines the life
of women. The study of women's oppression, then, must
deal with both sexual and economic material conditions if
we are to understand oppression, rather than merely understand economic exploitation. the historical materialist
method must be extended to incorporate women's relations to the sexual division of labor and society as producer
and reproducer as well as to incorporate the ideological
formulation of this relationship. Only then will her existence be understood in its true complexity and will species
life be available to her too.

ANTITHESIS: WOMAN AS SEX

1. Patriarchy and the Radical Feminists

Although the beginnings of radical feminism are usually considered to coincide with the beginnings of the recent women's liberation movement—around 1969-1970—radical feminism in fact has important historical ties to the liberal feminism of Mary Wollstonecraft, Elizabeth Cady Stanton, and Harriet Taylor Mill, women who spoke of sexual politics long before Kate Millett. These women understood in their own fragmented way that men have power *as men* in a society organized into "sexual spheres." But while they spoke of power in caste terms, they were only beginning to understand the structure of power enforced upon them through the sexual division of labor and society. The claims of these feminists remained reformist because they did not make the necessary connections between sexual oppression, the sexual division of labor and the economic class structure.

Radical feminism today has a much more sophisticated understanding of sexual power than did these feminist forebears and has thus been able to replace the struggle for the vote and for legal reform with the revolutionary demand for the destruction of patriarchy. It is the biological family, the hierarchical sexual division of society, and sex roles themselves which must be fundamentally reorganized. The sexual division of labor and society expresses the most basic hierarchical division in our society between masculine and feminine roles. It is the basic mechanism of control for patriarchal culture. It designates the fact that roles, purposes, activity, one's labor, are determined sexually. It expresses the very notion that the biological distinction, male/female, is used to distinguish social functions and individual power.

Radical feminists have not only found the analysis of Wollstonecraft, Stanton, and Taylor incomplete, but they have, in much the same way, found the politics and theo-

ries of today's left insufficient: existing radical analyses of
society also fail to relate the structure of the economic
class system to its origins in the sexual class system. Sexual, not economic, power seemed to be central to any
larger and meaningful revolutionary analysis. These women
were not satisfied with the Marxist definition of power, or
with the equation between women's oppression and exploitation. Economic class did not seem to be at the center
of their lives. History was perceived as patriarchal, and its
struggles have been struggles between the sexes. The battle lines are drawn between men and women, rather than
between bourgeoisie and proletariat, and the determining
relations are of reproduction, not production.

For radical feminists patriarchy is defined as a sexual
system of power in which the male possesses superior
power and economic privilege. Patriarchy is the male hierarchical ordering of society. Although the legal-institu-
tional base of patriarchy was more explicit in the past, the
basic relations of power remain intact today. The patriarchal system is preserved, via marriage and the family,
through the sexual division of labor and society. Patriarchy
is rooted in biology rather than in economics or history.
Manifested through male force and control, the roots of
patriarchy are located in women's reproductive selves.
Woman's position in this power hierarchy is defined not in
terms of the economic class structure but in terms of the
patriarchal organization of society.

Through this analysis, radical feminists bridge the dichotomy between the personal and the public. Sex as the
personal becomes political as well, and women share their
position of oppression because of the very sexual politics
of the society. The structuring of society through the sexual division limits the activities, work, desires, and aspirations of women. "Sex is a status category with political
implications.". . .

The connections and relations between the sexual class
system and the economic class system remain undefined
in the writings of radical feminism. Power is dealt with in

terms of half the dichotomy. It is sexually based; capitalism does not appear within the theoretical analysis to define a woman's access to power. Similarly, interactions between patriarchy as a system of power and woman's biology are also kept separate. Instead of seeing a historical formulation of woman's oppression, we are presented with biological determinism. The final outcome of this dichotomization is to sever the relationship between these conditions and their supporting ideologies. As a result, neither Marxists nor radical feminists deal with the interrelationships between ideas and real conditions sufficiently. If reality becomes segmented, it is not surprising that ideological representations of that reality become severed from the reality as well.

Synthesis Social Feminism

1. Exploitation and Oppression

Marxist analysis seeks a historical explanation of existing power relationships in terms of economic class relations, and radical feminism deals with the biological reality of power. Socialist feminism, on the other hand, analyzes power in terms of its class origins and its patriarchal roots. In such an analysis, capitalism and patriarchy are neither autonomous systems nor identical: they are, in their present form, mutually dependent. The focus upon the autonomous racial dimensions of power and oppression, although integral to a socialist feminist analysis, falls outside this discussion. As can be seen from the discussion of oppression below, race is viewed as a key factor in defining power, but my discussion focuses only on the relations between sex and class as a first step in moving toward the more inclusive analysis of race.

For socialist feminists, oppression and exploitation are not equivalent concepts, for women or for members of minority races, as they were for Marx and Engels. Exploitation speaks to the economic reality of capitalist class relations for men and women, whereas oppression refers to women and minorities defined within patriarchal, racist, and capitalist relations. Exploitation is what happens to men and women workers in the labor force; woman's oppression occurs from her exploitation as a wage-laborer but also occurs from the relations that define her existence in the patriarchal sexual hierarchy—as mother, domestic laborer, and consumer. Racial oppression locates her within the racist division of society alongside her exploitation and sexual oppression. Oppression is inclusive of exploitation but reflects a more complex reality. Power—or the converse, oppression—derives from sex, race, and class, and this is manifested through both the material and ideological dimensions of patriarchy, racism, and capitalism. Oppression reflects the hierarchical relations of the sexual and racial division of labor and society.

My discussion will be limited to understanding the mutual dependence of capitalism and patriarchy as they are presently practiced in what I have chosen to call capitalist patriarchy dated from the mid-eighteenth century in England and the mid-nineteenth century in America. Both of these periods reflect the developing relationship between patriarchy and the new industrial capitalism. Capitalist patriarchy, by definition breaks through the dichotomies of class and sex, private and public spheres, domestic and wage labor, family and economy, personal and political, and ideology and material conditions.

As we have seen, Marx and Engels saw men's oppression as a result of his exploited position as worker in capitalist society. They assumed that woman's oppression paralleled this. They equated the two when they suggested that domestic slavery was the same, in nature and essence, as wage-slavery. Marx and Engels acknowledged that woman was exploited as a member of the proletariat if she worked in the labor force; if she was relegated to domestic slavery she was seen as a nonwage slave. Capitalism was seen to exploit women, but there was no conception of how patriarchy and capitalism together defined women's oppression. Today, especially with the insights of radical feminism, we see that not only is the equation of exploitation and oppression problematic, but that if we use Marx's own categorization of productive labor as wage labor, domestic slaves are not exploited in the same way as wage slaves. They would have to be paid a wage for this to be true.

The reduction of oppression to exploitation, within Marxist analysis, rests upon equating the economic class structure with the structure of power in society. To the socialist feminist, woman's oppression is rooted in more than her class position (her exploitation); one must address her position within patriarchy—both structurally and ideologically—as well. It is the particular relation and operation of the hierarchical sexual ordering of society within the class structure or the understanding of the class structure within the sexual ordering of society which focuses upon human activity in capitalist patriarchy. They exist together and cannot be understood when falsely isolated. In dealing with these questions, one must break down the division between material existence (economic or sexual) and ideology, because the sexual division of labor and society, which lays the basis for patriarchy as we know it, has both material form (sex roles themselves) and ideological reality (the stereotypes, myths, and ideas which define these roles). They exist in an internal web.

If women's existence is defined by capitalism and patriarchy through their ruling ideologies and institutions, then an understanding of capitalism alone (or patriarchy in isolation) will not deal with the problem of women's oppression. As Juliet Mitchell has written, "the overthrow of the capitalist economy and the political challenge that effects this do not in themselves mean a transformation of patriarchal ideology."[35] The overthrow does not necessitate the destruction of patriarchal institutions either. Although practiced differently in each place, the sexual division of labor exists in the Soviet Union, in Cuba, in China. The histories of these societies have been different, and limitations in the struggle against patriarchy have been defined in terms of the particularities of their cultures. There has been real progress in women's lives, particularly in China and Cuba. But it would be inaccurate to say that a sexual division of labor and society does not exist in these countries. Only recently in Cuba has the sexual division of labor been tackled as a particular problem for the revolution. Patriarchy is crosscultural, then, by definition, though it is actualized differently in different societies via the institutionalizing of sexual hierachy. The contours of sex roles may differ societally but power has and does reside with the male.

Both radical feminists and socialist feminists agree that patriarchy precedes capitalism, whereas Marxists believe that patriarchy arose with capitalism. Patriarchy today, the power of the male through sexual roles in capitalism, is institutionalized in the nuclear family. Mitchell ties this to the "law of the prehistoric murdered father." In finding the certain root of patriarchy in this mythic crime among men at the dawn of our life as a social group, Mitchell risks discussing patriarchy more in terms of the ideology patriarchy produces, rather than in connecting it to its material formulation in the confrontation between man and woman. She roots the Oedipus complex in the universal patriarchal culture. However, culture is defined for her in terms of an exchange system which primarily exists in ideological form today. For Mitchell, patriarchy precedes capitalism through the universal existence of the Oedipus complex. I contend, however, that patriarchy precedes capitalism through the existence of the sexual orderng of society which derives from ideological and political interpretations of biological difference. In other words, men have chosen to interpret and politically use the fact that women are the reproducers of humanity. From this fact of reproduction and men's political control of it, the relations of reproduction have arisen in a particular formulation of woman's oppression. A patriarchal culture is carried over from one historical period to another to protect the sexual hierarchy of society; today the sexual division of society is based on real differences that have accrued from years of ideological pressure. Material conditions define necessary ideologies, and ideologies in their turn have impact on reality and alter reality. There is a two-way flow: women are products of their social history, and yet women can shape their own lives as well.

For socialist feminists, historical materialism is not defined in terms of the relations of production without understanding its connection to the relations that arise from woman's sexuality—relations of reproduction. And the ideological formulations of these relations are key. An understanding of feminist materialism must direct us to understanding the particular existence of women in capitalist patriarchal society. The general approaches of both Marxists in terms of class and radical feminists in terms of sex obfuscate the reality of power relations in women's lives.

2. Pioneers in Feminist Materialism: de Beauvoir and Mitchell

Simone de Beauvoir confronts the interrelationship between sexuality and history in *The Second Sex*. While for her "the division of the sexes is a biological fact, not an event in human history," nevertheless she says "we must view the facts of biology in the light of an ontological, economic, social, and psychological context." She understood that women were defined by men and as such cast in the role of the "other," but she also realizes that the sexual monism of Freud and the economic monism of Engels are inappropriate for the full analysis of woman's oppression. De Beauvoir's initial insights were further developed by Juliet Mitchell, who offered in *Woman's Estate* a rigorous criticism of classical socialist theory, criticizing it for locating woman's oppression too narrowly in the family. She rejected the reduction of woman's problem to her inability to work, which stresses her simple subordination to the institutions of private property and class exploitation.

Instead, woman's powerlessness in capitalist society is rooted in four basic structures, those of production, reproduction, sexuality, and socialization of children. Woman's biological capacity defines her social and economic purpose. Motherhood has set up the family as a historical necessity, and the family has become the woman's world. Hence, woman is excluded from production and public life, resulting in sexual inequality.

The family under capitalism reinforces woman's oppressive condition. The family supports capitalism by providing a way for calm to be maintained amidst the disruption that is very much a part of capitalism. The family supports capitalism economically by providing a productive labor force and supplying a market for massive consumption. The family also performs an ideological role by cultivating the belief in individualism, freedom, and equality basic to the belief structure of society, although they are at odds with social and economic reality. Mitchell concludes that by focusing on the destruction of the family alone, woman's situation will not necessarily be substantially altered. For Mitchell "socialism would properly mean not the abolition of the family but the diversification of the socially acknowledged relationships which are forcibly and rigidly compressed into it."

The importance of Mitchell's analysis lies in the fact that she focuses on the powerlessness that women experience because they are reproductive beings, sexual beings, working individuals, and socializers of children—in all the dimensions of their activities. She makes it clear that woman's oppression is based in part on the support the family gives the capitalist system. Power is seen as a complex reality. We are still left, however, with the need to clarify the relationship of the family and the political economy in capitalist patriarchal society. What Mitchell has supplied us with is an understanding of the family in capitalist society.

3. The Sexual Division of Labor and Society in Capitalist Patriarchy: Toward a New Feminist Theory

. . . Presently class categories are primarily male-defined, and a woman is assigned to a class on the basis of her husband's relation to the means of production; woman is not viewed as an autonomous being. According to what criteria is a woman termed middle-class? What does it mean to say that a middle-class woman's life is "easier" than a working-class woman's life when her status is significantly different from that of a middle-class male? What of the woman who earns no money at all (as houseworker) and is called middle-class because her husband is? Does she have the same freedom, autonomy, or control over her life as her husband, who earns his own way? How does her position compare to that of a single woman with a low-paying job?

> Clearly a man who is labeled upper- or middle-class (whatever, precisely, that may mean) has more money, power, security, and freedom of choice than his female counterpart. Most women are wives and mothers, dependent wholly or in part on a man's support, and what the Man giveth, he can take away.

I do not mean by these questions to imply that class labels are meaningless, or that class privilege does not exist among women, or that housewives (houseworkers) are a class of their own. I do mean to say, however, that we will not know what our real class differences are until we deal with what our real likenesses are as women. I am suggesting that we must develop a vocabulary and conceptual tools which deal with the question of differential power among women in terms of their relation to men and the class structure, production and reproduction, domestic and wage labor, private and public realms, etc. Only then will we see what effect this has on our understanding for organizing women. We need to understand our likenesses and differences if we are to be able to work together to change this society. Although our differences divide us, our likeness cuts through to somewhat redefine these conflicts.

A feminist class analysis must begin with distinctions drawn among women in terms of the work they do within

the economy as a whole—distinctions among working
women outside the home (professional versus nonprofes-
sional), among houseworkers (houseworkers who do not
work outside the home and women who are houseworkers
and also work outside), welfare women, unemployed
women, and wealthy women who do not work at all. These
class distinctions need to be further defined in terms of
race and marital status. We then need to study how women
in each of these categories share experiences with other
categories of women in the activities of reproduction,
childrearing, sexuality, consumption, maintenance of home.
What we will discover in this exploratory feminist class
analysis is a complicated and varied pattern, whose multi-
grid conceptualization mirrors the complexity of sex and
class differentials in the reality of women's life and experience.

	Reproduction	Childrearing	Maintenance of home	Sexuality	Consumption
Unemployed women					
Welfare					
Houseworkers (housewives)					
Working women outside of home—nonprofessional					
Working women outside of home—professional					
Wealthy women who do not work (even in own home)					

This model would direct attention to class differences within the context of the basic relationship between the sexual hierarchy of society and capitalism. Hopefully, the socialist feminist analysis can continue to explore the relationships between these systems, which in essence are not separate systems. Such a feminist class analysis will deal with the different economic realities of women but will show them to be defined largely within the context of patriarchal and capitalist needs. Women as women share like economic status and yet are divided through the family structure to experience real economic class differences. Such an examination should seek to realize woman's potential for living in social community, rather than in isolated homes; her potential for creative work, rather than alienating or mindless work; her potential for critical consciousness as opposed to false consciousness; and, her potential for uninhibited sexuality arising from new conceptions of sexuality. . . .

CORNEL WEST (1950–   )

In the abstract, socialists have historically tended to side with the racially oppressed, but they defined that oppression in terms of class. Marx, for example, sympathized with the colored peoples of the world who, in his view, were victims of global capitalism. (However, in his private writings, he was not above using violent epithets against these same people.) Before World War I, Western socialists wrote very little on the race issue. Some prominent American socialists such as Jack London and Victor Berger were racists, their animus directed mostly against Chinese and Japanese Americans. For its part, the Soviet Union directly addressed the race issue in its campaign against Western imperialism. In the United States it supported the formation of a separate black republic which would be created from the states comprising the black belt. To their credit, American communists preached and practiced the equality of the races, not a very popular idea in the 1920s, 30s, and 40s. By then, several outstanding African Americans such as W. E. B. DuBoise, A. Philip Randolph, Paul Robinson, and Richard Wright counted themselves as socialists. It is obvious that, during the last years of his life, socialism figured in Martin Luther King's hope for a society free of racism. None of these men, however, attempted to demonstrate theoretically why socialism better than any other ideology assured racial equality. Cornel West has made that attempt in his ambitious book, *Prophesy Deliverance! An Afro-American Revolutionary Christianity* (Philadelphia: The Westminster Press, 1982), from which the passage below is drawn. It is appropriate that an African American scholar (he teaches philosophy and religion at Princeton University) should make the American experience universally relevant, that is wherever race and class are inseparably joined.

PROPHESY DELIVERANCE! AN AFRO-AMERICAN
REVOLUTIONARY CHRISTIANITY
THE EVOLUTION OF BLACK THEOLOGY

In this section, I shall examine briefly the evolution of the prophetic Christian tradition in the Afro-American experience—which I refer to here as black theology—and suggest that the present expression of this tradition in postmodern times is black theology as critique of capitalist civilization.

The first stage can be viewed roughly as "Black Theology of Liberation as Critique of Slavery." This stage, lasting approximately from the middle of the seventeenth-century to 1863, consisted of black prophetic Christian viewpoints and actions that were grounded in the black slave experience and were critical of the institution of slavery. Many petitions of black Christians during the first two centuries of slavery expressed this prophetic viewpoint. For example, black Christian slaves wrote in 1779 to the General Assembly of Connecticut:

We perceive by our own Reflection, that we are
endowed with the same Faculties with our masters,
and there is nothing that leads us to a Belief, or
Suspicion, that we are any more Obliged to serve
them, than they us, and the more we Consider of
this matter, the more we are Convinced of our Right
(by the laws of Nature and by the whole Tenor of
the Christian Religion, so far as we have been taught)
to be free.

The prophetic Christian view that the gospel stands un-
equivocally opposed to slavery led, in some cases, to unsuccessful slave revolts spearheaded by black Christians.
In 1800, a young twenty-five-year-old black prophetic
Christian named Gabriel Prosser appealed to the Samson
story in the Old Testament, understood himself as the
divinely elected deliverer of black people, and subsequently engaged in the first thoroughly planned and overtly
revolutionary attempt to liberate black people from slavery. According to conservative estimates, this attempt involved over six thousand black Christians and non-Chris-
tians. Like most other slave insurrectionists, young Gabriel
was executed. The famous examples and executions of
Denmark Vesey (leader of a slave insurrection in 1822)
and Nat Turner (leader of a slave insurrection in 1831) also
exemplify the cost that black prophetic Christians were
willing to pay in their Christian-inspired fight for liberation.

The major codified theological expression during this
stage is found in David Walker's "Appeal to the Coloured
Citizens of the World," which appeared in 1829. Walker's
Appeal, as it came to be known, is one of the most powerful theological critiques of slavery to emanate from the
black Christian tradition. Gayraud Wilmore, a noted black
Christian social ethicist and historian, goes as far as to
state:

Walker's Appeal is steeped in Biblical language
and prophecy. It is certainly one of the most re-

markable religious documents of the Protestant era,
rivaling in its righteous indignation and Christian
radicalism Luther's "Open Letter to the Christian
Nobility of the German Nation," published in Wit-
tenberg in 1520.

In his theological antislavery text, Walker proclaims that
slavery,

> is ten thousand times more injurious to this country
> than all the other evils put together; and which will
> be the final overthrow of its government, unless
> something is very speedily done; for their cup is
> nearly full.—Perhaps they will laugh at or make
> light of this; but I tell you Americans! that unless
> you speedily alter your course, you and your Coun-
> try are gone!!!!!! For God Almighty will tear up the
> very face of the earth!!!

The second stage can be viewed as "Black Theology of
Liberation as Critique of Institutional Racism." This stage,
which occupied a little over a century (1864–1969), found
black prophetic Christians principally focusing attention
on the racist institutional structures in the United States
which rendered the vast majority of black people politically powerless (deprived of the right to vote or participate
in governmental affairs), economically exploited (in dependent positions as sharecroppers or in unskilled jobs),
and socially degraded (separate, segregated, and unequal
eating and recreational facilities, housing, education,
transportation, and police protection). This period contains
the vicious lynchings of hundreds of black people alongside the historic refusal of President Woodrow Wilson to
sign an antilynching law in 1916; there was also the migra-
tion of millions of job-hunting black people into rat-in-
fested dilapidated ghettos in the urban North, which triggered the historic race riots of 1919, 1943, 1964, 1967, and
1968.
    It is no accident that many of the salient black prophetic

Christian leaders—such as Bishop Henry McNeal Turner and Marcus Garvey—favored during this stage a return of black people to Africa. They were led to this viewpoint from their theological critiques of institutional racism in the United States. They held that this institutional racism so deeply pervaded and permeated U.S. society that only emigration to the black homeland could rid black people of their immediate oppression.

The most effective black prophetic Christian leader during this stage was, of course, Martin Luther King, Jr. Upon the strength of the black prophetic church and liberal white allies, he mobilized and organized black and white people against blantant institutional racism and waged a successful struggle for black civil rights—integrated transportation, eating and recreational facilities, and, most important, the right to vote. The tragic murder of King in 1968 triggered not only some of the worst race riots the United States had ever witnessed, and included the National Guard protecting the White House for the first time since the Civil War. King's death, along with the Black Power movement led by Stokely Carmichael and H. Rap Brown, also precipitated a great wave of the academic expression of black theological reflection.

Except for pioneer works by Benjamin Mays, Howard Thurman, George Kelsey, and a few others, black prophetic Christians had not systematically codified their theological viewpoints. But with the publishing of Albert Cleage's *The Black Messiah* (1968) and James Cone's *Black Theology and Black Power* (1969), a third stage commenced: "Black Theology of Liberation as Critique of White North American Theology." In this stage, which lasted less than a decade (1969–1977), we witnessed the first fullfledged academic expression of liberation theology in general and black theology of liberation in particular in the United States. James Cone's second book, *A Black Theology of Liberation* (1970), deepened a theological discourse in which many black theologians played a crucial role, including figures such as Cecil Cone (James Cone's brother),

Major Jones, William Jones, Charles Long, J. Deotis Roberts, Joseph Washington, Leon Watts, Preston Williams, and Gayraud Wilmore.

This particular stage was an intellectually creative one— partly in response to the spontaneous rebellion of black people in the streets, the more disciplined political praxis of Black Power groups, and the paralysis of most white North American theologians. Yet the conception of black theology was, in retrospect, understandably narrow: it focused principally on the failings of white North American theology, especially its silence on racial justice and the white racism within mainstream establishment churches and religious agencies. In response to this criticism, echoed partially by Cecil Cone, Charles Long, and Gayraud Wilmore, James Cone attempted in his next two books—*The Spirituals and the Blues* (1972) and *God of the Oppressed* (1975)—to broaden his focus by delving into black cultural sources for theological reflection, such as the spirituals, blues, folktales, sermons, and stories. As Cone notes:

I have learned much from this discussion on Black religion and Black Theology, because there is a basic truth in the critiques of Long, Cone, and Wilmore. . . . If the struggle of the victims is the only context for the development of a genuine Christian theology, then should not theology itself reflect in its speech the language of the people about whom it claims to speak? This is the critical issue. When this assumption is applied to Black Theology, I think that Black religion or the Black religious experience must become one of the important ingredients in the development of a Black Theology.

The fourth stage—and the stage that black prophetic theologians are presently transcending—can be viewed as "Black Theology of Liberation as Critique of U.S. Capitalism." With the presentation of two papers at the Black Theology Conference in Atlanta, Georgia, in 1977, black theological reflection focused on U.S. capitalism as a major enemy of black people. The one paper, "Message to the Black Church and Community," was that of the Black Theology Project, which is part of a progressive interethnic, interracial, interdenominational Christian organization called Theology in the Americas; the other, James Cone's essay "Black Theology and the Black Church: Where Do We Go from Here?" In the section entitled "The Roots of the Crisis," the Black Theology Project collectively stated:

> The issue for all of us is survival. The root problem is human sinfulness which nurtures monopolistic capitalism, aided by racism and abetted by sexism. Our crisis is spiritual, material and moral. Black people seem unable to effectively counter disruptive forces that undermine our quality of life. We seem unable to collectively define our situation, discover the nature of our problems, and develop sustained coalitions that can resolve our dilemmas.
>
> Exploitative, profit-oriented capitalism is a way of ordering life fundamentally alien to human value in general and to black humanity in particular. Racism and capitalism have set the stage for despoliation of natural and human resources all around the world. Yet those who seriously challenge these systems are often effectively silenced. We view racism as criminality and yet we are called criminals. We view racism as a human aberration, yet we are called freaks. The roots of our crisis are in social, economic, media and political power systems that prevent us from managing the reality of our everyday lives.
>
> It is this intolerable, alien order that has driven us to Atlanta seeking a word from the Lord out of the wellsprings of black theological tradition.

And in his essay, Cone explicitly notes:

> There is a little in our theological expressions and church practice that rejects American capitalism or recognizes its oppressive character in Third World countries. The time has. come for us to move be-

yond institutional survival in a capitalistic and racist society and begin to take more seriously our
dreams about a new heaven and a new earth. Does
this dream include capitalism or is it a radically
new way of life more consistent with African socialism as expressed in the Arusha Declaration in Tan-
zania?

This focus was deepened and sharpened by two of my
own essays—"Black Theology and Marxist Thought" (1979)
and "Black Theology and Socialist Thought" (1980)—which,
in a sense, initiated a dialogue between black prophetic
theologians and progressive Marxist thinkers, as well as
practicing socialists and communists. James Cone's latest
essay, "The Black Church and Marxism: What Do They
Have to Say to Each Other?" pursues this crucial dialogue.

Yet the prevailing conception of black theology of liberation remains inadequate. I believe that a new conception
of black theology of liberation is needed which preserves
the positive content of its earlier historical stages, overcome its earlier (and inevitable) blindnesses, and makes
explicit its present challenges. The positive content of the
earlier conceptions of black theology of liberation is as
follows:

1. The theological claim (or faith claim) that God sides
with the oppressed and acts on their behalf.

2. The idea that religion of the oppressed can be either
an opiate or a source of struggle for liberation.

3. The idea that white racism is a cancer at the core of
an exploitative capitalist U.S. society.

The limitations and shortcomings of earlier conceptions
of black theology are:

1. Its absence of a systemic social analysis, which has
prevented black theologians from coming to terms with
the relationships between racism, sexism, class exploitation, and imperialist oppression.

2. Its lack of a social vision, political program, and concrete praxis which defines and facilitates socioeconomic
and political liberation.

3. Its tendency to downplay existential issues such as death, disease, dread, despair, and disappointment which are related to, yet not identical with, suffering caused by oppressive structures.

The present challenge to black theologians is to put forward an understanding of the Christian gospel in the light of present circumstances that takes into account the complex ways in which racism (especially white racism) and sexism (especially male sexism) are integral to the class exploitative capitalist system of production as well as its repressive imperialist tentacles abroad; and to keep in view the crucial existential issues of death, disease, despair, dread, and disappointment that each and every individual must face within the context of these present circumstances. This theological perspective requires a move into a fifth stage: "Black Theology of Liberation as Critique of Capitalist Civilization." In short, black theological reflection and action must simultaneously become more familiar with and rooted in the progressive Marxist tradition, with its staunch anticapitalist, anti-imperialist, antiracist, and antisexist stance and its creative socialist outlook; and more anchored in its own proto-Kierkegaardian viewpoint, namely, its proper concern with the existential issues facing individuals.

So black theologians and Marxist thinkers are strangers. They steer clear of each other, content to express concerns to their respective audiences. Needless to say, their concerns overlap. Both focus on the plight of the exploited, oppressed, and degraded peoples of the world, their relative powerlessness and possible empowerment. I believe this common focus warrants a serious dialogue between black theologians and Marxist thinkers. This dialogue should not be a mere academic chat that separates religionists and secularists, theists and atheists. Instead, it ought to be an earnest encounter that specifies clearly the different sources of their praxis of faith, yet accents the possibility of mutually arrived at political action.

The primary aim of this encounter is to change the world, not each other's faith; to put both groups on the offensive

for structural social change, not put black Christians on the
defensive; and to enhance the quality of life of the dispossessed, not expose the empty Marxist meaning of death. In
short, both black theologians and Marxist thinkers must
preserve their own existential and intellectual integrity
and explore the possibility of promoting fundamental social amelioration together.

Black theology and Marxist thought are not monolithic
bodies of thought; each contains different perspectives,
distinct viewpoints, and diverse conclusions. Therefore it
is necessary to identify the particular claims put forward
by black theology and by Marxist thought, those claims
which distinguish each as a discernible school of thought.
Black theology claims:

1. The historical experience of black people and the
readings of the biblical texts that emerge therefrom are the
centers around which reflection about God evolves.

2. This reflection is related, in some way, to the liberation of black people, to the creation of a more abundant
life definable in existential, economic, social, and political
terms.

Marxist thought contains two specific elements: a theory
of history and an understanding of capitalism. These two
elements are inextricably interlinked, but it may be helpful to characterize them separately. The Marxist theory of
history claims:

1. The history of human societies is the history of their
transitional stages.

2. The transitional stages of human societies are discernible owing to their systems of production, or their
organizational arrangements in which people produce goods
and services for their survival.

3. Conflict within systems of production of human societies ultimately results in fundamental social change, or
transitions from one historical stage to another.

4. Conflict within systems of production of human societies consists of cleavages between social classes (in those
systems of production).

5. Social classes are historically transient, rooted in a particular set of socioeconomic conditions.

6. Therefore, the history of all hitherto existing society is the history of class struggles.

The Marxist theory of capitalist society claims: Capitalism is a historically transient system of production which requires human beings to produce commodities for the purpose of maximizing surplus value (profits). This production presupposes a fundamental social relationship between the purchasers and the sellers of a particular commodity, namely, the labor power (time, skill, and expertise) of producers. This crucial commodity is bought by capitalists who own the land, instruments, and capital necessary for production; it is sold by producers, whose labor power is needed for production. The aim of the former is to maximize profits; that of the latter, to ensure their own survival.

I shall claim that black theology and Marxist thought share three characteristics. First, both adhere to a similar methodology: they have the same way of approaching their respective subject matter and arriving at conclusions. Second, both link some notion of liberation to the future socioeconomic conditions of the downtrodden. Third, and most important, both attempt to put forward trenchant critiques of liberal capitalist America. I will try to show that these three traits provide a springboard for a meaningful dialogue between black theologians and Marxist thinkers and possibly spearhead a unifying effort for structural social change in liberal capitalist America.

DIALECTICAL METHODOLOGY: UNMASKING FALSEHOODS

Black theologians have either consciously or unconsciously employed a dialectical methodology in approaching their subject matter. This methodology consists of a three-step procedure of negation, preservation, and transformation; their subject matter, of white interpretations of the Christian gospel and their own circumstances. Dialectical methodology is critical in character and hermeneutic in content. For black theologians, it is highly critical of dogmatic viewpoints of the gospel, questioning whether certain unjustifiable prejudgments are operative. It is hermeneutic in that it is concerned with unearthing assumptions of particular interpretations and presenting an understanding of the gospel that extends and expands its ever-unfolding truth.

Black theologians have, for the most part, been compelled to adopt a dialectical methodology. They have refused to accept what has been given to them by white theologians; they have claimed that all reflection about God by whites must be digested, decoded, and deciphered. The first theological formulations by Afro-Americans based on biblical texts tried to come to terms with their white owners' viewpoints and their own servitude. Since its inception, black theology has been forced to reduce white deception and distortion of the gospel and make the Christian story meaningful in the light of their oppressive conditions.

The reflection by black theologians begins by negating white interpretations of the gospel, continues by preserving their own perceived truths of the biblical texts, and ends by transforming past understandings of the gospel into new ones. These three steps embody an awareness of the social context of theologizing, the need to accent the historical experience of black people and the insights of the Bible, and the ever-evolving task of recovering, regaining, and repeating the gospel.

Black theologians underscore the importance of the social context of theological reflection. Their dialectical methodology makes them sensitive to the hidden agendas of the theological formulations they negate, agendas often guided by social interests. Their penchant for revealing distortions leads them to adopt a sociology of knowledge approach that stresses the way in which particular viewpoints endorse and encourage ulterior aims.

An interpretation of the black historical experience and the readings of the biblical texts that emerge out of this experience constitute the raw ingredients for the second step of black theological reflection. By trying to understand the plight of black people in the light of the Bible, black theologians claim to preserve the biblical truth that God sides with the oppressed and acts on their behalf. Subsequently, the black historical experience and the biblical texts form a symbiotic relationship, each illuminating the other.

Since black theologians believe in the living presence of God and the work of the Holy Spirit, they acknowledge the constant unfolding process of the gospel. Paradoxically, the gospel is unchanging, yet it is deepened by embracing and encompassing new human realities and experiences. The gospel must speak to every age. Therefore it must be recovered and repeated, often sounding different, but in substance remaining the same. For black theologians, it sounds different because it addresses various contexts of oppression; it remains the same because it is essentially a gospel of liberation.

Marxist thinkers, like black theologians, employ a dialectical methodology in approaching their subject matter. But they do so consciously and their subject matter is bourgeois theories about capitalist society. The primary theoretical task of Marxist thinkers is to uncover the systematic misunderstanding of capitalist society by bourgeois thinkers; to show how this misunderstanding, whether deliberate or not, supports and sanctions exploitation and oppression in this society; and to put forward the correct understanding of this society in order to change it.

Marxist social theory is first and foremost a critique of inadequate theories of capitalist society and subsequently a critique of capitalist society itself. The subtitle of Marx's magnum opus, *Capital*, is "A Critique of Political Economy," not "A Critique of Capitalism." This work takes bourgeois economists to task for perpetuating falsehoods, which then results in revealing the internal dynamics of capitalism and the inhumane consequences. For Marx, a correct understanding of capitalist society is possible only by overcoming present mystifications of it; and this correct understanding is requisite for a propitious political praxis.

Marxist thought stresses the conflict-laden unfolding of history, the conflict-producing nature of social processes. Therefore it is not surprising that Marxist thinkers employ a dialectical methodology, a methodology deeply suspicious of stasis and stability, and highly skeptical of equilibrium and equipoise. This methodology, like that of black theologians, is critical in character and hermeneutic in content. It is critical of perspectives presented by bourgeois social scientists, questioning whether certain ideological biases are operative. It is hermeneutic in that it is obsessed with discovering the correct understanding underneath wrong interpretations, disclosing latent truths behind manifest distortions. For Marx, to be scientific is to be dialectical and to be dialectical is to unmask, unearth, to bring to light.

This conception of science, derived from Hegel, attempts to discern the hidden kernel of an evolving truth becoming manifest by bursting through a visible husk. The husk, once a hidden kernel, dissolves, leaving its indelible imprint upon the new, emerging kernel. This idea of inquiry highlights the moments of negation, preservation, and transformation. By presenting his theory of history and society from this perspective, Marx provided the most powerful and penetrating social criticism in modern times. Dialectical methodology enabled him to create a whole mode of inquiry distinctively his own, though often appearing hermetic and rigid to the untutored and the fanatic.

Despite the similar procedure that black theologians and Marxist thinkers share, there has been little discussion about it between them. This is so, primarily because a dialectical methodology is implicit, hence underdeveloped and often unnoticed, in black theology. This failure to examine the methodological stance embodied in black theological reflection obscures its similarity with that of Marxist thought.

LIBERATION: ITS CONSTITUTIVE ELEMENTS

Black theologians all agree that black liberation has something to do with ameliorating the socioeconomic conditions of black people. But it is not clear what this amelioration amounts to. There is little discussion in their writings about what the liberating society will be like. The notion and the process of liberation are often mentioned, but, surprisingly, one is hard put to find a sketch of what liberation would actually mean in the everyday lives of black people, what power they would possess, and what resources they would have access to.

There are two main reasons for this neglect among black theologians. First, a dialectical methodology discourages discussions about the ideal society and simply what ought to be. Instead, it encourages criticizing and overcoming existing society, negating and opposing what is.

The second reason, the one we shall be concerned with in this section, is the failure of black theologians to talk specifically about the way in which the existing system of production and the social structure relate to black oppression and exploitation. Without a focusing upon this relationship, it becomes extremely difficult to present an idea of liberation with socioeconomic content. In short, the lack of a clear-cut social theory prevents the emergence of any substantive political program or social vision.

Aside from James Cone in his latest writings, black theologians remain uncritical of America's imperialist presence in Third World countries, its capitalist system of production, and its grossly unequal distribution of wealth. Therefore we may assume they find this acceptable. If this is so, then the political and socioeconomic components of black liberation amount to racial equality before the law, equal

opportunities in employment, education, and business, and
economic parity with whites in median income.

Surely, this situation would be better than the current
dismal one, but it hardly can be viewed as black liberation
It roughly equates liberation with American middle-class
status, leaving the unequal distribution of wealth relatively untouched and the capitalist system of production,
along with its imperialist ventures, intact. Liberation would
consist of including black people within the mainstream of
liberal capitalist America. If this is the social vision of
black theologians, they should drop the meretricious and
flamboyant term "liberation" and adopt the more accurate
and sober word "inclusion."

Marxist thought, like black theology, does not elaborate
on the ideal society. As we noted earlier, a dialectical
methodology does not permit this elaboration. But the brief
sketch that progressive Marxist thinkers provide requires
a particular system of production and political arrangement—namely, participatory democracy in each. Human
liberation occurs only when people participate substan-
tively in the decision-making processes in the major institutions that regulate their lives. Democratic control over
the institutions in the productive and political processes in
order for them to satisfy human needs and protect personal
liberties of the populace constitutes human liberation.

Progressive Marxist thinkers are able to present this sketch
of human liberation primarily because they stress what
people must liberate themselves from. They suggest what
liberation is for only after understanding the internal dynamics of the society from which people must be liberated.
Without this clear-cut social theory about what is, it is
difficult to say anything significant about what can be. The
possibility of liberation is found only within the depths of
the actuality of oppression. Without an adequate social
theory, this possibility is precluded.

SOCIAL CRITICISM: CLASS, RACE, AND CULTURE

Black theology puts forward a vehement, often vociferous, critique of liberal capitalist America. One of its most attractive and alluring characteristics is its theological indictment of racist American society. An undisputable claim of black theology is America's unfair treatment of black people. What is less apparent is the way in which black theologians understand the internal dynamics of liberal capitalist America, how it functions, why it operates the way it does, who possesses substantive power, and where it is headed. As noted earlier, black theologians do not utilize a social theory that relates the oppression of black people to the overall makeup of America's system of production, foreign policy, political arrangement, and cultural practices.

Black theologians hardly mention the wealth, power, and influence of multinational corporations that monopolize production in the marketplace and prosper partially because of their dependence on public support in the form of government subsidies, free technological equipment, lucrative contracts, and sometimes even direct transfer payments. Black theologians do not stress the way in which corporate interests and the government intermesh, usually resulting in policies favorable to the former. Black theologians fail to highlight the fact that in liberal capitalist America one half of 1 percent own 22 percent of the wealth, 1 percent own 33 percent of the wealth, the lower 61 percent own only 7 percent of the wealth, and the bottom 45 percent own only 2 percent of the wealth. Lastly, black theologians do not emphasize sufficiently the way in which the racist interpretations of the gospel they reject encourage and support the capitalist system of production, its grossly unequal distribution of wealth, and its closely connected political arrangements.

Instead of focusing on these matters, black theologians draw attention to the racist practices in American society.

Since these practices constitute the most visible and vicious form of oppression in America, black theologians
justifiably do so. Like the Black Power proponents of the
'60s, they call for the empowerment of black people, the
need for black people to gain significant control over their
lives. But neither Black Power proponents nor black theologians have made it sufficiently clear as to what constitutes this black control, the real power to direct institutions
such that black people can live free of excessive exploitation and oppression. The tendency is to assume that middle-
class status is equivalent to such control, that a well-paying
job amounts to such power. Surely, this assumption is fal-
lacious.

The important point here is not that racist practices should
be stressed less by black theologians, for such practices
deeply affect black people and shape their perceptions of
American society. What is crucial is that these practices be
linked to the role they play in buttressing the current
mode of production, concealing the unequal distribution
of wealth, and portraying the lethargy of the political system. Black theologians are correct in relating racist practices to degrees of black powerlessness, but they obscure
this relation by failing to provide a lucid definition of what
power is in American society. Subsequently, they often
fall into the trap of assuming power in American society to
be synonymous with receiving high wages.

Marxist social criticism can be quite helpful at this point.
For Marx, power in modern industrial society consists of a
group's participation in the decision-making processes of
the major institutions that affect their destinies. Since institutions of production, such as multinational corporations, play an important role in people's lives, these institutions should be significantly accountable to the populace.
In short, they should be democratically controlled by the
citzenry; people should participate in their decision-making processes. Only collective control over the major institutions of society constitutes genuine power on behalf of
the people.

For Marx, power in modern industrial society is closely related to a group's say over what happens to products produced in the work situation, to a group's input into decisions that direct the production flow of goods and services. The most powerful group in society has the most say and input into decisions over this production flow; the least powerful group does not participate at all in such decisions. In liberal capitalist America, the former consist of multiple corporate owners who dictate policies concerning the mass production of a variety of products produced by white- and blue-collar workers who receive wages in return. The latter consist of the so-called underclass, the perennially unemployed who are totally removed from the work situation, precluded from any kind of input affecting the production flow, including negotiation and strikes available to white- and blue-collar workers.

Racist practices intensify the degree of powerlessness among black people. This is illustrated by the high rate of black unemployment, the heavy black concentration in low-paying jobs, and inferior housing, education, police protection, and health care. But it is important to note that this powerlessness differs from that of white- and blue-collar workers in degree, not in kind. In human terms, this difference is immense, incalculable; in structural terms, this difference is negligible, trifling. In other words, most Americans are, to a significant degree, powerless. They have no substantive control over their lives, little participation in the decision-making process of the major institutions that regulate their lives. Among Afro-Americans, this powerlessness is exacerbated, creating an apparent qualitative difference in oppression.

This contrast of the social criticism of black theologians and Marxist thinkers raises the age-old question as to whether class position or racial status is the major determinant of black oppression in America. This question should be formulated in the following way: whether class position or racial status contributes most to the fundamental form of powerlessness in America.

Racial status contributes greatly to black oppression. But middle-class black people are essentially well-paid white- or blue-collar workers who have little control over their lives primarily because of their class position, not their racial status. This is so because the same limited control is held by white middle-class people, despite the fact that a higher percentage of whites are well-paid white- and blue-collar workers than blacks. Significant degrees of powerlessness pertain to most Americans and this could be so only if class position determines such powerlessness. Therefore, class position contributes more than racial status to the basic form of powerlessness in America.

I am suggesting that the more black theologians discard or overlook Marxist social criticism, the farther they distance themselves from the fundamental determinant of black oppression and any effective strategy to alleviate it. This distancing also obscures the direct relationship of black oppression in America to black and brown oppression in Third World countries. The most powerful group in America, those multiple corporate owners who dictate crucial corporate policies over a variety of production flows, are intimately and inextricably linked (through their highly paid American and Third World white-collar workers and grossly underpaid Third World blue-collar workers) to the economies and governments of Third World countries, including the most repressive ones. Marxist social criticism permits this relationship to come to light in an extremely clear and convincing way.

The social criticism of black theologians reflects the peculiar phenomenon of American liberal and radical criticism. This criticism rarely has viewed class position as a major determinant of oppression primarily because of America's lack of a feudal past, the heterogeneity of its population, the many and disparate regions of its geography, and the ever-increasing levels of productivity and growth. These facts make it difficult to see class divisions, and, along with other forms of oppression, make it almost impossible. But, like protons leaving vapor trails in a cloud chamber, one is forced to posit them in the light of the overwhelming evidence for their existence. Only class divisions can explain the gross disparity between rich and poor, the immense benefits accruing to the former and the depravity of the latter.

Region, sex, age, ethnicity, and race often have been considered the only worthy candidates as determinants of oppression. This has been so primarily because American liberal and radical criticism usually has presupposed the existing system of production, assumed class divisions, and attempted only to include marginal groups in the mainstream of liberal capitalist America. This criticism has fostered a petit bourgeois viewpoint that clamors for a bigger piece of the ever-growing American pie, rarely asking fundamental questions such as why it never gets recut more equally or how it gets baked in the first place. In short, this criticism remains silent about class divisions, the crucial role they play in maintaining the unequal distribution of goods and services, and how they undergird discrimination against regions, impose ceilings on upward social mobility, and foster racism, sexism, and ageism. As has been stated above, with the exception of James Cone in his most recent writings contemporary black theologians suffer from this general myopia of American liberal and radical criticism.

Despite this shortsightedness, black theologians have performed an important service for Marxist thinkers, namely, emphasizing the ways in which culture and religion resist oppression. They have been admirably sensitive to the black cultural buffers against oppression, especially the black religious sources of struggle and strength, vitality and vigor. They also have stressed the indispensable contribution the black churches have made toward the survival, dignity, and self-worth of black people.

Contrary to Marxist thinkers, black theologians recognize that cultural and religious attitudes, values, and sensibilities have a life and logic of their own, not fully accountable in terms of a class analysis. Subsequently, racist practices are not reducible to a mere clever and successful strategy of divide and conquer promoted by the ruling class to prevent proletarian unity. Rather, racism is an integral element within the very fabric of American cul ture and society. It is embedded in the country's first collective definition, enunciated in its subsequent laws, and imbued in its dominant way of life.

The orthodox Marxist analysis of culture and religion that simply relates racist practices to misconceived material interests is only partially true, hence deceptive and misleading. These practices are fully comprehensible only if one conceives of culture, not as a mere hoax played by the ruling class on workers, but as the tradition that informs one's conception of tradition, as social practices that shape one's idea of social practice.

The major objection to the orthodox Marxist analysis of culture and religion is not that it is wrong, but that it is too narrow, rigid, and dogmatic. It views popular culture and religion only as instruments of domination, vehicles of pacification. It sees only their negative and repressive elements. On this view, only enlightenment, reason, or clarity imposed from the outside can break through the cultural layers of popular false consciousness. Therefore, the orthodox Marxist analysis refuses to acknowledge the positive, liberating aspects of popular culture and religion, and their potential for fostering structural social change. . . .

SAMIR AMIN (1931–   )

Nothing socialists had previously written on imperialism and colonialism came close to anticipating what has happened to the third world countries after their liberation. The economic disparity between North and South, the industrialized nations and the impoverished ones, bids fair to be the central issue of the next century. For socialism, with its appeal to universal equality, it is an issue of great moment on which much has been written from every point of view on the ideological spectrum, mildly reformist to militantly revolutionary. But socialist in our opinion has dealt with the relations between North and South on as high a theoretical level as Samir Amin, an Egyptian economist. The number of books he has written is daunting, many of them translated into the major languages of the world. The following passages, which give a summary account of his views, are taken from a recent work, *The Future of Socialism* (Harare: SAPES Trust, 1990).

It is surely time to raise the issue of the future of socialism once again. Since the beginning of the 1980s the ideological offensive of the ultra-liberal right has been such that the predominant social-dramatic forces of the Western left have found it necessary to fall broadly into line. In the Third World, the burgeoning of the relatively autonomous development has been systematically undermined in favour of total surrender to the demands of world-wide capitalist expansion. Last but not least, the sudden collapse of Eastern European regimes paves the way for a possible restoration of capitalism through social and economic integration of these countries into the same capitalist world system. Triumphant liberal ideology proclaims the definitive failure of socialism.

For those who believe, as we do, that socialism offers a system of values never "achieved", and in no way a "constructed model" on show in any particular place, the issue is infinitely more complex. I would say quite frankly that today's real danger is that the illusions affecting the peoples of the West, East and South can only mean that the inevitable failure of triumphant liberalism could be traumatic for the popular classes once they are ideologically and politically disarmed. More than ever, I would urge that the choice lies between "socialism or barbarism".

It might be helpful to begin this analysis with a critique of the three fundamental bases of the fashionable liberal thesis.

First liberal axiom: the "market" represents an economic rationality *per se* outside any specific social context.

This erroneous postulate is no more than an expression of
the economistic alienation essential for ideological legiti-
mation of capitalism. The "market" does not in fact determine social relations: on the contrary, the framework of
social relations determines how the market will operate.
From an alienated economist stand-point, economic laws
are analogous to laws of nature and exert external forces
on every human action, and the economy is the product of
determinate social behaviour. There is no economic rationality per se, but merely the expression of the demands of
a social system at the level of economic management. No
such social system is rational from a humanist point of
view if it fails to meet the need of the human beings
subject to it: unemployment, polarisation in world development, ecological waste are manifestations of the iration-
ality of this system—really existing capitalism. These negative phenomena are purely and simply necessary products
of the "market": the rationality of the market reproduces
the irrationalities of the social system.

Second liberal axiom: an interchangeable formula of
capitalism-democracy and equation of democracy = capitalist. This is mere trickery.

Contemporary trends of opinion, broadly typified by Anglo-American evolutionism and pragmatism, impoverish
the debate by treating democracy as a gamut of narrowly
defined rights and practices, independent of the desired
social outlook. This democracy can then stabilise the society, by leaving "evolution" to "objective forces". The latter are, in the last resort, deemed to be governed by science and technology operating regardless of human will;
hence the functional role of the revolutionary process in
history can be played down. . . .

If what are known as the Third World countries have
almost never seen their political systems in a genuinely
democratic form, this is not a hangover from their "traditional culture". What I call "really existing capitalism",
that is, capitalism as a world system and not as a mode of
production taken at its highest level of abstraction, has to

date always generated polarisation on a world scale (the "centres/peripheries" contradiction). Unfortunately, this dimension has always been underestimated in socialist thought of all forms, including Marxism. International polarisation inherent in this expansion brings in turn a manifold internal social polarisation: growing inequality in income distribution, widespread unemployment, marginalisation, etc. Making the world system the key unit of analysis responds to a social factor of crucial importance for an understanding of what is at stake in the struggles, namely that the essential reserve army of capital is to be found in the peripheries of the system. Hence instability is the rule in the political life of the peripheries. The background of vicious dictatorship (military or not as may be) broadly amenable to the demands of the world expansion of capital is occasionally shaken by explosions that challenge the dictatorships. Such explosions rarely lead to any semblance of political democracy. The commonest model is a "populist" response. This means regimes that genuinely address at least some aspects of the social problem and contemplate a development strategy capable of reducing the tragic consequences of peripherisation.

There is a middle ground between dictatorships of the right and/or populist moments on to which "petty democracy" can sometimes sneak. We mean regimes that recognise the principle of multi-party elections, and grant a measure of free speech, but fall short of addressing fundamental problems and/or challenging relations of dependence and subjection to the world system. These "democracies" are little more than an expression of the crisis of the usual despotic system of capitalism. Latin America, Korea, the Philippines provide examples of contradictions unresolved by the regimes. Democratic systems imposed in such circumstances face a striking dilemma. An either-or. Either the democratic political system accepts surrender to the demands of world "adjustment": it could not then consider any substantial social reform and the democracy would not be slow to reach crisis (as is already the case in Argentina). Or the popular forces take hold of the democracy and impose the reforms: the system would then come into conflict with dominant world capitalism and must shift from the national bourgeois project to a national and popular project.

The areas of the periphery most affected by capitalist expansion are in a more desperate plight. The history of capitalist expansion should cover not only the "development" it has engendered. Capitalism has a destructive side too often omitted from flattering portrayals of the system. Here the "usual" pattern of power is the Tontons Macoutes in Haiti, Somoza in Nicaragua and a disturbing number of dictatorships of the same stamp in contemporary Africa.

Third liberal axiom: a wide open door to the world system is an "unavoidable" constraint, the *sine qua non* of any "development". The underlying theoretical hypothesis is that ' development" depends essentially on internal circumstances peculiar to each society, with its integration into the world economy a potentially positive factor (if one knows how to use the opportunities it provides). This thesis is not only contradicted by the history of five centuries of capitalist expansion—incessant polarisation reproduced and intensified to date and for the foreseeable future—but is also scientifically unsound. The "world market" in question is truncated and restricted to goods and capital, whereas—despite international migrations—there has never been any suggestion of a "world labour market" (and no prospect of one). Liberal economics demonstrates that mobility of a single factor of production (capital) while two other factors (labour and natural resources) are imprisoned by natural and political geography can not lead to homogeneous productivity levels and social conditions.

In such circumstances, the world-wide law of value can only produce and reproduce polarisation (the centres/peripheries contradiction). In this sense the "external factor" (integration in the world system) is of its nature disfavourable and increasingly so. I have argued this thesis on intu-

itive evidence: a few decades were enough to allow the
19th century Germany to "catch up" with England; how
long would Brazil need to "catch up" with the United
States? Undoubtedly, the forms and content of the polarisation have evolved over time. From the industrial revolution to the Second World War, it was a distinction between
industrialised and non-industrialised countries. Accelerated industrialisation of some areas of the Third World
does not, in my view, raise a question mark over polarisation as such but merely over its forms. The mechanisms of
the new polarisation are founded on various forms of domination; financial (new forms of world-wide finance capital); technological (in relation to the new scientific and
technological revolution); cultural (with the growing influence of the media); and military. In this context, the "newly
industrialised countries" are not "semi-peripheries" on the
way to crystalising into new centres, but the true peripheries of tomorrow.

By contrast the countries of the so-called "Fourth World"
are not true peripheries but similar to the areas destroyed
by capitalist expansion in its earlier forms. The parlous
condition of the "Fourth World" is not the outcome of a
refusal to integrate within the international division of
labour and a "failed" attempt to delink. In fact the "Fourth
World" that is talked of as something new is a consistent
feature of capitalist expansion. A clear but lamentable example of this former Fourth World is provided by the areas
of slave labour in the Americas in the period of mercantil-
ism: North-East Brazil, the West Indies (including Haiti).
These areas were regarded as "prosperous" in their day;
and they were the heart of the periphery corresponding to
the system of the time. Later the new structures of capitalist development marginalised these areas, and they are
today among the most grievously wretched parts of the
Third World. Is Africa not now on the road to exclusion
from the world division of labour by a system that has
consigned the continent to specialisation in agriculture
and mining through extensive exploitation of the soils un-

til they are exhausted, and the technological revolution
that provides substitutes for some raw materials? Fourth
World societies subject to a passive delinking through rejection cannot, by definition, solve their problems through
open door policies. Recolonisation, sweetened by charity,
is surely trying to conceal the explicit failure of the neo-
liberal solution?

From the stand-point of the various peoples of the earth,
unification of the world system in the unilateral concern of
the market is undesirable. It is not even the most likely
outcome of the evolution under way, so bitter are the conflicts inexorably provoked by submission to the unilateral criterion of the "market" operating in a world of "Darwinism". The ideological discourse of the West, which has
opted for this strategy, aims to conceal the bitterness of
these conflicts. The values of socialism have their scientific (and not merely moral) justification in a rejection of
the three blunders in bourgeois thought described above.
All currents of socialist thought are keen to go beyond the
philosophy of the Enlightenment seeking to establish a "rational" society to endure for all time. Socialism comes from
an analysis of the historical limits of the "rationality" in
question, namely capitalism. Socialism therefore offers a
project of a qualitatively more advanced society, aiming at
a more complete mastery of human beings over their social
destiny. Here again the Marxist theory of alienation returns to the centre of the stage: the project of the society
in question implies liberation from the economistic alienation peculiar to bourgeois ideology. The project cannot
be defined more precisely in advance. Although it would
be possible to be precise as to what must be "abolished"
(such as private ownership of the means of production
obviously), it would not be possible—in the absence of
any social praxis—to delineate in advance new methods of
social management. Any attempt to do so would militate
against the methodology of the socialist project for liberation whereby responsibility for shaping destiny can lie

only with the succeeding generations who will be making
their own history. . . .

In these circumstances the scale of the crisis of the societies of the East is not a great surprise to us, even if like
everyone else we have been astounded by its suddenness.
These societies currently face a triple option that I briefly
summarise under the following three headings:

(i) Evolution towards a bourgeois democracy or progress beyond it by the strengthening of the social power of
workers in the management of the economy?

(ii) Restoration of an out-and-out "market economy" or
effective progress in carefully controlled resort to market
forces through democratic planning?

(iii) An unguarded door wide open to the exterior or
guarded relations with the surrounding capitalist world,
albeit on the basis of increased trade?

The confused theoretical debate and political disputes
causing shudders throughout the Eastern countries come
in part because ideological labelling as "socialist" has ob-
scured the genuinely "national and popular" character of
historical revolutions establishing each of the regimes. But
more pertinent is the fact that the conflictual forces of
capitalism and socialism are meeting within genuine
struggles. The forces anxious to "restore capitalism" propose unilateral acceptance of the "market" (as a springboard for the restoration of private ownership) and of "an
open door to the exterior", with or without democracy (in
the Western sense of the word) according to the tactical
requirements of their project. If the socialist forces dither
in their resistance to the project, and if they find it difficult
to articulate a coherent alternative (on the lines sketched
above), it is because the lack of democratic debate and the
ideological fallacy indicated earlier are major impediments
to action. I would add that the Western ideological offensive, orchestrated by powerful media, is flocking entirely
to the pro-capitalist, albeit anti-democratic, forces.

A response to the three questions posed above would

lead to intensive internal class struggle, already (silently)
under way. A significant minority (20%?) in the Eastern
countries might benefit from the restoration of capitalism.
But, in the light of the inadequate levels of development
and international competitiveness achieved by the socialist countries, this minority would never attain the Western
standard of living that fuels their aspirations, except by
grinding down the mass of the people. . . .

The initiative for "change" in the East is in fact taken
top-down by the ruling class itself. This class is constituted
on the basis of "statism" that has been the way of dealing
with the capitalism/socialism contradiction within the national and popular construct. It hopes now to be rid of the
constraints of the popular dimension of the system and opt
four-square for capitalism. The "scuttling" of the system to
which it lends itself to a degree astonishing to Western
commentators is not really surprising at all: it is the logical
terminus of its evolution, and was perfectly foreseen by
Mao. This class, in attacking its own system, adopts all the
outworn prejudices of the critique of socialism by bourgeois ideology, but refrains from pointing out that the system it is abandoning has been quite effective in making
possible its own constitution as a bourgeoisie!

We may add that the confusion is certainly accentuated
by the grafting of internal national conflicts (USSR and
Yugoslavia) and external (Germany/Poland, Hungary/Ro-
mania) on to the internal social struggles.

The question of the future of socialism is not subsumed
in possible advances or retreats in the countries of the
East.

We turn to the countries of the Third and Fourth World—
true peripheries and societies destroyed by capitalist expansion—where development capable of meeting the material needs of all social strata of the nation appears impossible within the framework of capitalism, and it becomes
necessary to consider the substitute of alternative development outside surrender to global constraints. This is the
meaning of the expression delinking. Delinking is not a

recipe but rather a principled choice: that of delinking the criteria of rationality of internal economic choices from those governing the world system, namely freeing oneself from the constraint of world-wide value by substituting a law of value of national and popular reference. If the bourgeoisie are incapable of delinking, and if only a popular alliance must and can be persuaded that this is an ineluctable requirement for any development project worthy of the name, the social dynamism must lead to seeing this popular project in a form that we can only describe as socialist. It is understood that socialism in question remains a project for society, well before us, and not a "constructed model" on show in any particular place that has merely to be copied. The current changes in the world economy and political and cultural situation are not expected to attentuate the polarising character inherent in really existing capitalism, but can only heighten the contradictions through which it is expressed. The policies of surrender to world unification through the market—described as "adjustment" for the peripheries (I describe it as unilateral, although one speaks of "restructuring" when the centres are concerned!)—one cannot "neutralise" the new polarisation. They are not, therefore, an acceptable alternative to the national and popular rupture that is still necessary, and more than ever so. The national bourgeoisies of the Third World who had co-opted the national liberation movement to their own advantage, have already been largely turned into compradors by the evolution of the world system. They are therefore incapable of mediating the new world-wide phcnomenon to the advantage of their own country. The popular classes subject to the evolution are still at a moment of confusion following the exhaustion of the former national liberation movement. Hence it is difficult to forecast the precise next step in an uninterrupted popular revolution that still threatens the globalisation of upheavals in the peripheries of the system that will for a time remain as "flash points".

In the short term, the responses of the peoples of the

Third World seem generally as inadequate as in the past. The revival of culturalist expressions heralded in the fundamentalist religious movements here and there is in itself a symptom of the crisis and not an adequate response to its challenge. . . .

The contours of a potential new capitalist globalisation remain quite vague. The configuration will follow the conflicts that will inevitably occur despite the ideological discourse of liberalism. Meanwhile on the absurd hypothesis that the national and social forces in dispute will agree to sacrifice their crucial divergent interests to surrender to the strict logic of "globalisation by the market", the reshaped world will be formidable. Hence the future remains open to various possibilities and there is no justification for abandoning the thought and struggle to promote a better world project: it is not a case of voluntarist subjectivity for the political options underlying the projects for the future are integral to historical objectivity. Exploration of the various possibilities would require consideration of the alternative parameters in regard to three orders of evolution:

(i) the centres/peripheries contradiction governed by the logic of the system;

(ii) West-East relations;

(iii) intra-Western competition.

I have attempted to do so briefly from the starting point of the logic of unilateral unification by the market that constitutes the essence of the Western project.

More than ever, therefore, the forces of the left have a duty to promote a credible alternative to this disastrous option. I shall not dwell here on the possible features of this alternative, some aspects of which I have discussed elsewhere.

Firstly, the only strategy meaningful for the progressive forces on world scale, on the basis of which an internationalism of the peoples of the three areas (West, East and South) could draw new breath, must look to the prospect of building a "polycentric" world. The various component areas must be articulated in a flexible way allowing the implementation of specific policies required by varying levels of development and objective circumstances.

It must be acknowledged at the outset that the problems the peoples of the world have to solve differ from one area to another; it is therefore essential that the world system be such that the peoples have the autonomy to promote their own interests; there must be a balance between "general interdependence" and this legitimate concern for autonomy; the logic of mutual and reciprocal adjustment must be substituted for unilateral adjustment by the weakest and pursuit of expansion for the exclusive benefit of the strongest.

Secondly, polycentrism means that the countries of the East and the South pursue development policies that are delinked in the sense I have given the word (subjection of external relations to the requirements of internal progress and not the converse that forms the essential of unilateral adjustment by the market). This strategy looks to the prospect of possible advances towards socialism (through democratisation and strengthening of the national and popular aspect), and not of a "restoration of capitalism" in the countries of the East, and to that of a refusal by the countries of the South to become compradors. It must, likewise, allow progressive advances in the countries of the West, through the opening up of non-market social spaces and through other reforms based on socialisation of economic management founded on respect for diversity of circumstances, one poles apart from the aggressive vision of "roll back".

Thirdly, with particular reference to the Third World, this strategy favours the concept of progress (in the organisation of the forces of production) albeit to the detriment of immediate "international competitiveness". It puts at the top of the agenda the objectives of an agricultural revolution marked by the maximum of equality (in such a way as to slow the uncontrolled drift to the towns and take into account the narrow limits of international emigration), transformation of the exploited and dependent informal sector into a popular transitional economy. It calls for an effective combination of planning and market forces, as the foundation for a democratisation concerned to bring the people social benefit. The vision of polycentrism it inspires gives the countries and regions of the Third World a margin of autonomy denied them in the model of world unification by the exclusive means of the market and in that of regionalisation governed by the principal competing poles of development.

Fourthly, as regards tasks towards international cooperation for general interdependence, the strategy aims to encourage the development of embryos of a "democratic world government" (as opposed to the "seven-power economic summit") and, for example, the introduction of a world tax to be spent on ecological protection measures. It also proposes to reduce the tensions produced by the arms race, notably by the superpowers. It aims finally to breathe new life into the democratic institutionalisation of world management through a revival of the UN.

Let me say, in conclusion, that the construction of a polycentric world affording prospects for new socialist advances implies an awareness of the universalist cultural dimension of the project for the future. . . .

BIBLIOGRAPHY

A full bibliography on the history of socialist thought would require volumes. We shall suggest only a few of the better introductory works in English. The indispensable general study is G. D. H. Cole's *A History of Socialist Thought* (5 volumes in 7, New York: St. Martin's Press, 1953–1958). Edmund Wilson's *To the Finland Station* (New York: Doubleday Anchor Books, 1953) is a dramatic and engagingly written account of socialist thought from its genesis in the eighteenth century to the Bolshevik Revolution. George Lichtheim's *Marxism: An Historical and Critical Study* (New York: Frederick Praeger & Co., 1961) is a sophisticated survey of the entire socialist tradition—with special emphasis on Marx of course—down to the present.

Kingsley Martin's *French Liberal Thought in the Eighteenth Century* (Boston: Little, Brown, 1925) provides a lucid summary of French radical philosophy, including Morelly's, in the second half of the century. The number of books on Rousseau continues to burgeon; but one of the few general studies in English of his political theory and its implications is Alfred Cobban's *Rousseau and the Modern State* (London: Allen and Unwin, 1934). David Thomson's *The Babeuf Plot* (London: K. Paul, Trench, Trubner, 1947) is a brief history of the uprising and of the later fate of the movement.

Emile Durkheim's *Socialism and Saint-Simon* (Yellow Springs, Ohio: Antioch Press, 1958) is by far the best work on utopian socialism in general. Few books on the utopians themselves are available. On Fourier there is nothing but an old, though adequate, biography: Charles Pellarin, *The Life of Charles Fourier* (New York: 1848). G. D. H. Cole's *Robert Owen* (Boston: Little, Brown, 1925) is a fine study.

One will search in vain for literature in English on Blanc and Blanqui. There are studies of Proudhon, however; the best of them in our opinion is George Woodcock's *Pierre-Joseph Proudhon* (London: Routledge and Kegan Paul, 1956). The British have carefully covered the Chartist movement, but G. D. H. Cole's *Chartist Portraits* (London: Macmillan, 1941), especially the first chapter, is the best introduction to the subject.

On early German socialism Sidney Hook's *From Hegel to Marx* (Ann Arbor: Ann Arbor Paperbacks, 1962) is trenchant. This should be supplemented by the appropriate sections of Lichtheim's book.

The number of books on Marx and Marxism is prohibitively large. Two may be recommended along with Lichtheim's: Isaiah Berlin's Karl Marx (London: Oxford University Press, 1948) and Franz Mehring's *Karl Marx* (Ann Arbor: Ann Arbor Paperbacks, 1962).

E. H. Carr's *Michael Bakunin* (New York: Vintage Books, 1961) is an outstanding biography. Peter Kropotkin is perhaps best approached through his autobiography, *Memoirs of a Revolutionist* (New York: Doubleday Anchor, 1962). French syndicalism is authoritatively discussed in an early work: Lewis Lorwin's *Syndicalism in France* (New York: Columbia University Press, 1914). The best work on Guild Socialism is still G. D. H. Cole's *Guild Socialism Restated* (New York: Frederick A. Stokes, 1921).

Volume three of Cole's *History of Socialist Thought* is quite good on revisionism and reformism and the problems of the Second International. The section on Lassalle in Edmund Wilson's book is one of the best summaries available in English. Peter Gay's *Dilemma of Democratic Socialism* (New York: Columbia University Press, 1952) discusses the problems raised by Bernstein in the German

Socialist Party before World War I. No comparable study of French socialism is available in English.

From the mountain of books on Bolshevism we recommend the following: Bertram Wolfe's *Three Who Made a Revolution* (Boston: Beacon Press, 1955); Isaac Deutscher's *Stalin* (New York: Vintage Books, 1960) and his excellent biography of Trotsky, of which two volumes have appeared, *The Prophet Armed* (New York: Oxford University Press, 1954) and *The Prophet Unarmed* (New York: Oxford University Press, 1959); and Leonard Schapiro's *The Origins of the Communist Autocracy* (Cambridge: Harvard University Press, 1955).

The history of contemporary socialism remains to be written, but the last chapter of Lichtheim's study contains a cogent portrayal of its current condition.